A Parent's Guide™ to
The Best
Children's
Videos
DVDs &
CD-ROMs

2nd Edition

Mars Publishing
Los Angeles, California
www.marspub.com

MARS
PARENT'S
GUIDES

This book, and all titles in the Parent's Guide series, are available for purposes of fund raising and educational sales to charity drives, fund raisers, parent or teacher organizations, schools, government agencies and corporations at a discount for purchases of more than 10 copies. Persons or organizations wishing to inquire should call Mars Publishing at 1-800-549-6646 or write to us at **sales@marspub.com**.

Every effort has been made to bring you an error-free, informative collection of information. If you find an error, or wish to simply comment to the author or publisher, please email us at **kidvid@marspub.com**.

A Parent's Guide to the Best Children's Videos, 2nd Edition
ISBN: 1-931199-04-3

MARS
PUBLISHING
www.marspub.com

Edwin E. Steussy, CEO and Publisher
Lars W. Peterson, Editor
Michael P. Duggan, Graphic Designer

Contents

Introduction
to the Second Edition

By Ranny Levy
Founder & President,
Coalition for Quality Children's Media — Kids First!

As we former children know, movies are more than just entertainment; they introduce us to our heroes and heroines, show us new places, help us sort out our emotions, and fuel our imaginations. A good movie stays with us long after we walk out of the theater. It's like an old friend we can visit and revisit. How many times do you find yourself reminiscing with friends after a good meal about some scene that touched you? At the same time, how many times have you been appalled by a movie that was more violent, full of sexual images, or foul language than you expected and found yourself wanting to have a face to face conversation with the person who mis-marketed the film? Never fear, your sigh of relief is this book!

We're delighted to bring you the second edition of the KIDS FIRST! *Parent's Guide to The Best Children's Videos*. This guide is the result of many hours of diligent video, DVD and CD-ROM screening by the KIDS FIRST! juries of child media critics. Our juries are composed of more than 3,000 children from diverse cultural backgrounds and 300 child development specialists, child media specialists, librarians, teachers and other professionals. This is a selective guide, giving you a list of the crème de la crème of children's media. More than 800 new titles have been added since the first edition of this book, and every title in this book has received a thumb's up from kids and adults alike. Further, every movie, video, DVD and CD-ROM in this book meets the KIDS FIRST! baseline criteria for endorsement. This means they're free of gratuitous violence or inappropriate sexual behavior, contain no negative gender, racial, cultural and religious stereotypes, do not glamorize physical or verbal abuse, do not promote unsafe behavior and do not condescend to children. You'll find frank comments about every title drawn from our child and adult juries. Most importantly, these titles are not only safe, but we know kids will like them because our kid jurors have told us so!

How to Use This Book

The book is divided into chapters suitable for a specific age group, from infant to adult. You can find a movie that will make your fifth grader jump for joy, or your pre-teen or teen cry over. Maybe you're looking for a video that captivates your toddler's attention while you find a few precious minutes to cook dinner. Because the needs of a two-year-old are quite different from those of twelve-year-old, or even a six- or seven-year-old, KIDS FIRST! screens each program with different age groups of children to determine age appropriateness. How I wish there had been a service like this when my kids were little. Some titles overlap age groups, and these are listed with a full review only once, in the chapter for the youngest age, and later cross-referenced in the chapter for the older age. Each age-specific chapter is then sub-divided by subject, from educational/instructional to music to special interest. This makes your search ever so much easier. Finally, the CD-ROMs are listed first, and the videos and DVDs are grouped together, alphabetically under each subject heading.

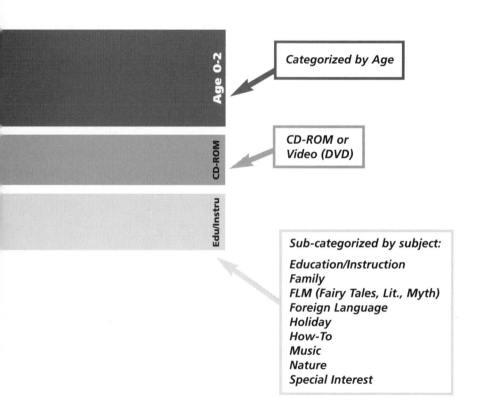

Age 0-2

Categorized by Age

CD-ROM

CD-ROM or Video (DVD)

Edu/Instru

Sub-categorized by subject:

Education/Instruction
Family
FLM (Fairy Tales, Lit., Myth)
Foreign Language
Holiday
How-To
Music
Nature
Special Interest

Here's what you'll find in each review: a brief summary of the program, the series title, the producer or supplier's name, the manufacturer's suggested retail price, the age recommendation, and feedback from both adult evaluators and child jurors. Each title is rated one, two or three stars. The three stars constitute our "All-Star" rating. These titles have received the highest ratings by both adult and child jurors. They are outstanding and appeal to a broad audience. Two stars indicate good, not exceptional. One star indicates good but may appeal to a special audience. The jurors' summary will support the rationale for the "Star" rating. We've also included Indices for easy reference, especially to help you find programs that address special topics such as cultural diversity or feature intriguing role models, conflict resolution, or problem-solving skills.

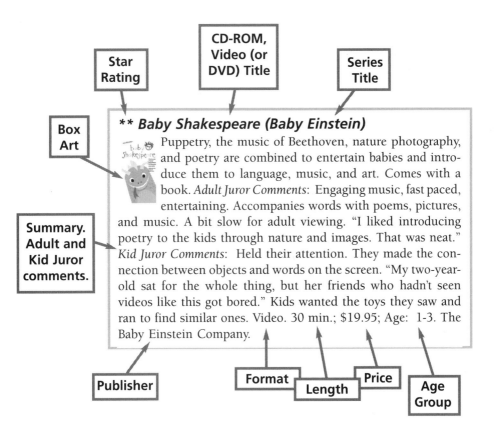

Star Rating

CD-ROM, Video (or DVD) Title

Series Title

Box Art

Summary. Adult and Kid Juror comments.

** Baby Shakespeare (Baby Einstein)

Puppetry, the music of Beethoven, nature photography, and poetry are combined to entertain babies and introduce them to language, music, and art. Comes with a book. *Adult Juror Comments*: Engaging music, fast paced, entertaining. Accompanies words with poems, pictures, and music. A bit slow for adult viewing. "I liked introducing poetry to the kids through nature and images. That was neat." *Kid Juror Comments*: Held their attention. They made the connection between objects and words on the screen. "My two-year-old sat for the whole thing, but her friends who hadn't seen videos like this got bored." Kids wanted the toys they saw and ran to find similar ones. Video. 30 min.; $19.95; Age: 1-3. The Baby Einstein Company.

Publisher

Format

Length

Price

Age Group

Who Made This Book?

Many people have contributed literally hundreds of thousands of hours to make this book a reality. More than 3,300 adult and child jurors from all around the United States, the wonderful, dedicated Coalition for Quality Children's Media staff, the producers of the programs, and our publishers at Mars Publishing all worked hard to bring this book to you. I'd like to personally acknowledge my children, Samsunshine and Alanna Nevada Levy, who have truly put KIDS FIRST! in my life and who both have contributed untold hours to the Coalition for Quality Children's Media and this book. CQCM staffers Deborah Cool, Suzanne Farley, Elizabeth McCann, Lorilei Songy and Liz Wirth have worked tirelessly on this project and without whom this second edition would not exist. The Coalition for Quality Children's Media's National Board members and Trustees who provide the guidance and support to keep this organization going are without a doubt, some of the most important contributors, especially Bruce Apar, Ann Church, Gay Dillingham, Rosanne Azarian, Nancy Kenney, Jere Rae-Mansfield and Harold Weitzberg.

Where to Find These Titles

Before setting you loose with this book, a few last words to help you. To find these programs, visit your local retailer, video rental store or your public library. Oder titles or those from independent producers will be more difficult to find and your chances of finding them are greater at a specialty store or on a web site. The Coalition's web site, **http://www.kidsfirstinternet.org**, has links to many of the independent producer's sites. Our website adds new reviews every month so it's a good source to find new titles that we've just endorsed. We also have articles on media literacy, public policy updates, and links to other advocacy organizations.

Ranny Levy, Founder and Executive Director: Taught at the elementary, middle school and university level. From 1980 - 91, Levy produced and marketed educational media. In 1991 Levy founded CQCM. Ms. Levy is a frequent speaker on children and media, presenting at Vice President Gore's Family Re-Union IV: The Family and The Media Conference, Video Software Dealers' Association Convention, the National Governor's Association Conference on Quality in Education, the Head Start Research Conference, and Marketing to Kids Report. She is the mother of two children ages 27 and 30 and a brand new grandmother.

Parent's Guide Choice Awards

The 30 titles that have been given this distinction are those selected as semi-finalists in the KIDS FIRST! Best Children's Film, Video or DVD of the Year Award. The competition was part of the KIDS FIRST! Film Festival 2001. To qualify, a title had to be released in either film, video, or DVD during the previous year and been awarded "All-Star" status from both child and adult KIDS FIRST! jurors. Titles that qualify for All-Star status are rated on their educational, production, and social values as well as how they enhance a child's personal competence. Various aspects in each of these four areas are examined, as follows:

Production Value
- The title is engaging and entertaining for both adults and children.
- It is appropriate for the child's age and developmental level.
- It is esthetically pleasing and technically proficient.
- It enriches the child's life experiences.
- It generates interest in creative expression and an appreciation for the arts.
- It provides a window on the world, exposure to diverse ethnic population.

Personal Competence
- The title enhances a child's self-esteem or assists in developing a more accurate self-concept.
- It encourages assertiveness skills so a child can stand up for what he or she believes.
- It helps to develop good decision making skills.
- It enhances planning skills and the ability to understand their own lives in a wider context.
- It offers positive role models.
- It encourages children to make connections to their own lives.
- It helps work through problems and emotional issues using humor or sensitivity.
- It offers a positive view of the future.
- It promotes admiration and love both of family and neighbors.

Social Value

- It values helping other people.
- It creates interest and concern about world issues such as hunger, environment, or animal and human rights.
- It values other people's feelings.
- It values appropriate sexuality.
- It promotes acceptance and respect of diverse cultures, lifestyles and individuality.
- It provides positive role models for interpersonal relationships such as good friendship making skills or non-violent means of conflict resolution.
- It improves communication between different groups of people such as parents and children, care-givers, and teachers.
- It values making judgements based on actual experience and interaction rather than hearsay or appearances.

Educational Value

- The title stimulates curiosity and creativity.
- It encourages a child to think, reason, question, and experiment.
- It helps develop cognitive and intellectual skills.
- It stimulates language development.
- It provides accurate information.
- It models good health, safety, and nutritional practices.
- It heightens a child's educational aspirations, promotes the importance of education, and values personal achievement.
- It provides appropriate social, personal, and educational challenges.
- It demonstrates how knowledge is applied.

Parent's Guide Choice
Award Winners for 2001

AGES: 0-2

Title	Publisher	Page
Baby Music School: Classical	The Baby School Company Inc.	13
Mozart Nature Symphonies	Munchkin, Inc.	29
Teletubbies: Bedtime Stories and Lullabies	The Itsy Bitsy Entertainment Co.	22
Teletubbies: Christmas in the Snow	The Itsy Bitsy Entertainment Co.	25

AGES: 2-5

Title	Publisher	Page
Bear in the Big Blue House: A Berry Bear Christmas	Columbia Tristar Home Video	123
Bear in the Big Blue House: Halloween & Thanksgiving	Columbia Tristar Home Video	124
Bear in the Big Blue House: Visiting The Doctor with Bear	Columbia Tristar Home Video	75
Blue's Clues: Blue's Big Musical Movie	Paramount Home Video	51
Dragon Tales: Follow the Clues	Columbia Tristar	79
Farm Country Ahead	Fred Levine Productions	149
George and Martha: Best Of Friends	Sony Wonder	54
Goodnight Moon and Other Sleepytime Tales	HBO	118
Theodore Tugboat: Nighttime Adventures	Warner Home Video	103

Chapter One

Ages 0-2

By Dr. Irving Lazar

It was inevitable that the video industry would turn its attention to infants. Video has become the baby-sitting tool of choice for many parents and child care providers. Be aware that while some videos for infants and toddlers are worthwhile, some should be avoided.

By the age of four, most kids can differentiate between reality and make-believe. They have an adequate repertoire of words and experiences to place a pictorial story in its context. They are able to turn off the TV or VCR and walk away. Infants are quite different. Current estimates are that only about 15% of the brain is "hardwired" at birth. Whatever learning has taken place before birth simply addresses physical survival. What the baby experiences in the first two years of its life directly affects how its brain files, stores, and recovers information.

Here's how it works: When the baby encounters a multi-sensory experience, its brain files the visual elements in one place, the auditory components somewhere else, and the other sensory inputs in still other places of the brain. These elements are connected to each other by nerve cells. The more senses excited by an event, the richer the network of cells that store that event. The wider the network, the more pathways are created for the baby to recall, making it more likely the baby will relate the event to other events. How experiences are filed, how they relate to future experiences, and how they are available for recall are determined to a large degree by what happens in the first year of life when the brain's filing system is being constructed. This means that the more multi-sensory an experience is, the more widely it is filed and the more readily it will be recalled.

What kinds of multi-sensory experiences are we talking about? Listening to Bach or Mozart or the Beatles from a recording stimulates only one sense—hearing. It does not promote a complex filing system. Watching a video stimulates sight and sound. Its influence is greater, but hardly the best. What is the richest experience? The perfect one is a mother breast-feeding her baby. Touch, taste, smell, motion, hearing, sight, and pressure are all combined into a single multi-sensory pleasurable experience.

Babies need human contact. They learn from complex human interaction in settings that offer rich stimuli for all the senses. Rich does not mean overwhelming; it means complexity and interrelationship. A mother (or father, or caregiver) can increase the sensory impact of a video by holding the baby while talking, dancing, or singing along. Recently, I have seen videos supposedly made for babies and toddlers that simply show lots of pictures of babies. Because an infant cannot interact with the pictured babies, he or she soon becomes bored. This may later discourage social interactions with real babies. Other videos attempt to teach infants vocabulary unsuitable for this age.

These programs are not educational in any real sense and may have a negative effect if they are used as substitutes for interactions with real people or doing real things. However, if parents or caregivers are willing to watch videos with their infants or toddlers and engage in play with them, they can increase both the child's pleasure and learning. Some videos aimed at babies and parents can be useful. For example, a video title you'll find in this chapter, *So Smart!* is designed to give a parent or care-giver audiovisual tools for playing with a baby. Using simple moving designs accompanied by gentle music, it provides instructions for playing with an infant, giving the infant stimuli at a comfortable pace, and responding to the baby's limited attention span. Another good example, *Exercise with Daddy and Me*, instructs fathers in exercises that make them comfortable holding and playing with their babies. This video introduces elements of infant massage, and its discussion with a group of fathers about the adjustments that a new baby demands may encourage them to share their feelings with their wives.

Irving Lazar, Professor Emeritus, Cornell University, is a resident scholar at the Kennedy Center, Vanderbilt University. He has conducted large-scale research demonstrating the long-term positive effects of infant and preschool services.

Chapter One • Infants

Format—CD-ROM

Category—Education/Instruction

*** Sesame Street: Baby & Me (Sesame Street)

Join Sesame Street friends in twelve interactive activities that include sing-along songs, cause and effect explorations, and introductions to colors, shapes and animals. *Adult Juror Comments*: Very easy to use. "The quality was excellent and the controls were well thought out." Requires adult participation. "Loved the follow me and peek-a-boo activities." "I was very surprised at how well this works for babies." They made fun noises. *Kid Juror Comments*: A big hit. The babies loved it. Lots of wide-eyed expressions and smiles. Hummed and tried to talk to Elmo and the gang. The kids chanted, "Melmo, Melmo" (for Elmo) when they wanted to play. Babies returned to the keyboard often. CD-ROM. WIN/MAC; $29.95; Age: 0-2. Sony Wonder.

Format—Video/DVD

Category—Education/Instruction

** Baby About Town - Friendly Faces, Baby Places (Baby About Town)

Shows happy expressive faces in familiar surroundings to delight and entertain your baby. Exposes viewers to people of all races, sizes, shapes and ages. *Adult Juror Comments*: Adequate production quality, minor soundtrack problems. Good pace. All encounters are positive, with friendly and happy people. It would hold an infant's attention briefly. Rural infants would be exposed to a diverse population they wouldn't normally see. *Kid Juror Comments*: Voices and faces attracted their attention, but held it only briefly and intermittently. Some became bored, others over-stimulated by the background noises. None cried while it was on. Video. 28 min.; $14.95; Age: 1-2. Baby About Town / Talibecca Productions.

** Baby Bach (DVD) (Baby Einstein)

Introduces infants to the music of J.S. Bach and to eight foreign languages, using concerts, flash cards, and study tracks to develop reading and listening skills. *Adult Juror Comments*: Engaging, colorful, well-produced and well-paced for the audience. Wonderful music. Facilitates language development. Contains a "flash card" section which jurors thought wasn't developmentally appropriate. Can be viewed in segments. *Kid Juror Comments*: Captivated. "Kids never seemed to tire of seeing the images." "The toddlers were quite proud of themselves for identifying the objects in the language lab and beamed when proven correct." Children danced with the music. DVD. 172 min.; $24.98; Age: 0-2. The Baby Einstein Company.

** Baby Doolittle Neighborhood Animals (Baby Einstein)

Introduces young children to animals that can be found close to home. Hosted by Pavlov the Dog, the program features fun puppet shows accompanied by beautiful footage of animals in their natural environment, accented with classical music. Adult Juror Comments: Professional production that perfectly coordinates music with joyful antics of puppets, toys and animation. Distinctive style intelligently groups subjects, logically breaks for viewing in segments. Visual cues allow children to anticipate changes. Kid Juror Comments: Everyone enjoyed dancing and moving to the music - even parents. Older kids pointed to the animals they recognized. All responded well to familiar animals and toys. Very enjoyable watching. Video. 30 min.; $14.98; Age: 0-3. The Baby Einstein Company.

* Baby Einstein (DVD) (Baby Einstein)

Introduces the sounds of eight foreign languages to infants, using interactive flash cards, familiar nursery rhymes, and classical music pieces. *Adult Juror Comments*: Well-produced with highly saturated colors and wonderful music. Images and words don't match. The multiple languages are confusing and detract from the visuals. *Kid Juror Comments*: Mixed. The preschoolers wanted to show their friends the language lab. The pictures in the theater captured their attention. Youngest kids lost attention with the flash card section. DVD. 162 min.; $24.98; Age: 0-3. The Baby Einstein Company.

** Baby Language School: Spanish (Baby Language School)

Using animation and nursery songs, Spanish-speaking hosts introduce infants to the Spanish language. *Adult Juror Comments*: Thoughtfully produced. Good balance of songs and images. Offers early exposure to the Spanish language. Graphics and vocabulary don't always correlate. Animation is smooth and gentle. Best viewed in segments. *Kid Juror Comments*: Would watch again. Lots of laughter and pointing at familiar objects. Kids mimicked the vocabulary and enjoyed following the birds across the sky and watching the creation of the sun. Had a soothing effect. Video. 30 min.; $14.95; Age: 0-3. The Baby School Company Inc.

Chapter One • Infants

*** *Baby Let's Play*

 Takes toddlers on a ride aboard a diesel engine; shows children in a gym daring to swing twenty feet in the air; jumping; climbing with balls, parachutes, and bubbles. Original music. *Adult Juror Comments*: Delightful music, charming children. Well-paced, interesting, good flow between activities and images. Good modeling for mothers and caregivers. *Kid Juror Comments*: Combination of music and children at play is excellent, good attention grabber. Kids asked to see it again immediately. All seemed to enjoy it, although it may be too long for one sitting. Video. 30 min.; $12.95; Age: 1-3. Little Ones Productions.

** *Baby Mozart (DVD) (Baby Einstein)*

 Introduces infants to the music of Mozart and eight foreign languages. Using an interactive format, Baby Mozart contains flash cards, pronunciations by native speakers, and study tracks to develop reading skills. *Adult Juror Comments*: Beautiful resolution and wonderful images. "Theater portion is wonderful." "Flash card section is dry and monotonous." Easily viewed in segments. Supports language development. Great music with a soothing quality. *Kid Juror Comments*: Inconsistent. Kids really tuned into the theater sections, but the language area lost their attention. Responded well to the music, moving their bodies and focusing in on the image on the screen. DVD. 170 min.; $24.98; Age: 0-3. The Baby Einstein Company.

*** *Baby Music School: Classical (Baby Music School)*

 Bold, brightly colored animals and classical music are brought together to encourage language development and facilitate creative thinking. *Adult Juror Comments*: Beautifully produced. Artfully blends images with engaging music. "I love the way each animal is assigned a musical instrument." "Offers a wonderful exposure to music and instruments." Easily viewed in segments. Includes parents' guide. *Kid Juror Comments*: Delighted. "The babies laughed, cooed, and clapped their hands." "They smiled and touched the screen." Kids liked guessing which animal was coming next. They called out the shapes and danced and played while watching. Video. 30 min.; $14.95; Age: 0-3. The Baby School Company Inc.

** Baby Shakespeare (Baby Einstein)

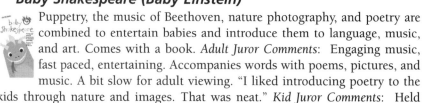

Puppetry, the music of Beethoven, nature photography, and poetry are combined to entertain babies and introduce them to language, music, and art. Comes with a book. *Adult Juror Comments*: Engaging music, fast paced, entertaining. Accompanies words with poems, pictures, and music. A bit slow for adult viewing. "I liked introducing poetry to the kids through nature and images. That was neat." *Kid Juror Comments*: Held their attention. They made the connection between objects and words on the screen. "My two-year-old sat for the whole thing, but her friends who hadn't seen videos like this got bored." Kids wanted the toys they saw and ran to find similar ones. Video. 30 min.; $19.95; Age: 1-3. The Baby Einstein Company.

*** Baby's First Impressions, Vol. 1: Shapes (Baby's First Impressions)

Takes an infant's view of four basic geometric shapes and uses a cinematic approach to find those basic shapes in everyday items familiar to an infant or toddler. *Adult Juror Comments*: Diverting and attractive. Good pace. Beautifully done. Keeps their interest. Lends itself to ooh's and ah's. Variety of shape movements on-screen is visually stimulating. Adults were riveted! *Kid Juror Comments*: Youngest children watched as they were playing. Held attention of two- and three-year-olds. Older kids retained learning best. Video. 32 min.; $14.95; Age: 0-2. Small Fry Productions.

*** Baby's First Impressions, Vol. 2: Colors (Baby's First Impressions)

Takes an infant's view of colors. Uses a cinematic approach to find colors in common items an infant or toddler is familiar with to reinforce the educational impact. *Adult Juror Comments*: Eye-catching. Shows wonderful variety of images, music and children. Quick pace and content keeps infants' attention. Helps teach colors in different settings. A definite favorite, kids will watch it. *Kid Juror Comments*: One fourteen-month-old actually watched for five to eight minutes, intrigued by the colors. Four- and five-year-olds followed along exceptionally well. "I liked everything. I felt like I was inside the video." Video. 32 min.; $14.95; Age: 1-4. Small Fry Productions.

Chapter One • Infants

*** Baby's First Impressions, Vol. 7: Sounds
(Baby's First Impressions)

 Open your children's ears to the world out there. Video is designed to sharpen listening skills and develop cognitive abilities through games such as guessing what sounds are. Sounds are accompanied by imaginative visuals. *Adult Juror Comments*: Here's a different type of video for preschoolers. The clear sounds and color appeal to the youngest toddler. Older kids enjoy guessing the sounds. Helps children identify sounds around them through a collection of common items. *Kid Juror Comments*: Kids responded to the different sounds. They enjoyed trying to figure out which phone sounded familiar. The barnyard animals made the children laugh. Then they imitated their sounds. Learned some new words and enjoyed the scenes of friendship. Video. 32 min.; $14.95; Age: 1-3. Small Fry Productions.

** Baby's Smart Start (Babyscapes)

 Classical music arrangements are accompanied by computer-generated black, white, and red geometric shapes. These high contrast colors and shapes move and dance to the rhythm and beat of each piece of music. *Adult Juror Comments*: Soothing music, captivating geometrical shapes with bold colors. "Hypnotic." Some found it boring. Includes instruction book that encourages interaction between parent and child. Can easily be viewed in segments. *Kid Juror Comments*: Provides a soothing backdrop for toddler play. Graphics caught their attention. Babies wanted to touch the images. Elicited conversation about paint, balls, and colors. "Balls?" Some children swayed to the music. Babies cooed and smiled. Video. 30 min.; $14.95; Age: 0-2. Keri Mann.

** Brainy Baby: Left Brain (Brainy Baby)

 A two-volume set that addresses both the right and left brain method of thinking. Volume two looks at the development of the left brain and focuses on areas of math, language, and logic. Explores language by introducing words in French and Spanish. *Adult Juror Comments*: Production well done. Good, clear language. Introduces basic concepts such as cause and effect. Addition and subtraction may be inappropriate for this age group. Best viewed in segments. *Kid Juror Comments*: Engaging. They smiled, clapped their hands, and tapped their toes. Responded well to other babies in the program. "My daughter couldn't help chiming in with her own guesses on the color and shape names." Video. 32 min.; $15.95; Age: 1-3. Small Fry Productions.

** Brainy Baby: Right Brain (Brainy Baby)

A two-volume set that addresses both the right and left brain methods of thinking. Volume one addresses the right brain and focuses on creativity, imagination, and perception. *Adult Juror Comments*: Moving objects are captivating. Visually engaging. Production well done. "It is respectful of children's emotional capacity." "The peek-a-boo activities are excellent." "The use of rhyme is beneficial in the language process." *Kid Juror Comments*: Interesting images and soothing music held children's attention. "My baby couldn't take her eyes off the set." Kids chimed in with guesses about colors, shapes, and object names. Narrator provided answers too soon for many children. Video. 32 min.; $15.95; Age: 1-3. Small Fry Productions.

** Baby Van Gogh Video with CD (Baby Einstein)

Designed to enrich a baby's learning process. A new approach is utilized to teach colors in the context of Van Gogh's paintings with classical music by Bizet, Offenbach, Strauss and Tchaikovsky. Adult Juror Comments: Enjoyable. Soundtrack perfectly coordinated to movement. Van Gogh paintings, puppets and toys are presented one at a time. Colors are the only words used on screen. Logical breaks allow for viewing in segments. Kid Juror Comments: Little ones laughed and moved with the music, pointed at familiar objects on the screen. Older ones were mesmerized and identified colors. All enjoyed the puppet movements and musical interludes. Video. 30 min.; $15.98; Age: 0-3. The Baby Einstein Company.

** Celebration of Color (Baby Scapes)

Showcases seven classical music pieces and introduces primary and secondary colors. Images move to the music. *Adult Juror Comments*: Joyous music. Exceptional graphics with clear crisp colors. The music sections were too long. "The paint combinations were interesting at first, but the repetition seemed tedious." "Great for discussion of color." *Kid Juror Comments*: Enjoyed the music and bright colors. The initial fireworks caught their attention, but many lost interest after that. Prompted discussion about color, shape, and motion. Children called out colors by name. Babies pointed and smiled. Video. 30 min.; $14.95; Age: 0-3. Keri Mann.

Chapter One • Infants

** In Their Favorite Places (Babies at Play)

Toddlers enjoy watching young children visit the zoo, toy store, grandma's house, and other great places. *Adult Juror Comments*: Good at showing parents participating in activities. Use of single words is instructive but not obtrusive. Choices of favorite places are universal: merry-go-round, ice cream parlor, etc. Shows beautiful variety of children. *Kid Juror Comments*: An interesting video for children to observe parent/child interactions. Kids loved the fair and climber parts. One five-year-old made a toy store afterwards. Kids found the sound track difficult to sing along with. Video. 39 min.; $12.98; Age: 1-3. Warner Home Video.

* Jump Jump Jazzy

This odyssey full of live animals, stimulating images, and classical art features original and soothing jazz music written just for babies and toddlers. Introduces the instruments played in the music. *Adult Juror Comments*: Introduces kids to instruments and jazz. Weak production qualities. Uses vibrant colors, great works of art, and live animals. Images do not always relate to the music or the theme. Too many images and animals are unfamiliar even to adults. Disjointed. *Kid Juror Comments*: Required significant interaction with an adult to keep them satisfied and interested. They liked seeing familiar animals such as ducks and bears. Some pretended to play the instruments and named the different shapes and objects. Video. 36 min.; $14.95; Age: 0-3. Zooknowlogy Learning Company, LLC.

** Miracle of Mozart: Teaching Your Child Numbers & Shapes (Babyscapes)

Introduces children to numbers and shapes with state-of-the-art graphics, while carefully chosen classical selections of Mozart play in the background. *Adult Juror Comments*: Shapes, colors, and techniques are exciting and pleasing to the eye. Provides lots of repetition, though some segments are a little long. "The segment where the numbers shoot up like a rocket and then burst into the number shape was fun." *Kid Juror Comments*: Did not hold kids' attention well. They liked the animation best, such as when the shapes splashed into the water. "I want to see the 'choo choo' carry shapes again." Kids danced or moved to the music. Video. 30 min.; $14.95; Age: 0-3. Keri Mann.

** My Best English, Vol. 2: Colors (My Best English)

An entertaining teaching aid to facilitate language-learning while prompting a positive learning environment. Teaches ten colors via live images, animation, and classical music. *Adult Juror Comments*: Cute concept, very bright and fun to watch. Good use of music and sound. Slow pace appropriate for targeted age. Younger viewers learn the colors; older kids start learning the words for the colors. Nicely done. *Kid Juror Comments*: Had fun with it. Repeated the words and made a game out of guessing colors. "I want to watch it again, again." "So many new colors." "It was okay. I already knowed my colors." Video. 24 min.; $16.95; Age: 1-3. Image Factory, Inc.

*** So Smart! Vol. 1: Stimulating Sights and Sounds (So Smart!)

An infant stimulation video that uses images based on research related to babies' visual and auditory preferences and early cognitive development. Beautifully animated in black and white and complementary colors. Set to classical music. *Adult Juror Comments*: High quality, excellent visual and aural training for infants. Beautiful music. Carefully instructs parents on proper use. One adult juror said, "If accompanied by an adult, it's the only infant video I'd recommend." *Kid Juror Comments*: Excellent timing, very stimulating for infants. "Even my toddler sat and watched and told his baby sister what he saw on the screen." Video. 30 min.; $14.95; Age: 0-3. The Baby School Company Inc.

*** So Smart! Vol. 2: All About Shapes (So Smart!)

Exposes babies to geometric shapes and objects through clever transformations of Cecil Circle, Suzie Square, and Traci Triangle. Words appear on-screen, creating a new way for parents to read to their toddlers. *Adult Juror Comments*: Good introduction which explains how to use the video, recommended interaction with adult. Wonderful classical music, bright colors and movement suitable for infants. "I thought this would be boring, but it captivated all the kids for a long time." *Kid Juror Comments*: Adults were amazed at how long it actually engaged babies from three to fifteen months. The older ones watched for twenty-five minutes. Even the shyest said the name of a letter or object out loud. Toddlers and preschoolers chatted among themselves. Video. 30 min.; $14.95; Age: 0-3. The Baby School Company Inc.

Chapter One • Infants

*** So Smart! Vol. 3: All About Letters (So Smart!)*

Exposes babies to the shapes and forms of each letter of the alphabet. Older children begin to see the relationship between letters, words, and images. Parents can teach their child as each letter forms in a creative way. *Adult Juror Comments*: Letters are displayed individually and in the usual order. Excellent sound, animation, and editing. Simplicity appeals to young children. Offers potential for learning beyond what it presents such as playing memory games with the children. *Kid Juror Comments*: Children loved the "walking" shapes. Kids smiled and talked back to the video throughout the screening. Even one- and two-year-olds can benefit. Some got up and danced to music. Video. 30 min.; $14.95; Age: 1-3. The Baby School Company Inc.

** Toddler Takes (Toddlers at Play)

 Features dozens of children in natural settings delighting in their own achievement, falling down and bouncing back, learning to take turns at play, venting anger, sharing, and overcoming fears. *Adult Juror Comments*: Nice shots of toddlers being toddlers. Very appealing to children and adults. Entertaining, soothing, fun, and visually well done. Good discussion of toddler issues: anger, sharing, and talking. Little diversity is shown. *Kid Juror Comments*: Kids tuned in. The lack of excessive verbiage was appreciated by the children. The children responded by laughing and interacting with one another. Video. 25 min.; $12.95; Age: 1-5. Tow Truck Productions.

** Toddler Treasury, A

 Developed by the creator of Nickelodeon and Pinwheel for children under the age of three. Animated songs, stories, rhythms, and rhymes invite participation and creative play. *Adult Juror Comments*: Charming collection of nursery rhymes and tunes. Enjoyable; clear images; simple, familiar songs; suitable pacing. Good repeat viewing value. "The kids had more fun watching this program than I had expected." *Kid Juror Comments*: Children thoroughly enjoyed it and were actively involved and engaged in the songs and pictures. Good music choices—kids loved the familiar songs. Even a seven-month-old watched. Video. 18 min.; $14.95; Age: 1-3. Paragon Media.

** Under A Blue, Blue Sky (Babies at Play)

Explores the park, some puppies, a carnival, and other sunny places. Shows real toddlers in live-action segments. *Adult Juror Comments*: Good child-centered activities for this age. Nice ending segments on nap and sleep. Great for modeling play. Key words on screen are lost on younger preschoolers. Limited cultural diversity shown. *Kid Juror Comments*: Captured children's attention and left room for questions. Kids liked the songs and responded well to the activities. Comments and narration are age-appropriate. Series title "Babies at Play" is misleading. Kids shown are toddlers, not babies. Video. 38 min.; $12.98; Age: 1-3. Warner Home Video.

Category—Family

** Baby Bach (Baby Einstein)

Introduces infants and toddlers to Bach and other classical music in a whimsical presentation based on research in music therapy and its positive effects on children. *Adult Juror Comments*: Wholesome and aesthetically pleasing with a steady flow of music and objects. Somewhat slow. Well-produced, occasionally fragmented. Some toys shown are too sophisticated for babies to understand. Lacks cultural diversity. *Kid Juror Comments*: Liked the interaction with the puppets and the visuals of the young children. They identified several objects and knew what the objects were doing. Babies lost interest after a while. Best shown in segments. Video. 30 min.; $15.95; Age: 0-2. The Baby Einstein Company.

** Baby Einstein (Baby Einstein)

Addresses the theory that children exposed to different languages in the first year find it easier to learn foreign tongues later on. Stresses the alphabet, counting, and nursery rhymes. Uses real-world objects and phrases in foreign languages. *Adult Juror Comments*: Large pictures, colorful, gentle voices. Exposure to multi-ethnic sounds. A little slow-moving and choppy at times. Some visual scenes did not match the audio content. "I'd like to know how different languages at such short length help little ones." *Kid Juror Comments*: Babies enjoyed seeing familiar objects; some sat for at least half an hour, but some kids got very bored. Kids responded best to the English-language sections. Video. 30 min.; $15.95; Age: 0-2. The Baby Einstein Company.

Chapter One • Infants

* Baby Faces the Video (Baby Faces)

Shows 30 minutes of toddlers and children. Comes with an audio cassette with twenty nursery rhymes. *Adult Juror Comments*: Simple production with appealing photography and a variety of music. Suggests opportunities for adult/toddler interaction. Babies enjoy looking at other babies' faces. Although this has no value in terms of child development, it is entertaining. *Kid Juror Comments*: Most babies loved watching the other babies. The songs are appealing, but overall the video is long, slow, and non-engaging because it lacks structure. Video. 30 min.; $9.99; Age: 0-3. Brentwood Home Video.

*** Baby Mozart (Baby Einstein)

Infants and toddlers view a parade of colorful objects—simple visuals accompanied by the music of Mozart in arrangements designed to appeal to youthful ears. *Adult Juror Comments*: The toys, animals, and movements are captivating. Creative use of objects draws attention to the wonderful music of Mozart. Very age-appropriate. *Kid Juror Comments*: Lots of laughter. Children seemed attentive to Mozart and requested replays. "I know that song!" At the end of the tape children requested more "dance" music. Video. 30 min.; $15.95; Age: 0-2. The Baby Einstein Company.

** Good Morning Good Night: A Day on the Farm (Bo Peep)

Enjoy a day on the farm. Wake up with a little child and watch how all the farm animals get up. Everyone has something to eat. Then it's time to play. Did you know that pigs play ball? After all the fun, it's time to sleep. Accompanied by folk songs. *Adult Juror Comments*: Gentle and positive, though some camerawork is overexposed or underexposed. Shows good clips of farm animal behavior. Simple production, with upbeat music and a slow pace. Helpful resources are included - a songbook and recommended activities. *Kid Juror Comments*: Children moved along to the music, though some thought it was boring. They liked seeing the muddy pig and the boy feeding the dog. The younger kids pointed out which animals they recognized and compared them to others they had seen. Video. 17 min.; $14.95; Age: 1-3. Bo Peep Productions.

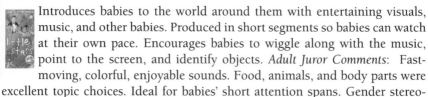

Age 0-2

Video

Family

* Little Stars

Introduces babies to the world around them with entertaining visuals, music, and other babies. Produced in short segments so babies can watch at their own pace. Encourages babies to wiggle along with the music, point to the screen, and identify objects. *Adult Juror Comments*: Fast-moving, colorful, enjoyable sounds. Food, animals, and body parts were excellent topic choices. Ideal for babies' short attention spans. Gender stereotyping when portraying babies in adult roles is unsuitable and disturbing. *Kid Juror Comments*: Smiled, pointed, and clapped their hands. The part about making friends and fitting into a group was well received and informative. Some wanted to watch it again. "Some children were spellbound—swaying, trying to dance." Video. 25 min.; $17.95; Age: 1-3. Big Chief, Inc./Tim Miller Entertainment.

*** Teletubbies: Bedtime Stories and Lullabies (Teletubbies)

It's bedtime for the Teletubbies. They grab their tubbytronic blankets and tuck themselves in with lullabies. Tinky Winky, Dipsy, Laa-Laa, and Po listen to the Itsy Bitsy Spider, Hey Diddle Diddle, and other lullabies and bedtime stories. *Adult Juror Comments*: Great. Bright colors, slow pace, nice transitions, fun jazz band. Encourages napping, going to bed, and teaches manners when somebody else is sleeping. Shows a preschooler help care for a sibling. Age-appropriate. Great diversity. Good parent guide. *Kid Juror Comments*: Familiar music a big hit. Kids loved singing along, doing the actions, and dancing. Shouted when they saw their favorite characters. "It was fun to look at." "Teletubbies treat each other right." Repeating the live characters was a plus. Video. 70 min.; $14.95; Age: 0-3. The Itsy Bitsy Entertainment Co.

*** Teletubbies: Big Hug (Teletubbies)

When a magic door appears, each Teletubby knocks and finds a big hug. Children are invited to sing and dance along. *Adult Juror Comments*: Wonderfully bright, crisp colors, soothing music. Engages kids in everyday behavior such as opening doors and knocking. Slow pace and repetition are very age-appropriate. Exhibits good diversity. Easily viewed in segments. *Kid Juror Comments*: Loved it. They hugged one another when they saw the Teletubbies hugging. Kids laughed out loud and shouted when the sun appeared. "I liked it so much because it's so funny." "Can we watch it again?" "I like how they're so nice to each other." Video. 60 min.; $14.95; Age: 0-3. The Itsy Bitsy Entertainment Co.

*** *Teletubbies: Dance with the Teletubbies (Teletubbies)*

A charming video about movement and play. As children interact with this video, they will clap their hands, stomp their feet, and wiggle their toes one at a time. *Adult Juror Comments*: Colorful, sweet, fun, childlike, well-produced. Predictable and consistent, which is age-appropriate for young children. Structured to encourage child's dancing and singing. Great modeling of sharing and taking turns. Little diversity. *Kid Juror Comments*: Appealing. Younger children responded enthusiastically to music: clapping, dancing, and squealing with laughter. At the end one child shouted, "More!" An older child commented—"If babies want to watch TV, Teletubbies is the best." Video. 60 min.; $14.95; Age: 1-3. Warner Home Video.

*** *Teletubbies: Favorite Things (Teletubbies)*

 Dance along with Dipsy and his hat. Help Laa-Laa find her ball. Sing a song with Tinky Winky and his magic bag. Take a ride with Po on her scooter! *Adult Juror Comments*: Bright, high contrast colors and simple, silly plot appealed to the youngest viewers. "Finding a scooter in a tree is hysterical to a toddler." Characters are helpful and kind to each other. Too long for one sitting. *Kid Juror Comments*: Enthralled them. Watched with delight from start to finish with lots of clapping and laughing. Almost all sang and danced along at every opportunity. Liked the repetition. "Do they wear diapers or underwear?" "Watch again." Video. 60 min.; $14.95; Age: 1-3. The Itsy Bitsy Entertainment Co.

*** *Teletubbies: Funny Day (Teletubbies)*

What happens when a puffy cloud comes indoors? Or, when a big ball of string appears in Teletubbyland? Uh-oh, there's a Teletubby mess! And lots of surprises are in store for Noo-Noo. *Adult Juror Comments*: Excellent production. Easily viewed in segments. "I love this video. It's charming, sweet, and age appropriate." Exposes children to new words. Models sharing behavior, curiosity, and fun. Repetition is used in a positive, relaxing way. *Kid Juror Comments*: Loved it. They sang, danced, giggled, and wanted to blow bubbles along with the kids on-screen. Wanted to watch it again. "We want to watch more Tubbies!" "I love La La." "I like how the Teletubbies take turns." "Where's Noo Noo?" "I like the bunnies." Video. 60 min.; $14.95; Age: 0-3. The Itsy Bitsy Entertainment Co.

Age 0-2

Video

Family

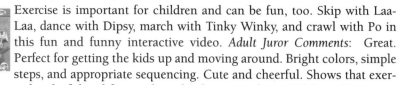

Age 0-2 · **Video** · **Family**

*** *Teletubbies: Go! Exercise with the Teletubbies (Teletubbies)*

Exercise is important for children and can be fun, too. Skip with Laa-Laa, dance with Dipsy, march with Tinky Winky, and crawl with Po in this fun and funny interactive video. *Adult Juror Comments*: Great. Perfect for getting the kids up and moving around. Bright colors, simple steps, and appropriate sequencing. Cute and cheerful. Shows that exercising can be playful and fun, and can be done anywhere. *Kid Juror Comments*: Kids exuberantly copied the movements, clapping and laughing. Watched it over and over. "It was fun fun." "We like to run and jump." "We did the exercises with them." "We learned to stand on one foot." "Ready-steady-go!" Video. 79 min.; $12.95; Age: 1-3. The Itsy Bitsy Entertainment Co.

*** *Teletubbies: Here Comes the Teletubbies (Teletubbies)*

The series was created to enhance a child's early development and creativity. When the wind blows, a magic windmill brings pictures from far away and the Teletubbies are joined to the world of real children celebrating the joy of play. *Adult Juror Comments*: Cute, endearing characters; simple story lines; well-presented. Age-appropriate use of predictions, math concepts, recall, and identification. Story lines are very simple and perfect for preschoolers. Music is catchy. *Kid Juror Comments*: Captivating. Kids wanted to watch it again. Viewers were enticed to pay attention by guessing what was going to happen next. Kids were fascinated; some vocalized, laughed, pointed, and mimicked. "I loved everything." Video. 60 min.; $14.95; Age: 1-3. Warner Home Video.

*** *Teletubbies: Nursery Rhymes (Teletubbies)*

Sing favorite nursery rhymes with the Teletubbies. Tinky Winky, Dipsy, Laa-Laa, and Po bring "Little Miss Muffet," "Jack and Jill," "Twinkle, Twinkle Little Star and other favorite nursery rhymes to life. *Adult Juror Comments*: Vivid colors. Filled with things toddlers love. Rhyme patterns promote language development. Encourages parents to sing and dance with kids. "Loved the repetition of songs and the real bunnies coupled with the story-board." *Kid Juror Comments*: Enjoyed the characters, bright colors, and noises. Engaging. They laughed, hummed, and sang along. "During Jack and Jill, when Jack falls down, all of the toddlers fell down." Eighteen month- to two-year-olds enjoyed it most. Video. 60 min.; $14.95; Age: 1-3. The Itsy Bitsy Entertainment Co.

Category—Holiday

*** Teletubbies: Christmas in the Snow (Teletubbies)

The Teletubbies have fun playing in the snow when it falls over Teletubbyland, covering all their favorite things. Tinky Winky, Dipsy, Laa-Laa, and Po build a snow tubby and take a peek at how children around the world celebrate Christmas. *Adult Juror Comments*: Conveys a peaceful and loving atmosphere. Even when it is snowing, the sun is shining. Great segments of different countries and Christmas traditions. "Too cute for words." *Kid Juror Comments*: Loved it. They danced, clapped, and sang along. Even the babies enjoyed watching the snow fall and pointed to the snowman. Older kids were curious about the different languages spoken. Best for this age when broken into smaller viewing segments. Video. 90 min.; $29.95; Age: 1-3. The Itsy Bitsy Entertainment Co.

*** Teletubbies: Magic Pumpkin and Other Stories, The (Teletubbies)

One day in Teletubbyland, a magic pumpkin appears. In keeping with the season, Tinky Winky, Dipsy, Laa-Laa, and Po watch children catch leaves. A fall wind takes Dipsy's hat for a ride. *Adult Juror Comments*: Great production, age appropriate lessons about seasons. Good Halloween program that's not scary. Teaches *please* and *thank you*, and uses a Jack O'Lantern to teach the names of facial features. Comes with a useful parents' guide. *Kid Juror Comments*: Smiles, laughter, clapping, and bouncing. "I want to watch it again pleeeease." "Now I want to make a pumpkin with leaves and glue." "I liked the way they made the pumpkin face." Video. 60 min.; $14.95; Age: 0-3. The Itsy Bitsy Entertainment Co.

Category—Music

** Baby Songs: Baby Rock (Baby Songs)

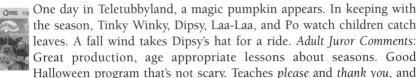Kids dance to rock and roll favorites. Ten song-filled, toe-tappin' vignettes include: Fats Domino's "I'm Walkin," Little Eva's "Locomotion," "Woolly Bully," and "Twist & Shout." *Adult Juror Comments*: Great tunes. Children enjoyed participating. Works best when viewed in segments. Appropriate use of language. Some safety concerns on this title, such as a child jumping on a bed near a window. *Kid Juror Comments*: Very colorful. Children enjoyed the character Baby Rock. Not all children appreciated the rock and roll music. Video. 30 min.; $12.98; Age: 1-5. Anchor Bay Entertainment.

*** Baby Songs: Baby Songs (Baby Songs)

Playfully portrays familiar themes for little people learning about the big world. *Adult Juror Comments*: Invites child/parent participation. Excellent photography. Zeroes in on what's important to children. Encourages joining in normal, natural activities by providing good examples. The cartoons shown before each song are particularly enjoyable. *Kid Juror Comments*: Children became very interested and engaged. They related to activities in the video: sleeping through the night, using the potty, and security blankets. Kids swayed to music, imitated the action, and identified with subject matter and characters. Video. 30 min.; $12.98; Age: 1-5. Anchor Bay Entertainment.

*** Baby Songs: Baby Songs Good Night (Baby Songs)

Contains ten original songs by Hap Palmer with live-action toddler shots. Lullabies and gentle songs designed to appeal to toddlers and parents. *Adult Juror Comments*: Super, well-produced. Sweet and calming, well-paced. Appropriate mix of fantasy and reality from dancing bears to real children playing with dolls. Age-appropriate images shown, such as sleeping, playing with parents, parents leaving and returning. *Kid Juror Comments*: Three- and four-year-olds sang and danced to the songs. Even two- and four-month-olds watched for fifteen minutes. All enjoyed the on-screen babies. One three-year-old wanted to watch it again immediately. Video. 30 min.; $12.98; Age: 1-5. Anchor Bay Entertainment.

*** Baby Songs: Even More Baby Songs (Baby Songs)

These Hap Palmer songs celebrate a child's everyday world, from getting up, eating and dressing, to everyone's favorite activity - playing. *Adult Juror Comments*: Very clever and lively, shows nice range of images, animation, live action, and graphics. Each song is introduced by engaging animation. One could view one segment at a time. Best for three-, four-, and five-year-olds. *Kid Juror Comments*: Very appealing. Music is fast, but it keeps their attention. Children giggled at the teddy bear. Video. 32 min.; $12.98; Age: 1-5. Anchor Bay Entertainment.

Chapter One • Infants

*** Baby Songs: Hap Palmer's Follow-along Songs (Baby Songs)

Imaginative, wonderful, joyful songs by Hap Palmer that invite kids to clap their hands, stamp their feet, dance, and act out the lyrics. Introduces colors and the alphabet and shows how to make musical instruments from ordinary things like bottle caps. *Adult Juror Comments*: Creatively inviting. Movement included children, held their attention. Music is great and lots of fun. Encourages participation even without guidance. Suggests activities and good songs to sing. *Kid Juror Comments*: Actively involved. Those familiar with the music were enthralled. Kids enjoyed acting like "monsters," tapping sticks and clapping. Video. 30 min.; $12.95; Age: 1-5. Anchor Bay Entertainment.

** Baby Songs: John Lithgow's Kid-Size Concert (Baby Songs)

 John Lithgow, with his infectious good humor, performs favorite children's songs, inviting the audience to sing along. From "She'll Be Coming Round the Mountain" to the story of "The Runaway Pancake," Lithgow delights with whimsy and song. *Adult Juror Comments*: Gentle and loving, Lithgow's a natural for kid songs. He's quiet, subtle, and relaxed. Child centered, child sensitive. Induces kids to sing along. *Kid Juror Comments*: Excellent choice of songs—toe-tappers and hand-clappers—and they come alive. Video. 32 min.; $12.98; Age: 2-8. Anchor Bay Entertainment.

*** Baby Songs: More Baby Songs (Baby Songs)

 Continues the energy of the original hit, "Baby Songs," with more playful songs. *Adult Juror Comments*: Great songs and lovely images of kids engaged in a variety of activities. Material is intelligent and sweet. The witch segment is not age-appropriate. *Kid Juror Comments*: Fun! Kids liked this and enjoyed repeated viewings, except for witch segment. Kids danced and attempted to sing along. Video. 30 min.; $12.98; Age: 1-5. Anchor Bay Entertainment.

** Baby Songs: Super Baby Songs (Baby Songs)

 From the creators of "Baby Songs" with irresistible sing-along songs from Hap Palmer, this upbeat collection contains such titles as "When Daddy Was a Little Boy," "Chomping Gum," "Hurry Up Blues" and "When Things Don't Go Your Way." *Adult Juror Comments*: Entertaining and well-produced. Great introductory song. Includes some nice role reversals and wonderful songs. Has some inappropriate behavior models for toddlers, balanced diversity. It's more for toddlers than "babies." *Kid Juror Comments*: The music was lovely. Kids tapped and sang along. A little long for attention spans of youngest kids. The claymation section (animation done with clay figures) moves pretty fast. Video. 30 min.; $12.98; Age: 3-7. Anchor Bay Entertainment.

* Infantastic Lullabyes (Infantastic Lullabyes)

Presents ways to communicate, educate, and entertain. Shapes, primary colors, animals, and easily recognizable objects are animated and set to familiar nursery songs, including "Row Your Boat" and "Rock-A-Bye." *Adult Juror Comments*: Beautiful images, visually appealing, and good music score make this an overall favorite. Useful for learning and entertaining. Jurors recommended using the program in small segments and encouraged active participation with parent or caregiver. *Kid Juror Comments*: Some kids liked this a lot, while others were so-so. The music captured their attention. This was an overall favorite with youngest children. They loved singing along. Video. 25 min.; $14.98; Age: 1-3. V.I.E.W. Video.

** On a Fun Rainy Day (Babies at Play)

Come in from splashing to enjoy a dressy tea party, baking cookies, fuzzy friends, and more. Shows real babies and toddlers at play. *Adult Juror Comments*: Well-paced, good interpretation of music and images. Well-produced. Perfect for age group. Kids are natural and appealing. Activities selected are age-appropriate. Good diversity shown. A little too long. *Kid Juror Comments*: "Cute babies." They loved the songs and the colorful images and clapped their hands while they watched. Stimulated discussion afterwards from older kids. Video. 37 min.; $12.98; Age: 1-3. Warner Home Video.

Category—Nature

** Kittens in the Country (Manitoulin Images)

Experience the sights and sounds of a farm as seen through the eyes of playful barnyard kittens. Contains footage of natural surroundings accompanied by gentle sounds and music. *Adult Juror Comments*: Lovely cinematography. Moves at a slow and soothing pace. Has a dreamlike quality. Farm animals are appealing. "Teddy bear swirling on the pond is a little surreal." "You can hear the birds sing and the cats purr. It's sweet." *Kid Juror Comments*: Captured their attention. They were intrigued by the lambs and the silly teddy bear in the water and talked about them afterwards. Kids giggled and pointed and meowed like the kitties. "My papa has ducks." "Pretty butterfly; see butterfly again?" Video. 36 min.; $19.95; Age: 0-2. Kids and Nature Videos.

*** Mozart Nature Symphonies (Video Soup)

  A soundtrack of Mozart accompanies scenes from nature and the animal world. *Adult Juror Comments*: Well produced, nice cinematography. Relaxing music. "Enjoyable, calming." Offers opportunities to discuss animal species and their habitats. *Kid Juror Comments*: Kids were both entranced and calmed. The images fascinated them, evoked pointing, smiling and swaying along to the music. "Can I see the elephant again?" Kids moved in and out of play as specific images caught their eye. Video. 32 min.; $12.95; Age: 0-3. Munchkin, Inc.

** Nature Babies (Video Soup)

 Shows lots of baby animals and their parents accompanied by jazzy instrumentals and soothing lullabies. *Adult Juror Comments*: Well-produced, familiar music. Quality visuals show variety of natural environments from jungle to snow and lots of different animals. Simple, repetitive content helps develop language skills. Parents are encouraged to watch with their babies. *Kid Juror Comments*: Kids watched intermittently. Long; best viewed in segments. Some children responded to the animals by touching the screen and smiling. The music didn't get them to sing or dance along. Video. 28 min.; $12.95; Age: 0-2. Munchkin, Inc.

Category—Special Interest

* Beach, The (Elbee's Babies Playing Series)

A non-scripted, non-narrative, action-oriented production showing babies between infancy and four years. Outdoor activities are filmed with natural sounds and music. It is simple and fun, showing contentment and joy. *Adult Juror Comments*: Good shots of babies walking, eating, and playing. Shows happy, positive emotions. Babies putting sandy things into their mouths disturbed some. Not much diversity. Jurors objected to the description on the box calling the tape a "baby-sitter." *Kid Juror Comments*: Evoked some interest, but not a great deal. They wandered in and out while viewing, which is a natural response for this age. Kids asked why there was only music, no talking. Program could be used to prepare for or reminisce about a trip to the beach. Video. 30 min.; $14.95; Age: 0-3. Elbee Productions.

Age 0-2

Video

Spec Int

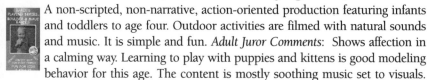

* Boulder & Maui Babies (Elbee's Babies Playing Series)

A non-scripted, non-narrative, action-oriented production featuring infants and toddlers to age four. Outdoor activities are filmed with natural sounds and music. It is simple and fun. *Adult Juror Comments*: Shows affection in a calming way. Learning to play with puppies and kittens is good modeling behavior for this age. The content is mostly soothing music set to visuals. Offers little educational or developmental value. *Kid Juror Comments*: Okay. Limited interest to babies - does not hold their interest for long. Toddlers wander in and out of room. Some ignored it completely. This could be useful for quiet time/nap/bedtime. Video. 30 min.; $14.95; Age: 0-2. Elbee Productions.

* Hi Daddy! (Hi Daddy!)

Captures the magic created when dads play with their babies. Babies will hear familiar tunes, watch laughing faces similar to their own, and tumble with their fathers. *Adult Juror Comments*: Dads who watched this were amused, but not eager to watch again. Songs were familiar. Shows good racial diversity and a pleasant interaction between parent and child. Poor production quality and nothing to hold a baby's attention. *Kid Juror Comments*: Even older children were delighted to see the daddies for short periods of time. Initially there was a lot of pointing and bouncing to the music, but overall they were easily bored. The children enjoyed the music and laughed at times. Video. 30 min.; $12.95; Age: 0-2. ELC Productions, LLC.

* It's Potty Time (The Duke Family Series)

Makes toilet training something it's never been: FUN. Demonstrates ideal manners portrayed by boys and girls attending a birthday party. Uses songs to capture and keep children's attention. *Adult Juror Comments*: Simple, straightforward handling of the subject matter that has a creative slant. An entertaining approach to potty etiquette. The sing-along is effective; the Raggedy Ann story was a good addition. At times, talks down to children and is too silly. *Kid Juror Comments*: Kids age two related to it best. It's not appropriate for children much older or younger. Video. 30 min.; $14.98; Age: 1-5. Learning Through Entertainment, Inc.

* It's Sleepy Time (The Duke Family Series)

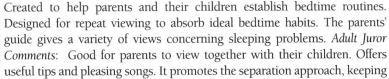

Created to help parents and their children establish bedtime routines. Designed for repeat viewing to absorb ideal bedtime habits. The parents' guide gives a variety of views concerning sleeping problems. *Adult Juror Comments*: Good for parents to view together with their children. Offers useful tips and pleasing songs. It promotes the separation approach, keeping children out of parents' beds whatever the situation, and portrays a very middle-class lifestyle. *Kid Juror Comments*: Most appropriate for parents when it fits within their value structure. Kids thought it was okay, but didn't stay with it. It's best viewed with parents. Children thought the songs were bossy. "It made me think about being nice." Video. 30 min.; $14.98; Age: 1-6. Learning Through Entertainment, Inc.

** Let's Dance on the Farm (Let's Dance)

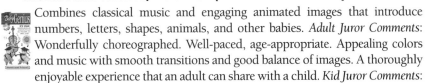

Visits the "Adventure Farm" and introduces preschoolers to farm animals through song and dance. *Adult Juror Comments*: Simple production. Contains good content on natural world. Used by parents and children together, it maximizes the opportunity for children to play along. *Kid Juror Comments*: Okay. Two's and three's loved it and tried their hardest to move along with it. Even crawlers enjoyed moving to it. Video. 30 min.; $14.95; Age: 1-4. Dance Adventure Entertainment.

*** Mozart and Friends, Volume I (Mozart and Friends)

Combines classical music and engaging animated images that introduce numbers, letters, shapes, animals, and other babies. *Adult Juror Comments*: Wonderfully choreographed. Well-paced, age-appropriate. Appealing colors and music with smooth transitions and good balance of images. A thoroughly enjoyable experience that an adult can share with a child. *Kid Juror Comments*: Captivated them. Kids were glued to the screen and readily responded to familiar objects. They pretended to be airplanes and responded to the animals with animal sounds. "They begged to see it again. I couldn't rewind it fast enough." Video. 36 min.; $12.98; Age: 0-2. Genius Products.

** Mozart and Friends, Volume II: Sleepytime (Mozart and Friends)

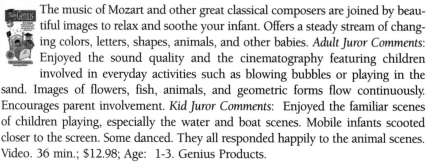

The music of Mozart and other great classical composers are joined by beautiful images to relax and soothe your infant. Offers a steady stream of changing colors, letters, shapes, animals, and other babies. *Adult Juror Comments*: Enjoyed the sound quality and the cinematography featuring children involved in everyday activities such as blowing bubbles or playing in the sand. Images of flowers, fish, animals, and geometric forms flow continuously. Encourages parent involvement. *Kid Juror Comments*: Enjoyed the familiar scenes of children playing, especially the water and boat scenes. Mobile infants scooted closer to the screen. Some danced. They all responded happily to the animal scenes. Video. 36 min.; $12.98; Age: 1-3. Genius Products.

* Playground, The (Elbee's Babies Playing Series)

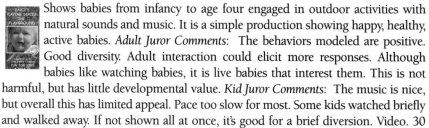

Shows babies from infancy to age four engaged in outdoor activities with natural sounds and music. It is a simple production showing happy, healthy, active babies. *Adult Juror Comments*: The behaviors modeled are positive. Good diversity. Adult interaction could elicit more responses. Although babies like watching babies, it is live babies that interest them. This is not harmful, but has little developmental value. *Kid Juror Comments*: The music is nice, but overall this has limited appeal. Pace too slow for most. Some kids watched briefly and walked away. If not shown all at once, it's good for a brief diversion. Video. 30 min.; $14.95; Age: 0-2. Elbee Productions.

Chapter Two

Preschool (Ages 2-5)

By Dr. Bettye Caldwell

My tennis club has a wonderful child-care center in full view of the courts. As an inveterate (and professional) child-watcher, I never pass it without pausing to look at the children and their play-school equipment: climbing bars, a maze appropriate for preschoolers, various hoops and balls of different sizes, a see-saw, and even a small merry-go-round. Mounted on one wall is—you guessed it—a television/VCR set. Whenever I walk by, it's always turned on. Of the approximately 20 children in the play school, about 15 are on the floor, watching whatever is on the monitor. The maze is empty, just like all the other equipment. If I spot one brave little soul wandering around with a ball in hand, that is unusual.

The message is clear: the power of our television screens is so great that it can nullify the best designed, most attractive play equipment available—the kind that children used to pine for and which can still provide important benefits. Preschoolers need to exercise their muscles as much as their mothers and fathers do on the tennis court! They need to be involved in active, not passive, learning most of the time. Because the "moving picture" dominates today's pop culture, throbbing with compelling images and attractive sound and color, we cannot be indifferent to what our children observe. Note that I didn't write "watch," the verb we generally use when talking about television and videos. For children do much more than watch: they listen, they process images and sounds, they respond with body movements and emotional and verbal expressions. And they absorb and retain for a long time the impressions that profoundly influence their developing brains, their interests, and their emerging values.

Interestingly, children don't have to *learn* to receive television and video messages the way they must *learn* to read and write. There is no television code to crack in order to comprehend and remember what appears on the screen, no motor movements to be mastered. If a child is born with the usual complement of sensory receivers—good eyes and ears—and a brain capable of making connections between these sensory systems, they are able to "receive" television and video shortly after birth. This built-in receptivity demands that parents and adults who supplement parental care with children's media be acutely sensitive to the format and content of the programs their young children observe. This kind of adult awareness requires vigilance; they need to "screen" what their young children will see on the small screen as carefully as they screen books and other experiences they want their children to either encounter or avoid.

So much for playing defense. Playing offense multiplies the benefits. When parents watch a video or a program on television or play with a CD-ROM together with their child, the benefits are tremendous. Let's be honest. Videos, TV, or CD-ROMs can be a godsend when we are trying to prepare dinner, make an important telephone call, or have an intimate adult conversation. At such times, a wisely selected program can give you just the break you need. But be sure you also take the time to watch programs with your child as often as you can. Not only does that give parent and child an opportunity for emotional closeness and perhaps physical contact, it also communicates to the child your conviction that his or her interests are valid. Moreover, it naturally opens the door to something as simple as further conversation—the questions and answers and comments that are a vital part of growing up, discovering ideas, and exploring new worlds.

The Coalition for Quality Children's Media has provided a wonderful set of tools for parents of preschoolers and for early-child-care professionals. This chapter offers an invaluable guide to videos and CD-ROMs appropriate for preschoolers. Preschool children themselves have found the selections entertaining. The evaluations don't tell parents what to do or buy or how many hours to allow for television; it simply gives them accurate and informative guidelines that enable them to make their own good choices. And good choices are what we all want to make and what our children need from us.

Dr. Bettye Caldwell is a professor of Pediatrics and Child Development and Education at the University of Arkansas Children's Hospital. A former president of the National Association for the Education of Young Children, Dr. Caldwell has published more than 200 articles and received many awards, including the 1990 National Governors' Association Distinguished Citizen Award.

Chapter Two • Preschool

Format—CD-ROM
Category—Education/Instruction

Age 2-5

** A to Zap!

 Teaches letters and words. Explores concepts such as over and under or quick versus slow. Offers 26 different activities. *Adult Juror Comments*: Easy to use. Fun, interactive approach. Good characters. Kids liked the orchestra at the beginning and the variety of activities. It does require small-muscle coordination, making it somewhat difficult for the youngest users. *Kid Juror Comments*: Really nice, especially the orchestra section at the beginning and the various activities throughout. Kids said they would play it at least once or twice. CD-ROM. WIN/MAC; $14.95; Age: 3-7. Sunburst Technology/Houghton Mifflin.

CD-ROM

Edu/Instru

** Alphabet Adventure with Digby and Lydia (Learning Ladder)

 Teaches the alphabet through storytelling, music, and animation. Using Quicktime movies, songs, and interactive tests, kids find hidden letters and learn word association and the alphabet. Rewards spelling, reading, and perception. *Adult Juror Comments*: Simple presentation. Great characters, good developmental level. Comes with good adult handbook. Voice-overs are respectful, instructive, and reassuring. "Click-and-point friendly." Minimal choice of levels. *Kid Juror Comments*: Story held interest of five- and six-year-olds; three- and four-year-olds liked the games. Unless computer literate, help is needed to fully utilize the program. Kids liked the lively music and printing out the awards. CD-ROM. WIN/MAC; $34.95; Age: 3-5. Panasonic Interactive Media.

** Alphabet Band (My First Interactive Story Book)

See the jazzy jaguars jog the trails with jingle bells around their tails. Look at Piggy play piano songs while penguins lead the sing-along. Join Puppy in this interactive program and storybook that introduces letters of the alphabet. *Adult Juror Comments*: Cute pictures and engaging rhymes. Installs easily. Does not hold player's place or offer multiple skill levels. Screen changes slowly. Jurors had some technical problems. Puppy gives positive praise such as, "Terrific, you did that in a snap." *Kid Juror Comments*: Loved the music and the games. Stimulated interest in musical instruments. "I want to find the hidden music clues so I can sing along." "I want to play a tuba like the tiger does." "I like the puzzles and printing out the pictures I made." CD-ROM. WIN/MAC; $9.99; Age: 2-5. Publications International, LTD.

** Arthur's Reading Race

Takes children on a walk around town with Arthur and his little sister, D.W. Children are encouraged to learn words throughout the story and through three additional activities. *Adult Juror Comments*: Slick, high-quality production. Excellent graphics, fun games. Develops word recognition, increases vocabulary, reading comprehension, computer literacy. "Great early-learning title." Jurors thought Arthur and D.W. were at times rude to each other. *Kid Juror Comments*: Kids enjoyed playing the "let me write" games, because they make nonsense sentences. They also like the clickable window and ice cream section and enjoyed playing it with their friends. Works best in a situation where kids can play repeatedly. CD-ROM. WIN/MAC; $29.95; Age: 3-6. Learning Company.

*** Bear in the Big Blue House:
Bears Sense of Adventure (Playzone)

Features Bear and his friends from the TV show with twenty activities, five adventures, and lots of songs. Teaches problem-solving, creativity, sharing, self-awareness, and imagination. Storybooks are printable. *Adult Juror Comments*: Easy to use. Great sound and graphics. Five missions are provided to introduce the five senses. Other activities address concentration skills, creativity, and problem-solving. Offers different levels for different age and skill level. *Kid Juror Comments*: Younger children had some difficulties; older kids loved the whole thing. They enjoyed playing together and helping one other. They loved searching for things the program asks for. Having the Bear showing up after each game became annoying. CD-ROM. WIN; min.; $30; Age: 2-8. Knowledge Adventure.

*** Blue's Clues: 1, 2, 3 Time Activities (Blue's Clues)

Practice pre-math and problem-solving skills with multi-level learning games. Teaches logical thinking, deductive reasoning skills, and recognition of complete patterns. Strengthens early math skills as kids help Blue win. *Adult Juror Comments*: Easy to use. Emphasizes good manners. Instills pride in achievement. Accurate facts and information. Reinforces counting skills. Characters are cute and colorful. Has areas for different age groups. Difficulty increases automatically. Good diversity. *Kid Juror Comments*: Enjoyed it. Most kids wanted to play it again...tomorrow. "Do I have to stop? When is it my turn again?" Difficult for some. "They are happy." "Blue is my friend." "It was fun. I won a lot, but it's okay to lose, you still get money." CD-ROM. WIN/MAC; $19.99; Age: 3-6. Humongous Entertainment.

Chapter Two • Preschool

*** Disney's Animated Storybook, Winnie the Pooh and the Honey Tree (Disney's Animated Storybook)*

 Read, sing, and play along with Winnie the Pooh. A friendly bear and a familiar story offer a jump into Pooh's world for exciting adventures. Pooh, Piglet, Tigger, and the gang make reading lively and fun. *Adult Juror Comments*: Makes an excellent first CD-ROM for children. It is well-organized, easy to use, and encourages independence. Familiarity with characters and art add to its appeal. Content and material are age-appropriate though they lack depth. *Kid Juror Comments*: Kids enjoyed the characters. They liked hearing the book in Spanish as well as in English. Games section is perfect for preschoolers. Kids weren't interested in playing the storybook section more than once. CD-ROM. WIN; $29.95; Age: 2-6. Disney Interactive.

*** Disney's Ready for Math with Pooh (Disney's Learning Series)*

 In the heart of the 100 Acre Wood, math is an adventure. Pooh and friends guide children through activities that reinforce beginning math skills. Fun rewards are used to build their own gardens. Counting, sorting, adding, and subtracting are covered. *Adult Juror Comments*: Excellent production quality. Quite creative and fun to do. Adorable use of characters in imaginative setting. Reinforces problem-solving, critical thinking, and visual and motor skills. Holds place when play is interrupted. *Kid Juror Comments*: Very easy for child to operate. Kids loved this. Easy to use without much assistance. "The characters were awfully polite to each other." "Rabbit wasn't so grumpy today." Praises the children—definitely a confidence booster. CD-ROM. WIN/MAC; $39.99; Age: 3-7. Disney Interactive.

*** Disney's Ready to Read with Pooh (Disney's Learning Series)*

 Pooh and friends guide children through activities that stimulate imagination and reinforce critical skills. Offers lots of surprises as kids learn to read through play and collecting fun rewards. Includes alphabet, phonics, spelling, and rhyming. *Adult Juror Comments*: Adorable. Excellent graphics, good variety of characters, imaginative setting, flows easily. Reinforces pre-writing skills. Sometimes difficult. A loving, polite group of animals help provide good role models for self-esteem and friendship. *Kid Juror Comments*: "It's magic." Characters and music help hold kids' interest. They can navigate without much help. Kids wanted to play over and over again. They stayed in at lunch, recess, and after school to play. CD-ROM. WIN/MAC; $39.99; Age: 3-7. Disney Interactive.

** Do You Wish You Could Fly?

This compilation of original songs by Kathy Byers is intended for children and caregivers alike with each playback and performance. *Adult Juror Comments*: Good production with lyrics that work well. Fun songs that lend themselves to creative movement. Integrates themes such as brushing teeth, fear of darkness, and the sounds of nature. Some Christian content. *Kid Juror Comments*: Enthusiastic. Would listen to the songs again. "I was sad when someone got hurt and no-one wanted to kiss their boo-boos." "My mommy teaches me to brush my teeth too." "It was fun to pretend to make rain sounds." CD-ROM. 20 min.; $15.99; Age: 3-6. 2 Media.

*** Dr. Seuss Kindergarten (Dr. Seuss)

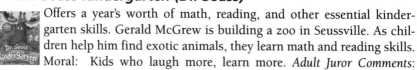 Offers a year's worth of math, reading, and other essential kindergarten skills. Gerald McGrew is building a zoo in Seussville. As children help him find exotic animals, they learn math and reading skills. Moral: Kids who laugh more, learn more. *Adult Juror Comments*: Superb. Fantasyland draws child in, offers breaks and playtime. Learn, participate, watch, listen, and sing along. Gets progressively harder. "I wish all CD-ROMs were as entertaining, educational, and engaging." Creative, well-planned. *Kid Juror Comments*: Kids loved this. They enjoyed checking their progress throughout the game. They didn't want to stop playing and were inspired to read the books. "Dr. Seuss put me in the mood to do math. It's like solving a puzzle. I felt good when I got it right." CD-ROM. WIN/MAC; $19.99; Age: 3-7. Learning Company.

*** Dr. Seuss Preschool (Dr. Seuss)

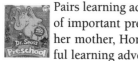 Pairs learning activities with a guided adventure. Offers a year's worth of important preschool skills. While helping baby Elma Sue look for her mother, Horton the faithful elephant leads children on a delightful learning adventure. *Adult Juror Comments*: Appealing. Keeps with the spirit of Dr. Seuss' stories with classic characters, great content, and good reinforcement for number, letter, and color recognition. Appropriately challenging. "I have played many kids' CD-ROMs and this is one of the best." *Kid Juror Comments*: Definitely a hit. A three-year-old could do it with little assistance. "The kids were spellbound from the beginning." Children remained involved with the characters and enjoyed learning material. Great value for home learning. "They're funny." CD-ROM. WIN/MAC; $19.99; Age: 3-5. Learning Company.

* Dr. Seuss's ABC

The magic of Dr. Seuss' books comes to life in this introduction to reading. *Adult Juror Comments*: Very cute and a pleasure to play. Requires high-level vocabulary for alphabet learning. Has limited educational value. Jurors weren't crazy about "alphabet" programming, but using the Dr. Seuss characters, a perennial favorite, made it palatable. *Kid Juror Comments*: Some children adored it, particularly those who are Seuss fans. Humor is catchy. Did not hold most children's interest through to the end. CD-ROM. WIN/MAC; $29.95; Age: 2-5. Learning Company.

** Fisher-Price Ready for School - Toddler

Join the Little People characters on a magical journey of learning and discovery created just for toddlers. Disk One includes 20 activities, carefully planned to help toddlers discover the world around them. Disc Two is a parenting guide. *Adult Juror Comments*: Positive, clear linear presentation, child-centered, encourages self-esteem. Variety of music, cultures, and experiences. Animated flash cards and worksheets offer minimal educational fare. Information on nutrition and breast-feeding are excellent. *Kid Juror Comments*: Quite enchanting. Wanted to play again. Easy, though child still needs adult help. Has two levels of difficulty. Requires direct parent involvement. CD-ROM. WIN/MAC; $20; Age: 3-6. Knowledge Adventure.

** Fisher-Price Time to Play Pet Shop (Fisher-Price CD-Roms)

 Children are invited to run their very own pet shop, selecting cute dogs, cats, fish, reptiles, hamsters, bunnies, and other critters. Six activities allow them to care for, groom, and feed the animals. Offers a unique experience each time they play. *Adult Juror Comments*: Good combination of cute animals and catchy songs. Easy installation. Reinforces the need to take care of pets, introduces various types of pets, and encourages decision-making. Mouse response is overly sensitive. Overuses the phrase "real good." *Kid Juror Comments*: Riveting for younger children. Preschoolers wanted to play this over and over. Instructions are very clear. Kids enjoyed the selection of items they can print. They came away with a renewed interest in taking care of animals. It was a favorite. CD-ROM. WIN/MAC; $20; Age: 3-6. Knowledge Adventure.

** Franklin Goes to School (Franklin the Turtle)

Invites children to accompany Franklin and his friends on their school journey. Teaches early curriculum skills using eight activities with three levels of difficulty. Parents are able to monitor and evaluate their child's progress. *Adult Juror Comments*: Educational, fun activities with clear, vivid colors and charming graphics. Easy to install. Great role models—characters are all kind to one another. Encourages critical thinking and problem-solving. Offers positive rewards. *Kid Juror Comments*: Loved it, laughed a lot, wanted to play it all the time. Kids particularly enjoyed the theater game. They played it several times. Children wanted to know what color and shape things are. Those who aren't mouse proficient were not able to play. CD-ROM. WIN; $30; Age: 2-5. Knowledge Adventure.

** Fun with Numbers (My First Interactive Story Book)

Solve a puzzle. Connect the dots. Match the pairs. Read along with Puppy in this interactive CD-ROM and storybook and explore the fun of starting to count. Uses interactive story screens, sing and learn songs, and problem-solving games. *Adult Juror Comments*: Easy to use. Characters are cute with appealing colors and personalities. Offers a variety of games. Lacks skill levels. "It impressed me that everything in the book was on the CD, only interactive." "Feedback was positive and genuine." *Kid Juror Comments*: "It was so great I didn't want to eat dinner. My mom let me finish playing after I ate—I ate fast." "I liked the funny things like the bouncing bubbles and singing fish." " My friends can play this when they come over." "I liked singing along." CD-ROM. WIN/MAC; $9.99; Age: 3-6. Publications International, LTD.

*** I Spy Junior (I Spy)

Based on the award winning "I Spy" book series. Can you figure out where to park the airplane? Visit the block farm or the nature area and use your magnifying glass to find hidden objects. Features over 70 picture riddles, puzzles, and games. *Adult Juror Comments*: Installs easily. Bright, clear graphics. Provides many opportunities for developing problem-solving skills in an exciting and interesting format. A fun feature is finding the player's name hidden throughout the games. *Kid Juror Comments*: They did not want to stop playing. Proficiency with a mouse is required. "It's cool. It's awesome." "I like all the games." "Oh! I see my name!" "The magnifier is the best." "I learned how to sort and match patterns." "My brother will love this!" CD-ROM. WIN/MAC; $29.95; Age: 2-5. Scholastic Entertainment.

*** Jumpstart: Baby Ball (Jumpstart)

 Peripheral to Jumpstart Baby CD-ROM that provides an alternative to the keyboard and mouse, making computer play easier and more comfortable for toddlers. Presents eight play areas designed to stimulate visual and auditory development. *Adult Juror Comments*: Easy to use. Brightly colored, cute songs, gentle narration with supportive language and adorable bear. Very supportive, kind, positive language used. "My 16-month-old learned to use the baby ball and now plays and enjoys the game frequently." *Kid Juror Comments*: Kids loved it, were mesmerized. They danced along. "A friendly bear I can dance and sing with." "I like the Teddy Bear and the colors." "My four-year-old took over the program after my one-year-old tired of it after 15-20 minutes. CD-ROM. WIN/MAC; $30; Age: 1-3. Knowledge Adventure.

Chapter Two • Preschool

*** *Jumpstart: Kindergarten Reading (Jumpstart)*

A grade-based reading program that gives kindergartners an early start in their reading efforts by teaching ten fundamental reading concepts and reinforcing these concepts with extended activities in printable color and written pages. *Adult Juror Comments*: Good songs, engaging games, enticing rewards. Gives gentle suggestions to try different sections. Contains a bonus section for adults that enables them to check each child's progress. *Kid Juror Comments*: Good variety of activities, music and graphics, but kids found that sometimes the program requested things they didn't know, such as "What is a vowel?" CD-ROM. WIN/MAC; $33; Age: 4-6. Knowledge Adventure.

*** *Jumpstart: Preschool (Jumpstart)*

 Join animal pals as they explore a colorful classroom of ten interactive play areas covering more than 20 preschool skills such as colors, shapes, letters, numbers, pre-reading, music, and listening. *Adult Juror Comments*: Easy to install, excellent levels of difficulty. Much better than the previous version, better graphics, lots of positive feedback, one click to move, low frustration factor. "Assesses difficulty and moves it up, but parent can also choose levels." *Kid Juror Comments*: "I loved it." Gave children confidence for activities at their own levels. Instills pride in personal achievement. CD-ROM. WIN/MAC; $20; Age: 2-5. Knowledge Adventure.

*** *Jumpstart: Spanish (Jumpstart)*

 Designed for preschool kids when they are most receptive to learning and retaining a new language. Kids explore ten activities introducing more than two hundred words and conversational phrases, providing a solid bilingual foundation. *Adult Juror Comments*: Stimulates language development. Audio is awesome, satisfying, and gratifying—everything a learning program should be. Easy to install and use. *Kid Juror Comments*: Great. "Let's do this again." Kids were so occupied with the activities they didn't realize they were learning how to say words in Spanish. Couldn't wait to take turns. A little frustrating for some. CD-ROM. WIN/MAC; $30; Age: 3-6. Knowledge Adventure.

*** *Jumpstart: Toddlers (Jumpstart)*

 Offers interactive activities designed specifically for toddlers where they can explore colors, numbers, letters, and shapes. *Adult Juror Comments*: Critical thinking skills are used throughout the program. Stimulates language development while improving communication. Encourages polite behavior and cooperation. Has two very different levels for toddlers. *Kid Juror Comments*: Enjoyable. The mouse is set up for usage by a young child. Kids liked the music section that allowed them to add instruments to the piece that is already playing. Their favorite parts were grandma's house, coloring, the alphabet game, and singing. CD-ROM. WIN/MAC; $20; Age: 2-5. Knowledge Adventure.

** Let's Go Read! An Island Adventure (Let's Go Read)

Develops reading, comprehension, and vocabulary skills while interacting with friendly characters and a colorful environment. Multi-leveled activities with interactive books allow children to choose the ending they prefer. *Adult Juror Comments*: Reinforces and encourages fundamental reading, thinking skills, and cooperative behavior. Develops beginning reading skills and other fundamental skills such as matching and discrimination. Does not allow the player to bypass certain tasks. *Kid Juror Comments*: Kids enjoyed how the characters encouraged each other. "If I learn to read, you can too." Parts were frustrating for kids. Technically difficult. Child cannot bypass certain tasks, must complete before moving on. Too slow for kids who are readers. CD-ROM. WIN/MAC; $44.95; Age: 3-6. Edmark.

** Magic Letter Factory, The

A challenging romp through an introduction to reading. Brimming with interactive pre-reading adventures and Hap Palmer songs and videos. Includes four Hap Palmer alphabet songs that can be played on any CD player. *Adult Juror Comments*: Very cute, but a little slow. Best for pre-readers developing early reading skills. Pace good for this audience. Voices are irritating and a little hard to understand. *Kid Juror Comments*: Most children found transition difficult and slow. One two-year-old loved this. Challenging content for three-year-olds, while some four's and five's were eager to demonstrate the parts they liked best. CD-ROM. WIN/MAC; $29.95; Age: 2-5. Educational Activities, Inc.

*** Microsoft Actimates Early Learning System

The system captivates children with fun, educational activities using preschooler character, Barney, as a 16-inch plush toy, accompanied with software and videos. *Adult Juror Comments*: Potential as a teaching tool is fantastic. Respectful of children and diversity. Paced well with gentle, non-threatening appeal. Large vocabulary. Responds to signals by external media such as TV. "This doll has endless possibilities." *Kid Juror Comments*: "My son enjoyed the Barney doll by itself and was fascinated with the interactivity between the video and CD-ROM. It increased his computer skills." When the doll is not receiving any stimuli, it announces it's "tired" and turns itself off. CD-ROM. WIN; $99.99; Age: 3-7. Microsoft.

Chapter Two • Preschool

*** *Microsoft Actimates Interactive Teletubbies* (*Microsoft Actimates*)

 Modeled after the characters in the television program, Actimates Teletubbies are interactive dolls which teach about cause and effect. The more children play with them, the more complex the interactions become. Requires some instruction by parents. *Adult Juror Comments:* Wholesome and appropriate, this is a cheerful and loving toy. The games are interesting and educational. Good sound quality and not too loud. Although the manual promotes it as self-teaching, jurors found initial instruction from an adult most beneficial. *Kid Juror Comments:* Children hugged and kissed Po, watched to the maximum of their attention spans, and were reluctant to give him up. "I know the colors and could say the names of the shapes!" They were having so much fun they returned to it again and again. CD-ROM. TOY; $59.95; Age: 2-4. Microsoft.

** *Microsoft My Personal Tutor*

A comprehensive learning solution for families with children ages three to seven. Contains hundreds of activities, games, tutorials, and songs that encourage confidence, exploration, and a love of learning. *Adult Juror Comments:* Well-designed with a variety of information. Good graphics with clear and vivid colors. User-friendly, good pace, age-appropriate vocabulary. Levels of difficulty are gradual enough for child to be successful. There are "no wrong answers." *Kid Juror Comments:* Most children liked this program and asked to play it again. Five-year-olds could navigate on their own with occasional help. Kids really enjoyed the graphics. CD-ROM. WIN; $54.95; Age: 3-7. Microsoft.

*** *Millie and Bailey Kindergarten* (*Millie and Bailey Early Learning*)

 Features well-structured activities designed to build a solid foundation in basic skills that support a child through kindergarten and beyond. Covers math, reading, language arts, science, problem-solving, and critical thinking. *Adult Juror Comments:* Excellent, very appealing. Works smoothly and mistakes are handled thoughtfully. The "discovery mode" is particularly good, stimulating exploration. Promotes critical thinking and problem-solving skills. Little diversity. *Kid Juror Comments:* Children learn while they're having fun. They enjoyed the question-and-answer section best. Younger children may need adult help. Encourages kids' self-esteem. Rewards correct answers, gently corrects errors. Kids learn from their mistakes. CD-ROM. WIN/MAC; $29.95; Age: 3-6. Edmark.

** *Phonics Adventure with Sing-Along Sam (Learning Ladder)*

Animated program teaches basic phonic skills with fifteen tunes and twelve sequenced lessons. Teaches letter and sound recognition, consonant and vowel blends, and simple sentence structure. At the end, child's name is included in the "Hall of Fame." *Adult Juror Comments*: Good tool that develops early reading skills. Wonderful for beginners. Some thought it dragged a bit. Feedback doesn't emphasize the positive. Easy to install. *Kid Juror Comments*: Good program. Most kids enjoyed it. Those who didn't, at first, were later drawn into playing with the game. CD-ROM. WIN/MAC; $34.95; Age: 4-6. Panasonic Interactive Media.

* *Phonics Fun (My First Interactive Story Book)*

Read along with Puppy in this interactive CD and storybook. Puppy will teach basic phonics skills with ten interactive story screens, five sing-and-learn songs, and five problem-solving games. *Adult Juror Comments*: Easy to install. Runs slow. Bright colors, cute characters, and simple story. Activities are challenging. Gives positive feedback, but has no help or skill levels. Doesn't intuit when a child needs help. "For a computer game, it's a bit ignorant." *Kid Juror Comments*: Some were reluctant to play again. "It was okay. I liked making pictures and printing them." "These matching games are hard." "I liked how the dog says nice things when you are done." "I want to find out more about lady bugs." CD-ROM. WIN/MAC; $9.99; Age: 3-6. Publications International, LTD.

** *Pound Puppies Interactive Storybook & Activity Ctr*

The player becomes the star. After a puppy is adopted from the pound, the puppy follows the child throughout the story. Teaches basic reading skills at multiple skill levels. Includes a paint program. *Adult Juror Comments*: Stimulates awareness about pets and veterinarians. Challenging game levels. Great coloring book, entertaining story. Good for inexperienced users. Some feedback is lost on non-readers. Contains some gender stereotyping. Doesn't hold child's place. *Kid Juror Comments*: They liked seeing their names in the story. The puzzles, picking the puppy, painting with the rainbow, and the puppy theme were favorite parts. Pre-readers found it difficult. Girls enjoyed it best. Some kids were quickly bored. CD-ROM. WIN; $19.95; Age: 3-6. El-ko Interactive.

Chapter Two • Preschool

*** Reading Blaster: Ages 4-6 (Blaster)*

 A brightly colored world filled with friendly fish helps kindergart-ners in a reading adventure. Kids can choose from nine activities that will build their reading abilities and introduce them to 750 vocabu-lary words. *Adult Juror Comments*: Teaches beginning reading skills through positive reinforcement, trial and error, and listening to instructions. Music, voices, and animation are excellent. Sustains attention throughout. *Kid Juror Comments*: Enjoyed the activities including the difficult sections. Installation and levels required adult assistance. "Gives stars when everything is right." Kids enjoyed the letter bubbles, stories, mazes, and the treasure hunt. "Makes me want to read." CD-ROM. WIN/MAC; $30; Age: 4-6. Knowledge Adventure.

*** Reading Fun (My First Interactive Story Book)*

 Learn to read with a puppy. CD-ROM and accompanying book teach basic reading skills through interactive story screens, songs, and problem-solving games. Contains more than 200 words. Has minimal computer memory requirements. *Adult Juror Comments*: Easy to use, although difficult to exit. Catchy music. Games have progressive learn-ing levels and positive reinforcement. Very age-appropriate. "Many wonderful fea-tures—builds vocabulary with animated definitions and a friendly speaker." *Kid Juror Comments*: Children loved the puppy instructor. "They didn't want me to turn it off." Kids had a great time learning to follow the maze and use the mouse. "More puppy games!" Children said they would play it again. CD-ROM. WIN/MAC; $9.99; Age: 3-6. Publications International, LTD.

*** Sesame Street: Elmo's Reading: Preschool & Kindergarten (Sesame Street)*

More than forty reading activities introduce children to letter recognition, phonics, word building, spelling, vocabulary, early sentence structure, and com-prehension. *Adult Juror Comments*: Quality production, smooth transitions—activities flowed well. "Makes phonics and other reading activities fun." "Wow—this CD-ROM really comes through—it's a great learning tool." *Kid Juror Comments*: Engaging. Pre-reading activities and Elmo's Adventures held their attention. Repeat play value was high. "I liked playing 'Elmo Through the Looking Glass,' a lot." "I liked making words in Super Grover's comic book." "Everything was fun." CD-ROM. WIN/MAC; $29.95; Age: 2-5. Sony Wonder.

** Sesame Street: Get Set to Learn (Sesame Street Home Video)

Integrates preschool skills that develop critical thinking and problem-solving skills. Features more than 25 essential skills, 20 activity combinations, and four skill levels. Skill levels adjust, based on child's progress. *Adult Juror Comments*: Nice reinforcements, ties in with well-known Sesame Street characters. Scored high with kids. Overly chatty characters slow down child's pace. *Kid Juror Comments*: Big Bird's counting the best part. The size game is the least liked. Kids didn't have adequate time to answer questions and complete the tasks before the characters interrupted them. CD-ROM. WIN; $39.95; Age: 4-6. Learning Company.

*** Sheila Rae the Brave (Sheila Rae the Brave)

 A sing-along adventure, an interactive storybook based on the children's book by the Caldecott Award-winning author Kevin Henkes. *Adult Juror Comments*: "Makes a good book even better." Songs are ideal. Female role model is excellent. Shows respect for family members. Instructions are clear, though adults experienced some technical problems in the map section. *Kid Juror Comments*: Big hit when a favorite book comes to life. Taps into three- and four-year-old humor. Kids stuck with it through to the end and played it again right away. Loved the music. CD-ROM. WIN/MAC; $40; Age: 2-7. Learning Company.

Category—Family

* Baby Wow!

Interactive software to be used with child and parent. Includes photographs and vocabulary in eight different languages. *Adult Juror Comments*: Easy to use. Pictures and sounds are bright and appealing. "A parent can use this like a picture book to reinforce concepts and vocabulary." "I'd like to see various skill levels offered for the different activities." "The peak-a-boo game was tedious." *Kid Juror Comments*: Kids younger than age two lost interest quickly, but enjoyed playing with the keyboard. Music and photos were a hit with the older children. CD-ROM. $14.99; Age: 2-4. Bow Wow House.

Chapter Two • Preschool

Category—Music

** Stella and the Star-Tones

 Living among the stars in the night sky, Stella and her cast of whimsical constellations come alive as you play their music. Contains 21 illustrated screens with animated characters, each hosting an original musical score from blues to jazz to polka. *Adult Juror Comments*: Great learning tool with lots of variety. Introduces musical awareness by giving children free rein to create their own concerts. Provides positive and encouraging support. Simple and fun. Lacks different levels of difficulty. *Kid Juror Comments*: Captivating, easy to use. Holds interest. Nothing you do on the computer is wrong in this program. Kids loved creating their own songs. Younger kids were dancing in their seats. Appeals most to kids interested in music. Comes with a star poster. CD-ROM. WIN/MAC; $25; Age: 2-5. Bohem Interactive.

Format—Video/DVD

Category—Education/Instruction

* 1, 2, 3 Come Count with Me

 Counting Cat introduces the world of numbers. Children can sing and play along with parachuting kangaroos, buzzing bees, and purple porcupines while learning to count. *Adult Juror Comments*: The presentation and content are suitable to make learning pleasant. Provides counting exercises with unusual objects, using questionable techniques. Repetitive. May be more effective when viewed in segments. The "real" face inserted seems strange. *Kid Juror Comments*: Just okay. They lost interest by number five, although counted straight through. Only some stayed for the entire program. A little too long for one sitting. Video. 22 min.; $29; Age: 2-6. Kideo Productions, Inc.

** 1, 2, 3 Count with Me (Sesame Street Home Video)

Ernie, Elmo, and The Count make learning numbers and counting a musical treat. Ernie shows everyone just how useful learning to count can be. Stars the Muppets. Musical numbers include: "Count With Me," "Seven Goldfish," and "Counting Vacation." *Adult Juror Comments*: Excellent techniques for teaching numbers. It's fun, musical, and has lots of repetition. Appeals to adults and children. Well-produced, high-quality sound and visuals. *Kid Juror Comments*: Reinforces counting. One four-and-a-half-year-old practiced her numerical skills after watching. Two hyperactive kids sat and watched the whole program. "I really like Elmo." Video. 30 min.; $12.98; Age: 2-5. Sony Wonder.

** ABC's & Such (Rusty & Rosy)

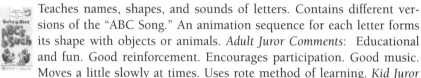

Teaches names, shapes, and sounds of letters. Contains different versions of the "ABC Song." An animation sequence for each letter forms its shape with objects or animals. *Adult Juror Comments*: Educational and fun. Good reinforcement. Encourages participation. Good music. Moves a little slowly at times. Uses rote method of learning. *Kid Juror Comments*: Good for three- to five-year-olds. Has lots of repetition and is easy to understand. Interaction required of kids is well done. Video. 35 min.; $24.95; Age: 2-6. Waterford Institute.

*** Alphabet Game, The (Sesame Street Home Video)

Sunny Friendly is the host of a new game show with prizes and surprises. The contestants are Big Bird, Gary Grouch, and Dimples the Dog. The object of the game is to be the first to find something that starts with the letter of the alphabet shown. *Adult Juror Comments*: Visually appealing, silly game show format. Funny puppets, lively songs, guest appearances by Kermit, Grover, Cookie Monster, Oscar, and Big Bird. Sesame Street follows through with humor and lots of color. *Kid Juror Comments*: "I liked it very much." "I liked the talking 'S,' he was funny." "I like watching for the letters." "I know my ABC's." Kids sang the Alphabet Song after watching the video. Video. 30 min.; $12.98; Age: 3-5. Sony Wonder.

* Alphabet Soup (Look & Learn)

This sing-along uses flying pictures and flipping words to help reinforce and retain the alphabet. Jaunty rhymes, spirited music, and charming pictures. *Adult Juror Comments*: Helpful for children who are learning the alphabet. Some words too difficult for audience. Stretches learning in a positive way. Simple production. Starts slow with lots of verbal information, making this best viewed in segments. *Kid Juror Comments*: A little slow-moving, especially at the beginning. Some kids asked to see it again. Others said they sang the ABC song "wrong." Content suitable for elementary age. Video. 30 min.; $14.98; Age: 3-6. V.I.E.W. Video.

*** Alphabet Zoo, The

Teaches the alphabet through bright, interactive songs and colorful scenes of animals in their natural habitat. Teaches letter recognition with visuals and sounds. *Adult Juror Comments*: Multi-sensory with interesting animals. Good repetition and content. Excellent suggestions for parents or caregivers that reinforce the lessons. Attractive settings, good pacing. Stimulates participation. *Kid Juror Comments*: They sounded out the letters, made animal sounds, and learned a lot about the animals after repeated viewings. One of the best alphabet tapes, great for zoo trips. Video. 25 min.; $14.95; Age: 3-7. Dolphin Communications.

* Alphabetland (Redbook Learning Adventures)

The magic power of letters and words through songs and games. Includes other lessons about patience, friendship, and imagination. *Adult Juror Comments*: Reinforces learning alphabet. Songs are creative and catchy. Program links letters to words. Gets off to a slow start and the presentation is jumbled. *Kid Juror Comments*: Kids listened as soon as the music started. Story line is a little difficult and complicated to follow. They didn't understand references in the songs. Some older children sang the ABC song afterwards. Video. 30 min.; $12.98; Age: 2-6. Video Treasures.

*** Baby's First Impressions, Vol. 10: Food Fun (Baby's First Impressions)

Learning about food was never this much fun. Produce comes to life on-screen, teaching children how to identify a multitude of fruits and vegetables while emphasizing table manners and good nutrition. Includes recipes kids can make themselves. *Adult Juror Comments*: Bright vivid colors. Great multi-cultural mix of children. "They related to the foods they know and got a kick out of those they were unfamiliar with or had never tried." Learning potential is excellent. Production well done. *Kid Juror Comments*: Stimulated and intrigued children. "The children shouted out the names of the foods presented. Many asked to watch it over again." While watching the section on fruits, one girl said, "I want a bite!" Children danced and laughed to the music. Video. 32 min.; $14.95; Age: 2-5. Small Fry Productions.

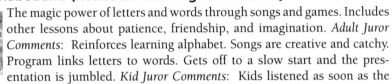

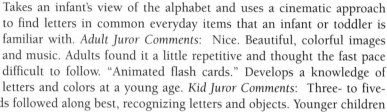

** Baby's First Impressions, Vol. 3: Letters
(Baby's First Impressions)

Takes an infant's view of the alphabet and uses a cinematic approach to find letters in common everyday items that an infant or toddler is familiar with. *Adult Juror Comments*: Nice. Beautiful, colorful images and music. Adults found it a little repetitive and thought the fast pace difficult to follow. "Animated flash cards." Develops a knowledge of letters and colors at a young age. *Kid Juror Comments*: Three- to five-year-olds followed along best, recognizing letters and objects. Younger children watched in segments. Video. 32 min.; $14.95; Age: 2-5. Small Fry Productions.

** Baby's First Impressions, Vol. 4: Numbers
(Baby's First Impressions)

Helps preschoolers learn their numbers by using object association and repetition. *Adult Juror Comments*: Good diversity. Good pacing for the count-and-answer segment. Helps motivate children to learn how to count. *Kid Juror Comments*: Fine. Children enjoyed the objects selected for counting. Children who are speaking benefit most from this video. Video. 32 min.; $14.95; Age: 2-5. Small Fry Productions.

*** Baby's First Impressions, Vol. 5: Opposites
(Baby's First Impressions)

Inspires and challenges creative kids' minds. Interesting visuals to show differences like up and down, left and right, hot and cold. *Adult Juror Comments*: Insight into difficult concepts using repetition to reinforce learning. Minimal comprehension for under age two. Beautiful visuals, music, and voices. Culturally diverse, good aspects for English as a Second Language preschool learning. *Kid Juror Comments*: Children watched enthusiastically, repeating opposite words and sharing gestures as well as their own opposite words. Viewing this program calmed children. "My infant loved it." Video. 32 min.; $14.95; Age: 1-5. Small Fry Productions.

** Baby's First Impressions, Vol. 6: Animals
(Baby's First Impressions)

Shows all types of animals, even some insects, interacting with children. Names of animals are spelled on the screen and each section has a recap learning period. *Adult Juror Comments*: Good pace, visually captivating, excellent diversity. Invites involvement with animal costumes and sounds. Reinforces concepts and stimulates responses. Some words difficult for audience. Educational value is more applicable to over-two's. *Kid Juror Comments*: Evoked questions about animal facts. Even the older kids learned something new, like how fast an emu can run. Good link to familiar songs. Infants and eighteen-month-olds loved it! A little long, but can be viewed in segments. Video. 32 min.; $14.95; Age: 1-5. Small Fry Productions.

Age 2-5

Video

Edu/Instru

Chapter Two • Preschool

** Baby's First Impressions, Vol. 8: Seasons
(Baby's First Impressions)

Teaches the differences between the four seasons: fresh winter snow, spring flowers, summer sunshine, and fall colors. Many holidays are explained so the child can learn connections between holidays and seasons. *Adult Juror Comments*: Colorful, but very slow pace. Depicts children in the garden, at the beach, other playful activities. Not much diversity in discussing traditional Christian Easter, Thanksgiving, and Christmas. *Kid Juror Comments*: Enthusiastic. Children were moving around and pretending to smell the flowers along with the on-screen kids. They liked seeing the different seasons. "We could grow flowers." "There is no snow here, we could make sand angels instead." Video. 32 min.; $14.95; Age: 2-5. Small Fry Productions.

** Baby's First Impressions, Vol. 9: Head to Toe
(Baby's First Impressions)

Teaches how to make learning connections as on-screen children demonstrate how a hand can do many things, like hold, touch, or clap. Encourages interaction from children. Exercise demonstrations included. *Adult Juror Comments*: Looks great. Shows realistic pictures of children and their body parts. Very clear images and simple music. May help kids identify their own body parts and develop a sense of self. Repetition becomes a little annoying after a while. *Kid Juror Comments*: Children enjoyed finding their body parts and following along with what they saw. Good exercises. Some kids lost interest and wandered off. "I liked the sit-ups." "I liked the jumping jacks." Video. 32 min.; $14.95; Age: 1-4. Small Fry Productions.

*** Blue's Clues: Blue's Big Musical Movie (Blue's Clues)

In his first feature movie, Blue plans a backyard musical show with Steve and their friends. Introduces Blue's new friend, Periwinkle, and six new songs. Stars Steve Burns and features the voices of Ray Charles and The Persuasions. *Adult Juror Comments*: Wonderful story. Well thought-out. Colorful characters, beautiful colors, and good music. Encourages interactivity. Musical concepts are explained well. For example, tempo is compared to the speed of a train. "I wanted to learn to make my own music." *Kid Juror Comments*: Actively engaging. "Everyone has a good time with Blue. Steve always does something fun, and you learn something too." Inspired kids to plan a show, starting with a checklist. "We want to write our own music and make our own tempo." Video. 75 min.; $19.95; Age: 2-7. Paramount Home Entertainment.

* Busy Day, A (Lil' Iguana)

A busy day at Lil' Iguana's house means making huge bubbles, unpacking special delivery boxes, cleaning out the refrigerator, deciding whether to put jelly dough-nuts on pizza, and figuring out a mixed-up story, not necessarily in that order. *Adult Juror Comments*: Well-produced. Quirky subject matter. The timing is too fast for significant audience participation. The characters and stories are appealing, but some content is slow and uneven. Seems a little forced and stilted. *Kid Juror Comments*: They liked learning bubble making, inventing the pizza, and the "day at the beach" sections best. Kids liked using "yum" and "yuck" as descriptors. Some children really responded to the iguanas. "The adults taught us good things about fresh food." Video. 30 min.; $12.95; Age: 3-5. WABU-TV 68 Boston.

*** Circus of Colors and Shapes, The

 Energetic music videos, a magic show, and clown antics teach children primary and secondary colors and basic shapes. *Adult Juror Comments*: Good pace, sequencing and humor. Straightforward information for learn-ing names of colors and shapes while encouraging creative activities. Additional parent follow-up activities are outstanding. *Kid Juror Comments*: Absorbing. Afterwards, they pointed out shapes around them. They touched the screen during the shapes quiz. Some kids requested watching the video every day for a week so they could memorize the songs and point out the shapes. Video. 22 min.; $14.95; Age: 2-5. Dolphin Communications.

** Cleared for Takeoff (Fred Levine's Original)

Follow a family through Chicago's O'Hare International airport as a pilot shows them the control tower, baggage handling, takeoffs and landings of giant jets. *Adult Juror Comments*: Interesting production, well-paced, with realistic photography and an extensive vocabulary. Nice music. Appropriate for age group. They will relate to the story line. Some found the plane information insufficient. *Kid Juror Comments*: They wanted to know more. One child didn't realize that planes take off and land; she thought they just flew around. Children were disappointed when the video didn't show the final destination (Grandma in her house). Video. 30 min.; $14.95; Age: 2-5. Fred Levine Productions, DBA Little Hardhats.

*** Clifford's Fun with Numbers (Clifford the Big Red Dog)

With Emily, Elizabeth, and Clifford—her big red dog—this episode teaches number recognition and mathematical vocabulary. An activity booklet gives parents or teach-ers additional content. *Adult Juror Comments*: High-quality production, brings char-acters to life for active viewing. Teaches kindness to animals. Children learn basic concept of number recognition. *Kid Juror Comments*: Attentive and interacted with the tape, counting out loud and anticipating each segment. Older kids taught younger ones. Kids asked to see it repeatedly. Video. 27 min.; $12.98; Age: 3-7. Artisan/Family Home Entertainment.

Chapter Two • Preschool

*** *Count with Maisy (Maisy)*

 Maisy and her friends embark on a counting adventure aboard a train. Maisy drives the train and makes stops to pick up various numbers of animals. *Adult Juror Comments*: Well-produced—bright and friendly. Reinforces counting one through ten. Shows healthy foods from the garden and safe driving practices. Very age appropriate with lots of playful learning for the little ones. *Kid Juror Comments*: Youngest kids had a lot of fun with the counting section. "We love getting better in counting!" "It made us count different things in our own house; you can count everything!" "I wanted to learn more numbers, and Maisy only counts to ten." Video. 32 min.; $12.98; Age: 2-5. Universal Studios Home Video.

*** *Discover Spot (Spot)*

 Spot the curious puppy embarks on a song-filled journey of discovery. In 13 stories based on the books by Eric Hill, Spot learns about making breakfast, brushing teeth, cleaning up, and much more. Includes live-action vignettes of preschoolers learning. *Adult Juror Comments*: Charming, lovable, simple songs. A bit long for one sitting. Each story is followed by a live action sequence reinforcing concepts from the story. Covers everyday themes such as cleaning up, taking turns, and eating breakfast. Great diversity. *Kid Juror Comments*: Enjoyable. Generated long-term interest in some of the activities. A four-year-old said, "I love that there are many Spot stories all together." "I want to play with Spot." "I don't think any kid could really be as nice as Spot is all the time." Video. 75 min.; $19.98; Age: 1-4. Buena Vista Home Entertainment/Disney.

*** *Do the Alphabet (Sesame Street's Kids' Guide to Life)*

Get ready to sing, dance, and laugh all the way from A to Z! It's 26 times the fun when you learn the alphabet with Big Bird and friends! *Adult Juror Comments*: Learning in the best of Sesame Street tradition. Great combination of children and characters. "Alphabet Blues" is really cute. The alphabet support group is clever. *Kid Juror Comments*: A winner! They cheered when Baby Bear got to "Z." An eight-year-old said, "I wish they had invented great alphabet songs like this when I was a kid." Video. 45 min.; $12.98; Age: 2-5. Sony Wonder.

*** *Doing Things—Eating, Washing, in Motion (Live Action Video)*

Compares children and animals engaged in everyday activities of eating, washing, and playing. Non-narrated with musical accompaniment. *Adult Juror Comments*: Delightful! Good production, fun to watch. What a beautiful variety of children, the diversity is really a treasure. Kids enjoy watching animals and people do the same things. *Kid Juror Comments*: "That's awesome." "That was fun." The two's were ready to see it again right away. Video. 27 min.; $14.95; Age: 2-5. Bo Peep Productions.

* Exploring Colors & Shapes of the Deep Blue Sea (Redbook Learning Adventures)

Fluffy Duffy and his friends are off on their greatest adventure yet: a voyage beneath the sea, where they learn all about colors and shapes. *Adult Juror Comments*: A meaningful video. The actors did a good job, but the story seems contrived. The story and jokes are given more emphasis than teaching shapes and colors. Simple production, developmentally appropriate. *Kid Juror Comments*: Funny characters. Story line is a little over the heads of the younger ones, yet the educational goals are geared for them. Video. 30 min.; $12.98; Age: 2-5. Video Treasures.

* Fire and Rescue (Fred Levine's Original)

A behind-the-scenes look at the life of firefighters, from the training academy to the firehouse. Provides fire safety tips. *Adult Juror Comments*: Stimulating for older children. Good introduction to fire safety, equipment, and procedures. Inspires admiration for firefighters. Toddler appearing to play near burning building evoked safety concerns. Recommend adult facilitation. *Kid Juror Comments*: Attentive. Good for fire department field trips. Boys were most interested. Some parts are very scary for this age. Video. 30 min.; $14.95; Age: 2-5. Fred Levine Productions, DBA Little Hardhats.

*** George and Martha: Best Friends (Doors of Wonder)

Animated story, based on books by James Marshall. George and Martha, two hippos, have an enduring friendship that addresses consideration for others, resolving conflicts, and solving problems. Features the voices of Nathan Lane and Andrea Martin. *Adult Juror Comments*: Wonderful, lighthearted, fun, with lovable funny characters. Messages are gentle, voices are quiet, and dialogue is simple. Brings the books to life. Reinforces forgiveness—even best friends have good times and bad times. *Kid Juror Comments*: Adored the characters and understood the lesson on forgiveness. "We all sometimes get mad at our friends, but it showed us how to work things out." "First they got mad at each other, but then they were nice because they love each other and I love them." Video. 45 min.; $9.98; Age: 2-5. Sony Wonder.

** Heart of Antarctica

Personal, entertaining and informational introduction to Antarctica. Based on an actual scientific expedition to the interior, including the South Pole. Covers history and geography. *Adult Juror Comments*: Delightful. Respectful of elderly people. Reinforces the idea of helping others. Stories tell of daily life in a small English village. The slow pace weaves lovely little tales with darling puppets. Women's roles are stereotypical. *Kid Juror Comments*: Fascinating. Kids had lots of questions. "Why do they have to heat the refrigerators?" "Why does it stay dark for such a long time?" They liked the penguins and noticed there were no black people there. Video. 40 min.; $19.95; Age: 2-5. La Sonrisa Productions.

* Hello Numbers (Look & Learn)

Interactive games and sing- and count-alongs teach children to count from one through 100. *Adult Juror Comments*: Educational and interesting. Repetition and encouragement are from robot host. Simple production shows that kids don't need high-tech presentation to learn educational concepts and be entertained. Some jurors objected to war toys as counting objects. *Kid Juror Comments*: Cute. Children participated by singing and following instructions such as touch your nose. The counting by ten's was too fast to follow. Liked the music. Too slow for some children. Video. 30 min.; $14.98; Age: 2-5. V.I.E.W. Video.

** Hey! That's My Hay

Geraldine, a talking cow, is eager to show how hay is made on her farm, and other things about farm life. Peter, the farmer, shows farm machinery and the tractors and horses that pull them. *Adult Juror Comments*: Though some segments were fascinating, program is too dry and long. Using a talking cow as a teacher is a cute idea, but the explanations are way beyond the child's comprehension. Humor is effective. Spurs interest in caring for animals. *Kid Juror Comments*: They liked the animals, but got tired of all the machinery. Lots of questions, such as "Where do the animals go in the winter?" "The talking cow was fun to watch and listen to." "We liked seeing hay being made." Video. 30 min.; $12.95; Age: 3-6. Blackboard Entertainment.

Age 2-5

Video

Edu/Instru

** *Jitter the Critter's Barnyard Adventure (Jitter the Critter)*

Jitter the Critter introduces Farmer Fred's Fun Farm, an imaginative place where animals love to sing. Everyone is happy until Fred's brother has a secret plan to take Fred's farm and turn it into a shopping mall...then everyone pitches in to save the farm. *Adult Juror Comments*: Well-produced, lively music, good pace. Encourages audience participation through songs and music that invite you to get up and dance and sing. Teaches lessons about telling the truth and being kind to animals. Had some audio problems. *Kid Juror Comments*: Enjoyed the singing—especially the song about the pickles. "I danced and danced." "I was glad when Evil Ed became nice and didn't turn the farm into a shopping mall." "Farmer Fred was kind to the mice. They were good friends." Video. 30 min.; $14.99; Age: 2-5. Jitter the Critter Productions.

*** *Learning to Share (Sesame Street's Kids' Guide To Life)*

 Special program featuring Katie Couric helps make growing up a lot more fun and gives parents tips for teaching kids to share. *Adult Juror Comments*: Demonstrates good conflict-resolution strategy in very real situations, including a child in wheelchair. Elmo is perfect character to take on the "it's mine" attitude. *Kid Juror Comments*: All the children loved the characters and story. "You learn special rules in this tape." Kids wanted to know why Elmo wouldn't share. "I danced along for a minute, a couple times." Video. 45 min.; $12.98; Age: 2-5. Sony Wonder.

* *Love (New Zoo Review)*

Freddie discovers that love is giving, so he sells his beloved record player to buy a community swing that everyone loves to use. Featured songs: "I Love Most Everyone and Everything," "L.O.V.E.," and "A Little Love." *Adult Juror Comments*: Slow-moving, but animals are cute and colorful. "Made in 1971 and looks it." It's a little condescending. Women are shown in stereotypical roles. Some songs are lip-synched and awkwardly integrated into rest of show. *Kid Juror Comments*: "Boring." "Silly." "I liked how they danced." Kids liked the messages about learning to be nice and share. For the most part, they enjoyed the singing and the characters. "The hippo sang bad." Video. 25 min.; $9.95; Age: 3-5. Blackboard Entertainment.

Chapter Two • Preschool

*** Maisy's Bedtime (Maisy)

 Maisy the lovable mouse gets ready for bed by saying goodnight to her friends, washing up, changing her clothes, and reading a bedtime story. She finally goes to sleep after visiting the bathroom again, of course. *Adult Juror Comments*: Bright, cheerful and colorful production. Features day-to-day activities which young children can relate to, such as bathing, playing with friends, and eating . Shows excellent pro-social behavior. Can be easily viewed in segments. *Kid Juror Comments*: Entranced. "Maisy is my favorite mouse. She has a lot of friends." "My favorite part is when she went to the park and fed all the animals." "Maisy is always doing something fun." "Maisy shows kids what to do at night to get ready for bed." Video. 38 min.; $12.98; Age: 2-5. Universal Studios Home Video.

* Moo Moo Mozart

Conductor Moo Moo Mozart introduces babies and toddlers to classical music, animals, and art and landmarks from around the world. *Adult Juror Comments*: Enjoyable music selections though visuals don't connect with the music. Repetitive; lacks continuity. Moves too fast. Mediocre production quality. Useful for introducing young ones to classical music. *Kid Juror Comments*: Partially engaged them. Those that watched, enjoyed it. Most liked "Moo." Some liked the fast moving images, and some liked the music. Many images are unfamiliar to the children and consequently, they don't relate to them. Video. 34 min.; $14.95; Age: 2-3. Zooknowlogy Learning Company, LLC.

*** More Preschool Power (Preschool Power)

 Preschool-age "teachers" show how to tie shoes, brush teeth, make fruit salad, and play with shadow puppets. Packed with songs, music, jokes, and tongue twisters. *Adult Juror Comments*: This is a great child-centered tape. Excellent choice of activities, well-produced. Segments are the perfect length for this age. *Kid Juror Comments*: Fabulous. Kids loved watching others their own age, dancing, playing, and being nice to one another. Good diversity and lovely songs. Kids responded throughout and afterwards talked about brushing teeth and the shadow finger animals they made. Video. 30 min.; $14.95; Age: 2-5. Concept Associates.

** My Alphabet

Teaches letter and word recognition while introducing characters Alexander G. Bear and a cast of others who explore the alphabet together. *Adult Juror Comments*: Straight-forward, pleasant learning. Fine premise for letter recognition as reinforcement; rote knowledge is not as important during the preschool years as is active exploration. Contains some static images. *Kid Juror Comments*: Children liked singing the songs afterwards. They recognized the letters and responded by thinking up other words. Some chose to watch this based on the box cover. Video. 22 min.; $34.95; Age: 2-5. Kideo Productions, Inc.

** Numbers Express, The

A friendly engineer on a turn-of-the-century steam engine introduces numbers, number relationships, and counting, with catchy songs and games. *Adult Juror Comments*: The train ride is fun. Too many types of enumeration are mixed together. Introduces counting, sorting, sequencing. Encourages parent involvement. Good length, but not a lot of trains. *Kid Juror Comments*: Very nice, especially for the younger ones who enjoyed the songs and counting along. Video. 24 min.; $14.95; Age: 2-5. Dolphin Communications.

** Our World of Wheels

Designed to teach early skills in visual tracking, shape recognition, pre-reading readiness, sight and sound association. Portrays different vehicles in motion, such as fire engines, trains, motorcycles, police cars, and airplanes. *Adult Juror Comments*: Simple and fascinating. Lots to watch for. Authentic sounds are good. Good video for language development, recognition and labeling of objects. The lack of narration makes this a good teaching tool without interruption. *Kid Juror Comments*: Interesting sounds and vehicles. They relaxed on the floor and discussed what they recognized as it came on the screen. Children seemed to like the "realness" of the video. Video. 25 min.; $9.95; Age: 2-5. Top Shelf Productions.

** Pinatta's View: A Trip to the Dentist (Pinatta's View)

Join Pinatta and her puppet band inside the big oak tree as they use music, boggle-goggles, and a child's perspective to practice going to the dentist. Journey with them as they take a real trip to the dentist. *Adult Juror Comments*: Fun characters, bright colors, catchy music. Shows a real dentist's office with sounds, tools, and procedures. Suited for preschoolers who will be seeing the dentist for the first time to help them feel secure. Stimulates interest in tooth care. *Kid Juror Comments*: "My 3-year-old watched it ten times. She loved it!" Teaches good dental hygiene practices and encourages kids not to be afraid of the dentist. Kids enjoyed the humor and music, but were antsy during the explanation sections. Video. 29 min.; $12.98; Age: 3-5. Boggle-Goggle Enterprises.

*** Preschool Power #3 (Preschool Power)

 Preschoolers learn to do things for themselves: putting on gloves, making a paper fan, sweeping up spills, making French bread, blowing giant bubbles, setting up dominoes. Imagination and cooperation are emphasized. *Adult Juror Comments*: Great series with Montessori-designed activities in a music video format. Well-produced, good diversity. *Kid Juror Comments*: Tops! KIDS FIRST! has put the videos into waiting rooms of health clinics, where the staff and clients enjoy them equally. Video. 30 min.; $14.95; Age: 2-5. Concept Associates.

*** Preschool Power: Jacket Flips & Other Tips (Preschool Power)

 How to button, buckle, zip, wash hands, put on jackets, tidy rooms, make snacks, and pour without spilling a drop. Featuring the proven methods of Maria Montessori. Preschoolers will learn the lasting gift of self-reliance. *Adult Juror Comments*: A great musical series. Activities are age-appropriate, well-executed and fun. Very child-centered and well-produced. "It's great to see what kids are capable of doing, because parents sometimes forget." *Kid Juror Comments*: They immediately imitated the behaviors they saw on-screen, and asked questions about what the kids were doing. Video. 30 min.; $14.95; Age: 2-5. Concept Associates.

Age 2-5

Video

Edu/Instru

** *Richard Scarry's Best ABC Video Ever!*
(Richard Scarry's Best Videos Ever!)

Huckle Cat and his classmates present the alphabet in 26 charming stories. *Adult Juror Comments*: Great alphabet video with little cultural diversity in the voices. Characters are appealing. Some jurors don't like using it with children under four, since they may not understand the relationship between a letter symbol and a sound. *Kid Juror Comments*: Excellent. They laughed at the jokes, called out each others' names when their letter came up. Works well with the Scarry books. Video. 30 min.; $9.98; Age: 2-6. Random House Video.

*** *Richard Scarry's Best Counting Video Ever!*
(Richard Scarry's Best Videos Ever!)

Children will love helping Lily Bunny count from one to 20. On her counting adventure, she meets Lowly Worm, Wrong-Way Roger, Bananas Gorilla, and other Richard Scarry characters who help her find funny things to count. *Adult Juror Comments*: Good animation, dialogue, songs. Promotes learning in a pleasant way. Perhaps a little too long for youngest kids—good to break it up into segments. *Kid Juror Comments*: Kids love Richard Scarry. They relate well to the animal characters. Some older kids requested it again. Video. 30 min.; $9.98; Age: 2-6. Random House Video.

** *See It! Say It! Sing It! Play It!*
(Primalux Video Educational Series)

Teaches word association, object recognition, and counting, through familiar images and the sounds they make. Includes counting games and songs such as "ABC's," "Ten Little Fingers," and "Eensy Weensy Spider." *Adult Juror Comments*: Entertaining and encourages basic reading readiness. Good use of different ways to learn: music, words, visuals. Concrete examples. *Kid Juror Comments*: Appealing across the board. From one-year-olds to the "just-turned-four" kids, especially the boys. Children sang along with the songs. "I liked that the kids were funny." Video. 25 min.; $14.95; Age: 1-6. Primalux Video.

* *Silly Willy Workout (Silly Willy Series)*

Contemporary musical activities enliven this well-rounded program. It offers relaxation techniques and encourages activity. Lessons should last a lifetime. *Adult Juror Comments*: Looks dated and lacks cute characters. Explanation of aerobics and warming-up is well-done, but the transitions do not flow well. It only shows kids who look like they're already in pretty good shape. Comes with helpful parent guide. *Kid Juror Comments*: Most liked the music and repeated the songs afterwards. "The pretend horse ride was fun." "I wish I knew the songs because I like to sing when I exercise." "I wonder if my dad knows where his heart is?" "Exercise is fun." Video. 25 min.; $19.95; Age: 3-5. Educational Activities, Inc.

Chapter Two • Preschool

* Sounds of Letters (Reading Lesson)

How do the letters of the alphabet sound? Animated characters help the child take the first steps into the world of reading. *Adult Juror Comments*: Sounds and visuals are effective and appropriate for introducing the alphabet, but rather dry and slow-moving. Presents the alphabet simply. *Kid Juror Comments*: For children who do not know their alphabet, this tape will have the appeal of repeat playing. Older children who know their ABC's will be less interested. Video. 32 min.; $29; Age: 2-5. Attainment Company, Inc.

* Spot Goes to School (Spot)

Spot the curious puppy and his friends prepare for the first day of school. They learn how to play safe at the playground, decorate a cake, and put on hats and mittens for a cold day. Includes live-action preschoolers who learn along with Spot. *Adult Juror Comments*: Cute, simple, fun. Easy to follow story and pictures. Gives a warm, secure feeling. Encourages going to preschool and playing with friends. Art lesson lacks creativity; kids playing Indian by patting hand to mouth calling whoo whoo is inappropriate. *Kid Juror Comments*: Younger ones are most responsive. They were ready to mimic Spot's activities. "I want to go to school." "Let's make a snowman. Let's go to the park." "Spot is fun." They were interested in learning more about hippos and going to school. Video. 35 min.; $19.98; Age: 2-5. Buena Vista Home Entertainment/Disney.

** Spot Goes to the Farm (Spot)

Spot the curious puppy and his friends meet baby animals, pack their bags for a sleepover, meet a circus clown, fly a kite, and take turns on the swing while at the farm. Includes live-action cast of preschoolers who learn along with Spot. *Adult Juror Comments*: Simple, even paced production, good music, vivid colors. Cute animation. Its simplicity is its best asset. Introduces children to farm animals and numbers. Good diversity. For very young children, adult supervision is recommended for these activities. *Kid Juror Comments*: Engaged and wanted to watch again. "Spot and his mom and dad are very nice." "We love Spot because he is so cute...just like a real puppy." "Spot can balance a ball on his nose." "The games were really fun and we want to go to the farm like Spot." Video. 33 min.; $19.98; Age: 2-5. Buena Vista Home Entertainment/Disney.

** Tractors, Combines and Things on the Grow

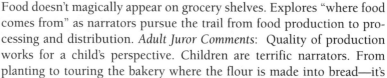

Food doesn't magically appear on grocery shelves. Explores "where food comes from" as narrators pursue the trail from food production to processing and distribution. *Adult Juror Comments*: Quality of production works for a child's perspective. Children are terrific narrators. From planting to touring the bakery where the flour is made into bread—it's all there. Shows how hard farmers work. A little long for this audience *Kid Juror Comments*: Favorite segments: time-lapse photography of plant growth, watching closeups of the big machines in action. Older kids enjoyed this best. Video. 30 min.; $19.95; Age: 2-8. Just Our Size Videos.

*** True Friends (The All New Captain Kangaroo)

Joey gets a pet turtle and thoughtlessly builds a house for it using the Captain's hat. He learns to be more responsible. Joey tells a fib about messing up the Captain's garden and learns the importance of telling the truth. *Adult Juror Comments*: Appealing, gentle, nice atmosphere. "Children are so captivated that it's a pleasure to view with them." Good variety of reality and fantasy. Positive and respectful of the way kids think. Language play is fun. Great blending of characters and media. *Kid Juror Comments*: Enthralling. A two-year-boy stated, "I LOVE Captain Kangaroo." "Why is he a Captain?" Kids liked Mr. Moose's jokes. Video. 54 min.; $12.98; Age: 2-11. Twentieth Century Fox Home Entertainment.

* We Can Get Along (Treasure Attic)

Children discover the secrets to building lasting friendships. Promotes the idea that "there is no need to compare, each of us is very needed and special." The song "Little Things" shows how even small deeds of kindness can reap big results. Adult Juror Comments: Teaches the importance of trying hard and appreciating differences. Live action mixed with animation offers good messages divided into short, sometimes choppy, segments. Addresses new neighbors and self-acceptance. Excessively sweet. Kid Juror Comments: Kids continued to draw the flowers and trees from this video afterwards. Five-year-old girls enjoyed watching it a second time. Their favorite parts were seeing the kitten rescued and the art lesson. Video. 25 min.; $14.95; Age: 3-7. Family Care Foundation.

** Where's Spot? (Spot)

Based on the books by Eric Hill, Spot the curious puppy and his friends play hide 'n' seek, take a nature walk, celebrate a birthday, and jump in rain puddles. Includes live-action preschoolers learning along with Spot. *Adult Juror Comments*: Fun, interesting, respectful. Charming animation and whimsical, familiar stories based on the Spot books. Simple, slow and easy pace. Mix of animation and live-action. Interactive activities relate to interests of preschoolers and hold their attention. *Kid Juror Comments*: Youngest sat and watched the entire program. The stories were familiar, and they repeated the dialogue. "Spot was nice. He had a birthday. That was nice." They liked the hide 'n' seek part and wanted to play afterwards. "The animals are fun to watch." Video. 34 min.; $19.98; Age: 2-4. Buena Vista Home Entertainment/Disney.

* You Can't Win 'Em All (The Huggable Club)

Being a good sport is the focus of this music-packed video. Do your best, play by the rules, play it safe, learn to share. Kids will learn they can't always be the winners. *Adult Juror Comments*: Very sweet, with good discussions about playing fair. Demonstrates positive social behaviors. Some parts moved slowly. Actors were stiff and artificial and empathizing with them was difficult. Lively songs. *Kid Juror Comments*: Music had children moving in their seats. Some were singing the songs long after the tape had ended, but some children had lost interest. "I'm thinking about the different characters and the poor sport, Sally." Video. 27 min.; $12.98; Age: 2-5. Huggabug Productions, Inc.

Category—Family

* Adventure to Kids TV (The Enchanted Dollhouse)

A magic dollhouse transports two sisters into an imaginary land peopled with puppets. Presents activities such as dancing, spelling, and baking. *Adult Juror Comments*: Production has a home video look to it. The puppets are cute, though simple in design. Addresses social issues such as not lying and sharing and encourages children to use their imaginations in a positive way. *Kid Juror Comments*: Kids were concerned that there were no consequences for characters that wandered off by themselves. "The bears were not real, but I still liked it, especially when the bears shared their cookies." "We liked the puppets and the dancing." Some danced along. Video. 30 min.; $12.98; Age: 2-5. Millennium Entertainment Group.

** Adventures of Elmo in Grouchland, The

 Elmo loves his blanket more than anything in the world. When a tug-of-war with Zoe sends his blanket into a far-away land, Elmo summons all of his courage to undertake a rescue mission and is plunged into Grouchland. *Adult Juror Comments*: Excellent production quality. Holds interest from start to finish. Combines compelling music with friendly characters who makes the audience feel like they're part of the action. There is a continuous sense that everyone is looking out for Elmo. *Kid Juror Comments*: Kids relate to Elmo. "He is so cute. I was sad when the mean man took his blankie." "Huxley is a bad guy with no manners." "The fireflies helped Elmo in the dark." "I liked the song with the Grouches, 'Welcome to Grouchland, Now Scram.'" DVD. 73 min.; $24.95; Age: 2-5. Columbia Tristar Home Entertainment.

** And Baby Makes Four (The Huggabug Club)

Maria is concerned about the new baby coming into her family. The Buggsters learn how special it is to be a brother or a sister and the importance of families. *Adult Juror Comments*: Helps children cope with becoming an older brother or sister. Entertaining costumes and music. Some vocabulary is beyond the comprehension of preschoolers. Some segments focus on negative aspects of the new baby such as crying and funny smells. *Kid Juror Comments*: Children respond by talking about their siblings and families, and some even drew pictures of their families. "I want my mom to have a baby." "I liked the baby songs." Video. 30 min.; $10.95; Age: 2-6. Huggabug Productions, Inc.

*** Animal Alphabet

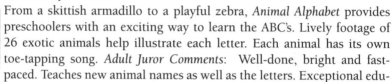

From a skittish armadillo to a playful zebra, *Animal Alphabet* provides preschoolers with an exciting way to learn the ABC's. Lively footage of 26 exotic animals help illustrate each letter. Each animal has its own toe-tapping song. *Adult Juror Comments*: Well-done, bright and fast-paced. Teaches new animal names as well as the letters. Exceptional educational value. Kids learn through songs and repetition. Older kids will continue to enjoy the animals even after they've learned their ABC's. *Kid Juror Comments*: Seeing a wide range of animals was wonderful. Kids learned their names and songs to go with them. They danced, sang, and asked for the animal names to be repeated for the animals they were unfamiliar with. "You shouldn't eat butterflies!" Video. 44 min.; $12.99; Age: 2-5. Time Life Home Video.

** Animal Numbers

Join this musical safari as *Animal Numbers* introduces children to the numbers zero through ten. *Adult Juror Comments*: Good production and cinematography. "Teaches counting and classification skills by focusing on lots of different eyes, tails, ears, and noses of animals." Catchy tunes, though songs seem longer than necessary and are hard to learn. *Kid Juror Comments*: High repeat value. Most asked to see again. They danced, counted with the narrator, and called out the names of familiar animals. "Look at the bird riding on the alligator's back." "I saw lots of tails." "The kitties were my favorite." Video. 40 min.; $12.99; Age: 2-5. Time Life Home Video.

Chapter Two • Preschool

*** *Arthur Gets Lost (Arthur)*

Includes two stories. Arthur is ready for his first solo ride on the public bus. He has his book to read and the exact fare. But then he falls asleep and wakes up in a strange part of town. Will he find his way home, and will D.W. forgive him? *Adult Juror Comments*: Arthur is a great role model. Tells anecdotes that adults can relate to. Teaches valuable lessons about being lost and civic mindedness. Teaches assertiveness skills; enhances self-esteem and positive self-concept. *Kid Juror Comments*: Remained attentive throughout and wanted to watch it again. "Everybody loves Arthur. I was afraid when he was lost." Some parts were scary. "It taught us things. I learned that I have to pick up garbage. Let's go clean the playground." Video. 30 min.; $12.99; Age: 2-5. Sony Wonder.

*** *Arthur's Baby (Arthur)*

Arthur is not sure he's ready for a new baby in the house. As the months fly by, Arthur imagines how his life is about to change—and it isn't a pretty picture. When the baby arrives, it seems as if she doesn't like Arthur very much—or does she? *Adult Juror Comments*: Excellent production, good content. Deals with jealousy, anxiety, and safety. Insightful and well-paced. The section with opinions by "real" children is excellent. Useful for families expecting a new baby. *Kid Juror Comments*: "My kids laughed so much it made me laugh." Kids with siblings really responded well. One five-year-old said, "Everything they say is very, very true." Stories capture kids' thoughts and feelings. The characters respected each other. Video. 30 min.; $12.98; Age: 2-7. Sony Wonder.

** *Arthur's Teacher Troubles (Arthur)*

Arthur's biggest fear has come true: Mr. Ratburn is his third grade teacher. The man is rumored to eat nails for breakfast, to turn into a vampire at night, and give homework every day! *Adult Juror Comments*: Good subject matter about misconceptions—handled well, good content. Some vocabulary not age-appropriate. *Kid Juror Comments*: Enjoyed it, especially the child comments between the programs. The three-year-olds didn't understand the concept of false impressions. They like the fact that the characters are all different animals. Video. 30 min.; $12.98; Age: 3-6. Sony Wonder.

*** Baby Songs: ABC, 123, Colors & Shapes (Baby Songs)

Ten, live-action, finger-snapping Hap Palmer songs that entertain while introducing letters, numbers, colors, and shapes. *Adult Juror Comments*: A wonderful combination of music and learning. Encourages critical thinking. Children use the whole body while learning concepts. "I found my toes tapping on more than one occasion. It really pulled me into all the fun they're having." *Kid Juror Comments*: Kids danced and sang along. Wanted to watch several more times. The "Tap the Stick" song was very popular and encouraged children to play together. Everyone wanted to play with bean bags after the "Alphabet Bean Bag" song. "It made me dance silly." Video. 30 min.; $12.95; Age: 2-6. Backyard Productions.

*** Barney Goes to School (Barney Home Video)

Barney joins the Backyard Gang at school for finger-painting and to learn numbers, letters, colors, and shapes. Barney discovers why the children love to go to school. *Adult Juror Comments*: Quality production. Songs, fantasies, and school lessons are fun, hands-on, and well-presented. Promotes learning at school. Introduces water and pretend play. The patriotism is a little overdone and conformist. *Kid Juror Comments*: They smiled and danced to the music. Responded well to the combination of learning and fun. Video. 30 min.; $14.95; Age: 2-5. Lyrick Studios.

*** Barney in Concert (Barney Home Video)

Barney and the Backyard Gang hold a live musical extravaganza at the Majestic Theater in Dallas. Features traditional songs that encourage interaction and audience participation. Introduces Baby Bop, a forever two-year-old. *Adult Juror Comments*: Enjoyable for intended audience. Songs and skits encourage participation. Shots of the audience are delightful. *Kid Juror Comments*: "My two-year-olds really enjoyed this tape. They were dancing, clapping, and screaming." It held their interest. Video. 45 min.; $14.95; Age: 2-5. Lyrick Studios.

*** Barney Live! In New York City (Barney Classic Collection)

Barney appears on stage in New York for an imaginative and lively musical extravaganza. Barney, Baby Bop, and BJ teach the importance of having friends and sharing. *Adult Juror Comments*: Even Barney critics enjoyed this show. Nice awareness of gender roles such as the changing song that includes both mom and dad. It's entertaining for young and old to sing childhood songs with Barney and friends. Audience shots shows good diversity. *Kid Juror Comments*: Smash success. Children got up and danced, sang along. Kids were entranced, particularly younger ones. Barney makes them feel good. "Winkster is a fun character." Some wanted to watch it again. Video. 75 min.; $19.99; Age: 2-5. Lyrick Studios.

Chapter Two • Preschool

*** Barney Safety (Barney Home Video)*

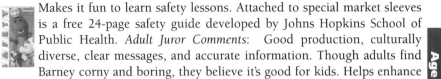 Makes it fun to learn safety lessons. Attached to special market sleeves is a free 24-page safety guide developed by Johns Hopkins School of Public Health. *Adult Juror Comments:* Good production, culturally diverse, clear messages, and accurate information. Though adults find Barney corny and boring, they believe it's good for kids. Helps enhance children's sense of self-esteem. Demonstrates love and friendship. *Kid Juror Comments:* Great. Barney is always a hit. Children immediately identify with character. Kids loved this and watched it again the next morning. Provoked discussion about disabilities. Video. 45 min.; $14.95; Age: 2-7. Lyric Studios.

*** Barney's Adventure Bus (Barney)*

Bus driver Barney takes the gang to some favorite imaginary destinations—a castle where Brett can rule; Barney's Purple Pepperoni Pizzeria; a rootin', tootin' ride into the Wild West, and a stop at the circus—all filled with fun and music. *Adult Juror Comments:* Attempts to appeal to older audience, but is more suitable for preschoolers. Emphasis on careers encourages kids to think about their future. Well-produced. Pace is too fast at times. Sets are unoriginal; messages a little simplistic. Good Diversity. *Kid Juror Comments:* Great. Preschoolers recognize and enjoy Barney and the other characters. They loved the music and fantasy parts, especially making pizza, the tight rope scene, and "all the adventures." It's a little on the long side, best viewed in segments. Video. 50 min.; $14.95; Age: 2-5. Lyric Studios.

*** Barney's Best Manners (Barney & Friends Collection)*

Barney and friends picnic and have a bubble splash party with Baby Bop. Songs reinforce saying "please" and "thank you," taking turns, opening and closing doors for friends. *Adult Juror Comments:* Offers exceptional reinforcements for using good manners. Relative naturalness of children is appealing. Activity guide offers appropriate, engaging suggestions. Pacing is a little slow. Overall feeling is positive. *Kid Juror Comments:* Two levels of satisfaction: Terrific or super-terrific. Enjoyed the songs that reinforce politeness, and imitated such behavior afterwards. All the kids enjoyed the bubble scene. Video. 30 min.; $14.95; Age: 2-5. Lyric Studios.

*** Barney's Big Surprise (Barney)

Barney the Dinosaur is planning a Super-Dee-Duper surprise party for BJ. It's going to be a musical extravaganza with Professor Tinkerputt, Mother Goose, and others. Includes "Barney Is a Dinosaur," "If You're Happy and You Know It," and other songs. *Adult Juror Comments*: Lively, entertaining combination of old and new songs. Enthusiasm is contagious. Mother Goose section explains what rhyming is. Even the kids who thought they'd outgrown Barney enjoyed the video. *Kid Juror Comments*: Children broke out into smiles and giggles. "If kids like Barney, they will like this." "The Humpty Dumpty rhyme part was my favorite." Stimulated questions about acting, theater, and production. Kids wanted to perform with Barney. Video. 78 min.; $19.99; Age: 2-5. Lyrick Studios.

*** Barney's Birthday (Barney Home Video)

For Barney's birthday, his friends throw the best party ever. Introduces birthday customs from other parts of the world. *Adult Juror Comments*: A pleasant, happy experience. Birthdays always appeal to kids. Portrays cooperation, creativity, and making your own party materials. Shows social skills representing different cultures. *Kid Juror Comments*: Love that Barney, especially the girls. They sang along and asked to see it again. Every child spoke about their own birthdays—what they would do and who they would invite. Video. 30 min.; $14.95; Age: 2-5. Lyrick Studios.

* Barney's Campfire Sing-Along (Barney Home Video)

The children meet all sorts of woodland creatures, study the stars, learn forest safety lessons, and discover the delights of using their imaginations. *Adult Juror Comments*: The content, songs, and concepts are more suitable to school-aged children than the preschool audience Barney attracts. The studio forest set looks phoney. The solutions to problems are too easy; kids are not encouraged to find solutions. *Kid Juror Comments*: This video is a little long for the intended audience. Children always like singing along to the familiar songs. The Barney doll advertisement is distracting. Video. 40 min.; $14.95; Age: 2-5. Lyrick Studios.

Chapter Two • Preschool

*** *Barney's Good Day Good Night (Barney)*

It's a warm, sunny day, and Barney and his friends are soaking up some wonderful fun. When Robert wishes that just once he could stay up all night long, Barney uses his special "Night Timer" to create "night" during the day. *Adult Juror Comments*: Cheerful, with limited adult appeal. Well-produced, colorful, nice songs. A pleasant look at the simpler side of day and night—wind, crickets, and fireflies. Barney gives children lots of praise for their thoughts and ideas. *Kid Juror Comments*: Liked the music and the songs. "There were silly parts like the moon getting dressed up." "Everyone was nice." Learned some new flower names. Two's and three's like this best. Even a one-year-old watched, clapped, and laughed along with Barney. Video. 50 min.; $14.95; Age: 2-5. Lyrick Studios.

*** *Barney's Halloween Party (Barney)*

Barney and his friends decorate the school gym for a party. BJ and Baby Bop prepare their costumes for a night of trick-or-treating. Although the trick-or-treaters come up empty-handed, their friends have goodies and friendship to share. *Adult Juror Comments*: Wow, a Halloween theme without the scariness. Colorful, good special effects, cheerful music encourages cooperation, good manners, and diversity. Well-produced with an overall good feeling that encourages participation, but doesn't challenge kids. *Kid Juror Comments*: Appealing, especially Barney's teal-and-purple pumpkin. "It had lots of funny parts." "It showed how to dance and sing." "They were having so much fun." A boy who said he hated Barney before watched the whole video and enjoyed it. Video. 50 min.; $14.95; Age: 2-5. Lyrick Studios.

* *Barney's Home Sweet Home (Barney & Friends Collection)*

There's no place like home. Barney's friends discover that there are many kinds of homes in the world, for animals as well as for people. *Adult Juror Comments*: Good tips for parents. Adult intervention helps expand on concepts in video. "A bit didactic. Barney is stiff and artificial-looking. Character interaction too contrived. Children in video overact." *Kid Juror Comments*: Enthusiasm wavered throughout; didn't hold their attention. Video. 30 min.; $14.95; Age: 2-5. Lyrick Studios.

*** Barney's Magical Musical Adventure (Barney Home Video)

A great adventure to a real castle. On the way, the troupe travels through a magical forest and discovers Twynkle the elf. *Adult Juror Comments*: Different themes and the music make this very appealing. Has good learning potential and age-appropriate language. Nice diversity. *Kid Juror Comments*: Totally absorbed. Watched intently and asked to see it over and over. "Magical Barney" had kids glued to their seats and promoted further discussion of Barney's adventure, as well as spontaneous clapping. Video. 40 min.; $14.95; Age: 2-5. Lyrick Studios.

*** Barney's Musical Scrapbook (Barney)

Remember when Barney and his friends sailed to Coco Island? Or when the wind came along and blew BJ's hat away? Aaaah, the memories. One look through Barney's scrapbook and you'll be reminded of some of the best Barney moments ever. *Adult Juror Comments*: Appealing and educational stories motivate parent and child to sing, dance, and play together. Vivid colors, friendly characters, multi-cultural, entertaining with lots of love, laughter, and lessons about respect and feelings. *Kid Juror Comments*: Great. Children don't just sit and watch, they get up and dance, sing, and clap. It prepares them for reading by teaching pre-reading skills using songs and language. "Let's do what they are doing. It's fun and has silly parts." Video. 50 min.; $14.95; Age: 2-5. Lyrick Studios.

** Barney: All Aboard for Sharing
(Barney & Friends Collection)

BJ, Baby Bop, and the children are left a host of surprises by trains passing through the playground. Barney, however, must wait for his surprise. Finally, it arrives: Stella the Storyteller recounts the story of "The Little Engine That Could." *Adult Juror Comments*: Nice imaginative play sequences have a sharing theme, although the sharing theme doesn't come across as well as expected. Adults thought the children in video were too perfect and not real enough. *Kid Juror Comments*: Barney is lovable in every form. Most of the child jurors sing and dance along. Some children were uncomfortable with the "feeling" songs. Younger kids enjoy it most. Video. 30 min.; $14.95; Age: 2-5. Lyrick Studios.

Chapter Two • Preschool

** Barney: Barney Rhymes with Mother Goose
(Barney & Friends Collection)

A bookworm has eaten the pages of Mother Goose's book. Barney and friends help Mother Goose remember her favorite nursery rhymes. Features songs, dances, puzzles, and puppets. *Adult Juror Comments*: Barney is child-centered, caring and encouraging. This tape comes with an activity guide recommending follow-up activities to reinforce message. Adults found inadequacies in the forced puppetry, heavy-handed diversity, and lack of musicality. *Kid Juror Comments*: Younger kids loved this and wanted to watch it again, some found it too long for one sitting and were easily distracted. Kids sang and danced along. They discovered Mother Goose rhymes are fun to say but thought that "Barney was not real." Video. 30 min.; $14.95; Age: 2-5. Lyrick Studios.

*** Barney: Camp Wanna Runna Round (Barney)

After a forest ranger visits the school, Jake decides he wants to be a ranger when he grows up. There's only one problem, he's never been in a real forest. With a little imagination and some help from Barney, Jake soon learns about the outdoors. *Adult Juror Comments*: Appeals to a large audience. Encourages children to use their imagination and be respectful of others. Well-produced. Bravo for putting promos at end of the show and not at the beginning. Good safety and environmental lessons. *Kid Juror Comments*: Excited by singing the songs and doing the exercises afterwards. Watched it twice. Prompted discussion about their camping experiences. Kids liked watching the child actors. Video. 50 min.; $14.95; Age: 2-5. Lyrick Studios.

*** Barney: Families Are Special (Barney & Friends Collection)

Barney and his friends celebrate and explore the uniqueness of individual families. Ella Jenkins makes a guest appearance. *Adult Juror Comments*: Entertaining, invites participation, nice songs. Subject is treated well, although all the families are two-parent families. Positive lyrics value uniqueness and encourage self-esteem. Ella Jenkins is a fabulous addition. *Kid Juror Comments*: Good stuff. Kids sang and danced along, especially with Ella Jenkins and the "Boppity Bop" song. Good pace for two- to five-year-olds. Stimulated discussion about twins. Video. 30 min.; $14.95; Age: 2-5. Lyrick Studios.

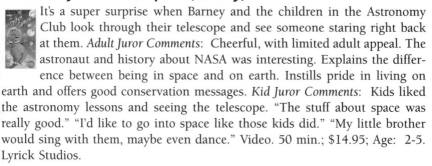

*** *Barney: In Outer Space (Barney)*

It's a super surprise when Barney and the children in the Astronomy Club look through their telescope and see someone staring right back at them. *Adult Juror Comments*: Cheerful, with limited adult appeal. The astronaut and history about NASA was interesting. Explains the difference between being in space and on earth. Instills pride in living on earth and offers good conservation messages. *Kid Juror Comments*: Kids liked the astronomy lessons and seeing the telescope. "The stuff about space was really good." "I'd like to go into space like those kids did." "My little brother would sing with them, maybe even dance." Video. 50 min.; $14.95; Age: 2-5. Lyrick Studios.

*** *Barney: It's Time for Counting (Barney)*

When Stella the Storyteller loses the numbers from her magic clock, it's up to Barney and his friends to help her find them. Their number search leads them straight to the library for some good old-fashioned storytelling fun. *Adult Juror Comments*: Thoroughly enjoyable. Humor is age-appropriate, shows good diversity, story moves well. Emphasizes importance of books and the library. "Barney is great at teaching social skills such as self-esteem." *Kid Juror Comments*: Children readily participated. Enjoyed finding the numbers, going on the treasure hunt. "He makes learning easy and makes me feel good." Kids wished they could play in the on-screen tree house. Two's and three's liked it best. Video. 30 min.; $14.95; Age: 2-5. Lyrick Studios.

** *Barney: Making New Friends (Barney & Friends Collection)*

Children learn that making new friends and attending a new school can be fun. *Adult Juror Comments*: Contains good topics related to friendship, old friends, new friends, and a new school. Language concepts clear, simple and entertaining. *Kid Juror Comments*: Most children can relate to having new friends at school. This is a popular topic. Barney fans loved this and were excited just to see Barney on the screen. Video. 30 min.; $14.95; Age: 2-5. Lyrick Studios.

* Barney: My Party with Barney (Barney)

Features the child of your choice starring Barney and Friends in a personalized video about your child's birthday party. Barney says the child's name and appears on-screen along with Barney, BJ, and Baby Bop. Lots of songs and animation. *Adult Juror Comments*: Music and visuals foster positive self-concept and social skills. Personalization feature is a real plus. Contains cheerful, catchy rhyming music, good visuals, and animation. Overall, the production is very choppy. *Kid Juror Comments*: The music motivated them to get up and dance. One song says, "You can tie your shoes," but most this age can't, and they noticed it. Competitive games are portrayed, which are inappropriate for this age. Video. 18 min.; $34.95; Age: 3-5. Kideo Productions, Inc.

** Barney: Rock with Barney (Barney Home Video)

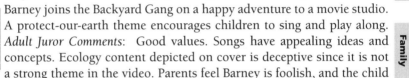

Barney joins the Backyard Gang on a happy adventure to a movie studio. A protect-our-earth theme encourages children to sing and play along. *Adult Juror Comments*: Good values. Songs have appealing ideas and concepts. Ecology content depicted on cover is deceptive since it is not a strong theme in the video. Parents feel Barney is foolish, and the child actors seem too old and unnatural for targeted age group. *Kid Juror Comments*: Captivated by music and dancing. They clapped and swayed, especially the girls. Children like Barney for his soft, appealing, comfortable look and his behavior, which honors them. And they love Baby Bop! Video. 30 min.; $14.95; Age: 2-5. Lyrick Studios.

*** Bear in the Big Blue House, Vol. 1: Home Is Where the Bear Is (Bear in the Big Blue House)

Bear tours the Big Blue House, introduces his friends, and together they point out their favorite things about each room. After all "Home is where your favorite stuff is." *Adult Juror Comments*: Excellent, engaging production down to the most minute details. Colorful characters. Presentation taps into kids' natural curiosity about other people's homes. Offers many opportunities for learning new words through songs and language. *Kid Juror Comments*: Very interested in discussing different types of houses. Liked the idea of creating their own pretend spaces. "Can we visit Bear's house?" "Can we play mail carrier?" "We want to write letter." Video. 50 min.; $9.95; Age: 2-5. Columbia Tristar Home Entertainment.

*** Bear in the Big Blue House, Vol. 2: Friends for Life (Bear in the Big Blue House)

Bear and his friends explore friendship and what it means to be someone's friend. Ojo learns to make new friends while still keeping all his old friends. *Adult Juror Comments*: Delightful. "Combines high-quality production and cuddle-cute characters with solid educational values. Shows children how to care for one another and demonstrates kindness." Adults found characters to be loud and obnoxious. *Kid Juror Comments*: Great. "Bear and his friends are very kind to each other." "We like the puppets." "Bear is big but friendly." Older kids didn't like the screechy voices. Younger ones weren't bothered by them. Most were familiar with the characters. Video. 50 min.; $9.95; Age: 2-5. Columbia Tristar Home Entertainment.

*** Bear in the Big Blue House, Vol. 3: Dancin' the Day Away (Bear in the Big Blue House)

Bear demonstrates different dances such as the Bear Cha-Cha-Cha, a jig, and a waltz. Bear teaches Tutter to dance because, after all, everybody can dance, even a little mouse. *Adult Juror Comments*: Tunes into child's world with a variety of colorful puppet characters who speak directly to the children. Excellent role models. Introduces new words. Offers many opportunities for learning. *Kid Juror Comments*: Music is a big attraction. Kids clapped and danced along. "Tutter is my friend." "I could watch this every day." "I want to dance like Bear." "We like the puppets." Older children sang the goodbye song. Video. 50 min.; $9.95; Age: 2-5. Columbia Tristar Home Entertainment.

*** Bear in the Big Blue House, Vol. 4: I Need a Little Help Today (Bear in the Big Blue House)

Bear has a case of the sniffles, and he's taking some quiet time. Everyone is helping to make him feel better, and with all the help, Bear will be back on his feet in no time. *Adult Juror Comments*: Characters are friendly and sincere. Plots are simple and well-paced. Shows self-respect and compassion. Colorful production without being garish. Careful listening is required to develop language and problem-solving skills. *Kid Juror Comments*: Appealing. Humor perfectly suited to children's sensibilities. Variety of characters and expressive features make them attractive but not cutesy. "I could watch this every day." Video. 50 min.; $9.95; Age: 2-5. Columbia Tristar Home Entertainment.

*** *Bear in the Big Blue House: Visiting the Doctor with Bear (Bear in the Big Blue House)*

  Going to the doctor is a scary proposition for a child. Bear visits the doctor's office in two episodes to show what happens and what can be done to ease the anxiety of a doctor visit. *Adult Juror Comments*: Wonderful. Outstanding songs and puppets. Speaks well to the child. "I especially enjoyed how well it explains what doctors do." "Good role models for overcoming fear." Easily viewed in two 25-minute segments. *Kid Juror Comments*: Enjoyed it, would watch again. "Bear helped Ojo. I love Bear." "It teaches everyone not to be afraid to go to the doctor." "I wonder if my doctor likes to go to the doctor?" "I thought the little rats getting their checkups were cute." Video. 50 min.; $12.95; Age: 2-5. Columbia Tristar Home Entertainment.

*** *Bedtime Stories*

 Timeless stories promise only the sweetest of dreams. These eight beautifully animated films are in the tradition of classic childhood favorites. *Adult Juror Comments*: Charming, lovely stories with real childhood bedtime rituals and issues. Comforting and fun to watch. Well-illustrated and colored. Wonderful pace. "This is one of the best videos for young children I have seen." *Kid Juror Comments*: Attentive, calm and smiling. Asked to see it again and again. "Everyone was very interested in commenting on their own bedtime rituals and feelings." "I like this one." "It's pretty." Video. 44 min.; $12.99; Age: 2-5. Time Life Home Video.

** *Berenstain Bears Vol. 2 (Berenstain Bears)*

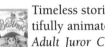 Contains three episodes, "The Berenstain Bears and the Truth," "The Berenstain Bears Save the Bees," and "The Berenstain Bears in the Forbidden Cave." *Adult Juror Comments*: Stories are great, with just enough conflict to provide interest, but not enough to distress a toddler. Characters are easy to identify with, though the father is often presented as foolish. Production is attractive, simple, and reassuring. *Kid Juror Comments*: Related easily to the message: Telling the truth is always better than lying. "I liked the characters." "It was fun to watch." "How did they get the flowers to eat the bees?" "They argued a lot, but in the end, they got along." Video. 36 min.; $9.95; Age: 3-6. Columbia Tristar Home Entertainment.

* Berenstain Bears Vol. 3 (Berenstain Bears)

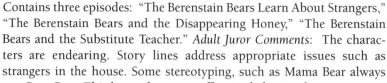

Contains three episodes: "The Berenstain Bears Learn About Strangers," "The Berenstain Bears and the Disappearing Honey," "The Berenstain Bears and the Substitute Teacher." *Adult Juror Comments*: The characters are endearing. Story lines address appropriate issues such as strangers in the house. Some stereotyping, such as Mama Bear always deferring to Papa Bear. Third story has some offensive behavior that goes unrecognized. *Kid Juror Comments*: Attentive. They recognized the characters and their traits from the books and asked to watch it again. "I liked Sister Bear." "I think everyone except bullies will want to watch this tape." Video. 36 min.; $9.95; Age: 2-5. Columbia Tristar Home Entertainment.

*** Best of Elmo, The (Sesame Street Home Video)

Elmo presents his greatest hits, from "Happy Tapping" to "Elmo's Song." Whether he's dancing on stage, explaining heavy and light to Telly, or singing along with Ernie, Elmo makes you smile. Whoopi Goldberg makes a guest appearance. *Adult Juror Comments*: Excellent, really holds kids' attention. Perhaps a little long for youngest kids, but can be viewed in segments. *Kid Juror Comments*: Fast pace. Kids love Elmo for his child-like qualities and enjoy singing along with him. Kids were attentive; particularly enjoyed music. Video. 29 min.; $12.98; Age: 2-5. Sony Wonder.

** Best of Kermit on Sesame Street
(Sesame Street Home Video)

Kermit the Frog has been named "Frog of the Year." It couldn't have happened to a nicer amphibian. Kermit's old pal Grover is on hand to host a special tribute to Kermit's most memorable moments on Sesame Street. *Adult Juror Comments*: Kermit is everyone's favorite. Exciting, bouncy, a little too chaotic at times. Encourages discovery, fosters learning, offers variety of musical styles, diversity, and silly humor. Front-loaded with commercials and inappropriate physical behavior. *Kid Juror Comments*: "It was fun." Kids were upset that Grover hit the pigs to get rid of them. "I'd like to talk to Kermit." "I liked the ABC song the best." Some children found the pace too slow and lost interest. Kids enjoy the familiar Sesame Street characters. Video. 30 min.; $12.98; Age: 2-5. Sony Wonder.

*** *Birthday Stories*

Captivating stories celebrate the wonder and anticipation of every child's birthday. These seven beautifully animated films are in the tradition of childhood classics. *Adult Juror Comments*: Visually interesting, great graphics. Offers a lot for kids. "I loved the stories. The colors, music, and voices were calming." British accents were fine, but kids will not understand some British words. Addresses social values such as sharing. *Kid Juror Comments*: Enjoyed what they saw and talked about the program afterwards. "Can we have a birthday party?" "I learned how to share and help each other." "I want it to be my birthday." Video. 44 min.; $12.99; Age: 2-8. Time Life Home Video.

** *Buzz Lightyear of Star Command*

The world's bravest Space Ranger takes on the evil Emperor Zurg in an intergalactic struggle. Zurg has invaded the Planet of Little Green Men, and Buzz and his fearless team of Space Ranger Cadets are the only ones who can save the day. *Adult Juror Comments*: Fun and interesting. Language is appropriate, the aliens not too scary, and in the end, good wins over evil. Amusing spoof on popular intergalactic war movies. *Kid Juror Comments*: Enjoyed by all, held their attention throughout...even those who had seen it already. Understood the lesson in teamwork. "They learned they needed to work together because Buzz needed help and couldn't do it alone." "What planet was that?" Video. 70 min.; $24.99; Age: 2-5. Buena Vista Home Entertainment/Disney.

** *Case of the Giggles, A (Hello Mrs. Cherrywinkle)*

Kitty is upset when she loses her stuffed puppy dog, and to make matters worse, one sniff of a giggle-lily has given everyone an unstoppable case of the giggles. Mrs. Cherrywinkle soothes ruffled feelings and saves the day. *Adult Juror Comments*: Colorful, fun-loving characters. Teaches lessons about sadness, happiness, and hurt feelings. "There tends to be a lot of yelling." Creative craft project is woven into the story, though some felt it was too rushed. "Hectic pace is fun but exhausting." *Kid Juror Comments*: Kids sang and danced along. They wanted to see the "ho-down" dance several times. "I liked the laughing flower." "Lets pretend we're a giggle-lily." "We want to make more things." Elicited empathy. "Poor kitty, she feels sad because she lost Sox." Video. 30 min.; $12.99; Age: 2-7. Time Life Home Video.

Age 2-5

Video

Family

Age 2-5

Video

Family

* Cat's Meow, The

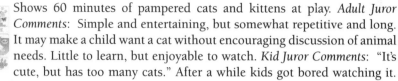

Shows 60 minutes of pampered cats and kittens at play. *Adult Juror Comments*: Simple and entertaining, but somewhat repetitive and long. It may make a child want a cat without encouraging discussion of animal needs. Little to learn, but enjoyable to watch. *Kid Juror Comments*: "It's cute, but has too many cats." After a while kids got bored watching it. The only ones who stayed with it were those with cats at home. Video. 60 min.; $9.99; Age: 3-6. Brentwood Home Video.

*** Daisy Head Mayzie by Dr. Seuss

Mayzie McGrew wakes up to find a daisy sprouting from her head. Faced with ridicule, she acquires the hard-won knowledge that love is more important than fame and glory. *Adult Juror Comments*: Colorful, fun, rhyming, great music, with a moral—the kids sing along. Brings an adventurous old-fashioned Dr. Seuss story to life. Some adults didn't quite understand the point. *Kid Juror Comments*: Fascinated. They joined in with the chant, "Daisy Head Mayzie" and were singing the song all day. Video. 23 min.; $12.95; Age: 2-9. Warner Home Video.

*** Dragon Tales: Big Brave Adventure (Dragon Tales)

Emmy and Max go on three adventures with magical talking dragons. First, Cassie learns that bringing something familiar to sleepovers makes them a lot more fun. Next, Zak learns that doctors want to help us. Then Ord learns not to be afraid of the dark. *Adult Juror Comments*: Wonderful production, beautiful scenery, brightly colored characters. Good "crisis-proofing" for potential crises like sleepovers, doctor visits, and darkness. Good role models for sharing feelings and working through fears with play. *Kid Juror Comments*: Loved it. They danced and sang along and immediately identified with the characters. "I slept over at my grandma's house and I was scared too." "Lets pretend we're going to the doctor's office." "The dragon had a thorn in his foot." Video. 40 min.; $12.95; Age: 2-5. Columbia Tristar Home Entertainment.

*** *Dragon Tales: Follow the Clues (Dragon Tales)*

Max and Emmy go on three adventures in Dragon Land. In the first, Doodle Fairy shows how pictures can help explain things. Next, Number Gnome shows how to count from 1 to 10. Then everyone learns that everything has its own special sound in Dragon Land. *Adult Juror Comments:* Super presentation. Fun music, clear voices, good graphics. Lively and positive. Pushes critical thinking and promotes pro-activity instead of re-activity. Great introduction into exploring and investigating. "Shows characters using their brains." *Kid Juror Comments:* Mesmerized, watched it from start to finish. Danced and sang along. Especially enjoyed the Silly Sounds Song and imitated the silly sounds. Dot-to-dot exercise held their interest. "We liked the silly songs and giggly flowers." Video. 40 min.; $12.95; Age: 2-5. Columbia Tristar Home Entertainment.

*** *Dragon Tales: Let's All Share (Dragon Tales)*

Go to Dragon Land with Max and Emmy on three different adventures. First, Ord learns how to share. Next everyone helps Cassie baby-sit baby Kiki. Then Cassie learns that being selfish is lonely, and sharing lets everyone play together. *Adult Juror Comments:* Entertaining. Story is perfect for this audience. Emphasizes friendship and teamwork. Teaches kids to see and understand simple concepts. No one is judged whether he or she is a human or dragon. They're all friends. *Kid Juror Comments:* Enjoyed the stories and the dancing. "My friends will love the magic crayon just like me." "I like to see Ord. He is so silly." "The dragons and the kids all treated each other so nice." "All the girls will like this. The boys won't like it so much." Video. 40 min.; $12.95; Age: 2-5. Columbia Tristar Home Entertainment.

*** *Dragon Tales: You Can Do It! (Dragon Tales)*

Go with Max and Emmy on three adventures in Dragon Land. First, Zak goes swimming for the first time. Next, Cassie learns how to roller-skate. Then, Ord tries to ride a bike, and finds out how hard it is. *Adult Juror Comments:* Playful. Delightful collection of stories, songs, kind characters. Shows friends being supportive and positive as younger characters learn new skills. Presented in segments with breaks in between that allow the kids to dance and sing. *Kid Juror Comments:* Loved the stories; related to the characters. "When the dinosaur learns to ride his bike, it taught us to keep trying even when you can't do something." "It makes me happy to see the dragons help each other." "The songs are fun." Video. 40 min.; $12.95; Age: 2-5. Columbia Tristar Home Entertainment.

** Elmo Says Boo! (Sesame Street Home Video)

Elmo drops by The Count's castle to stir up some scary fun. Lots of jokes, songs, and spooky surprises—even a visit from Julia Roberts as everybody's favorite furry red monster in the first-ever Sesame Street Halloween special. *Adult Juror Comments*: Excellent graphics, good jokes and riddles to engage everybody. Repetition well-used. Content is age-appropriate. Counting with the Count is well done. Kids enjoyed going inside his house. A little spooky for littlest ones. *Kid Juror Comments*: "It was just a little scary." Kids liked the songs, jokes, and Elmo—a perennial favorite. Afterwards, kids pointed out the bones in their own skeletons. Some found the "baby talk" disturbing. Video. 30 min.; $12.98; Age: 2-5. Sony Wonder.

* Emily and Happiness (A Creative Imagination Series)

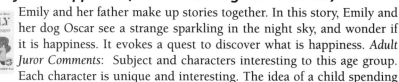

Emily and her father make up stories together. In this story, Emily and her dog Oscar see a strange sparkling in the night sky, and wonder if it is happiness. It evokes a quest to discover what is happiness. *Adult Juror Comments*: Subject and characters interesting to this age group. Each character is unique and interesting. The idea of a child spending time with a parent, making up stories, is commendable. Too bad it's slow-moving with poor sound quality. Little diversity. *Kid Juror Comments*: Kids thought it moved slowly, but liked the stories. "I like that they're nice to each other." "It got me interested in drawing pictures." Video. 30 min.; $12.95; Age: 2-5. Interama, Inc.

* Emily and Her Friends (Emily)

Two animated stories from Finland. In one, twin brothers receive a new bathtub boat they must share. In the other, Emily lives in the middle of an apple tree forest in which the trees are mysteriously disappearing. *Adult Juror Comments*: Uniquely introduces environmental awareness and encourages imaginative thinking and listening skills. Portrays good parent/child relationship. Slow pace, simple animation, poor sound quality. *Kid Juror Comments*: Inspired by family interaction: father and daughter making up stories together. Seven- to eight-year-olds created their own stories afterwards. Stimulated a discussion about conservation. Three- to four-year-olds liked the bathtub boat. Video. 30 min.; $12.95; Age: 3-6. Interama, Inc.

Chapter Two • Preschool

*** Family Tales (Maurice Sendak's Little Bear)*

Contains four episodes addressing family relationships based on books by Else Holmelund Minarik, illustrated by Maurice Sendak. Addresses Little Bear's adventure on an overnight camping trip, a surprise breakfast, and assurance from the howling wind. *Adult Juror Comments:* Very enjoyable and positive. Deals with emotions and behavior in clear, concrete ways. Great quality and appropriate for age group. Promotes further inquiry. Resolution of problems are clever and insightful while conveying a feeling of warmth. *Kid Juror Comments:* Funny. It also made them think and explore feelings. They were intrigued by the production. "How did they get the characters to walk?" "I like this movie!" "We like all of the movies of Little Bear!" Video. 34 min.; $9.95; Age: 2-6. Paramount Home Entertainment.

** Fire Trucks in Action*

Fire trucks and firefighters in action on the job. Demonstrates how equipment works and includes safety rules for children. Appropriate for home or school. *Adult Juror Comments:* Well done and informative. Great question and answer format. The accident scene may be a little scary. Lacks cultural diversity and female firefighters. Some kids were glued to the program for the entire time. *Kid Juror Comments:* Absorbing, especially watching the firefighters at work. Surprisingly, one child who has serious fears of fire loved it. "They showed stop, drop, and roll." Good job! Video. 25 min.; $14.95; Age: 2-5. High Profiles.

** Fishy Tale, A (Mumfie)*

Mumfie, an elephant, and his best friend, Scarecrow, win a goldfish at the local fair. Sadly, they learn they can't keep it, set out to find the perfect home for it, and end up helping others along the way. *Adult Juror Comments:* Cute, friendly, good animation. Appropriate content about sharing, cooperating, families, and caring for animals. Approaches emotional aspects of issues. "Why is the cloud sad?" Humor is more suited to adults than kids. Refers to past shows. *Kid Juror Comments:* Fun, good music. Kids enjoyed the friendship theme and related to the characters. They asked why an elephant, pig, and scarecrow would be friends. Despite the title, only the first story is about a fish. They kept asking to see the fishy video. Video. 45 min.; $12.98; Age: 2-5. BMG Home Video.

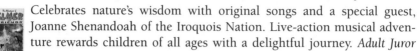

** Freedom Rocks (The Adventures of Elmer & Friends)

Celebrates nature's wisdom with original songs and a special guest, Joanne Shenandoah of the Iroquois Nation. Live-action musical adventure rewards children of all ages with a delightful journey. *Adult Juror Comments*: Discusses equality, acceptance, and purpose. Fosters insightful thoughts on Native American traditions. A cheerful production with scenic shots of animals, fun songs, respectful behavior. Mixed race, culture, and gender. Contains Christian overtones. *Kid Juror Comments*: Understood the humor. Younger kids enjoyed dancing to the songs and music. "I like the forest part. The puppets and the different animals are great. We liked learning about how Native American sports compare to our sports." Video. 30 min.; $14.95; Age: 3-6. Featherwind Productions.

** Good Advice, Captain! (The All New Captain Kangaroo)

Unsuccessful at building his new Billiwompis machine without following the directions, Joey learns the value of following directions. He also learns the value of safety rules after skateboarding inside the Treasure House and getting hurt. *Adult Juror Comments*: Good messages, songs. Sets are fanciful and colorful. Very age-appropriate. Lots of action and variety, yet all focused on topic. Just enough silliness to hold interest. Teaches difference between fantasy and reality. Little diversity. *Kid Juror Comments*: Valued the pleasant attitudes of the characters and the puppets. "We learned to help each other and follow directions." "Next time we make a cake, we should follow the directions." They enjoyed singing along and watching the animals. Video. 54 min.; $12.98; Age: 2-5. Twentieth Century Fox Home Entertainment.

* Grumpy Tree, The

Animated story about a tree who never wants to share. The tree is unkind to everyone and never realizes how lonely he is. When he's attacked by termites, the kindness of the forest animals helps him discover the meaning of true friendship. *Adult Juror Comments*: Teaches friendship and idea of working together. Starts slowly, picks up later. Addresses issues of personal competence, forgiveness, sharing, and friendship. Tree is a little too aggressively grumpy. The presenter's guide is excellent. *Kid Juror Comments*: Well with watching, despite slow beginning. Stimulated a discussion about friendship afterwards. "The drawings are pretty." "It made me think about being grumpy." Video. 13 min.; $9.95; Age: 2-6. Pauline Books and Media.

Chapter Two • Preschool

** Happy Birthday Mrs. C! (Hello Mrs. Cherrywinkle)

Murry, kitty, and fish conspire with Neddy and Captain Dinghy to stage a surprise birthday party for Mrs. Cherrywinkle, but they keep the secret so well that Mrs. C. begins to think they have forgotten her birthday. *Adult Juror Comments*: Bright colors with positive and age-appropriate content. Good diversity. Engaging songs invite participation. Many jurors would prefer that craft projects be demonstrated, not simply explained. Role models are cooperative and caring. *Kid Juror Comments*: They loved the birthday party theme. "I want to have a surprise party for my birthday." "I love all the balloons." They felt empathy and concern for characters. "I felt sad too, when I thought they forgot my birthday." "The fish-cake was funny." Video. 30 min.; $12.99; Age: 2-7. Time Life Home Video.

* Happy Ness Vol II

Join the McJoy children—Halsey, Haden, and Hanna—as they discover the magical land of Happy Ness that dwells far beneath the infamous Loch Ness. With their Scottish guide, Sir Prize, they meet the most lovable monsters of all time. *Adult Juror Comments*: Has upbeat, clear format most suitable for younger children. Too long for one sitting. Tends to offer simple solutions to improbable situations. *Kid Juror Comments*: Stayed with it, though a little scary at times. They related to "darkness" and "happiness." Some found it extremely slow-moving; others watched quietly and attentively. Some requested to see it again right away. Video. 95 min.; $19.95; Age: 2-5. Just For Kids Home Video/Celebrity Home Entertainment.

** I Love Toy Trains, Part 6 (I Love Toy Trains)

The seven-year-old narrator guides a tour of a steam engine museum, explains how steam works to power trains, how tracks are repaired, and about the different bridges used by trains. *Adult Juror Comments*: Engaging and informative about popular topics—trains, transportation, and bridges. Excellent real-life footage. Songs appeal to younger kids. Technical explanation of steam engines is unique and suitable to older kids. *Kid Juror Comments*: Liked singing along. Intrigued with how steam engines work. Child narrator was a hit. "I'd like to play with some trains now." Slow-moving for some. Five-year-olds said, "It's good for little kids, but we were bored." Video. 30 min.; $12.95; Age: 3-6. TM Books and Video.

Age 2-5

Video

Family

** Imagine with Us (Big Bag)

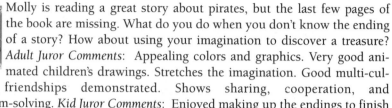

Molly is reading a great story about pirates, but the last few pages of the book are missing. What do you do when you don't know the ending of a story? How about using your imagination to discover a treasure? *Adult Juror Comments*: Appealing colors and graphics. Very good animated children's drawings. Stretches the imagination. Good multi-cultural friendships demonstrated. Shows sharing, cooperation, and problem-solving. *Kid Juror Comments*: Enjoyed making up the endings to finish the stories. It was slightly difficult to follow. May be best viewed in segments. Video. 60 min.; $12.95; Age: 3-5. Warner Home Video.

*** It's Itsy Bitsy Time (It's Itsy Bitsy Time)

This collection of animated children's shows includes the Animal Shelf, Budgie, Charley & Mimmo, and 64 Zoo Lane. All emphasize educational and social values. Features arts, crafts, and sign language for the hearing impaired. *Adult Juror Comments*: Highly rated. Enjoyable, value-based animated story segments are accompanied by a cheerful, bouncy soundtrack. Portrays patience and gentle interaction between adults and kids. "There is soooo very much to work with here." *Kid Juror Comments*: Kids sat up and clapped, sang, and snapped their fingers. They watched it over and over. "Can I make a leaf book too?" "How do hibernating animals know when to wake up?" "I like it better than Barney!" Video. 60 min.; $0 (Fox Family Network); Age: 2-7. The Itsy Bitsy Entertainment Co.

** It's the Pied Piper, Charlie Brown (Peanuts Classic)

What do you do when your town is overrun with soccer-playing, river-dancing mice? Charlie Brown calls Snoopy, the Pied Piper, to the rescue. Includes an interview with the Peanuts creator, Charles Schulz. Inspired by the Pied Piper fairytale. *Adult Juror Comments*: Well-produced, lots of singing and dancing. Emphasizes the importance of keeping promises. Some jurors objected to the use of the word "stupid" throughout the story. Classic story is retold in a childlike fashion. *Kid Juror Comments*: Mixed reviews. "Snoopy was funny." "I liked it when Charlie Brown read to his sister." "I liked the basketball playing scenes." Many kids objected to using the word stupid. "The grownups didn't keep their promise. That was not good." Video. 25 min.; $14.95; Age: 3-8. Paramount Home Entertainment.

Chapter Two • Preschool

** Jay Jay's First Flight (Adventures of Jay Jay the Jet Plane)

Join Jay Jay and friends on an aerial adventure on which they overcome fears, use their imaginations, follow the rules, and never give up. *Adult Juror Comments*: Good format with four stories, best viewed in segments. Good story lines and characters with expressive personalities. Children relate to the humor and other emotions. The ideas for discussion at the end of each segment are helpful and appropriate. *Kid Juror Comments*: Children relate to the characters, especially the planes. Kids laughed out loud at the funny parts, although some younger kids lost attention. It's better for them to watch individual stories separately. Video. 30 min.; $12.95; Age: 2-5. Kidquest.

* Jungle Jamboree

Combines a playful mix of puppets, costumed characters, and live-action performers to create a show full of song and learning. *Adult Juror Comments*: Somewhat slow, but catchy tunes contain good messages that promote a good sense of self-awareness. Content is age-appropriate. Segment about strangers gives mixed messages about trusting strangers and safety. *Kid Juror Comments*: Video okay, but not the songs. Set and characters appealed to kids. Discussion followed about being nice and being mean. Video. 138 min.; $19.95; Age: 2-5. Just for Kids Home Video/Celebrity Home Entertainment.

*** Lady and the Tramp II: Scamp's Adventure

Along with their well-behaved girl puppies, Lady and Tramp are raising Scamp—who is always in the doghouse. Scamp meets a stray named Angel, who introduces him to the Junkyard Dogs. Scamp is torn between a world of adventure and family life. *Adult Juror Comments*: Lively, colorful, and fast paced. Great animation. A fun and well-developed story that playfully coaches children in making the right choices. Shows positive parenting: concern and discipline when necessary; but always love, even when the child does wrong. *Kid Juror Comments*: Related very well to the characters and the conflict. "It is better to have a home than be part of a group." "It taught me to come home. Home is the best place." "I sometimes feel like Scamp, but I wouldn't run away." "Do dogs really eat spaghetti?" Video. 70 min.; $26.99; Age: 2-10. Buena Vista Home Entertainment/Disney.

Age 2-5

Video

Family

*** Let's Go Fly a Kite (Mumfie)

Mumfie and Scarecrow are having a tough time flying their special homemade kite, when suddenly the kite gets tangled in the tree. They learn a valuable lesson. *Adult Juror Comments*: Pleasant with a touch of reality in a light-hearted way. Mumfie shows empathy, is respectful and cooperative. Teaches kindness and concern for diversity of individuals. They enjoy their adventures. Vocabulary is a little sophisticated. *Kid Juror Comments*: Splendid musical interludes. Kids noticed how kindly the characters treated each other. They loved the flying piggy with the squeaky voice. Even two-year-olds were toe-tapping to the songs. Video. 45 min.; $12.98; Age: 2-5. BMG Home Video.

*** Little Bear Movie, The (Little Bear)

Feature-length, animated movie starring Little Bear and his friends as they explore friendship, family, adventure, and differences that make us special. Based on the children's book by Else Holmelund Minarik, illustrated by Maurice Sendak. *Adult Juror Comments*: Light, fun. Contrasts Little Bear's domesticated lifestyle with the lifestyle of a wild bear, encouraging the acceptance of diversity. Characters are considerate, calm, and relaxed. Love and respect between family members is exemplary. *Kid Juror Comments*: Found it funny and good. "It's so good I can't stop watching it!" "I liked seeing everyone sleeping in Cub's den and Duck was all spread out over Poppy and Pete." "Can we go camping with our families?" Video. 75 min.; $15; Age: 2-9. Paramount Home Entertainment.

** Little Engine That Could, The

This beloved children's story is retold this time as an animated feature. *Adult Juror Comments*: Nice adaptation. Simple production. The female character is determined, confident, and presents a positive message for girls. Lesson is portrayed without much imagination and by stereotypical characters, perhaps to make the point clear. *Kid Juror Comments*: A winner. Most are familiar with the story and love seeing it come to life. They giggled and listened. Video. 30 min.; $12.98; Age: 3-6. Universal Studios Home Video.

*** Lost & Found (Jane Hissey's Old Bear Stories)

Join Old Bear and his friends in a bit of mystery and intrigue as they band together in some puzzling situations. Based on the classic "Old Bear" storybooks by Jane Hissey. Includes "Little Bear Lost," "Little Bear's Trousers," and "Jigsaw." *Adult Juror Comments*: Engaging, with appropriate humor and images. Stop-motion animation works well. Discusses trust and the harmony of working together, as well as respect for adults. Accurately paced and simple, yet very engaging. Some vocabulary is too advanced. *Kid Juror Comments*: Calming yet captivating. Children enjoyed the stories, loved the puppets and the jigsaw puzzle. "My two-year-old watched it two times, start to finish! He giggled at the silly parts." Video. 30 min.; $9.98; Age: 2-6. Sony Wonder.

* Magical World of Trains, The (Train Adventure For Kids)

The magical engineer, Smoky Jones, examines trains both big and small. From passenger to freight, engine to caboose, Smoky shares the excitement of railroading. *Adult Juror Comments*: Appealing to children. Encourages creativity, exploration, and imagination. Relates experiences with explanations of safety issues. Good format and music. Concerns about strangers and kids going places with them. *Kid Juror Comments*: Okay. Video. 30 min.; $12.95; Age: 2-10. Goldhill Home Media.

*** Maisy's Colors and Shapes (Maisy)

Maisy, the lovable mouse, takes her friends on adventures with colors and shapes. Maisy and Cyrill buy balloons and find that it is not so easy to keep them from flying away. *Adult Juror Comments*: Vivid, beautiful colors, great animation, and upbeat music. Demonstrates sharing and friendship. Interacts with children. Encourages critical thinking and language development. Teaches directions. Best viewed in segments. *Kid Juror Comments*: Kids loved this. "Can we see it again...now?" "I laughed a lot. I love Maisy." The "Wheels on the Bus" song was a hit. Children danced and sang along. "Maisy is funny." "It made me think about sharing." "The animals were nice to each other." Video. 32 min.; $12.98; Age: 2-5. Universal Studios Home Video.

*** Maisy's Friends (Maisy)

Join Maisy the lovable mouse and all her friends for adventure and good times. Includes several stories about friendship including "Pool" and "It's a Very Hot Day." *Adult Juror Comments*: Beautiful colors. Simple, bright animation with big shapes and clear sounds. Characters are expressive, but nonverbal. Narrator's voice is calming and affectionate. Fosters discussion on topics such as sharing, helping, and cleaning up. *Kid Juror Comments*: Enthralled. Kids laughed a lot. "I'd like to watch it over and over everyday." "It made me want to read Maisy's books." "Maisy helped the elephant with his ouchee." "They hold hands and play ring-around-the-rosy just like me and my friends do." Video. 38 min.; $12.98; Age: 2-5. Universal Studios Home Video.

Age 2-5

Video

Family

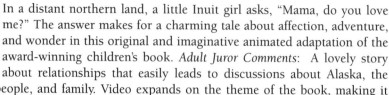

*** Mama Do You Love Me? (Doors of Wonder)*

In a distant northern land, a little Inuit girl asks, "Mama, do you love me?" The answer makes for a charming tale about affection, adventure, and wonder in this original and imaginative animated adaptation of the award-winning children's book. *Adult Juror Comments:* A lovely story about relationships that easily leads to discussions about Alaska, the Inuit people, and family. Video expands on the theme of the book, making it even more enjoyable. Excellent portrayal of Eskimos and their respect for animals. *Kid Juror Comments:* "It was great." "I want to know more about Alaska and sled dogs." "I thought about love and how I treat people." "Mother showed she really loved her daughter even when she was mad." Video. 30 min.; $12.98; Age: 3-8. Sony Wonder.

*** Max's Chocolate Chicken (Children's Circle)*

The Easter Bunny is watching to see if Max will play by the rules when he and his sister compete for the chocolate chicken. Directed by Michael Sporn. Includes three more book-based titles: "Each Peach Pear Plum," "Picnic," and "The Circus Baby." *Adult Juror Comments:* Thumbs up! Wonderful, lovely, engaging video based on award-winning children's literature. Inspired kids to seek out these books. Animation is touching. *Kid Juror Comments:* Big Success. Kids relate to animal themes and were taken by the characters. They liked the lead story and "Picnic" best, but truly enjoyed the whole program. Video. 36 min.; $14.95; Age: 2-7. Scholastic/Children's Circle.

** Me and My Tugboat (Me and My Series)*

A little boy loses his model tugboat in a creek and dreams about a colorful adventure on a real tugboat. Warm and humorous with fascinating people and awesome machines. It's about children's dreams that do come true. *Adult Juror Comments:* Captain Bob's acting seemed so real. The comparison to Christopher Colombus was distracting. Not a lot going on, best for kids interested in boats. Pleasant background music. *Kid Juror Comments:* The calypso-style music went over fine. Didn't understand the Columbus comparison. Definitely for younger children; older kids felt talked down to. Video. 34 min.; $19.95; Age: 2-8. Tony Artz Supreme Video Works.

Chapter Two • Preschool

*** Meet Little Bear (Maurice Sendak's Little Bear)*

One of the most cherished characters in all of children's literature, Little Bear, comes to life in these four stories full of warmth, humor, and mischief. Includes "What Will Little Bear Wear?" "Hide and Seek," and "Little Bear Goes to the Moon." *Adult Juror Comments:* Characters are charming, delightful, and pleasant to watch. Story line is easy to follow. The language is simple and age-appropriate. Reinforces good behaviors and emotions of preschoolers. Encourages adults to hug children. Stories are true to book. *Kid Juror Comments:* Terrific reception. Related to such activities as playing in the snow, fishing, and pretend play. Many children recognized the story. "The baby bear was cuddly." They liked the fish soup story best. Video. 34 min.; $9.95; Age: 2-5. Paramount Home Entertainment.

*** Mouse House*

Behind the tiny brown door of the Mouse House live five adorable mice: Betsey, Lester, Kevin, Max, and Primrose. Whether playing, cleaning house, making music, or adopting strays, they learn a lot about sharing, caring, and ups and downs of friendship. *Adult Juror Comments:* Gives you warm fuzzies. Very creative and simple. Nine story segments, each deals with an issue relevant to preschoolers, and each problem is handled sensitively. Adults loved this. The mice have British accents which kids tried to imitate. *Kid Juror Comments:* Loved it. With arms outstretched, one child said, "I liked it that much." "I love to say that poem with the Mom mouse." "I like bugs too. What's a sunbug? Do we have those in our yard?" "Can we watch it again?" Best viewed in segments. Video. 60 min.; $14.98; Age: 2-5. Twentieth Century Fox Home Entertainment.

** MRN: Circus Fun (Mister Rogers' Neighborhood)*

 The circus is fascinating, full of interesting people with unusual talents. Mister Rogers and Lady Aberlin visit the circus where they go backstage to visit performers and learn how much practice it takes to be a performer. *Adult Juror Comments:* Imaginative, informative, realistic presentation. A variety of characters and locations. Circuses can be fun but scary too. The animals were fascinating, although the caged tigers stimulated discussion about the treatment of circus animals. *Kid Juror Comments:* Children enjoyed it and wanted to do face-painting afterwards. They liked the way Nancy's friends helped her feel better about herself. Video. 28 min.; $9.98; Age: 3-6. Family Communications, Inc.

*** MRN: Going to School (Mister Rogers' Neighborhood)*

Children often wonder what school will be like for the very first time or when they start a new school year. Mister Rogers takes a ride on a real school bus and helps children realize that there are many caring teachers who will help them learn. *Adult Juror Comments*: Enjoyable. By the end of the tape even adults sang along. Structure helps explain what happens in school and then shows what it's like to actually ride a bus. Emphasizes the importance of caring, and teaches children not to be afraid. Great music. *Kid Juror Comments*: Children got excited about going to school. Loved the puppets, sang along with the songs, and moved to the music. They wanted to ride a school bus. Particularly helpful to kids who are just starting kindergarten. Video. 28 min.; $9.98; Age: 2-5. Family Communications, Inc.

*** MRN: Kindness (Mister Rogers' Neighborhood)*

Being kind means responding to the needs of others. Mister Rogers helps children know that when they are kind to others, they'll discover something worthwhile about themselves. *Adult Juror Comments*: Engaging, entertaining, and educational. Simple, comfortable, welcoming. Reinforces importance of teachers. Discusses need to practice (music, for example) everyday. Adult discussion helps to reinforce concepts. *Kid Juror Comments*: Children wanted to learn more about the accordion and the trolley. They liked the music and songs and clapped along with the rhythm band. Moved too slowly at times. "I like Mister Rogers, he is very nice." Video. 28 min.; $9.98; Age: 2-5. Family Communications, Inc.

*** MRN: Learning Is Everywhere!*
(Mister Rogers' Neighborhood)

Mister Rogers helps children know that the world is full of lots of things to wonder about, and that learning is everywhere when we're with people who care about us. *Adult Juror Comments*: Gentle but funny. The songs and music are slow and comforting. Mister Rogers asks lots of questions, talks about things he's doing, and is very conscious about demonstrating how both sexes—and all ethnic groups—can do everything. *Kid Juror Comments*: "I like Mister Rogers because he does nice things." "I want to find out about everything in this video." "It was too short." Most importantly, the show encourages young children to explore and learn about their environment and broaden their horizon. Video. 28 min.; $9.98; Age: 2-5. Family Communications, Inc.

Chapter Two • Preschool

*** MRN: Monsters and Dinosaurs
(Mister Rogers' Neighborhood)

 Mister Rogers, everybody's trusted neighbor, helps young children understand scary monsters. Visits a dinosaur exhibit and offers reassurances about scary dreams. *Adult Juror Comments*: Well-paced, not flashy, but very solid and child-centered. Encourages listening skills. *Kid Juror Comments*: An all-time favorite. Because it's long, most adults played it in segments, which worked well. Subject matter held children's attention. Video. 64 min.; $12.95; Age: 2-7. Family Communications, Inc.

*** MRN: Our Earth: Clean and Green
(Mister Rogers' Neighborhood)

 Mister Rogers helps children appreciate the wonderful beauty of our world. There's a visit from a real live goat and some ideas for making playthings from things that might have been thrown away. *Adult Juror Comments*: "Mister Rogers can do no wrong in my book." Subject of recycling is great. A little slow at times. Creates parent/child craft activities using simple things found at home such as a shoebox. Teaches that everything has a purpose. *Kid Juror Comments*: Very attentive, especially enjoyed seeing the goats. "I liked the shoebox being turned into a train." "Can we do that?" "I want to make puppets too." "Will we see the two puppets he made again?" Video. 28 min.; $9.98; Age: 2-5. Family Communications, Inc.

*** MRN: The Doctor, Your Friend
(Mister Rogers' Neighborhood)

 Children can better manage difficult experiences such as going to the doctor when they know what to expect. Mister Rogers visits a pediatrician during a young girl's routine checkup and lets children know that doctors care about them. *Adult Juror Comments*: Good cultural diversity. "Mister Rogers' warmth makes you feel like you're watching a friend." Briefly mentions private areas of the body and what to do if touched there. *Kid Juror Comments*: Elicited comments from the children about their experience with doctors. Most of the children watched closely; some didn't. The big favorite was Mister Rogers himself. A little slow-paced, but compelling. "How can I be a doctor?" Video. 28 min.; $9.98; Age: 3-5. Family Communications, Inc.

*** MRN: What about Love (Mister Rogers' Neighborhood)

Love is never easy to understand, especially when people who love each other get angry. Program helps kids appreciate love and other feelings that accompany it. "It's the people we love the most who can make us gladdest and maddest." *Adult Juror Comments*: It's thought-provoking with a simple, easy-to-understand style, and a clear and compassionate tone. Provides a supportive emotional video environment for kids. Very age-appropriate. Mister Rogers speaks slowly and clearly. *Kid Juror Comments*: Presentation allows time to stop and reflect. Appealed to older four- and five-year-olds. They responded best when questioned by an adult about the content. One child said, "I like everything Mister Rogers does." Video. 51 min.; $12.95; Age: 2-7. Family Communications, Inc.

** Old Oscar Leads the Parade and Other Stories (Adventures of Jay Jay the Jet Plane)

Model airplanes come to life in the storybook land of Tarrytown. In four short stories, Jay Jay discovers why it's always best to be "True Blue." Teaches respect for others. *Adult Juror Comments*: Addresses important social issues in ways that children can understand. "Presents idea that everyone is equally important, and you don't always have to win first place." Could be more diverse about culture, race, and gender. *Kid Juror Comments*: Thoroughly enjoyable. They found the plane characters entertaining. "Jay Jay told a fib and he was blue. He should have told the truth first." Video. 35 min.; $12.95; Age: 2-5. Kidquest.

** Paper Bag Players on Top of Spaghetti, The

Laugh, dance, and sing along with The Paper Bag Players in its first video. A runaway meatball, a heroic plumber, and a dreamy postman play parts in the stories, plays, and songs that make up this silly show. *Adult Juror Comments*: Entertaining stories that address issues such as sharing and making up for wrongdoing. Uses a theatrical structure to present eight different skits, but it's a little too simple for today's child. Like other plays, when videotaped, it loses its luster. *Kid Juror Comments*: Laughed loud and often. Liked the content, but most were unimpressed by the delivery. Only one group did not respond positively. "It was funny." "I like singing." "My friends would love this." Video. 57 min.; $15; Age: 3-7. The Paper Bag Players.

Chapter Two • Preschool

** *Play Along with Allegra and Friends (Allegra's Window)*

Stand up and join the fun as the Hummingbird Gang offers nine get-up-and-sing numbers. *Adult Juror Comments*: Sets and characters are appealing. Allegra is very pleasant. Transitions well-timed and entertaining. Nice diversity. Appropriate characterization of competitive game behavior. Music is age-appropriate. Over stimulating, visually cluttered. *Kid Juror Comments*: "Good singing." Enjoyed the mix of people and characters. They liked the flying horse, the sharing, and the flashback effect, and thought there were some good ideas. They noticed that the cat always wanted to win. Video. 29 min.; $9.95; Age: 2-5. Paramount Home Entertainment.

** *Play Along with Binyah and Friends (Gullah Gullah Island)*

Teaches a variety of different games: pretend, clapping games, team sports. Includes "I love a Haircut," a barbershop sextet that makes Simeon's first haircut memorable. *Adult Juror Comments*: Offers role models from multi-cultural age groups, preschoolers to seniors. Emphasizes positive ways to deal with mistakes: "Continue practicing and try your best." Games invite audience participation. Binyah's voice is hard to understand. *Kid Juror Comments*: Three- to six-year-old kids loved the songs, games, and Binyah character though they thought the kids weren't really singing along in the video. Video. 30 min.; $12.98; Age: 2-6. Paramount Home Entertainment.

*** *Pooh's Grand Adventure (Winnie the Pooh)*

On the last day of summer, Christopher Robin can't bear to tell Pooh he is going to school, so he leaves a note that Pooh, Piglet, Tigger, and Rabbit misunderstand—they think he has gone to skull! The adventure begins when they go to rescue him. *Adult Juror Comments*: Loved it. One the best Pooh films yet. A great lesson in personal strengths and learning about yourself and your fears. Beautiful animation, silly Pooh fun. "Everyone can find something to like." *Kid Juror Comments*: Pooh Bear is always a hit, and this adventure kept them on the edge of their seats. They sang and hummed the tunes. "Christopher Robin said I am smarter than I think." "It was so much fun to watch, it had such nice music in it, we really loved it." Video. 70 min.; $24.99; Age: 2-11. Buena Vista Home Entertainment/Disney.

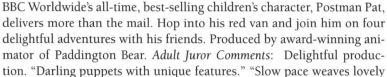

** Postman Pat Takes the Bus (Postman Pat)

BBC Worldwide's all-time, best-selling children's character, Postman Pat, delivers more than the mail. Hop into his red van and join him on four delightful adventures with his friends. Produced by award-winning animator of Paddington Bear. *Adult Juror Comments*: Delightful production. "Darling puppets with unique features." "Slow pace weaves lovely little tales." Shows respect for the elderly and people helping other people. Depicts everyday life in a small English village. Stereotypes females. *Kid Juror Comments*: Watched attentively and noticed details. "Postman Pat lets everyone on the bus." "I liked it a lot, especially his truck." "The puppets all have big noses." "How come the mail boxes aren't blue?" "My mom lost her ring too and boy, was she sad." Video. 75 min.; $19.95; Age: 2-5. Just For Kids Home Video/Celebrity Home Entertainment.

*** Quiet Time (Sesame Street Home Video)

Big Bird's not sure what to do when his Granny Bird tells him it's quiet time. Fortunately, Oscar, Telly, Rosita, and his other Sesame Street friends have plenty of great ideas, like reading stories and playing quiet games. Features Daphne Rubin-Vega. *Adult Juror Comments*: Great subject. Adults love Sesame Street too. Perfect four- to five-year-old humor! Excellent choice of vocabulary level, selected experiences, activity breaks, and music. Interracial mix of kids. *Kid Juror Comments*: Endearing and fun. "It was silly." Kids liked suggested activities: touching tongues to nose and balancing spoons. Kids offered their ideas about appropriate quiet-time activities. Video. 30 min.; $12.98; Age: 2-5. Sony Wonder.

* Raggedy Ann & Andy: The Pixling Adventure (Adventures of Raggedy Ann and Andy)

Raggedy Dog finds a baby in a basket. The baby is Prince Luke, heir to the Pixling throne. To be crowned, he must reach the Pixling Castle by nightfall. *Adult Juror Comments*: Contains a scary stalker, inappropriate language, and baby's crying is constant and irritating. It's intense and frightening to young viewers. Little diversity. Shows teamwork, humor, adventure, suspense, and resolution. *Kid Juror Comments*: Kids asked why baby was always crying. Younger viewers had a hard time understanding the finer points of the story line. "Grouchy bear is mean, but sometimes he does help." Video. 28 min.; $9.98; Age: 3-7. Twentieth Century Fox Home Entertainment.

** Rainbow Fish (Doors of Wonder)

 With his coat of sparkling scales, he was the most beautiful fish in the sea. He was so proud that his selfishness left him feeling very alone. But as he is about to discover, the best feeling of all comes from sharing the things you care about most. *Adult Juror Comments*: Good message about teamwork and sharing. Production features colorful, special effects. Some messages are too mature for this age group, and they were not adequately resolved. *Kid Juror Comments*: A keeper! Three-year-olds were very responsive. They loved the fish and the story. "I'm glad rainbow fish learned how to make friends." Video. 30 min.; $12.98; Age: 3-6. Sony Wonder.

*** Richard Scarry's Best Busy People Video Ever! (Richard Scarry's Best Videos Ever!)

All the Richard Scarry Busytown characters take turns answering every child's favorite question: "What do you want to be when you grow up?" Shows children what it's like to be a farmer, a firefighter, a teacher, or a truck driver. Original music. *Adult Juror Comments*: Fun, book-based title. Shows better cultural and gender roles than the original books do. Music is catchy, easy to learn. Exceptional use of language. Promotes children's interest in literature. *Kid Juror Comments*: Fast-moving, holds children's interest. Kids wanted to view it again. Identified with the characters and sang along. Generated discussion on what boys and girls wanted to be when they grew up. Video. 30 min.; $9.98; Age: 2-6. Random House Video.

*** Rock Dreams (Puzzle Place, The)

 Puppet-kids learn to solve life's little problems. Native American figure, Red Thunder, shows how music can help harmonize your life. *Adult Juror Comments*: Attractive characters, cooperation, and problem-solving. Excellent puppetry and real people playing instruments. Social issues are seldom portrayed as insightfully as this. Adults loved the Boys Choir of Harlem. Best viewed in segments. *Kid Juror Comments*: Really liked singing along. "This is really good at showing people from different places," one six-year-old commented. Children played their own instruments afterwards. Video. 55 min.; $9.98; Age: 2-7. Sony Wonder.

*** *Rolie Polie Olie: A Rolie Polie Christmas* (Playhouse Disney)

Rolie and his sister Zowie spread holiday cheer in these three stories. They meet up with Klanky Klaus in "Starry, Starry Night" and see a snowman come to life in "Snowie." Then in "Jingle Jangle Days Eve," Olie's family gathers for a Christmas adventure. *Adult Juror Comments*: Cute Christmas spoof. Adorable short segments suits attention span of audience. Colorful story, appealing music. Charming robot characters in a magical and intriguing world. Fun, extended family interacts respectfully. Handles difficult situations well. *Kid Juror Comments*: Held the kids' attention. They related to the young characters having fun, loving snow, sometimes having an accident. "I loved the snow story." "I love to think about things in the future. Maybe we'll all have robot families in our families." Video. 24 min.; $19.98; Age: 2-5. Buena Vista Home Entertainment/Disney.

** *Rolie Polie Olie: Happy Hearts Day (Rolie Polie Olie)*

There's a new girl in Polieville, and pals Olie and Billie act pretty silly when she's around—until they learn a loving lesson in courtesy and friendship on Gooey Hearts Day! *Adult Juror Comments*: Interesting, unusual style. Good color, sound, and movements. Wonderful role models and good silliness. Supportive situations and mischief all in one. Characters are made of geometric shapes. Some jurors found the voices irritating. *Kid Juror Comments*: Genuinely liked it. Enjoyed the bright colors and songs and appreciated the relationships between characters. "They are all good to each other because they are getting love." "Zooey made her dad's boo-boo better." "It was good to teach us manners." Video. 24 min.; $12.99; Age: 2-5. Buena Vista Home Entertainment/Disney.

*** *Rosie's Walk & Other Stories (Children's Circle)*

"Rosie's Walk" stars an overeager fox and the hen he is stalking. Includes: "Charlie Needs a Cloak" by Tomie de Paola, "The Story about Ping," and "The Beast of Monsieur Racine." *Adult Juror Comments*: Wonderful stories, great music that fits the mood of the stories. Good choices for discussion starters. The "Ping" story may work better for older children; younger ones didn't like the animation on this story. *Kid Juror Comments*: A hit, especially among the younger ones. Elicits participation. "I like Rosie a lot." Video. 32 min.; $14.95; Age: 2-8. Scholastic/Children's Circle.

** Rupert

"Rupert the Bear" has been Britain's most beloved comic strip since 1920. Video contains 12 delightful stories featuring Rupert and his friends, Bill Badger, Tiger-Lily, and Jack Frost. *Adult Juror Comments*: Not full animation, but nicely illustrated. May have too little action for kids today. Appealing and friendly characters. Charming rendition of story book style. Likely to encourage reading of similar stories. The rhyming is fun. *Kid Juror Comments*: "That was a good one." "I liked the magic ball." Narration was too fast for kids to understand, maybe a little too long. Video. 57 min.; $9.98; Age: 2-5. Twentieth Century Fox Home Entertainment.

** Rupert and the Runaway Dragon

Join Rupert and his friends Bill Badger, Tiger-Lily, and Jack Frost on an enchanted journey containing seven stories. Rupert the Bear has been Britain's favorite comic strip for almost 80 years. *Adult Juror Comments*: Entertaining and unusual stories, but not full animation. "This video is like reading stories from a book." Narration was read too fast. Length of episodes and video well done. *Kid Juror Comments*: Children enjoyed the video for the first twenty minutes, then became restless. "Rupert is nice." "He plays with friends." Kids had a hard time keeping up with the narrator. Video. 36 min.; $9.98; Age: 2-5. Twentieth Century Fox Home Entertainment.

** See What I Can Do (Gregory and Me)

The viewer becomes the star of the show. Gregory Gopher, inventor, explorer, adventurer—leads the viewer on many adventures, discovering new ideas for projects, travels, shows, and parties. *Adult Juror Comments*: Well-paced, though the "personalized" segments are primitive. Encouragement messages are clearly presented, focusing on thinking through problems. Characters are polite. Contains some gender stereotyping and is crammed full of commercials. *Kid Juror Comments*: "They watched, got up and down, and followed the characters' actions." Music is hummable. Good mixture of real and pretend. "The bird yells a lot." Children wanted to be included in the tape. Video. 25 min.; $34.95; Age: 2-5. Kideo Productions, Inc.

** Sesame Street: Elmo's Sing Along Guessing Game
(Sesame Songs Home Video)

Elmo hosts Sesame Street's wackiest TV game show. Guess the answer to Elmo's questions with the help of some sing-along video clues. Features favorite songs like Big Bird's "My Best Friend," Kermit's "I Love my Elbows," and more. *Adult Juror Comments*: Scored high with adults. Themes of cooperation and friendship are excellent. Has good diversity and mix of age groups. Beginning is a little confusing. *Kid Juror Comments*: Okay. Thrilled to see their favorite Sesame Street characters. Story line a little difficult for younger kids to follow. Video. 30 min.; $12.98; Age: 2-5. Sony Wonder.

*** Sesame Street Visits the Firehouse
(Sesame Street Home Video)

 When Oscar's trash-can barbecue gets a little too smoky, the Sesame Street gang gets a visit from some firefighters who invite them back to the firehouse for a tour. Big Bird, Elmo, and Gordon learn all about fighting fires. *Adult Juror Comments*: Informative, full of safety tips and great learning potential. Kids see the equipment, are exposed to procedures, noises, and terminology. Closed-captioned for hearing-impaired. *Kid Juror Comments*: Children love to laugh at Elmo's antics. Really held their attention and stimulated continued play with firefighter props. Interacted with the dialog in the video. "We need to have a fire drill." A little scary for younger ones. Video. 30 min.; $9.98; Age: 2-5. Sony Wonder.

*** Sesame Street's 25th Birthday: A Musical Celebration
(Sesame Street Specials)

An hour-long collection of favorite Sesame Street songs, such as "C is for Cookie," "Bein' Green," "Monster in the Mirror." Ernie sings a medley of Duckie songs, and Big Bird leads a rousing finale of "Sing." *Adult Juror Comments*: Lively, contains lots of songs and shows excellent cultural diversity. Wonderfully ethnic! Great for active parent or teacher involvement: dancing, sing-along, creative movement. Long and best viewed in segments. *Kid Juror Comments*: Children clapped and danced, loved the singing and music—especially the African songs and singers. Video. 60 min.; $12.98; Age: 2-5. Sony Wonder.

*** Sesame Street: Kids Favorite Songs
(Sesame Street Home Video)

Elmo is getting ready for his Top Ten Countdown on the radio, and everyone on Sesame Street wants him to play their favorite songs! But with so many great songs to choose from, how will Elmo pick which ones to play? *Adult Juror Comments*: A lighthearted video, fun for parents and kids alike. "Not only did the video play music that kids liked, but they learned to count, too!" Upbeat, lively sing-alongs. "Watching with a child is a great excuse to act like a kid." *Kid Juror Comments*: Great enthusiasm. Sang loudly to all of the songs, and frequently giggled. "I know all the songs so I can sing EVERYTHING!" "I want a radio that plays all these songs." Had the kids counting along. "Let's do our ABC's." Video. 30 min.; $12.98; Age: 2-5. Sony Wonder.

*** Sesame Street: Let's Eat (Sesame Street Home Video)

Grover, the waiter, has a new job working at Planet Storybook. When his favorite customer comes in, Grover becomes a monster with a mission—to introduce this picky eater to all the fabulous foods that he could be enjoying. *Adult Juror Comments*: Funny, witty characters, charming story line, attractive multi-faceted presentation. An entertaining, well-made, colorful and culturally diverse show. All complex ideas and words are explained in a kid-friendly manner. Great cultural diversity. *Kid Juror Comments*: Kids were riveted throughout the entire program. "Yes, we would watch it again because it is so funny." "It taught us about vegetables. We didn't know there were so many." Children sang and danced. "I don't like broccoli." Video. 30 min.; $12.98; Age: 2-5. Sony Wonder.

*** Sesame Street: The Alphabet Jungle Game
(Sesame Street Home Video)

Elmo, Zoe, and Tell explore the Alphabet Jungle, where letters grow on trees. Every letter from A to Y leads them on an animated adventure, but Zoe's favorite letter is missing. What will happen if Zoe can't find the letter Z? *Adult Juror Comments*: Imaginative, interesting, invites participation. "Fun to watch with my grandchild." Rhythmic pace, eye-catching too. Occasionally inconsistent: skipped definitions for letters Q, R, S, and V. *Kid Juror Comments*: Fabulous, especially the ending, in which they had to find what started with "Z." "The alphabet party was fun." They recognized lots of words and wanted to see it again. "I love Elmo and Zoe." Video. 30 min.; $12.98; Age: 2-5. Sony Wonder.

Age 2-5

Video

Family

*** Sesame Street: The Great Numbers Game (Sesame Street Home Video)

With a push of the start button, Elmo and friends find themselves transported to a magical forest filled with hidden numbers. Each one they find leads them to one of Sesame Street's classic counting cartoons, but will they make it to number 20? *Adult Juror Comments*: Cute characters, engaging video clips, and lively colors. Made by people who truly understand kids. Emphasizes how numbers are sequential. Discusses time, using clocks, and days of the week. *Kid Juror Comments*: "I would like everyone to like it." "Number 14 is my favorite!" "I'd like more videos about numbers." Children asked to see this again, immediately after first viewing. Video. 30 min.; $12.98; Age: 2-5. Sony Wonder.

*** Share with Us (Big Bag)

Molli and Chelli learn to share crayons. Chelli's not sure he wants to share, so it's up to the viewer to convince him that it's the right thing to do. Invites the viewer to find out how great it feels to help a friend. *Adult Juror Comments*: Very cute, likable characters. Nice mix of animation and puppets, imaginary and real-life characters, with catchy music and wonderful songs. Subject is age-appropriate. Many ethnic groups positively represented. Shows difficulty in sharing. *Kid Juror Comments*: Promotes friendship between people, characters, and animals of all genders, races, shapes, and sizes. Reinforces feelings and emotions respectfully. Gives the viewer a sense of control. "My friends would like everything about this video." Video. 60 min.; $12.95; Age: 2-5. Warner Home Video.

*** Sharing Is Caring (The All New Captain Kangaroo)

Two stories: In the first one, Bunny wins a prize and hoards his prize carrots. He ends up learning the importance of sharing. In the second, Moose, Bunny, and Joey learn to take turns, listen to each other, and create music as a band. *Adult Juror Comments*: Attractive, interesting, and helpful themes—taking turns and sharing. Respectful of other people and animals. Good variety of characters. Concepts may be difficult for children under three. Reinforces idea that learning can be fun. *Kid Juror Comments*: Appealing and repeatable. Kids especially liked the live animal segments. Also liked the Captain. He laughs a lot instead of getting angry. Good environmental awareness. Video. 54 min.; $12.98; Age: 2-5. Twentieth Century Fox Home Entertainment.

*** Small Is Beautiful (Allegra's Window)*

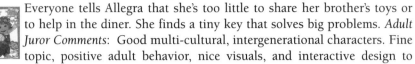

Everyone tells Allegra that she's too little to share her brother's toys or to help in the diner. She finds a tiny key that solves big problems. *Adult Juror Comments*: Good multi-cultural, intergenerational characters. Fine topic, positive adult behavior, nice visuals, and interactive design to demonstrate key concepts. Incorporates reading skills. *Kid Juror Comments*: Easily related to the human-like puppets. More appropriate for five- and six-year-olds. Video. 28 min.; $9.95; Age: 4-6. Paramount Home Entertainment.

** Spot Goes to a Party and Other Delightful Stories (Spot)*

Based on the books by Eric Hill. Spot the curious puppy goes to a party and a fair. Spot also follows his nose, goes on his first picnic, and swims at the beach. *Adult Juror Comments*: Cute stories. Multiple themes cover lots of familiar activities for preschoolers. Inspires imagination and discussions about make believe. Some scenes may need adult reinforcement about safe behavior. *Kid Juror Comments*: Engaged and delighted them. Kids can relate to Spot and his preschool-like antics. "They had a birthday cake at the party just like me." "It was funny when Spot's friend pretended to be a horse and gave Spot a ride." "Dress up is fun." Video. 30 min.; $19.98; Age: 2-5. Buena Vista Home Entertainment/Disney.

** Story of Joseph and His Brothers, The (The Beginner's Bible)*

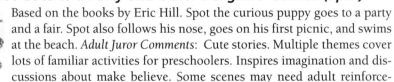

Joseph's jealous brothers throw him down a well. He is captured and taken to Egypt, where he becomes a favorite with the Pharaoh and finds himself sitting in judgment over his brothers. He must choose between vengeance and divine forgiveness. *Adult Juror Comments*: Appealing, with good handling of sibling rivalry, jealousy, spirituality, and lying. Egyptian symbols are instructive. Story is harsh for this age, promoting faith without enriching the themes. Christian overtones are prominent. *Kid Juror Comments*: Good songs and characters, particularly for four-year-olds. Whether or not children learn lasting lessons about lying or rivalry is questionable. Some scenes are scary for younger kids. Video. 30 min.; $12.98; Age: 3-6. Sony Wonder.

Age 2-5

Video

Family

** Sue's Birthday Adventure (Grandpa's Magic Shoebox)

Barely out of the egg, Sue the alligator sings instead of hisses—unheard of for an alligator. Exiled from her jungle home, Sue rises to fame and stardom as a singer. *Adult Juror Comments*: Good production quality, simple story. Jurors enjoyed the message about Sue's struggle to fulfill her dream to become a singer. It teaches kids to believe in themselves. Story is somewhat long for younger children and too simple for older kids. *Kid Juror Comments*: The story provoked questions from the kids about the character's motives and actions. "Paper trees are easy to make, and the puppets are cool." Video. 44 min.; $12.95; Age: 3-7. Barry Simon Productions.

* Tale of the Bunny Picnic (Tale of The Bunny Picnic)

Bean Bunny learns that he is worthwhile even though he seems too insignificant to be of much help to anyone. *Adult Juror Comments*: Engaging characters and story. Younger kids will enjoy the puppets but have difficulty comprehending the moral of the story. Long, slow-moving, poor audio, some inappropriate language. Toddlers won't understand the farmer's cruelty to the dog. *Kid Juror Comments*: Farmer's bad language is excessive and bothersome to preschoolers. They enjoyed the bunnies and the songs. Kids sang along and clapped. "It was funny when the bunnies scared the dog." Video. 51 min.; $9.95; Age: 2-5. Columbia Tristar Home Entertainment.

** Teo

Teo is a redheaded, restless, curious, kind, and good-natured four-year-old. In his company, the viewer is introduced to various situations and characters related to family, friends, and animals. *Adult Juror Comments*: A simple, well-paced production with good music, art, and age-appropriate vocabulary. What two- to five-year-old doesn't relate to a walk in the park? Lacks diversity in characters and shows some gender stereotypes. Reinforces safety issues. *Kid Juror Comments*: Stimulated discussion about parks and family outings. Children liked the simple music and presentation. They commented on the British accents. The program is short and left kids wanting to see more. "The mommy and daddy are nice." Video. 30 min.; $14.95; Age: 2-5. B.R.B. Internacional, S.A.

** *Theodore Helps a Friend (Theodore Tugboat)*

 Boats take on character and names in these stories that tell how Northumberland, the Sleepy Submarine, makes himself surprisingly scarce when another boat visits the big harbor. Bedford Buoy puzzles everyone when he wants to leave the harbor. *Adult Juror Comments*: Character and stories teach good value lessons about respect while building vocabulary. Social interactions are well done, if long-winded. Helping others, keeping friends, and dealing with conflict are all addressed. Shows little diversity. *Kid Juror Comments*: The children sang along and wanted to play in the water afterwards. Boys really enjoyed the boats. They were particularly interested in the submarines. They liked the different characters. Video. 43 min.; $12.95; Age: 3-6. Warner Home Video.

*** *Theodore Tugboat: Nighttime Adventures*

 Theodore Tugboat and friends set out for nighttime fun and adventure on Big Harbor. *Adult Juror Comments*: "Pleasant characters and good story lines for all three stories." "The narrator's voice is soothing." Running time of each is the right length for preschoolers. The stories are preschooler issues: nighttime fears, nobody's perfect, and staying up late. *Kid Juror Comments*: "I like to sing along with boats and ocean creatures." "One boat was grumpy, but said she was sorry." "A favorite was when the boats turned off their lights and told Hank about the Big Dipper." "I want to know how they found things on the ocean floor." Video. 45 min.; $12.95; Age: 2-5. Warner Home Video.

** *Theodore Tugboat: Underwater Mysteries (Theodore Tugboat)*

 Tugboats with different personalities work with Theodore to solve mysteries. More importantly, acting as a team, the tugboats learn to resolve personality issues—such as bragging and bossiness—amongst themselves. *Adult Juror Comments*: Simple, enjoyable presentation. Boats have appealing expressions and strong color contrasts. Models social skills such as team work and conflict resolution. The stories are engaging, full of adventure, and easily viewed in segments. *Kid Juror Comments*: Most enjoyable. "I want to watch this everyday, even when I'm 100 years old." "I liked that the stories were mysteries that weren't too scary." "I couldn't wait to see how the story ended." "It made me think about other people." Video. 44 min.; $12.95; Age: 2-6. Warner Home Video.

** Theodore's Friendly Adventures (Theodore Tugboat)

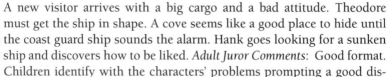 A new visitor arrives with a big cargo and a bad attitude. Theodore must get the ship in shape. A cove seems like a good place to hide until the coast guard ship sounds the alarm. Hank goes looking for a sunken ship and discovers how to be liked. *Adult Juror Comments*: Good format. Children identify with the characters' problems prompting a good discussion on cooperation and problem-solving. Contains fine themes, good voices, personalities. Boats are appealing, with large eyes, happy faces, and color contrast. *Kid Juror Comments*: Compelling stories and characters, although the kids were bothered by the story about poor listening ears and bad behavior. Children could relate to the feelings and emotions of Theodore and his friends. A bit slow, they wanted to watch it again, Video. 43 min.; $12.95; Age: 2-5. Warner Home Video.

** Thomas the Tank: Better Late Than Never
(Thomas the Tank Engine & Friends)

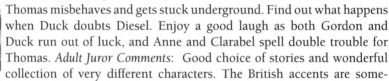 Thomas misbehaves and gets stuck underground. Find out what happens when Duck doubts Diesel. Enjoy a good laugh as both Gordon and Duck run out of luck, and Anne and Clarabel spell double trouble for Thomas. *Adult Juror Comments*: Good choice of stories and wonderful collection of very different characters. The British accents are somewhat difficult to follow. The three sections are best viewed together, although each one warrants its own discussion. *Kid Juror Comments*: Threes and fours liked watching this. However, school-aged kids understand the stories and messages better. Boys were attracted to the trains. Their interest in mechanical things was higher than most of the girls. Many were familiar with the TV show. Video. 40 min.; $12.98; Age: 3-8. Anchor Bay Entertainment.

** Thomas the Tank: Daisy & Other Stories
(Thomas the Tank Engine & Friends)

More escapades of Thomas the Tank Engine and Friends: Daisy, a classy, sassy passenger diesel; Trevor, the very useful tractor engine, and others. *Adult Juror Comments*: These simple stories are effective two and easy for kids to understand. They're well presented and age-appropriate. Though the trains have little action, their humanized faces make very appealing expressions. *Kid Juror Comments*: Readily identified with the characters. It's surprising how appealing this is to children who often don't enjoy programs with so little movement. Thomas is a big hit with both preschoolers and younger school-aged children. Video. 37 min.; $12.98; Age: 3-8. Anchor Bay Entertainment.

** *Thomas the Tank: James Goes Buzz Buzz*
(Thomas the Tank Engine & Friends)

Still more adventures with Thomas and friends. Meet Bulgy, the devious double-decker bus. Watch Bertie make a mad dash to rescue a tardy Thomas. See James brave a swarm of buzzing bees, and giggle while Percy puffs his way into a sticky predicament. *Adult Juror Comments*: This is a pleasure. Nicely produced. Helps develop good listening skills. Adults were concerned about lack of attention to safety. They ride over a broken bridge because they're in a hurry. *Kid Juror Comments*: Quite appealing and will watch again and again. Kids love learning the identity of each character. They remember them in subsequent viewings. The bee story was a quick favorite. For this age group, it's best viewed in segments. Video. 37 min.; $12.98; Age: 3-8. Anchor Bay Entertainment.

** *Thomas the Tank: James Learns a Lesson*
(Thomas the Tank Engine & Friends)

With a peep of his whistle and a puff of steam, Thomas chugs merrily along, pulling the passengers safely behind him. Thomas and friends always learn lessons that get them back on track. *Adult Juror Comments*: The settings and landscapes are very well done, the narrative is simple. Extremely well-done, both in terms of production value and the story content. British accent may be a problem for some children. *Kid Juror Comments*: Captivated by the trains. They would watch it repeatedly, especially when viewed in segments. Kids recognize and relate to Thomas. Prompted discussions afterwards about the characters and their individual traits. Video. 40 min.; $12.98; Age: 3-8. Anchor Bay Entertainment.

** *Thomas the Tank: Percy's Ghostly Trick*
(Thomas the Tank Engine & Friends)

Percy has Thomas thinking he's just seen a ghost. On their next escapade, the tables turn when Percy puffs away into a giant pile of hay. The seven stories can be watched independently. *Adult Juror Comments*: Entertaining and imaginative. The content is most appropriate for school-age children, whereas the presentation is more suitable for preschoolers. The narration is appropriately paced and works for both ages. *Kid Juror Comments*: Liked the narrator's voice and related to the characters, although keeping them separate is a little confusing at first. Boys are particularly responsive; not many female roles. Video. 37 min.; $12.98; Age: 3-8. Anchor Bay Entertainment.

** Thomas the Tank: Races, Rescues & Runaways (Thomas the Tank)

Alec Baldwin narrates new stories featuring races, rescues, and runaways with Thomas and his friends. Watch what happens to Percy when some runaway freight cars cause a near-disaster. Cheer Harold as he comes to the aid of troubled Toby. *Adult Juror Comments:* "I surprised myself by thoroughly enjoying this video." "Excellent narration; good use of intonation." Introduces new vocabulary. There is some teasing among the characters. Every story ends happily. Lacks gender diversity. *Kid Juror Comments:* Appeals to kids' imagination and sense of fairness. Children asked lots of questions. "What's a lorry?" "Where do the trains sleep?" Evoked empathy. "Thomas had a bad day." "The helicopter helped the train." "My friends would like it." Video. 37 min.; $12.98; Age: 2-5. Anchor Bay Entertainment.

** Thomas the Tank: Rusty to the Rescue & Other Thomas Stories (Thomas the Tank Engine & Friends)

This tape includes six stories and a music video. Thomas meets his new friend Rusty for fun and adventure on the Island of Sodor. *Adult Juror Comments:* Jurors liked the moral issues in the story, but thought it was too complicated for some viewers. Still, it's a great way to introduce new and different vocabulary to preschoolers. *Kid Juror Comments:* Thomas was particularly attractive. It's surprising how much they respond to him. Too long for the youngest viewers, but the stories can be watched separately. Video. 44 min.; $12.98; Age: 4-8. Anchor Bay Entertainment.

*** Thomas the Tank: Thomas and His Friends Get Along (Thomas the Tank Engine & Friends)

This compilation features some of the best Thomas stories on how to get along with one another, work together, and develop trust. *Adult Juror Comments:* Contains great stories with excellent messages about caring and sharing, friendship, and how to treat one another. Well-produced though little diversity is shown. "Children will definitely be engaged in the stories." Contains great stories with excellent messages about caring and sharing, friendship and how to treat one another. Well produced though little diversity is shown. "Children will definitely be engaged in the stories about Thomas and his friends." *Kid Juror Comments:* This was a group favorite that motivated discussion on sharing and caring. "Most kids loved this video." The sets provided strong visual appeal for the youngest kids, and the stories appeal to the four- and five-year-olds. Video. 56 min.; $12.98; Age: 2-5. Anchor Bay Entertainment.

** *Thomas the Tank: Thomas Breaks the Rules*
(Thomas the Tank Engine & Friends)

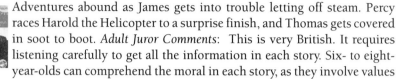 Adventures abound as James gets into trouble letting off steam. Percy races Harold the Helicopter to a surprise finish, and Thomas gets covered in soot to boot. *Adult Juror Comments:* This is very British. It requires listening carefully to get all the information in each story. Six- to eight-year-olds can comprehend the moral in each story, as they involve values and discrimination, among others. Best viewed in segments. *Kid Juror Comments:* Liked Thomas and the different train characters with their varied personality types. The four- and five-year-olds especially enjoyed this. There was lots of train playing afterwards. Video. 40 min.; $12.98; Age: 3-8. Anchor Bay Entertainment.

** *Thomas the Tank: Thomas Gets Bumped*
(Thomas the Tank Engine & Friends)

Harold thinks he can deliver the mail better than the others. Edward and Trevor prove they are useful despite being older, and a VIP engine visits the yard. The storyteller is George Carlin. *Adult Juror Comments:* Delightful stories with simple lessons that build interpersonal skills. The short segments are appropriate. A great vehicle to introduce new vocabulary to preschoolers and even early elementary-age children. *Kid Juror Comments:* Adults wondered whether kids would have difficulty understanding the British accent, but they had no problem with it. High appeal to boys. Video. 37 min.; $12.98; Age: 3-8. Anchor Bay Entertainment.

** *Thomas the Tank: Thomas Gets Tricked & Other Stories*
(Thomas the Tank Engine & Friends)

All aboard for a trainload of fun with Thomas and friends. This trip tours the Island of Sodor with Thomas, Gordon, Edward, Percy, Toby, Annie, and Clarabel. Narration is by Ringo Starr. *Adult Juror Comments:* "One of the best in the series." Great role models for relating with one another and treating people well. Ringo Starr's storytelling is a joy. Some gender stereotyping. *Kid Juror Comments:* Quietly enjoyed watching. Appropriate for both preschoolers and younger school-age children. Surprisingly, the kids got very attached to the individual train characters. Video. 40 min.; $12.98; Age: 3-8. Anchor Bay Entertainment.

** *Thomas the Tank: Thomas, Percy & the Dragon* (Thomas The Tank Engine & Friends)

Watch for miles of smiles from Thomas, Percy, and the gang on the Island of Sodor. Percy meets a dragon. James handles an embarrassing situation. Donald and Douglas rescue Henry, and some silly freight cars cause trouble. Storyteller is George Carlin. *Adult Juror Comments*: These simply produced stories promote positive values and role models. The length of these sweet vignettes is very age-appropriate. The relation of male to female trains seems a bit sexist. *Kid Juror Comments*: Fixated for the whole program. Children relate well to Thomas as well as the other characters. This tape prompted a discussion about fears afterwards. Video. 37 min.; $12.98; Age: 3-8. Anchor Bay Entertainment.

** *Thomas the Tank: Trust Thomas* (Thomas the Tank Engine & Friends)

Mavis, a young diesel engine, puts Toby on the spot. Percy keeps his promise. The engines help Henry rescue the forest. *Adult Juror Comments*: These stories lead to clarification of values and early moral development. The characters have well-defined traits and problems. However, children not fluent in English may find it difficult to understand. It's very language-dependent. *Kid Juror Comments*: Children responded well to these stories, especially when the engines move. Boys like them better than the girls. The stories are best viewed in segments and discussed afterwards. Video. 40 min.; $12.98; Age: 3-8. Anchor Bay Entertainment.

** *Three Little Pigs, The (Toddler Tales)*

Designed for use by parents as well as kids. By incorporating toddler issues such as learning to "use your words," children enact the traditional story with a toddler twist. *Adult Juror Comments*: It's enjoyable to see a child-acted play. Shows many positive behaviors such as sharing, working together, taking turns, using words to solve problems and communicate feelings. Low production level, poor sound, entire program is shot in a back yard. *Kid Juror Comments*: Kids enjoyed this. Humor is just right for this audience. "I liked it when the first pig built her house." "Why were all the pigs girls?" Kids dressed up and began role-playing afterwards. Video. 20 min.; $14.95; Age: 2-5. Toddler Tales.

Age 2-5

Video

Family

Chapter Two • Preschool

*** Tigger Movie (Winnie The Pooh)*

When everyone gets annoyed with Tigger's counterproductive bouncing, Rabbit suggests that Tigger go outside and find other tiggers to bounce with—a ridiculous notion to the "onliest" Tigger. He begins on a journey to find his family. *Adult Juror Comments*: Wonderful production. Aesthetically pleasing. Cute story with sweet, heart-warming characters. Depicts tender friendship role models. Offers an up-close look at real-life feelings and interpersonal relationships. *Kid Juror Comments*: Loved it. "I love Tigger! He is so funny." "It was sad to find out that Tigger didn't have a family. Then, we found out that all his friends are his family and that is great." "This story is about helping others when they are lonely and sad." Video. 77 min.; $19.98; Age: 2-8. Buena Vista Home Entertainment/Disney.

** Toothbrush Family, The: Visit from the Tooth Fairy, A (Toothbrush Family, The)

The bathroom world of the Toothbrush Family is full of surprises such as mischievous dinosaurs, runaway clothespins, dancing shoes, and even a tooth fairy. In their world of make-believe, anything can happen. *Adult Juror Comments*: Entertaining and engaging. Easily breaks into segments. Provides many examples of problem-solving skills and cooperation. "Encourages beneficial health practices by making the bathroom a fun and exciting place." "Fanciful." *Kid Juror Comments*: Enthusiastic. Kids liked the sharing and friendship. "Backwards land was great. Let's play backwards land." "I liked when they helped each other play in the water." "The dinosaur was the best." "Let's brush our teeth." "My brother would like it." Video. 85 min.; $19.95; Age: 2-5. Just For Kids Home Video/Celebrity Home Entertainment.

*** Tots TV: The Tots and the Great Big Light (Tots TV)

Find out what happens when the Tots go on a seashore adventure and discover a lighthouse. Listen as Tilly tells the Tots about three mischievous elves. And laugh at Tom's silly new game. *Adult Juror Comments*: Great puppetry. Characters are lovable and cute. An excellent opportunity to learn respect for different cultures and languages, including an introduction to Spanish. Good-quality production. Colors, animation, and detail all excellent. *Kid Juror Comments*: Children were deeply engaged, enjoyed the songs, and loved learning Spanish. Prompted good discussion about the fear of thunder and how to handle it. They wanted to share the themes of friendship. Video. 31 min.; $12.98; Age: 2-5. The Itsy Bitsy Entertainment Co.

Age 2-5

Video

Family

*** Tots TV: The Tots and the Lovely Bubbly Surprise (Tots TV)

Tiny's Bolsa Magica (magic bag) contains a gift for the giraffe. Discover who can build the tallest Tot's Tower. Smile as Tilly, Tom, and Tiny discover the magic of bubble making. *Adult Juror Comments*: Interesting and humorous. Tots' antics bring back childhood memories. Reinforces positive themes that children recognize such as respect, sharing, and playing with others. Colors are warm and realistic, voices are gentle. Lots of diversity. *Kid Juror Comments*: All thumbs up! Children talked about bubbles, blew bubbles, and stacked towers all the next day. Lots of conversation about what they could use for bubbles and safe things to stack. "I have never seen a giraffe." Video. 35 min.; $12.98; Age: 2-5. The Itsy Bitsy Entertainment Co.

*** Tots TV: The Tots Find a Treasure Map (Tots TV)

In a secret magical cottage live the Tots—Tom, Tiny, and Spanish-speaking Tilly. Finding lost things is the Tots' specialty. In doing so, they reunite a lost girl with her mom, track down Donkey when he gets loose, and find a secret map. *Adult Juror Comments*: Main characters are quite entertaining. They sang, gardened, and played together, imparting a feeling of warmth and concern for one another. Offers good insight on getting lost, doing business, and problem-solving. Good introduction to Spanish. *Kid Juror Comments*: Children loved this and wanted to watch again. They watched intently when the child got lost in the grocery store. "How do they know what Tilly is saying?" (Tilly speaks Spanish only.) "I know they are good friends because they help each other." Video. 31 min.; $12.98; Age: 2-5. The Itsy Bitsy Entertainment Co.

*** Tots TV: The Tots, the Moon, & the Happy House (Tots TV)

Three characters live in a magical cottage. Mixes live action and puppetry. One tot, Tilly, speaks only Spanish. *Adult Juror Comments*: It's delightful, with cute characters, good production values and well-paced story. Excellent way to introduce Spanish and keep children interested. Very positive. Portrays cooperative family relationships, care and respect for living things. *Kid Juror Comments*: Wonderful! Cute! Kids were mesmerized. Liked the fantasy world and the kittens. They enjoyed the different languages. "I learned how to say uno, dos, tres which means 1, 2, 3." "I liked the Spanish. I tried to learn some words." Video. 31 min.; $12.98; Age: 2-5. Anchor Bay Entertainment.

*** Tots TV: Tilly's Magic Flute (Tots TV)*

 In a secret magical cottage in the woods live the Tots—Tom, Tiny, and Spanish-speaking Tilly. In this episode, the Tots go on an adventure, see a musical instrument constructed out of wood, and listen to Tilly play her magic flute. *Adult Juror Comments*: Lively and engaging with cute and diverse characters. Production uses puppets and live action to address a musical theme. Shows curiosity as positive, respect for others, the importance of friends, and a love for nature. Reinforces art appreciation. *Kid Juror Comments*: Happily lapped up all the information and asked lots of questions about the instruments. The music was catchy and inspired them to dance. They wanted to play with musical instruments afterwards. "This is one of my favorites." Video. 31 min.; $12.98; Age: 2-5. The Itsy Bitsy Entertainment Co.

** Tracy's Handy Hideout & Three Other Stories (Adventures of Jay Jay the Jet Plane)*

 Contains three stories addressing the importance of taking care of the things you love, how teamwork works in a stormy situation, and how sharing can solve problems. All this plus a magical flight through the clouds. *Adult Juror Comments*: Simple production, somewhat repetitive, with appealing characters and worthy story lines about friendship and elders. Lacks diversity and has some gender stereotyping. *Kid Juror Comments*: Liked the stories which are short and easy to follow. Children related to the different plane characters. Some thought the faces were scary; others thought they were all smiling. Two- and three-year-olds liked it best. Video. 32 min.; $12.95; Age: 2-5. Kidquest.

*** Veggie Tales: Are You My Neighbor? (Veggie Tales)*

Loving thy neighbor is the theme, featuring two funny stories that help kids understand and celebrate the many differences that make people unique. The first story is based on the Good Samaritan tale; the second story is a Star Trek spoof. *Adult Juror Comments*: A well-animated, comical program. Promotes kindness and understanding differences. Christian overtones. "Made me smile." "Tunes are catchy, colors are vivid, and use of spaceships and faraway lands attracts all ages." *Kid Juror Comments*: Liked the characters. They thought it was fun to dance and sing along. "They were talking nicely and being nice, I like that." "I liked the tomatoes and spaceships and how they made them fly." "What a fun video." Video. 30 min.; $12.99; Age: 2-8. Big Idea Productions, Inc.

** Veggie Tales: Madame Blueberry (Veggie Tales)

A very blue berry delivers a message about thankfulness. Madame Blueberry has everything she needs, but she's not satisfied. She and her friends learn that "being greedy makes you grumpy, but a thankful heart is a happy heart." *Adult Juror Comments*: Excellent production: music is catchy, animation is flawless, has brilliant colors, and is very imaginative. Humorously teaches a lesson about greed and thankfulness. Helps kids explore their emotions. *Kid Juror Comments*: Learned that you don't need a whole lot of stuff to be happy. They were amused when Madame Blueberry bought so many things, her house crashed. They noticed representations of people of different cultures. Loved the humor and the music. Video. 30 min.; $12.99; Age: 3-8. Cushman/Amberg Communications.

** Veggie Tales: Rack, Shack & Benny (Veggie Tales)

Kids learn to resist peer pressure in an engaging way. Even when they get permission to eat as many chocolate bunnies as they want, Rack, Shack, and Benny remember what their parents taught them. They do what's right even when their friends don't. *Adult Juror Comments*: Veggies have individual characteristics, a sense of humor and wit, moral development, and are lively and personable. Shows excellent examples of peer pressure. Respects kids' thinking. Some stereotypes; Christian overtones. *Kid Juror Comments*: Children loved the perfectly silly songs, singing and dancing at the end. It simplifies some big issues for kids. "I liked how the girl carrot saved her friends and God put the fire out in the furnace." Kids learned why "sissy" is a mean word. Video. 30 min.; $12.99; Age: 3-8. Big Idea Productions, Inc.

*** Waiting for Grandma (Allegra's Window)

Allegra can't seem to wait for anything. It's even harder knowing that today is the day of the "Hummingbird Alley Holiday Happy Hoopla" and the day her grandma is coming to visit. *Adult Juror Comments*: Puppets are wonderful. A great tribute to grandmas everywhere with positive messages of cooperation, helping others, family tradition, memories. "This is one swinging, modern grandma!" Emotional themes explored thoughtfully. "A feel-good program." *Kid Juror Comments*: A sweet and lively story about grandmothers and grandchildren. Kids admired the characters and related well to them. "This movie's about waiting and Christmas celebrations. I just loved Grandma." Video. 30 min.; $12.98; Age: 2-5. Paramount Home Entertainment.

** When Nino Flew

Inspired by Mayan legends. Maria flies on her winged burro to get a feather from the old serpent of the mountain to cure her sick baby brother. Includes adventures, an epic battle, and triumphant return. Demonstrates love, selflessness and courage. *Adult Juror Comments*: Simple production demonstrates bravery, sibling love, and positive values. Promotes idea that anything is possible. Features a female heroine. Touching story invites discussion. Simple, child-like illustrations give it a "real" quality. *Kid Juror Comments*: Very well appreciated. Kids liked the dragon and the sense of danger without being scary. An Ojibwa girl who is very proud of her cultural heritage thought this was a great film and was inspired to create a film of her own. Video. 25 min.; $14.95; Age: 3-7. West Hill Press, Inc.

*** Which Way Weather? (Live Action Video)

A group of children explore seasonal weather conditions and related activities, from puddle stomping to ice skating. Includes a songbook. *Adult Juror Comments*: Wonderful, child-centered, hands-on. Good for stimulating thinking and imagination. Makes weather exciting, gives kids good ideas and concepts. A multi-cultural mix of children. *Kid Juror Comments*: The children on screen were very attractive. Prompted discussion about what they had done or wanted to do like the kids in the video. Stimulated interest about the weather. Video. 30 min.; $14.95; Age: 2-5. Bo Peep Productions.

** Wide Awake at Eureeka's Castle (Eureeka's Castle)

The sun's gone down but Batly and Magellan don't want to go to bed—ever again. Who wins the contest to stay awake as Eureeka guides the viewer on a tour of the castle? *Adult Juror Comments*: Colorful, cute, and fast-moving. Creative ways to combat anti-bedtime behavior. Promotes respect and cooperation. Deals with "night noises." A little overdone with outrageous and "loud" characters. Adults objected to excessive commercial trailers. *Kid Juror Comments*: Older kids thought it was for younger kids, but watched and laughed anyway. Young kids enjoyed it a lot and asked to see it again. Children wanted to sing along with the songs but couldn't. Video. 35 min.; $12.98; Age: 2-5. Paramount Home Entertainment.

Age 2-5

Video

Family

** William's Wish Wellingtons (William's Wish Wellingtons)

William is a small boy with a big imagination and a pair of magical red boots. Whenever William wants something special, he puts on his wonderful red Wellingtons, makes a wish and "poof," he's on a new adventure. From the creators of "Sesame Street." *Adult Juror Comments*: A delightful and endearing adventure. Portrays helpful behaviors. Some jurors objected to the use of the word stupid. Inspires wonder and imagination. Great music. Can be viewed in segments. Positive values portrayed when the trophy is returned. *Kid Juror Comments*: Loved it, would definitely watch it again. Encouraged them to play imaginatively. "I want a pair of wishing boots." They found old shoes and made them wishing shoes. Some worried that William made the alien cry. Kids danced to the music. Video. 65 min.; $14.98; Age: 2-6. Twentieth Century Fox Home Entertainment.

*** Wimzie's House: It's Magic Time!

 Wimzie makes scary masks and becomes a magician's apprentice. Grandmother Yaya helps Wimzie with her "anti-nightmare" trick when Wimzie becomes afraid. Wimzie learns never to tell how the magician's tricks work. *Adult Juror Comments*: Entertaining for children, with a message: how to help a friend and overcome fear. The children care about one another. Young children learn that it's okay to make a mistake. "It addresses important issues." *Kid Juror Comments*: "It's scary fun, and I like magic tricks." "It made me want to learn magic tricks too." Wimzie helped LouLou to not be afraid. Everyone was nice to Wimzie when she was scared." Video. 55 min.; $9.98; Age: 2-5. Sony Wonder.

*** Wimzie's House: You're Special

Wimzie is the bright, extroverted progeny of a mixed marriage between a bird and a dragon. In a daycare run by grandmother, Wimzie is a natural leader. Everyone learns to be themselves. Kids argue about gender and learn to celebrate differences. *Adult Juror Comments*: Cute characters taught valuable lessons to kids with song, humor, and example. "Puppets speak to kids in their language." The concepts of cooperation and equality are discussed and illustrated. *Kid Juror Comments*: The puppets are fun and funny. "It teaches that boys and girls are both good; neither is better than the other." "Everybody can be themselves." Video. 55 min.; $9.98; Age: 2-5. Sony Wonder.

* Winnie the Pooh

Contains four of the famous A. A. Milne stories animated in the original animation style. *Adult Juror Comments:* Faithful to the book, characters encourage acceptance and diversity. Adults enjoyed the illustrations. *Kid Juror Comments:* Though children liked the stories, the British accent was a little difficult for preschoolers to understand. They thought it had too much talking. The animation style did not appeal to those familiar with the more current film version of Pooh. Video. 57 min.; $14.98; Age: 2-5. Twentieth Century Fox Home Entertainment.

*** Winnie the Pooh: Winnie the Pooh and a Day for Eeyore (Winnie the Pooh Storybook Classics)

Based on the books by A.A. Milne. Eeyore is especially sad when it appears that no one has remembered his birthday. Pooh Bear, Piglet, Rabbit, Owl, and the rest of Christopher Robin's menagerie do their best to cheer up their down-hearted pal. Animated. *Adult Juror Comments:* Tender, endearing story about friendship. The characters have silly, playful ways to make a birthday special. Even after 30 years, it still can get preschoolers to stand up and sing along. Tigger is a delightful scamp like many preschoolers. *Kid Juror Comments:* Loved it. They said they'd watch it a million times. "I want to walk to the creek and play that stick game." "I'm going to have a cake for my party like Eeyore." "Tigger was sad when he pushed Eeyore into the water." "This was great." Video. 25 min.; $19.98; Age: 2-8. Buena Vista Home Entertainment/Disney.

*** Winnie the Pooh: Winnie the Pooh and the Blustery Day (Winnie the Pooh Storybook Classics)

Based on books by A.A. Milne. Beginning on "Windsday" in the Hundred Acre Wood, a strong breeze blows Pooh on a fur-raising adventure involving bouncy Tigger, a spooky dream, and timid Piglet who performs a noble deed worth celebrating. Animated. *Adult Juror Comments:* Topnotch production. Clever lyrics with tunes that make you want to hum along. Very positive behaviors showing concern and caring for one another. There is not a single thing that could make this movie better—it is one of the best. *Kid Juror Comments:* Beloved Pooh is always a hit. "It is my favorite movie." "It was colored really pretty." "It made me want to do my ABC's and read the pages in the movie book." "It was funny." "I want to know how the songs go." Video. 25 min.; $19.98; Age: 2-5. Buena Vista Home Entertainment/Disney.

*** *Winnie the Pooh: Winnie the Pooh and the Honey Tree (Winnie the Pooh Storybook Classics)*

Based on the books by A.A. Milne. Pooh gets into a big jam when he climbs to the top of a honey tree and meets a swarm of bees who disapprove of his "bee"havior. Now it's up to his Hundred Acre pals to save their sweet-toothed friend. Animated. *Adult Juror Comments*: Heartwarming tale, endearing characters, whimsical story about friends helping friends. Colors and pace are perfect for young children. Loved the music. Some even found themselves humming along. *Kid Juror Comments*: Would watch this again and again. "I just love ole Pooh Bear." "I can sing the 'Pooh Song,' want me to show you?" "My friends would like to see Pooh fly up in the air with the balloon." "It was funny when he got stuck in the rabbit hole." Video. 25 min.; $19.95; Age: 2-8. Buena Vista Home Entertainment/Disney.

*** *Winnie the Pooh: Winnie the Pooh and Tigger Too (Winnie the Pooh Storybook Classics)*

Tigger sings, "The wonderful thing about Tiggers is Tiggers are wonderful things." Unfortunately, Tigger's bouncing is driving Pooh and his friends crazy. Soon, they realize bouncing is one of the wonderful things about Tigger. Animated. *Adult Juror Comments*: Great story for the young and the young at heart. Excellent. Wonderful songs and animation. Deals with everyday friendship issues and concerns. The characters are positive role models for friendship and problem-solving. *Kid Juror Comments*: Enthusiastic. "Even my Dad loves this!" "I think that Rabbit is a little bit tired and grumpy." "We like Tigger and the 'Bouncy-trouncy' song." "Tigger is a bouncy tiger." "This is so much fun. I want to watch it over and over again." Video. 25 min.; $19.98; Age: 2-8. Buena Vista Home Entertainment/Disney.

*** *Winter Tales (Maurice Sendak's Little Bear)*

Join Sendak's beloved Little Bear and a menagerie of friends in a frosty, glistening winter wonderland in these four snowy tales. *Adult Juror Comments*: It's playful, well-paced and kindhearted. Main character is funny, curious, and endearing. Beautifully produced. Emphasis is on family and traditions. Motivates interest in using a compass and introduces new vocabulary. Good seasonal entertainment. *Kid Juror Comments*: Lots of questions about the snow. "My two- and four-year-olds have been playing the story of the winter tree, ring around the rosy, and making snow angels." Good discussion starter about what to do with grumpy behavior. Video. 32 min.; $9.95; Age: 2-7. Paramount Home Entertainment.

Age 2-5

Video

Family

Chapter Two • Preschool

** Wubbulous World of Dr. Seuss
(Wubbulous World of Dr. Seuss)

The "Wubbulous World of Dr. Seuss" takes place in the wildly decorated house of the Cat in the Hat, where the colorful cast of characters has a good time while learning how to face daily dilemmas. *Adult Juror Comments*: Well-produced. Characters are true to the spirit of the original. Adults enjoyed the animation and rhymes. Enriches children's imaginations through creative play. The mini-stories, running one after another, make it hard to follow the story. *Kid Juror Comments*: Mixed response. Some sang along with the opening song, and others thought it was slow and boring. "We could be friends with these cats." "I wish I had a wubbulouscope and could see magical things too." Video. 50 min.; $12.95; Age: 2-5. Columbia Tristar Home Entertainment.

Category—FLM (Fairy Tales, Literature, Myth)

** Dragon Tales: Keep on Trying (Dragon Tales)

Follow the adventures of six-year-old Emmy and her four-year-old brother, Max, who find a dragon scale in their playroom. When they hold it and chant a poem, it transports them to Dragon Land, where they meet fantastic—but human-like—dragons. *Adult Juror Comments*: Simple themes presented in quiet tones teach good lessons in small bites. Cute dragons are like loveable kids. Language is appropriate but challenging. Playing with rope and use of the word "stupid" caused concern. Provides wonderful Hispanic role model. *Kid Juror Comments*: Danced, stretched, and sang to the "fun music." Learned how to keep on trying…and how to have fun even if you don't win. "The kids and the dragons all help each other. They helped Max and gave him encouragement to tie the knot." Video. 40 min.; $12.95; Age: 2-5. Columbia Tristar Home Entertainment.

*** Dragon Tales: Let's Play Together (Dragon Tales)

Follow the adventures of six-year-old Emmy and her four-year-old brother, Max, who find a dragon scale in their playroom. When they hold it and chant a poem, it transports them to Dragon Land, where they meet fantastic—but human-like—dragons. *Adult Juror Comments*: Lovely, colorful, catchy music. Teaches patience and waiting your turn—universal themes that are hard for little ones to master. Shows good manners: one dragon burps and says excuse me. Never speaks down to audience. Equal treatment of boys and girls. *Kid Juror Comments*: All smiles. Related to the characters and their challenges. "One kid got mad, and a bad fairy grew bigger as he got madder. But his friends helped him to get unmad and then the fairy got small." "Can we make our own stories?" Video. 40 min.; $12.95; Age: 2-5. Columbia Tristar Home Entertainment.

*** Goodnight Moon and Other Sleepytime Tales*

Children and stars come together to present classic bedtime stories and lullabies in an animated format. Children offer wise and witty reflections on a host of sleepytime topics, including "blankies," dreamcatchers, monsters, and nightmares. *Adult Juror Comments*: Great music and super illustrations. Cute and soothing. Addresses nighttime anxieties and stimulates interest in dreams. Children get to see their peers explain their feelings. Shows many cultures and races. *Kid Juror Comments*: Connected with the story, loved the music and the lyrics. "We watched it three times in a row." "Can I watch it before bed?" "I like the music." "I like the bunny." "I love the monster." "I learned about dreams." Video. 30 min.; $9.95; Age: 2-5. HBO.

*** Video Buddy™: Blackout/ High Spirits (Salty's Lighthouse)*

Two interactive stories set in a seafaring town that challenge children to overcome fear and learn to work together. Used with VIDEO BUDDY™ handset. *Adult Juror Comments*: The handset is engaging, and it seemed to increase attentiveness to the video, though it was hard to keep up with. The 'stop-action' section frightened some children. Teaches positive social skills and respectful sibling relations. *Kid Juror Comments*: Children enjoyed the stories. "I'd watch it again because I like the songs." "I'd watch it a hundred million more times." "The boy shared his flashlight when the lights went out." "I liked the octopus and the sharks." Video. 45 min.; $12.99; Age: 3-6. Interactive Learning Group.

*** Video Buddy™: Can't Wait to Paint (Once Upon a Tree)*

It's hard to wait for something you really want to do. Kids are invited to join the animals in this interactive program as they think of activities to do while they wait for their turn to paint pictures. To be used with VIDEO BUDDY™ handset. *Adult Juror Comments*: Story is enjoyable, and the video buddy is easy to operate. Puppet characters are neat, especially the trees. Some adults objected to using food for painting. Encourages critical thinking skills. *Kid Juror Comments*: Enjoyed it. "I liked it a whole bunch." "I want to learn more about llamas." "The llama had a broken leg." "They all played together." "Pushing the buttons is fun, but it's hard to wait for your turn when only one can use it at a time." Video. 38 min.; $12.99; Age: 2-5. Interactive Learning Group.

*** *Video Buddy™: Carrot Caper, The (Once Upon a Tree)*

A charming and interactive tale about who stole the carrots from Jenny's garden that covers lessons about honesty and asking permission. To be used with the VIDEO BUDDY™ handset. *Adult Juror Comments*: Encourages positive social behavior, enhances vocabulary, teaches compassion through respect for others' things. Articulate, enthusiastic characters accept each other's faults and learn from their mistakes. *Kid Juror Comments*: Kids commented on the gardening tips, they wanted to make potato prints as shown in the video. They enjoyed the interactive format and wanted to watch it again. They noticed when characters were nice to one another. Video. 45 min.; $12.99; Age: 3-7. Interactive Learning Group.

** *Video Buddy™: Let's Try Sharing (The Big Comfy Couch)*

Although sometimes it is hard to share, Loonette and Molly learn that cooperating with others makes everyone feel good. To be used with the VIDEO BUDDY™ handset. *Adult Juror Comments*: A bit campy, but sweet. Teaches social skills using simple language and humor. Stories and anecdotes address emotional situations that are age-appropriate. "This was a little bit silly, but enjoyable nevertheless." *Kid Juror Comments*: Kids focused on the story in order to answer questions posed by the video buddy. "It wasn't nice for Loonette to put the basketball net on Molly's head." "Too bad there is only one video buddy machine." "I love Loonette and Molly." Video. 45 min.; $14.99; Age: 2-6. Interactive Learning Group.

** *Video Buddy™: Let's Wing It/Taking My Turn (Salty's Lighthouse)*

Two stories each featuring themes related to teamwork and cooperation. In the first, Sadie the Seagull has a sprained wing, but still finds ways to help out. In the second, the Lighthouse Friends team up for a Calypso party. Use with VIDEO BUDDY handset. *Adult Juror Comments*: Imparts strong messages about perseverance and keeping a positive attitude. Addresses the issues of being small, which kids can relate to. Jurors felt that the correlation between the real-life segments and the cartoons were hard to follow. *Kid Juror Comments*: Inspired some kids. They loved the Calypso music. "I danced with the music." "I loved the song, 'Taking My Turn.' " The story line was sometimes difficult for kids to follow. Most found the tugboat part boring. "Can we sponge paint, like in the video?" Lori Video. 45 min.; $12.99; Age: 3-6. Interactive Learning Group.

** Video Buddy™: My Best Friend (The Big Comfy Couch)

Loonette has a new best pal and through trial and error must learn to balance her friendship with her current best friend and with her new best friend. To be used with VIDEO BUDDY™ handset. *Adult Juror Comments*: Bright, bold images. Addresses simple, yet important, concepts such as coping with jealousy. Time to answer the questions is sometimes too short. "I especially liked the positive comments and compliments." *Kid Juror Comments*: "Made me smile." Kids found they needed to listen carefully to the questions. "I liked when the Video Buddy asked me to sing along." "I liked Molly and the Dust Bunnies because they were so funny." "The Banana's dance song made me get up and move around." Video. 45 min.; $14.99; Age: 2-6. Interactive Learning Group.

** Video Buddy™: Scooter's Hidden Talent (Muppet Babies)

It's Nanny's birthday and the Muppet Babies are making her a special present. Scooter is not in the mood to help because he does not feel talented enough. In the end, it is Scooter's talent that makes the present work. Use with VIDEO BUDDY™ handset. *Adult Juror Comments*: Cute story, promotes critical thinking skills. The interactive part re-caps portions of the story before asking the questions. Vocabulary is a bit advanced for preschoolers and the Muppet babies' slap-stick humor is more suitable for adults. *Kid Juror Comments*: Kids related to the story, but their attention wandered. "I liked pressing the buttons on the video buddy." "Animal broke Scooters card castle. He was sad." "The baby tore up Gonzo's book. That wasn't a good thing to do." Video. 45 min.; $14.99; Age: 3-6. Interactive Learning Group.

** Video Buddy™: Sticks and Stones (The Big Comfy Couch)

Play pick-up sticks with Loonette and Molly. Make up names for everything in Granny Garbanzo's garden and then learn that silly nicknames sometimes are not nice. To be used with the VIDEO BUDDY™ handset. *Adult Juror Comments*: Sound and colors are clear and vibrant. Works as a learning tool, encourages concentration, memory, and listening and provides positive feedback. "I enjoyed watching the video with the children because the social value of name-calling was presented." *Kid Juror Comments*: Would watch again. Kids protested when a character said "You can call me ugly" in one of the songs. "Loonette hugged Molly; a hug is a good thing." "Loonette didn't know that 'clumsy' was a mean thing to say." Interactive pace was a little too fast. Video. 45 min.; $14.99; Age: 2-5. Interactive Learning Group.

** Video Buddy™: What Do You Want to Be When You Grow Up (Muppet Babies)

When it comes to what the Muppet Babies want to do when they get older, the sky is the limit. When Baby Kermit wonders about this question, his friends set out to help him figure it out. Use with the VIDEO BUDDY™ handset. *Adult Juror Comments*: Well-produced with bright, appealing colors and endearing characters. Shows good role models and some inappropriate behavior such as turning up the volume on headphones way too loud. Stimulates critical thinking. *Kid Juror Comments*: Enjoyed the topic and ensuing conversation. "I love the Muppet Babies." "Molly showed the babies a book with lots of different jobs." "I can be what ever I want when I grow up." "Kermit couldn't decide; he was silly." "I want to be a fireman too." Video. 45 min.; $14.99; Age: 4-6. Interactive Learning Group.

*** Video Buddy™: What If the Dinosaurs Came Back (Once Upon a Tree)

Could there really be a dinosaur in the magical forest? Our animal friends get a big surprise and learn something about believing in one another too. To be used with the VIDEO BUDDY™ handset. *Adult Juror Comments*: Great production. Wonderful, appealing, puppet characters. "I greatly enjoyed this video." Encourages assertiveness skills, and problem-solving. Respectful of children's thinking skills. Video buddy brought it all together. *Kid Juror Comments*: Kids had a blast. "The animals and the trees talk." "I love the dinosaur." "My favorite part was when he gave the dinosaur carrots." "I'd watch it 500 more times." "I love it when I get the answer right." Video. 45 min.; $12.99; Age: 2-5. Interactive Learning Group.

*** Video Buddy™: What's New at the Zoo (Muppet Babies)

The Muppet Babies learn that the zoo protects animals and helps people think about the environment through an imaginary expedition. Use with VIDEO BUDDY™ handset. *Adult Juror Comments*: Helps kids think critically about the purpose of zoos. Encourages imagination and awareness of feelings and expands vocabulary. Excellent question and answer sessions. Credits kids for their feelings. *Kid Juror Comments*: The contrast between cartoon and real-life segments sparked and kept kids' interest. They wanted to score each others' cartwheels after watching the Olympics scene. "I wouldn't like to be in a cage." Video. 45 min.; $14.99; Age: 3-6. Interactive Learning Group.

** Video Buddy™: Who Took My Crayons / Guilty Gull (Salty's Lighthouse)

When Salty looses his crayons and Ten Cent loses his engine parts, the blaming begins. Luckily everything works out okay. To be used with the VIDEO BUDDY™ handset. *Adult Juror Comments*: The first story taught a lesson about blame and the second story the importance of listening. Respects kids' ability to tell right from wrong, speaks to a child's sense of ownership. Stresses the importance of friends, compassion, and being truthful. *Kid Juror Comments*: Kids' faces lit up when they saw the video buddy on the screen. It's a great way to help them remember the story. They enjoyed thinking and answering questions about the characters and story. "Salty learned to say sorry." Video. 45 min.; $12.99; Age: 3-6. Interactive Learning Group.

Category—Foreign Language

** Bilingual Baby: Volume 2, Spanish

Teaches early language skills to young children, introducing different sounds, syntax, and sentence structures. *Adult Juror Comments*: Well-produced, flows easily. Presents Spanish in a fun and interesting way. Most effective viewed with an adult. Contains a lot of information but doesn't allow much time for assimilation and answering the questions. *Kid Juror Comments*: Mixed reviews. Some kids gravitated toward the show and were motivated and attentive. Others lost interest quickly. "We can practice saying words in Spanish." "I want to learn Spanish so I can talk to my Spanish-speaking friends." Video. 45 min.; $16.95; Age: 2-6. Small Fry Productions.

*** Eres Tu Mi Mama? (Are You My Mother?)
(Beginner Book Video Series)

Spanish adaption of P. D. Eastman's classic about a baby bird who sets out to find his mother, asking everyone he meets along the way "Are you my mother?" *Adult Juror Comments*: Good video to show to young children who are learning their first words. A great tool to integrate a group of multi-cultural kids. Adults used the books as a follow-up to the video. Can be used to teach Spanish to very young children. *Kid Juror Comments*: Mostly silly, but fun. Bilingual children adored it, and Spanish-speaking children also enjoyed it tremendously. English-speaking children were interested, but worked hard to understand. Overall, a fun viewing experience. Video. 30 min.; $9.98; Age: 2-6. Random House Video.

* Professor Parrot Speaks Spanish Learning System

Teaches Spanish by having children sing, dance, and play games. Introduces 150 Spanish words. Includes a 30-minute video, a parent/caregiver guide, and an audio cassette of sing-along songs. *Adult Juror Comments*: It's a crisp, clear production with good introductory teaching techniques. Characters are visually appealing and likable. The short songs make learning Spanish fun for children. Requires repeat viewings to benefit from the Spanish lessons. *Kid Juror Comments*: Learned some Spanish phrases, loved the songs and the puppets. Younger kids danced and sang along. The Goldilocks story was difficult for kids to understand. Video. 30 min.; $19.95; Age: 3-5. Sound Beginnings.

Category—Holiday

*** Allegra's Christmas (Allegra's Window)

Allegra learns the true meaning of Christmas giving when she finds out that one of Santa's helpers expects to spend Christmas alone. Allegra to the rescue! *Adult Juror Comments*: Colorful characters. Engaging, thoughtful story. Wonderfully instructive in showing how to be happy about simple things. Good message about giving. Good color and amusing puppets. Appropriate language. Pace and visuals at times too fast. *Kid Juror Comments*: A nice Christmas message for kids. Prompted discussion among kids afterwards. Allegra is very lovable. The children sang along and laughed and talked about what they saw. Some dialog scenes are somewhat long. Video. 47 min.; $9.95; Age: 2-7. Paramount Home Entertainment.

*** Bear in the Big Blue House: A Berry Bear Christmas (Bear in the Big Blue House)

Bear and his friends learn about the various winter holidays: Christmas, Chanukah, Kwanzaa, and Winterberry. After helping a homeless dog find a home, Bear and his friends learn that there is more to the holidays than receiving presents. *Adult Juror Comments*: First-rate production, quality couldn't be better. Playful way of teaching children about sharing and helping. Homelessness is gently broached with a homeless dog that Bear kindly brings into the house. Sends a subtle message of diversity and good will. *Kid Juror Comments*: "I love the big Bear!" "It was so nice to see how Bear helped that dog and the dog got his wish and found a home to live in." "Bear made us think about helping others during Christmas, that it's better to give." "I would like to see a Kwanzaa." Video. 50 min.; $12.95; Age: 2-6. Columbia Tristar Home Entertainment.

*** *Bear in the Big Blue House: Halloween & Thanksgiving* (Bear in the Big Blue House)

Bear and his friends discover dressing up in costumes and trick-or-treating for Halloween. Then, everyone comes together to create a Thanksgiving Day meal and pageant for friends. They sing many songs and learn how fun it is to celebrate their blessings. *Adult Juror Comments*: Colorful, enriching, exciting presentation. Wouldn't any parent want Bear as a substitute caregiver? Original and creative, nothing is being copied here. Characters are great friends for any young viewers. "I think I may enjoy it as much as the children." *Kid Juror Comments*: Awesome! "We like Bear." "I like it when Bear smells." "I like the songs and characters." "We want to make our own pumpkins and decorate for Thanksgiving." "I learned about Thanksgiving. I'm going to tell the story next Thanksgiving." Video. 50 min.; $12.95; Age: 2-6. Columbia Tristar Home Entertainment.

** *Christmas Adventure, The* (Adventures of Raggedy Ann and Andy)

Everybody's favorite rag dolls discover someone has stolen Santa's reindeer, his sleigh, and all of the children's toys! By following clues, Raggedy Ann and Andy meet their old friends and discover who's behind the Christmas-napping. *Adult Juror Comments*: Children enjoy stories about Christmas. This one presents a dramatic situation with a satisfying resolution. Displays good teamwork. Teaches children to think and care about others. Adults disliked aggressive language and behavior. *Kid Juror Comments*: Generated lots of comments about Christmas, reinforces the myth of Santa. Most of the children watched the entire video. "It's a good show. I like the camel. But they can't really fly, only reindeer can." Video. 25 min.; $9.98; Age: 3-7. Twentieth Century Fox Home Entertainment.

*** *Christmas Eve on Sesame Street* (Sesame Street Specials)

As everyone is getting ready for Christmas on Sesame Street, Oscar asks a disturbing question, "How does Santa, who is built like a dump truck, get down those skinny chimneys?" While solving the riddle, they discover the true meaning of Christmas. *Adult Juror Comments*: A lovely Christmas story with nice focus on giving. Sign language portion is a nice addition. Some parts are a little slow. One scene in which Oscar flies out of the skating rink and falls down a stairwell is unnecessary and unsafe. *Kid Juror Comments*: Great ice skating. Very attentive, enjoyed the singing. It's a little long for younger children. Good to show in sections. They sing "Feliz Navidad." Video. 60 min.; $12.98; Age: 2-5. Sony Wonder.

*** Christmas Presents (Old Bear Stories)

 Three lighthearted holiday tales starring a cast of whimsically animated playroom toys brought to life through animation. Based on the books by Jane Hissey. *Adult Juror Comments*: Characters are appealing, simple, inventive, and creative. They show concern, sharing and friendship. Enjoyable mix of animation and real environments. Artfully understated. Contains message: "Sharing is the true meaning of giving." *Kid Juror Comments*: The old-fashioned quality was wonderful, and the children requested several reruns. They wanted to hold stuffed bears while they watched. One seven-year-old said it gave her ideas of things to make. Video. 32 min.; $14.95; Age: 2-5. Sony Wonder.

* Christmas Tree Train, The (Chucklewood Critters)

Buttons and Rusty accidentally board the Christmas Tree Train on a delivery run to the big city. A wise owl befriends them, telling them all about the city, and Santa comes to their rescue. *Adult Juror Comments*: Old-fashioned style of animation has marginal entertainment value. Adults didn't find any special qualities in this program. The cubs' mischievous nature creates situations that are alarming, but not addressed. *Kid Juror Comments*: The Christmas theme spurred an animated discussion about Santa, what the kids wanted for Christmas, and getting lost from one's parents. Video. 25 min.; $9.98; Age: 3-6. Unapix/Miramar.

*** Country Mouse and the City Mouse:
A Christmas Story, The

 When Emily, the country mouse, visits her worldly cousin, Alexander, for the holidays, they discover the true meaning of Christmas—love and family. Based on an Aesop's fable. Animation by Michael Sporn. Voices by Crystal Gayle and John Lithgow. *Adult Juror Comments*: Good, consistent, understandable story line. Strong in showing values of friendship, relationship, non-materialism, respect for differences. Appeals more to younger kids, although the older kids enjoyed it just as well. *Kid Juror Comments*: "Excellent, great, really good, funny, super-cute—we liked it a lot!" Kids had sympathy for the mouse lost in New York City and delight over the "welcome home Christmas gifts." Video. 25 min.; $9.95; Age: 2-6. Random House Video.

Age 2-5

Video

Holiday

** First Easter Egg, The

Easter-themed animated tale of a bunny named One who searches for a gift for his mother and starts a worldwide tradition! *Adult Juror Comments*: Simple story with cute animation, vivid colors, cheerful music, and a mix of familiar characters. The message is a playful explanation of the Easter egg's origin. Some language is grammatically incorrect, and characters make fun of one another. *Kid Juror Comments*: The Easter theme was appealing. "The chickens were silly, and the pigs were really silly." Some liked the bunny, others thought his speech was too babyish. He was polite, though. Video. 30 min.; $9.99; Age: 2-5. Anchor Bay Entertainment.

* He Ain't Scary. He's Our Brother (Casper)

Casper refuses to go spooking with the other ghosts, planning instead to trick-or-treat dressed as a real boy. *Adult Juror Comments*: The moral of the story teaches that ghosts can't hurt you. Vocabulary level is uneven. The "ghosts" have poor enunciation. The resolution of the story is not quite credible. *Kid Juror Comments*: Casper can't miss, especially the music and songs. Four-year-olds were interested, three's wandered around. Even the two-year-olds watched for a while. Video. 25 min.; $9.98; Age: 3-6. Warner Home Video.

* Night Before Christmas, The (Enchanted Tales)

Magical tale about a young orphan boy and his cat who discover a miracle on Christmas Eve. *Adult Juror Comments*: Not very believable, odd mixture of songs and music. Addresses sharing, giving, and caring. Uses "Nutcracker" soundtrack in a peculiar way. The mouse character is appealing. Animation is average, some characters are mean. *Kid Juror Comments*: Mixed reaction. Some didn't really pay attention to the story, while others enjoyed it. Provoked discussions about sharing, giving, and caring. Video. 48 min.; $9.98; Age: 5-8. Sony Wonder.

** Noddy Gives A Birthday Party (Noddy)

To earn money for a birthday present for Big Ears, Noddy takes a delivery job and gets all mixed up. Meanwhile, the cake he made burns to a crisp. Mrs. Tessie Bear saves the day with a new cake. Includes two additional episodes. *Adult Juror Comments*: Well-produced, teaches kindness and handling life when things aren't perfect. Outstanding production with good diversity. Noddy is constantly getting himself out of messes. Characters' inappropriate and at-times-rude behavior goes uncorrected. *Kid Juror Comments*: Noddy amused the kids by flying around or singing songs. Enjoyed the story, especially the two-year-olds. All wanted to watch it again. "It seemed real because they used toys." Kids noticed the respect shown at times. Video. 30 min.; $12.95; Age: 2-5. U.S.A. Home Entertainment.

Chapter Two • Preschool

*** Sharon, Lois & Bram: Candles, Snow & Mistletoe (Sharon, Lois & Bram)

An original musical fantasy that combines the familiar warmth, wit, and magic of Sharon, Lois, and Bram with the hijinks of their adorable pal, Elephant. Full of new songs as well as familiar classics about discovering the true meaning of Christmas. *Adult Juror Comments*: "Bigger than life" characters are very entertaining. Well-produced, entertaining. The holiday season comes across with song and movement. *Kid Juror Comments*: Enjoyed the songs and sang along, but also thought it moved a little slowly and was a little long. Best viewed in segments. Video. 50 min.; $9.98; Age: 2-6. Video Treasures.

* Tales & Tunes: Christmas Tales & Tunes (Tales & Tunes)

The creators of "Baby Songs" presents a holiday assortment of Christmas stories and songs for young viewers. Video disc jockey K. J. narrates. *Adult Juror Comments*: Nice mix of animation and live action. The puppet story promotes values of friendship and giving. It's very silly and somewhat fragmented. Talks down to kids at times and has some name-calling. *Kid Juror Comments*: Songs are catchy. Kids sang along the first time they viewed it. Gets off to a slow start, but then captures their attention. Children thought it was a bit jumbled, though. Video. 30 min.; $12.98; Age: 2-6. Video Treasures.

** Tales & Tunes: Hanukkah Tales & Tunes (Tales & Tunes)

The creators of "Baby Songs" present an assortment of Hanukkah stories and songs, hosted by video disc jockey K. J. *Adult Juror Comments*: This video is well done and conveys important information in an interesting and exciting way. The music and dance numbers with children are appealing. Production quality is low and slow-paced. *Kid Juror Comments*: The children liked to watch the kids in the video dancing. They got up and joined in! Kids liked all of the Hanukkah music and learning about the holiday. Video. 30 min.; $12.98; Age: 5-8. Video Treasures.

** Thomas the Tank: Thomas' Christmas Party (Thomas the Tank Engine & Friends)

The Island of Sodor is covered with snow, including Mrs. Kindly's house. Will someone rescue Mrs. Kindly in time for Sir Topham Hatt's Christmas Party? Thomas is missing with the Christmas Tree, and Terence the Tractor helps save the day. *Adult Juror Comments*: Enjoyable and well-produced with creative sets. "Henry's Forest" has great environmental messages. There is some stereotyping of gender portrayed. For example, the more important train cars have male names while lesser ones have female names. *Kid Juror Comments*: The four- and five-year-olds loved it. Kids recognize Thomas from TV and respond to the characters. They enjoy imitating the characters afterwards as they play train. Video. 42 min.; $12.98; Age: 3-8. Anchor Bay Entertainment.

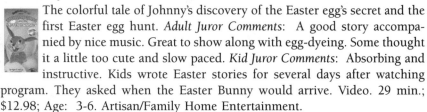

** Thumpkin & the Easter Bunnies

The colorful tale of Johnny's discovery of the Easter egg's secret and the first Easter egg hunt. *Adult Juror Comments*: A good story accompanied by nice music. Great to show along with egg-dyeing. Some thought it a little too cute and slow paced. *Kid Juror Comments*: Absorbing and instructive. Kids wrote Easter stories for several days after watching program. They asked when the Easter Bunny would arrive. Video. 29 min.; $12.98; Age: 3-6. Artisan/Family Home Entertainment.

* Twas the Day Before Christmas (Chucklewood Critters)

Buttons and Rusty prepare for the gala Christmas celebration by gathering ornaments and other goodies from the forest. There's a monster lurking in Chucklewood, which the cubs learn is imaginary. *Adult Juror Comments*: Although the cubs' mischief-making goes unnoticed, there is positive content. The animals work together for the good of the whole group. Enforces the joy of celebrating Christmas without the emphasis on presents. "Too much emphasis on monsters." *Kid Juror Comments*: Motivated questions from the kids about the characters and their actions. It's long for the intended age group. Most kids were not interested in seeing it a second time. Video. 25 min.; $9.98; Age: 3-6. Unapix/Miramar.

** Veggie Tales: The Toy That Saved Christmas (Veggie Tales)

It looks like the worst Christmas ever until brave little Buzz-Saw Louie doll takes matters into his own hands. Teaches children messages about the true meaning of Christmas. *Adult Juror Comments*: Offers easy-to-understand message about the value of giving. Lessons employ positive role models. Encourages problem-solving. Animation is unique and inviting. Contains some stereotyping. Christian overtones. *Kid Juror Comments*: Sang along with the songs and found the animation inviting. "At first I was sad when I thought Christmas would be ruined, but then I was happy when the penguins and the toy saved Christmas." "I liked the song about 'It's okay to be different.'" Video. 30 min.; $12.99; Age: 3-8. Big Idea Productions, Inc.

*** Wee Sing the Best Christmas Ever! (Wee Sing)

The Smith family travels to Santa's workshop to help solve an elfin problem and sees that challenges can be overcome with the help of friends. *Adult Juror Comments*: Great holiday viewing. Entertaining, magical, and fun. Good ethnic diversity. Addresses maintaining friendships, respect, honesty, and manners. *Kid Juror Comments*: Lots of laughter. Sang along, danced, and clapped their hands. Video. 60 min.; $12.98; Age: 2-8. Universal Studios Home Video.

Chapter Two • Preschool

Category—How-To

** I Can Build! (Can Too!)

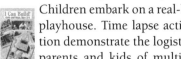 Children embark on a real-life adventure designing and building a dream playhouse. Time lapse action and whimsical three-dimensional animation demonstrate the logistics of building. *Adult Juror Comments*: Shows parents and kids of multiple ages and skills working together. Talks directly to kids. Computer graphics were popular and helpful in illustrating the building process: how everything comes together from start to finish. Music is repetitive. *Kid Juror Comments*: Great to discover that they could be a part of a building project. Sparked interest in building. Provoked lots of conversation about making things. "I'm going to draw a picture, so that I can make a castle too." Video. 25 min.; $14.95; Age: 2-8. Can Too! Tapes/Bellman Girls, L.L.C.

Category—Music

* Another Great Day for Singing, with James Durst (Sidewalk Songs)

 Features 14 melodic songs—many familiar—performed with guitar accompaniment. Several are enhanced with digital effects, including duets with guests "Eb and Flo" and an introduction to the orchestra with "Old King Cole." *Adult Juror Comments*: Light, catchy, lively American folk songs. Encourages imagination. Simple, clear presentation. Durst has a soothing voice and friendly appearance. Lyrics are easily repeated. Best viewed in two sessions or for quiet time. Format is a bit dull. *Kid Juror Comments*: While this engaged some children, others were bored. "There weren't a lot of songs with pictures." Some kids readily sang along, laughed, and participated with hand gestures. Overall, it was too long to hold their interest throughout. Video. 37 min.; $12.98; Age: 3-7. Sidewalk Productions.

*** Baby Songs: Animals (Baby Songs)

 Lively Hap Palmer music is accompanied by scenes of cute, cuddly animals and toddlers at the zoo, farm, and pet store. *Adult Juror Comments*: Appealing, engaging. Excellent production—clear images and audio. Blends animation and live action. Encourages creative movement, language development, and curiosity. Shows multi-cultural cast and diverse geographic locations. *Kid Juror Comments*: Entertaining. Kids enjoyed the activities and games shown and many played them afterwards. "I would watch it again because I like animals." "I can run, jump and skip like the animals do." "I learned to hold the kitty softly." Video. 32 min.; $12.98; Age: 2-5. Anchor Bay Entertainment.

** Baby Songs: Baby's Busy Day (Baby Songs)

Original live action musical about a baby's day. Contains ten new songs by Hap Palmer that explore a toddler's world. *Adult Juror Comments*: Beautiful songs with catchy lyrics combined with fast-moving, colorful pictures. Shows nifty self-help skills. Stereotypes adult jobs by gender and shows unsafe images such as a child jumping into a tub. Good diversity shown. *Kid Juror Comments*: Kids were hungry for more. "Play it again!" Inspired kids to play dress-up afterwards. Promoted many happy feelings and giggles. Kids danced and clapped along with the music. They liked "pet the ducky" and watching the kids on-screen. Video. 30 min.; $12.98; Age: 2-5. Backyard Productions.

** Baby Songs: Play Along Songs (Baby Songs)

With two new songs and other popular tunes, Hap Palmer's songs inspire children to be creative and imagine, move, and sing along to the music. Includes ideas for musical playtime fun and scenes of children moving to the music. *Adult Juror Comments*: Cute, upbeat pace, funny original songs and catchy tunes. Age-appropriate except calling it "baby songs" turns off the five-year-olds. Encourages interactive play between parents and children. Great diversity and respectful of generations and gender. *Kid Juror Comments*: Really enjoyed it. Kids sang and danced along. "I love to dance." "I want to be the girl with the baton." "The drumming on the pots and pans was fun." "My favorite game is follow the leader." "I hope Grandma gives me this movie." Video. 30 min.; $12.98; Age: 1-5. Anchor Bay Entertainment.

** Baby Songs: Rock & Roll (Baby Songs)

Features rock 'n' roll classics by the original artists who made them hits. A collection of hip-shakin,' smile-makin' tunes for kids and their parents to enjoy together. *Adult Juror Comments*: Well-made. Upbeat music familiar to most adults. Encourages kids to get up and dance. "Silliness of songs like Blue Suede Shoes and Wooly Bully appeals to kids." Promotes positive attitudes. Some objected to fast-paced, MTV-style cuts. Good diversity. *Kid Juror Comments*: Liked it a lot. Held their interest and they danced along. Girls liked it better than boys. One four-year-old said, "I could watch it all day long." Kids would watch for 15 minutes, wander off, and check back every few minutes. Video. 30 min.; $12.98; Age: 2-5. Anchor Bay Entertainment.

Chapter Two • Preschool

** Bedtime (Stories to Remember)

 Judy Collins invites young viewers on a gentle journey into dreamland with a collection of best-loved lullabies: "Hush Little Baby," "Lullaby and Good Night," and "The Land of Nod." Adapted from Kay Chorao's *The Baby's Bedtime Book*. *Adult Juror Comments*: Parents who are Judy Collins' fans are thrilled to share this charming production with their kids. Moves from fast-paced songs to slow, sleepy ones. *Kid Juror Comments*: It works well. One adult juror commented, "My six-month-old baby went to sleep with it right away." Video. 26 min.; $9.95; Age: 1-5. Stories to Remember.

** Big & Little Stuff (Sidewalk Songs)

A sing-along with original songs by Jim Scott, offers authentic music for kids celebrating friendship, nature, and the good feeling you get by simply breathing in and out. Scott, a former Paul Winter Consort member, sings in Spanish and English. *Adult Juror Comments*: Offers fun songs with important and meaningful messages such as environmental issues, taking care of each other, respect, and independence. Songs are simple and easy to learn. Simple production that shows good diversity. *Kid Juror Comments*: "My friends like to sing, and they could sing a lot with this video." "I liked the pictures that went with the songs." "My favorite part was learning the hand movements with the songs." "The songs talked about friends and nature." Video. 30 min.; $12.98; Age: 2-6. Sidewalk Productions.

*** Concert in Angel-Land

 Children take a magic journey to Angel-Land where song and dance abound. Whimsical angels and children from many cultures sing along with recording artists Megon McDonough and Victor Cockburn. *Adult Juror Comments*: Teaches respect through simple songs, stories, and games. Presented at a child's level, it simplifies ideas that reassure young children. Simple production, showing the diversity of children's artwork. *Kid Juror Comments*: Fabulous music, great storytelling. One leader had to sneak the tape away after viewing. Children were totally engaged by the material and the angels. Video. 25 min.; $10.95; Age: 2-8. MVP Home Entertainment, Inc.

** *Fingerplays and Footplays*

Focuses on activities that develop coordination, concentration, and listening skills. Everything can be performed while standing, seated in a chair, or with legs crossed on the floor. *Adult Juror Comments*: Basic production values, repetitive. Songs and characters are simple and easy to follow. Good balance of kids, adults, and pictures. Ideal for preschoolers who pick up the tunes quickly. Nice diversity. Clear instructions. *Kid Juror Comments*: Danced along and did movements. Some fingerplays were familiar. Older kids suggested it for their younger brothers and sisters. Video. 30 min.; $19.95; Age: 2-5. Educational Activities, Inc.

* *Friends (The Parables of Peter Rabbit)*

The adventure of a lifetime begins when four unsuspecting children stumble upon the burrow of Peter Rabbit. Based on the parable of the Good Samaritan and what it means to be a friend. *Adult Juror Comments*: Friendship concepts are presented within Christian framework. Though not overstated, presents God and the Bible throughout. Good child acting, catchy music, but really corny. *Kid Juror Comments*: Remained interested, though they didn't like the lip singing. They did like seeing the girl teaching the boy to play catch. Kids thought it was too long, but enjoyed the message: "Friends are really important." Video. 30 min.; $14.95; Age: 3-6. Brentwood Music.

** *Great Day for Singing, A (Sidewalk Songs)*

A colorful sing-along introducing 25 well-known nursery rhymes and children's songs in a relaxed setting. Features James Durst on acoustic guitar in studio and on a 19th-century working farm with kids and barnyard animals. *Adult Juror Comments*: Pleasant songs and varied backgrounds with appeal for both boys and girls. Good transitions between songs showing the title and the children's art work depicting that title. Good sound quality. No multi-cultural children or songs. *Kid Juror Comments*: Kids enjoyed the singing and the music. The simplicity inspires imagination and conversation, some dancing. "I liked the spider song." "I didn't want it to end." Started a discussion about farm animals. Video. 30 min.; $12.98; Age: 2-5. Sidewalk Productions.

** *In Search of the Lost Note (Lil' Iguana)*

A missing musical note leaves Lil' Iguana and Buk feeling unharmonious. After forming an impromptu conga band, Lil' Iguana and friends try adding a quarter-note to end their rendition of "The Silly Song" on key. *Adult Juror Comments*: The live segments are well done. Encourages cognitive and intellectual skills. Provides an introduction to musical elements—notes, tunes, instruments, rhythm, and melody—at a basic level. Entertaining for preschoolers. *Kid Juror Comments*: Mixed reaction. Some children were attentive while others walked away. The kids who attend music lessons enjoyed it the most. Liked the art project that showed them how to make a tambourine. Video. 25 min.; $12.95; Age: 3-5. WABU-TV 68 Boston.

** *Jungle Jamboree Sing-a-Long*

Hosted by Gus the gorilla. Features an array of other jungle animals and their human friends, Pancho and Denise. Kids can discover something about themselves by singing these songs of self-awareness. *Adult Juror Comments*: Fun, engaging, lively songs have potential for further discussion about self-awareness. Some skits had positive messages, though lack transitions that further explain subject matter. Cluttered sets. Method to engage audience was distracting. *Kid Juror Comments*: Some children danced to the music, joined in with the singing, but the reaction was mixed. Some kids love watching it repeatedly, others were less responsive and didn't pay much attention. Video. 35 min.; $9.95; Age: 2-5. Just for Kids Home Video/Celebrity Home Entertainment.

** *Kids Make Music (Lynn Kleiner Series)*

Full of activities: singing, dancing, rhyming, and clapping. Orff Schulwerk's approach to music education directs children's natural instincts into an active process teaching music by making music. *Adult Juror Comments*: A good teaching video with many examples of music activities. Encourages active participation, creativity, and self expression. If possible, have musical instruments available for kids' use. Simplified for those with no musical background. *Kid Juror Comments*: Three- to four-year-olds loved this approach. Inspires an interest in musical instruments. Video. 45 min.; $14.95; Age: 2-5. Headbone.

Age 2-5

Video

Music

* Kids Make Music Too! (Lynn Kleiner Series)

Teaches music through active participation using language, movement, rhythm, and melodies in game and story format. *Adult Juror Comments*: Pleasant, simple production, slow paced. Children with instruments will benefit most from this. The teacher is polite and encouraging. Musical terms are defined simply. "This basically shows a music class with puppets added." *Kid Juror Comments*: Kids' interest waned after twenty minutes because they didn't have the instruments or a way to actively participate in the lesson. They enjoyed learning the names of the instruments and wanted to play and sing along. Video. 43 min.; $14.95; Age: 2-5. Headbone.

** Kidsongs: Meet the Biggles (Kidsongs)

Invites viewers to join in the fun as Billy and Ruby Biggle use their special powers to take their friends, the KidSongs Kids, to magical Biggleland for a musical adventure. *Adult Juror Comments*: This program has a selection of good songs sung competently by a group of cheerful children and puppets in relentlessly cheerful settings. The performers dance in an exhausting prepubescent jubilation. *Kid Juror Comments*: Songs are enjoyable, kids sang and danced along. Kids pointed out that all the kids on-screen looked like they were from middle-to-upper-class families with nice clothes, room full of tapes, big houses. Little diversity shown. They liked the songs. Video. 30 min.; $12.98; Age: 2-5. Sony Wonder.

* Let's Sing (Sing Along with John Langstaff)

Invites children to clap, move, and sing with master music educator and Pied Piper John Langstaff. Designed for children to watch alone or in groups. *Adult Juror Comments*: Good content. Easy to learn, but challenging at the same time. Format could become boring if watched all in one sitting. Jurors found it useful to view in segments. Excellent diversity, songs from different regions. *Kid Juror Comments*: Best when showed in segments. Some songs were difficult for children to hear, follow, and sing along with. Video. 45 min.; $19.95; Age: 3-5. Langstaff Video Project.

* Little Music Makers Band

Combines music and movement while introducing children to rhythm instruments. Teaches through traditional songs with creative new arrangements. *Adult Juror Comments*: Colorful environment for introducing music. On-screen children do not appear engaged. Instruments used are well selected. Demonstrates cooperation. Lacks diversity. *Kid Juror Comments*: Not much of a grabber. Motivated physical activity from some kids—swinging, tapping, and playing their own instruments. It did not hold the attention of all. Video. 26 min.; $9.95; Age: 2-5. B & D Enterprises.

Chapter Two • Preschool

* Mommy Songs: Everyone Can Sing

 The focus is on mom, Beth Klarreich Corwin, teaching songs with accompanying movements. *Adult Juror Comments*: Simple production with comfortable setting, but offers little interaction. Does not teach songs as much as it shows them. Good mix of familiar and new songs. Objected to "Little Bunny Foo Foo" which may encourage kids to hit each other on the head. *Kid Juror Comments*: Liked the animated gestures of the host. Provides a springboard for adult and child interaction. Two's and three's sang and danced; older children were a bit bored. Best if viewed with an adult who knows the songs and can help repeat them. Video. 22 min.; $14.95; Age: 3-5. Stargate Pictures.

* Movin' & Groovin' Vids for Kids (The Learning Station)

 The Learning Station performs their most requested songs in music video format. Includes a memory and observation quiz. *Adult Juror Comments*: Enthusiastic, silly, and fun. Uneven pace and quality. Featured songs encourage audience participation. The sets and costumes are a little funny. Quiz and outtakes are over the heads for the targeted age. *Kid Juror Comments*: Upbeat, happy response to the songs. Lots of foot-tapping. "The songs were fun, but the people were sort of funny." "I liked singing the songs because I knew the words." "I liked it because it was silly." Video. 34 min.; $19.95; Age: 2-5. On-Line Video Design, Inc.

*** MRN: Music and Feelings (Mister Rogers' Neighborhood)

Celebrates the many ways music touches our lives. Visits with cellist Yo-Yo Ma and folk singer Ella Jenkins. Explores how bass violins are made. *Adult Juror Comments*: Informative, delightful, moving, at times slow. Mister Rogers excels in his child-centered approach. Contains a lot of information useful for music classes. Ella Jenkins is great. *Kid Juror Comments*: Exciting, especially the making of the violin. Stimulated lively discussion and interest in music as a follow-up activity. Children hummed with the pitch pipe, like the song "Head and Shoulders." Video. 65 min.; $12.95; Age: 2-7. Family Communications, Inc.

*** MRN: Musical Stories (Mister Rogers' Neighborhood)

Two musical, whimsical adventures dealing with themes important to children. In one, a cow learns to feel good about himself. The other celebrates a family reunion. *Adult Juror Comments*: Meaningful messages for children. Mister Rogers offers quality entertainment without a lot of flash. Pace appropriate for this age, encourages children to engage in the material. It's long. Jurors recommend viewing individual stories separately. *Kid Juror Comments*: Scored high. Kept their attention and led to discussion afterwards. Video. 59 min.; $12.95; Age: 2-7. Family Communications, Inc.

* Nursery Songs & Rhymes (Rusty & Rosy)

A collection of 26 favorite nursery rhymes, songs, and chants teach many vital pre-reading concepts. Reinforces learning letters, names, shapes, and sounds. *Adult Juror Comments:* Good for reinforcement, as secondary to active learning. Somewhat static, music more lively than pictures. *Kid Juror Comments:* Children liked this better than adults. Held their attention. Helpful for early readers to have the words on the screen. Kids sang along. Video. 37 min.; $24.95; Age: 2-6. Waterford Institute.

*** Richard Scarry's Best Learning Songs Video Ever! (Richard Scarry's Best Videos Ever!)

Huckle Cat and friends put on a backyard show full of songs and surprises. Characters from Busytown sing about letters, shapes, and numbers. *Adult Juror Comments:* Cheerful preschool activity. Nice incorporation of known subjects with new materials. Easy to absorb information, songs, and characters. Very effective teaching tool to learn shapes and the alphabet. Stimulates interest in the Scarry books. *Kid Juror Comments:* Charming. The songs and characters went over big. "My son was riveted to the screen and identified letters and objects." All of the children asked to watch it again. Video. 30 min.; $9.98; Age: 2-6. Random House Video.

*** Sharon, Lois & Bram: One Elephant Went Out to Play (Sharon, Lois & Bram)

Children of all ages sing with the trio, lighting up their eyes with pleasure. *Adult Juror Comments:* Excellent. It's full of life and good spirits: playful, cheerful, and active. Appealing audio: great music, good variety of songs. Fabulous program. Unfortunately, box cover lacks appeal. Breaks between segments disrupt continuity. *Kid Juror Comments:* Enthusiastic response. Enjoyed the familiar songs, especially the four- and five-year-olds. They sang along with most songs. Video. 60 min.; $9.98; Age: 2-6. Video Treasures.

* Sharon, Lois & Bram: Sing A to Z (Sharon, Lois & Bram)

Sharon, Lois and Bram, along with their fuzzy elephant friend, sing and dance, teaching every letter of the alphabet. *Adult Juror Comments:* Entertaining introduction of the alphabet with many familiar songs. Some adults felt this was very entertaining; others said it was a little monotonous. *Kid Juror Comments:* Okay. It was a little hard for them to follow which letter they were on. Long, best viewed in segments. Video. 50 min.; $9.98; Age: 2-5. Video Treasures.

*** *Sing Along with Binyah Binyah (Gullah Gullah Island)*

 Contains eleven popular songs, including "Eensy Weensy Spider," "B-I-N-G-O," and "Loop de Loop." *Adult Juror Comments*: Familiar songs for children are presented in an entertaining, compassionate way. Great cultural mix, good movement activities, and appropriate pace encourage interactive viewing. *Kid Juror Comments*: A winner! They sang along and wanted to watch again. Great interactions from kids. Video. 30 min.; $12.98; Age: 3-6. Paramount Home Entertainment.

*** *Sing Along with Eureeka (Eureeka's Castle)*

 A special collection of eleven favorite songs from the television series "Eureeka's Castle." *Adult Juror Comments*: Lively, colorful, funny puppets—a fun fantasy with lots of musical variety. *Kid Juror Comments*: Enraptured. They were singing along, tapping their feet, and bopping their heads. Wanted to watch again. Video. 30 min.; $9.95; Age: 2-5. Paramount Home Entertainment.

** *Sing Me a Story: Rabbi Joe Black in Concert*

 Rabbi Joe Black in concert explores stories and songs from the Jewish tradition, such as looking for the Afikoman, and lighting the Chanukah menorah. Original and favorite songs celebrate and entertain at the same time. *Adult Juror Comments*: Great songs. Lots of toe-tapping, humming, and singing along. Special appeal to Jewish kids. A great way to expose non-Jewish children to this culture. "Definite educational value. Mr. Black is a good performer; he appeals to children." *Kid Juror Comments*: A hard time understanding the unfamiliar words. Would work best with activity book or lesson. "Our two-year-olds hung in there for the entire 45 minutes!" Video. 45 min.; $15.95; Age: 2-8. Lanitunes.

*** *Sing Yourself Sillier at the Movies*
(Sesame Street Home Video)

Hosts Telly and Oscar review the silliest movies you've ever seen, with the silliest songs you've ever heard! Will these daffy ditties rate a "wow" or a "phooey?" They can't seem to agree. Contains: "Eight Balls of Fur," "Hey Diddle Diddle," and more. *Adult Juror Comments*: Good catchy songs from Sesame Street. Clever production techniques. Artistic excellence, great humor, engages children and adults. Good for parent/child interaction and developing critical thinking skills. May stimulate dramatic play. *Kid Juror Comments*: Sang and danced along to the songs. Liked Telly and Oscar as the hosts. Kids familiar with Sesame Street identify readily with it. Video. 30 min.; $12.98; Age: 2-5. Sony Wonder.

Age 2-5

Video

Music

** Singing Time (Stories to Remember)

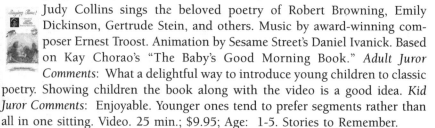

Judy Collins sings the beloved poetry of Robert Browning, Emily Dickinson, Gertrude Stein, and others. Music by award-winning composer Ernest Troost. Animation by Sesame Street's Daniel Ivanick. Based on Kay Chorao's "The Baby's Good Morning Book." *Adult Juror Comments*: What a delightful way to introduce young children to classic poetry. Showing children the book along with the video is a good idea. *Kid Juror Comments*: Enjoyable. Younger ones tend to prefer segments rather than all in one sitting. Video. 25 min.; $9.95; Age: 1-5. Stories to Remember.

*** Something Special

Fast-moving animation, expressive children, and colorful art bring these Hap Palmer favorites to life. Selections from the popular Walter and Sally albums help students increase vocabulary while having fun. *Adult Juror Comments*: Promotes good self-image while stimulating children to respond to the music by dancing and moving about. Helps develop gross-motor skills and ability to follow directions. Culturally diverse. *Kid Juror Comments*: Great fun to dance and sing along! It's silly and made them feel happy. Shows lots of different people, including good cartoon monsters. "I can pretend to do things like throw a rope and ride a horse." " It's fun and you can dance to it." Video. 25 min.; $19.95; Age: 2-6. Educational Activities, Inc.

*** Stepping Out with Hap Palmer

Hap Palmer is an innovator in using music and movement to teach basic skills: shapes, days of the week, counting, and movement. Encourages the use of imagination. His music has been widely used in schools and day care centers for over 20 years. *Adult Juror Comments*: Palmer's songs suit child's developmental level perfectly. Activities are fun, varied, and easy. Number learning is incidental and very well integrated. Shows excellent representation of handicapped kids and diverse cultures. *Kid Juror Comments*: Enthusiastic, especially the music and movement. One kids' jury commented, "We didn't watch it—we did it!" Video. 30 min.; $19.95; Age: 2-6. Educational Activities, Inc.

*** Storytime (Stories to Remember)

Legendary singer-songwriter Arlo Guthrie brings his whimsical wit and music to storytelling: "The Three Little Pigs," "Henny Penny," and "Little Red Riding Hood." Animation by Michael Sporn. Adapted from Kay Chorao's "The Baby's Story Book." *Adult Juror Comments*: Fun and funny. Arlo Guthrie fans were anxious to share it with their kids. *Kid Juror Comments*: Kids get a kick out of Guthrie's manner and love seeing and hearing their favorite stories. Video. 26 min.; $9.95; Age: 1-5. Stories to Remember.

*** *Storytime Sing Along (Allegra's Window)*

Poco wants Allegra and Lindi to read him a story, but they don't know how to read yet. Instead, they tell stories and draw pictures of their friends. By the end, they've created a beautiful book of their own. *Adult Juror Comments*: Contains easy-to-follow, colorful, catchy tunes. Prompts creativity, making up new words to songs, expression through music. Teaches reflection and storytelling through pictures. *Kid Juror Comments*: Three- and four-years-olds particularly enjoyed it. Children wanted to sing the songs afterwards and asked to hear specific selections. Video. 30 min.; $12.98; Age: 2-5. Paramount Home Entertainment.

** *Tales & Tunes: Original Tales & Tunes (Tales & Tunes)*

A collection of whimsical stories and music for young children guided by a spunky little character named K. J. Contemporary tales and upbeat tunes are combined with live action, animation, and puppetry. *Adult Juror Comments*: Funny. Adults liked the overall content. Kids were interested in the "William Small" section. In one section, children behave in an adult fashion. In another, mothers are stereotyped. *Kid Juror Comments*: Enjoyed observing other children, particularly the "silliness." They followed along with everything, enjoyed singing and joined in. Too long for younger kids without breaking it up; older ones loved it. Video. 30 min.; $12.98; Age: 2-8. Video Treasures.

** *Tales & Tunes: Silly Tales & Tunes (Tales & Tunes)*

From the creators of "Baby Songs" comes this assortment of comical stories and sing-along songs. Video disc jockey K. J. hosts this collection of rib-tickling tales, kooky cartoons, laugh-packed tunes, and non-stop fun. *Adult Juror Comments*: Nice variety of elements to keep young viewers interested: animation, live action, jokes, stories, and songs. Some cultural stereotyping and not such good role models. For example, wearing high heels on monkey bars. *Kid Juror Comments*: Very nice, especially the music and sing-along songs. "I want to see that one again." Age-appropriateness changes, humor and content best suited for older kids. Video. 30 min.; $12.98; Age: 2-8. Video Treasures.

* *Tubby the Tuba*

Tubby is a member of a great orchestra, but he's unhappy with his monotonous "oompah" sound and envious of the other instruments. Tubby leaves the orchestra in search of a tuneful melody, and his wanderings bring success, failure, and heartbreak. *Adult Juror Comments*: A sweet classic story. Tuneful but not stellar music. Fairly old-fashioned, and slow-moving for today's audience. *Kid Juror Comments*: Okay. They especially liked the elephant dance scene. The beginning is a little sad. Video. 81 min.; $12.98; Age: 3-7. Sony Wonder.

** Veggie Tales: Silly Sing-Along 2: The End of Silliness? (Veggie Tales)

A fast-paced sing-along collection that finds Larry the Cucumber drowning his sorrows in the ice cream parlor. Features songs from the Veggie Tales Series and asks the question, "Is this the end of silliness?" *Adult Juror Comments*: Definitely silly, colorful, and bright. The humor, fast music, and funny characters are age-appropriate and enjoyable. "I loved watching the children watch it." The rapid speech is difficult to follow. Relates slightly to Bible stories. *Kid Juror Comments*: The children laughed and sang along. "If you don't watch this kind of movie, your heart will be broken." Some kids wanted to watch it again, tomorrow. Video. 30 min.; $12.99; Age: 3-7. Big Idea Productions, Inc.

** Wee Sing Favorites: Animal Songs (Wee Sing)

Wee Sing characters Singaling and Warbly guide the audience through an assortment of fifteen favorite animal songs, including "Mary Had a Little Lamb" and "Eency Weency Spider." *Adult Juror Comments*: Material drawn from previous productions still works. Demonstrates minimal cultural diversity and is very fast-paced. Simple production work for this age group. Characters are appealing, animation is eye-catching. Gives good points for discussion. *Kid Juror Comments*: A hit! Good length that readily engaged their attention. Kids hummed along to their old favorites. They loved the animals and costumes. Video. 33 min.; $9.98; Age: 2-5. Universal Studios Home Video.

** Wee Sing in Sillyville (Wee Sing)

Songs, dances, and an uplifting story show that the world is a better place when people of all colors (blue, green, and purple) live together in happiness. *Adult Juror Comments*: Magical, full of fun, silly, and colorful. Addresses discrimination and cooperation. Little diversity. Children love the silly creatures as they work to become friends again. Humorous music. *Kid Juror Comments*: Enjoyable. Kids participated by singing and dancing along. Program is long for this age, good to watch in segments to enjoy the whole thing. Video. 60 min.; $12.98; Age: 2-8. Universal Studios Home Video.

** Wee Sing in the Big Rock Candy Mountains (Wee Sing)

A zany romp in a land of food and fun teaches children about the importance of friendship, recycling, and nutrition. *Adult Juror Comments*: Very cute, lively, and colorful. Addresses excluding others and cooperation. Morals, riddles, and humor are for older children. Honesty, good eating habits, and imagination are emphasized. Little cultural diversity. *Kid Juror Comments*: Thoroughly enjoyable, with lots of laughter. Participated by singing, dancing, and clapping. A bit long for this age, best viewed in segments. Video. 60 min.; $12.98; Age: 2-8. Universal Studios Home Video.

** Wee Sing in the Marvelous Musical Mansion (Wee Sing)

Sing and dance with Alex, Kelly, and Benji. Solve a baffling mystery while learning about music, self-esteem, and friendship. *Adult Juror Comments*: Good production, great learning potential. Incorporates musical knowledge into story: scales, names of notes, and instrument names. Wonderful incorporation of musical knowledge and informative story content. Little diversity. *Kid Juror Comments*: Wonderful. Great story and music. Kids joined in singing and dancing. Held kids' attention all the way. Stimulated discussion. "I wish I could watch it a hundred times." Song booklet a plus. Video. 60 min.; $12.98; Age: 2-8. Universal Studios Home Video.

** Wee Sing Together (Wee Sing)

Join Sally for her birthday party and celebrate the fun of music and the joy of friendship. *Adult Juror Comments*: Acknowledges valid feelings. Adults find these too long for one sitting. *Kid Juror Comments*: Good, especially the familiar songs. Kept their attention, and they danced while watching. Video. 60 min.; $12.98; Age: 2-8. Universal Studios Home Video.

*** Wee Sing Train, The (Wee Sing)

Takes children on singing and dancing adventures through the old West, a fairy tale castle, and other exciting lands. Imagine playing with a toy train and suddenly becoming a passenger! This can only happen in the land of make-believe. *Adult Juror Comments*: Children's voices are particularly enjoyable. Fun and silly. Some cultural diversity. *Kid Juror Comments*: Exceptional. All age groups were very attentive to this, best with two's and three's. Enjoyed the story, music, and singing along. Lots of fun and just enough silliness. Video. 60 min.; $12.98; Age: 2-8. Universal Studios Home Video.

** Wee Sing Under the Sea (Wee Sing)

Takes children to a place they've never been—under the sea. Sing, dance, and swim along with the wet and wonderful characters. Experience the beauty and splendor of the world beneath the waves. *Adult Juror Comments*: Musical score is lively and suitable, but adults felt it was overly didactic in addressing the audience. Very little is creative or original. The exotic starfish puppet is campy but amusing. *Kid Juror Comments*: Pretty good. Kids liked the puppets. One boy, quite young, liked the big clam. Kids' jury was looking for more from the characters, wanted to know more about what is under the sea. A bit long. Video. 60 min.; $12.98; Age: 2-9. Universal Studios Home Video.

Age 2-5

Video

Music

** Wee Sing: Classic Songs for Kids (Wee Sing)

Introduces Wee Sing characters Singaling and Warbly. Features a compilation of favorite traditional songs from the Wee Sing collection including "Row, Row, Row Your Boat" and "Home on the Range." *Adult Juror Comments*: Lovely, simple, well-staged production which emphasizes cooperation children understand. Structure is a little unorganized and presentations seem artificial. Music does make children want to sing along. *Kid Juror Comments*: It didn't take long for them to join in. Some kids absolutely loved singing the songs. Several wanted to see it again. Video. 31 min.; $9.98; Age: 2-6. Universal Studios Home Video.

** Wee Sing: Grandpa's Magical Toys (Wee Sing)

Join Peter and his friends on their visit to the world's most wonderful grandpa and discover how important it is to be young at heart. *Adult Juror Comments*: Invites participation through familiar songs, different dance steps, movement songs, and partner hand-clapping games. Good values. Little diversity. *Kid Juror Comments*: Sang and danced with the video. They noticed that all the adults were Caucasian and there was only one African-American child. Too long for one sitting. Video. 60 min.; $12.98; Age: 2-8. Universal Studios Home Video.

** Wee Sing: King Cole's Party (Wee Sing)

At a royal, rollicking party for Old King Cole, children realize that the most precious gifts of all aren't jewels or gold, but ones that come from the heart. *Adult Juror Comments*: Imaginative and entertaining. Links familiar nursery rhymes. Effective plot, good message about non-materialism. Vocabulary is sometimes beyond level of audience. Little diversity shown. *Kid Juror Comments*: Okay, but it was too long for the younger ones. Kids noticed that all the people on screen were Caucasian. Video. 60 min.; $12.98; Age: 2-8. Universal Studios Home Video.

*** Weesingdom—The Land of Music and Fun (Wee Sing)

Enter a tuneful new land. Combining classic and original songs, a festive story, and a cast of favorite sing-along friends, this Wee Sing volume captivates young imaginations from the first note. *Adult Juror Comments*: Cute story, cute characters, and a lot of fun. It models cooperation; eye-catching and personable characters. Addresses making mistakes such as forgetting words to a song, but learning to have fun anyway. "Wee Sing tapes are like old friends." *Kid Juror Comments*: Even non-English-speaking children were mesmerized. Has great familiar old songs and fun new ones. A little long for some kids, but all ages danced along. Video. 64 min.; $12.98; Age: 2-5. Universal Studios Home Video.

*** Winnie the Pooh: Sing a Song with Pooh Bear (Winnie the Pooh)*

In the Hundred Acre Wood, Winnie the Pooh feels like he's missing something—his very own song. Pooh and his friends search for his song and discover lots of other songs along the way. Includes 12 songs with words that appear on screen. *Adult Juror Comments*: Terrific. Well-produced. Great music and dancing. Characters have distinct personalities. In a sense they represent a wide variety of people. Most personalities are represented from wise to fun to obnoxious. Yet, they are always respectful and helpful. *Kid Juror Comments*: All laughed and sang along. Kids really love Tigger. He's happy and easy to relate to. They liked the Kangaroo Hop and danced along. "It teaches kids about sharing." "I liked when Pooh found his song." One two-year-old watched it every day for two weeks. Video. 36 min.; $19.98; Age: 2-8. Buena Vista Home Entertainment/Disney.

*** Winnie the Pooh: Sing a Song with Tigger (Winnie the Pooh)*

Tigger bounces along memory lane as he pages through his scrapbook. He reminisces over magical moments and songs with his friends, like Roo's first bouncing lesson and when Tigger met Buddy-Boy. 12 songs and Tigger's tips on making a scrapbook. Animated. *Adult Juror Comments*: Excellent. Great graphics and music. Bouncy and cheerful. Having the words on screen makes it easier to learn the songs. Encourages child's imagination, a spirit of adventure and the love of family and friends. *Kid Juror Comments*: Delighted and engaged. "I liked this because of the bouncing and because of the wizard." "We watched the 'I Wanna Scare Myself' song four times." "Tigger has a lot of friends." "Great songs." Video. 31 min.; $19.98; Age: 2-8. Buena Vista Home Entertainment/Disney.

** Yodel-Ay-Hee-Hoo! (Cathy and Marcy's Song Shop)*

 Cathy and Marcy lead children and adults in singing, signing, dancing, and yodeling. Filled with uncommon instruments and vocal styles. *Adult Juror Comments*: Enjoyable. Great music, great role models, rich in diversity, lots of interactive shots. Hosts are very genuine. Invites participation. *Kid Juror Comments*: Favorites: storytelling and sign language. Everyone tried to sing along. Kids liked hearing familiar songs. Video. 30 min.; $14.95; Age: 2-8. Community Music, Inc.

Category—Nature

** Animal Antics: Summer (Animal Antics-Seasons)

Follows a year in the lives of wild, farm, and domestic animals over the four seasons in and around the old schoolhouse where they live. The series of short stories are narrated in a humorous way. *Adult Juror Comments*: Humorous production that introduces children to a variety of wild animals such as ferrets, voles, and hedgehogs. Excellent cinematography. Short story format makes it easy to view in segments—ideal for this age. It covers the life cycle of a frog. *Kid Juror Comments*: Would definitely watch again. "I know my friends will like this, just like me." "Why do some animals eat other animals?" "The big pigs were scary." "I wonder what our birds are talking about?" "I loved the frogs, can we get a book about them?" Video. 45 min.; $12.95; Age: 2-5. Just for Kids Home Video/Celebrity Home Entertainment.

** Animal Quest (Adventures with Baaco)

Baaco, a friendly visitor from the planet Baacia, magically transports Mr. Dean and his science class to the international zoo, where they learn about animals from around the world. Eet-oot, earthlings! *Adult Juror Comments*: Good information with simple, lively music. The review at the end was helpful. Dancing segments were an unnecessary interruption. *Kid Juror Comments*: Much to the adults' surprise, children enjoyed integrating the dancing and singing with a trip to the zoo. They were interested to learn about the animal facts. Video. 32 min.; $9.95; Age: 2-8. Kids Trek Productions.

** At the Zoo (Picture This Sing-a-Long)

Toe-tapping, hand-clapping songs about monkeys, elephants, giraffes, zebras, meerkats, aardvarks, sea lions, polar bears, and dolphins. *Adult Juror Comments*: Good content. Interesting footage of animals at the zoo. The learning potential is high, especially when used with other materials or experiences. *Kid Juror Comments*: Really good. Talked about the animals afterwards and danced to the songs, including the three-year-olds. Repeat viewings would be needed in order for children to learn songs. Video. 25 min.; $14.95; Age: 3-8. Goldsholl: Learning Videos.

** At the Zoo: 2 (Picture This! Sing-a-Long)

An exciting, educational, fun-filled visit to the zoo, with original songs and interesting animals, starring: bears, otters, piglets, gorillas, woodpeckers, kangaroos, reptiles, ibex, water loving animals, and the rain forest. *Adult Juror Comments*: Delightful. Interesting selection of animals. Songs are fun, children could pick them up after just a few viewings. Stimulates further inquiry, some advanced language. "Ties animals to habitats very well, emphasizing the beauty of nature." *Kid Juror Comments*: Lots of toe-tapping and head-bobbing to the fun songs that kids picked up right away. "Let's go on a field trip to the zoo." Children wanted to see it again. Led to a discussion about animals. Video. 30 min.; $14.95; Age: 2-7. Goldsholl: Learning Videos.

*** Bugs Don't Bug Us! (Live Action Video)

Fascinating look at children observing insects, spiders, and other common invertebrates in a friendly, amusing way. Observes detailed motions and eating habits of these creatures. *Adult Juror Comments*: "One of the best." Has superb cinematography and nice musical choices. Sequence with butterflies is excellent. Shows good ethnic diversity among children, who act naturally and are a pleasure to watch. Excellent resource; good repeat viewing value. *Kid Juror Comments*: "It was great." Kids were active, commenting, and questioning. They responded by going on a bug hunt. Naturally educational, kids asked to see it again. Video. 35 min.; $14.95; Age: 2-5. Bo Peep Productions.

** Camouflage, Cuttlefish, and Chameleons Changing Color (Geokids)

Looks at nature's camouflaged animals, including three-toed sloths, arctic foxes, hermit crabs, and octopi. Bobby and Sunny discover that chameleons like Uncle Balzac can change color with their mood. *Adult Juror Comments*: Good resource. Great teaching supplement for animal theme. Shows good examples of natural camouflage. Some felt that this imposes adult ideas on children watching. *Kid Juror Comments*: Very informational; children became interested in finding the camouflaged animals. Held most kids' attention. The "Mood" song dragged a bit. Video. 40 min.; $14.95; Age: 2-10. Nat'l Geographic Home Video.

*** Chomping on Bugs, Swimming Sea Slugs & Stuff That Makes Animals Special (Geokids)*

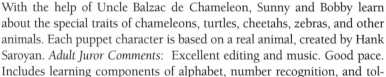

With the help of Uncle Balzac de Chameleon, Sunny and Bobby learn about the special traits of chameleons, turtles, cheetahs, zebras, and other animals. Each puppet character is based on a real animal, created by Hank Saroyan. *Adult Juror Comments:* Excellent editing and music. Good pace. Includes learning components of alphabet, number recognition, and tolerance for different living situations. Information and presentation are suitable for younger kids; sophisticated enough for older kids. *Kid Juror Comments:* Watching the animals was terrific. Different voices held their attention. A little too long for one sitting, especially for younger ones. "The animal acrobat section is great!" Video. 35 min.; $14.95; Age: 2-10. Nat'l Geographic Home Video.

** Creepy Critters (Professor Iris)*

Snakes, bats, bugs, and bees are some of the creatures that come out to play when Professor Iris investigates his attic. Don't be afraid, they're all quite friendly and fascinating, as the Professor will show you. *Adult Juror Comments:* Good program. Promotes comparisons in thinking on children's part. *Kid Juror Comments:* The songs and the humor were nice. They discussed many of the concepts and facts afterwards. Video. 40 min.; $12.95; Age: 2-6. Discovery Communications.

** First Look at Mammals, A (Nature's Way)*

When most people think of mammals, they think of dogs, cats, or horses. Nevertheless, beavers, otters, whales, dolphins, and bats are mammals too. Explores the common characteristics of mammals whether they live on land, in water, or fly through the air. *Adult Juror Comments:* Good content. It's most suitable for library collections. Format is good for learning, but it's visually flat. Most shots are stationary. Quality appears old, lacks action. *Kid Juror Comments:* Well-focused, good length. Some giggled at nursing animals. Most suited for one-time viewing. Not highly entertaining. Video. 13 min.; $29.95; Age: 2-5. Aims Multimedia.

** Let's Explore...Furry, Fishy, Feathery Friends (Let's Explore)*

Seven-year-old McKenzie showcases frogs, birds, snakes, rabbits, lizards, and more: what they eat; how they sleep; and other behaviors. *Adult Juror Comments:* Great introduction to the world of pets—both usual and unusual. Main character is appealing. It's very informational, but brings up some safety issues. *Kid Juror Comments:* Wonderful. Discussed proper names for animals and which ones bite. Some kids didn't like how the animals were picked up and hugged. Beware: children might want a pet after watching this video. Video. 30 min.; $14.95; Age: 2-8. Braun Film and Video, Inc.

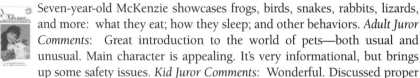

Chapter Two • Preschool

** Meet Your Animal Friends

 Lynn Redgrave hosts this wonderful visit with baby animals, to the delight of infants and toddlers who giggle with glee at the funny antics of sheep, deer, horses, dogs, and other species. *Adult Juror Comments*: Wonderful selection of animals: bunnies, rheas, swans, cows, kangaroos, puppies, kittens, and fat pigs. Narration is age-appropriate, informative, and invites commentary from the kids. Good camera work, some footage is a little washed out and dated. *Kid Juror Comments*: "I loved the kittens, they're so cute. I liked watching the funny things that the animals do. Rheas are funny looking birds." Inspired the kids to want to go to the zoo. Video. 54 min.; $14.95; Age: 1-6. JSK Enterprises.

* Mommy, Gimme a Drinka Water

 Child's point of view portrayed in songs, words, and pictures. Stars Didi Conn and Stacy Jones of "Shining Time Station." *Adult Juror Comments*: Good theme, fun presentation. Beautiful inclusion of senior citizens. Didi Conn is believably childlike. Songs are hard to follow. Objection to the "Don't Tickle Me" song: children should be respected and listened to. Little cultural diversity. *Kid Juror Comments*: Okay. Liked the songs, although some of the words were hard to follow. Favorites: "Playing on the See-Saw" and "I'm Hiding." Video. 35 min.; $14.95; Age: 3-6. White Star Video.

* More Zoofari

 Sir Arthur Blowhard and his assistant, Smythe, head out on an adventure, visiting different members of the animal kingdom on an exciting "zoofari." *Adult Juror Comments*: Excellent production quality. Informative and factual—good introduction to animal study. Lacks human diversity. Pace is slow and difficult to follow. "Wacky tour guides are a fun approach." *Kid Juror Comments*: Nothing special. "It's like visiting the zoo, only the animals are close-up instead of far away." Stimulated discussion afterwards, especially with kids interested in animals. Video. 30 min.; $14.95; Age: 4-6. White Tree Pictures, Inc./Venture Entertainment Group.

* My Amazing Animal Adventure (Gregory and Me)

 Your child is the star of the show in this combination of live-action, puppets, and animation. Your child travels the world with Gregory, visiting animals big and small, returning with a big surprise. *Adult Juror Comments*: Good information, fun antics, and factual tidbits. Parts are not suitable for non-readers. Notion of personalized video is appealing— good idea for families. Humor and vocabulary are not always age-appropriate. *Kid Juror Comments*: Features kids' favorite animals, sparks some toe-tapping. Children enjoyed it, but not many wanted to watch it again. Gregory and his sidekicks were a big hit! Video. 25 min.; $34.95; Age: 2-5. Kideo Productions, Inc.

*** *Tadpoles, Dragonflies, and the Caterpillar's Big Change (Geokids)*

A pod hanging from a branch is a sort of sleeping bag, where a caterpillar becomes a butterfly in a big change called metamorphosis. Curiosity leads an exploration of other big-change artists. *Adult Juror Comments*: A beautifully photographed nature discovery, it gives children a good picture of the environment. "It's the best nature series I've seen." *Kid Juror Comments*: It all was great, from the music to the movement of the plants. They thought it was fast-paced and packed full of information about growth and development. Video. 40 min.; $14.95; Age: 2-10. Nat'l Geographic Home Video.

Category—Special Interest

*** *Big Trains, Little Trains*

An interesting, amusing look at trains of all sizes, from toy trains to an incredible miniature backyard railroad with tunnels, bridges, and a cliff-top ocean view. Includes a giant outdoor model run by remote control. *Adult Juror Comments*: Trains are a favorite topic with children. Content is self-contained, with good, accurate information. Great resource tool. "I loved the two child hosts!" Shows little diversity. *Kid Juror Comments*: Little boys particularly enjoyed this one. Children under four years of age did not stay with it. "I love trains, I want to play trains." Video. 27 min.; $14.95; Age: 2-8. Sandbox Home Videos.

** *Classic Nursery Rhymes*

Offers a collection of nursery rhymes produced with original musical arrangements and captivating computer-animated visuals appealing to children and adults. *Adult Juror Comments*: Visually interesting and original, but at times the visuals seem poorly integrated with the story. The three-dimensional presentation tends to be more important than the nursery rhymes and images. Pacing is too fast at times. *Kid Juror Comments*: High-scoring appeal. Some characters will be scary for sensitive viewers. Video. 32 min.; $14.95; Age: 3-6. M3D Inc.

* *Daycare Live!*

Features a day visiting a day care center. Viewers are invited to participate in a typical day that includes arrival, mealtimes, singing, structured play, swimming, nap-time, and a birthday celebration. *Adult Juror Comments*: This is a good model for day care providers with recommended developmental activities. Jurors' objections to use of balloons, popcorn as snack, and multiple use of wading pool. *Kid Juror Comments*: Fun! Two's and three's liked it best. They smiled, sang, clapped, and giggled. "I liked the children walking around barefoot on the cushioned floor." Video. 39 min.; $9.99; Age: 2-5. Mother's Helper Inc.

* Dr. Bip's New Baby Tips

Dr. Bip, an animated character, explains to young children what to expect when Mommy and Daddy bring home a new baby. Addresses the emotional aspects and some practical, common sense tips for kids. *Adult Juror Comments*: Deals with jealousy, responsibility, and safety. May motivate questioning by siblings. Bip is appealing to some, but many found his rhyming annoying. The language used is not always age-appropriate. Some gender stereotypes. Lacks diversity. *Kid Juror Comments*: Appeals to those who are expecting a brother or sister. Kids remembered the safety tips: "Never let go and never pick up the baby without an adult. It's slippery." Kids didn't care for the rhyming, and content was sometimes missed due to the rhyming. Video. 14 min.; $14.95; Age: 3-6. Kidz-Med, Inc.

*** Farm Country Ahead (Little Hardhats)

 Takes kids for a close-up view of the tools and big machines that grow and harvest foods. Includes a behind-the-scenes look at how peanut butter, jelly, bread, and potato chips are made. *Adult Juror Comments*: Fun, educational. Shows how each food in the host's lunchbox is made as well as the hard work and the many steps involved in growing and preparing food. "Teachers could use this with the first grade social studies curriculum." *Kid Juror Comments*: Prompted lots of interest and discussion. "We learned how peanut butter is made." "Can we make potato chips?" "I saw how they used cow poop!" "Can I go to a real farm and ride on a tractor?" Video. 46 min.; $14.95; Age: 3-6. Fred Levine Productions, DBA Little Hardhats.

*** Franklin and the Secret Club (Franklin)

When Porcupine, jealous of Franklin's popularity, creates a secret club for the sole purpose of keeping him out, Franklin teaches her the true meaning of friendship. *Adult Juror Comments*: Content is refreshingly meaningful. Issues of friendship, belonging, and honesty are dealt with appropriately and relevantly in situations common to preschoolers—teasing, exclusion, and sharing. High learning potential. *Kid Juror Comments*: Captivating. They wanted to see it again immediately. Kids seemed sensitive to Franklin's feelings. "We could watch it together and laugh." "Made me think about being nice." Video. 25 min.; $12.95; Age: 2-5. U.S.A. Home Entertainment.

Age 2-5

Video

Spec Int

** Grandpa Worked on the Railroad

Combines songs and activities easy for young children to learn. Includes demonstrations of actual steam trains. Teaches some basic skills that grown-ups use at work: teamwork, communication, and working with machines. *Adult Juror Comments*: Trains seem to have an eternal appeal, and this story is engaging. Very informative though somewhat hokey. Would be effective as part of a unit. *Kid Juror Comments*: Absorbing. Prompted lots of discussion about trains. Some information too technical for three-to-five age group. Video. 30 min.; $14.95; Age: 2-8. Phoenix Media.

** Heavy Equipment Operator
(What Do You Want to Be When You Grow Up?)

Spotlights construction workers working with big machinery. Features bulldozers, ringer cranes, scrapers, excavators, and back hoes moving mountains of earth and lifting tons of steel. *Adult Juror Comments*: Fascinating footage especially for the little ones. Safety tips are good. Motivates discussions about safety issues. *Kid Juror Comments*: Enthusiastically watched the machines work and listened to the explanations of how they work. The young boy's excitement captured the viewer's interest. Prompted a discussion about the heavy equipment kids are familiar with or have seen. Video. 30 min.; $14.95; Age: 2-8. Big Kids Productions, Inc.

** Here We Go Again

Hosted by Lynn Redgrave, takes youngsters on close inspection of vehicles such as tow trucks and jets, police cars and trolleys, subways and construction cranes. *Adult Juror Comments*: Shows a wide variety of vehicles and situations, from tow trucks to the Concorde to a cable car to boats of various sizes. Second-guesses kids' questions with informative narrative. *Kid Juror Comments*: It made kids want to travel somewhere so they could ride on a plane or on a cable car. "It's too long for me. I can't watch it all at once." "Ooh, I want to live on a barge." Video. 60 min.; $14.95; Age: 2-5. JSK Enterprises.

** Here We Go, Volume 1

Take an action-packed voyage on some of the most exciting vehicles ever, capturing a child's fascination with such diverse conveyances as steam locomotives, ocean liners, fire engines, blimps, and more. Narrated by Lynn Redgrave. *Adult Juror Comments*: Great exploration of various modes of travel, from helicopters to bulldozers to hovercrafts. Gives very child-centered explanations of how the vehicles work. *Kid Juror Comments*: They were fascinated by the amphibious hovercraft. "It looks like a spaceship. I wonder how many cars it holds." Video. 32 min.; $14.95; Age: 2-5. JSK Enterprises.

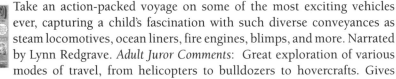

Chapter Two • Preschool

** *Here We Go, Volume 2*

 This show takes children on a musical adventure on different modes of transportation, such as helicopters, bulldozers, dump trucks, bicycles, fire engines, and an aerial tramway. Narrated by Lynn Redgrave. *Adult Juror Comments*: Excellent production, showing various modes of travel from double-decker buses in London to a cruise ship, a hydrofoil, and a fire truck. *Kid Juror Comments*: "Where's London? Can we go there? I want to ride a double-decker bus." Kids loved the swimming pool on the cruise ship. Kids thought some of the British terminology was funny and noticed that they didn't lock up their bikes. Video. 34 min.; $14.95; Age: 2-5. JSK Enterprises.

** *Hey, What About Me*

 A warm, straightforward talk to preschoolers about adjusting to new siblings. Teaches games, lullabies, and rhymes. *Adult Juror Comments*: Addresses sibling rivalry in a fun way. Great for showing kids they have a role to play when the new baby comes. Shows other kids helping with the baby, singing to him, playing with him, being quiet when he is sleeping. *Kid Juror Comments*: Related to the subject matter quite well. "The girl was mad because there was a new baby coming." "I learned to be nice to babies and to rock them." "I sing to my baby brother." Video. 30 min.; $14.95; Age: 2-6. Kidvidz.

** *House Construction Ahead (Fred Levine's Original)*

Shows house construction, from site-clearing and excavation to blasting at rock quarries. Also, harvesting timber and a visit to the sawmill. *Adult Juror Comments*: Informative. Nice camera work, with many close-ups. Illustrates parallels between kids' play and house construction. Lacks diversity and solid safety guidelines. *Kid Juror Comments*: The language is too advanced for preschoolers. Kids didn't understand sections. Stimulated kids' thinking about houses and how they're built. The backward explosions were a big hit with boys. "It made me think about how many parts go into a house." Video. 30 min.; $14.95; Age: 3-6. Fred Levine Productions, DBA Little Hardhats.

* *How to Be a Ballerina*

Most little girls dream of becoming a ballerina. Their dreams are encouraged in this informative program that demonstrates some simple but beautiful ballet movements that can be learned at home. *Adult Juror Comments*: Well done visually and organizationally. Instructional value most appropriate for six- and seven-year-olds. Instructor is stern but reassuring. Introduces children to the idea that dance requires discipline and practice. *Kid Juror Comments*: The girls were crazy about the video, dancing and hopping around afterwards. Boys were not as engaged; no boys are shown in the video. May be too long for children under four. "My friends who study ballet would like this." Video. 40 min.; $9.98; Age: 3-7. Sony Wonder.

** *Kids Love the Circus (Kids Love)*

Elephants help put up the tent at the old-fashioned Clyde Beatty-Cole Bros. Circus. Children take center stage and imagine themselves taming lions and walking the high wire at the backyard circus. *Adult Juror Comments*: A wonderful, catchy musical extravaganza! Encourages children to use their imagination for a backyard circus and offers behind-the-scenes information. Encourages creativity. *Kid Juror Comments*: Terrific, especially seeing how to stage a circus and the old circus footage. The songs held children's interest. "I'm going to try to balance on the floor just like they did." Video. 40 min.; $14.95; Age: 2-8. Acorn Media Publishing Inc.

* *Kids on the Block (Early Learning Series)*

The "Kids on the Block" puppets bring 20 years of experience in teaching children about disabilities and differences. Includes important lessons on aggression, compassion, and perseverance for young audiences. Includes suggested follow-up activities. *Adult Juror Comments*: Offers positive examples of good social skills and concrete ideas for dealing with anger. Excellent diversity but low production values. Prompts good discussion. Messages sometimes unclear. Slow pace. *Kid Juror Comments*: Mixed reactions. Enjoyed the characters, although their attention drifted. Information was good, but messages were a little bit unclear to young children. Video. 30 min.; $39.95; Age: 3-5. Kids on the Block, Inc.

** *Let's Create for Preschoolers (Let's Create)*

An opportunity to introduce preschoolers to the world of art. Teaches about colors and shapes while working on six projects. *Adult Juror Comments*: Clever instructional ideas for parents or caregivers who want to enrich child's artistic abilities by engaging in art activities. Jurors objected to the product-versus-process approach. Makes a good instructional tool for parents and teachers. *Kid Juror Comments*: Mixed reactions. Best shown in segments. Some kids objected to doing exactly what the instructor did and wanted more creative freedom. Video. 45 min.; $24.95; Age: 2-5. Let's Create, Inc.

* *Look What Happens...at the Car Wash (Look What Happens)*

Shows in detail exactly how the car wash works, from start to finish. Teaches key words through soapy action and clean fun. *Adult Juror Comments*: Entertaining and silly; interesting comparison between hand washing and a car wash. *Kid Juror Comments*: Loved the humor, but overall not particularly appealing. Children got a kick out of the reverse segment and watching the police car get washed. They weren't interested in watching it again. Too long, and they lost interest. Video. 25 min.; $19.95; Age: 3-6. Informedia.

** Mighty Construction Machines

Puts you in the operator's seat of some powerful, earth-shaking construction machines. Diverse musical interludes, realistic sound effects, awe-inspiring power of machines-at-work, delightful surprises in an interactive format. *Adult Juror Comments*: Creative video techniques. Good demonstrations, replicates hands-on-learning. Visually appealing. Provides insight for curious minds into different types of equipment. Excellent multi-ethnic and gender roles portrayed. Music works well with video. *Kid Juror Comments*: Involving. They wanted to draw the machines. They liked the women truck drivers and the teen-age female narrator. "Look, he's pushing over a mountain!" "I've been on a backhoe before." "My little brother would like this." Video. 33 min.; $14.99; Age: 3-6. Bang Zoom! Entertainment.

** Miss Christy's Dance Adventure (Miss Christy's Dancin)

As an introduction for younger children, it teaches the basics of ballet, tap, and jazz through visuals and demonstration. *Adult Juror Comments*: Encourages interest in dance and use of imagination. A pleasant way to learn some dance steps. Children pictured dancing were appealing and real. Miss Christy shows love and respect for the students. Best used in addition to a dance class. *Kid Juror Comments*: Fabulous. Preschoolers went crazy over this video! Children got up to join in the dancing. Some kids had a hard time following the steps. "I'd like to watch this again." Video. 35 min.; $12.98; Age: 2-5. PPI / Peter Pan, Inc.

* Mr. Tibbs & the Great Pet Search

Personalized video invites child on an adventure in search of the perfect pet. Travels to a farm, the jungle, and the ocean. *Adult Juror Comments*: Cute animal story. Concept of including a child in the video is clever, but the image gets tiresome. May be a nice touch for families. The rhyming narration works well. *Kid Juror Comments*: Okay. Wanted to see the image of the child move. Two-year-olds enjoyed the whole video. Afterwards, kids drew pictures of animals with their own photo included. Kids showed little interest in watching again. Video. 22 min.; $34.95; Age: 2-6. Kideo Productions, Inc.

*** MRN: When Parents Are Away
(Mister Rogers' Neighborhood)

Helps deal with the anxieties that arise when parents are away. Visits a child care center and a graham cracker factory while addressing lots of feelings about being apart. *Adult Juror Comments*: Great content and subject. Well-paced. Mister Rogers relates to children most effectively. He is clear, takes his time, and treats subject in a sensitive way. *Kid Juror Comments*: Top marks. Prompted discussion later. "I get scared, but I like my babysitter." A little long for this audience, best viewed in segments. Video. 66 min.; $12.95; Age: 2-7. Family Communications, Inc.

Age 2-5

Video

Spec Int

Chapter Two • Preschool

*** New Baby in My House, A (Sesame Street Home Video)

 Mrs. Snuffleupagus reads her children a fairy tale about a prince who feels neglected when his baby sister arrives. It helps Snuffy realize that even though he's not the only child anymore, everyone still loves him just the same. *Adult Juror Comments*: Deals with an issue that is meaningful to children—sibling rivalry. Humorous, thought-provoking presentation. Presents the same theme in several ways as a story within a story. Has a good mix of animation and live action with lively, simple songs. *Kid Juror Comments*: Funny, loved upbeat songs. Message is delightful and authentic. Children with special needs are included. "My brother gets on my nerves too." A little advanced for two-year-olds. Video. 30 min.; $9.98; Age: 2-5. Sony Wonder.

* Nounou Time: Good Night Volume One (Nounou Time)

Nounou the bear and Timothy Timekeeper help parents at bedtime. Eight segments prepare children for bed with lullabies and goodnight kisses while teaching good manners and habits. Contains original music. *Adult Juror Comments*: Liked the puppets. The individual segments are short with good songs and messages. Openings and credits run before and after each segment which is quite distracting. Best viewed in segments, ideally, as a daily bedtime routine. *Kid Juror Comments*: "The puppets were cute. I liked Nounou best." Kids responded well to the music and identified with the characters and situations. They kept thinking the tape was over each time the credits ran. " It's too short." Lacks ethnic diversity. Video. 30 min.; $12.99; Age: 2-5. Benny Smart.

* Railroaders (What Do You Want to Be When You Grow Up?)

Conductors, engineers, and workers teach all about steam, freight, and passenger trains. Learn about engines, boxcars, flat cars, hoppers, and tankers, working on the railroad every step of the way. *Adult Juror Comments*: Has fascinating footage of train movies. Great music, excellent for train presentations. Jurors felt the acting was not respectful to children and promoted some stereotyping. *Kid Juror Comments*: Scored well. Ready to go on a train ride. A great subject for little ones. Video. 30 min.; $14.95; Age: 3-6. Big Kids Productions, Inc.

** Rhymin' Time (Stories to Remember)

Mother Goose, welcome to the 90s. Phylicia Rashad, star of "The Cosby Show," sings a collection of great nursery rhymes. Animation based on Kay Chorao's "The Baby's Lap Book;" music by composer Jason Miles. *Adult Juror Comments*: This book-based title can be complemented by sharing the book with your child as well as the video. Combining book with video exposure encourages reading. *Kid Juror Comments*: Good to hear their favorite nursery rhymes especially "This Little Pig," "Old King Cole," "Humpty Dumpty," and "Twinkle, Twinkle Little Star." "I liked the constellations that the stars made." "All the music was my favorite." Video. 26 min.; $9.95; Age: 1-5. Stories to Remember.

Age 2-5

Video

Spec Int

** Richard Scarry: The Best Birthday Party Ever (Busy World of Richard Scarry, The)

There's a birthday disaster in Busytown. Kenny and Lynnie are going to throw birthday parties on the same day. Their friends plan to get everyone into the same room so it's a big surprise. Lynnie and Kenny end up having the best birthday ever. *Adult Juror Comments*: Excellent. The story characters seem human and come to life. Plot stimulates creative interpretations and problem-solving. Sharing qualities are displayed. Suggests good follow-up activities. *Kid Juror Comments*: Interested, attentive, and enjoyed the film. They love Richard Scarry books, were inspired to read more. "I liked thinking about the animals in the story and how real animals solve problems. I laughed when he borrowed the bulldozer." Video. 25 min.; $9.95; Age: 2-5. U.S.A. Home Entertainment.

** Road Construction Ahead (Fred Levine's Original)

Shows every step in a road construction project, from surveyors staking out the job site to blasting rock to the first car traveling down the finished highway. *Adult Juror Comments*: Good overview of large pieces of machinery. Nice cuts to children playing with toy trucks. Background music a little overpowering at points. Good safety tips. Little diversity, no female role models. *Kid Juror Comments*: Most kids enjoyed watching, especially the boys who were captivated throughout viewing this program. Favorite part: the explosives. Video. 30 min.; $14.95; Age: 2-5. Fred Levine Productions, DBA Little Hardhats.

** Sounds Around (Live Action Video)

Explores sounds made by toys, machines, animals, people, and musical instruments. Varied children listen to and imitate these sounds. Helps understand differences and similarities. *Adult Juror Comments*: Great, lots of information. The real animal sounds contrast with sounds that adults usually attribute to animals. Offers a variety of mechanical and natural sounds. Lends itself to active viewing—extending the activities beyond the video. *Kid Juror Comments*: Very appealing, especially seeing the animals and hearing the sounds they make. They danced to the music and recognized each sound. Lots of information. Kids requested this one repeatedly, enjoyed it every time. Video. 28 min.; $14.95; Age: 2-5. Bo Peep Productions.

* Telling the Truth (Sesame Street: Kids Guide to Life)

Telly learns that even when you mean to tell the truth, a little lie can balloon into a big problem. He learns a lesson after he lies to impress his friends by telling them his uncle (Dennis Quaid) is a ringmaster at the circus. *Adult Juror Comments*: Age-appropriate subject. Opens up many opportunities for discussion about "telling the truth." High-quality sound and visuals. Good for day care or families. "There's lots to talk about in this video." *Kid Juror Comments*: Initial enthusiasm dissipated. Action was too slow for younger kids. Older ones stayed with it better. Needs an adult facilitator to work well. Video. 30 min.; $12.98; Age: 2-5. Sony Wonder.

* Those Doggone Dogs and Puppies (Doggone Dogs)

Shows perky young puppies at play and carefree canines. *Adult Juror Comments*: Cute but extremely long. Lacks substance and depth and has virtually no learning benefits. Photos fit the musical selections. "I love dogs, but had a hard time watching sixty minutes of non-stop dogs." *Kid Juror Comments*: Kids say okay, but a little redundant. Cute dogs overall, but too long. Beware: may inspire children to want a dog. Video. 60 min.; $9.99; Age: 3-6. Brentwood Home Video.

* Tik Tak Volume One (Tik Tak)

Bright, colorful forms, familiar objects, playful movements, and music make up the essential elements of this production. Set to quiet background music, pieces of puzzles appear and disappear, gradually revealing completed images. *Adult Juror Comments*: "Lots of color, very different than most videos." Not suitable for under two's because it's illogical, random, and therefore confusing. Language doesn't support visuals. Cognitive value is limited, but it's fun. Best viewed with an adult. No diversity. *Kid Juror Comments*: Kids often asked, "What is that?" Made them curious though did not create opportunities for direct interaction. Under two's were not engaged. Elicited few responses from children. Only some seemed to enjoy it and would watch it again. Video. 30 min.; $12.99; Age: 3-4. Benny Smart.

** Vrrrooommm-Farming For Kids

Look, listen, and learn how the food we eat is grown. Explores how modern farm equipment is used in food production. Tractors, combines, and cultivators are shown from planting to harvesting. *Adult Juror Comments*: Good visuals—shows equipment kids don't often see unless they live on a farm. Low-budget production, inexperienced narrator, but offers interesting perspective on farming. Family picnic segment was great. *Kid Juror Comments*: Urban kids wanted to know more about how everything on a farm works—how plants grow and what the farm machinery does. Some terminology is too advanced for younger children. Video. 30 min.; $14.95; Age: 5-8. Rainbow Communications.

Chapter Two • Preschool

** Wacky Dogs (Wacky Animals)

 A hilarious and educational journey into the wonderful world of dogs. See 51 breeds of adorable canines doing funny, unusual, and often amazing things. *Adult Juror Comments*: Entertaining and very cute. Gives good pointers on taking care of one's pet. "I loved it!" Has a lot of information about dogs, but the information is not reinforced. The dialogue gives personality to the animals. The kid hosts were good. *Kid Juror Comments*: Depends on the child. Those with dogs enjoyed it best and wanted to watch it repeatedly. Those who don't have dogs didn't understand the humor. "I thought the dogs were funny when they 'talked.'" Video. 33 min.; $9.95; Age: 2-10. Clovernook Communications.

** Walk, Ride, Fly (Picture This Sing-A-Long)

 Explores many unusual and everyday forms of transportation: hot-air balloons, airplanes, space shuttles, windsurfing, wheels, and even feet! Filled with exciting visuals and original toe-tapping, hand-clapping music and lyrics. *Adult Juror Comments*: Music is easy to sing, keeps a momentum, and the camera works effectively for subject matter. Shows a wide variety of vehicles. Adults felt that it lacked a theme and had mediocre music. *Kid Juror Comments*: Entertaining. Presents useful introduction about these familiar and appealing objects in children's lives. Younger ones watched on-and-off. They liked the balloon section as well as the feet, wheels, and trucks. Video. 30 min.; $14.95; Age: 2-9. Goldsholl: Learning Videos.

* We're Goin' to the Farm with Farmer Dan

 Farmer Dan and his friends journey to a farm full of animals and music. The animals get fed, the cows herded, and the hay baled. *Adult Juror Comments*: Presents good information about farms. Music is catchy. Farmer Dan seems artificial and has minimal interaction with kids. Video seems patched together, but it's fun. Shows little diversity. *Kid Juror Comments*: Identifying the animals was fun. They did not respond well to Farmer Dan. Kids tapped their feet to the music. Interest recaptured when the farm footage reappears. Video. 30 min.; $19.95; Age: 3-5. Shortstuff Entertainment, Inc.

** *Where the Garbage Goes (Fred Levine's Original)*

Children see how the operations of the haulers, grinders, dozers, loaders, and compactors used at a state-of-the-art waste-handling facility. Shows how materials are sorted, crushed, and compacted. Explains why recycling is so important. *Adult Juror Comments:* Typical of this genre of videos, "the fascination of big machines." The production values are suited to the audience, but it has no story line or depth. Provides a good introduction to environmental and recycling issues in a realistic presentation. *Kid Juror Comments:* Large machines keep kids interested, but they would rarely watch it a second or third time. Boys responded best. Kids asked questions, enjoyed the music. They lost interest in non-narrative parts. Kids spotted recycling truck next time they saw it. Video. 30 min.; $14.95; Age: 3-6. Fred Levine Productions, DBA Little Hardhats.

*** *Yoga Kids*

Adventuresome yoga activity for children, introduces safe and simple movements which are imaginative and fun. Children learn balance and coordination as they stretch like dogs, roar like lions, and stand like flamingos. *Adult Juror Comments:* Excellent! Nice explanation and illustration of movements. Engaging and child-centered, it values imagination, good health, and self-esteem. Generates interest in enriching a child's life, stimulates creativity, language,, and cognitive development. *Kid Juror Comments:* Works best with younger kids, relaxing for quiet time. Even shy children joined in. "It was neat to try to be the animals." "I learned new ways to exercise. We decided to watch this once a week as a class." Video. 30 min.; $9.98; Age: 3-6. Livingarts.

Chapter Three

Elementary (Ages 5-8)

By Martha Dewing

Five-year-olds vary in their understanding about how their favorite TV shows are delivered. They understand that Barney and Mr. Rogers aren't actually inside the TV set, but when questioned further, it is clear that they are not certain about what's real and what's not in the videos and CD-ROMs that they watch. Programs that might create anxieties about injury or abandonment are frightening to most of them, sometimes producing nightmares. While they are less frightened by a scary story than when they were four, five-year-olds benefit from the reassurance of a happy ending. They may experience some fear during the program, but by the story's ending, they feel a sense of accomplishment and bravery for having stuck with it. Videos and CD-ROMs that celebrate friendship, independence, and exploration offer hope and reassurance to this age group. School forces kindergartners to do things on their own and to be accountable for their own actions. Themes of independence coupled with a child's need for security are appealing to this age group. Many of the video and CD-ROM titles in this chapter feature stories about characters who undertake a journey and return home feeling ever-so-proud of their accomplishments. At this age, children adore stories about characters who, like themselves, are members of a family and are learning about friendship, problem-solving, and conflict resolution.

Chapter Three • Elementary

For five-year-olds, school is also about learning and work. You will find a variety of programs here with familiar characters that challenge and engage while reinforcing important academic principles, such as *Captain Kangaroo: Life's First Lessons* and *Disney's Animated Storybook, Mulan*. The appropriateness of the educational content is an important part of the Coalition for Quality Children's Media's evaluation process. However, not every title you'll find here offers educational value. Some are just plain fun, like *Dennis the Menace Strikes Again!* And even when they score high on entertainment, they show respect for others, feature a variety of cultures, and avoid promoting stereotypes.

In first grade, children are learning to read and appreciate a good story. This chapter includes beautiful adaptations of favorite books, classic mythology, and folk tales, such as *The Snow Queen* and *Ivan and His Magic Pony* as well as superb live-action documentaries such as *The Big Park*. The fact that a child is just learning to read does not mean that he or she cannot follow a complex story line. Children this age can readily identify with many of the selections here that offer challenging characters and situations such as *The Land Before Time VI: The Secrets of Saurus Rock*.

Six- and seven-year-olds are gaining in physical competence and developing gross motor skills as well as an interest in games, rules, sports, and hobbies. Programs such as *You Can Ride a Horse*, *Nutcracker on Ice*, and *New Soccer for Fun and Skills* enhance their new skills in ballet, baseball, soccer, and horseback riding and introduce them to the rigors and romance of their newfound interests.

By second grade, children often think they are old enough to watch the more sophisticated programming that their older siblings are enjoying. They are savvy to the ways of school and are developing interests of their own, separate from their families. Although they appear independent, many would benefit from programs such as *Sometimes I Wonder* or *The Morris Brothers Live in Concert* that offer them comfort and hope as they struggle with such issues as sibling rivalry, peer pressure, death, and divorce.

Third graders are generally grounded in what's real and what's not. Although eight-year-olds know when the story is just a story, they are still interested in knowing whether it's based on fact or fantasy. Children are extremely curious about the world outside their own community. Videos and CD-ROMs that tap into their love of animals, the natural world, and the environment reinforce their innate curiosity, broaden their knowledge, and allow them to explore new information at their own pace. Some excellent choices include *Babe*, *Balto*, *Buddy*, *Ferngully 2: The Magical Rescue*, and *Lassie Come Home*.

Martha Dewing, a former elementary-school teacher, has a B.S. in education from New York University and a Ed. M. in educational media and interactive technology from Harvard University. She published Children's Video Report for many years.

Format—CD-ROM

Category—Education/Instruction

** *Adiboo: Discover Music, Melody & Rhyme (Adiboo)*

Children join Adiboo, their whimsical and inquisitive playmate, on an exciting journey to explore magical play and learning lands. Investigates music, melody, and rhyme. *Adult Juror Comments*: Good visuals, format, content. Music and endearing characters an added bonus. Provides good feedback, but relies on the help icon too much. "Kids don't want to read help files, and parents don't want to either." *Kid Juror Comments*: Liked it, easy to operate and follow. "It was fun, and had cool stuff to do." Liked composing music and printing their own artwork. Didn't like the aggressive monster. "We had trouble with the puzzles, but it tried to help us." CD-ROM. WIN/MAC; $30; Age: 5-8. Knowledge Adventure.

*** *All Dogs Go to Heaven Activity Center*

Teaches language skills, vocabulary, and counting, using the characters from the movie and TV series as guides. Develops critical thinking skills, memory, and hand/eye coordination. Features multiple skill levels. *Adult Juror Comments*: Well-organized, lots of variety, interactive and entertaining things to do and learn. Some educational benefits are well disguised as games. Visually inviting. Nice introduction to art. Very child-appropriate, kids should enjoy this. *Kid Juror Comments*: Really fun. Kids enjoyed the different activities, particularly the chase game. Easy to install and play. The dog videos were particularly appealing. "It made me really think." "There are so many things to do. It's the best CD-ROM I have ever used." CD-ROM. WIN/MAC; $29.95; Age: 5-11. MGM/UA Home Entertainment.

** *Ariel's Story Studio*

Children create, learn, and play with characters from *The Little Mermaid* while building skills in reading, vocabulary, and critical thinking. Encourages creativity in music and writing in an enjoyable learning situation. *Adult Juror Comments*: Program is very entertaining, educational, and not at all didactic. Wholesome and life-affirming. Excellent tool for increasing vocabulary while building general reading skills. Allows children to be creative in an enjoyable manner. *Kid Juror Comments*: Kids enjoyed making up stories and their own music, the animation, and learning about sea life. They noticed the stereotypical nasty, bad guys and were frustrated because "You have to go through the same story each time you play." Appeals to girls. CD-ROM. WIN/MAC; $35; Age: 5-8. Disney Interactive.

Age 5-8

CD-ROM

Edu/Instru

** Arthur's Computer Adventure (Arthur)

Arthur wants to play "Deep Dark Sea" on the computer every chance he gets. When his mom leaves for work and asks him not to touch the computer, Arthur can't resist. Disobedience leads to disaster. Will Arthur be able to fix the computer? *Adult Juror Comments*: Colorful and child-friendly, though the characters seem stiff compared to those on TV. Offers lots of rewards and treasures. May open discussion about obedience to parents. The game never rises above drill and practice. *Kid Juror Comments*: Easy to play, except that kids had trouble getting out of some parts. Children could use it on their own. Great graphics, color, and special effects. Much variety. "I want to try all the page activities. There are lots of hidden surprises." CD-ROM. WIN/MAC; $29.95; Age: 4-8. Learning Company.

** Babes in Toyland: An Interactive Adventure

Offers an enchanting magical world inspired by animated, musical film. Join Humpty Dumpty, Jack and Jill, and other favorite nursery-rhyme characters for action-filled music, games, and puzzles that entertain while teaching valuable early-learning skills. *Adult Juror Comments*: Child-friendly, but not very imaginative. Good variety of animals, music, different cultures. Everything was very clear and colorful. Allows child time to think. Develops coordination skills. Reviews nursery-rhyme characters. *Kid Juror Comments*: Good graphics, but a little too simple. Most kids didn't want to play it again. "The music was putting me to sleep." Children really liked Humpty Dumpty and the puzzles. "I think it's the best CD-ROM for little kids, and it's okay for me (eleven)." CD-ROM. WIN/MAC; $29.95; Age: 3-8. MGM/UA Home Entertainment.

*** Baby Felix Creativity Center

Baby Felix helps children learn the basics of art, music, shapes, and colors while being entertained. This three-level program was developed by child educators. *Adult Juror Comments*: The music and piano sections are excellent. Requires auditory memory skills as well as visual. Immediate feedback, thorough tutorial, bright colors. Installs easily and quickly. *Kid Juror Comments*: Seven-year-olds stayed with it. It took them over an hour to get an entire song complete, but they wanted to play it again. Paint-and-draw portion is engaging and easier than music section. CD-ROM. WIN/MAC; $19.98; Age: 4-8. Twentieth Century Fox Home Entertainment.

** *Captain Kangaroo: Life's First Lessons (Captain Kangaroo)*

 On a treasure hunt with Captain Kangaroo, children find out how much fun helping a friend can be. Discover hidden objects, learn the responsibilities of taking care of pets and plants, and be treated to Captain Kangaroo's story. *Adult Juror Comments*: Great animation and songs. Easy to run. Allows kids to select how the story evolves. Shows positive role models; good rhyming for preschoolers. Printer option had glitches. Only four game choices. Little diversity. *Kid Juror Comments*: It's cute; it's simple; it's not that varied. Kids sang and bobbed along with the music. Lively enough to keep children's attention while allowing them to control the pace. "I like it a lot. Can I play it again?" CD-ROM. WIN/MAC; $20; Age: 4-8. Knowledge Adventure.

** *Chitty Chitty Bang Bang: Adventures in Tinkertown*

 Kids can put the pedal to the metal on a delightful journey in a fantasy world with oversized appliances and household items in need of repair. Refrigerators and telephones magically come to life, as children learn how they work. *Adult Juror Comments*: No apparent logic, which is frustrating and irritating. Promotes concepts about space and time. Enhances memory and counting skills. Good pace, aesthetically pleasing, engages children's interest, but instructions didn't answer kids' questions. *Kid Juror Comments*: They had a good time with this. "I did well and repaired everyone in Tinkertown." "I liked Louie (screwdriver) best." Program froze at one point. "It was hard at first, but I learned the difference between many tools." CD-ROM. WIN; $19.95; Age: 5-8. MGM/UA Home Entertainment.

** *Danny and the Dinosaur*

 This activity center helps children learn beginning reading skills based on the book, "Danny and the Dinosaur." The five animated games and friendly characters make reading exciting for everyone. *Adult Juror Comments*: Pace is slow and not very inspiring. Clear and simple games are visually appealing. Focus is on pre-reading "decoding." Offers good reinforcements for word and sound recognition. Three difficulty levels provide a range of options. *Kid Juror Comments*: Liked the games and were anxious to get to different skill levels. "Danny and the boy are very polite." "The Dinosaur captivated the boys." "They would follow him anywhere." CD-ROM. WIN/MAC; $19.98; Age: 4-8. Twentieth Century Fox Home Entertainment.

Age 5-8

CD-ROM

Edu/Instru

Age 5-8

CD-ROM

Edu/Instru

*** Disney's Active Play, The Lion King II (Disney's Active Play)

Kids join Kiara and Kovu and a jungle filled with playful activities, arts and crafts, sing-alongs and more. *Adult Juror Comments*: One of the best CD-ROMs we've seen for young children. Graphics are dazzling and ultra-contemporary. Sing-alongs are ideal for preschool and kindergarten ages. Contains a state-of-the-art paint box with more flexibility than most. Appropriate humor. *Kid Juror Comments*: Most kids needed help getting started. "Colorful and I can change the pictures." "Animals are funny. I like the music." "I learned how to print the pictures out." It sometimes takes a few clicks to move from place to place. CD-ROM. WIN; $29.99; Age: 4-7. Disney Interactive.

*** Disney's Animated Storybook, Mulan (Disney's Animated Storybook)

 A legendary reading adventure packed with games and activities. Mulan's amazing story unfolds as kids play learning games and discover the power of the mind. *Adult Juror Comments*: Beautifully designed with strong entertainment value and challenging games. Supports girls' independent thinking. Mulan's decisions result in disobedience to family and breaking the law. The outcome justifies these actions, but some may object. *Kid Juror Comments*: A big hit. Those who saw the movie will enjoy the video. "I liked it, but I needed help five times." "If you liked the movie, you will like this." Very colorful. Sometimes frustrating. "You don't get bored easily. There are a lot of things to do." CD-ROM. WIN/MAC; $29.99; Age: 6-10. Disney Interactive.

** Disney's Math Quest with Aladdin (Disney's Learning Series)

 Uses math skills in a challenging adventure to save Agrabah from Bizarrah, an evil genie. Features eighteen activities designed with leading math educator Marilyn Burns. Addresses standards set by the National Council of Teachers of Mathematics. *Adult Juror Comments*: The activities are very creative. Most kids do not notice that most of the activities are math. Well-done with good music. May require good math and patterning skills. Does not offer a lot of interactivity. Considerable talking. *Kid Juror Comments*: The games were fun, helpful in learning basic mathematical concepts. Enjoyable and entertaining, but "It took almost 20 minutes to get to the first math problem." Advancing in program may be difficult and frustrating for some children. CD-ROM. WIN/MAC; $39.99; Age: 5-9. Disney Interactive.

** Disney's Reading Quest with Aladdin (Disney's Learning Series)

Teaches essential reading skills including phonics, vocabulary, and reading comprehension with the help of Genie, Jasmine, and Iago. Presents twelve activities in which players help free Aladdin, along with three skill-level options. *Adult Juror Comments*: Easy to use, though pace is too advanced for the audience. Even the lowest level had words too difficult for six- and seven-year-olds. Production quality high, helps initiate and build on reading skills. Excellent use of multiple play levels. *Kid Juror Comments*: "It was fun." Some words in the program were too difficult for children. Kids didn't like that they had to complete the activity before they could move on. Some directions are difficult for kids to understand, required an adult. CD-ROM. WIN/MAC; $29.99; Age: 6-9. Disney Interactive.

*** Disney/Pixar's Active Play, A Bug's Life (Active Play)

Kids discover the world from a bug's eye-view. Explore and create with Flik and the gang through activities, adventures, and printable board games and puppet shows. *Adult Juror Comments*: Entertaining program that provides occasions for good thinking. Easy for kindergarten to grade-two students to use on their own, though portions will require adult assistance. We experienced some technical problems. *Kid Juror Comments*: They liked to play this together, taking turns. "Everyone would like this game. It's fun." "The graphics looked cool." "The good thing about this program is that you get to play different things, and you learn from them." CD-ROM. WIN; $29.99; Age: 5-8. Disney Interactive.

** Fraction Attraction

Helps children develop fundamental concepts about fractions, including ordering equivalence, relative size, multiple representations, and locations of fractions on a number line. *Adult Juror Comments*: Good teaching tool, but somewhat boring. Variety of games is limited. Each exercise has depth that extends its use. "Offers a year's worth of fractions that can be reviewed to stretch math skills." The "whacking" game was somewhat violent. *Kid Juror Comments*: Learned a lot, fast. They liked the pictures and the music. Not as fun as some games, but it still makes learning fractions a pleasure. Sound effects are great. Adult needed to set skill level. "Better than flashcards by a mile." CD-ROM. WIN/MAC; $19.95; Age: 6-11. Sunburst Technology/Houghton Mifflin.

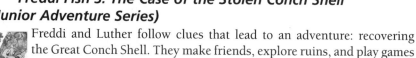

** *Do You Wish You Could Fly? See Page 36.*

***** *Freddi Fish 3: The Case of the Stolen Conch Shell
(Junior Adventure Series)***

Freddi and Luther follow clues that lead to an adventure: recovering the Great Conch Shell. They make friends, explore ruins, and play games in a tropical paradise. Children piece clues together to solve who's responsible for this underwater caper. *Adult Juror Comments*: Well-produced. Great graphics. Promotes teamwork and models positive behaviors. Helps develop critical thinking and problem-solving skills. Highly entertaining, great music and activities. Characters are likable and intelligent. *Kid Juror Comments*: Enjoyed playing and figuring out the mystery. "It's interesting. You get to search for things and find suspects." "I like it because it's fun to play." Children may need some adult instruction. CD-ROM. WIN/MAC; $29.99; Age: 5-8. Humongous Entertainment.

** *Frog and Toad Are Friends - Fox*

Frog and Toad make practicing reading skills more fun and exciting than ever. Based on the best-selling book, this program lets children learn and improve reading essentials with their favorite characters. *Adult Juror Comments*: Good variety of activities. Pace is a little slow for some adults and children. Excellent graphics, good value for children who are at the reading level. *Kid Juror Comments*: Enjoyable. More appealing for boys than girls. Children who cannot read yet became frustrated. They could not figure out how to play. Readers loved the characters and the music, especially when Frog wakes up Toad. CD-ROM. WIN/MAC; $19.98; Age: 6-8. Twentieth Century Fox Home Entertainment.

*** *Green Eggs and Ham by Dr. Seuss*

The classic comes to life through cutting-edge animation and silly sound effects. As children explore the story and activities, they learn word recognition, phonic skills, and computer literacy. *Adult Juror Comments*: High-quality production works well with children learning to read. Encourages confidence in accomplishment. Learning games with multiple levels are engaging. *Kid Juror Comments*: Children smiled a lot. The games that pop up during the story were fun and helped keep children engaged and on track. They like the voices of the characters. Sometimes kids wanted the program to run faster. CD-ROM. WIN/MAC; $29.95; Age: 5-7. Learning Company.

** Hello Kitty Creativity Center

 Helps children master essential learning skills easily and more enjoyably through lively animation and friendly voice and text prompts. The challenging three-level program was developed with child educators to encourage learning. *Adult Juror Comments*: Simple, but nicely done with good graphics. Adults found it slow-moving. The math section is uninspired, but the "build your own story" book section is great. "Simple drill practice on the computer." "A bit bland." Requires adult assistance to play. *Kid Juror Comments*: Not very complex or fast-paced. Appealed more to girls than boys. Kids like the music, the vegetable section, and making up their own story. CD-ROM. WIN/MAC; $19.98; Age: 4-7. Twentieth Century Fox Home Entertainment.

*** I Spy Spooky Mansion (I Spy)

 Explore ten creepy rooms filled with picture riddles and multi-leveled games while building skills in problem-solving, reading, vocabulary development, and creativity. The more riddles you solve, the closer you come to the game's finale. *Adult Juror Comments*: A thoroughly enjoyable program. Very easy to navigate, excellent graphics. Increasing levels of challenge keep excitement and interest high. Rewards positive efforts and holds place in the game. "It was very motivating to try and solve the puzzles." *Kid Juror Comments*: Enthusiastic. "I loved finding information in the wings of the butterfly!" "The haunted house was cool. The skeleton wasn't scary, but I learned a lot, and it made me think hard." "We used a flashlight in the attic to find clues." CD-ROM. WIN/MAC; $29.95; Age: 5-12. Scholastic Entertainment.

*** Interactive Math Journey (Reader Rabbit)

Journey through math lands with 25 sequenced activities: interactive storybooks, open-ended exploration, challenging games, and songs. Makes sense of math by building a child's comprehension. Included as a bonus in Reader Rabbit's Math CD-ROM. *Adult Juror Comments*: Covers a lot of material. Encourages more than one way to get a correct answer. Presents basic as well as complex math skills. The activity book is a great supplement. Difficult to play with touch pad. *Kid Juror Comments*: Liked the puzzle style of problem-solving. Their favorite parts were "Measurement Land," the dancing frog, the music, and singing. "I like how the characters talk and play." "Gets a little repetitive." CD-ROM. WIN/MAC; $29.95; Age: 5-8. Learning Company.

*** Jumpstart: 1st Grade (Jumpstart)*

 Children explore a enchanting schoolhouse with Frankie and friends that teach more than 40 essential first grade skills. Children travel to faraway places with Frankie and learn about different cultures, languages, and money systems. *Adult Juror Comments:* Entertaining and educational. Ease of use makes it enjoyable. High quality software - very smooth graphics and audio. Content parallels most first grade curricula. "Very good tool for parents to help their children develop skills." *Kid Juror Comments:* Enjoyed by all. Some had minor problems exiting from the middle of a program. "You had to listen to the story to know what to do." "The animal teachers always tell you, 'you did great!' when you do something right." "I liked learning how to count money." CD-ROM. WIN/MAC; $30; Age: 5-8. Knowledge Adventure.

*** Jumpstart: Kindergarten (Jumpstart)*

 Children explore an interactive kindergarten classroom where fun, music, and games are the rewards for curiosity. This new version of the original classic has updated graphics and animation, new phonics activities, a printable workbook, and more. *Adult Juror Comments*: Nice mix of content for developing critical thinking, interpersonal behavior, visual-motor skills, and problem-solving. Well-organized, clearly presented, motivating, and easy to use. Facilitates learning in an entertaining manner. *Kid Juror Comments*: Fun and interesting. Kids like the coloring book activity. All the children enjoyed it. Good kindergarten program, covers variety of material. CD-ROM. WIN/MAC; $30; Age: 4-6. Knowledge Adventure.

Age 5-8

CD-ROM

Edu/Instru

** Jumpstart: Phonics Learning System (Jumpstart)

Features state-of-the-art voice recognition technology in a comprehensive suite of early literacy software, videos, and workbooks designed to help children build confidence and encourage a love of reading. *Adult Juror Comments*: Easy to use. Clever and fun way to learn and practice phonics skills using videos, CD-ROMs, and audio recordings. Offers high level of involvement and interaction, but requires letter recognition. Jurors experienced some difficulties with the microphone. *Kid Juror Comments*: In general, kids like the games. They were excited about the score sheet and seeing their name show up on progress reports. "It was like a real arcade game." Some parts were too difficult for the kids to do without help; they got discouraged. CD-ROM. WIN/MAC; $60; Age: 4-6. Knowledge Adventure.

*** Let's Explore (Junior Field Trips)

Kids learn about hundreds of plants, animals, and machines as they explore and create. Packed with games featuring Buzzy the Knowledge Bug, and an illustrated tour of farms, airports, and jungles. *Adult Juror Comments*: Entertaining. Covers spelling, vocabulary, and animal identification. Adapts to child's skill level. Shows women in non-traditional jobs. Contains lots of information. Designed for individual play. Includes workbook and stickers. *Kid Juror Comments*: Kids particularly enjoyed games, trivia, matching, and paint box. Best for reader, although Buzzy "reads" to you. "I liked all the neat stuff it does. It's very challenging—especially the trivia and spelling sections at the difficult level. CD-ROM. WIN/MAC; $19.95; Age: 5-8. Humongous Entertainment.

* Lift Off to the Library

Host VIRG, Very Important Robotron Guide, leads children on an interactive, bibliographic journey with games, graphics, video, and audio clips. Introduces different parts and products of a library. *Adult Juror Comments*: While this had an admirable goal, the program adds little knowledge to most children's understanding of a library. Very limited; games and activities only have one or two versions, so most kids would not spend much time with the program. *Kid Juror Comments*: Most thought it was too easy. Making their own library was the best part. Kids needed frequent help. "I liked the games with the mazes." Kids enjoyed the graphics and the robot. They were frustrated when the program froze up on them. CD-ROM. WIN/MAC; $40; Age: 5-8. Library Video Network.

*** Lion King, The - Disney's Activity Center

Explore a king-sized world of games, puzzles, and art activities while building memory, matching, and spelling skills. Paint in the art studio, watch film clips from the hit movie, play with a friend or a favorite Lion King character. *Adult Juror Comments*: Appealing program young kids can use independently—an important growth step. Material is interesting and age-appropriate, but demanding on the computer. Appropriate for non-readers and beginning readers, although artwork is coloring-book style. *Kid Juror Comments*: Really good. They'd play it again many times. Enjoyed by a wide range of kids, from gifted to challenged. Both loved it and worked together. They like Simba and the puzzle games. CD-ROM. WIN; $19.98; Age: 5-8. Disney Interactive.

*** Math Blaster: 1st Grade (Blaster)

Teaches addition, subtraction, logic skills, and telling time. Animal trading cards and number stones make math problems and puzzles fun. *Adult Juror Comments*: Excellent. Helps strengthen and solidify math skills and explores the Internet. Pace is easy to control. Kids can make stickers as a reward—cool. Gives good hints when the kids get stuck. Great audio track. *Kid Juror Comments*: Easy to use, connects to the Internet, lots of different activities. "Making the sticker awards was awesome." "It's a fun way to practice what we learn in the classroom." Some of the reading was difficult. "Characters and music were neat." CD-ROM. WIN/MAC; $30; Age: 5-8. Knowledge Adventure.

*** Math Blaster: 3rd Grade

Glasternaut and GC need the viewer's help to solve a galaxy full of addition, subtraction, multiplication, and division problems. As they master basic math skills, they save the planet Moldar. Includes six difficulty levels in ten different subjects. *Adult Juror Comments*: Easy to install and use. Should get kids excited about math. Offers a wide variety of mathematical skills and helps them to understand basic concepts. Waits for user to correct answer. *Kid Juror Comments*: Easy to play. Liked the way it looked and enjoyed the games and the space ships. Kids didn't like that they had to get the answers right before they could play the games. Shooting games and arcade are geared more towards boys than girls. CD-ROM. WIN/MAC; $35; Age: 6-10. Knowledge Adventure.

*** Mia 2: Romaine's New Hat (Mia)*

Blends a story about Mia's quest to retrieve her mother's hat with a variety of science activities covering a wide range of topics. Features a unique navigational system that enables real-time control over Mia. The game varies with each new start. *Adult Juror Comments*: Topnotch. Easy to use, sophisticated 3-D graphics. Teaches and tests both physical and life sciences. Packed with information about the planets, weather, and more. Teaches problem solving skills. "Has long-lasting playability." *Kid Juror Comments*: Captivating story, boys enjoyed more than girls. Kids liked solving the problems and being rewarded. "I liked figuring things out for myself instead of the teacher telling me what to do." "The villains were scary but fun." CD-ROM. WIN/MAC; $29.95; Age: 5-8. Kutoka Interactive.

** Multiplication Tour with Mike and Spike (Learning Ladder)*

Journey on a concert tour that teaches basic multiplication skills and takes players around the world. Twelve lessons take children to twelve cities in eleven countries accompanied by concerts and songs. Games reward success with newly learned skills. *Adult Juror Comments*: Introduces multiplication and other math concepts. Offers math skill-building practice in an age-appropriate fashion. Adults disliked narrator's voice. *Kid Juror Comments*: Kept their attention. They liked the music, the characters Mike and Ike and loved getting the answers right. Challenges kids and encourages continued participation. The speed is frustrating at times. "The stone-hopping taught me a lot." CD-ROM. WIN/MAC; $34.95; Age: 6-9. Panasonic Interactive Media.

*** Nick Jr. Play Math*

Entertaining and curriculum-based, teaches early math skills to preschoolers. Children join a play-group of animated friends in 25 activities. Different features track child's progress. *Adult Juror Comments*: Good blend of tasks and entertainment. Parents can easily check child's progress. Offers polite feedback. Includes manual with follow-up exercises and suggestions for parents. "Our three-year-old adores this and stayed with it for over an hour." *Kid Juror Comments*: Program can be set to child's level of understanding. "I am becoming really good with the mouse because of my love of this program. I was introduced to patterns that now I look for in other places," commented a three-year-old. CD-ROM. WIN; $29.95; Age: 3-8. Virgin Interactive.

*** Putt-Putt Enters the Race (Putt-Putt)

Takes kids to Cartown where Putt-Putt wants to enter the Cartown 500 auto race. Kids help Putt-Putt and Pep find objects to make Putt-Putt a true racing machine. *Adult Juror Comments*: Easy to operate. Engaging characters, vividly colored graphics, variety of activities. Excellent for developing critical thinking and problem-solving skills. Activities, length of play is up to kids. Lacks adequate on-screen instruction. *Kid Juror Comments*: Loved the animation, sound effects, variety of activities, and the funny animals popping out of trees. Some needed more assistance than was given. "The game includes helping others on the way to the race." CD-ROM. WIN/MAC; $29.99; Age: 5-8. Humongous Entertainment.

** Reader Rabbit's Interactive Reading Journey 2 (Reader Rabbit)

Strengthens reading skills of five- to eight-year-olds while following the adventures of Reader Rabbit, Sam the Lion, and others through fifteen imaginary lands with multi-level activities. Included as a bonus in Reader Rabbit's Reading CD-ROM. *Adult Juror Comments*: Enjoyable and well-designed. Develops reading confidence and language skills. Great sound and animation. Some parts too difficult for pre-readers. *Kid Juror Comments*: Favorite parts were recording their own voices and reading a story and hearing it played back. Rhyme Time was a hit, as were the fun characters and the sound sorter. CD-ROM. WIN/MAC; $29.95; Age: 5-8. Learning Company.

** Reading Adventure with Kenny Kite (Learning Ladder)

Learn to read short sentences while attending Kenny Kite's flight school. Increases reading and problem-solving skills. Learners rewarded when they graduate flight school and are listed in the Hall of Fame. *Adult Juror Comments*: Good scaffold for developing language skills. Progresses at a good pace. Requires basic reading skills. Players must listen carefully to songs to answer the questions. Easy installation. *Kid Juror Comments*: Five- to seven-year-olds learned the material, liked the pace. Slower readers felt rushed. Kids liked the screen displays, characters, and expressive voices. "Kenny helped me when I needed it." "I liked finding my way home." CD-ROM. WIN/MAC; $34.95; Age: 5-8. Panasonic Interactive Media.

*** Reading Blaster 3rd Grade
(Reading Blaster Learning Series)

Takes kids through an exciting, space-age game show that builds early reading skills including phonics, spelling, vocabulary, reading, and comprehension. Features over two thousand vocabulary words and six action-packed activities. *Adult Juror Comments*: Entertaining and easy-to-use. Excellent rewards. Features printable stories that can be read later. Offers good choices of difficulty levels. Recommend using adult supervision. The vocabulary and spelling sections work with older kids as well. *Kid Juror Comments*: Great! Very interesting. The space blaster part was overwhelmingly popular. Favorite parts included the puzzle section, the quizzes, and the relay races. CD-ROM. WIN/MAC; $35; Age: 6-10. Knowledge Adventure.

** Reading Mansion CD-ROM

Reading Mansion teaches reading by having children search through mansions. Activities include letters, phonics, word recognition, sentence skills, and following directions. Features student tracking and tutorials. Customizes for ages three to eight. *Adult Juror Comments*: Engaging, good coaching for basic reading and phonics' skills. Develops critical thinking and problem-solving skills. Educators loved the extensive levels, but felt it was somewhat repetitive. Runs poorly on older computers. Not particularly playful. *Kid Juror Comments*: Easy to use. Younger kids will need help. Children enjoyed the format and liked how it praised their success. "I got a reward. I'm going to put it on my wall." Most children chose to play it again and challenged themselves by choosing harder levels. CD-ROM. WIN/MAC; $40; Age: 5-8. Great Wave Software.

* Richard Scarry's How Things Work in Busytown (Busytown)

Through hands-on exploration of Busytown's eight interconnecting playgrounds, teaches the importance of working together in a community while gaining valuable early-learning skills. *Adult Juror Comments*: Shows how people with different jobs help others. They learn who takes care of certain problems. It's mouse-dependent, which is difficult for a four-year-old. Information lacks depth. *Kid Juror Comments*: Okay, but problems with the mechanics of using the mouse. Inspired interest in reading about the book characters. CD-ROM. WIN; $49.99; Age: 4-8. Virgin Interactive.

*** *Scholastic's Magic School Bus Explores the Ocean (Scholastic's The Magic School Bus)*

Wacky science teacher Ms. Frizzle and her inquisitive class go on an amazing adventure through the ocean. Join the "Friz" and her class as they explore seven distinct ocean zones to discover and solve clues in their search for the sunken treasure. *Adult Juror Comments*: Wonderful new information. Requires some reading skills. Includes entertaining video sections with a strong environmental awareness. Activity booklet makes a great tool for parent or teacher. Saving is tricky. Some games have many levels. *Kid Juror Comments*: They liked the bus, were confused in some parts, amused in others, and overall, loved playing the program. "This taught me a lot about sea animals. I learned that sailfish are the fastest fish in the ocean." "Hints were easy to understand." CD-ROM. MAC; $44.95; Age: 6-10. Scholastic Entertainment.

*** *Stellaluna*

Based on the popular children's book by Jane Cannon. Stellaluna, a young fruit bat, is adopted by a family of birds after she becomes separated from her mother. *Adult Juror Comments*: Kindhearted story demonstrates individual differences. Games based on the original story are enhanced by the narrative. Gorgeous animated illustrations. Software loads easily and offers a variety of learning benefits. *Kid Juror Comments*: Captivating. Children liked many of the different activities, such as the Bat Quiz, Bat Game, and the Ice Cream section. Kids learned about trust, love, and self-reliance. Kids interested in animals expressed particularly keen interest. CD-ROM. WIN/MAC; $29.95; Age: 5-8. Learning Company.

*** *Storybook Weaver Deluxe*

Imaginative writing tool where students create their own stories with pictures and words. Features graphics, voice record and playback, text-to-speech capabilities, and the ability to copy and paste scanned images. Bilingual in Spanish and English. *Adult Juror Comments*: Empowers pre-readers, outstanding for all skill levels. Good team activity. Ideal for budding writers. "One of the best learning programs I've seen to date." Helpful to read "Getting Started" before beginning the story mode. Some stereotypes. *Kid Juror Comments*: "Once kids learned the program, they all loved making up their own stories." Inspired imaginations and developed literacy skills. Their favorite parts were the story starters, graphics, music, pictures, and objects. CD-ROM. WIN/MAC; $29.95; Age: 6-13. Learning Company.

*** *Sunbuddy Writer*

Youngsters learn to write with the lovable Sunbuddies. All the favorite *A to Zap!* pals—Hopkins, Tiny, Max, Cassie, and Shelby—are back with an easy-to-use writing tool designed especially for young writers. *Adult Juror Comments*: Great for beginning writers. The teacher's guide outlines activities, collaborative stories, and more. Simple installation, although there are some difficult procedures. *Kid Juror Comments*: Liked the program at the start of the story. Preferred watching in groups. "No blank-page syndrome." Players enjoyed the "word necklace" and "word finder." Best used by kids who are familiar with the keyboard. CD-ROM. WIN/MAC; $19.95; Age: 5-8. Sunburst Technology/Houghton Mifflin.

*** *Super Radio Addition with Mike and Spike (Learning Ladder)*

Guides children through basic concepts of addition as they play the role of disc jockeys at a radio station. Teaches addition through songs and games. Upon completion, children receive recognition in the "Hall of Fame." *Adult Juror Comments*: Captivating learning tool. Highly challenging for age group, allows for quick advancement. Requires fast action. Encourages kids to keep trying. Even adult jurors liked the music. *Kid Juror Comments*: As kids improve, the fun increases. Kids liked the humor, the frog named Mike, the bubbleloids, and the music. "They really have a hit with this one." CD-ROM. WIN/MAC; $34.95; Age: 5-8. Panasonic Interactive Media.

*** *Thinking Games (Madeline)*

Explore Madeline's mansion and uncover challenging and fun games in every room. Kids practice spelling and keyboarding in the classroom, learn French and Spanish vocabulary, decorate Madeline's bedroom, and create music in the studio. *Adult Juror Comments*: What a great interactive adaptation of this well-loved character! Clever animations, good sequencing, clear sound, and delightful music. A low-key approach and a refreshing change of pace, starring a girl. *Kid Juror Comments*: Loved seeing one of their favorite book characters, especially girls and those familiar with Madeline. Entertaining and educating and provokes creative thought. Liked decorating rooms the best. "Better than sliced bread." CD-ROM. WIN/MAC; $39.95; Age: 4-10. Learning Company.

Category—Family

*** Backyard Baseball (Junior Sports)

Sports designed for kids. Features 30 of the funniest boys and girls from the neighborhood, each with a unique personality. Choose your team and pick your players for non-stop thrills and action-packed games. *Adult Juror Comments*: Entertaining and well-produced. Great animation and sound. Teaches a variety of life skills in a variety of ways. Multi-cultural and special-needs diversity. Can be troublesome to install. *Kid Juror Comments*: Loved this game. Offers "stealth learning" such as studying statistics for the best pitcher and learning to bat and catch. Fun for all ages, girls and boys, even adults. "I liked choosing my team, then taking our picture. Cool characters." CD-ROM. WIN/MAC; $29.99; Age: 6-12. Humongous Entertainment.

** Disney's Animated Storybook, Pocahontas (Disney's Animated Storybook)

Enter Pocahontas's world and share her adventures as she romps through the woods with Meeko and Flit. Lively storytelling, exciting activities and games, rich animation and music from the film make interactive magic with the click of the mouse. *Adult Juror Comments*: Fun, easy to use. Cute games develop eye-hand coordination and matching skills. Shallow and predictable in content area; "Tastes great, but leaves you hungry." Although it's good entertainment, the vocabulary is limited. *Kid Juror Comments*: Fun and challenging. They liked the archery and storytelling. New readers enjoyed the reading skills practice section. Several boys did not want to try it, but once they started playing, couldn't stop. CD-ROM. WIN; $34.99; Age: 4-8. Disney Interactive.

*** Disney's Magic Artist

Transform your computer into the ultimate art studio. Create works of art with realistic tools like paints that smear and crayons that look waxy. Spray your drawings with special effects. Includes 300 Disney characters, props, and backgrounds. *Adult Juror Comments*: Sophisticated program. Superior, appealing, excellent production. Entertaining, easy drawing lessons. The Minnie Mouse section is great. Children can produce their own high-quality work. Younger ages may need some help. *Kid Juror Comments*: Appeals to most, not just game players. Suitable for various ages. Very popular in the classroom. "Easy." "I loved it." "I'm going to ask my Mom for this because it is really fun." "Can I skip recess to do this?" CD-ROM. WIN/MAC; $35; Age: 5-12. Disney Interactive.

*** *Freddi Fish 2: The Case of the Haunted Schoolhouse* (Junior Adventure Series)

A ghost has invaded the schoolhouse and is stealing all the guppies' toys. Freddi and Luther's job is to build a trap to capture the ghost and reclaim the toys. *Adult Juror Comments*: Excellent for building critical thinking and memory skill. Engaging graphics, sound effects, and music. Great for school readiness. Encourages teamwork for children at different levels. Colorful graphics are realistic and pleasing. *Kid Juror Comments*: Chasing a ghost is very interesting. Children enjoyed helping each other remember where things were. The game changes to keep children's interest. They liked the fact that the program talks to them while playing. Kids wanted to play this again. CD-ROM. WIN/MAC; $39.95; Age: 4-8. Humongous Entertainment.

*** *Freddi Fish 4: The Case of the Hogfish Rustlers* (Junior Adventure Series)

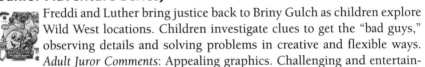

Freddi and Luther bring justice back to Briny Gulch as children explore Wild West locations. Children investigate clues to get the "bad guys," observing details and solving problems in creative and flexible ways. *Adult Juror Comments*: Appealing graphics. Challenging and entertaining brain exercise. Age-appropriate. Freddi and Luther are great role models. Freddi always got ahead by helping others solve their problems. Introduces cowboy lingo vocabulary. *Kid Juror Comments*: Easy to use. More difficult than the previous versions. "Some things were hard, but I figured them out." "I like it because it keeps changing. "Kids loved the multiple game paths and said they would play the game again. CD-ROM. WIN/MAC; $29.99; Age: 5-8. Humongous Entertainment.

*** *Freddi Fish and the Case of the Missing Kelp Seeds* (Junior Adventure Series)

Players help Freddi Fish and her friend Luther search for Grandma Grouper's missing kelp seeds. An underwater adventure rich in discovery, laughter, and learning with exciting surprises, enchanting characters, and rich animation. *Adult Juror Comments*: In addition to cooperative learning and problem-solving, teaches spatial relationships, geography, logic, and reasoning. Demands memory skills and concentration. The math section has multiple skill levels that start with counting. *Kid Juror Comments*: Loved the challenges, songs, and their ability to make things happen with the program. Kids learned what the bottom of the sea looks like. CD-ROM. WIN/MAC; $39.95; Age: 5-8. Humongous Entertainment.

* Gamebreak! Timon and Pumbaa's Jungle Games (Gamebreak!)

Timon and Pumbaa are the hosts in five arcade-style games of speed, skill, and indigestion. Loaded with hundreds of wacky sound effects and a two-player option. *Adult Juror Comments*: Challenging, fun to play repeatedly. Kid humor unappealing to adults (belching and gas), but kids love it. Develops eye-hand coordination. Pinball is the best self-explanatory game. *Kid Juror Comments*: They would play it again. "It's fun and there's lots to do." CD-ROM. WIN/MAC; $29.95; Age: 6-12. Disney Interactive.

** Little Wizard, The (Kidtainment)

Join the Little Wizard on his quest to find a special friend. Journey beyond his home deep into the Eartail Forest to strange and mystical lands. Teaches reading, math, and decision-making skills. Helps improve memory recognition and keyboard skills. *Adult Juror Comments*: Programming is excellent, but they need to hire an early-childhood professional to consult on story line, which is uninspired. The games, special effects, and interactivity are well done. Child needs to be able to read well to participate. *Kid Juror Comments*: The games, especially the number game, were terrific, but kids were bored with the story. Easy to use. Great graphics. Kids liked clicking the same object to get different actions. "I liked making the trees sing." CD-ROM. WIN/MAC; $29.95; Age: 5-8. Gizmo Gypsies.

*** Pajama Sam in No Need to Hide When It's Dark Outside (Junior Adventure Series)

Pajama Sam is afraid of the dark until he turns into the world's youngest Super Hero and sets out to confront fear. Kids must help Pajama Sam find his way through adventures in a fantastic world of talking trees, dancing furniture, and more. *Adult Juror Comments*: Good problem-solving exercises. Colorful and fun, comic book-like animation. Suitable for many different skill levels. Kids intuitively know how to play this game and enjoyed the variety of sound effects. Non-readers can play along with readers. *Kid Juror Comments*: Loved the surprise ending and the "darkness" character. Deals sensitively with a common fear. Six- to eight-year-olds adored the "Calvin and Hobbes"-type humor. CD-ROM. WIN/MAC; $39.95; Age: 5-8. Humongous Entertainment.

*** *Putt-Putt Saves the Zoo (Junior Adventure Series)*

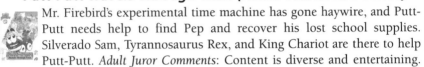

When the baby animals are missing from the Zoo, it's up to Putt-Putt to save them. Kids develop problem-solving and critical-thinking skills while seeing how their decisions change the world around them. *Adult Juror Comments*: Game is challenging, but the same solutions work every time. Variety of interactive diversions offers a break from problem-solving: ice hockey, tag, and making monkey rhymes. *Kid Juror Comments*: Happily spent at least two hours in the first session trying to save the baby animals. They loved this Putt-Putt program the best. The little kids needed help from adults or older kids. Once solved, the games are easy to replay. CD-ROM. WIN/MAC; $39.95; Age: 5-8. Humongous Entertainment.

*** *Putt-Putt Travels Through Time (Junior Adventure Series)*

Mr. Firebird's experimental time machine has gone haywire, and Putt-Putt needs help to find Pep and recover his lost school supplies. Silverado Sam, Tyrannosaurus Rex, and King Chariot are there to help Putt-Putt. *Adult Juror Comments*: Content is diverse and entertaining. With so much to do, children forget what they are out to find. Develops basic skills of math, counting, matching, eye-hand coordination, and memory. Gracefully free of gender stereotypes. *Kid Juror Comments*: The future setting and the pet-food maker were among the highlights. The Dinosaur Age was also a hit. Funny and entertaining. They thought Putt-Putt was a great role model who takes pride in school performance. Enjoyed the different levels of play. CD-ROM. WIN/MAC; $39.95; Age: 4-8. Humongous Entertainment.

*** *Toy Story – CD-ROM (Disney's Animated Storybook)*

Share the exciting adventures of Woody, Buzz, and the rest of the gang from *Toy Story*. You can be a part of their world as toys come to life and the magic begins. Exciting activities, games, rich animation, and lively storytelling. *Adult Juror Comments*: Familiar family fun. Good characters, challenging, excellent play value, and beautiful graphics. Content is shallow and lacks depth. Slightly difficult to install and set up for younger kids. *Kid Juror Comments*: Great, especially the escape from Sid's House, seeing the character Buzz Lightyear, and playing the crane game. They got a kick out of bringing the toys to life. Younger kids had a difficult time navigating the program. CD-ROM. WIN; $34.95; Age: 4-9. Disney Interactive.

Age 5-8

CD-ROM

Family

Category—Foreign Language

*** Kids! Spanish

Interactive fun with wacky monsters hosting over 35 activities at five progressive levels. Teaches more than 400 Spanish words and phrases for sports, animals, food, time, colors, and family members. Covers letters, numbers, and everyday expressions. *Adult Juror Comments*: Good resource. Teaches nouns, alphabet, and numbers. Good educational tool. An adult needs to install program and interpret feedback. Reinforces memory skills. Contains varied levels for different abilities. *Kid Juror Comments*: Though some words were hard, kids learned a lot and found this entertaining. "I can teach my friends when we play school." Kids missed seeing written words on screen. They loved the playback feature and learning new words in Spanish. CD-ROM. WIN; $30; Age: 6-10. Syracuse Language.

Category—Music

** Beethoven Lives Upstairs (Classical Kids)

Journey through a magical world of music, games, and artistic inspiration with Ludwig van Beethoven as your musical guide. Through a wide range of goal-oriented games and creative activities, children learn all aspects of music. *Adult Juror Comments*: Wonderful for musical play and training. Extremely creative and well-presented, a fun way to introduce kids to Beethoven. We had difficulty installing and working—freeze-ups and crashes were common. Age appropriate, interesting variety of content. *Kid Juror Comments*: "This was cool." Had to read instructions, but it was not difficult to install and play. "There was so much to do." Frustrating to kids because it kept crashing. "I clicked everywhere, but I couldn't do it." CD-ROM. WIN; $29.98; Age: 6-12. The Children's Group.

Category—Nature

** Yellowstone Journey
(Trekinteractive Young Naturalist Series)

Photographic exploration of Yellowstone National Park and its ecosystem. Filled with vivid photographs and field-guide facts about the geysers, hiking, and fishing of this spectacular park. Quick Time 2.1 is required. *Adult Juror Comments*: Good reference and teaching tool. Informative, engaging, and eye-catching. Encourages further investigation into ecosystems. Lacks adequate instructions on use or understanding of material. Child narrator is a plus. *Kid Juror Comments*: Liked it for awhile, but became bored. Good resource for school assignments. Grizzly bear pranks were a hit. Kids enjoyed the silly songs, photos, and the geysers. Functionality was a problem. Disk does not self-boot. CD-ROM. WIN/MAC; $24.95; Age: 6-12. T.I. Multimedia.

Chapter Three • Elementary

** Alligator Tale, An (Amazing Voyages of Nikki Piper)

 Two young explorers and a cast of puppets go on an adventure to Alligator Island. After one of the crew gets into trouble with an alligator, the others travel to Gatorland to learn all they can from a gator specialist. *Adult Juror Comments*: The video incorporates factual material into the story, providing good background and resource material about alligators. Reading is necessary. Good diversity and a female role model. Jurors disliked kids traveling without their parents' permission. *Kid Juror Comments*: They watched it again and again. It provoked questions. Liked the fact that it shows respect. "It's sort of fake, but still fun." Some thought that Captain Crab was rude. "It would be cool to live on an island." Video. 32 min.; $14.95; Age: 5-7. New Discoveries, Inc.

* Alphabet Train, The

From A to Z, children learn vocabulary and phonics skills while exploring aspects of real trains and concepts such as in and out, over and under, teamwork, off and on. *Adult Juror Comments*: Concepts are too advanced for two-year-olds, yet the production is too slow for older kids. Has lovely scenery and great footage of trains. Language is not age-appropriate. Limited appeal, no story line, too boring for younger kids. *Kid Juror Comments*: Boys liked it better than girls. "I like trains." Older children need more of a story to hold their attention. Video. 60 min; $19.95; Age: 4-7. Superior Promotions/Home Video, Inc.

*** Amaizing Miracle Workshop, The
(Children's Self-Awareness and Self-Defense Video)

Offers suggestions for peaceful conflict resolution, forming friendships, awareness of strangers, and self-defense in a relaxed way. *Adult Juror Comments*: Gives tools to deal with problems kids encounter daily. Covers scary issues in a positive way. Presentation lacks pizzazz. Having children act out scenes offers good reinforcement. Respectful of race, culture, and gender. *Kid Juror Comments*: High interest in self-defense, solving problems, and recognizing potential dangers such as with strangers, bullies, and e-mail. "It made me think about difficult things and talk about them." Children all tried the self-defense part. Video. 44 min.; $19.95; Age: 5-8. Maiz Productions.

** Be Cool, Play It Safe (Children's Safety Video)

Using humor and music to enhance learning and retention, this program shows kids how cool it is to be safe. Topics include motor vehicle, pedestrian, gun, water and bicycle safety, fire prevention, and more. Includes an activity book. *Adult Juror Comments*: Well-done. The adult leader gets the kids' attention about safety issues. Catchy music, simple rules. The drug segment, though well-meaning, seemed to point at African-Americans and rap music as part of the drug culture. *Kid Juror Comments*: In a school setting, kids wanted to watch it again. It helped reinforce the various safety rules. Kids related to the fire safety, but some were scared by the gun safety section. They liked the songs and graphics and loved the dog wearing shoes. Video. 43 min.; $19.99; Age: 5-10. EMP America, Inc.

*** Big Airshow, The (Big Adventure Series)

Shows a wide variety of planes from passenger planes to fighter jets. Take-offs, landings, history, and "why planes fly" are shown in a factual, fun narrative. *Adult Juror Comments*: Excellent presentation, loaded with facts and history. Shows planes from all angles. Teaches about flight in an appealing way while encouraging you to follow your dreams. Good mix of live action and animation. Good child narrator. *Kid Juror Comments*: Most enjoyable. Loved learning about all different types of airplanes and afterwards wanted to see an air-show or become a pilot. The cartoons were a big hit. "I loved the acrobatic flying." "I'd like to know about the plane my grandpa flew in WWII." Video. 50 min.; $14.95; Age: 5-12. Little Mammoth Media.

** Big Auto Plant, The (Big Adventure Series)

Watch a car being made in different countries around the world, beginning in a design studio and engine plant in Stuttgart, Germany, to the ultra-modern assembly plant in Tuscaloosa, Alabama. Includes an animated section on how an engine works. *Adult Juror Comments*: Offers a fascinating look into how automobiles are made. Very detailed. Appealing to kids who are really into cars. Shows people from two continents working together and emphasizes teamwork. Moves logically through the process of building a car. *Kid Juror Comments*: Kids interested in cars enjoyed this a lot, others didn't. They were fascinated by the robotics and the crash dummies. "It was interesting to see all the steps involved and how many people work on it. It showed the importance of teamwork." Video. 50 min.; $14.95; Age: 5-12. Little Mammoth Media.

*** Big Boom, The (Big Adventure Series)

Explores things that go boom. Shows active volcanoes in Hawaii, an expert demolition team imploding a 22-story building, and explains why jets make sonic booms. *Adult Juror Comments*: Provides advanced and detailed information in a cohesive presentation with explanations and demonstrations. Enjoyable live footage and child narrator. Great for science classes. Challenges kids to think. *Kid Juror Comments*: Most kids loved it, asking questions and counting along with the explosions. They loved seeing the action of a building demolition in reverse. "It's cool. I liked watching the volcanoes and learning how the lava makes islands." "Too much like school." Video. 50 min.; $14.99; Age: 5-12. Little Mammoth Media.

* Big Cable Bridges

Have you ever wondered how cable-stayed bridges are built? Young hosts examine the action-packed construction that creates impressive structures such as the Sunshine Skyway Bridge in Tampa, Florida. *Adult Juror Comments*: Offers a good look at a subject kids are curious about, and addresses the technical components of bridge-building. The female engineer-narrator is a bit stilted. Shows little gender diversity. *Kid Juror Comments*: Very excited. Boys delighted at seeing the big machines and the computer segment. They thought the helmets looked phony. Five-year-olds got a little restless at the end. Video. 30 min.; $19.95; Age: 5-8. Segments of Knowledge.

** Big Hotel, The (Big Adventure Series)

Shows how a staff of over 2,000 people work together to make the Banff Hotel in the Canadian Rockies work. Offers a behind-the-scenes look into the facility and shows the outdoor activities available from snowshoeing to dog sledding. *Adult Juror Comments*: Well-produced travelogue with detailed explanations of every aspect of hotel life accompanied by employee anecdotes. Shows multi-cultural visitors to hotel. It looks a bit like an infomercial or a tourist ad, but it's still fun. *Kid Juror Comments*: Kids liked that it was a real story about a real place. They watched it many times. "I want to go see the castle in the mountains." "The people who work in the kitchen must be happy to work there, but they wash lots of plates." "Kids were playing golf." Video. 50 min.; $14.95; Age: 5-8. Little Mammoth Media.

Age 5-8

Video

Edu/Instru

* Big Newspaper, The (Big Adventure Series)

 All about a unique newspaper- USA Today. Follow reporters to the White House, to a big league ball game, and on the road to test a new sports car. *Adult Juror Comments*: Looks at reporting and printing. Excellent graphics illustrate concepts. Covers a variety of subjects, but with gender bias. Of eleven personnel, only two were female and their segments are the shortest. Lacks cultural diversity. *Kid Juror Comments*: More academic than entertaining. Boys liked the rockets, planes, and sports cars. "I'd like to be the guy who tries all the cars and then writes about them." Girls were bored and found it way too long. Video. 50 min.; $14.95; Age: 6-10. Little Mammoth Media.

** Big Train Trip, The (Big Adventure Series)

 This segment covers travel across Canada on the Trans-Canadian Railway. It winds through the Rocky Mountains from the perspective of being in a dome car or riding in the locomotive with the engineer. *Adult Juror Comments*: Good for getting ready to take a train trip, but quite long. "The entire trip with all the meals did not need to be shown to get the idea." Great photography. Accurate facts are presented, though it lacks diversity. *Kid Juror Comments*: Kids enjoyed learning about train travel. "I didn't know you could shower on the train." "Wow. A restaurant on the train." "It's hard to work as a waiter on a train because it's moving." "The tunnel was awesome." Kids thought it was too long. Video. 50 min.; $14.95; Age: 5-10. Little Mammoth Media.

*** Brett the Jet (I Wonder...)

  Brothers Cody and Tyler learn the value of sharing and teamwork when they are taken behind the scenes with stunt flyers at the airfield. *Adult Juror Comments*: Fast-paced. Well-produced: good lighting, color, and set design. "Motivates viewers to develop plans and work together as a team." Generates interest in planes and flying. "It's like being at an air show." Lacks gender and ethnic diversity. *Kid Juror Comments*: Awesome! Enjoyable. Kids appreciated the aspects of teamwork and respect. Boys enjoyed it most. "Wow. I liked seeing the planes fly in patterns." "It taught us something." "Now I know how planes work and fly in the Air Force." Video. 28 min.; $11.99; Age: 6-12. Kid ROM, Inc.

*** Carousel, The (Reading Rainbow)

Sisters discover their mother's legacy while on a magical carousel ride. LeVar Burton extends the story and explores the power of tradition with quilt-makers and Harlem school children who are making a carousel for their community legacy. *Adult Juror Comments*: Bright and appealing. Reinforces adopting new family values and traditions, or expanding existing ones. Effectively deals with loss and death. Encourages social interaction between generations within a family. *Kid Juror Comments*: Kids generally loved this. They grasped the concepts, and many wanted to start legacies of their own right away. "I really liked the book. It was magic." "Made me want to learn about sewing." "It might make my friends sad." Video. 29 min.; $19.95; Age: 5-8. GPN.

* Chicken Fat and the Youth Fitness Video

Children's exercise video based on the song written by Meridith Willson (composer of "The Music Man,") for President Kennedy's Council for Physical Fitness. *Adult Juror Comments*: Repetitious. Exercises are taught to accompany one song, "Chicken Fat." Format is military-style and adult-directed. Instructions are clear but outdated. Shows good cultural diversity. *Kid Juror Comments*: Kids were slow at responding. Kids in general like exercising to music, but they disliked the name of this tape and the theme song. Video. 23 min.; $14.95; Age: 5-10. Chicken Fat Enterprises.

** Dance! Workout with Barbie

Barbie is the star of her own dance video. Teaches over a dozen dance routines with fun steps such as "The Barbie Basic," "Hot Foot," and "Jammin' Jogger." Features original songs by Jennifer Love Hewitt. Designed to get kids interested in fitness. *Adult Juror Comments*: Well-produced, emphasis on proper technique. Light, lively, encourages young girls to engage in positive exercise and health practices. The young couch potato might be inspired to see exercise as fun. *Kid Juror Comments*: Girls loved it, boys did not. They enjoyed the dance instructor. "Everyone was so energetic." "I loved it when Barbie showed up." "It helped me get my muscles working." "The dance steps were a little hard to learn because it went so fast." Video. 30 min.; $14.99; Age: 6-12. Looking Glass Productions.

* Digging for Dinosaurs

 Professor Fossilworth, a rather unconventional scientist, searches for fossils that give more clues about what happened to dinosaurs. This program offers information about different types of dinosaurs and shows what they looked like. *Adult Juror Comments*: The live scenes with the kids are well done. The information is sometimes suitable for younger kids, sometimes older. The content is a bit weak. It's a good introduction to general vocabulary concepts about dinosaurs. Shows little diversity. *Kid Juror Comments*: Inspired to dig afterwards, but they definitely thought the program didn't teach them enough. The humor is perfect for this age group. "It was fun. The guy was goofy, and the dog is great!" Kids found some parts too slow and a bit dry. Video. 35 min.; $14.95; Age: 5-10. Dolphin Communications.

** Ei Ei Yoga

Provides children with a balanced and enjoyable practice session, combining 25 yoga postures to create strength, balance, and flexibility. Designed to get everybody off the couch and moving. Encourages children and adults to sing, dance, and play. *Adult Juror Comments*: Gives clear, accurate instructions in a very child-appropriate presentation. Shows a variety of poses, all taught by children of diverse cultures. We recommend that an adult assist at least in the initial viewings of this program. *Kid Juror Comments*: Enjoyed finding a new way to exercise, stretch, and relax. Some language too difficult. Kids participated readily and wanted to know more about movement. They liked the songs. Video. 38 min.; $14.95; Age: 5-8. Mystic Fire Video.

** Extremely Goofy Movie, An

 Goofy's son Max sets off for college, but Goofy misses Max so much he literally falls down on the job. Goofy shows up, leisure suit and all, to finish college alongside Max and his friends. Goofy and Max must learn how to live their own lives…together. *Adult Juror Comments*: Cute story, wonderful animation. Depicts positive life lessons about finding yourself and respecting your parents. Offers strong message about focusing on what you want and working hard to achieve it. Characters are college students. *Kid Juror Comments*: Enjoyed the music, dancing, and Goofy's antics. They related to the story. One child said, "I got in with some bad kids at school, and I can see where I was wrong." "The pictures were realistic and made me feel like I was part of the story." Video. 76 min.; $19.98; Age: 6-10. Buena Vista Home Entertainment/Disney.

Chapter Three • Elementary

*** Families of Japan (Families of the World)

Spend a day with Seichi's and Ayako's farm and city families, and take in Sports Day, a silent piano, feeding chickens, grocery shopping, an engagement ceremony, rice planting, and calligraphy. How are kids in Japan similar or different from us? *Adult Juror Comments*: Well-paced, educational presentation. Shows the respect Japanese children have toward one another and their high regard for education and self-responsibility. Children exploring geography and other cultures will find this particularly interesting. *Kid Juror Comments*: Welcomed learning that Japanese children play the same things they do, such as tug-of-war, basketball, and tennis. They noticed that they have more letters to learn. They particularly enjoyed seeing Sports Day, sumo wrestlers, and a day in school. Video. 29 min.; $19.95; Age: 5-10. Arden Media Resources.

*** Families of Sweden (Families of the World)

Evelina and Matthew take you through a day in their lives—a birthday party, computer games, history class, pony ride, feeding ducks, swimming lessons, and eating moose steak. An intriguing introduction to another culture. *Adult Juror Comments*: Discusses other lands, traditions, and family backgrounds. Shows both boy's and girl's perspective. Children's opinions are recognized, and their needs are respected. Raises environmental awareness. Slow-moving. Good educational content. *Kid Juror Comments*: Kids enjoyed comparing their experiences to those of the Swedish children. Intrigued by the Swedish kids taking off their shoes when they come into a house and learning that their favorite stories are enjoyed by the Swedish kids as well. Video. 29 min.; $19.95; Age: 5-10. Arden Media Resources.

* Fit for a King: The Smart Kid's Guide to Food & Fun

Teaches the basics of good nutrition: how nutrition and physical activity go hand-in-hand; how adding grains, vegetables and fruits to your diet decreases fat; and how healthy eating can mean discovering new foods. *Adult Juror Comments*: Gives good information. Good diversity. Production is somewhat flat and didactic. Best used in a classroom setting. Some kids will already know most of the information. *Kid Juror Comments*: A good introduction to nutrition for children, though it's not particularly entertaining. "It was just right. I think it has special virtues." Many children liked the use of the fairy tale. Video. 9 min.; $19.95; Age: 5-10. A.A. Pediatrics

* Freddy's School of Fish

Hosted by an animated fish named Freddy, the video covers the basics of fishing from rod-and-reel operation to casting, tying knots, boat terminology, and safety. *Adult Juror Comments*: Good information for a child interested in fishing (and for adults, too). Little cultural diversity. *Kid Juror Comments*: Eight- to twelve-year-olds enjoyed this best. One six-year-old said, "I felt wonderful fishing." It could be scary for younger kids. One child commented, "I didn't like the fish with sharp teeth." Video. 40 min.; $19.95; Age: 6-12. Just Fish It, Inc.

** Happy and Healthy (Treasure Attic)

Teaches how to cope with sickness and encourages good habits in health and nutrition, as well as a healthy positive attitude. Mr. Protein and company spring to life in the "Nutrition Song," which also encourages good eating habits. *Adult Juror Comments*: Entertaining format that encourages healthy eating, exercising, and taking care of oneself. Cute production, though it does have some lip-sync problems and primitive sets. Good diversity and deals well with health-related situations. *Kid Juror Comments*: Appealing. "This would be a good movie for our PE teacher to show us." Kids enjoyed the music, but sometimes it was difficult for them to understand the words to the songs. Video. 25 min.; $14.95; Age: 4-7. Family Care Foundation.

* Hola Amigos, Volume 1 (Hola Amigos)

Teaches the basics of Spanish, with Paco and his friends from Veracruz as hosts. The songs and action that fill their trips help kids recognize and recall numbers, letters, colors, and everyday words. *Adult Juror Comments*: A little academic but appealing, particularly to children interested in foreign languages. Its strength is the choice of words and phrases. Portrayal of the Hispanic family is stereotypical, as are the gender roles. Animation is simple. *Kid Juror Comments*: Excited about learning Spanish, though they found this was a little slow-moving. Video. 55 min.; $19.95; Age: 5-8. Monterey Home Video.

* Hospital Trip with Dr. Bip, A

Dr. Bip, an animated character, guides a child through a true-to-life visit to the hospital for an operation. Dr. Bip explains pre-operative and post-operative routines with bouncy rhymes and light music. *Adult Juror Comments*: The simple messages work well. Showing actual hospital equipment is useful. Good for preparing kids for a hospital visit, although the language is too advanced. Misleading, promotes the idea that "everything's going to be fine, it won't hurt." *Kid Juror Comments*: Helpful in telling them what to expect when you visit the doctor or hospital. They liked the doctors and nurses, but some didn't care for the cartoon character Dr. Bip. The program brought up a lot of questions afterwards. Video. 12 min.; $14.95; Age: 4-7. Kidz-Med, Inc.

* Importance of Trees

Describes how trees grow and their benefits to the environment—as a source of material, food, oxygen, and air-conditioning. Illustrates the role of trees in fighting pollution, preventing soil erosion, and more. *Adult Juror Comments*: An important and current topic. Production value is low, and child actors slightly amateurish. Some film clips were dated, but text flows well. Shows great shots of different cultures with trees. Creates awareness of the need to care for our trees. *Kid Juror Comments*: Hard to get kids interested initially; once they started, it captured their attention, particularly for saving trees. Pictures were blurry at times and sound difficult to hear. Kids thought music was corny. They learned a lot about trees. Video. 30 min.; $59.95; Age: 6-10. Filmus/Benjamin Goldstein Productions LTD.

** In Tune with Keyboards (Instrumental Classmates)

Examines keyboards of every shape and size from grand, upright, and player pianos to digital keyboards. Shows how learning a keyboard can be fun and simple. Series sold as a five-video set only. *Adult Juror Comments*: Engaging format, but sometimes corny. Jumps from serious to silly. Would be useful in a music classroom. Great visual examples and captions for new vocabulary. *Kid Juror Comments*: Held children's attention by combining humor with fact. Liked the music, costumes, and the humor. "It is funny, but I still learned a lot about pianos." Some lost interest. Video. 30 min.; $149.95; Age: 5-10. Warner Bros. Publications.

** In Tune with Percussion (Instrumental Classmates)

 Introduces various percussion instruments and explains the difference between pitched and non-pitched instruments. Explains importance of percussion instruments within the ensemble. Series sold as a five-video set only. *Adult Juror Comments*: A clever and humorous introduction to percussion instruments. Good ethnic diversity. "Surfer-dude-type" host was annoying with his "valley girl" dialect. The repetitive short reviews worked well to reinforce concepts. Presentation flowed well. *Kid Juror Comments*: The drumming was a big hit. "I want to play the Congo drums." "I didn't know a piano was like a drum." "You can play music anywhere with percussion." The review sections were too educational and too much like school. Video. 30 min.; $149.95; Age: 5-10. Warner Bros. Publications.

** In Tune with Strings (Instrumental Classmates)

 Introduces members of the string family. Gives examples of rock, jazz, and classical music. Demonstrates the versatility of string instruments and how sound resonates in the bodies of the instruments. Series sold as a five-video set only. *Adult Juror Comments*: Provokes critical thinking and introduces viewers to unusual instruments. Combination of mystery story and educational format works well together. Lacks gender diversity. Introduces new vocabulary. Upbeat, colorful, and somewhat silly. *Kid Juror Comments*: Enjoyed the mystery format and were excited about making their own instruments. "I want to hear a symphony—so I can hear the strings." Children were impressed with the children's band. "The detective is funny." "Harps sound beautiful." Video. 30 min.; $149.95; Age: 5-10. Warner Bros. Publications.

** In Tune with Woodwinds (Instrumental Classmates)

 Introduces the two different groups of woodwind instruments: the reeds and the flutes. Demonstrates the unique sounds that the woodwind instruments produce and shows how to make reeds for a woodwind instrument. Series sold as a five-video set only. *Adult Juror Comments*: Interesting and educational. Lots of humor holds interest. Introduces a variety of instruments and musicians. Science experiments illustrate points. Production quality was okay. *Kid Juror Comments*: Really enjoyed the bottle sounds in the science experiment. "I learned that the reeds are what make the sounds." "Practicing everyday is important to become a good musician." "Let's watch it again." "I might try a clarinet." Video. 30 min.; $149.95; Age: 5-10. Warner Bros. Publications.

Chapter Three • Elementary

* Keeping Kids Safe! A Guide for Kids and Their Families (The Personal Safety Series)

 Encourages children to solve problems about personal safety through open communication. Informative and non-threatening. Designed for families to watch together. *Adult Juror Comments*: Though this is a valuable educational tool; adults should definitely watch it with their children, or it could be too frightening. Shows good interaction between the kids. Addresses an important topic that lends to discussion after the viewing. *Kid Juror Comments*: Learned a lot. Appreciated having the kids do the interviews. It's too frightening for five-year-olds to watch without an adult. Video. 27 min.; $14.95; Age: 5-10. PSI Productions.

* Learning to Save (Adventures of Two Piggy Banks)

Two piggy bank puppets escape from a toy store, are adopted by a school classroom, and teach children the important concepts of saving and sharing. Features original songs as sing-alongs such as "I'm glad I'm a Piggy Bank." *Adult Juror Comments*: The first ten minutes are slow and don't engage the audience. Overall, it's a good vehicle to prompt discussion about savings. It offers good tips, is age-appropriate and child-friendly. *Kid Juror Comments*: The piggy bank characters got a favorable response. One kids' jury was just completing a unit on money, and found this provided good ancillary materials to what they had just learned. It's a good discussion-starter. Video. 30 min.; $14.95; Age: 4-7. Raindrop Entertainment.

* Morris Brothers Live in Concert, The (The Morris Brothers)

 A live performance by the Morris Brothers reinforces positive character traits and teaches better ways to deal with peer pressure and handle conflict. Fosters friendship, encourages cooperation, and promotes unity. *Adult Juror Comments*: The video addresses accepting others, how to act in school, and believing in yourself. Promotes the idea that you can change the inner you; it's doable. The Morris Brothers' nerd attire and behavior is not appealing to all audiences. *Kid Juror Comments*: Some thought the Morris Brothers were smart and funny. Others thought it was long and boring. Some would watch it again. Kids liked the phrase "Give yourself a big hand." They liked the part about how to say no to drugs. Video. 55 min.; $14.99; Age: 5-8. Funimation Productions, Inc.

*** *Mrs. Katz and Tush (Reading Rainbow)*

 A young African-American girl and a lonely Jewish widow develop a friendship that bridges differences between age and culture. Host LeVar Burton expands the concept of cross-cultural relationships by visiting a Jewish grandmother and baking challah bread. *Adult Juror Comments*: Beautifully produced. A touching story. Explores Jewish holiday traditions. Emphasizes the value of older people and expounds on the value of inter-generational relationships. The topic of death is looked at in a very gentle and caring way. *Kid Juror Comments*: Loved it. "My favorite part was when they braided the bread dough." "I make bread with Mama just like that." "My mama and papa and tia will like this too. Can I just take it home?" "It's kind of sad, but it made me think of my own bubbie so far away." Video. 28 min.; $19.95; Age: 5-12. GPN.

** *My Body Belongs to Me*

 Good information for preventing sexual abuse and showing how kids can get help. A family therapist acts as a friend and counselor to a puppet. Simple, repetitive safety lessons are presented entertainingly. *Adult Juror Comments*: Excellent teaching of difficult and delicate material. The information is clearly presented at the intended audience age level. We recommend adult facilitation because of the sensitivity of the subject. *Kid Juror Comments*: Enjoyed the puppets' humor. The boys were clearly embarrassed. The girls watched closely. "It's good what they talked about." Kids' attention strayed toward the end. Most appropriate for in-school or similar settings. Video. 24 min.; $24.95; Age: 5-8. CNS Communications.

*** *My Life with the Wave (Reading Rainbow)*

Based on the story by Latin American writer, Octavio Paz, this magical tale tells about a boy who brings home a wave. Host LeVar Burton explores the beauty of water and meets with people who are working to save endangered sea life. *Adult Juror Comments*: Visually attractive, enthusiastic narration, great instructional tools. Piques interest without being teachy or preachy. Generates concern about the ocean environment. Factual content is presented in the form of "magical reality." *Kid Juror Comments*: Mostly positive responses. Kids who live by the coast enjoyed it most. The manatee and surfing dog were big hits across the board. "I learned a lot from the movie." "I didn't know coral is alive. I wonder what else looks dead that isn't." Video. 29 min.; $19.95; Age: 5-8. GPN.

** No Body's Perfect...Everybody's Special!

 Profiles three kids coping with different disabilities. Olivia has a visual impairment. Tristan is deaf. Emily lost a leg in a farm accident. Encourages viewer to accept differences as essential to growing up. *Adult Juror Comments*: Very accessible. Features attractive, articulate kids. One gets a sense of their lives and acceptance of their disabilities. Good content that is geared toward kids. Studio setting is nicely integrated with kids' visits. Some camera work is poor. *Kid Juror Comments*: Kids liked seeing children their own age learning to deal with their disabilities. It gave them insight into the feelings that disabled children have about being different. Kids showed appreciation for their bravery. Video. 21 min.; $89; Age: 5-10. Attainment Company, Inc.

*** Owl Moon and Other Caldecott Classics (Children's Circle)

 Includes "Owl Moon," about a girl and her father looking for the Great Horned Owl; "Make Way for Ducklings," where the mallards find a new home; "In The Night Kitchen," where dough airplanes fly, and "Strega Nonna" with the magic pasta pot. *Adult Juror Comments*: These book-based stories are like old friends. Color, narration, and stories are captivating. "It's a great way to increase children's interest in books." "Filled with imagination." Some felt it moved too slowly. *Kid Juror Comments*: "It's neat that they used real books." Most kids would watch it again. Some wanted more action. "I'm just like Stega Nona." "I didn't like when the boy got stirred into the cake batter." "I want to find an owl and hoot." Video. 34 min.; $19.95; Age: 4-7. Weston Woods Studios/Scholastic.

* Peepers and Penny (Treasure Attic)

 Filled with lively songs that help develop positive sibling and peer relationships. Penny learns to overcome shyness and fear of rejection. The music drama "A Man, a Boy and a Donkey" teaches character building—do what is right. *Adult Juror Comments*: Concept of the program is good, but the age level of the intended audience is not clear. Did not hold attention of the adults. Needs polishing. Purposeful and offers good lessons such as teaching how to draw puppets. Good ethnicity. *Kid Juror Comments*: Most children lost interest. Some parts caught the children's attention and enticed them to follow along. "My mom listens to that kind of music." Kids seemed to enjoy the musical part best. Video. 25 min.; $14.95; Age: 4-7. Family Care Foundation.

*** Rainy Day Magic Show, The

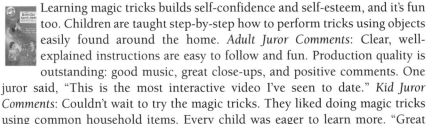

Learning magic tricks builds self-confidence and self-esteem, and it's fun too. Children are taught step-by-step how to perform tricks using objects easily found around the home. *Adult Juror Comments*: Clear, well-explained instructions are easy to follow and fun. Production quality is outstanding: good music, great close-ups, and positive comments. One juror said, "This is the most interactive video I've seen to date." *Kid Juror Comments*: Couldn't wait to try the magic tricks. They liked doing magic tricks using common household items. Every child was eager to learn more. "Great for would-be magicians. We tried every one." Video. 25 min.; $14.95; Age: 5-12. Dolphin Communications.

** Red's Musical Misadventure, Episode 1 (Four Fish Fly Free)

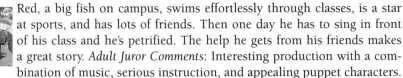

Red, a big fish on campus, swims effortlessly through classes, is a star at sports, and has lots of friends. Then one day he has to sing in front of his class and he's petrified. The help he gets from his friends makes a great story. *Adult Juror Comments*: Interesting production with a combination of music, serious instruction, and appealing puppet characters. Audio is poor. Portrays the school principal as negative and bossy. Accurately addresses children's fears and emotions. *Kid Juror Comments*: Related to the fish who was afraid to sing. They felt the characters were kind and supportive toward one another. "It teaches you to try and try again." "It helped me to want to read the words to the songs." "Can we watch it again, now?" Video. 30 min.; $14.95; Age: 4-7. Four Fish Productions.

* Rhythms of Peace 2 (Rhythms of Peace)

Subtitled, "When Your Argument Goes Bust," this material helps children learn to solve conflict. Teaches values and skills to create a more peaceful world. Includes topics on cooperation, empathy, making friends, and choosing heroes. *Adult Juror Comments*: Refreshing, encourages group discussions. Segments appeal to different audiences. Well-organized. Good understanding of theme and content. The repeated use of the word "stupid" overshadows the peace theme. Study guide is a real asset. *Kid Juror Comments*: Tells a great story about a father and son building a canoe together. "Mr. Fredd was goofy and strange." "I learned that working together is better than working alone." "Too long, too boring, too much like school." Some fell asleep. Video. 35 min.; $34.95; Age: 6-10. Mennonite Media.

** Rope Around the World

What's more fun than jumping rope? Getting fit and feeling great. Learn jump-rope tricks with both adults and kids from cities all around the world. *Adult Juror Comments*: Lively, informative, instructional. Addresses health and wellness issues as well as jump-rope tricks. Fun to watch children from a variety of international cities learning to jump-rope. Lacks gender diversity. *Kid Juror Comments*: Delighted. Will recommend to friends. "The teacher can even jump-rope sitting down." "Jump-roping while doing an Irish Jig was awesome." "I learned a lot of cool new jump-rope tricks such as the crossover jump." Video. 30 min.; $14.95; Age: 6-12. Hip Hopper Inc.

* Saints for Kids, Volume 1 (Saints for Kids)

Educational and inspiring. Each four-minute animated story shows extraordinary real men and women as outstanding role models. Features Francis of Assisi, Elizabeth, Zechariah, Martin, and others. Includes discussion guide. *Adult Juror Comments*: Production value is poor and distracting. Sound doesn't always match mouth movement. Stories are accurate, but it is perhaps most appropriate for religious-educational use. Well-presented with an excellent study guide. Price is high for its length. *Kid Juror Comments*: Good, but most appropriate for use at Sunday school. "It taught me things I did not know—to look at life differently." "It was okay." Sometimes it was hard for children to understand the voices. Video. 14 min.; $12.95; Age: 5-8. Pauline Books and Media.

* Saints for Kids, Volume 2 (Saints for Kids)

Educational and inspiring. Each four-minute animated story shows extraordinary real men and women as outstanding role models. Features saints including Nicholas, Stephen, Anne, and Joachim. Includes discussion guide. *Adult Juror Comments*: Respectful and appropriate, but slow-paced. Limited audience appeal for a Christian audience, but provides a good teaching tool. Lacks cultural diversity. Promotes helping others, preserving faith, and other excellent general values. *Kid Juror Comments*: They didn't like the mean people. They did like the pictures and the music. It was short and interesting. "It would be good for church." "I liked learning about St. Nicholas." "It says Stephen was a martyr, but doesn't show it." Video. 14 min.; $12.95; Age: 5-8. Pauline Books and Media.

Age 5-8

Video

Edu/Instru

** Saints for Kids, Volume 5 (Saints for Kids)

A series of four-minute animated stories. Kids discover ordinary men and women as outstanding role models. Features Mary (the mother of Jesus), Paul, and Rita. Includes discussion guide. *Adult Juror Comments*: Well–produced. Soft colors and clear audio. "I was drawn into the stories. They convey family values such as love and caring." "Shows people from ordinary backgrounds making a difference in the world." Contains Christian references. *Kid Juror Comments*: Engaging. Would watch again. "I'm going to tell these stories to my mom and dad when I get home." "It teaches you about history and religion." "I want to learn more about Mary. She was sad for Jesus." "Can people today become saints?" Video. 19 min.; $12.95; Age: 5-8. Pauline Books and Media.

** Saints for Kids, Volume 6 (Saints for Kids)

Four enchanting and inspiring animated stories in which kids discover extraordinary real men and women as outstanding role models. Features Joseph, Catherine of Siena, Cecilia, and Benedict. *Adult Juror Comments*: Appealing animation; religious history. Educational and inspirational for those of a Christian orientation. Excellent blend of male and female role models. Saints are shown in a humanistic fashion. *Kid Juror Comments*: Enjoyed it. Would watch again. "I learned that Saints were real people." "I liked each short story. They were all very different." "It helped me understand what I learned in church." Video. 19 min.; $12.95; Age: 5-8. Pauline Books and Media.

*** Shaman's Apprentice, The (Reading Rainbow)

 LeVar Burton and Mark Plotkin, an enthno-botanist, visit the Tirio village in the Amazon rainforest and meet with the shaman Kamanya to search for healing plants and learn about the Tirio people. *Adult Juror Comments*: Well-produced. Age appropriate. Great introduction to tribal medicine and an examination of the origins of modern medicine. "I will use this in my classroom in both life sciences and social studies." Respectful of culture. *Kid Juror Comments*: Riveted. "The people grew plants, and the shaman knew how to use them to make sick people well." "My favorite part was when the sick boy got well." "We want to learn more about the rainforest now." "Can I take this to school for show and tell?" Video. 29 min.; $19.95; Age: 5-12. GPN.

Chapter Three • Elementary

* Smart Start Guitar

 Demonstrates a new approach to teaching the guitar to young children. Starts kids off with an open tuning method that enables them to play a chord even before they learn left-hand fingering. *Adult Juror Comments*: Gives simple, clear instructions. Best use is with motivated students wanting to play the guitar. Audio quality and production values are not great, and it's a little long for this intended audience. *Kid Juror Comments*: Held the children's interest. Initially, the kids thought the explanations were too complex. Later, they made sense. Kids objected to using baby names for fingers. Video. 50 min.; $19.95; Age: 5-8. Homespun Tapes.

** Snow Jam (Avenue E)

Butch wants it to snow so much that he can feel it in his bones. But if the weatherman is right and Whiz's computer is on target, Avenue E won't see snow for quite some time. So, Butch comes up with a special plan to make his snow dream come true. *Adult Juror Comments*: Encourages kids to think of solutions to problems and believe in their dreams. Enhances self-esteem for minority children and reinforces persistence. Older kids tease Butch initially, but help him later. Adult representations are not always positive. *Kid Juror Comments*: Liked the different kinds of music; felt that it represented harmony between different races. They liked the idea of finding snow at the library and using their creativity and imagination to make it happen. "I learned not to make fun of other people." Video. 30 min.; $14.95; Age: 5-12. C&C Films.

* Stay Safe! (Video Adventures of Lost and Found)

 Demonstrates safety lessons through an adventure with four children who encounter danger at every turn. Features songs about hot stoves, strangers, and street safety. The message is: "Watch Out! Stay Safe!" *Adult Juror Comments*: Entertaining, although it presents safety and danger information in an unusual manner. The production quality is good, the characters silly and overacted, detracting from the message. We recommend viewing with an adult and follow-up discussion. *Kid Juror Comments*: Some kids enjoyed the funny music and sang along. They had a hard time staying with the entire program and found the characters confusing. "Watch out Willie" looks like a happy face, but tells you there's danger somewhere. Video. 25 min.; $14.95; Age: 5-8. Media Guild.

* There Goes a Dump Truck (Real Wheels)

Shows giant road construction vehicles at work building and fixing roads. These wrecking and building machines crush, dig, move, pull, lift, scrape, hammer and spin. Includes rock crushers and cement mixers in action. *Adult Juror Comments*: Accurate information about the world of construction. Combines verbal and visual demonstrations. Narrator's silly monologues and slap-stick behavior were lost on kids, and he confused them by getting into trouble. Emphasis on safety. *Kid Juror Comments*: Held the attention of older boys best. They loved the explosions and made associations between garbage trucks, fire trucks, and other trucks. "I liked the Kamatzzu 930E because it was huge." "The conveyer belt is like a roller coaster." No diversity. Video. 30 min.; $9.95; Age: 4-7. Power to Create.

** There Goes a Farm Truck (Real Wheels)

Dave wonders where all the food we eat comes from, which leads him on a journey to fields far and near, filled with crops. From mowing, plowing, planting, and harvesting, Dave finds plenty of machinery to enjoy. *Adult Juror Comments*: Educational and entertaining. Teaches kids fundamentals of harvesting in a fun, comedic fashion. Attuned to how kids think and attend, never too much detail. A nice balance of noisy machines and impressive on-the-spot photography. Follows logical format. *Kid Juror Comments*: Enjoyed it. "It is a fun video and you can learn practical stuff." "Dave has to hurry a lot, but he took us to cool places like fields and carrot factories." "I liked the carrots flying, I liked it all." "The big trucks are the bomb!" Video. 30 min.; $9.95; Age: 4-7. Power to Create.

** There Goes a Tractor (Real Wheels)

Dave discovers that, even for one day, being a rancher or a farmer is a lot harder than it looks…and the tractor is the busiest piece of machinery around. Whether it's dragging a plow or pulling feed for the cows, the tractor makes things happen. *Adult Juror Comments*: Jam-packed with farm scenes and information that interest the whole family. Takes the viewer right into the action. Good narration, very matter-of-fact format. "I never knew there were so many kinds of tractors." *Kid Juror Comments*: Fascinated and amazed. "I want to milk cows and make chocolate milk." "I am definitely going to be a farmer!" "We never get to see this stuff in my country, which is a big city." "I don't think kids drive tractors, but I want to." "We can dig up dirt!" Video. 30 min.; $9.95; Age: 4-7. Power to Create.

Chapter Three • Elementary

** *Toby the Tugboat (I Wonder…)*

Set in New York City, aboard a real tugboat, two children travel through the harbor with Toby the Tugboat. Toby shows them how small tugboats move big boats and that no matter how big or small one is, it's what's on the inside that counts. *Adult Juror Comments*: Well-produced. Catchy tunes. Educational and entertaining. Good balance of animation with live action. Emphasizes teamwork and confidence in one's self, no matter how big or little you are. *Kid Juror Comments*: Loved it. "We love Toby. It was fun to learn about tugboats." "The men on the tugboats work really hard." "Everyone treats each other with respect, even the children on the playground." "Now I know what tugboats are used for. I want to ride on one." Video. 28 min.; $11.95; Age: 5-9. Kid ROM, Inc.

*** *Trav's Travels - Geography for Kids (United States of America)*

Teaches the geography, history, culture, and wildlife of the United States, including a range of metropolitan areas, rural towns, and farmlands. Trav, the host, makes learning interesting. *Adult Juror Comments*: An overview of U.S. cities and farmland with beautiful photography at a fast pace. The vocabulary used is challenging. Good cultural diversity and respect for both people and animals. Could motivate interest and discussion in travel. *Kid Juror Comments*: Loved it. They enjoyed seeing the volcanoes, appreciated the cultural diversity, and enjoyed learning things even their teachers didn't know. "I wanted to learn more." "We want to visit some of the places." "It made me want to take a vacation." Video. 23 min.; $14.99; Age: 6-12. IVN Entertainment.

*** *Visit with Tomie Depaola, A*

An inside look at the life and art of Tomie dePaola. Follows Tomie through his home and studio, highlighting home movies featuring the young Tomie creating his art. A comprehensive and personal perspective is meant to inform and entertain kids. *Adult Juror Comments*: An excellent visit with a successful artist. Viewers will want to explore their own forms of creativity. Excellent production quality; length is just right. Familiarizes kids with a fascinating array of his work. *Kid Juror Comments*: Enjoyed watching dePaola drawing in his studio and telling stories. "I like his house and all the beautiful things in it." "I want to become an artist too!" Best for seven- to eight-year-olds or those interested in illustration. Video. 25 min.; $39.95; Age: 6-12. Whitebird, Inc.

*** When Aunt Lena Did the Rhumba (Reading Rainbow)

 A young girl plans to bring Broadway to her Aunt Lena who's in bed with a sprained ankle after she fell practicing the rhumba. Narrated by Lucie Arnaz. Includes a backstage tour with Lanie Ackerman from CATS and the Harlem Boys Choir. *Adult Juror Comments*: Well-produced, totally engaging. Develops appreciation for the arts and the learning process. "Good introduction to alternative thinking for youth—such as when the boy chooses singing to drugs." *Kid Juror Comments*: Really liked learning about performance arts. "Cool dances, jokes, and makeup." "Now I know how a comedian falls." Most were inspired to try some kind of performing. "I want to talk to my mom and dad about acting." Video. 29 min.; $19.95; Age: 6-12. GPN.

** Who Is an American?

Cultivates awareness of America's multi-ethnic heritage by fostering an appreciation of the contributions of various cultures, exploring the origin of cultural traditions, and learning about the process of becoming a citizen. *Adult Juror Comments*: Straightforward, accurate information that reinforces the message of inclusion. Appropriate for studying diversity. Has little entertainment value. Opens discussion of race and nationality issues. Values contribution by immigrants. *Kid Juror Comments*: Kids were somewhat bored. It contains good information about constitutional rights, and the quiz section got them involved and searching for answers. Advanced vocabulary was a bit challenging. Kids learned: "There is no one type of American." Video. 26 min.; $89; Age: 6-10. Educational Activities, Inc.

*** You're Always Welcome! (Values Through Music)

 What can you do if you feel lonely, rejected, hurt, or sad? Join the Lonely Club where they deal with arguments, being bored, helping each other learning respect, and how to make decisions that make them feel good about themselves. *Adult Juror Comments*: Very authentic. Sets and costumes seem very realistic. Good reminder to play fair, take care of the environment, and respect one another. Emphasizes the importance of listening. Offers positive role models for interacting with your peers. Good diversity. *Kid Juror Comments*: Kids enjoyed seeing how problems were solved, liked the use of music, and thought it encouraged them to "use their brains." "I liked how they stopped the fight by talking." "It told us things we knew in a different way." Video. 30 min.; $29.95; Age: 5-8. Values Through Music Productions, Inc.

Category—Family

** 102 Dalmatians

Animated sequel to the popular 101 Dalmatians. Full of fun new characters like Oddball, who searches for his rightful spots, and Waddlesworth, the delusional macaw who thinks he's a rottweiler. *Adult Juror Comments*: Well-done with enjoyable musical score. Contains suspense, action, romance, and humor. "Great resolution to conflict that makes everyone cheer right in their own living-room." Portrays some men as stereotypically foolish. *Kid Juror Comments*: Loved it and can't wait to see again. "I saw it three times at the theater." "There were some scary parts with scary music." "My favorite part was when the puppies made Cruella into a cake." "I want a dog like Oddball." Video. 90 min.; $24.99; Age: 5-12. Buena Vista Home Entertainment/Disney.

* Adventures for Children: Thru a Dog's Eyes

Follows a day in the life of a dog as seen from the dog's point of view, about two feet from the ground. The dog takes a car ride and a trip to a farm and visits the zoo, the vet, and a pet store. Features original music. *Adult Juror Comments*: An unusual perspective and the photography is well-done, but the unusual camera angle (from a dog's eye-level) disoriented some jurors. *Kid Juror Comments*: Interested in seeing things from a dog's perspective. They were particularly fascinated when the dog chased the farm animals. "This is pretty silly." The production is slow and more appropriate for younger children. Video. 25 min.; $14.95; Age: 5-8. Made-For-Dog Videos, Inc.

** Adventures of Curious George

Contains two stories of the world's favorite monkey. One follows the Man with the Yellow Hat to the jungle, where he finds Curious George and brings him to the big city. The other tells how Curious George winds up in the hospital and makes friends. *Adult Juror Comments*: Nicely produced, good narration. Unlike the book, George takes on human qualities. Good discussion of right versus wrong, good versus bad. Could be used to prepare child for a hospital visit. One adult said, "This was by far my favorite video." *Kid Juror Comments*: Thoroughly enjoyable. Lots of spontaneous laughter and comments about George's silliness. Kids watched George actively, anticipated events, and discussed the consequences of his actions. "I wish I was George." Video. 30 min.; $12.95; Age: 3-8. Sony Wonder.

*** Adventures of Flower the Arson Dog (Animal Bootcamp)*

 Takes children behind the scenes to show how animals are trained and used for different vocations here and abroad. Flower assists fire fighters in the search for gas leaks and other fire hazards. *Adult Juror Comments*: Excellent. Offers a fascinating look at the world of a working dog. Explains arson without the scare factor. Best viewed with an adult. Emphasizes respectful interaction with animals. *Kid Juror Comments*: Enthusiastic. Generated discussion about the topics presented. "All the dog training was so great. I didn't know that dogs could be so smart." "It was very cool to see how Flower learned to do her job." Video. 43 min.; $14.95; Age: 5-8. KHK Films, Inc.

** Air Bud: World Pup*

 Buddy competes with some of the top names in women's soccer. He also proves himself a capable father by adopting a litter of puppies he finds, whom he ultimately rescues from pup-nappers. *Adult Juror Comments*: Exciting. Adventure, intrigue, and humor on appropriate levels. Easy to follow but not pedantic. Beautifully filmed, engaging characters, music blends well with the action. "Soccer and dogs, what a great combination." *Kid Juror Comments*: Enjoyed it. "It's really funny and cool." "We liked when Buddy became a father and had to rescue the puppies." "It showed that girls can compete against boys and do good." "I'd watch it every night." Video. 83 min.; Rental Only; Age: 5-12. Buena Vista Home Entertainment/Disney.

* Aladdin and the King of Thieves*

 Everyone's third wish comes true in Aladdin's ultimate adventure. Features Robin Williams as the voice of Genie. *Adult Juror Comments*: Beautifully animated. Aggressive language, adult humor, lots of sword fighting, and stereotypical portrayal of Arabs. Glamorizes the initiation used to gain entry into the Forty Thieves Gang. Offers message: "You must fight or else be killed." *Kid Juror Comments*: Big hit. Wanted to watch it again right away. Kids enjoyed the production style and the characters. They did not understand much of the story. The content is more appropriate for older children. It's too scary for children under five. Video. 80 min.; $24.99; Age: 5-8. Buena Vista Home Entertainment/Disney.

*** *Aladdin and the Magic Lamp (We All Have Tales)*

From "A Thousand and One Nights," this story is about a young rogue and the genie who helps him win the love of the Sultan's daughter. Musician Mickey Hart weaves the rhythms of the Middle East. *Adult Juror Comments*: Scored high. This iconographic presentation is faithful to the original story, with excellent narration and music. It is perhaps a little slow-moving for some children, but visually it's beautiful. *Kid Juror Comments*: Enjoyed the story and the presentation. They were intrigued that it was not the Disney version. Kids liked the narrator, but wanted the characters to have motion. "I loved the music and the colors." "I learned to be kind and not selfish." Video. 30 min.; $8.95; Age: 5-12. Rabbit Ears Production.

** *Alice Through the Looking Glass*

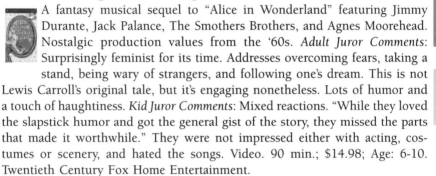

A fantasy musical sequel to "Alice in Wonderland" featuring Jimmy Durante, Jack Palance, The Smothers Brothers, and Agnes Moorehead. Nostalgic production values from the '60s. *Adult Juror Comments*: Surprisingly feminist for its time. Addresses overcoming fears, taking a stand, being wary of strangers, and following one's dream. This is not Lewis Carroll's original tale, but it's engaging nonetheless. Lots of humor and a touch of haughtiness. *Kid Juror Comments*: Mixed reactions. "While they loved the slapstick humor and got the general gist of the story, they missed the parts that made it worthwhile." They were not impressed either with acting, costumes or scenery, and hated the songs. Video. 90 min.; $14.98; Age: 6-10. Twentieth Century Fox Home Entertainment.

*** *All Dogs Go to Heaven*

Set in 1939 New Orleans, this colorful, song-filled story centers on Charles B. Barkin, a roguish German shepherd with the charm of a con-man and the heart of a marshmallow. *Adult Juror Comments*: A lively film that encourages cooperation and honesty. A well-told story with a good mixture of adventure and values. Teaches morality without being pedantic. It's one of the best cartoon movies our jurors have seen. *Kid Juror Comments*: Really enjoyed the characters. They reacted strongly to the emotional content, developing empathy for the orphan. They liked how it emphasizes building one's character and learning from mistakes. All said they'd watch this again. Video. 85 min.; $14.95; Age: 3-12. MGM/UA Home Entertainment.

** Alley Cats on Strike (Disney Channel)

A group of retro outsiders who love bowling become the focal point of an inter-school rivalry when it is announced that a bowling match will be the tie-breaker in the annual quest for the "Golden Apple" trophy. *Adult Juror Comments*: Upbeat, clever look at the world of high school sports that conveys a strong message about acceptance versus labeling. Fresh and crisp, believable sets and good music. Dialogue and slower pace might lose younger viewers. Unflattering portrayal of parents. *Kid Juror Comments*: Enjoyed it; responded well to the message of teamwork. "It taught us not to judge our friends." "The kids were like us. They could play basketball and bowl. They could win or lose the game." "Even if you are not popular you can win if you work as a team." Video. 88 min.; Rental Only; Age: 6-12. Buena Vista Home Entertainment/Disney.

*** Amazing Bone and Other Caldecott Classics, The

Contains three Caldecott classics—"The Amazing Bone," where a young pig finds a talking bone that gives her courage; "Where the Wild Things Are," where Max becomes king; "Goggles," where bullies are outsmarted; and the classic tale, "Stone Soup." *Adult Juror Comments*: Presents positive themes, whimsical characters, and creative learning potential. Brings up issues about walking alone, encountering strangers, running from older children, and helping those in need. Encourages kids to think about their own behavior. *Kid Juror Comments*: Well-received. Best part: when the bedroom turns into a forest. They didn't like the mean kids in "Goggles;" that led to a discussion about bullies. "Stone Soup was hilarious, it made all the kids laugh." Would watch again and re-read the books. Video. 36 min.; $19.95; Age: 5-12. Weston Woods Studios/Scholastic.

*** Amazing Grace and Other Stories (Children's Circle)

Features three stories adapted from popular children's picture books: "Amazing Grace," "Flossie & the Fox," and "Who's in Rabbit's House?" *Adult Juror Comments*: Outstanding music and narration. This thematic grouping of beautiful stories is tastefully done and a great springboard for discussions about history, language, countries, and culture. Shows excellent multi-cultural mix. "Should be in every library." *Kid Juror Comments*: Very attentive and polite while viewing. "We liked all of the stories." The presentation "Amazing Grace" was a little slow. Kids liked the first story best. Video. 35 min.; $14.95; Age: 5-8. Scholastic/Children's Circle.

** An American Tail: Fievel Goes West (An American Tail Series)

In this adventure, brave little Fievel is lured west by evil double-dealer Cat R. Waul, who plans to turn the settlers into mouseburgers. With help of his friend Tiger, Fievel joins forces with lawdog Wiley Burp to stop a sinister scheme. *Adult Juror Comments*: Animation, music, and story are engaging, but it does glamorize gun-shooting scenes. "Story line helps learn about new habitats and adapting to environments." *Kid Juror Comments*: Swell. Fievel is a likable, active role model. "The cats were bad when they tried to eat the mice." More kindness is shown than meanness, though. "I loved when the dog is teaching the tiger." "It made me think about the desert habitat." Video. 75 min.; $19.98; Age: 4-8. Universal Studios Home Video.

*** An American Tail (An American Tail Series)

A delightful animated tale of Fievel, the brave little mouse, who journeys from Russia to America with his family seeking a new life free from cat persecution. Fievel's adventure begins after he's lost at sea and washes ashore in New York City. *Adult Juror Comments*: This engaging story is well-animated with catchy songs and lovable characters. Viewers are drawn into Fievel's journey. It addresses friendship, death, and separation. Can be scary for younger kids. Motivates discussion about emigration and cultures. *Kid Juror Comments*: They were rooted to their seats. Loved Fievel's sweetness. Older kids liked the action and the suspense. Kids resonated to ideas such as: "Never give up, keep trying." "America is a place to find hope." "Not all cats (people) are bad." Video. 81 min.; $19.98; Age: 5-10. Universal Studios Home Video.

* Anastasia (Enchanted Tales)

A young princess finds her life changed forever by the tide of revolution in Czarist Russia. When the evil Rasputin betrays the royal family, Anastasia is forced to flee for her life, aided by the dashing young soldier Alexander. *Adult Juror Comments*: A charming tale, though the story is too complex for the youngest ones and is sometimes scary. This version is more historically accurate than others, though it contains implied violence and has too simple a resolution. *Kid Juror Comments*: Kids four and up liked this, even though they didn't understand the story line. It's hard to know what held kids' attention. "I don't know why Anastasia forgot everything." "I like the little birds." Video. 48 min.; $9.98; Age: 5-8. Sony Wonder.

Age 5-8

Video

Family

** Angels in the Infield (Wonderful World of Disney)

A big league pitcher on a losing streak gets help from his daughter, who prays to restore his confidence. Her prayer is answered by an African-American angel who is in the process of earning his wings, but the angel has never played baseball. Rental Only. *Adult Juror Comments*: Humorous and engaging. Great visual effects, like showing fast pitches. Some scenes have a video game quality. Many laughs—"The silly scenes were really silly." Religious and spiritual undertones. "We are taught to believe in ourselves and our skills." *Kid Juror Comments*: Enjoyed it. "It was hilarious." "I'd watch it again." "The praying thing was kind of strange. I didn't get it about the devil." "The devil was bad, but I think he has to be." "Why do they always have to have a smoochie part?" "Ballet was funny." Video. 94 min.; rental only; Age: 6-10. Buena Vista Home Entertainment/Disney.

* Animals and Their People Friends (Animal Crackups)

Animals and people have been living together on Earth for millions of years. Now you can join ZAK and C-MOR as they explore the lighter side of our relationship with our furry friends. Includes animal tricks. *Adult Juror Comments*: Good cinematography. Cute but somewhat fragmented. Does not flow well. The anthropomorphizing of animals is trite, and the interactions with humans border on exploitation. *Kid Juror Comments*: Kids liked the animals, but thought it was too long. "It was funny to see a chicken taking care of bunnies." "How does a parrot roller skate?" "It showed diversity by having a disabled dog in the story." "My favorite animal was the panda." Video. 30 min.; $14.99; Age: 5-8. E-Realbiz.

* Animaniacs: Wakko's Wish (Animaniacs)

A feature length animated musical with magical mayhem as the Animaniacs race to the wishing star and try to make all their dreams come true. *Adult Juror Comments*: Non-stop action, lots of music and sound effects. Clever rhyming and quick wit. Lots of cartoon humor of the head-bopping sort. Shows compassion, tolerance, and diversity. The ice sculpture made out of spit was interesting . *Kid Juror Comments*: Amused and entertained. "They're silly. We like it when the Animaniacs trick grown-ups." "I liked the way the brothers took care of their sister." "The bad guys were really mean." "It's like a fairy tale." Video. 80 min.; $19.96; Age: 6-10. Warner Home Video.

** Annie Oakley (American Heroes and Legends)

Recalls the life and sharpshooting exploits of America's favorite cowgirl, and a star of Buffalo Bill's famous Wild West Show. Narration is by Keith Carradine. Music is by Los Lobos. *Adult Juror Comments*: Entertaining biography of a female protagonist. Handles attitudes toward Native Americans delicately, if not accurately. Animation is thoughtfully beautiful, though slow. Los Lobos' music is lively and engaging. *Kid Juror Comments*: Entertaining as well as informative. Kids loved the story, character, and narration and asked to see it again. They loved the music and seeing a girl hero! "We want to keep this one." Video. 30 min.; $19.95; Age: 5-12. Rabbit Ears Production.

*** Aristocats

A Parisian millionaire wills her fortune to her "family"—adorable high-society cats. But the butler tries to thwart her plans by catnapping the cat heirs and dumping them in the French countryside where their rough and tumble adventure begins. *Adult Juror Comments*: Superb quality. Classic family video: cute characters, sad parts, and a happy ending. Bright animation and colorful characters keep the story swinging and full of life. Good triumphs over evil. Differences are set aside to help each other. *Kid Juror Comments*: Danced and sang at the end. "I love this movie!" "I love cats!" "I want to be a cat!" Identified with the characters and teamwork. "It teaches you how to be good to people." "The dogs teased each other like I do my friends. They were just having fun." Video. 79 min.; $22.99; Age: 4-12. Buena Vista Home Entertainment/Disney.

** Arthur Writes a Story (Arthur)

Struggling with a school assignment, Arthur decides that with a little imagination he can make his life sound more interesting than it really is. He crosses the line when the story of how he got his puppy starts to involve invisible elephants. *Adult Juror Comments*: Good story, inspiring and well-produced. Arthur teaches in a gentle yet thorough way. Filled with practical writing tips. Most adults loved Arthur. *Kid Juror Comments*: They enjoy Arthur as a rule. He's very realistic and deals with issues they relate to. Also, good music and animation. Commented on the negative interaction between the siblings. Video. 30 min.; $12.98; Age: 4-8. Sony Wonder.

Age 5-8

Video

Family

** Arthur's Eyes (Arthur)

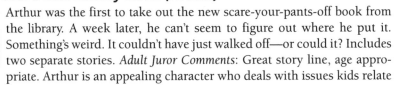

For some reason, Arthur isn't doing very well in school anymore. Maybe he just needs glasses? The problem is he doesn't want to be seen wearing them. It appears as if Arthur has started a trend. *Adult Juror Comments*: Good content for discussing differences. It's true to the book, with captivating animation and adorable characters. Realistically shows children's responses to attitudes. Some segments would benefit from adult explanation. *Kid Juror Comments*: Great discussion-starter about feelings. Children disliked the name-calling, though it's addressed in a suitable manner. Kids didn't understand all of the concepts involved. They liked the live segments at the end best. Video. 30 min.; $12.98; Age: 4-8. Sony Wonder.

** Arthur's Lost Library Book (Arthur)

Arthur was the first to take out the new scare-your-pants-off book from the library. A week later, he can't seem to figure out where he put it. Something's weird. It couldn't have just walked off—or could it? Includes two separate stories. *Adult Juror Comments*: Great story line, age appropriate. Arthur is an appealing character who deals with issues kids relate to. He teaches social values without being preachy. It does have some inappropriate vocabulary. *Kid Juror Comments*: "I love Arthur." "Do you have any more Arthur tapes?" This held the children's attention. Kids wanted to see it again. Kids talked about what scares them afterwards. Video. 30 min.; $12.98; Age: 3-8. Sony Wonder.

** Arthur's Pet Business (Arthur)

How can Arthur prove to his parents that he's responsible enough to take care of his very own puppy? "Get a job," suggests D.W. Within two days, Arthur's pet business has its first client. Can Arthur really care for a canine with her own pet? *Adult Juror Comments*: Beautiful stories, dealing with typical issues in an entertaining way. Arthur is strong, appealing, silly, and age-appropriate. The sibling relationship is negative and doesn't really get resolved. *Kid Juror Comments*: Cute. Kids love Arthur. They relate to the moral of each story. This one motivated discussion afterwards about responsibility, caring for pets, and helping out in their family. Kids familiar with the TV show were big fans even before the tape played. Video. 30 min.; $12.98; Age: 4-8. Sony Wonder.

Chapter Three • Elementary

** Arthur's Tooth (Arthur)

Everyone in class has lost a tooth except Arthur, and they keep teasing him about it. Will Arthur have to go through life with a mouthful of baby teeth? *Adult Juror Comments*: Upbeat, fast-moving, cheerful music and animation. The mystery of the Tooth Fairy is a common topic for children this age. Some name-calling. Arthur's relationship with his sister is realistic, but not always positive. *Kid Juror Comments*: "Arthur is so funny." Kids like all the different things Arthur does, like soccer, basketball, and swimming, that are fun to watch." "Francine is mean." "I don't like the way D.W. and Arthur fight." "Don't force your teeth out." Video. 30 min.; $12.98; Age: 5-8. Random House Video.

*** Arthur's Treasure Hunt (Arthur)

After Buster digs up an ancient arrowhead, everyone wants to hunt for buried treasures. How can Arthur become a famous discoverer of lost civilizations if his mom won't let him dig up the back yard? Includes two stories. *Adult Juror Comments*: Engaging and interesting for adults as well as children. Realistic characters, strong female role models, age-appropriate. Addresses accepting responsibility and maintaining positive relationships with parents, friends, and siblings. *Kid Juror Comments*: Loved it. "Arthur's family will always love him and D.W., even when they argue." "I learned you're supposed to do the right thing even if you first did the wrong thing!" "I want to dig in my yard to find something old." "We watched it three times." Video. 30 min.; $12.99; Age: 4-8. Sony Wonder.

** At the Airport

Explores a busy airport from the ticket counter to the cockpit, baggage handling to jet fueling. Visit to pilots and air traffic controllers. *Adult Juror Comments*: Shows female pilots and air traffic controllers. An informative production about airports and planes, great for kids taking a field trip to the airport or preparing for a plane ride. *Kid Juror Comments*: Well-traveled children particularly loved it because they are familiar with the subject. "I liked that they showed different kinds of airplanes." Older children enjoyed it best. Video. 25 min.; $14.95; Age: 3-8. Papillion Productions.

*** Babar Returns (Babar)*

Babar shares a tale with a lesson about concentrating on our strengths rather than our weaknesses. Years after the wicked hunter separated Babar from his family, he meets him again, defeats him with his knowledge of man's ways, and is crowned king. *Adult Juror Comments*: Nicely animated with a good story that's appealing and creative. Delivers positive messages about home, family, and helping others take charge. *Kid Juror Comments*: Babar is always a favorite. Wanted to watch it repeatedly. Babar's separation from his parents may be frightening for the youngest children. It's best that they view this with their parent present. Video. 49 min.; $12.98; Age: 3-12. Artisan/Family Home Entertainment.

** Babar's First Step (Babar)*

Babar tells his son Alexander about an event from his childhood: when a hunter terrorized the elephant herd and Babar realized that he must face his fears to conquer them. This uplifting adventure explores the meaning of friendship and family. *Adult Juror Comments*: Good animation and simple, appealing characters. Showing Babar losing his mother could be disturbing for younger viewers. Discussion is required to bring home the point of the story, which is "being yourself." *Kid Juror Comments*: Big hit. Children laughed at Babar's silliness. Very attentive and curious to see what would happen next. Younger children did not understand why Babar's mom died. This title is more suitable for ages six to eight. Video. 49 min.; $12.98; Age: 6-8. Artisan/Family Home Entertainment.

** Babar's Triumph (Babar)*

When deadly hunters threaten, Babar helps the animals join forces to protect themselves and their homes. *Adult Juror Comments*: Colorful video brings a favorite Babar story to life. Great learning potential for discussion of peace and conflict resolution. The story does include the use of guns and provides an ideal opportunity to discuss them. *Kid Juror Comments*: Several children were disconcerted by the segment in which the turtles fought with the hunters. Babar and his family were very appealing to the kids, who wanted to live where Babar lives. "Teaches unity and tolerance." Video. 51 min.; $12.98; Age: 6-12. Artisan/Family Home Entertainment.

* Babar: The Movie (Babar)

 Full-length feature movie based on the charming French classic about Babar, the King of the Elephants. *Adult Juror Comments*: Well-produced with appealing music. It has the standard good-versus-bad scenario with battle scenes. It is violent in parts, though not particularly graphic. Gender roles are fairly rigidly defined, and older people are portrayed as slightly senile. *Kid Juror Comments*: Prompted an animated discussion of the movie and the issues of good versus bad that it raised. Video. 79 min.; $12.98; Age: 6-12. Artisan/Family Home Entertainment.

*** Babe

A very special pig turns Hoggett's orderly farm on its ear. A naive newcomer, Babe boldly forges friendships among all the animals and convinces the entire farm that only in the absence of prejudice can one truly be free to soar. *Adult Juror Comments*: Great. Fabulous. This story respects differences between characters and their abilities. Challenges the notions of solving problems with violence. Babe is a model of goodness. *Kid Juror Comments*: "I liked how nice the talking animals were." Particularly enjoyed seeing Babe save the sheep. All the animals were adored by the kids, especially the singing mice. They wanted to watch it again. One took it home and watched it five times. Video. 92 min.; $14.98; Age: 4-12. Universal Studios Home Video.

** Bach and Broccoli (Les Productions La Fête)

Fanny, an eleven-year-old orphan, brings love to her lonely uncle, a middle-aged bachelor whose passion is the music of Bach. *Adult Juror Comments*: Excellent drama, colorful music. The British accent was distracting for some. The main characters were very realistic and dealt with real issues and a range of emotions. Children may not understand the tension between uncle and mother. *Kid Juror Comments*: Related to the story and the emotional range experienced by the main characters. They enjoyed the scenes with the animals and thought the men were mean and grumpy, and the women were kind. Many kids asked to see it again. Video. 96 min.; $14.98; Age: 4-12. Productions La Fête.

* Balloon Farm (Wonderful World of Disney)

Harvey, a new farmer in a drought-ravaged town, has a knack for growing an unusual crop—balloons! The townspeople believe the balloons are a sign of hope, but as the drought persists, they turn on Harry. Find out who sets things right. *Adult Juror Comments*: Creative story and aesthetically pleasing production. A bit of drama, a touch of mystery, and a whole lot of fantasy make this a cute family video. Portrays some ethnic stereotypes, and adults argue excessively. *Kid Juror Comments*: Would watch again. "My favorite was the magical field of balloons." "There was a lot of fussing between the grownups." "I learned about the importance of rain for farmers." "It shows the magic of believing in the simple things." Video. 88 min.; $14.99; Age: 5-10. Buena Vista Home Entertainment/Disney.

*** Balto

 Balto, an outcast sled dog, becomes a hero when he saves the children of Nome, Alaska from an epidemic. A team of sled dogs, carrying medicine, races six hundred miles through a blizzard. Features voices of Kevin Bacon, Bridget Fonda, and Bob Hoskins. *Adult Juror Comments*: Excellent, action-packed production. Good adaptation of a true story, demonstrating the idea to "keep trying, don't quit." Children identified with rejection and praise. Encouraged reading the book. More educational than expected. *Kid Juror Comments*: "Really great." "Exciting." Animal lovers responded particularly well. Kids were curious to know more about the real story. Stimulated discussion afterwards about the role of huskies in everyday life. "Dogs are more than just pets." Video. 78 min.; $14.98; Age: 5-12. Universal Studios Home Video.

** Bartok the Magnificent

 Bartok the Magnificent enjoys performing acts of heroism in front of crowds in Moscow, but it's only an act. When Prince Ivan is kidnapped, a real hero is needed. Bartok must find the courage to save the prince before an evil regent takes the throne. *Adult Juror Comments*: Story line is logical and consistent. Bartok keeps the scariest places from being taken too seriously. Teaches the moral that looks can be deceiving. Contains adult language and humor, female stereotypes, and a wicked queen who mistreats slaves. *Kid Juror Comments*: Children danced along with the songs. They discussed how Bartok kept trying, without giving up, and became the hero he always wanted to be. Kids had trouble understanding what Bartok was saying. "Even though Bartok was little, he did big things." Video. 71 min.; $19.98; Age: 6-10. Twentieth Century Fox Home Entertainment.

** Beauty and the Beast
(Stories to Remember)

 Classic enchantment and romance. To save her beloved father, a beautiful young girl agrees to become the companion of a brutish and unhappy beast. As time passes, love works a miraculous change in their lives. Narrated by Mia Farrow. *Adult Juror Comments*: A beautifully illustrated work of art though not full-range animation. The ending here more accurately reflects the original story than some major studio releases. *Kid Juror Comments*: Expecting to see the Disney version, kids were surprised with this one. They didn't like that the characters' mouths didn't move. Generated a discussion about how stories can be told differently. Video. 27 min.; $9.95; Age: 5-12. Stories to Remember.

** Being Responsible (You Can Choose!)

 Takes an interesting approach to youth guidance by combining comedy, drama, music, peer-education, and role modeling into a lively format to challenge young viewers. *Adult Juror Comments*: This kind of program—"have fun with personal change"—is often seen as stupid in the nervous eyes of teens. This one is well-done, though the content is best suited for older children and the format best for younger kids. *Kid Juror Comments*: Appreciated having guidelines on how to behave. They enjoyed the conversation and discussion among the children in the program. Kids had a hard time admitting to one another that they enjoyed the video. Video. 28 min.; $59.95; Age: 6-11. Live Wire Media.

** Ben's Dream and Other Stories (Fun in a Box)

 The lead story is based on the book by Chris Van Allsburg in which a young boy dreams about an imaginary trip around the world. Next, a mile-a-minute train ride on the famous Cannonball Express. Last, a little girl and her escapades. *Adult Juror Comments*: The title story, "Ben's Dream," based on a Caldecott award-winning book, is true to the original: delightful and imaginative visits to world-famous landmarks in a geography-induced dream. *Kid Juror Comments*: Although they enjoyed "Ben's Dream," the other two stories were not as compelling. They talked about the landmarks afterwards. Some were familiar with the Eiffel Tower and Mount Rushmore. One asked, "Are these famous places I should know about?" Video. 30 min.; $14.95; Age: 4-12. Made to Order Productions/Rainbow.

Age 5-8

Video

Family

** *Big Harbor Bedtime (Theodore Tugboat)*

Features Theodore, a stout-hearted tugboat, and his many friends in the Big Harbor. Anthology includes "Emily and the Sleep Over," "Theodore's Bright Night," and "Foduck and the Shy Ship." *Adult Juror Comments*: Simple production with characters who are friendly, amusing, and unusual. The content and language are very age-appropriate. Encourages respectful behavior. Although long, it can be broken up easily for viewing in four segments. *Kid Juror Comments*: Liked the short stories and narration, the peer interaction, and the showing of emotions. "My seven-year-old watched attentively." "My two-year-olds sang along, pointed at the tugboats, asked questions and imitated words." Video. 43 min.; $12.95; Age: 4-7. Warner Home Video.

** *Birthday Dragon*

Every night, Emily is secretly visited by a lovable dragon. Together they play and fly through the skies. Her birthday is coming, and what she wants most is for him to be a part of her celebration, but two dragon hunters stand in her way. *Adult Juror Comments*: A good birthday choice, entertaining and unusual, even though it's simply produced and somewhat slow. *Kid Juror Comments*: Lots of laughter from attentive audience. The humor is just right for five-year-olds! Kids were confused about how the dragon got out of the net and the bad guys were caught. Video. 26 min.; $9.98; Age: 5-8. Artisan/Family Home Entertainment.

* *Blue Bird, The (Shirley Temple)*

Shirley Temple longs to see the world outside her doorstep, but soon discovers there's no place like home. *Adult Juror Comments*: Confusing story and dated special effects. Content is somewhat scary. Despite moral ending, lacks diversity, reflecting its cultural era. *Kid Juror Comments*: The fairy-tale quality was appealing. They thought the dog and cat were funny. Lead to discussions about trustworthiness, luxury, and being happy with what one has. Held kids' attention throughout. Video. 83 min.; $14.98; Age: 5-8. Twentieth Century Fox Home Entertainment.

Age 5-8

Video

Family

*** Boy & His Car, A

A young boy finds his heart's desire, a remote-controlled car, loses it, and goes on a quest through the streets and subways of New York City to get it back. Features the chorus of St. John the Divine. *Adult Juror Comments*: A lovely film. Shows good multi-cultural mix, social themes, and examples of cooperation. Charmingly original, creative, and intriguing, though the ending is awkward. Introduces kids to choir music and religion. Teachers loved it. *Kid Juror Comments*: Some kids absolutely loved this. The mix of music with an original story are good, but a little difficult for kids to follow. Sparks interesting discussion. One boy remembered it from a previous screening where it made a lasting impression. Video. 25 min.; $14.95; Age: 3-10. Anne Richardson Productions.

* Boy Named Charlie Brown, A

The animated Peanuts gang faces the start of the baseball season and a pitcher's mound overgrown with dandelions. *Adult Juror Comments*: The Peanuts Gang's adventures are imaginative and enjoyable. Explores baseball, friendships, and spelling bees. Children may find the presentation slow. Shows little diversity and stereotypical gender portrayal of characters. *Kid Juror Comments*: Liked the interactions between Lucy and Charlie Brown. Snoopy, of course, was a hit. "Poor Charlie Brown, everything always happens to him." "Snoopy and Lucy have all the good luck." "Charlie Brown always keeps trying." Video. 85 min.; $14.98; Age: 5-8. Twentieth Century Fox Home Entertainment.

** Brer Rabbit and Boss Lion (American Heroes and Legends)

When mean old Boss Lion threatens the folks of Brer Village, Brer Rabbit teaches him a lesson he'll never forget. Narration is by Danny Glover. Music is by Dr. John's Bayou. *Adult Juror Comments*: Delightful and amusing, with great music and story line. Excellent addition to any collection of folk tales. Danny Glovers' voiceover is perfect. Brer Rabbit is an example of resourcefulness. *Kid Juror Comments*: Kids loved Brer Rabbit's character. Responded well to Danny Glover's narration and the music. "I like the rabbit because he comes up with good plans." "I wish I could think of things like that." Video. 30 min.; $19.95; Age: 5-12. Weston Woods Studios/Scholastic.

** Brink (Disney Channel)

A group of amateur skaters from the beach dares to go head-to-head with the hottest team of sponsored skaters on the circuit. *Adult Juror Comments*: Entertaining, fast-paced production with a solid message about conflict resolution. Favorable portrayal of parent-child relationship. Skaters are "macho" and engage in risky behavior. "I had to sit through the whole movie to see the redeeming factor." *Kid Juror Comments*: Particularly appealing to middle-school boys. "It told a good story about how a lie can get you into trouble." "The music and the filming made the story suspenseful." "They tried too hard to make it 'cool.'" "I don't like kids being so mean." Video. 89 min.; rental only; Age: 8-12. Buena Vista Home Entertainment/Disney.

** Buddy

Rene Russo stars in this family adventure about a woman who opens her home and her heart to a household of creatures including the adorable baby gorilla Buddy. Based on a true story. *Adult Juror Comments*: Well-produced, slow-moving, lags in the middle, sad at times, but the resolution redeems it. Good range of emotions and whimsical yet realistic sets and costumes. *Kid Juror Comments*: Entertaining. Girls liked it; boys were bored. Prompted discussion about zoos and pets. Kids agreed they would want to have a pet gorilla. "The animals looked healthy and well-kept." "I liked when they got into trouble." Video. 85 min.; $14.95; Age: 5-13. Columbia Tristar Home Entertainment.

*** Bug's Life, A

On behalf of "oppressed bugs everywhere" an inventive ant named Flik hires warrior bugs to defend his colony from a horde of freeloading grasshoppers. But Flik's cavalry turns into a group of ragtag flea circus performers and comic confusion follows. *Adult Juror Comments*: Dynamic film with superb structure and style. Flawless production. Characters are lively and unique. Encourages kids to look at things differently, even to value the life of a bug. Good stuff. *Kid Juror Comments*: Positively entranced them. They laughed, got scared, cheered, and even cried. "They were trying to work together, but it was like when we tried to learn square dancing." "I did not know bugs were so smart." Enthusiastic thumbs-up from everyone. Video. 95 min.; $22.99; Age: 6-12. Buena Vista Home Entertainment/Disney.

** Bugs Bunny Superstar

This classic is narrated by Orson Welles and highlighted by live action and behind-the-scenes interviews with cartoon geniuses Bob Clampett, Tex Avery, and Friz Freleng. *Adult Juror Comments*: Interesting documentary survey of cartoon-making. Shows kids how a character such as Bugs Bunny came to be. Engages kids' awareness of the material on two levels: how animation is made and how characters are created. *Kid Juror Comments*: Passive reaction at first, but the historical information about cartoon-making and character creation caught their interest, and their attention level increased. Interesting as a documentary, but not geared toward children. Video. 91 min.; $14.95; Age: 6-12. MGM/UA Home Entertainment.

** Building Skyscrapers

This construction video visits busy building sites with giant jackhammers, flash welders, and excavations. Set among skyscrapers in New York City, Chicago, and Hong Kong, viewed from a helicopter. *Adult Juror Comments*: Informative, well-presented, with a good child narrator. Well-produced, with good aerial shots. It's very age-appropriate. Parents liked it too. Glamorizes explosives and demolition. *Kid Juror Comments*: Appealed to boys; girls specifically said they did not like it. The boys liked the explosions particularly well. Several preschoolers and their parents enjoyed this, though they found it too long for younger kids. Video. 40 min.; $19.95; Age: 4-10. David Alpert Associates, Inc.

** Cabbage Patch: The Screen Test (Cabbage Patch Kids)

The Cabbage Patch Kids decide to team up to make a film for a school project about heroes. They learn anyone can be a hero. *Adult Juror Comments*: Cute. Quality production, engaging music, good messages about cooperation, self-worth, and teamwork. Characters are believable and distinct, though it shows some gender stereotypes. *Kid Juror Comments*: "Loved it, especially the songs and the silly twins." Kids liked seeing a resolution. Even older children enjoyed it. Girls liked it better than boys. Video. 30 min.; $12.98; Age: 5-8. BMG Home Video.

* Captain January (Shirley Temple)

A mean truant officer attempts to take Shirley Temple, an orphan, away from a kindly lighthouse keeper. Features the song "The Codfish Ball." *Adult Juror Comments*: Offers lessons on values, family interactions, and problem-solving. The social generalizations lack cultural or gender sensitivity, and the characters' argumentative and name-calling behaviors offer poor role models. *Kid Juror Comments*: Kids were bored and thought it was too long. Most kids thought the sea captain "baby" scene was funny. Younger ones found the story too complex to follow. Video. 76 min.; $14.98; Age: 5-10. Twentieth Century Fox Home Entertainment.

Age 5-8

Video

Family

*** Caring and Sharing with Friends (Rupert the Bear)

Rupert and his friends embark on magical, globe-trotting adventures while offering gentle and humorous lessons about growing up. *Adult Juror Comments*: Entertaining and well-produced. Brings up good issues surrounding responsibility and friendship. Some of the behaviors border on being unsafe. *Kid Juror Comments*: "Funny. I'd watch more of these programs." Sparked conversations about younger siblings and friendship. One child scooted over and affectionately put her arm around her friend. Video. 48 min.; $9.98; Age: 5-8. Sony Wonder.

** Case of the Hotel Who-Done-It, The (The Adventures of Mary-Kate and Ashley)

A frantic call from a frazzled hotel manager sends the pint-sized Mary-Kate and Ashley to the Hilton Hawaiian Village, a Honolulu resort hotel that has been plagued by a string of "disappearances." *Adult Juror Comments*: The twins explain how they solve the mystery, which helps illuminate the audience. Catchy tunes and visuals. Bike ride to Hawaii is irrelevant, although wearing helmets is a plus. Filled with gender stereotypical behavior and "stupid" portrayal of adults. *Kid Juror Comments*: Kids asked questions about the Navy ship and said they didn't understand the hotel manager. "The songs and clothes were cool. I would give this video for a birthday present." Video. 30 min.; $12.95; Age: 5-8. Warner Home Video.

** Case of the Logical I Ranch, The (The Adventures of Mary-Kate and Ashley)

The Olsen and Olsen Mystery Agency is hired to explore the missing cattle at the Logical I Ranch. *Adult Juror Comments*: Corny but cute. Very middle-class. Well-produced, predictable, but suitable for this age and for kids who like to solve mysteries. *Kid Juror Comments*: A hit. Afterwards, kids talked about the research the girls did in the library. Much to our surprise, both boys and girls liked it equally, even memorizing some of the songs. This went over best with early elementary-aged kids. Video. 30 min.; $12.95; Age: 5-9. Warner Home Video.

** Case of the Mystery Cruise, The
(The Adventures of Mary-Kate and Ashley)

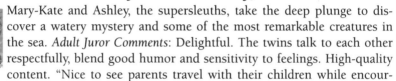

The pint-sized gumshoes board a cruise ship to soak up some sun and fun and find themselves engaged in crime-solving on the high seas. Along with their dog Clue, Mary-Kate and Ashley promise to "solve any crime by dinner time." *Adult Juror Comments*: This action-filled story kept kids engaged and guessing. The depiction of the parents is rather stereotypical. Mom is frivolous and Dad the worker. *Kid Juror Comments*: Video motivated kids who came to America by ship to talk about their trip. They tried to figure out the mystery as the story moved along. Kids loved the songs, memorizing the words and singing along. Video. 30 min.; $12.95; Age: 5-9. Warner Home Video.

* Case of the Sea World Adventure, The
(The Adventures of Mary-Kate and Ashley)

Mary-Kate and Ashley, the supersleuths, take the deep plunge to discover a watery mystery and some of the most remarkable creatures in the sea. *Adult Juror Comments*: Delightful. The twins talk to each other respectfully, blend good humor and sensitivity to feelings. High-quality content. "Nice to see parents travel with their children while encouraging their creativity." Humor is well-suited for this age. *Kid Juror Comments*: Suspenseful. Inspired kids to solve mysteries on their own. "I want to find a mystery to solve." Prompted a discussion about working at Sea World. Kids liked the Miami song, the costumes, and the boat. "I wish my Mom and Dad talked to dolphins." Video. 30 min.; $12.95; Age: 5-8. Warner Home Video.

** Case of the Shark Encounter, The
(The Adventures of Mary-Kate and Ashley)

Mary-Kate and Ashley, the adventurous twosome, take on the undersea case of three pirates who swear that the sharks are actually singing. *Adult Juror Comments*: Theatrical, goofy, and girlish. Demonstrates problem-solving skills, gives accurate information about sharks, and introduces good vocabulary words. Glorifies pirates as thieves. "I liked that Sharlene Fish, the shark expert, was African-American." *Kid Juror Comments*: Kids like singing along with the girls. They like the spy stuff and learning about sharks. "Some parts sound like nonsense and some like they're real detectives. I'm not sure how they figured out fishing poles made music." "It's a girls' movie." Video. 30 min.; $12.95; Age: 5-8. Warner Home Video.

Age 5-8

Video

Family

** Case of the U.S. Navy Adventure, The
(The Adventures of Mary-Kate and Ashley)

 Join Mary-Kate and Ashley as they travel to the edge of space, where a fleet of UFOs has been flying over earth every 93 minutes. The twins use their knowledge, and, with a little help from the Navy, solve the mystery. *Adult Juror Comments*: A good transition movie for young girls. Concepts offer opportunity for discussion about the use of an atlas, satellites, UFOs, time, and the armed services. The twins use clear thinking, show respect for adults. Overacting (at times) is the only drawback. *Kid Juror Comments*: Kids love being detectives and following clues. Enjoyed the costumes, dancing, singing, and humor. They commented on the stereotypical portrayal of science nerds. Video. 30 min.; $12.95; Age: 5-8. Warner Home Video.

** Case of the U.S. Space Camp Mission, The
(The Adventures of Mary-Kate and Ashley)

 Mary-Kate and Ashley are called in to help the Space Program and Mission Control aided by Alan Bean of Apollo XII, the fourth astronaut on the moon. Unless they solve the mystery of the unknown ticking sounds, the space shuttle cannot lift off. *Adult Juror Comments*: Good cinematography. Lacks continuity and jumps from scene to scene. Useful information on space camp and flight training, but it's a digression from the mystery. Offers lessons on bravery and critical thinking. *Kid Juror Comments*: Kids liked the footage from outer space. Opened discussion about how the girls solved the mystery by using their minds to make deductions and conclusions. "Girls can be astronauts too." Video. 30 min.; $12.95; Age: 5-8. Warner Home Video.

** Case of the Volcano Mystery, The
(The Adventures of Mary-Kate and Ashley)

 The case begins with a frantic call from three marshmallow-mining prospectors who have been terrorized by a claim-jumping, snowball-throwing monster. In a wild, volcanic wilderness like Jelly Jungle, what kind of monster can the twins be up against? *Adult Juror Comments*: Includes many volcano facts and a realistic jungle. The vulcanologist adds credibility to the story. The rural minors were obnoxiously stereotyped. Story line is age-appropriate, but adults generally didn't care for it. Good-quality production. *Kid Juror Comments*: Kids like the mystery story. "It was fun and we learned a lot too." Girls enjoyed it more than boys and were "genuinely enthralled." They commented that "The girls are real smart and almost as good as superheroes." Some boys refused to watch. Video. 30 min.; $12.95; Age: 5-8. Warner Home Video.

Chapter Three • Elementary

** Case of Thorn Mansion, The
(The Adventures of Mary-Kate and Ashley)

 Mary-Kate and Ashley try to find the ghost in a haunted mansion in Transylvania. With their dog Clue, they promise to "solve any crime by dinner time." *Adult Juror Comments*: This mystery is filled with great music, and it's well suited for this age. Kids relate to the true-to-life situations the girls get into. It's fun figuring out the mystery from the clues. The treatment of the younger sister is not very good. *Kid Juror Comments*: Girls loved this and watched it again to learn the songs. Kids objected to the idea that you can cross the ocean on a bike. They learned that there is usually an explanation for everything. It could be scary for those under five years of age. Video. 30 min.; $12.95; Age: 5-9. Warner Home Video.

* Casper, A Spirited Beginning

Casper is on the run from Kibosh, king of spooks. Like his uncles, Casper skips spectral training and finds a friend and teacher in a little boy. Casper discovers his powers, saves a town from the wrecking ball, and reunites the boy with his father. *Adult Juror Comments*: Good final message, but poorly acted. Shows poor adult role models, kids playing with knives, and food processors, and behaviors by the mean ghosts which are offensive and negative. The Green Monster is particularly violent, both verbally and physically *Kid Juror Comments*: The ghost train was too scary for youngest kids. The father's behavior, when he ignored his kid, bothered them. They were glad at the end when the father finally realizes his kid needs him. Video. 90 min.; $19.98; Age: 6-12. Twentieth Century Fox Home Entertainment.

** Children's Favorites: Five Fables (Children's Favorites)

Animated fables about greedy and quarrelsome birds who learn a lesson, along with three well-known fables by Aesop: "Town Mouse and City Mouse," "Lion and the Mouse," "The North Wind," and "The Sun." *Adult Juror Comments*: Visually interesting with beautiful graphics and music. Requires explanation of background and cultural context. Vocabulary is too sophisticated. Kids will benefit from a little coaching that encourages them to examine the artistry. *Kid Juror Comments*: Liked it, but were bothered by absence of narrative. Related to some characters: County Mouse and City Mouse. "The pictures are nice." "I like the music." Video. 26 min.; $19.95; Age: 4-7. Nat'l Film Board of Canada.

** *Children's Favorites: Tales of Wonder (Children's Favorites)*

Three engrossing tales of magic and love are rendered in colorful animation. Includes "The Boy and the Snow Goose," "The Long Enchantment," and "The Magic Flute." *Adult Juror Comments*: Good content and aesthetics. "I enjoyed the images and colors." Appeals to imagination, asks audience to interpret the actions and emotions for themselves. As always, high standards from the National Film Board of Canada. *Kid Juror Comments*: Needed coaching to get beyond the non-narrative nature of the program. Those accustomed to standard TV fare didn't "get it." Those that did said, "Great! We really liked the drawings." Lacking diversity. Good discussion about fantasy. Video. 30 min.; $19.95; Age: 4-8. Nat'l Film Board of Canada.

** *Children's Stories from Africa - Vol. 1 (Children's Stories from Africa)*

Charming original songs and delightful African fables entertain and teach youngsters. Enchantingly told by Nandi Nyembe and features dancers from the Mahlatsi Preschool. *Adult Juror Comments*: Good storytellers, beautiful sets and music, excellent pace. Stories are recounted with such mirth that it's contagious. Opportunity for cross-cultural learning. Featuring a native speaker was a plus. *Kid Juror Comments*: "The young dancers, the songs, and the storyteller were appealing highlights." "I liked that the storyteller didn't read from a book." "It told us how to be friends and to not laugh at anyone because they're different." Video. 26 min.; $12.95; Age: 3-8. Monterey Home Video.

** *Chitty Chitty Bang Bang*

Dick Van Dyke stars as inventor Caractacus Potts, who creates an incredible car that drives, flies, and floats his family into a magical world of pirates and castles. *Adult Juror Comments*: It's funny, fast-paced, and lively. The simplistic storytelling and the special effects are somewhat dated. *Kid Juror Comments*: Good story. Kids enjoyed watching with their parents. Many retold the story. Some found it pretty corny. Young kids have trouble with the story line, older kids found it old-fashioned. Appeals to seven- to ten-years-old. Video. 147 min.; $14.95; Age: 4-10. MGM/UA Home Entertainment.

** *Cinderella, Cinderella, Cinderella*

All-time favorite retold three ways—making it three times as entertaining. One is a traditional interpretation illustrated in watercolors, another features animated crayon drawings by fifth-grade students. *Adult Juror Comments*: Delightful Canadian film demonstrates outstanding artistry. Can be used in the classroom or at home. Presentation demonstrates how styles have changed over the years. Some objected to the portrayal of the prince as a moron in the last story. *Kid Juror Comments*: Kids enjoyed it, especially the last story. It probably would not be played repeatedly. Kids didn't care for the music. The penguin story was everyone's favorite. "Different Cinderellas than the one we know." Video. 27 min.; $19.95; Age: 5-10. Nat'l Film Board of Canada.

** *Circus Champions (Barnyard Buddies)*

 The Barnyard Buddies are off on an exciting adventure to the circus. They steal the show when they discover an old barn filled with circus memorabilia. Narration by Sally Struthers. *Adult Juror Comments*: This is rather an endearing story. Sally Struthers' narration is perfect. Stimulated questions in younger children about the circus. The animation is well-done, with original music. Kids really related to the animals. *Kid Juror Comments*: The characters, music, and story were very good. They wanted to play circus afterwards. The introduction went over children's heads unless they were familiar with the circus. "We liked to see the animals working together." Video. 56 min.; $12.95; Age: 5-8. Stardom Company, LTD., The.

*** *Clubhouse, The (Cabbage Patch Kids)*

The Cabbage Patch dolls come to life. The boys are in for a big surprise when they challenge the girls to a clubhouse-building competition. *Adult Juror Comments*: Well-produced with good message that discourages gender stereotyping. Straight-forward, interesting, and thoughtful. Stimulates critical thinking skills. "All the characters have memorable personalities that we enjoy." *Kid Juror Comments*: Fun to watch. They enjoyed the songs, wanted to see more. Kids liked the good examples of working together. Some kids thought the doll animation was too babyish. Video. 30 min.; $12.98; Age: 4-8. BMG Home Video.

** Cooperation (You Can Choose!)

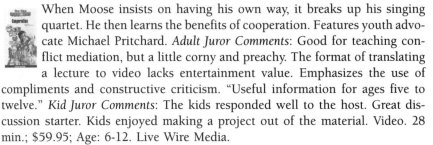

When Moose insists on having his own way, it breaks up his singing quartet. He then learns the benefits of cooperation. Features youth advocate Michael Pritchard. *Adult Juror Comments*: Good for teaching conflict mediation, but a little corny and preachy. The format of translating a lecture to video lacks entertainment value. Emphasizes the use of compliments and constructive criticism. "Useful information for ages five to twelve." *Kid Juror Comments*: The kids responded well to the host. Great discussion starter. Kids enjoyed making a project out of the material. Video. 28 min.; $59.95; Age: 6-12. Live Wire Media.

** Corduroy and Other Bear Stories (Children's Circle)

Features three stories. Corduroy, the toy store teddy bear who longs for a real home, is dramatized in a live-action performance. "Panama," the crate discovered by Little Bear, and "Blueberries for Sal," from the Caldecott award-winning book. *Adult Juror Comments*: This is a nice thematic presentation of children's classics. "Corduroy" is excellent; shows good problem-solving skills. Adults liked lead title best, though the security guard appeared threatening. *Kid Juror Comments*: Held children's interest. They enjoyed seeing books they knew in animated form. Liked the special effects. Encourages reading and literacy. Children who know the books are intrigued by the videos; those who see the videos want to read the books. Video. 38 min.; $14.95; Age: 3-8. Scholastic/Children's Circle.

*** Courage of Lassie

Loyal Lassie stars in the story of Bill, a pup who becomes separated from his family and is accidentally wounded. Elizabeth Taylor plays Kathie Merrick, the young girl who rescues Bill, nurses him back to health, and helps him see what an asset he is. *Adult Juror Comments*: This classic is a great family film. Lassie's experience may be harder for adults to handle than children. It's quite traumatic. "Lassie the collie is a legend and holds up well over time." Scenes of family life are stereotypical of the 1950s. *Kid Juror Comments*: Appealing. Wanted to watch again. Opening scenes drew them in immediately. Kids truly love Lassie. Some parts may be scary to younger children. Girls enjoyed it most. Even though it's somewhat old-fashioned, it has lasting values. Video. 93 min.; $14.95; Age: 6-12. MGM/UA Home Entertainment.

Age 5-8

Video

Family

** Curly Top (Shirley Temple)

Shirley Temple and Rochelle Hudson are orphans who adore the rich, young, and handsome trustee of their orphanage. When he falls in love with Hudson, Temple plays matchmaker. *Adult Juror Comments*: By today's standards, the story line is so unrealistic that even the children noticed it. However, Shirley is still adorable to watch, and the sisters' relationship is affectionate. Some empathized with being orphaned. Little cultural diversity. *Kid Juror Comments*: Younger children were not able to identify with the orphanage setting. They thought Shirley was too perfect, but enjoyed seeing her sing and dance. Girls liked it much more than boys did. They noticed there were no people from different cultures. Video. 74 min.; $19.98; Age: 5-10. Twentieth Century Fox Home Entertainment.

*** Dance Along with the Daise Family (Gullah Gullah Island)

Features an African-American family, and this episode celebrates the culture and language of Gullah Gullah, an island off South Carolina. Kids learn about life issues through interactive singing, dancing, and play. *Adult Juror Comments*: Great tunes with ethnic variety—lots of different danceable beats. "I like that the focus of the program is on an African-American family." Engaging actions stimulated creative movement and encouraged all to "dance their own special way." *Kid Juror Comments*: Enthusiastic response with singing and dancing. They commented on the variety of interesting ethnic characters. "I danced my feet off!" They loved Binyah Binyah Pollywog. "They're awful good at dancing." Video. 30 min.; $9.95; Age: 3-8. Paramount Home Entertainment.

*** Day Jimmy's Boa Ate the Wash and Other Stories, The (Children's Circle)

When Jimmy brings his pet on a field trip, one uproarious incident leads to another. Animated by Michael Sporn. Includes three more book-based titles: "Monty," "The Great White Man-Eating Shark," and "Fourteen Rats & the Rat Catcher." *Adult Juror Comments*: All great stories with good humorous morals, which stimulate an interest in reading the original books. Adults enjoyed watching the programs as much as the kids. *Kid Juror Comments*: Loved it! Appealing absurdity. Each story teaches a lesson. Younger kids like the shark story best. They especially liked the colors, the characters' wording, and the shark trick at the beach. Video. 35 min.; $14.95; Age: 4-9. Scholastic/Children's Circle.

* Dennis the Menace Strikes Again

America's favorite menace is back. When Dennis' grandfather moves in, Mr. Wilson feels he must keep up with his rival. Wilson is conned by bogus ways of regaining his youth. Dennis saves the day by getting Mr. Wilson into precarious situations. *Adult Juror Comments*: Adults had mixed reactions to this title. Contains name-calling, lying, cheating, gender bias, inappropriate language, and bad behavior. Shows characters' concerns for one another, but the slapstick humor often crosses the boundaries of good taste. *Kid Juror Comments*: Dennis makes a lot of trouble for everyone, and kids commented, "Dennis gave us some fun ideas." They appreciated that Dennis tries to do the right thing and be nice, but commented, "The girls are disrespected and older people are treated as stupid." Video. 75 min.; $19.94; Age: 6-12. Warner Home Video.

** Dig Hole Build House (Real World Video)

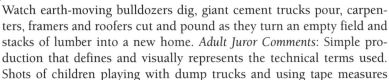

Watch earth-moving bulldozers dig, giant cement trucks pour, carpenters, framers and roofers cut and pound as they turn an empty field and stacks of lumber into a new home. *Adult Juror Comments*: Simple production that defines and visually represents the technical terms used. Shots of children playing with dump trucks and using tape measures encourages kids to mimic these in their play. Shows good cultural mix. *Kid Juror Comments*: Some terminology is too advanced for this age. It's too long to hold kids' attention, better viewed in segments. Children were interested in building something of their own after viewing this. Video. 30 min.; $14.95; Age: 3-10. Real World Video.

** Doing the Right Thing (You Can Choose!)

Doing what's right feels better than doing what you can get away with. When a lost wallet is found on the playground, it brings up the question of what is right. *Adult Juror Comments*: This is a well-produced program, a little long-winded at times, with the right amount of moralizing. It's a good catalyst for discussing honesty and respect. Appropriate for target age group, it's most suited to a school setting. *Kid Juror Comments*: It took some encouragement from the adult leader to get children engaged with the program to discuss it afterwards. Some kids laughed and liked the singing and drama. Others did not. Video. 28 min.; $59.95; Age: 6-12. Live Wire Media.

Chapter Three • Elementary

** Double Double Toil and Trouble
(The Adventures of Mary-Kate and Ashley)

 Make way for spells, witches, wizards, and adventure. It's Halloween, but for Lynn and Kelly Farmer, something scarier could happen. They could lose their home, unless the spirited twins find a way to save it. *Adult Juror Comments*: Amusing. Good family film, especially the black-and-white flashback scenes. Led to discussion about make-believe, safety, and getting along. The girls running off from their parents is not a good role model. Very age-appropriate and appealing. *Kid Juror Comments*: Kids enjoyed a magic word the twins used to make a guy spin. Four- and five-year-olds thought it was scary and the witch was mean. The best part: when the twins dress up as mice. Kids responded to the messages about kindness, love, and caring. Video. 93 min.; $14.95; Age: 5-8. Warner Home Video.

** Dr. Desoto and Other Stories (Children's Circle)

Kindhearted Dr. DeSoto, the mouse dentist, outfoxes a fox. Anthology also includes "Curious George Rides a Bike," "Patrick," and "The Hat." *Adult Juror Comments*: Dr. DeSoto is carried out with glee. The classical music really fits "Patrick." The length is perfect. They are all true to the original. Curious George is iconographic but timeless. *Kid Juror Comments*: Terrific, especially for kids who are familiar with the stories in book form. Dr. DeSoto was their runaway favorite; "Curious George"—second. They were mesmerized by "Patrick." In "The Hat," younger kids were upset by the fire in the baby buggy. Video. 35 min.; $14.95; Age: 3-9. Scholastic/Children's Circle.

* Duke, The

 A dog, Hubert, inherits the royal title of Duke when his owner dies, and he and his companions have silly mishaps. *Adult Juror Comments*: Enjoyable with some reservations. The animals' personalities exude charm, heroism, loyalty, and a sense of justice. The comedy definitely appeals to teens, however it borders on rude and crass behavior. Has some gender stereotyping. *Kid Juror Comments*: Loved seeing animals as the stars of the movie. Hubert the dog is personable with a range of emotions. "Seeing a dog saving the family jewels made me laugh." "My friends liked Daisy and Duke getting married." Video. 88 min.; $19.99; Age: 6-12. Buena Vista Home Entertainment/Disney.

** Elbert's Bad Word/Weird Parents

 "Elbert's Bad Word" is a lesson about how an inadvertent nasty remark can get out of control. Narrated by Ringo Starr. "Weird Parents" teaches the values of tolerance and understanding; narrated by Bette Midler. *Adult Juror Comments*: These are fun and thought-provoking, though the visuals lack dynamics. Younger kids didn't understand why the bad words looked like an insect. The commercial at the beginning was too long and distracting. *Kid Juror Comments*: Funny. They laughed out loud. "Weird Parents" provoked a lot of discussion. "That's just like my parents." Kids accepted this at face value. Video. 30 min.; $12.98; Age: 5-8. Universal Studios Home Video.

*** Elmopalooza (Sesame Street)

Elmo, Big Bird, and the rest of Sesame Street Muppets take over Radio City Music Hall for an all-star show. Rosie O'Donnell, Gloria Estefan, Jon Stewart, Chris Rock, and more join the celebration of thirty years of songs and laughs on Sesame Street. *Adult Juror Comments*: Funny and entertaining. Music makes everyone want to dance. Great humor, superb mix of learning. Kids are exposed to a variety of rhythm and music, plus interesting facts. *Kid Juror Comments*: Entranced and entertained. "I want to hear more songs." "I can mambo now!" "I liked when the Cookie Monster eats the script." "I like to dance with this." Video. 55 min.; $12.98; Age: 5-8. Sony Wonder.

* Emperor's Nightingale

Based on the classic tale by Hans Christian Andersen, tells the story of how a young boy, the Emperor of China, is liberated from his palace of rules and rituals by the beauty of a nightingale's song. *Adult Juror Comments*: This is a beautiful story, though slow-paced for today's kids. The production quality appears dated. The Chinese characters are stereotypically dressed and portrayed. *Kid Juror Comments*: Appealing, but not all kids stayed with it. Considered slow-moving and "kinda dark." Video. 70 min.; $24.95; Age: 6-12. Rembrandt Films.

** Enchanted Tales: Legend of Su-Ling, The (Enchanted Tales)

A Far East fairy tale classic springs to life in this richly animated tale of a handsome prince, the peasant girl he is forbidden to love, and the tiny nightingale who holds the key to their happiness. *Adult Juror Comments*: Teaches values of love, work, and family. Shows a strong female character and sensitive male hero. Songs were catchy. The language is too sophisticated for the audience. Discusses happiness, history, and culture. *Kid Juror Comments*: Enjoyed Su-Ling's character but commented, "I think they were making fun of how Chinese people talk." "Chinese people have fairytales too." "Girls can protect their families too, not just men can be strong." Video. 48 min.; $9.89; Age: 6-10. Sony Wonder.

** Enough Already!
(A Beloved Folktale About Being Grateful)

Brings to life a beloved Jewish tale. "Smooze" is a poor but happy farmer who brings one after another of his barnyard animals into his crowded house. The result is a hilarious lesson in togetherness. *Adult Juror Comments*: Appealing, cute animation, good lessons. Kind and lifelike characters. Good graphics. Some religious content, but it doesn't detract from the story, which is perhaps a little pedantic and outdated. *Kid Juror Comments*: Liked the songs and sang them afterwards. Some kids had trouble understanding the rabbi. It is slow-moving and long for younger viewers. "It's good because I love songs." Video. 26 min.; $14.95; Age: 5-8. Roseberry Entertainment.

*** Ewok Adventure, The

The furry creatures from *Return of the Jedi* crash-land on the planet Endor, befriend a magical Ewok, and search for their missing parents. *Adult Juror Comments*: Cinematography is beautiful and creative. Entertaining family viewing that truly appeals to both children and adults. Grabs and holds your attention. Separation from parents, possibly permanently, is a difficult subject for younger ones. *Kid Juror Comments*: "Children always love animals, real or make-believe." It's surprising how preteen boys were spellbound and openly expressed their fondness for Ewok. The kids really enjoyed the Ewok fight with spiders, and when the Ewoks rescued the parents. Video. 96 min.; $14.95; Age: 4-15. MGM/UA Home Entertainment.

*** Ewoks Battle for Endor

When an army of evil marauders attacks the Ewok village and a young Ewok is kidnapped, his friends set out for the castle fortress of the evil King Terak to rescue him. Thrilling adventure. Story by George Lucas. *Adult Juror Comments*: This classic film of the 80s is visually and technically lavish and compelling. Though it shows violence as a solution, the jurors did not consider it to be gratuitous. *Kid Juror Comments*: Liked the adventure, found it exciting and would definitely want to see it again. "Star Wars" fans in particular adore the characters and story. Both girls and boys enjoy this equally. Video. 98 min.; $14.95; Age: 5-15. MGM/UA Home Entertainment.

Age 5-8

Video

Family

*** Face, The (Stories to Remember)*

Live-action retelling of a traditional Zen Buddhist story about a young boy, a dying storyteller, and the boy's desire to have the old man's magical story mask. The new owner must pass a test of integrity, to grow a plant from a magic seed. *Adult Juror Comments*: Led to intense and productive discussion about honesty. Kept children's attention. An example of storytelling invitingly translated to video. "I enjoyed the story myself, but watching with children was even more enjoyable." Nicely-paced. *Kid Juror Comments*: Funny, sad, and scary. "We liked that the face could see things." "This is a good teaching story. It shows the benefits of being honest." "I liked the fish and the face and how the old man taught the kids to be honest and truthful." Video. 20 min.; $19.95; Age: 5-12. Stories to Remember.

** Families of China (Families of The World)*

Chinese children tell about a typical day in a tea farming family and an urban professional family. The segments show real-life activities, people, and places. *Adult Juror Comments*: Educational, accurately portrays different cultures and lifestyles. Shows how Chinese children are taught consideration and respect at an early age. Well-suited for social studies curriculum. *Kid Juror Comments*: Kids enjoyed comparing the Chinese way of life with their own. They enjoyed learning how their peers in China live and play. They wanted to know more about raising butterflies and were curious about the cartoons the Chinese kids watched. Video. 29 min.; $19.95; Age: 6-12. Arden Media Resources.

** Families of Puerto Rico (Families of the World)*

Puerto Rican children tell about a typical day in the life of a banana-farming family and an urban professional family. Shows real-life activities, people, and places. *Adult Juror Comments*: Engaging and very real. Shows good family relationships between the main characters. Information is presented in a easy-to-follow format, using a child as the guide. Introduces new vocabulary. *Kid Juror Comments*: Enjoyed learning about life in Puerto Rico. Liked how it shows people working cooperatively. "I liked the mother who farmed bananas and flowers. I think I would like to farm too." Were fascinated by the hurricanes and frogs in the bathroom. Video. 29 min.; $19.95; Age: 6-12. Arden Media Resources.

** Famous Fred (Doors of Wonder)

Looks at the life of a cat named Fred, from kitten-hood through meeting of his mentor, Kenneth the Guinea Pig. He doesn't handle stardom well, and the price of fame catches up. Based on book by Posy Simmonds. Academy Award nomination, Best Animated Short. *Adult Juror Comments*: Illustrates the joy and challenge of owning a pet. Shows the making of a star through a little talent and a lot of glitter. Jurors had concerns about the music and Fred's "resurrection." Presented death in a tasteful, humorous, and age appropriate manner. *Kid Juror Comments*: Thought the British humor was funny. Kids liked dancing along with the rock 'n roll music. "Fred reminded me of my pet that died, but he had one life left that we wanted to know more about." "Makes you wonder what cats really talk about." Video. 30 min.; $12.98; Age: 4-10. Sony Wonder.

*** Fantasia 2000 (Mickey Mouse)

Beginning where the original Fantasia left off, in these seven segments, the images of flamingos bobbing yo-yos to a city in bluesy motion bring music to life. Includes "The Sorcerer's Apprentice" and classical music favorites. *Adult Juror Comments*: Wondrous animation accompanied by stupendous orchestral music. Great fantasy of images and sound. Encourages interest in the arts and creativity. Lots of room to explore one's imagination in interpreting the story. Respectful of race, gender, and culture *Kid Juror Comments*: Mesmerized. Loved the graphics. "This was really cool." "The Firebird Suite was really bright, and the music fit really well." "I loved the whale segment. I thought they were flying, then swimming. I guess you were supposed to think both." Video. 74 min.; $19.98; Age: 5-18. Buena Vista Home Entertainment/Disney.

*** Ferngully 2: The Magical Rescue

Return to the magical forest of Ferngully, where Batty, Crystal, Pips, and the Beetle Boys embark on a great adventure to save natural resources. *Adult Juror Comments*: Appealing. A modern fairy tale that explores environmental issues at a child's level. Very well-produced, with good role models. A wonderful discussion starter about the environment and kids' role in conservation. *Kid Juror Comments*: Big success. Provoked comments about respect for the environment as well as one another. They loved the animals, but they thought the "bad men" looked unrealistic. Video. 73 min.; $19.98; Age: 4-12. Twentieth Century Fox Home Entertainment.

*** Ferngully: The Last Rainforest

 In this brilliantly colored animated feature, a young man, joined by magical spirits of the rainforest, saves Ferngully from destruction. Based on a best-selling book from Australia. Includes Robin Williams, Sheena Easton, Raffi, Ton-Loc, and others. *Adult Juror Comments*: Age-appropriate. Heightens concern about environmental issues. Music and animation are delightful. Promotes compassion for living things. Forest creatures are respectful of one another. Lumberjacks are stereotyped as careless. *Kid Juror Comments*: Sat wide-eyed throughout the screening, laughing at everything Batty said. "We liked the girl hero." Danced and sang along. "The colors and sounds were beautiful." Asked questions about it for several days afterwards. Video. 76 min.; $14.99; Age: 6-12. Twentieth Century Fox Home Entertainment.

** Fingermouse, Yoffy, and Friends

In each sequence, Yoffy the puppeteer sends Fingermouse and some of his finger-puppet friends on various voyages. With each voyage his friends collect different objects and wisdom that are used to tell a story. *Adult Juror Comments*: This is delightfully simple, yet intriguing. Says a lot about the power of imagination and storytelling. It could motivate creative work after viewing or stimulate children's problem-solving skills. Probably appeals to a limited audience. *Kid Juror Comments*: The stories went over nicely. Wanted to make finger-puppets, discuss the stories, and write stories of their own after viewing. The first part was lengthy, but the rest of it held the kids' attention. They loved the music and watched it again. Video. 180 min.; $19.95; Age: 3-8. Applause Video.

** Fire Busters

 Explores the world of firefighting, in which helicopters, planes, boats, and trucks are the tools of the trade. Teaches the importance of teamwork and fire safety. Good song and dance. *Adult Juror Comments*: Simple production that shows examples of cooperation and teamwork. Promotes positive messages about recycling and cleaning up. Fire fighting footage provoked a lot of discussion after viewing the tape. The music is catchy; the host is appropriate. *Kid Juror Comments*: Fascinated. It held their attention and prompted many questions about safety issues. They asked to see the helicopter and sea plane section again. Video. 30 min.; $12.95; Age: 4-7. Azure Blues, Inc.

Chapter Three • Elementary

*** Flipper*

The film that brought world awareness to the amazing intelligence of dolphins in a story about a young boy who develops a unique friendship with a wounded dolphin and loves him as a friend. Stars Chuck Conners as the fisherman. *Adult Juror Comments*: Excellent family film with timely messages and positive role models. Content is great. Story is well-presented. Cinematography is beautiful. It's educational. Requires a good attention span and thinking skills. Parts are completely unrealistic. *Kid Juror Comments*: Stands the test of time. Older kids enjoyed it most. Younger kids ask lots of questions about the story details. Opening may be a little slow, but after becoming engaged, the kids responded well. Most appropriate for six- to ten-year-olds. Video. 91 min.; $14.95; Age: 3-11. MGM/UA Home Entertainment.

** Flipper's New Adventure*

Sandy and Flipper are threatened by the impending construction of a freeway to be built on their property. To avoid losing Flipper to the local aquarium, Sandy retreats to the sea with him. *Adult Juror Comments*: While the story is a bit corny, it's sweet. The talents of Flipper are fantastic. It starts out slowly, but gains momentum when they get to the island. "Flipper is the hero." Underwater photography is outstanding. *Kid Juror Comments*: Opening is slow and didn't pull children in. Once they became engaged in the story, they enjoy it. Kids love to watch Flipper's antics. Video. 95 min.; $14.95; Age: 4-12. MGM/UA Home Entertainment.

** Follow the Drinking Gourd (American Heroes and Legends)*

Based on the traditional American folk song, the compelling adventures of one family's escape from slavery via the Underground Railroad. Narrated by Morgan Freeman; score by Taj Mahal. *Adult Juror Comments*: Iconographic presentation. Shows the hardships of the journey to freedom. Follows the story book of the same title and shows strength of people believing in a better life. Uses story-telling and legends to teach history and life's lessons. *Kid Juror Comments*: "Why don't the pictures move?" Asked about the Underground Railroad. Commented that they liked learning history from cartoons. "I like how the slaves knew they had to be free, even though it was scary to escape. Everybody should be free." Video. 30 min.; $8.95; Age: 5-12. Rabbit Ears Production.

*** *Fool Moon and Other Stories, The (Jingaroo)*

 Follow a treasure map to a lost ship in the desert. What happens when the Groote gets a love letter by mistake? How does Victoria win her most important game? Find out with Jingaroo and his friends in these short stories and music videos. *Adult Juror Comments*: Engaging and challenging. Great animation and audio—catchy lyrics. Stories address friendship, recognition, and misunderstanding. "Diversity is presented so that the audience can relate to it." *Kid Juror Comments*: Kids related to the lessons taught in the stories and enjoyed the music. "They are very funny stories." "I thought the characters were honest and friendly with one another." "It taught me not to brag." "It's important to share and to get along." Video. 30 min.; $14.95; Age: 2-8. Beckett Entertainment.

*** *Fox and The Hound, The*

A lonely widow adopts an orphaned fox cub named Tod. The mischievous fox soon meets up with Copper, an adorable hound puppy. As the innocent pair grow up together in the forest, they become inseparable friends. But their friendship is soon tested. *Adult Juror Comments*: Excellent production of a timeless tale about friendship, caring, and loyalty. Loving, gentle, comforting style. Good, clear conflict and solid resolution. Powerful tool to teach children social skills. Vibrant animation, emotional expressions. *Kid Juror Comments*: Went from teary-eyed to smiling to laughing aloud. Unanimously said they'd watch it again. "Cool, lots of action and funny." "My friend was really nice to me, then really mean, then nice again—like Copper and Todd. People change over time." Video. 83 min.; $22.99; Age: 5-8. Buena Vista Home Entertainment/Disney.

*** *Franklin Plays the Game (Franklin)*

Franklin's soccer team loses every game, but he's still determined to be the best player on the team. He learns to put his team ahead of himself as he rallies them for the final game. Also includes the episode "Franklin and the Red Scooter." *Adult Juror Comments*: Great moral content, sweet characters. Franklin sorts through situations to find solutions, shows good sportsmanship and cooperation. Offers insight into familiar problems. "I loved that boys and girls both played soccer." *Kid Juror Comments*: Kids related enthusiastically to the theme of team spirit. Loved the cartoon turtle and friends of all different shapes and sizes. They learned about turning negative feelings into positive ones. "Sharing is nice." Video. 25 min.; $12.95; Age: 3-8. U.S.A. Home Entertainment.

Chapter Three • Elementary

** *Frog and Toad Are Friends (John Matthews Collection)*

 Frog and Toad star in five claymation short stories of friendship that are faithful to the book in letter, appearance, and wit. *Adult Juror Comments*: Outstanding claymation and music. Demonstrates cooperation, sharing, and friendship. Deals with relationships suitable for this age. Stimulated one child juror to write a letter as described in story. Slow-paced. *Kid Juror Comments*: Liked the stories a lot. Enjoyed seeing the book come alive and were fascinated by the technical demonstration on the claymation process. The second segment is more appropriate for older children than the first part. Video. 25 min.; $12.95; Age: 4-9. Sony Wonder.

* *Fruit & Jingles: A Learning Experience (Fruit & Jingles)*

In true clown fashion, transforms a series of adventures and misadventures into positive learning experiences: fair play, safety, sharing, cooperation, perseverance, and more. *Adult Juror Comments*: Funny situations are used to teach lessons. Discussion centers on safety, making friends, littering, and valuing differences. The pace is slow and the characters are so silly that they are irritating and even condescending. *Kid Juror Comments*: Funny clowns. "It made me want to find out if there are more Fruits and Jingle videos." "I learned it's good to share things and that you should wear a bike helmet." Kids said they understood everything and liked the music. Video. 30 min.; $19.95; Age: 4-7. Eye Candy Productions.

** *Fun and Fancy Free*

Two timeless tales are presented on the same video: "Bongo" and "Mickey and the Beanstalk." Features the voice of Walt Disney as Mickey, and combines live action with animation. *Adult Juror Comments*: Easy to watch. Lovely, upbeat production. Pleasant social interactions between characters. Somewhat old-fashioned. Bonus section on making the movie is worthwhile. *Kid Juror Comments*: Put them in a good mood. "I had never heard of it before, so I didn't want to watch it...but it was good!" "Some of the music was mushy, but the pictures were good. They looked pretty real." "I like that the bears slap each other for love. That was funny." Video. 73 min.; $22.99; Age: 5-8. Buena Vista Home Entertainment/Disney.

Age 5-8

Video

Family

** Fun House Mystery
(The Adventures of Mary-Kate and Ashley)

 The pint-size twins take a spin on spine-tingling amusement park rides and then team up with some hilarious pirates of the midway to catch the monster that lurks inside the freaky Fun House. *Adult Juror Comments*: Appeals to kids interested in youthful detective stories. Introduces the idea of using reference materials. Alliteration and tongue twisters abound. Non-violent and entertaining. Teaches the value of facing our fears. Songs are cute. *Kid Juror Comments*: Enjoyed the twins and their singing. Liked following the mystery and clues and solving the problem. "It was funny when they screamed at the orangutan. My friends would like the scary monster part." Video. 30 min.; $12.95; Age: 5-8. Warner Home Video.

** Funniest Animal Families (Animal Crackups)

Features animal parents and their babies playing, learning, and having fun. Zak and C-Mor show amazing animals from around the world such as gorillas and octopi. Full of cute, cuddly animals and songs. *Adult Juror Comments*: Interesting animal facts presented in a laugh-out-loud format. Beautiful underwater footage. Ideal for family viewing. Some jurors found the narrators disruptive to the continuity of the film because they interrupted and were rude. *Kid Juror Comments*: Slapstick humor a hit with the kids. Loved the silly narrators. "I didn't know octopi were so coordinated." "My favorite animals are in Africa." Kids said they'd watch it again. "I want my friends to see this." Video. 30 min.; $14.99; Age: 4-8. E-Realbiz.

* Garfields's Feline Fantasies

Garfield's ruminations take him in and out of creative, imaginative daydreams with inventive scenarios. With clever script and characters, Garfield's adventures take him all over the world. Encourages children to use their imaginations. *Adult Juror Comments*: Entertaining but sexist. Lots of name-calling, like "slobber-job" and "fatso." Displays positive messages such as "feeling good about yourself." Shows people drinking and smoking. Animation is appealing and the focus on imagination encouraging. *Kid Juror Comments*: Pretty silly. They liked watching Garfield in his many adventures. Most would watch it again. Some commented on the smoking and drinking. Video. 23 min.; $5.98; Age: 5-10. Twentieth Century Fox Home Entertainment.

Age 5-8

Video

Family

Chapter Three • Elementary

*** Goldilocks and the Three Bears

 Goldie, a ten-year-old orphaned city girl, is sent to live with her uncle, deep in a forest, where Goldie discovers three bears who can talk. The bears realize she is the new protector of their enchanted forest and find their work cut out for them. *Adult Juror Comments*: Well-made and appealing with good messages. Animals and environment are cute and friendly. Could generate interest and discussion about orphans, the environment, lifestyles, and personal relationships. It's well-paced and the perfect length. *Kid Juror Comments*: "The movie was creative, the acting was good, the forest is important." "I want to know how to stop people from cutting down trees." Kids also pointed out their awareness that "Bears can't really talk." Video. 85 min.; $19.95; Age: 6-12. Nexus Media International.

* Great Easter Egg Hunt, The (Golden Tales-Hallmark)

Whiskers, a bean bag rabbit, becomes the real Easter Bunny when he saves the life of a little boy named Peter. Intertwines themes of selflessness, giving, and Easter. *Adult Juror Comments*: Entertaining. Flows well and has a happy ending, but lacks originality. Many aspects of the story are drawn from the classic, "The Velveteen Rabbit." Lacks cultural diversity and stereotypes gender role models. *Kid Juror Comments*: Would watch again. "I liked the magic from the Easter Bunny." "It is important to help people you care about." "I liked the way the toys came to life." "It made me feel good when Peter found the gifts from the Easter Bunny." Video. 48 min.; $12.98; Age: 5-8. Golden Films.

* Great Land of Small, The (Les Productions La Fête)

When two children from New York spend a weekend with their grandparents, they befriend one of the little people, whose gold dust has been stolen. They journey to the Great Land of Small, where they meet some weird characters before all ends well. *Adult Juror Comments*: This imaginative fantasy is wonderfully creative, but slow-moving and dark. Special effects are well–done; the story is executed with care. Appeals to a limited audience. Adult characters are not well-developed. *Kid Juror Comments*: Some scenes seem staged, and the pace is at times tedious. The Land of Small goes on for too long. The scenes in which the children become immortal and can't return home are not comprehensible by the intended age group. Video. 91 min.; $29.95; Age: 4-10. Productions La Fête.

* Gulliver's Travels (Enchanted Tales)

This new adaptation of Jonathan Swift's classic adventure is filled with original songs and kooky characters, and stars Gulliver, the shipwrecked "giant," and the tiny Lilliputians who discover him. *Adult Juror Comments*: Good introduction to classical music. Singing and humor are suitable. Shows how being "good" brings rewards. May encourage kids to read this classic story. Animation quality is mediocre, and the program is front-loaded with commercials. *Kid Juror Comments*: Gulliver was a hero, especially to the younger ones. They did think it was a bit wordy and too silly. Older children followed the story best. They liked the music. Video. 48 min.; $9.98; Age: 6-9. Sony Wonder.

* Hansel and Gretel: An Opera Fantasy (Children's Cultural Collection)

This version of Engelbert Humperdinck's 1893 opera stars hand-sculpted dolls and lavish sets that create a fantasy land of eerie beauty. The soundtrack received a Grammy nomination. *Adult Juror Comments*: Although there is background noise, the music is lovely. Animation style is dated and pace seems slow. Hansel and Gretel have a babyish quality. *Kid Juror Comments*: Younger kids loved it and watched it again. The music and the puppets were a big hit. Some older kids found it too slow. It was difficult for sophisticated music listeners. Video. 72 min.; $19.98; Age: 6-12. V.I.E.W. Video.

*** Harold and the Purple Crayon (Children's Circle)

An anthology of adaptations of the books by Crockett Johnson, including: "Harold and the Purple Crayon," "Harold's Fairy Tale," and "A Picture for Harold's Room." *Adult Juror Comments*: The stories have universal appeal and lend themselves to imagination and fantasy on a child's part. The adaptations are true to the original books. *Kid Juror Comments*: Terrific! All ages enjoyed this. Six- to eight-year-olds made sense of Harold's crayon animation. Younger kids enjoyed it, but were confused. "My eight-year-old watched it off-and-on all weekend." Video. 30 min.; $14.95; Age: 3-8. Scholastic/Children's Circle.

* Hercules (Enchanted Tales)

Journey back in time to an age of mysteries, superhuman deeds, and mystical adventures. Hercules is a mortal with the strength of a god, destined to become one of the greatest kings ever. But first, he must thwart the plots of his enemies. *Adult Juror Comments*: The dialects and modernizing slightly obscured the story, making it a confusing representation of the myth. Mediocre animation, but the music is engaging. Theme is appropriate for this age. *Kid Juror Comments*: Because of its length, the kids had difficulty staying focused. The story went over the heads of younger children. For older children, it sparked an interest in Greek mythology. Video. 48 min.; $9.98; Age: 4-8. Sony Wonder.

Chapter Three • Elementary

** Herman and Marguerite (Jay O'Callahan)

 Herman, a fearful worm, befriends an equally anxious caterpillar, Marguerite. They learn to love and respect each other as they help bring spring to the earth. *Adult Juror Comments*: Wonderful storytelling, production requires viewers' imagination. Somewhat disappointing in parts.

Kid Juror Comments: Requires patience and attention. Some did not "get it" or understand the language. Others thought it was just beautiful. Video. 28 min.; $19.95; Age: 5-12. Vineyard Productions.

** Horton Hatches the Egg - Dr. Seuss
(Dr. Seuss Video Classics)

Horton the Elephant agrees to help Mayzie the lazy bird. While she takes a "short" vacation, he sits on her egg, enduring terrible snowstorms and jeering friends. Narrated by Billy Crystal. *Adult Juror Comments*: Good themes. Appropriate short-story length. Iconographic presentation lacks dynamics and doesn't compare with most contemporary titles which are fully animated. *Kid Juror Comments*: The rhyming verse went over well. This makes for a good introduction to the book and to reading for oneself. It's best viewed in two segments. Video. 30 min.; $6.98; Age: 4-8. Sony Wonder.

** How the West Was Fun
(The Adventures of Mary-Kate and Ashley)

 Mary-Kate and Ashley lead the battle of wits and wills to save the beloved ranch in this feature-length comedy. *Adult Juror Comments*: Fun, good production quality. Appealing characters although a simplistic plot. May create curiosity about mining, camping, nature, and solving problems as they arise. Shows kids working together for their family. Men were shown in a non-traditional light. *Kid Juror Comments*: Liked seeing the girls sing and dance, although they found the story line to be old fashioned. Favorite parts: the treasure hunt for gold and building a sand castle. "Lots of funny things happened at the ranch. It would be fun to live there." Video. 93 min.; $14.95; Age: 5-8. Warner Home Video.

* In Search of the Haunted Gold Mine (Adventures of Dave & Becky, The)

 Dave and Becky are reporters for the hottest children's newspaper in the country "The Daily Adventure." Their assignment: investigate rumors about a haunted gold mine deep in the woods. The adventure also includes safe camping tips. *Adult Juror Comments*: The safety tips provide valuable information for potential campers. Segment on caring for animals was well-done. Some adults disliked the humor and the gender stereotypes. It portrays a smart woman and a dumb man. *Kid Juror Comments*: Those who enjoy camping thought it was great, responding well to the hosts and their humor. "Good camping ideas. I learned about hypothermia." One five-year-old found some parts scary. Video. 37 min.; $12.99; Age: 6-11. Daily Adventure, LTD. Dave Hood Entertainment.

** In Search of the Willie T (Roundabout Tales)

A pirate who lost his ship heads out to search for it. He boards a schooner, a Coast Guard buoy tender, and a submarine. This tongue-in-cheek adventure has laugh potential for kids and adults. *Adult Juror Comments*: It should be made clear this is a documentary about vessels. Characters were enjoyable. Shows variety of ships, compares past technologies to today's. Covers water safety and other boating subjects. *Kid Juror Comments*: "This was interesting. I learned a lot about ships." "The captain was a nice pirate." Kids liked the songs. "We used to not know how submarines and torpedoes worked." Lots of interesting information is covered. Video. 25 min.; $11; Age: 5-8. Sobo Video Productions, Inc.

*** Indian in the Cupboard, The

Based on an award-winning, best-selling children's book, "Indian in the Cupboard" is a touching tale of nine-year-old Omri, who magically brings his three-inch toy Indian to life. Together they embark upon a fabulous adventure. *Adult Juror Comments*: Very engaging. This is a wonderful extension of the book series. Kids portrayed characters from the program for weeks after viewing. It offers respect for the Native American culture and kept the kids' attention. *Kid Juror Comments*: Fine, in general. Those familiar with the book responded particularly well. "There was a little bit of fighting between the characters, but good fighting." It motivated the children to further explore Native American culture. Video. 98 min.; $14.95; Age: 5-8. Columbia Tristar Home Entertainment.

** It Takes Two (The Adventures of Mary-Kate and Ashley)

What does it take to bring a single, attractive orphanage case worker and a widowed corporate zillionaire together? It takes sly maneuvers, crazy mix-ups, and clever switcheroos. Most of all it takes two Olsen twins. *Adult Juror Comments*: Positive story in which the girls resolve problems such as anger and conflict between themselves and the adults. Set in a real world with valid social pressures. Acting is believable and endearing. Stimulates kids and parents to communicate better. *Kid Juror Comments*: Captured attention for the entire story. Kids cheered the twins' success. They discussed how everyone is capable and worthy of love and how the girls worked together to make their wish come true. Best parts were New York City and summer camp. Video. 101 min.; $19.98; Age: 5-8. Warner Home Video.

*** It Was My Best Birthday Ever, Charlie Brown (Peanuts)

The Peanuts kids get together for their blanket-toting pal's birthday party. Linus wants all his friends to come to his party. Most of all, the birthday boy wants a very special guest to be there. He invites Mimi. *Adult Juror Comments*: Engages both kids and adults. Good cultural diversity, appropriate humor, and good manners. Sibling and safety issues are handled well. "I like the use of music, foreign language, and safety themes." "One of the best videos I've ever seen." *Kid Juror Comments*: Upbeat, fun, well-paced, and very enjoyable. Children love this video. Motivated discussions after about how to celebrate birthdays and the concept of an RSVP Kids sang along. "I'd like to take it home and share it with my family." Video. 25 min.; $12.95; Age: 4-9. Paramount Home Entertainment.

** It Zwibble: Earthday Birthday

Celebrate Earth Day with a comical clan of modern-day dinosaurs dedicated to protecting the planet. *Adult Juror Comments*: Somewhat convoluted story for this audience with a weak ending that seems abrupt. Mediocre animation. In the end, though, the characters are excellent role models and make the whole thing engaging. *Kid Juror Comments*: Good, although they noticed that it seemed somewhat fabricated. Some asked to watch again. Others didn't. Video. 30 min.; $9.98; Age: 3-10. Artisan/Family Home Entertainment.

*** Ivan and His Magic Pony
(Mikhail Baryshnikov's Stories from My Childhood)

Ivan, a simple country lad, and his magic pony encounter fantastic creatures and adventure in this classic Russian tale with award-winning animation and the voices of Rob Lowe and Hector Elizondo. *Adult Juror Comments*: Thoughtful, splendid animation with some adult humor. Ivan, the archetypal fool, triumphs in the end because he has good character. Some violence falls within the context of the tale. *Kid Juror Comments*: Great! "It was very funny when the king jumped into the milk." "My friend would think it was very good." "This movie was good for kids." "I love seeing the horses." Video. 60 min.; $19.98; Age: 5-8. Video Information Source.

** James Marshall Library, The (Children's Circle)

Contains four fully animated titles: "Wings: A Tale of Two Chickens," "Goldilocks and the Three Bears," "The Three Little Pigs," and "Red Riding Hood." *Adult Juror Comments*: The animation is charming, the humor appropriate, the pace slow. These three classics are all clever and a delight to watch. Inspired viewers to check the books out from the library. Some values from traditional fairy tales are inappropriate today. *Kid Juror Comments*: The humor held their attention. Enjoyed the repetition of "I'll huff and I'll puff." Kids made houses afterwards as an art project. Video. 43 min.; $14.95; Age: 4-8. Scholastic/Children's Circle.

** Joey Runs Away and Other Stories (Children's Circle)

Includes "Joey Runs Away," about a young kangaroo who ventures out of his mother's pouch, "The Cow Who Fell in the Canal," "The Bear and the Fly," and "The Most Wonderful Egg in the World." *Adult Juror Comments*: These timeless adaptations are charming stories, artfully told. Well-paced with wonderful music accompaniment. The length is fine for this age. Celebrates diversity. *Kid Juror Comments*: Many stories were new to them, and those familiar with the books loved watching them as videos. Kids not familiar with the books were inspired to read them. Video. 28 min.; $14.95; Age: 3-8. Scholastic/Children's Circle.

** John Henry (American Heroes and Legends)

Denzel Washington recalls the legend of John Henry, who single-handedly defeated a steam drill in a steel-driving competition. Score is by B.B. King. *Adult Juror Comments*: Iconographic production, lacks full motion. Inspiring music. The visuals are artistically executed, and the narration is poetic. One juror commented, "I felt like I was sitting on a front porch admiring the Spanish moss." *Kid Juror Comments*: Kids asked why the pictures didn't move. This tall tale, new to many of the kids, was great. It prompted discussions about literal exaggerations. They enjoyed Denzel Washington's narration and the music, but found it slow-moving. Video. 30 min.; $8.95; Age: 5-12. Rabbit Ears Production.

** Johnny Appleseed (American Heroes and Legends)

Retelling the story of the benevolent naturalist who roamed the Ohio Valley region in the 1800s, planting apple orchards and spreading good will. Read by Garrison Keillor. *Adult Juror Comments*: Iconographic presentation is slow-moving. Good introduction to a legendary American figure. Perfect blend of watercolor illustrations, narration, and music. Invites discussion about this complex frontiersman and the riches he brings to settlers. *Kid Juror Comments*: An unusual pleasure. Afterwards, they wanted to plant apple trees. They discussed the quality of this production compared to other, more commercial videos they have seen. Conclusion: artistically executed, but not always engaging and a little boring. Video. 30 min.; $8.95; Age: 6-12. Rabbit Ears Production.

** Johnny Tsunami (Disney Channel)

A teen surfing sensation who, with the help of some new friends, learns to master the art of snowboarding and thus ends a long-standing school rivalry. *Adult Juror Comments*: Enjoyable. An appealing contrast of climate, activities, and personalities. Spectacular surfing, snowboarding, and skiing scenes. Good parenting and good coping skills shown. Lots of risk-taking behaviors. *Kid Juror Comments*: Glued to it throughout, particularly the boys. Related well to the grandfather character and to peer situations. "They aren't like me, but have similar feelings and problems." "I try to please my father and make him proud of me, too." "Awesome snowboarding!" Video. 90 min.; rental only; Age: 6-12. Buena Vista Home Entertainment/Disney.

* Josie and the Pussycats: Chile Today, Hot Tamale

Josie and the Pussycats, the all-girl rock band, travel to Mexico for fiestas and south-of-the-border fun. Adult Juror Comments: Fun '70s cartoon show comes with some '70s baggage and skimpy clothes. Light fare with gender stereotyping. Choppy sequences and songs don't seem to work with story. Fighting scenes go on and on, designed to make kids laugh at the expense of others. Kid Juror Comments: Everybody had fun. Lots of dancing and singing. "I like to sing. I'm going to have a band when I grow up." "The Pussycats help each other, except Alexandria. But things never work out for her." "Sometimes the characters don't get along." Video. 95 min.; $14.95; Age: 5-10. Warner Home Video.

Age 5-8

Video

Family

* Josie and the Pussycats: The Melody Memory Mix-Up

Josie and the Pussycats, the all-girl rock band, go to Hawaii for an unforgettable tropical experience including a run-in with the evil mastermind, The Hawk, who is scheming to steal a secret force-field formula and take over the world. Adult Juror Comments: Fun and nostalgic if a little dated. Animation style gives hip retro appeal. Gender stereotyping, especially with a dumb blonde. Some explosions and guns, and some name calling. Scientific inaccuracies abound. Kid Juror Comments: Slapstick comedy cracked them up. Had fun trying to solve the mysteries. "The story is fun - the songs are kind of weird, though." "There are definitely good guys and bad guys." "We like that Sebastian is a cat who can understand everything!" Video. 95 min.; $14.95; Age: 5-10. Warner Home Video

** Journey Beneath the Sea (Oz Kids)

Jack Pumpkinhead wants to have an adventure in the worst way. The Oz Kids embark on a sea cruise in a leaky boat. Befriended by two mermaids, they explore the underwater world until their tour is cut short by sea devils and the evil Zog. Adult Juror Comments: Contains some good messages, such as "It takes too much time to hate." Too long for this age. The language, animation, and format are fine. "What child doesn't like an adventure with queens, castles, and mermaids?" Kid Juror Comments: First-rate animation and characters. "You could tell the story without sound because the animation was so good." Kids liked how the characters helped each other. Video. 66 min.; $12.95; Age: 5-8. Paramount Home Entertainment.

** Journey Home: The Animals of Farthingwood

Heroic Fox, dutiful Badger, shy Mole, playful Weasel, and their friends are on the move. These are the animals of Farthingwood, looking for a land free of bulldozers and humans—a safe place to call home. From best-selling children's books. Adult Juror Comments: Charming story but too long. Sad in parts, but great voices and enchanting characters. Death of the animals was a little too sad for those under six. Good humor, great message about how hard it is to work together. Kid Juror Comments: "You get the feeling it is a very long journey." "The animals are cute. I didn't like that they died." Kids liked the value of the animals of "mutual protection" helping the younger, small animals. Younger kids found it too long. Video. 120 min.; $14.98; Age: 5-10. Twentieth Century Fox Home Entertainment.

*** Kratts' Creatures: Checkin' Out Chimps (Kratts Creatures)

Swing around with Chris and Martin Kratts as they explore Africa and discover the wild chimpanzee. You'll see how chimps can be smart, playful, and a whole lot of laughs. Adult Juror Comments: "Yes, yes, yes!" Fascinating, hilarious, educational, and entertaining—surprising facts and new vocabulary. Excellent personal interaction and great messages about animal respect. Excellent teaching tool. *Kid Juror Comments*: Funny, sad, and informative. "Those chimps are cute." Kids love exploring with the Kratts brothers. The creatures fascinated them. "Animals are neat." "I didn't know they did all those things." Video. 25 min.; $12.95; Age: 5-11. U.S.A. Home Entertainment.

** Kristen's Fairy House

Join Kristen as she vacations on a small island off the New England coast with her aunt Tracy, an artist. Tracy is creating a picture book about "fairy houses" built in the woods by visiting children. A special relationship develops between them. *Adult Juror Comments*: Enjoyable, easy to watch, though very low-key. There is no conflict, no character development. There is a natural rapport between adult and child and a link between nature and art, imagination and life. Further inquiry is possible for make-believe. *Kid Juror Comments*: They liked how the pictures tell the story. Girls liked it more than boys. Some thought it too slow. Children were interested in building a fairy house. Video. 40 min.; $19.99; Age: 5-8. Great White Dog Picture Co.

*** Land Before Time I, The (The Land Before Time)

A young bracheosaurus suddenly finds himself alone in this prehistoric adventure. He meets up with four other young dinosaurs that join him on his quest for the legendary lush feeding grounds of Great Valley. *Adult Juror Comments*: Elegantly crafted, adventurous, suspenseful. Story easy to follow with a bit of hard truth. Littlefoot's mother dies early in the movie. Offers acceptable range of scary elements for this age and great lessons about friendship and acceptance of others. *Kid Juror Comments*: Enthralled. "My friends would like it because they like dinosaurs like me." "It's sad when Littlefoot's mommy dies." "Not all the dinosaurs liked Littlefoot at first. Later they became friends." "When Sharp tooth chased them into the cave, it was scary." Video. 69 min.; $19.98; Age: 4-10. Universal Studios Home Video.

*** Land Before Time II, The - The Great Valley Adventure (The Land Before Time).

The prehistoric pals Littlefoot, Cera, Spike, Ducky, and Petrie return in this new movie with original songs, colorful animation, and the beloved dinosaurs from "The Land Before Time." *Adult Juror Comments*: Tells a highly moral story without being preachy. Excellent, high-quality animation. Teaches kids to accept differences as well as how to get along with one another. A little too violent and scary for younger audiences. *Kid Juror Comments*: Entertaining. Grasped the message: Parents have reasons for the things they do and that they're not just trying to keep you from having fun. Two-year-olds found it too scary. Video. 74 min.; $19.98; Age: 4-10. Universal Studios Home Video.

*** Land Before Time III - The Time of Great Giving, The (The Land Before Time)

When a huge meteorite plunges into the Great Valley, it cuts off the water supply to the dinosaurs. Searching for more water, Littlefoot and his friends find a large trapped pool. They learn how they can move mountains by working together. *Adult Juror Comments*: A morality play that rewards cooperation, delivers environmental messages, and rewards good thinking. Shows how diverse groups can co-exist and become friends. "Virtue is rewarded, and kids are the heroes." The songs and music are engaging. *Kid Juror Comments*: The characters are wonderful. Many were familiar with them. "The raptors are cool." Some kids thought the songs were too long, others were mesmerized. "The long necks told the other dinosaurs to share. People should share also." Video. 71 min.; $19.98; Age: 4-8. Universal Studios Home Video.

*** Land Before Time IV - Journey Through the Mists, The (The Land Before Time)

Littlefoot, Cera, Spike, Ducky, Petrie, and shy newcomer, Ali, set off in search of a mysterious, healing flower that grows only in the Land of Mists. A song-filled, animated addition to the continuing story of The Land Before Time. *Adult Juror Comments*: Excellent, well-produced. Opportunities to discuss friendships, making new friends, and the impact of moving frequently. The characters are very sweet. Some scenes are scary. Teamwork is emphasized. Appealing songs support messages in story. *Kid Juror Comments*: Great happy ending. They empathize with Little Foot. "Little Foot is very brave and good to his friends because he can't do everything himself." Children wanted to watch this again and talked about it with one another. Video. 74 min.; $19.98; Age: 4-7. Universal Studios Home Video.

*** Land Before Time V: The Mysterious Island, The (The Land Before Time)

Beyond the Great Valley lies an island of beauty and mystery. In this wondrous place, Littlefoot, Cera, Spike, Ducky, and Petrie discover old and new friends, face exciting challenges, and share the adventure of a lifetime. *Adult Juror Comments*: Good animation, characters, music, and scenery. Teaches children to respect racial differences, emphasizes the importance of friends and family, and promotes the concept of collaboration. The earthquake, sharks, and carnivorous dinosaurs were scary. *Kid Juror Comments*: Very cute. It held everyone's interest. Kids wanted to watch it again with their friends. They thought some of the characters were frightening and mean. They liked Chomper best. "Good music." "I like when they got back with their mommy and daddy." Video. 74 min.; $19.98; Age: 4-10. Universal Studios Home Video.

*** Land Before Time VI: Secret of Saurus Rock, The (The Land Before Time)

 On a distant edge of the Great Valley stands mysterious Saurus Rock. The twin baby Threehorns, Dianah, and Dana have run away to find it. It's up to Littlefoot, Cera, Spike, Ducky, and Petrie to bring them back. *Adult Juror Comments*: Enjoyable family entertainment. Presents valuable concepts such as dealing with fears, family members as heroes, helping one another, and having faith in oneself. Animation is well-done. Provides a basis for a discussion about self-esteem. *Kid Juror Comments*: Excited to see a new adventure with their dinosaur friends. The songs captured the children's attention. One juror commented, "My daughter has been reading about dinosaurs for weeks now." "I want to draw dinosaurs." Video. 77 min.; $19.98; Age: 3-7. Universal Studios Home Video.

*** Lassie Come Home

Roddy McDowell stars as Joe, the young boy to whom Lassie is forever loyal. After Joe's father sells Lassie to a wealthy duke, she escapes and travels 100 miles to return to the boy she loves. This was Elizabeth Taylor's magnificent screen debut. *Adult Juror Comments*: Warm, touching story of human-animal devotion, the rewards of perseverance and loyalty, human kindness. Enormous evergreen appeal as a family film. *Kid Juror Comments*: Responded to the emotionality and suspense despite the old-fashioned feel. They cheered when Lassie escaped, cried when she was hurt, and thoroughly enjoyed themselves. This belongs in every library of children's classic films. Video. 89 min.; $14.95; Age: 6-12. MGM/UA Home Entertainment.

*** Linnea in Monet's Garden

Based on the book, blends imagination and education while teaching about the art and life of one of the 20th century's most important painters, Claude Monet. Story of a young girl and an old man, her neighbor, who visit Monet's garden. *Adult Juror Comments*: Beautifully produced. An inspiring, entertaining, and thoughtful story. A superb mixture of animation, photographs, and live action as well as an effective art education tool. All agreed, "It's one of the best we've seen." *Kid Juror Comments*: Fantastic! Glued to the screen, especially for the animated parts. They enjoyed the friendship between the old man and Linnea. "I loved this video; I want to be Linnea." "I'm an artist like Monet." They wanted to picnic in his garden. Video. 30 min.; $14.95; Age: 3-10. First Run Features.

Age 5-8

Video

Family

*** Little Men

Louisa May Alcott's classic novel comes to life in this film starring Mariel Hemingway as the matriarch of a rural family in the late 1800s. When two troubled boys join the house, one fits in fine, but the other can't leave behind his city ways. *Adult Juror Comments*: This is well-produced with beautiful footage and good costumes. Insight into human nature and empathy toward others. Demonstrates powerful moral lessons. Made students curious about other time periods and differences in their lives. *Kid Juror Comments*: Makes children think about the consequences of their actions. "Gambling, smoking, and lying are stupid." "It was good at explaining what not to do and what it was like growing up in that time period." "I wish I could watch this every day." Video. 97 min.; $19.94; Age: 6-12. Warner Home Video.

** Little Mermaid II, The: Return to the Sea (The Little Mermaid)

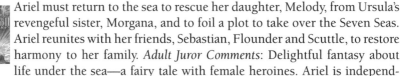

Ariel must return to the sea to rescue her daughter, Melody, from Ursula's revengeful sister, Morgana, and to foil a plot to take over the Seven Seas. Ariel reunites with her friends, Sebastian, Flounder and Scuttle, to restore harmony to her family. *Adult Juror Comments*: Delightful fantasy about life under the sea—a fairy tale with female heroines. Ariel is independent and follows her dream and makes a great role model. Good messages about communication and trust. Slapstick comedy is used a lot. *Kid Juror Comments*: Enjoyable. Kids related to the main character. "Melody didn't mind her mother and sometimes I get into trouble for not minding my mother." "I loved all the animals under the sea." "The music was great." There was some name-calling. Video. 75 min.; $19.98; Age: 5-12. Buena Vista Home Entertainment/Disney.

** Little Mermaid, The (Animated Classics)

Princess Lena, a beautiful and adventurous mermaid, has everything she could ever need but longs to travel to the ocean's surface and explore the world of humans. *Adult Juror Comments*: An engaging, favorite story. Compared to the Disney version, it's weak, with a lot of sexual stereotyping. *Kid Juror Comments*: Reenacted the story afterwards, sparking a discussion about the likelihood of witches. Questioned whether or not one could be mean and still be beautiful. Video. 50 min.; $19.95; Age: 4-8. Goodtimes Entertainment.

*** Little Nemo Collector's Set

Little Nemo journeys to Slumberland, where he encounters the world of Nightmares. He uses the magical royal scepter to free the King of Slumberland and put an end to Nightmare World. Nemo returns to a hero's welcome and flies away into the moonlight. *Adult Juror Comments*: It's somewhat scary with a basic good-versus-evil story line. The early twentieth-century time frame is a little confusing. *Kid Juror Comments*: Appealing. Some recommended it to others and asked to view it again. Afterwards, they used the cassette and drew pictures about the movie. Video. 84 min.; $29.95; Age: 4-8. Plaza Entertainment.

** Little Sister Rabbit

A whimsical journey through one day in the lives of a boy rabbit and his lovable but stubborn little sister. *Adult Juror Comments*: Sensitively deals with being an older sibling. There is a difficult scene of the burial of the rabbits' mother. Some negative stereotypes and name-calling. *Kid Juror Comments*: Likable story and characters. Prompted a lively discussion about siblings and helping out. Appropriate for ages five and up. Video. 25 min.; $12.98; Age: 4-8. Artisan/Family Home Entertainment.

** Little Witch (Doors of Wonder)

Liddy is a junior sorceress with good intentions who just wants to be a normal, everyday kid. The Little Witch stands out among her "evil" family as a good witch. Based on the best-selling book by Deborah Hautzig. *Adult Juror Comments*: Entertaining, colorful animation, attractive characters. Gives hope. Encourages one to be oneself. Addresses overcoming fears about making new friends. "The Little Witch is a model of cheerful kindness." Some couldn't show to kids due to witch subject. *Kid Juror Comments*: Kids thought it was fun. They liked the bet bat and spells and when the little witch made some friends. "I liked it how sparkled when she did a spell." "The Little Witch was un-witch like and a good neighbor." "It is okay to be yourself." Video. 30 min.; $12.98; Age: 5-8. Sony Wonder.

* Love Bug, The (Wonderful World of Disney)

Follows the adventures of Herbie, the love bug and vivacious VW Beetle, as he revs up romance for his new-found owner and a beautiful magazine reporter. *Adult Juror Comments*: Light, lively, action-packed, and humorous. Portrays stereotypes such as showing the "good" car as white and the "bad" car as black, as well as stereotypical gender roles. *Kid Juror Comments*: Engaging, especially the special effects. Boys loved it. "How did they get those cars to do wheelies? It's cool." "I want to invent a car that talks." "The black car was disrespectful and cruel." "How come the girlfriend never talks?" Video. 88 min.; $14.99; Age: 5-12. Buena Vista Home Entertainment/Disney.

** Madeline's Rescue (Madeline)

When Madeline tries to balance on a bridge rail, she plunges into the river and is saved by a special dog. The dog helps with lessons, sings, spells, and even selects her own name, Genevieve. *Adult Juror Comments*: Delightful adaptation of the book. The high-quality animation and music is charming and entertaining. The "bad man" who got rid of the dog is a sure discussion-prompter. Lacks cultural diversity. A good tie-in to the classic children's book. *Kid Juror Comments*: Afterwards, the younger ones reenacted the story, humming the music. The songs were a big hit. The accents took some getting used to for the children. Inner-city kids commented that they did not feel represented. Video. 25 min.; $12.95; Age: 3-9. Sony Wonder.

** Magic Map, The (The Adventures of Elmer & Friends)

 Imagine the thrill of finding an old treasure map, then finding yourself with the man who drew it, who happens to be the author of *Treasure Island*, Robert Louis Stevenson. "The Magic Map" reveals how easy it is to find a treasure in a book. *Adult Juror Comments*: Simple production that uses humor, imagination, dance, and song to present ideas about writing stories. The children were disappointed with the ending, which doesn't conclude with finding where the treasure map leads. Christian overtones. *Kid Juror Comments*: Lots to like: humor, dancing, songs, and a treasure map. It held their attention. "They treated each other well." "The crow was really silly." "I liked when they went to the beach." Video. 30 min.; $14.95; Age: 4-7. Featherwind Productions.

*** Making of Zoom, The (Zoom)

 A behind-the-scenes look at the cast and crew of the new Zoom that shows how they create the show. Contains audition clips and bloopers. *Adult Juror Comments*: Engaging. Inspirational for those interested in TV production. Generated interest in the arts. Science activities are age-appropriate. Shows how we learn from our mistakes. Provides good role models for working together. *Kid Juror Comments*: Kids were enthusiastic. They loved the "ubba dubba" language. "The bloopers were so funny." "It made me want to sing with them." "My friends will like this." "It was neat watching them learn to dance." "Everyone was friendly." Video. 45 min.; $12.95; Age: 6-10. WGBH.

** Margaret Mahy Video Library

Contains three titles: "The Three-Legged Cat," about a peg-leg cat's ride atop a bald head; "The Great White Man-Eating Shark," about a boy who resembles a shark; and "Keeping House," the tale of Lizzie Firkin who hates to clean. *Adult Juror Comments*: Very inventive production. Characters are quirky and appealing. Demonstrates that actions have consequences. Each story has cute animation and narration. "Captures your attention." Exposes children to classic literature with discussion topics. *Kid Juror Comments*: Engaged them, but most said they wouldn't watch it again. They liked the drawings and narrator. Kids learned to clean up after themselves. Their eyes were wide open while watching the shark story. British slang and humor were beyond some. Video. 30 min.; $19.95; Age: 4-7. Weston Woods Studios/Scholastic.

*** Mary Poppins

The lovable nanny drops from the sky into the home of a no-nonsense banker and his two mischievous children. She turns every chore into a game and every day into a whimsical adventure. *Adult Juror Comments*: "It's as wonderful now as I remember it being." Visual effects add to the story. Technologically dated, but it doesn't matter. Teaches kids key lessons in a humorous way. "I hope we never get too old or too sophisticated to enjoy a family gem like this." *Kid Juror Comments*: Enjoyed it and wanted to watch it again…"over and over. Liked learning the lessons. "You have to take the good with the bad…a spoonful of sugar helps." "It's gonna be one of my favorites." "It was supercalifragilistic…" Video. 139 min.; $22.99; Age: 4-12. Buena Vista Home Entertainment/Disney.

** Mary-Kate and Ashley Olsen: Our First Video (Mary-Kate and Ashley)

From the hit ABC series "Full House," this program contains seven music videos. The girls introduce each segment with wit and humor, providing a glimpse of life behind the camera. *Adult Juror Comments*: It's awfully cute, maybe too much so. Fans of the Olsen twins will appreciate it most. Variety of music is well-selected and appropriate. Good costumes. *Kid Juror Comments*: The Peanut Butter Band was a favorite. After the screening some children dressed up like Mary-Kate and Ashley had in the video. As expected, the Olsen twins' fans thought this was right up their alley. Video. 30 min.; $12.95; Age: 5-9. Warner Home Video.

Age 5-8

Video

Family

** Mary-Kate and Ashley Olsen: Our Music Video (Mary-Kate and Ashley)

Contains ten of the twins' favorite music videos from their Adventure and You're Invited series to dance and sing-along with. *Adult Juror Comments*: Cheerful. The girls are respectful to each other and have fun together. Songs cover a variety of subjects. Enhances self-esteem and provides positive role models for the appropriate age group. Main benefit is having a good time, laughing, and singing. *Kid Juror Comments*: Kids liked the jokes and how the girls dress for each occasion. They enjoyed learning the words to the songs, especially "Brother for Sale." Some thought they were trying to be too cool. "I learned to be nice to others." Video. 30 min.; $12.95; Age: 5-8. Warner Home Video.

*** Maurice Sendak Library (Children's Circle)

Includes the Caldecott Award-winner, "In the Night Kitchen" where bread-dough airplanes fly and everyone dances; "Where the Wild Things Are," the best-selling children's book; and profiles of author Maurice Sendak. *Adult Juror Comments*: This classic literary anthology features two of Maurice Sendak's best-known stories and stimulates a great discussion about fears of the unknown. The biography of Maurice Sendak is quite fascinating. *Kid Juror Comments*: Always a winner, in whatever medium. Most are familiar with Sendak's books, especially "Where the Wild Things Are" and love seeing it come to life. They talked afterwards about what scares them. Video. 35 min.; $14.95; Age: 5-12. Scholastic/Children's Circle.

*** Merlin and the Dragons (Stories to Remember)

Young Arthur doesn't understand why pulling a sword from a stone qualifies him for kingship. Merlin, the magician, guides him with inspiring stories and prophetic dreams that prepare him to become a magnificent king. Narrated by Kevin Kline. *Adult Juror Comments*: A wonderful slant on the classic story of King Arthur and his mentor, the incredible magician Merlin. Excellent role models for self-esteem, courage, and trustworthiness. *Kid Juror Comments*: Compelling and complex. Kids enjoyed the animation, though some scenes were scary for the youngest viewers. The older children were fascinated with it and talked about it later. Video. 27 min.; $9.95; Age: 5-12. Stories to Remember.

* Monkey Prince, The (Oz Kids)

Dorothy's son, Neddie, programs a computer belonging to the Wizard's son, Frank, to take him and Toto II to China. When the computer is stolen by the Monkey Prince, they will be stranded unless the other Oz Kids can find them. *Adult Juror Comments*: Amusing story with clearly presented messages about feelings and fears. Well-produced. It's very respectful of kids' thinking, feelings, and social skills. The monkey learns from his mistakes. *Kid Juror Comments*: Younger kids particularly enjoyed it. They loved the animal characters. Good discussion-starter about feelings, emotions, and possible fears. "It teaches you not to be mean to others." Video. 65 min.; $12.95; Age: 4-7. Paramount Home Entertainment.

*** Monkeys! Monkeys! Monkeys! (Animal Crackups)

Monkeys are wacky, fun, and always a barrel of laughs. This video catches all types of monkeys at their playful best. *Adult Juror Comments*: Simple, engaging film with good cinematography. Flows from topic to topic well. "I really liked that they covered primates from all over the world such as Sumatra and Japan." Fun and interesting. Touches on human evolution. *Kid Juror Comments*: Liked the songs and the monkeys. "My friends would think this movie is cool. I've never seen monkeys swim before." "I learned that monkeys can walk in the snow and take a hot bath." "I learned a lot. I liked the whole thing." Video. 30 min.; $14.99; Age: 5-8. E-Realbiz.

** Mouse Soup (John Matthews Collection)

A happy-go-lucky field mouse finds himself on the dinner menu of a dim-witted weasel and has to think fast. *Adult Juror Comments*: Well-produced, nicely animated. The attention to detail is exemplary. Addresses positive ways to resolve conflicts. Characters are courteous, kind, and funny. Faithful to the original book. Some stereotyping. *Kid Juror Comments*: Good fun. Worth repeating. They loved the songs and the characters' voices, and acted out the mouse dance steps afterwards. Video. 26 min.; $12.95; Age: 4-12. Sony Wonder.

*** Mowgli's Brothers

Based on Rudyard Kipling's immortal stories from *The Jungle Book*, a delightful tale of a small child who is raised in the jungle by a pair of wolves. Narrated by Roddy McDowall. Animated by Chuck Jones. *Adult Juror Comments*: Offers ideas about democracy in a literary style. Encourages reading the original story. Well-paced. Images of the tiger are scary for kids under six. *Kid Juror Comments*: Enthusiastic about seeing this story. Asked many questions about the people represented. Boys liked it more than girls. Kids thought some of the animated scenes were too grim. Video. 29 min.; $9.98; Age: 5-8. Artisan/Family Home Entertainment.

** Ms. Bear

 A direct-to-video, heartwarming family film featuring Ed Begley Jr., Shaun Johnston, Kaitlyn Burke, and an adorable brown bear. *Adult Juror Comments*: Storyline addresses animal safety, human values, respect, and forgiveness at a child's level. It's age-appropriate, engaging, and well-executed. Adults concerned that its portrayal of a female bear doesn't address how dangerous she is. *Kid Juror Comments*: Ms. Bear was funny and wonderful. "It made me feel happy, sad, and excited." Afterwards, it stimulated lots of discussion about forgiveness. Video. 95 min.; $12; Age: 5-12. Cabin Fever Entertainment.

** Mumfie, The Movie

 An extra-special little elephant searches for adventure. He joins his friends to recapture the Cloak of Dreams and return to a magical island of happiness. Fourteen sing-along songs move the story along. *Adult Juror Comments*: This plot weaves magic throughout, touching on loneliness and friendship. Delightful animation, songs, and darling characters. Contains some aggressive language. Visually it appeals to preschoolers, but the plot is geared for children five to eight. *Kid Juror Comments*: Mesmerized. Even though it was a bit long, kids became very involved in the story, the characters, and the outcome. There was never a dull moment. The kids wanted to watch it again. Video. 110 min.; $14.98; Age: 4-8. BMG Home Video.

** Muppet Treasure Island

Robert Louis Stevenson's classic adventure takes a new twist. Jim Hawkins inherits a pirate's treasure map, hires a ship with Captain Smollett (Kermit) and the evil Long John Silver (Tim Curry). Miss Piggy plays Benjamina Gunn, dressed to kill. *Adult Juror Comments*: The characters, both humans and puppets, interact well together and appeal to children. The introduction of the crew on-board ship is priceless. The story jumps around and is scary at times for younger kids. A little slow. *Kid Juror Comments*: Older kids loved the story and the singing. They stayed for the entire program. Kids were very excited to see Kermit and Miss Piggy, some perennial favorites. It was too scary for the younger ones. Video. 100 min.; $19.99; Age: 5-12. Buena Vista Home Entertainment/Disney.

*** Murder She Purred: A Mrs. Murphy Mystery (Wonderful World of Disney)

Mary Minor "Harry" Haristeen (Ricki Lake), is an amateur sleuth in a small Virginia town whose closest companions are her pet dog and cat. Unbeknownst to Harry, her pets can talk to each other and are her secret accomplices in solving the crime. *Adult Juror Comments*: Excellent production. Sound and lighting create a sufficiently scary mood. "A wonderful movie to watch." "Very intriguing. A murder mystery without excessive violence." Enhances critical thinking skills. *Kid Juror Comments*: Great. "I got it. This was so cool." Some children were frightened during the storm and graveyard scene. "It got so dark and creepy, but it was great." "I just found out that I really love mysteries." "It made me want to be the detective." Video. 87 min.; $14.99; Age: 7-12. Buena Vista Home Entertainment/Disney.

** My Neighbor Totoro

Japanese children's classic tells the magic of magical creatures who inhabit a tree trunk and the way they touch a child's life. *Adult Juror Comments*: Truly entertaining. Blends cultural and ethnic characteristics to show the similarities between people, but there is no way the characters look Japanese, and there are too many stereotypes: an old hag next-door and an imitation "Indian war dance." *Kid Juror Comments*: Prompted discussions about running away and how to handle fear or ghosts. Kids wanted to know who Totoro was. There was not a child in the group who didn't like it. "Tell them we just love it." Video. 87 min.; $19.98; Age: 5-8. Twentieth Century Fox Home Entertainment.

* Mystery Lights of Navajo Mesa (The Last Chance Detectives)

Four kids escape boredom in a small desert town by forming a detective agency and taking on unwanted and unsolved cases. Mysterious lights in the desert and a local museum heist draw them into a bigger plot than they expect. *Adult Juror Comments*: A compelling story, technically well-produced and good for family viewing. The characters and dialogue seem contrived at times. The story is slow to develop. Contains biblical references. *Kid Juror Comments*: The story went over the best. Most biblical references were over the heads of the kids, but they found the story exciting and loved the youth detective angle. Video. 50 min.; $19.99; Age: 5-10. Tyndale House Publishers.

Age 5-8

Video

Family

** *Namu, My Best Friend (Family Treasures)*

Hank Donner, a naturalist, studies whales in the Pacific Northwest. A dying killer whale beaches herself, and her heartsick companion refuses to leave her side. Donner tries to help, but the local fishermen are irate since they fear killer whales. *Adult Juror Comments*: Wonderful movie, stimulated lots of discussion. It is slightly dated and shows smoking by the main character. There is a distinct lack of people of color. Still, most families will enjoy this. *Kid Juror Comments*: Older kids enjoyed this tremendously. Stimulated lots of discussion about how things change over time, although it gets off to a slow start. Younger kids lost the meaning, but still found it intriguing. Video. 89 min.; $14.95; Age: 5-13. MGM/UA Home Entertainment.

*** *New Friends and Other Stories (Fun in a Box)*

Lead title is adapted from the book *Howard* by James Stevenson. Howard gets lost and ends up in New York City, where he is befriended by a frog and some nice mice. Contains three other shorts. *Adult Juror Comments*: Great adaptation of the book and true to the original story. For New Yorkers, it has particular appeal, opening up a discussion about friendship and life in the big city. Beautiful animation. *Kid Juror Comments*: Best story was the first one. Rural kids had questions about the scenes from New York. They liked how Howard's new friends took care of him and how, when he tried to leave them, he was motivated to return. Video. 30 min.; $14.95; Age: 4-12. Made to Order Productions/Rainbow.

*** *New Kid, The (Cabbage Patch Kids)*

The Cabbage Patch dolls come to life—singing and dancing—in this animated program. Norma Jean, the new kid, shows how everybody is special when she saves the day in the school talent show. *Adult Juror Comments*: Wonderful, thought-out story. Humorously deals with sensitive issues. Character development is excellent; language is reality-based. Addresses being picked on and cooperation. Content is suitable for older kids, but presentation suits younger ones. *Kid Juror Comments*: Readily identified with Norma Jean and her situation. They enjoyed the story and thought the music was cute and fit right in. Humor was right at their age level, though the boys thought the dolls were silly. Most would watch it again. Video. 30 min.; $12.98; Age: 4-8. BMG Home Video.

*** Noah's Ark (Stories to Remember)

 A moving drama with heartwarming emotion of Noah's heroic mission to rescue all creatures great and small. Based on the book by Peter Spier. Narrated by James Earl Jones. Music is by Stewart Copeland of "The Police." *Adult Juror Comments*: Great addition to any children's video library, well-produced and thoroughly engaging. James Earl Jones' narration is perfect for the story and makes it appealing to a contemporary audience. *Kid Juror Comments*: A big treat. Those familiar with the story were anxious to see if it was accurate to the version they knew. Video. 27 min.; $9.95; Age: 5-12. Stories to Remember.

* Noddy Makes a New Friend (Noddy)

Noddy meets a bunkey, claiming to be half-monkey, half-bunny. Noddy befriends the bunkey, who then causes trouble by taking the possessions of others and giving them to Noddy as thanks for his kindness. Includes three stories. *Adult Juror Comments*: Noddy's new friend's behavior—theft without consequence—is inappropriate. The production is charming with adorable animation and catchy tunes. Best viewed with an adult in order to discuss the bad behavior. *Kid Juror Comments*: bunkey was a hit. Liked Noddy's car and seeing Noddy help Pink Cat find her tail. They discussed bunkey's lying, disrespect for the police and stealing other people's belongings. Didn't like animation where characters' mouths didn't move. Video. 30 min.; $12.95; Age: 4-7. U.S.A. Home Entertainment.

** Once Upon a Dinosaur

Three tales of "once upon a time" to add to any child's collection of fairy tales: "How Dinosaurs Learned to Fly," "The Emperor's New Clothes," and "The Long Enchantment." *Adult Juror Comments*: Each story offers a unique style and presentation. Well-done with bright animation, intricate sets and costumes. The narrator is at times difficult to understand, and the morals are too advanced for the audience. *Kid Juror Comments*: On target, though they had some problems grasping all the concepts. "I didn't understand it until my Mommy explained it to me." "My daughter watched it three times." All of the programs evoked discussion from the children afterwards. Video. 26 min.; $19.95; Age: 3-7. Nat'l Film Board of Canada.

** Once Upon a Forest

Three Furling friends undertake a dangerous journey after a chemical spill destroys Dapplewood and a young friend becomes ill from its toxic fumes. Their wisdom pays off as they restore Dapplewood to its original splendor. *Adult Juror Comments*: Animals and animation are cute; characters are believable. The story includes a parent's death, which is a difficult issue for a child of this age. Should be viewed with an adult. *Kid Juror Comments*: The story heightened children's awareness about environmental issues and provoked questions about differences. Some parts were scary. Kids noticed and commented on how all the animals cooperate with one another. Video. 71 min.; $14.98; Age: 5-8. Twentieth Century Fox Home Entertainment.

* Operation: Secret Birthday Surprise (Adventures of Timmy the Tooth)

 Explore Flossmore Valley, where Timmy the Tooth lives with his best buddy Brushbrush and a neighborhood full of lovable characters. *Adult Juror Comments*: Well-produced with creative concepts and songs, but tries to cover too many things at once. Conveys a very commercial feeling and lacked adequate useful information about toothcare. Often the terms used related to health have no explanations. *Kid Juror Comments*: Enjoyed the muppet characters, but thought the program was too slow. Their attention wandered. Older kids thought it was too busy and too silly. They did not want to watch it again. Video. 30 min.; $12.98; Age: 3-8. Universal Studios Home Video.

*** Outback Grand Prix and Other Stories (Jingaroo)

 Features a loveable cast of friends who are unique and magical. Each of the three stories is six minutes long and has an original song and music video. *Adult Juror Comments*: Excellent. Very realistic 3-D animation. Cute characters, fun music, and interesting stories. Social skills such as good sportsmanship and speaking up when feelings are hurt are emphasized. "Generated interest in Australia." *Kid Juror Comments*: They'd watch it again. "You can still win even when you're not showing off." "I learned that I can feel safe at home when I have a bad dream." "The race car story was my favorite." "I felt like dancing to the music." Video. 30 min.; $14.95; Age: 4-9. Beckett Entertainment.

*** Owl Moon and Other Stories (Children's Circle)

 Haunting music and poetic narration underscore the special closeness between father and child as they search for the great horned owl. This book-based program includes three other literary stories. *Adult Juror Comments*: True to the original, though slow-moving at times. *Kid Juror Comments*: Kids liked the stories though they were disappointed that not all are fully animated. Video. 35 min.; $14.95; Age: 4-12. Scholastic/Children's Circle.

** Pagemaster, The

Richard Tyler enters an empty library and is swept away into the Pagemaster's magical world. Famous literary characters come to life, and young Richard must conquer his fears to return home. Stars Macaulay Culkin, Whoopi Goldberg, and Patrick Stewart. *Adult Juror Comments*: Well-animated story that provides a glimpse into some classic tales. It could motivate reading or encourage children's interest in libraries. Some parts are scary for younger viewers and depict unsafe behavior. *Kid Juror Comments*: Related to the child's change from being scared to being brave. Children enjoyed this adventure and the characters from the book. It prompted a discussion about feelings afterwards. Video. 76 min.; $22.98; Age: 5-12. Twentieth Century Fox Home Entertainment.

** Paper Bag Princess, The (A Bunch of Munsch)

 A clever princess has her kingdom toasted by a fire-breathing dragon that prince-naps Ronald. She finds out that every prince isn't charming, and she can make her own happily-ever-afters. *Adult Juror Comments*: This charming, modern fairytale has a female heroine. Takes a humorous look at royalty. Some vocabulary was a little over the head of the audience. Deviates from the original book. Some stereotyping. *Kid Juror Comments*: The story and the music were thoroughly appealing. They laughed at the antics of both the princess and the prince. Most were familiar with the story and the feminist messages. They loved the outcome: the dragon became a better friend in the end. Video. 25 min.; $12.95; Age: 5-12. Sony Wonder.

*** Party with Zoom (Zoom)

The "Zoom kids" show how to make any day or get-together a real party. Offers ideas for invitations, recipes, games, and more. *Adult Juror Comments*: Wonderful. Moves at a good pace, has excellent diversity, and is well-organized. "It really got me into the party spirit." "The magic tricks were terrific and offered thorough explanations." "We loved the cooking projects." *Kid Juror Comments*: Enthusiastic. Related to the on-screen children. Definite interest in watching it again. "I liked how respectful they were." "The backwards spelling game was difficult." "I want to learn how to cook." "I liked the cool party stuff." Video. 45 min.; $12.95; Age: 5-12. WGBH.

*** Pegasus (Stories to Remember)

 Follows the mythological Pegasus from birth to his battle with the multi-headed Chimera, his appointment by Zeus as thunder-bearer and his transformation into the constellation bearing his name. Narrated by Mia Farrow. Adapted by Doris Orgel. *Adult Juror Comments*: Beautifully animated and an excellent translation of the Greek myth. An engaging way to introduce children to mythology. *Kid Juror Comments*: After watching, the kids get really jazzed about mythology in general. Many were familiar with the story of Pegasus and enjoyed watching it on video. It stimulated a search in the library afterwards for more myths. Video. 25 min.; $9.95; Age: 4-12. Stories to Remember.

** Pet Forgetters Cure, The/Never-Want-to-Go-to-Bedders Cure (Shelley Duvall Presents Mrs. Piggle-Wiggle)

 Mrs. Piggle-Wiggle has a knack for helping kids and their parents out of the stickiest situations. She's a genius at finding uncommon solutions to the challenges of growing up. Stars Jean Stapleton, Ed Begley Jr., Shelly Duvall, and Phyllis Diller. *Adult Juror Comments*: Here's a silly fantasy with real people, based on the books by the same title, but not quite as entertaining. The individual segments are appealing. *Kid Juror Comments*: Six-year-olds and up enjoyed this the best. Under-fives had difficulty paying attention. The humor is pretty corny, even for kids, and it's way too verbal. It had a hard time holding kids' interest. Video. 57 min.; $12.98; Age: 3-10. Universal Studios Home Video.

** Pete's Dragon

Pete, a young orphan, runs away from his guardians to a Maine fishing town with his best friend, a sometimes-invisible dragon named Elliot. A kind lighthouse keeper and her father take them in, but Elliot's pranks get them into trouble. *Adult Juror Comments*: Creative, fanciful show. Lets your imagination grow. Charming mix of animation and live action. Shows how valuable it is to have friends you can count on when you need help. "Believing in children can help them accomplish many things." *Kid Juror Comments*: Liked the whole movie. Talked about kids needing a safe home to live in. "The Gogans were really mean and greedy. We're nicer to people." "We understood that Pete needed a friend to play with and someone to take care of him." "The dragon was cool." Video. 129 min.; $22.99; Age: 5-12. Buena Vista Home Entertainment/Disney.

** Peter and the Wolf

This timeless tale is brought to life with such stars as Kirstie Alley, Lloyd Bridges, Ross Mulinger, and the whole new cast of unforgettable animated characters from the legendary Chuck Jones. *Adult Juror Comments*: The story is wonderful, with lovely music and beautiful sets. Adults found the animation flat and dull. Little cultural diversity. The story is a little long. *Kid Juror Comments*: Delightful. The kids loved it and wanted to watch again. They enjoyed the music, the characters, and how they take care of one other. "We liked the part where the duck did a happy dance." Video. 60 min.; $14.98; Age: 5-8. BMG Home Video.

*** Peter Pan (Cathy Rigby)

Stars Cathy Rigby as Peter Pan, about the boy who refuses to grow up, in the filmed Broadway musical production. J.M. Barrie's classic tale is an adventure of lost boys, Indian maidens, and rogue pirates. *Adult Juror Comments*: Exceptional entertainment, splendid acting. Classic story shown in a unique stage production. Audible audience response helps develop an appreciation for the theater. Enduring qualities capture viewers of all ages. *Kid Juror Comments*: Riveted. Really appreciated the differences between the stage production and the animated version. "The person playing Peter Pan is a woman! That is so cool." "We like to pretend we're in a play too." "I liked the songs. We sing them all the time now." Video. 104 min.; $19.95; Age: 6-12. New Video Group, Inc.

** Pigs Plus "David's Father" (Bunch of Munsch, A)

Contains two stories. First, the pigpen gate is left ajar, opening the way to an adventure. In the second, a young girl who doesn't want to meet her new neighbors changes her mind when an ordinary boy introduces her to his extraordinary father. *Adult Juror Comments*: Great stories, cute story lines. Some of the music was difficult for kids to follow. The humor is odd at times. David's father was interestingly different. The story brings up the issue of being adopted. At times it makes fun of teachers. *Kid Juror Comments*: Much appreciated stories, and afterwards kids talked about people not being what they seem at first. Video. 25 min.; $12.95; Age: 4-12. Sony Wonder.

*** Pigs' Wedding and Other Stories, The (Children's Circle)

Porker and Curlytail invite all of their favorite friends to their wedding. Everyone comes, along with the rain. *Adult Juror Comments*: Good literary stories. Not all of the animation is full-range. Some stories are better-produced than others, but the content makes up for it. *Kid Juror Comments*: Stories were fine, but children disappointed when they were not fully animated. They talked about the stories afterwards, and wanted to watch the video again. Video. 39 min.; $14.95; Age: 5-12. Scholastic/Children's Circle.

** *Pinocchio (Animated Classics)*

Pinocchio longs to be a real boy. The Blue Fairy watching over Pinocchio helps him escape from danger. When the Blue Fairy becomes ill and Pinocchio assists her, she grants his wish as a reward. *Adult Juror Comments*: A good story with some modernized narration and some stereotypes. Teaches never to talk to strangers, not to lie, and to care for others. Animation is not equal to Disney's. Production and music are mediocre. *Kid Juror Comments*: A three-year-old watched it three more times. The length was just right for him. Video. 50 min.; $19.95; Age: 4-8. Goodtimes Entertainment.

** *Pirate Island (The Adventures of Elmer & Friends)*

 How would you like a treasure chest of valuable learning adventures? Benjamin Ouid, the pirate, his parrot, Yappy, and monkey, Mappy, help youngsters discover the rewards of unexpected acts of kindness and the priceless value of good friends. *Adult Juror Comments*: Corny production with pleasant scenery, songs, and respectful characters, but it's a bit slow and sappy and transitions are awkward. Encourages language, singing, and expressive movement. Language is age-appropriate. Christian content. *Kid Juror Comments*: The girls tended to like the music, the boys liked the pirate. "I wanted to learn the songs." "All the people were nice to each other." "We would love to find a buried treasure." They were captivated by the pirate and bored by the slower songs. Video. 30 min.; $14.95; Age: 3-7. Featherwind Productions.

*** *Pocahontas (Disney)*

The free-spirited daughter of Chief Powhatan develops a strong friendship with Captain John Smith when his boatload of English settlers arrive on the Virginia shoreline. When tensions mount between the two cultures, Pocahontas helps find a way for peace. *Adult Juror Comments*: Excellent production with beautiful animation. Good depiction of the fight against cultural bias. Portrays strong values regarding the importance of friendship. Stimulates discussion about American history. *Kid Juror Comments*: Loved it. "This was a very exciting story." "My favorite part was when Pocahontas sang to Grandmother Willow." "This story showed white people treating the Indians bad and then they treated them good." "The music was great." Video. 81 min.; $22.99; Age: 5-12. Buena Vista Home Entertainment/Disney.

Chapter Three • Elementary

** Pocahontas (Enchanted Tales)

The familiar tale of Pocahontas, a beautiful Indian princess, and the dashing English Virginia settler whose life she saves. *Adult Juror Comments*: Appropriate humor and well-selected classical music. Several inaccuracies, among them: use of gardening implements not available then, Pocahontas's appearance is not representative of the time. *Kid Juror Comments*: The animals won over hearts and minds. Many preferred this to the Disney version and thought it was a more complete story. They watched it over and over. Video. 48 min.; $9.98; Age: 5-12. Sony Wonder.

*** Pocahontas II: Journey to a New World

Pocahontas goes to London and is swept away by curious English customs. However, she must convince the king that her people are truly civilized in order to stop the armada moving against them...and make choices between her heart and her future. *Adult Juror Comments*: Top notch production. Songs are sweet and story is wonderful. Exciting way for kids to learn a little history. Doesn't water down the rigid cultural bias Pocahontas had to overcome. A good account of two different cultures meeting. *Kid Juror Comments*: Great. Awesome. "It was a good story because Pocahontas was a good person." "The Indians have brown skin like me." "It was funny." "I learned a little about Pocahontas; now I need to read and see what really happened and if the movie goes along with it." Video. 73 min.; $22.99; Age: 5-12. Buena Vista Home Entertainment/Disney.

** Pooch and the Pauper, The (Wonderful World of Disney)

The snobbish First Dog of the United States accidentally is switched with a street smart, look-alike dog from the wrong side of the tracks. *Adult Juror Comments*: Cute, funny, entertaining. Great dog voices and acting. White House setting gives insight into politics, the president, and taxes. Shows how a pet can make an adult more caring. Camera shots from dog's point of view are cool. *Kid Juror Comments*: Really tickled by it. "It was about money and the government, but it was silly." "It was funny watching the good dog and the snotty dog talk and trade places." "I liked seeing inside the White House." "I liked the escape from the Humane Society." Video. 88 min.; rental only; Age: 5-12. Buena Vista Home Entertainment/Disney.

Age 5-8

Video

Family

* Prince and the Pauper, The (Enchanted Tales)

Animated classic about a young prince who swaps identities with a look-alike beggar boy—an adventure tale that has lasted through the ages. *Adult Juror Comments*: Mediocre animation. The addition of vicarious talking objects who sing and dance is more distracting to the program than beneficial. *Kid Juror Comments*: Okay, but not funny. "I couldn't tell what those talking things were," commented one child. Video. 48 min.; $14.98; Age: 5-8. Sony Wonder.

* Raggedy Ann & Andy: The Mabbit Adventure (Adventures of Raggedy Ann and Andy)

The Mabbits have tried to keep their Book of Spells hidden from the evil wizard, but they are no match for his magic. As a last resort, they turn themselves into statues and Raggedy Ann, Raggedy Andy, and Sunny Bunny's magic pen saves the day. *Adult Juror Comments*: The structure of this story is complicated and seems contrived. It tries to show problem-solving skills. The characters sneak around a lot. It may encourage kids to get a pen pal. *Kid Juror Comments*: Children ages three to five loved the movie, though some found it difficult to follow. The older kids asked questions while viewing, which helped them understand what was going on. Video. 28 min.; $9.98; Age: 3-8. Twentieth Century Fox Home Entertainment.

* Raggedy Ann & Andy: The Perriwonk Adventure (Adventures of Raggedy Ann and Andy)

Playful Raggedy Andy runs off with Marcella's locket and lets Raggedy Dog bury it in the yard. When he goes to dig it up, it's gone. To find and retrieve the locket, the Raggedys must free the Perriwonks from a dragon whom they befriend as well. *Adult Juror Comments*: Really silly and contrived. The characters and the story line are appropriate for this age. Reinforces cooperation in solving problems and conflicts. The long names make it difficult to follow. Some name-calling. *Kid Juror Comments*: Cute. Children liked this story and wanted to see it again. Parts were scary for the younger kids. The kids found the story line difficult to follow. Video. 28 min.; $9.98; Age: 5-8. Twentieth Century Fox Home Entertainment.

* Raggedy Ann & Andy: The Ransom of Sunny Bunny (Adventures of Raggedy Ann and Andy)

Sunny Bunny is doll-napped. The Raggedys play right into the hands of the evil Cracklen, who needs the hair of Raggedy Dog to complete a spell. Raggedy Ann and Andy end up rescuing two of their best friends. *Adult Juror Comments*: Bright and lively, some cute scenes, a little drama. Contains some aggressive behaviors such as zapping, stealing, and sneaky pie-throwing. "I like the teamwork of the Raggedy team. Loved that the bunny participated in the cooking contest, and won." *Kid Juror Comments*: They wanted to make mud pies afterwards. The four- and five-year-olds loved it. They learned about caring for friends. There were some scary parts for the younger ones. The kids were concerned about the issue of kidnapping. Video. 28 min.; $9.98; Age: 4-7. Twentieth Century Fox Home Entertainment.

* Raggedy Ann & Andy: The Scared Cat Adventure (Adventures of Raggedy Ann and Andy)

A magic lamp spells adventure for the Raggedys when the genie of the lamp kidnaps Raggedy Cat. *Adult Juror Comments*: Standard good-versus-evil story-line. Egyptian theme is interesting. Has lots of chasing and running from collapsing buildings. Scary parts are good as discussion-starters. Contains some inappropriate language and attitudes. *Kid Juror Comments*: This title had mixed and limited appeal for children. The Egyptian story line is most suitable for children ages five to eight. Length is appropriate. Video. 30 min.; $9.98; Age: 5-8. Twentieth Century Fox Home Entertainment.

** Railway Dragon

 An ancient dragon emerges from beneath a railroad bridge and befriends a young girl. *Adult Juror Comments*: Adults thought the story was well–animated, but nothing special. They were concerned about the girl sneaking out at night. It may be understood better if the lesson of the story was explained beforehand. *Kid Juror Comments*: Appealing. It promoted discussion afterwards about imagination. Video. 27 min.; $9.98; Age: 4-10. Artisan/Family Home Entertainment.

*** Ram in The Pepper Patch, The (Between the Lions)

A girl from Mexico tries everything to stop a ram from eating all her peppers—until a tiny bee flies in to save the day. But run for cover! The ram escapes from his book and creates a ruckus in the library. Features the short "a" sound. *Adult Juror Comments*: Well-produced, fun, and lively. Combines puppets, animation, and live action to bring the world of books to life. A great tool for beginning readers. "The producers have gone all out on making a well-designed educational video." *Kid Juror Comments*: Sang along with the songs and sounded out words aloud with the tape. "I liked the people reading to me and I could see the words." "It makes learning to read fun, like a game." "I want to go to the library." Video. 30 min.; $12.95; Age: 4-8. WGBH.

Age 5-8

Video

Family

*** Ready to Run

A young girl and her mother find out that her father's death is not an end but a beginning. The girl's special gift with horses allows everyone to reach for their dreams and win. *Adult Juror Comments*: Great. Excellent example about persevering in pursuit of a goal. Appealing family programming. Does not sugar-coat the message. Light and bright; breezy rural atmosphere is refreshing. Strongly demonstrates respect for parent, family, and boss. *Kid Juror Comments*: Riveted them…especially the girls. Cheered for the underdog horse during the race. Talking horses really amused them: "The man kissed the horse and the horse said yuck!" "The horses watched the race on TV." "I like seeing the horse dance." Video. 89 min.; $14.99; Age: 6-10. Buena Vista Home Entertainment/Disney.

** Real Story of Humpty Dumpty, The (Real Story)

One day the misunderstood egg's luck changes. He foils Glitch the Witch's evil plan to poison Princess Allegra and becomes the town hero. Then…crack! Will the power of love save Humpty? *Adult Juror Comments*: Despite its loose relationship to the original story, it has many merits—a sense of humor, imagination, and fantastic characters. A happy and realistic ending. Some of the language is too aggressive and too advanced for the audience. *Kid Juror Comments*: The child-centered characters held their attention from beginning to end. The length is perfect. The kids related to the emphasis that "it's okay to be different." Video. 25 min.; $9.95; Age: 5-8. Sony Wonder.

* Rebecca of Sunnybrook Farm (Shirley Temple)

Shirley Temple sings, dances, and charms her way through this classic. Orphan Rebecca auditions for a radio show and doesn't get hired, so her stepfather sends her off to live with relatives while the show's talent agent searches frantically for her. *Adult Juror Comments*: Excellent opportunity to introduce kids to the book by Kate Douglas Wiggin. Discussion about the time period helps understand portrayal of minorities. *Kid Juror Comments*: Kids enjoyed the movie, especially Shirley Temple. Girls liked it best, though most of the kids enjoyed it. They thought Shirley was funny. Video. 81 min.; $14.98; Age: 6-12. Twentieth Century Fox Home Entertainment.

*** Rescuers Down Under

Deep in the Australian Outback, young Cody forges an incredible friendship with a golden eagle whom he tries to protect from a ruthless poacher. With Bernard and Bianca—the world's bravest mice—and Wilbur the albatross, the mission is possible. *Adult Juror Comments*: Excellent production. Intriguing story illustrates poaching and teaches subtle lessons about learning right from wrong, and about courage and teamwork. Charming supporting characters and novel setting. Fun animation, great music. Scary kidnapping scene. *Kid Juror*

Age 5-8 · Video · Family

Comments: Cool. "There was neat music, and the pictures were made really well." Understood the concept of animal rights. "I am like the boy and would try to save the eagle." "There are lots of great scenes. The good animals are brave and work together." Video. 77 min.; $22.99; Age: 6-10. Buena Vista Home Entertainment/Disney.

* Return of Mombi, The (Oz Kids)

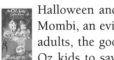

Halloween and witchcraft make for another exciting adventure in Oz. Mombi, an evil witch, has returned to Emerald City, kidnapping the Oz adults, the good witch Glinda, and the Nome King. Now it's up to the Oz kids to save Oz from Mombi's dark powers. *Adult Juror Comments*: Simply animated story with good narration. The concept is interesting and imaginative. Uses very age-appropriate language. Helpful if the viewer is familiar with the original story. Characters behave respectfully. Too long for some kids. *Kid Juror Comments*: Interesting characters, though one said, "You have to know the Wizard of Oz to get this." "Some parts are spooky." "It makes me want to learn magic." Most kids liked this video. It may be too slow for some. Video. 89 min.; $12.95; Age: 5-8. Paramount Home Entertainment.

** Return of The Sand Fairy, The

Four children visit their gruff aunt who doesn't like youngsters. Their lives are changed when they discover a lovable troll who grants all of their wishes. *Adult Juror Comments*: Charming story, but the length was formidable. Good interaction among siblings, accents hard to understand. Some parts seem a little contrived, the sand fairy character not very well developed. Lacked cultural diversity. *Kid Juror Comments*: Enjoyed the time travel and the characters becoming invisible, but thought the story was too long. "It was neat to see how people talked and dressed back then." "The troll complained a lot, and sometimes he was mean." Video. 139 min.; $29.98; Age: 6-10. Twentieth Century Fox Home Entertainment.

** Richard Scarry's Best Silly Stories and Songs Video Ever! (Richard Scarry's Best Videos Ever!)

Each hilarious adventure comes to life, as children laugh, learn, and sing along with the Richard Scarry characters Huckle Cat and Lowly Worm. *Adult Juror Comments*: Entertaining short stories are a good length for this age group. Contains very childlike, silly humor. Shows good gender role models. *Kid Juror Comments*: Immediate demands for repeat showing. Many recognized the characters and loved the songs. Inspired to visit the library and look for Scarry's books. Excellent teaching video for toddlers to age seven. Video. 30 min.; $9.98; Age: 3-8. Sony Wonder.

** Richard Scarry's Best Sing-Along Mother Goose Video Ever! (Richard Scarry's Best Videos Ever!)

While searching for Lowly Worm, Huckle meets lots of new friends. Includes "Mary Had A Little Lamb," "Hey Diddle, Diddle," and other sing-alongs. *Adult Juror Comments*: Well-produced with nice music. The characters are clearly identified and distinct and children relate to them. It's suitable for this age group, especially the four- and five-year-olds. Prompted discussion about the values of classic children's rhymes. *Kid Juror Comments*: Sang along and repeated rhymes with the tape. Five-year-olds said it was "too silly!" Even the three-year-olds understood "Looking for Lowly" because of the repetition. Video. 30 min.; $9.98; Age: 3-8. Sony Wonder.

* Robert McCloskey Video Library, The

Anthology includes: "Lentil," about a boy and his harmonica; "Make Way for Ducklings," the classic tale of ducks who find a new home; "Blueberries for Sal," the literature-based tale in which Sal gets lost and goes home with the wrong mother. *Adult Juror Comments*: Stories are charming with beautiful illustrations. The iconographic presentation and outdated themes and roles definitely limit its appeal. Time of Wonder is particularly slow, long, and dry. *Kid Juror Comments*: Children enjoyed the familiar stories best. Younger kids tuned in to the duck story and laughed at the bears in Blueberries for Sal. They asked questions about the past, discussed going to the beach and the effects of a storm. Video. 52 min.; $19.95; Age: 4-8. Weston Woods Studios/Scholastic.

** Robin Hood

England is at war and ruled by a phony king. Roguish Robin Hood and his band of merry men outfox the ruling royalty at every turn, not stopping until Robin has the hand of Maid Marian and King Richard is restored to the throne. *Adult Juror Comments*: Appealing presentation and engaging music. Endearing, adventurous characters. Funny noises and surprising sound effects. True to the classic tale so moral basis needs explaining, like stealing from the rich (even to feed the poor) and why there are taxes. *Kid Juror Comments*: Enjoyed it. Grasped the concept of class differences even if they could not explain it. "You understood how the poor felt when the king took their money." "We know you shouldn't take money from people." "It was just fun to watch. It made me laugh." Video. 83 min.; $22.99; Age: 5-12. Buena Vista Home Entertainment/ Disney.

** Rosemary Wells Video Library, The

Anthology includes "Noisy Nora," whose presence is heard at every turn; "Max's Chocolate Chicken," an Easter egg hunt; "Max's Christmas," where kids stay up to see Santa Claus; and "Morris's Disappearing Bag," a surprising last Christmas present. *Adult Juror Comments*: Deals directly with issues children typically face: fairness, self-esteem, and acceptance. Narration is pleasant, and the production has a storybook character. Some were concerned about the lack of consequences for one's actions. *Kid Juror Comments*: Identified with the characters and liked how images told the stories. They liked Morris when he got a chance to prove that he was responsible with others' possessions. Led to a discussion about how to treat siblings respectfully. Video. 26 min.; $19.95; Age: 3-9. Weston Woods Studios/Scholastic.

* Rotten Ralph, Volume 1 (Rotten Ralph)

Ralph is Sarah's rotten cat, but Sarah loves him anyway. Ralph can't understand why everyone gets so mad at him. Ralph's good ideas always end up getting him in trouble. Silly, messy Ralph sometimes needs to be bad before he figures out what's good. *Adult Juror Comments*: Clever story lessons told at a hyperkinetic pace. Simple "cardboard" animation is interesting and appealing. The short episodes are entertaining. Ralph, the two-dimensional book character, comes off as a real pain in the neck in animation. *Kid Juror Comments*: Enjoyed it. Liked the bright colors and music. "Ralph reminds me of kids I know." "Ralph wanted to protect his family." "We learned not to break things." Video. 60 min.; $19.95; Age: 6-9. Twentieth Century Fox Home Entertainment.

** Rotten Ralph, Volume 2 (Rotten Ralph)

Ralph is Sarah's rotten cat, but she loves him anyway. Ralph sometimes needs to be bad before he figures out what's good. Ralph has some bad habits, like eating junk food then keeping the whole family awake at night and teaching a lost kitten bad habits. *Adult Juror Comments*: Cute and hip if somewhat grating to adult tastes. Fast-paced activity; lessons are taught in 15-minute vignettes. Sophisticated, modern, and appropriate language for kids. "Ralph has no redeeming qualities—but he does get a taste of his own medicine." *Kid Juror Comments*: Amused by Ralph's antics, they "got" the lessons. "Ralph was naughty and sometimes we are naughty, too." "He's a joker. He's really funny." "It looks cool. We like the dance costumes and the designs." "We like the clay animation." Video. 60 min.; $19.95; Age: 5-8. Twentieth Century Fox Home Entertainment.

* Rudy Roo's Trains, Lots of Trains
(Rudy Roo's Library Adventure Series)

Rudy Roo, an animated kangaroo, and two young children learn all about trains as a result of their trip to the library. They ride on a train and visit a fabulous model train set-up. *Adult Juror Comments*: Tells a lot about trains, train history, and safety. The connection between books and real life is interesting. The train shots are great. The pace is too slow for older kids while the information is too complex for younger ones. *Kid Juror Comments*: Six-year-olds enjoyed it most. They followed up by playing train the next day. Boys definitely liked it better than girls. Rudy Roo was too corny for some kids. "I like trains." "I liked the songs." Video. 30 min.; $12.95; Age: 4-8. Meritage Productions, Inc.

** Runaway Reptar (Rugrats)

The Rugrats reptilian hero, Reptar, has turned naughty, smashing Tokyo as though it is made of toothpicks. How can the good-hearted dinosaur who saved humanity from aliens, cockroaches, and mole people be persuaded to change his ways. *Adult Juror Comments*: Definitely appealing to children of this age with good action and bright colors. Deals with things children fear, yet find intriguing. Promotes standing up for your beliefs. Good diversity, but shows unsafe behaviors. *Kid Juror Comments*: Funny and thought-provoking. "It's about raptors and things that I like." "Has unsafe behavior—adults don't let kids act this way." "Kids do not run around in diapers." "Angelica is a brat. She's loud and mean but still funny." Video. 59 min.; $12.99; Age: 5-10. Paramount Home Entertainment.

*** Scholastic's Magic School Bus: Rainforest
(Scholastic's Magic School Bus)

On a school field trip, kids solve the mystery of how cocoa trees, mud puddles, and tiny bugs are all part of nature's wondrous web of life. *Adult Juror Comments*: Enjoyable and well-produced. It's interesting to examine the interdependence of everything in the rainforest's ecosystem. Presentation is very age-appropriate and encourages kids to think for themselves and solve the mystery. Very respectful. *Kid Juror Comments*: Loved it and were attentive. They talked about how their mom makes hot chocolate and liked learning about where it comes from. "Cocoa beans turn into pods and then it makes chocolate, right?" "I liked how everyone solved the mystery together." Video. 30 min.; $9.95; Age: 4-8. Warner Home Video.

Chapter Three • Elementary

** Scooby-Doo and the Alien Invaders (Scooby-Doo!)

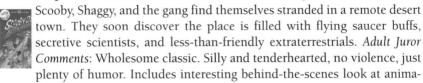

Scooby, Shaggy, and the gang find themselves stranded in a remote desert town. They soon discover the place is filled with flying saucer buffs, secretive scientists, and less-than-friendly extraterrestrials. *Adult Juror Comments*: Wholesome classic. Silly and tenderhearted, no violence, just plenty of humor. Includes interesting behind-the-scenes look at animation production. Encourages teamwork. Contains some stereotypical gender behaviors. *Kid Juror Comments*: Thoroughly enjoyed it. Stayed with it until the very end. "It was kind of scary, but I loved it." "Scooby and his friends help each other. Strangers are nice to them." "Shaggy and Scooby are extreme." Video. 80 min.; $19.96; Age: 6-10. Warner Home Video.

** Secret Garden, The - MGM/UA

Outstanding child actress Margaret O'Brien touches the heart in this classic adventure of a young orphan sent to live at the foreboding English estate of her uncle and his crippled son. *Adult Juror Comments*: Creates a magical world from a child's point of view. Shows how children can influence and affect events towards a positive outcome. Takes a healthy attitude on bereavement and taking a chance on love. Visually lush and evocative. Invaluable insight. *Kid Juror Comments*: Good story, but some commented, "Black and white is boring." Though it took time for them to get into it, provided an opportunity to discuss death, love, and friendship. Video. 72 min.; $14.95; Age: 6-14. MGM/UA Home Entertainment.

*** Secret of Nimh, The

A timid mouse becomes a heroine in spite of herself. Clara struggles to save her home from farmer Fitzgibbon's plow and gets help from an awkward crow, a wise owl, and intelligent rats. *Adult Juror Comments*: A fantastic story. Well-presented with beautiful colors, stirring adventure, and good values. Engaged kids empathetically and critically in discussions about courage and progress. Promotes multi-cultural awareness. *Kid Juror Comments*: Enthusiastic. They loved Clara. The story elicited a lot of discussion afterwards. Video. 83 min.; $14.95; Age: 3-12. MGM/UA Home Entertainment.

** *Simon the Lamb (Precious Moments)*

When Timmy the Angel drops some rainbow paint on Simon the Lamb, he turns from fleecy white to comical blue. The other lambs shun him, but Simon rescues the flock in a blizzard and winds up a hero. *Adult Juror Comments*: Deals with basic socialization concepts such as differences and helping one another. The teasing segment seems a little drawn-out. The story contains Christian overtones and is not particularly original. *Kid Juror Comments*: Kids enjoyed it. Girls liked it better than boys. The lost-in-the-woods section and the snowstorm parts were scary. Video. 25 min.; $12.95; Age: 3-8. Western Publishing.

** *Sinbad (Animated Classics)*

 Sail through the excitement of a lifetime in this classic tale. Explore the voyages, dangers and narrow escapes that await the legendary hero. *Adult Juror Comments*: The story is a winner, though the animation is mediocre and there are no female role models. Some characters seem harsh, but they're not, and the overall effect is calming. Very age-appropriate. *Kid Juror Comments*: Just loved the story, particularly those already familiar with it. Video. 50 min.; $12.95; Age: 5-8. Goodtimes Entertainment.

* *Six Stories about Little Heroes: Jay O'Callahan (Jay O'Callahan)*

This collection of original tales told by Jay O'Callahan features child heroes and heroines. The stories speak about trust, friendship, courage, and common sense. The stories stretch the imagination and inspire children to tell their own tales. *Adult Juror Comments*: O'Callahan is an engaging storyteller who dramatically acts out this collection of carefully selected stories. Though the stories are well-done, the translation to video lacks something that makes the live performances so engaging. *Kid Juror Comments*: Hard for kids to understand him. They wanted more interaction between the characters as well as more action. The video did not hold their attention and many walked away. Video. 38 min.; $19.95; Age: 5-12. Vineyard Productions.

Chapter Three • Elementary

** Smart House (Disney Channel)

 A boy wins a computer-run "smart house" which malfunctions and develops a motherly mind of its own. Rental only. *Adult Juror Comments*: Creative and fun, yet sensitive look at loss and single parenting. Colorful scenes, clear characters, and real-life situations are well-positioned on a futuristic background. Technology aids the functioning of a household, but falls short of replacing Mom. *Kid Juror Comments*: Enjoyed and would recommend to their friends. "It's very funny when all the oranges go crazy in the kitchen." "The special effects were cool." "It was scary when the house turned into the mean mother." Video. 82 min.; rental only; Age: 5-12. Buena Vista Home Entertainment/Disney.

*** Snoopy Come Home

This animated classic revolves around an incident in which Charlie Brown's beloved beagle turns up missing and the whole Peanuts gang springs into action. *Adult Juror Comments*: Wonderful family fun with hummable music and a feel-good ending. Shows cooperation between characters. *Kid Juror Comments*: Always a winner. Definitely held their interest, though they thought Linus and Snoopy were sometimes mean to one another, particularly when they fought over the blanket. Still, they found that funny. They love Woodstock. Video. 80 min.; $14.98; Age: 4-12. Twentieth Century Fox Home Entertainment.

** Snow Queen, The
(Mikhail Baryshnikov's Stories from My Childhood)

A brave young girl defies danger to save a dear friend from a cold but beautiful Snow Queen. Russian animation, with voices of Kathleen Turner, Kristen Dunst, and Mickey Rooney in the classic Anderson tale. *Adult Juror Comments*: Great model of perseverance and friendship. Somewhat confusing story line, stereotypical female characters. Beautiful illustrations. Lively characters. Good introduction to folk tales, fairy tales, and cultural legends. *Kid Juror Comments*: "Can I get this book?" "The Snow Queen looks mean. I don't want to watch." "The girl is so brave and loves her friend." "I wonder if that is why people get sad in the winter." Some children were so disturbed they wouldn't watch the whole thing. Video. 60 min.; $19.98; Age: 5-8. Video Information Source.

*** Snow Queen, The - Stories to Remember
(Stories to Remember)

Powerful tale follows a young girl's quest to rescue her playmate from the icy palace of the Snow Queen. Based on the Hans Christian Anderson folktale. Narrated by Sigourney Weaver. Music by Jason Miles. *Adult Juror Comments*: Beautifully animated with wonderful character voices and lovely music. Excellent role models. The characters express many emotions that children can relate to, such as caring enough for another to put oneself out for them. *Kid Juror Comments*: Absorbing. Kids enjoyed the characters' adventures, responded to the story, and loved the ending, which reunites the friends. They wanted to watch it again. Video. 30 min.; $9.95; Age: 5-12. Stories to Remember.

* Snow White (Enchanted Tales)

Classic fairy tale about a princess, a wicked stepmother, seven dwarfs and a handsome prince. *Adult Juror Comments*: A twist on the original story, because Snow White knows the prince she falls in love with. Animation quality mediocre, but the appealing, humorous characters and pleasant songs make it worthwhile. *Kid Juror Comments*: A dwarf by any other name...Kids found it entertaining that all the dwarves were named "Joe," and wanted to see it again. Not as scary as the Disney version, and they appreciated that. Good length. Video. 48 min.; $14.98; Age: 4-9. Sony Wonder.

** Snowy Day and Other Caldecott Classics, The
(Children's Circle)

Anthology includes: "The Snowy Day," where a boy enjoys the wonder of a city snow; "Blueberries for Sal," where a girl and a bear cub mix up their mothers; "Owen," who loses his beloved yellow blanket; "Goldilocks and the Three Bears," the classic. *Adult Juror Comments*: The stories reflect children's lives and emotional capacities and enhance positive self-concept. The teacher's guide is helpful to integrate the stories with activities. Shows good role models. *Kid Juror Comments*: Related to Owen and his favorite blanket and thought Goldilocks was funny. Their favorite part: when Dr. DeSoto took out the fox's tooth and when Owen's mom made the handkerchief. "Snowy Day" is slow. Kids said they would show the video to a friend. Video. 32 min.; $19.95; Age: 3-7. Weston Woods Studios/Scholastic.

*** Sometimes I Wonder*

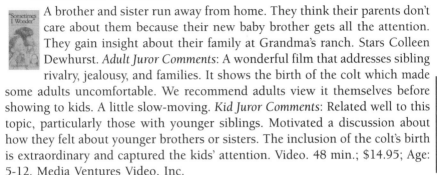

A brother and sister run away from home. They think their parents don't care about them because their new baby brother gets all the attention. They gain insight about their family at Grandma's ranch. Stars Colleen Dewhurst. *Adult Juror Comments*: A wonderful film that addresses sibling rivalry, jealousy, and families. It shows the birth of the colt which made some adults uncomfortable. We recommend adults view it themselves before showing to kids. A little slow-moving. *Kid Juror Comments*: Related well to this topic, particularly those with younger siblings. Motivated a discussion about how they felt about younger brothers or sisters. The inclusion of the colt's birth is extraordinary and captured the kids' attention. Video. 48 min.; $14.95; Age: 5-12. Media Ventures Video, Inc.

** Spin (Secret Adventures)*

An imaginative baby-sitter runs for class president. After some dirty campaigning, she learns about honesty while taking two of the children on a secret adventure. *Adult Juror Comments*: The story is realistic and exceptionally creative. The female teacher is a great role model. Contains Christian overtones that are not indicated on the packaging. At times the educational values overwhelms the story. *Kid Juror Comments*: Some enjoyed it a lot, while others found it to be too slow-moving to stay with. The Christian overtones seemed not to bother them. At least with those who tested this, they weren't affected by it. Video. 30 min.; $19.95; Age: 4-13. Taweel-Loos & Company.

*** Stories from the Black Tradition (Children's Circle)*

Contains four wonderful stories: "A Story, A Story," by Gail E. Haley; "Mufaro's Beautiful Daughters," by John Steptoe; "In the Village of the Round and Square Houses," by Ann Grifalconi; and "Goggles," by Ezra Jack Keats. *Adult Juror Comments*: Rich texture, warm feelings. The short stories, ten minutes each, can be shown in segments. Sensitive to fathers' relationships with daughters. All themes are centered on the community. *Kid Juror Comments*: "Magical, wonderful, and different." Kids enjoyed hearing the African accents. "Showed how African men and women appreciate one another." Referring to the story about mosquitoes, "I will never look at a mosquito the same way again." Video. 52 min.; $14.95; Age: 5-12. Scholastic/Children's Circle.

Age 5-8

Video

Family

* Story of Jonah and the Whale, The (The Beginner's Bible)

Jonah tries to escape God's command, runs away on a ship, and gets swallowed by a gigantic but friendly whale. Inside the whale's stomach, Jonah learns an astonishing lesson about God's love and forgiveness, even for those who disobey. *Adult Juror Comments*: Entertaining, with good role models. Best suited to a Christian audience. Borders on talking down to kids. *Kid Juror Comments*: A lot of information that five's and up can relate to and understand. Stimulated discussion afterwards. Some kids thought it was too preachy. The language used was too difficult for the younger kids. Video. 30 min.; $12.98; Age: 4-8. Sony Wonder.

* Story of the Prodigal Son, The (The Beginner's Bible)

To teach repentance, forgiveness, and love, Jesus tells about a son who refused to work on the family farm. He goes off to see the world where he encounters the glittering temptations of the city. When he returns, his father welcomes him with love. *Adult Juror Comments*: Good storybook quality and visually appealing. Teaches lessons by showing how to handle different behaviors. The vignettes lack continuity, and most characters are white. Best for Christian viewers. *Kid Juror Comments*: "That was a good cartoon." "It's better than church, where they just tell about it," commented one six-year-old. Some children didn't understand the meaning of the story. Others talked about their relationship with their parents. Video. 30 min.; $12.98; Age: 4-8. Sony Wonder.

** Stowaway (Shirley Temple)

Shirley Temple's Chinese missionary parents are killed, leaving her to fend for herself on the mean streets of Shanghai. *Adult Juror Comments*: Emphasizes traditional values and questions today's values. Addresses subjects of death, loss, and love. Content is serious, but dealt with in a lighthearted manner with simplistic solutions. The colorization makes it more appealing for today's kids. *Kid Juror Comments*: Children did not identify with characters. Stimulated interest in Chinese culture. "I wish I knew Chinese." Kids liked the way Shirley Temple was dressed. Held children's interest only in spurts. Video. 86 min.; $14.98; Age: 5-10. Twentieth Century Fox Home Entertainment.

Age 5-8

Video

Family

** Strega Nonna and Other Stories (Children's Circle)

Includes "Strega Nonna," the Chinese "Tikki Tikki Tembo," an African Folk Tale "A Story, A Story," and "Foolish Frog," a folk song by Pete Seeger. *Adult Juror Comments*: Interesting flavor promotes multicultural understanding. Beautifully done with great music. "Foolish Frog" is a fun sing-along. The stories can be viewed individually with discussion and activities in between. *Kid Juror Comments*: Older kids loved the stories, especially "Tikki Tikki Tembo" and "A Story, A Story." Younger kids paid more attention to the stories with songs. They liked the representation of many different cultures and asked questions afterwards. Video. 35 min.; $14.95; Age: 3-12. Scholastic/Children's Circle.

** Swan Princess, The

From the director of "The Fox and the Hound," this animated feature-length film stars John Cleese as Jean-Bob the Frog, Jack Palance as Rothbart, Sandy Duncan as the Queen, and Steven Wright as Speed the Turtle. *Adult Juror Comments*: Animation is excellent, with colorful characters and uplifting music. A simplistic version of the classic fairy tale and best suited for four- to ten-year-olds. *Kid Juror Comments*: Okay but not great. "It's a fairytale that turns out good." Video. 90 min.; $19.98; Age: 4-10. Warner Home Video.

*** Sword in the Stone, The

England is in the midst of a dark age and without a proper king. Young "Wart," an orphan squire-in-training, is content with kitchen duties in his foster home—until Merlin teaches him three life lessons about intellect, wisdom, and love. *Adult Juror Comments*: Quite entertaining. Classic tale of the under dog: good will prevails. Straightforward presentation and creative style make it an easy reference to Camelot and historical Europe. Fine production, although animation is not as expertly done as today's films. *Kid Juror Comments*: Kept them glued to the screen. All around great story, interesting, with laughs too. "It's different from new Disney movies. The jokes are different. Even my mom would like it." "I want to go and learn more about King Arthur. Were he and Merlin real?" Video. 79 min.; $22.99; Age: 5-10. Buena Vista Home Entertainment/Disney.

Age 5-8

Video

Family

*** Tale of Mrs. Tiggy-Winkle and Mr. Jeremy Fisher, The (The World of Peter Rabbit and Friends)*

Contains two stories. When Lucie loses her handkerchiefs, yet again, she never imagines that her search will end with kindly washerwoman, Mrs. Tiggy-Winkle. *Adult Juror Comments*: A wonderful production with excellent animation and soothing music. It is true to the original classic story and a little slow-moving, but it may promote an interest in reading the story. *Kid Juror Comments*: Girls liked it more than boys. Both were a little confused to find the two stories didn't relate to one another. Video. 30 min.; $14.95; Age: 3-12. Goodtimes Entertainment.

*** Tale of Peter Rabbit and Benjamin Bunny, The (The World of Peter Rabbit and Friends)*

Peter was very lucky to escape from Mr. MacGregor's garden without getting caught. When his cousin Benjamin suggests that they visit the garden again, Peter is more than a little nervous. *Adult Juror Comments*: Charming production retains the spirit of the original art while making the stories accessible to contemporary audiences. May promote an interest in reading. *Kid Juror Comments*: Kids loved it and asked for other Beatrix Potter books to read. "Good about safety." "I liked it because it's funny." Adults had problems with the British accents, but the kids didn't. They stayed with it all the way through. Video. 30 min.; $14.95; Age: 3-12. Goodtimes Entertainment.

** Tale of Peter Rabbit, The*

Beatrix Potter's classic comes to musical life through animation and the voice of Carol Burnett. *Adult Juror Comments*: Good story. The father's death is dealt with more than in the original story. Some stereotyping: girls are good and expected to "obey"; boys are naughty and it's okay for them to "explore" and be forgiven. *Kid Juror Comments*: A grand show, especially the funny parts. Afterwards, they asked to read the books. It's most appropriate for ages four and up. Video. 28 min.; $12.98; Age: 3-10. Artisan/Family Home Entertainment.

*** Tale of Samuel Whiskers, The (The World of Peter Rabbit and Friends)*

Samuel Whiskers the rat thinks that Tom Kitten could be made into an excellent roly-poly pudding for dinner. *Adult Juror Comments*: Excellent production with beautiful animation. Faithful to the book, with a compelling live-action opening sequence. May promote an interest in children's literature. *Kid Juror Comments*: Loved the kittens, the rat, and the mice. The English accents were occasionally difficult to understand. Video. 30 min.; $14.95; Age: 3-12. Goodtimes Entertainment.

*** Tale of Tom Kitten and Jemima Puddle Duck, The (The World of Peter Rabbit and Friends)

The farmyard garden is not the place for Tom Kitten and his sisters to play if they are going to keep their clothes clean for their mother's tea party. *Adult Juror Comments*: Superior production and animation retains spirit of original stories. Could stimulate interest in the books. *Kid Juror Comments*: Some kids went overboard for it. One child was ready to trade a "Barney" movie for this video. Video. 30 min.; $14.95; Age: 3-12. Goodtimes Entertainment.

** Tales from the Crib (Rugrats)

 Not yet two years old, Tommy Pickles is as mischievous and talkative as someone twice his age. Tommy and Chuckie find all kinds of trouble in a spooky toy store. *Adult Juror Comments*: The individual stories are clever. Appropriate humor for this age group. Animation has a clear contemporary feel to it. Little cultural diversity. *Kid Juror Comments*: Laughed throughout, enjoying the fantasy. Boys liked it better than girls. "In cartoons, they can do anything because it's not for real." Some kids thought this was too "loud." Video. 40 min.; $9.95; Age: 4-10. Paramount Home Entertainment.

** Tales of Beatrix Potter

Six classic stories, including "The Tale of Peter Rabbit," "The Story of Miss Moppet," and "Tale of Two Bad Mice." *Adult Juror Comments*: Good stories, separated by nursery rhymes. Includes activity book for parents. Faithful to original artwork. *Kid Juror Comments*: Okay but a little long. The sound wasn't always clear. Too sophisticated for younger children. Video. 44 min.; $12.98; Age: 4-10. Artisan/Family Home Entertainment.

* Tales of Beatrix Pottery, Volume 2

 Beatrix Potter's illustrations come vividly to life in this second volume of her classic fairy tales. Narrated by storyteller Sydney Walker, who guides the viewer on a journey into the world of Ms. Potter's beloved animal friends. *Adult Juror Comments*: Nicely animated with lively music and good narration. Use of a gun to chase the rabbit is objectionable. Addresses conflict resolution, friendship, and cooperation. The "Tale of Fierce Bad Rabbit" is too scary for younger ones. *Kid Juror Comments*: Children under five found the "real-life" experiences too scary. They liked the poems at the end, which helped them to read along. The slow pacing made kids a little drowsy. Best viewed in segments. Video. 46 min.; $12.98; Age: 5-10. Artisan/Family Home Entertainment.

** Teddy Bear's Picnic, The

For one magical day every year, the teddy bears of the world come alive to gather in the forest for food, fun, and games. *Adult Juror Comments*: This charming, lovely fantasy provides lots of opportunities to stop and ask questions. The characters are good role models. Opens the way to discuss emotions and cooperation. *Kid Juror Comments*: The bear fantasy was great. Video. 26 min.; $9.98; Age: 3-12. Artisan/Family Home Entertainment.

** Thirteenth Year, The (Disney Channel)

A boy learns that his birth mother is a mermaid after he begins to grow scales on his thirteenth birthday. *Adult Juror Comments*: Enjoyable family film, well-written and well-told. Lots of action and comedy with a serious ending. Fine scenery and quality photography; auditory accents enhance the drama. A contemporary version of old legends, showing real kids with real problems. *Kid Juror Comments*: Lots of good laughs. Related well to characters, especially the nerd who becomes the hero. "I liked the big explosion from the tuba when it fell in the pool." "It shows how it will be when we're teenagers, but we covered our eyes during the kissy part." Video. 89 min.; rental only; Age: 6-12. Buena Vista Home Entertainment/Disney.

* This Pretty Planet (Tom Chapin)

Tom Chapin sings thirteen songs from his award-winning recordings, which are enhanced with spectacular nature footage. *Adult Juror Comments*: Loved the music. This is better suited for activity than simply viewing. Although the message is important, the presentation is rather slow-moving. Culturally diverse. *Kid Juror Comments*: Though the kids got up and danced, they did not enjoy the music as much as they had hoped. They weren't anxious to see it again. Video. 50 min.; $14.98; Age: 4-10. Sony Wonder.

** Thomas the Tank: Thomas and the Magic Railroad (Thomas the Tank Engine & Friends)

Feature-length film. Lily, her grandfather, and Mr. Conductor join Thomas and his friends in a mission to rescue the magical gold dust supply from the evil Diesel #10. Stars Peter Fonda, Alec Baldwin, and Mara Wilson. *Adult Juror Comments*: Magical adventure. Beautifully done, animation and live action with stop action cinematography. Children are portrayed as competent contributors in relationships. Plot unfolds slowly, may lose youngest viewers. Diesel 10's meanness may be excessive. *Kid Juror Comments*: Entranced hard-core Thomas fans. "This will make my friends happy, happy, happy." "I want to learn about trains." "The diesel trains did a lot of name calling and were very mean to the steam trains." Youngest kids couldn't follow the intricate plot. Video. 84 min.; $22.96; Age: 4-8. Columbia Tristar Home Entertainment.

*** Three Musketeers, The (Animated Classics)

"All for one and one for all" is the motto of this animated tale of royal intrigue and swashbuckling adventure. D'Artagnan and the Three Musketeers battle to save France from the evil Cardinal Richelieu, bringing classic literature to life. *Adult Juror Comments*: Entertaining presentation of a classic novel. Beware that it does contain rather stereotypical portrayals of women: small voices, secretive, a willingness to be sacrificed. *Kid Juror Comments*: Really enjoyed it. They noticed that the fight scenes were not very graphic. Most asked if they could see the movie again. Children discussed parts of the movie as they watched it. Video. 50 min.; $12.95; Age: 6-12. Goodtimes Entertainment.

** Thumbelina (Animated Classics)

Based on the story by Hans Christian Andersen which follows the heroine, Thumbelina, and her efforts to save the Little People. *Adult Juror Comments*: Families will find this ageless tale enjoyable. Animation is mediocre. Shows how uncomfortable situations can be resolved without violence and fear. Could stimulate discussion about cooperation. *Kid Juror Comments*: Very special. Some wanted to watch it again immediately after it ended; others lost interest. Because of its length, it may be better-suited for younger kids to view in segments. Video. 50 min.; $19.95; Age: 4-8. Goodtimes Entertainment.

* Tom and Jerry's 50th Birthday Classics

From their debut in 1940, almost 60 years later Tom and Jerry are as funny as ever. This collection marks their half-century anniversary with seven classic cat-and-mouse contests. *Adult Juror Comments*: Like many golden oldies, this brings up issues concerning stereotypical portrayals, such as the African-American housekeeper and the cat-and-mouse behavior. Jurors passed this with some reservation. It provokes discussions about then and now. *Kid Juror Comments*: A barrel of laughs. The fast action and wildness grabbed their attention. Kids noticed the somewhat violent interaction between the cat and the mouse. "They could hurt someone." Video. 57 min.; $14.95; Age: 5-12. MGM/UA Home Entertainment.

*** Tom and Jerry: The Movie

The cat and mouse are at it again in an extravagant full-length musical adventure helping a young girl find her father. *Adult Juror Comments*: Production is well-done, and though the language is sometimes too sophisticated, it's still quite humorous. Relationship between Tom and Jerry is charming. The wordplay used in the songs is rich in meanings and rhymes. *Kid Juror Comments*: A big hit. The familiar characters are appealing and funny. Afterwards, kids discussed the nature of the wicked guardian and the cooperation and kindness shown by the rest of the characters. Video. 83 min.; $14.98; Age: 5-14. Artisan/Family Home Entertainment.

Age 5-8

Video

Family

*** Tom Sawyer

This film version of Mark Twain's classic story is set to music and features a first-rate cast: Johnny Whitaker as Tom; Jodie Foster as Tom's girlfriend, Becky; Celeste Holm as Aunt Polly; and Warren Oates as the boozy Muff Potter. *Adult Juror Comments*: Good introduction to the work of Mark Twain as a musical, which helps keep the kids interested. Encourages thinking about people's places within their community and community ethics. *Kid Juror Comments*: They noticed the dated look of the movie, but enjoyed the story anyway and loved the music. Injun Joe was too scary for some. The murder scene is disturbing, although it's not graphically depicted. It sparked an interest in reading more Twain. Video. 102 min.; $14.95; Age: 3-11. MGM/UA Home Entertainment.

** Tom Thumb

The classic adventures of a tiny boy in the Big World. *Adult Juror Comments*: Purists will be disappointed because it does not closely follow the original story. It's still a good story, simply produced. Jurors were disturbed that Tom's size was not consistent. *Kid Juror Comments*: Funny and cute. Best-suited to younger children, though it may have some frightening aspects. Video. 26 min.; $9.98; Age: 3-18. Artisan/Family Home Entertainment.

** Tomie DePaola Video Library, The

Anthology includes: "Charlie Needs a Cloak," Charlie's old one is torn; "Strega Nonna," featuring a magic pasta pot that Big Anthony discovers; and "The Clown of God," where a once famous juggler gives an unforgettable performance on Christmas Eve. *Adult Juror Comments*: The illustrations attract young and old alike. Each story explores animals, cooking, clothing, religion, and culture. DePaola's humor is magnified. "Strega Nonna tickles a child's imagination." Contains Christian messages. *Kid Juror Comments*: Liked every story. Enjoyed learning where wool comes from and how to make a cloak. They were interested in the juggling, although they didn't follow the meaning of the clown story. "Strega Nonna is magic." Video. 27 min.; $19.95; Age: 4-8. Weston Woods Studios/Scholastic.

** *Tommy Tricker and the Stamp Traveler (Les Productions La Fête)*

Ralph James shares his father's passion for collecting stamps. He makes the mistake of trading one of his father's favorite stamps to Tommy Tricker. A series of adventures follow, as Ralph tries to get his hands on a worthy replacement. *Adult Juror Comments*: An interesting story that stimulates an interest in geography. Some stereotyping, especially the portrayal of Chinese children. When Tommy steals, cheats and lies, his behavior is dismissed as 'tricks.'" *Kid Juror Comments*: Loved the story. Learning about the value of stamps intrigued them. They enjoyed the animation and a discussion about honesty followed the viewing. Video. 105 min.; $14.98; Age: 4-12. Productions La Fête.

* *Tommy Troubles (Rugrats)*

Includes four episodes. Tommy attempts to lead his friends away from the confinement of clothing; experiences the supermarket as an amusement park; acts up at the baseball game; anguishes when his favorite stuffed toy is thrown away. *Adult Juror Comments*: Well-produced with subtle learning tucked in. Looks at things from a child's perspective. The inclusion of older people is welcome. Angelica is not the best kid role model. Some sarcasm and stereotyping. *Kid Juror Comments*: Enjoyable viewing with kids. It's funny and easy to follow. Kids relate to it and find it interesting. The comedy is partly about kids in trouble and looks at it from their point of view. Video. 63 min.; $12.95; Age: 6-9. Paramount Home Entertainment.

* *Treasure Island (Enchanted Tales)*

Set course for the grandest pirate yarn ever, in this animated, song-and-laughter-filled version of Robert Louis Stevenson's swashbuckling classic. *Adult Juror Comments*: Entertaining and well–produced, but portrayal of characters is stereotypical. Shows disrespect of others as funny. Not true to original story, adding silly elements for the sake of humor, which don't help at all. *Kid Juror Comments*: Catchy songs, even if some kids were bothered that the mouths didn't match the animated characters. Boys liked it better than girls. Video. 48 min.; $9.99; Age: 5-8. Sony Wonder.

* *Trollies Musical Adventure (The Trollies)*

Exciting action and adventure is on the horizon for the Trollies as they thwart the Trouble Trollie Gang's attempt to steal the sun. *Adult Juror Comments*: Some stories are better than others. At times they are cluttered and confusing. "In a Different Light" is an excellent story. Too much emphasis is given to the bad Trollies and their negative behavior. *Kid Juror Comments*: Good narrative, but thought the songs were too long. Boys liked this better than girls. It was scary for younger kids. Video. 43 min.; $12.98; Age: 4-8. PPI/Peter Pan, Inc.

*** *Trouble on Planet Wait-Your-Turn (3-2-1 Penguins!)*

From the creators of "VeggieTales" comes a hilarious video series with faith, fun, and flightless birds: 3-2-1 Penguins! Twins Jason and Michelle learn about patience when they meet Zidgel, Midgel, Fidgel, and Kevin. *Adult Juror Comments*: Enjoyable. Excellent graphics. A trip to Grandma's with a moral lesson. Good length, color, and animation. Talks about how to behave, patience, and making the best of a bad situation. Quotes Bible verses, but not in a preachy way. *Kid Juror Comments*: Delighted. Kids related to the characters. "The kids were like me and my friends. We hate to wait." "I want to show this to my class so we can all learn to wait our turn." "I loved the penguins." "I want to go to outer space." Video. 30 min.; $14.95; Age: 4-8. Big Idea Productions, Inc.

*** *Trumpet of the Swan*

Louie is born without a voice—a tragedy for a trumpeter swan. Out of love, Louie's father steals a trumpet to give Louie a voice…but stealing is wrong, and Louie is committed to restoring his father's honor. Animated. *Adult Juror Comments*: Fabulous. A treat to watch. Excellent adaptation of the book. Parallels wildlife and mankind, with social and emotional complexities. Wonderful, theatrical wing-tossing and web-footed pacing. Rich language, touches of humor, delightful original score. *Kid Juror Comments*: Listened intently throughout. Shared their favorite parts over and over again. "I liked how Louie tried to get his father's honor back." "I loved when the swan father made those funny speeches and no one wanted to listen." "Sam Beaver was way, way cool." Video. 77 min.; rental only; Age: 5-12. Columbia Tristar Home Entertainment.

*** *Tuned In (The Puzzle Place)*

Teaches kids that there' more to life than what they see on TV! *Adult Juror Comments*: Cheerful, colorful, fast-moving, and humorous presentation. Helps kids examine different perspectives about TV-watching. Provoked discussion about TV-watching rules. The characters' personalities are believable, and the children relate to them. *Kid Juror Comments*: Totally absorbing from the get-go. They danced along while watching. Kids recognized these characters from TV. They talked about how TV shows are made. Animation held children's attention. They loved the puppets. Video. 55 min.; $9.99; Age: 4-7. Sony Wonder.

Chapter Three • Elementary

*** Uncle Elephant (John Matthews Collection)*

The parents of nine-year-old Arnie the elephant vanish, and his life abruptly changes. Arnie's Uncle Elephant tries to lift his spirits. Their new friendship tickles everyone. Arnie's parents are rescued and return to a rousing welcome. *Adult Juror Comments*: Has a wonderful story and fantastic animation. A sensitive exploration of emotion shows there can be laughter even during difficult times. A good connection between youth and elderly. Some sequences were quite surrealistic. *Kid Juror Comments*: Made some kids sad, and they needed to talk it through. When the parents are rescued, the resolution is comforting. The production values were appreciated. Video. 26 min.; $12.95; Age: 4-12. Sony Wonder.

** Urban Adventures (Hey Arnold!)*

These five big-city stories follow the adventures of Arnold, a nine-year-old boy, who's as vulnerable to heart-wrenching crushes as he is to head-squeezing bullies. For Arnold and his best friend Gerald, adventure is just a bus stop away. *Adult Juror Comments*: Excellent animated production. Shows good friendship role models of a diverse mix of children. Shows life in the big city. Some wisecracks are inappropriate. *Kid Juror Comments*: Fabulous, especially those familiar with Arnold. Sparked a curiosity among kids who don't live in urban areas to see people in big cities. One child commented, "Cities are really different from our area." "People were different and all sizes." Video. 55 min.; $12.95; Age: 6-9. Paramount Home Entertainment.

*** Veggie Tales: Dave and the Giant Pickle (Veggie Tales)*

Retells the Biblical story of David and Goliath. Junior Asparagus plays young David, who takes on a nine-foot pickle. Offers a lesson in self-esteem when Bob the Tomato and Larry the Cucumber teach kids that even little guys can do big things. *Adult Juror Comments*: Engaging and funny. Not a traditional retelling of the story. The characters are represented by talking vegetables. "It reminded me of something out of Monty Python." Maintains the basic theme of "everyone is special." Appeals to Christian audience. *Kid Juror Comments*: The message went over well. "It doesn't matter if you are small. You are still great." When asked, "Who would have thought to turn the characters into vegetables?" One eight-year-old responded, "Someone who liked Brussels sprouts when they were a kid." Video. 30 min.; $12.99; Age: 5-8. Big Idea Productions, Inc.

*** Veggie Tales: Esther...the Girl Who Became Queen (Veggie Tales)

Esther is the king's chosen queen, but she soon discovers that being queen takes more courage than she ever imagined. Filled with drama, humor, and great music. Esther teaches kids they "never need to be afraid to do what's right!" *Adult Juror Comments*: Fantastic graphics, toe-tapping music, and endearing characters. Unusual video concept that does a good job of bringing Bible stories to the younger set. Sophisticated, colorful animation. "Walking, talking vegetables...what's not to like?" *Kid Juror Comments*: Charmed by the whole package. "I liked how the movie looked. The computer animation was cool." "Neat songs." "It showed that you have to stand up for yourself." "Esther is really pretty." "I would like to learn more about what Esther did." Video. 36 min.; $12.99; Age: 4-8. Big Idea Productions, Inc.

** Veggie Tales: God Wants Me to Forgive Them (Veggie Tales)

Two stories teach children a lesson in forgiveness. In "The Grapes of Wrath," Junior Asparagus leans to forgive the grapes even after they've hurt his feelings. "Larry's Lagoon" is a spoof of "Gilligan's Island" in which passengers learn to forgive. *Adult Juror Comments*: Negatively stereotypes Appalachian people. Engaging, bright visuals and clear animation. Great starting point for discussing fairness and forgiveness. Contains Christian overtones and numerous references to God and Jesus. *Kid Juror Comments*: Terrific. A hoot. They really understood the concepts. "The veggies taught us to forgive." "I think it would be a great movie for preschoolers." Video. 30 min.; $12.99; Age: 5-8. Big Idea Productions, Inc.

*** Veggie Tales: Josh and the Big Wall (Veggie Tales)

Obedience is taught in this adaptation of a Bible story featuring vegetables. To get to the Promised Land, Larry the Cucumber, Bob the Tomato, and Junior Asparagus must go through Jericho first. It's not easy since a huge wall surrounds Jericho. *Adult Juror Comments*: Good animation. Using vegetables as characters is an amusing twist. Delightful music, brilliant colors, and realistic action. Biblical theme is very clear and done in a fun way that kids can understand. Contains Christian content. *Kid Juror Comments*: Much appreciated learning about a story they didn't know. Discovered what a narrator is. Sang along the second time. Were intrigued with the characters. "I learned that you need to listen to God." "I like how the vegetables talk." Video. 30 min.; $12.99; Age: 5-8. Big Idea Productions, Inc.

Chapter Three • Elementary

*** *Veggie Tales: King George and the Ducky (Veggie Tales)*

  Kids and parents alike will laugh along as they learn a lesson about selfishness. The kingdom is at war, and King George can think of only one thing; his beloved rubber duck bath toy. Yet, he must have little Thomas's ducky too. *Adult Juror Comments*: "Takes a common feeling of wanting something another has." The King learns to share. The gesture gives kids a basis for caring. "Good graphics of the humorous vegetable characters." Silly and fun sing-along-songs. *Kid Juror Comments*: "The king was not good at first because he did not share, but then he learned to share." "My friends would like Bob the Cucumber and Larry the Tomato because Bob and Larry sing silly fun songs." Video. 30 min.; $12.95; Age: 5-8. Big Idea Productions, Inc.

*** *Veggie Tales: Larry-Boy and the Fib from Outer Space! (Veggie Tales)*

A little fib turns into a big problem for Junior Asparagus. Junior is advised to cover his tracks with a little white lie. Junior learns that lies have a way of growing, and it isn't long before his "little fib" has grown into a 30-foot tall monster. *Adult Juror Comments*: Entertaining. Good animation with engaging characters, lots of action, well-paced. Promotes discussion about how lies perpetuate themselves. Reinforces the notion that to stop a lie one must confess and tell the truth. Promotes Christian values. *Kid Juror Comments*: "It's so silly, you have to watch it." Children related well to the characters. Big Fib was a bit scary. Children understood the growing lie. "I learned we shouldn't lie. Lies get bigger and bigger." "I liked it when he decided to tell the truth." Video. 30 min.; $12.99; Age: 5-8. Big Idea Productions, Inc.

*** *Veggie Tales: Where's God When I'm S-Scared? (Veggie Tales)*

 In "Tales from the Crisper," Junior Asparagus watches a movie that is too scary for him. With help from his friends, his fears are alleviated. In "Daniel and the Lion's Den," Larry the Cucumber finds himself in trouble with the king's conniving men. *Adult Juror Comments*: Well-done. Appealing in sound, sight, and theme. Good example of how to refocus emotions and handle fear. Addresses how not to be afraid of the dark. Biblical story is told in a non-threatening manner. Appeals most to a Christian audience. *Kid Juror Comments*: Children talked about their fears. Identified with the vegetable. "I would tell my friends to watch this." One child said she wouldn't be afraid of the dark anymore. They liked the song about God being bigger than the monsters. Video. 30 min.; $12.99; Age: 4-8. Big Idea Productions, Inc.

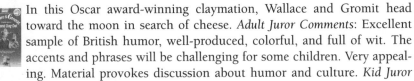

*** Wallace and Gromit: A Grand Day Out (Wallace & Gromit)

In this Oscar award-winning claymation, Wallace and Gromit head toward the moon in search of cheese. *Adult Juror Comments*: Excellent sample of British humor, well-produced, colorful, and full of wit. The accents and phrases will be challenging for some children. Very appealing. Material provokes discussion about humor and culture. *Kid Juror Comments*: Tons of fun. The dog character was a big hit. Kids loved that Gromit the dog is so smart and can read. "How exciting, let's watch it again!" Video. 25 min.; $9.98; Age: 4-10. Twentieth Century Fox Home Entertainment.

*** Water Tree and Other Stories, The (Jingaroo)

What's the best part of waking up in the morning? How do you get a stingy old desert tree to share? What's the hardest thing about being in a play? Watch Jingaroo in these three short stories and find out. *Adult Juror Comments*: Well-produced. "Best 3-D animation I've seen." Characters are appealing. Stories teach about the importance of teamwork, encouragement, and sharing. One story covers stage fright. Upbeat music and songs. *Kid Juror Comments*: Captivated them. They loved it. "The colors in the video were awesome." "The pancake machine was cool." "It's important to share so you'll have friends." "I felt afraid like Victoria, when I was in a play." "I liked the music videos." Video. 24 min.; $14.95; Age: 5-8. Beckett Entertainment.

* Weird, Wet and Wild (Animal Crackups)

Explores the world of animals that live in and around the water. Follows an incredible adventure with Zak and C-Mor as they find out what makes these animals different. *Adult Juror Comments*: Film footage is great. Lacks detail. Adults disliked the "wise-guy" narrator. "The animals are fascinating without the hoopla of the narrator." "The make-believe comments of the animals are humorous but misleading." *Kid Juror Comments*: Kids had trouble following the story. "Zak the narrator was all over the place without telling us where he was." "I didn't know fish spit." "The hippo was very funny." "The voices were cute." "The birth of the whale was gross." Video. 30 min.; $14.99; Age: 5-8. E-Realbiz.

Chapter Three • Elementary

*** *White Seal*

Roddy McDowall narrates this classic story from Rudyard Kipling's *Jungle Book*. Follows the adventures of a very special baby seal who grows up to save his tribe from the men who slaughter seals. Animated by Chuck Jones. *Adult Juror Comments*: Good story line. Encourages children to think for themselves, find solutions, and make an effort to care for their community. Starts discussion about endangered species. Some objected to the violence even though it furthers the story. *Kid Juror Comments*: Though kids enjoyed the video, they asked, "Why are the daddy seals so mean?" They also commented, "I never knew seals had to learn to swim." "Are there really white seals?" Video. 29 min.; $9.98; Age: 3-12. Artisan/Family Home Entertainment.

*** *Wild Swans, The (Stories to Remember)*

Princess Elise is exiled and her brothers transformed into wild swans by an envious Queen. Elise searches for her brothers. Although faced with a daunting task, she succeeds. Narrated by Sigourney Weaver from a tale by Hans Christian Andersen. *Adult Juror Comments*: This well-told, imaginatively animated classic makes a great addition to any child's video collection. The sibling relationship is an exemplary role model. Some aspects of the story may be frightening for younger kids. *Kid Juror Comments*: Completely focused on it and interacted with each other throughout the screening. "I loved this movie." "It was very entertaining." They noticed that "The mouths don't move when they talk." Video. 25 min.; $9.95; Age: 4-12. Stories to Remember.

*** *William Steig Video Library, The*

Anthology includes: "Sylvester and the Magic Pebble," Sylvester turns into a rock to escape a lion; "The Amazing Bone," a young female pig finds courage; "Doctor De Soto," the doctor relieves a fox's toothache; and more. *Adult Juror Comments*: Engaging humor. Stimulates language development with artistic excellence. Stories present problems that are positively resolved. "Steig presents fantasy and wonder at a child's level." Teachers found the activity guide useful. *Kid Juror Comments*: Thought the pictures were old-fashioned. They liked the stories about Dr. DeSoto outfoxing the fox best. "My favorite segment is Brave Irene." All of the children wanted to read the books again. Video. 45 min.; $19.95; Age: 4-8. Weston Woods Studios/Scholastic.

* William Wegman's Mother Goose (Sesame Street)

How will Mother Goose ever teach her son, Simon Goose, the art of rhyming? Who will carry on the great goose tradition of rhyming rhymes? Favorite children's rhymes are infused with Wegman's wry sense of humor and charm. *Adult Juror Comments*: Perfect subject for this age. The language is difficult for under fives. Presumes kids know the nursery rhymes and understand sarcasm and wit. Though Wegman's work is skillful, the dogs dressed in clothes are strange. *Kid Juror Comments*: Not a grabber. Kids wandered in and out during viewing. They liked the costumes and the visuals. Preschoolers didn't understand the sophisticated sense of humor, but the adults did. Video. 30 min.; $12.98; Age: 4-8. Sony Wonder.

** Winnie the Pooh: Seasons of Giving (Winnie the Pooh)

One day in the Hundred Acre Wood, Pooh, Piglet, Tigger, and Rabbit set out on a quest for winter—a favorite season they have missed—which leads to a wild search for the perfect ingredients for a festive holiday feast. *Adult Juror Comments*: Positive, light, and funny. Pooh is always adorable. Stories within the story led to a choppy presentation. Seemed a little long; characters seemed to plod along. *Kid Juror Comments*: Amused them, even if they had seen it before. They all love Pooh and his friends. "They are really nice friends." "Rabbit was kind of bossy, but he usually is. He wouldn't let Pooh be helpful." Video. 70 min.; $22.99; Age: 4-10. Buena Vista Home Entertainment/Disney.

** You Can Ride a Horse (You Can Video Series for Children)

Explores the world of horses and shows what it's like to work and play with them every day. Full of fascinating facts about horses and exciting stunt-riding scenes. *Adult Juror Comments*: Information and clear instructions. Shows that kids can ride a horse and enjoy riding lessons with other kids. Demonstrates cooperation and teamwork. Little cultural diversity. Pace is a little uneven. *Kid Juror Comments*: Girls liked it better than boys. Older kids liked it, but found it too simple. Kids appreciated inclusions of a person in a wheelchair and a child with glasses. Video. 29 min.; $12.95; Age: 4-9. Blackboard Entertainment.

** You Lucky Dog (Disney Channel)

A washed up dog psychic turned therapist is named guardian of a millionaire dog. Rental only. *Adult Juror Comments*: Entertaining and suspenseful. Well-produced. Flows well from scene to scene. Promotes acceptance of diversity and individual-ity. Great for dog lovers. Some name-calling and negative behaviors which have appropriate consequences. *Kid Juror Comments*: Enjoyed, would recommend to friends. "It's so silly, it's fun." "My friends would like to see a man acting like a dog." "I'd like to know if there is someone in the world who can really talk to animals." Video. 88 min.; rental only; Age: 6-12. Buena Vista Home Entertainment/Disney.

** You're Invited to Mary-Kate & Ashley's Ballet Party (You're Invited to Mary-Kate And Ashley's)

What's more exciting than a whirlwind trip to New York City? Mary-Kate and Ashley invite the viewer to join them at the ultimate ballet party at Lincoln Center. *Adult Juror Comments*: Provokes children's interest in professional ballet. Explains the moves and models the steps. Also addresses the rare overnight success as well as the need to practice to become better. With no story line, it's a little disjointed. *Kid Juror Comments*: Kids were impressed with the ability and agility of the ballet dancers. Girls were especially enthralled with the actors, the settings, and the music. The focus on the twins was at times distracting. "Ballerinas are beautiful. I love the tutus." Video. 30 min.; $12.95; Age: 5-8. Warner Home Video.

* You're Invited to Mary-Kate & Ashley's Birthday Party (You're Invited to Mary-Kate and Ashley's)

Mary-Kate and Ashley plan a birthday party filled with excitement and fun. With five new songs, it's geared up to be the biggest, most fantabulous birthday party in history. *Adult Juror Comments*: Well-produced. Presents many party ideas. Many gender stereotypes such as girls' fascination with makeup and clothes, boys causing mischief. Filled with mildly derogatory comments about boys throughout. Attention is overly focused on the twins. *Kid Juror Comments*: Girls thought it was fun. One boy said dejectedly, "I hate when they talk about boys." Sparked an interest in Six Flags' Amusement Park rides. The songs appealed to some. A favorite element was the outtakes at the end. Video. 30 min.; $12.95; Age: 5-8. Warner Home Video.

* You're Invited to Mary-Kate & Ashley's Campout Party (You're Invited to Mary-Kate and Ashley's)

Grab your knapsack, light your lantern, and take along your tent. Get ready for the outrageous antics in the great outdoors with Mary-Kate and Ashley. Includes several original songs with elaborate choreography. *Adult Juror Comments*: Girls display stereotypical behaviors such as their concern about what to wear and "creepy crawly" bugs. Some objected to the silliness and the overly materialistic nature of the program. *Kid Juror Comments*: Children split by gender on its appeal. Girls liked it—the music and the dancing—boys thought it was "dumb." All agreed that boys were poorly depicted. Kids were disappointed not to learn anything about camping. The electric tent was ridiculous. Video. 30 min.; $12.95; Age: 5-8. Warner Home Video.

* You're Invited to Mary-Kate & Ashley's Costume Party (You're Invited to Mary-Kate and Ashley's)

 Travel back in time with Mary-Kate and Ashley as they dress up for their costume party in styles from previous generations. *Adult Juror Comments*: Songs and dances are appropriate and tasteful. Demonstrates dances from the '50s through the '80s including country-western. Female stereotypes prevail—girls focusing on boys and appearance. Lip-synching by the twins is distracting at times. *Kid Juror Comments*: Responded well to the music and the kids on-screen. They enjoyed the twins and their friends. Prompted discussion about clothes from different eras. "The music was fun to dance to." Video. 30 min.; $12.95; Age: 5-8. Warner Home Video.

** You're Invited to Mary-Kate & Ashley's Hawaiian Beach Party (You're Invited to Mary-Kate and Ashley's)

Mary-Kate and Ashley join their friends in Hawaii for swimming, surfing, jet skiing, and singing. They build sand castles, visit a submarine, and dance the day away. *Adult Juror Comments*: Refreshingly healthy fun. Upbeat and bright. Beautiful footage introducing the sights of Hawaii. Appropriate language and content for this age range. Includes "surfer" lingo. *Kid Juror Comments*: Enjoyable. They learned a bit about Hawaii and surfing. "I want to go to the beach now or horseback riding. I want to sing the songs." "The sand castle looked great, but you know they didn't build it." "There's too much singing for me." Video. 30 min.; $12.95; Age: 5-8. Warner Home Video.

* You're Invited to Mary-Kate & Ashley's Mall Party (You're Invited to Mary-Kate & Ashley's)

 The twins sing, dance, and shop their way around the Mall of America. From roller coasters to bumper cars, the girls invite the audience to grab their shopping bags and join them in their imaginations. *Adult Juror Comments*: Entertaining production, though it promotes materialism. "This video works fine as a promo piece for the mall, but it's very shallow." Children playing at the mall without parents are poor role models. *Kid Juror Comments*: Girls liked it more than boys, but almost everyone thought the mall was a neat place. They liked the music and the amusement park the best. "It was fun, but kind of the same thing over and over." "Maybe Mama and Papa will take me shopping." Video. 30 min.; $12.95; Age: 5-8. Warner Home Video.

** You're Invited to Mary-Kate & Ashley's Sleepover Party (You're Invited to Mary-Kate and Ashley's)

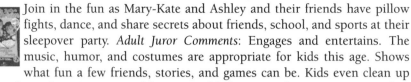

Join in the fun as Mary-Kate and Ashley and their friends have pillow fights, dance, and share secrets about friends, school, and sports at their sleepover party. *Adult Juror Comments*: Engages and entertains. The music, humor, and costumes are appropriate for kids this age. Shows what fun a few friends, stories, and games can be. Kids even clean up after themselves. Stereotypical boy vs. girl behavior. *Kid Juror Comments*: They liked watching the girls dress as monsters. All the kids wanted to have a sleepover party with their friends. Some kids sang along. "The fish pizza was disgusting." Video. 30 min.; $12.95; Age: 5-8. Warner Home Video.

* Young People (Shirley Temple)

Shirley Temple stars in this charming story about a show business couple who retire to a small town to give their daughter a normal life. Features footage from early Shirley Temple films. *Adult Juror Comments*: Very slow-paced. Footage of Shirley has great nostalgic appeal. The story is sometimes complex and gender stereotypes are rampant. The story emphasizes respect for differences. Contains aggressive language, name-calling, and parents slapping kids. *Kid Juror Comments*: Young children did not understand the story. Children watched part of the program and were not interested in seeing it again. The witches scared them and some had bad dreams afterwards. Led to discussion of different values from that time period. Video. 78 min.; $14.98; Age: 5-8. Twentieth Century Fox Home Entertainment.

** Zebra in the Kitchen, A (Family Treasures)

Hilarious chaos reigns when a well-intentioned but misguided twelve-year-old boy lets all the animals out of the zoo and into the backyards, bedrooms, and even bathrooms of the neighborhood. *Adult Juror Comments*: This is great for family viewing. Both adults and children enjoyed it. A little dated in its portrayal of zoos and how animals are kept. As a result, it prompted discussion about the care of animals and their zoo experiences. Slow-paced. *Kid Juror Comments*: Very funny, though dated. They followed the story and enjoyed watching with the adults. It prompted a discussion about zoos, caring for animals. It's a great introduction for a field trip to a zoo. Video. 92 min.; $14.95; Age: 5-12. MGM/UA Home Entertainment.

* Zenon: Girl of the 21st Century (Disney Channel)

The story of a free-spirited thirteen-year-old girl who lives most of her life on a space station. When she gets in trouble, her parents ground her, literally, back to Earth where she learns about life on the blue planet. *Adult Juror Comments*: Clever depiction of the future. Very kid-centric, humorously done. Children presented as forces of change. Questionable behavior, sassiness, loud rock music. "Potential for discussion about the future, but the subtler message may be that of taking risks." *Kid Juror Comments*: Older kids definitely related to the characters and story. "It was different because it showed the future from a kid's point of view." "It was about kids like us and problems growing up." "Cool clothes and expressions." "My mom would have yelled at them." Video. 97 min.; rental only; Age: 6-12. Buena Vista Home Entertainment/Disney.

** ZOOM: Best of the 70s (ZOOM)

Relive your favorite bits of ZOOM—the Emmy-Award-winning PBS kid's show from the 70s. In the first TV series inspired, written, and performed by kids, the cast uses material such as games, dancing, and cooking submitted by viewers. *Adult Juror Comments*: Great. "It was fun to see the styles from when I grew up." Excellent mix of cultures. Generates interest in creative expression. Promotes individuality, although it does show some gender stereotyping typical of the period. *Kid Juror Comments*: It was fun to see the 70s styles. "It showed the importance of being yourself." Some were intrigued, others were confused by the "ubbi dubbi" language. "I liked the dough-craft demonstration." Some found the repetition boring. Video. 40 min.; $19.95; Age: 6-12. WGBH.

Chapter Three • Elementary

Category—FLM

* Babar, King of the Elephants

 Children have read the classic tales of Babar for over sixty years. The stories of Babar and his jungle friends in this feature length film begin when Babar was orphaned in the wild, and culminate in Babar's becoming King. *Adult Juror Comments*: Epic presentation, coming-of-age story. Fanciful animation helps balance more serious undertones. Handles death and grieving. Soft and slow paced. Has both humorous elements and sad events, and ultimately a happy ending. *Kid Juror Comments*: Older kids were better able to handle the portrayal of death. "The elephant acted like a person, and I liked that." "I learned about being nice." "I knew hunting wasn't good, and this showed it." "Maybe the man who killed the mommy should be punished." Video. 78 min.; $19.98; Age: 6-9. HBO.

** Dr. Dolittle (Doctor Dolittle)

A musical masterpiece about a 19th century doctor who talks with animals in an imaginative world of endless imagination, music, dance, and special effects. Stars Rex Harrison as Dr. Dolittle, dubbed in Spanish. *Adult Juror Comments*: 1960s era film that appeals to the entire family. Cool special effects, especially the Giant Pink Snail. African islanders are portrayed as cultured, educated, and well-read. "I love every time Dr. Dolittle says good morning to the animals." *Kid Juror Comments*: Kids thought the music was corny, but still liked it. They related to Dr. Dolittle fulfilling his dream and how "Miss Fairfax wants to prove that she is more than what people prejudge her to be...I relate to that." "It made me want to study animals." Video. 145 min.; $14.98; Age: 5-12. Twentieth Century Fox Home Entertainment.

** Hansel & Gretel (Musical Classics)

Marionettes dramatize the children's version of Humperdinck's famous opera. *Adult Juror Comments*: Presents traditional and religious values from an old story in a new way. Adults liked this musical interpretation because it inspires appreciation. Parents demonstrate care even when children misbehave. Helps families work through problems. *Kid Juror Comments*: Great puppets, realistic backgrounds, and funny characters! Some kids were upset by slight changes to the story. They learned lessons about bad behavior. Kids tried using rhythm to create a spell to release Hansel. Favorite part: finding the candy house. Video. 40 min.; $14.95; Age: 5-8. Jim Gamble Puppet Productions.

Age 5-8

Video

FLM

* Ruby Princess Runs Away, The (The Jewel Kingdom)

 Roxanne is afraid to be crowned the Ruby Princess, so she runs away. In her adventures, she gains confidence in herself and learns that being the Ruby Princess is about being a good listener and a true friend. *Adult Juror Comments*: The Princess feels unworthy initially, but in the end finds the strength within herself to be a true princess. There is a magic quality throughout. Shows concern for others, respect of differences, accepting responsibility. *Kid Juror Comments*: Kids liked the powerful talking dragon. Taught them a lesson about helpfulness. Some kids thought there was too much singing and didn't like the graphics. They had a hard time understanding why a princess would run away. The darklings were scary for some. Video. 45 min.; $14.99; Age: 5-8. Where We Live Productions, LLC.

Category—Foreign Language

** Bonjour Les Amis, Volume One (Bonjour Les Amis)

 What, you don't speak French? Moustache teaches how to speak French while introducing his friends, singing songs, and visiting a magic show. *Adult Juror Comments*: Very slow-paced. Clever, innovative approach to teaching French. The lessons are short, challenging, and require concentration. The cats were great. "Good not great, not all-star, pretty static." *Kid Juror Comments*: Kids had trouble reading the French words on-screen. Using songs makes it much easier to learn another language than using straight vocabulary. Introduces kids to the intricacies of learning another language. Video. 48 min.; $19.95; Age: 4-10. Monterey Home Video.

** El Barco Magico (Juana La Iguana)

 A beach day becomes a fantastic experience for Pablo and Ana when they sail in a magic ship with Juana the Iguana. Through music and exploration, it conveys a message that learning can be a magical adventure. This is a Spanish language title. *Adult Juror Comments*: Nice mix of songs, good blend of eye-catching, live action and puppetry with engaging child performers. Imaginative and creative, stimulates a positive response. Poor sound-quality, background noise overshadows narrative. *Kid Juror Comments*: Kids go for make-believe. They sang along while learning new vocabulary words. Some four-year-olds found the pirate section scary. Older kids responded best. "This made all of us feel special," commented some Spanish-speaking kids. Video. 30 min.; $14.95; Age: 3-8. Iguana Productions.

Chapter Three • Elementary

* El Paseo De Rosita Y Otros Cuento De Animales (Children's Circle)

In Spanish. Stories: "Rosie's Walk," fox stalks an unsuspecting hen; "The Caterpillar and the Polliwog," about springtime; "Make Way for Ducklings," the story of Mr. and Mrs. Mallard; and "The Story About Ping," a lonely duck is befriended by a boy. *Adult Juror Comments*: Faithful adaptations of classics and some newer tales. Excellent narration, good pace, sweet and appealing. Animation is done in iconographic style. Inaccurately stereotypes Chinese people. Addresses being on time, safety of home and family. *Kid Juror Comments*: Imaginations were captured. "I love it in Spanish like we speak at home." "I was scared for the Ping duck, but I liked it all." "This is a great story time." "Let's get these books. I know they are at the library." Each child had a favorite story. Video. 35 min.; $19.95; Age: 3-7. Weston Woods Studios/Scholastic.

** Jorge, El Monito Ciclista Y Otras Historias (Children's Circle)

Four stories in Spanish. The first shows Curious George's adventures in a circus. Next, "Millions of Cats," where a man looking for a cat discovers trillions of cats. "Noisy Nora" makes her presence known in her house where everyone is too busy. *Adult Juror Comments*: Illustrations in "El Dia Nevado" are gorgeous, creative, colorful, and cozy. "Millions of Cats" is not as appealing. The Spanish vocabulary is a plus. "Kids need stories like these. George gets into trouble, but always saves the day at the end." *Kid Juror Comments*: Some were disappointed that the stories were not fully animated. "My friends might want the pictures to move like cartoons." Children liked "Curious George" best. One group of non-Spanish speaking kids found it difficult to follow in Spanish. Video. 35 min.; $19.95; Age: 3-8. Weston Woods Studios/Scholastic.

*** La Gallinita Roja Y Otros Cuentos Populares (Children's Circle)

Video adaptations, in Spanish, of four classic stories: "The Little Red Hen," "Stone Soup," "Why Mosquitoes Buzz in People's Ears," and "Charlie Needs a Cloak." Includes a curriculum guide for enhancing early language and literacy skills. *Adult Juror Comments*: Wonderful variety of styles. True to the original stories. Well-paced. Glimpses into different cultures, lifestyles, and experiences. Emphasizes cooperation and creativity. Enhances Spanish language fluency. *Kid Juror Comments*: Liked the vibrant colors, but could only understand a little of the Spanish. "I liked the mosquito story. I just read it in English in school." "It wasn't like science of math, but just good stories!" "Shows us that you reap what you sow." Video. 37 min.; $19.95; Age: 3-8. Weston Woods Studios/Scholastic.

** Max, El Prodigio Musical Y Otras Historias (Children's Circle)

Includes: "Musical Max," a story about practicing music; "Monty," who won't give his friends a ride to school; "Whistle for Willie," about a boy who learns to call his dog; and "Panama," the tale of two friends in search of their dreams. *Adult Juror Comments*: Appealing, good production values, true to original stories. Great supplement to a literature program. Discusses social values and achieving happiness in life. A great Spanish language program for non-native speakers. *Kid Juror Comments*: Appreciated having problems to solve and fantasies to live. Children were encouraged to make predictions and comment on events in the stories. "Really good stories—the kind we like to watch." "At last! Stories I love—in Spanish!" Video. 33 min.; $19.95; Age: 4-8. WFXT TV.

** More Spanish (Lyric Language)

Learning a foreign language is fun when it's combined with music and live-action adventures. Teaches Spanish through songs and images. Can be used to teach Spanish-speaking kids English as well. *Adult Juror Comments*: Songs were catchy and repetitive. The on-screen lyrics are useful, but the pace is so fast it's difficult to follow along. It's a good supplemental tool for learning either Spanish or English. Photography is creative and interesting. Stereotyping. *Kid Juror Comments*: Children who already speak Spanish respond to it best and are most motivated to stick with the tape. Nice songs—too fast to pick up easily. Everyone had a different favorite song or part. They also enjoyed the food and the clowns. Video. 35 min.; $14.95; Age: 4-12. Penton Overseas, Inc.

** Spanish (Lyric Language)

Learning a new language is fun when children listen and sing along to catchy tunes, easily learning new words and phrases. Lyrics are clearly subtitled on the screen in English and in Spanish. Animation features Family Circus characters. *Adult Juror Comments*: Colorful, engaging, and active with sing-along tunes. A good tool for teaching English to Spanish-speaking children or vice versa. The music and images work well together, reinforcing the lessons. Each song may be viewed individually. *Kid Juror Comments*: Good reception. The visuals help kids remember the words they're learning. Video. 35 min.; $14.95; Age: 4-8. On the Ball Video Productions.

Chapter Three • Elementary

Category—Holiday

*** All Dogs Christmas Carol, An (Family Entertainment)

Charlie, Itchy, and Sasha star in a canine version of the classic Charles Dickens' Christmas tale. When Carface the bulldog devises a corrupt plan to ruin Christmas, Charlie and his pals visit him as the ghosts of Christmas past, present, and future. *Adult Juror Comments*: Promotes Christmas spirit; good things come if we hold fast. Stresses good will toward others. Interesting spin on the classic story. Characters inspire compassion for animals. Adults objected to the zombie scene where they put a spell on the dogs. *Kid Juror Comments*: Great heroes, funny adventure. Enjoyed watching Charlie dance in the yellow suit and listening to the other dogs sing. "I like the magical things they do with cartoons." "Most characters behaved, some needed to learn to be nice." Video. 76 min.; $14.95; Age: 5-8. MGM/UA Home Entertainment.

*** Babar and Father Christmas (Babar)

Babar, that most regal of elephants, searches for the legendary Father Christmas, eager to make this Christmas a holiday his children will remember. He persuades Santa to take a holiday in the Land of Elephants and proves himself a worthy king. *Adult Juror Comments*: True to the spirit of the characters, and made a familiar book come alive. A great story with redeeming values. Animation and production is excellent. *Kid Juror Comments*: What's better than a happy ending and everyone gets what they want? Better-suited to those who have read the books. Video. 33 min.; $12.98; Age: 5-11. Artisan/Family Home Entertainment.

** Bear Who Slept Through Christmas, The (Christmas Classics)

While the rest of the world is getting ready for Christmas, all the bears in Bearbank are getting ready to go to sleep. That is, except Ted E. Bear who wants to find out just what Christmas is all about. *Adult Juror Comments*: Very good story overall, with few multicultural aspects. Prompted discussion after viewing about bears and hibernation. *Kid Juror Comments*: A very different approach to the traditional Christmas holiday story and very appealing. Video. 27 min.; $12.98; Age: 3-9. Artisan/Family Home Entertainment.

** Big Christmas Tree, The (Big Adventure Series)

Watch as the perfect Christmas tree is found by helicopter for the Rockefeller Center Tree Lighting Celebration. Gives the history about Christmas trees and visits a Christmas tree farm. *Adult Juror Comments*: Well-done, flows easily, offers facts in age-appropriate fashion. Concepts are both explained and demonstrated. Historical information is about trees, not the meaning of Christmas. "Personally, the focus on finding a perfect tree seems superficial." *Kid Juror Comments*: Captured kids' attention. They enjoyed learning about the Rockefeller tree and sang along to Christmas songs. They appreciated the child narrator. "I liked the people in the video." "The pictures made the story more clear." Video. 25 min.; $14.95; Age: 5-8. Little Mammoth Media.

** Case of the Christmas Caper, The (The Adventures of Mary-Kate And Ashley)

The sly sleuths are busy wrapping holiday gifts and learning carols when a call from the Three Wise Men sends them in search of the Spirit of Christmas. *Adult Juror Comments*: Promotes the spirit of giving and love. Characters are polite, helpful, accepting of others, and practice good manners. Both fantasy and realism used to entertain and inform. The lack of supervision for the girls concerned some adult jurors. *Kid Juror Comments*: Kids sang the songs long after viewing. Brevity of the video works well for this age group. Inspired their interest in mysteries. Kids discussed the safety issues and the vocabulary they didn't know. "I would like to be a detective and solve mysteries." Video. 30 min.; $12.95; Age: 5-8. Warner Home Video.

** Casper's First Christmas

On Christmas Eve, Casper and Hairy Scarey are house-hunting because Hairy's haunt has been condemned. Caught in a snowstorm, Yogi Bear, Boo-boo, and Huckleberry Hound take refuge in the haunted house. New friends are made in the spirit of the season. *Adult Juror Comments*: This is goofy yet engaging, with pleasant old-fashioned animation and nice music. Good entertainment value while teaching a lesson about selfishness. "What's the point of marketing these old cartoons?" *Kid Juror Comments*: Kids couldn't follow the plot and wandered off after five minutes. Some got into the spirit of the video, laughing and booing along the way. Kids recognized the familiar television-based characters. One child said, "It's too babyish." Video. 25 min.; $9.98; Age: 5-9. Warner Home Video.

** Chanuka at Bubbe's (Bubbe's Boarding House)

While this colorful group of puppet characters prepares for the holiday feast, the past comes alive as Bubbe relates the story of Chanuka—the fight between the Greeks and Maccabees and the miracle of the burning oil. *Adult Juror Comments*: Provides an excellent introduction to the story of Chanuka. Promotes cultural awareness for non-Jewish and Jewish children alike. Well-written and well-produced. *Kid Juror Comments*: Both Jewish and non-Jewish children enjoyed the puppets and learning about Chanuka. The kids were able to follow the story line. Video. 30 min.; $19.95; Age: 3-11. Monterey Home Video.

** Christmas Carol, A

A holiday story with a musical twist. An animated version featuring the voices of Whoopi Goldberg, Ed Asner, Michael York, Tim Curry, and Jodi Benson. *Adult Juror Comments*: Age-appropriate introduction to this classic. The vocabulary is right on target. Delivers positive messages about caring, being kind, and giving. Some great songs. Animated characters are very realistic. *Kid Juror Comments*: Imaginative animation; liked the singing and the story. "I liked the singing and the ghosts best." Received high points from younger kids. They enjoyed the lessons about kindness and how to act toward other people. Video. 72 min.; $19.98; Age: 6-12. Twentieth Century Fox Home Entertainment.

** Christmas Story, A (Doug)

Doug's dog is mistakenly accused of biting his friend Beebe during an ice-skating outing. *Adult Juror Comments*: Though the story resolves positively, it has little re-watching value. *Kid Juror Comments*: Kids liked this a lot. Some wanted to see it again, others said, "No thank you." Video. 30 min.; $9.98; Age: 4-11. Paramount Home Entertainment.

** Christmas Tree Story, The

From seedling to recycling, a magical, musical, and adventurous journey to discover where Christmas trees come from. Plants a seed of hope for the future of this Christmas tradition. *Adult Juror Comments*: Interesting and makes a good learning tool. The host was very natural and fun to watch. It's good to hear something good can be done with old Christmas trees. It's appropriate for library collections. Production value is mediocre. *Kid Juror Comments*: Interest in the life cycle of Christmas trees. Even those who do not celebrate Christmas thought it was informative and enjoyed watching. Has limited repeat value. "Now I know where Christmas trees come from and why they cost so much." Video. 25 min.; $14.95; Age: 5-8. Youngheart Video.

* Cinco De Mayo (The Holidays for Children Video Series)

The history of Cinco de Mayo, Mexico's independence celebration. Includes traditional Mexican folk songs and discusses the Mayan myth of creation. *Adult Juror Comments*: A simple production, short but well-done. The focus on traditional music is quite engaging. Good background on the culture and history of Mexico. The pace is just about right. The plot jumps around a bit. *Kid Juror Comments*: Highest score with children from Mexico and Central America, who liked the mural made by the children and the way the kids help to tell the story. Video. 25 min.; $29.95; Age: 5-12. Schlessinger Video Productions.

** Fun in a Box 3: The Birthday Movie (Fun in a Box)

Hosted by the Birthday Spirit, who knows all there is to know about birthday fun, and explores a multicultural mélange of birthday lore from Hispanic piñatas to Japanese rice cakes. *Adult Juror Comments*: Good production, though it moves around a lot. The inclusion of birthday traditions from other cultures is interesting. Some jurors objected to a scene of birthday spanking. *Kid Juror Comments*: Learning about other cultural traditions was interesting. Video. 30 min.; $14.95; Age: 6-12. Made to Order Productions/Rainbow.

* Halloween Tree, The

An adventure that reveals the magical secrets of past and present Halloweens. *Adult Juror Comments*: Encourages exploration into Halloween practices around the world. Might be too scary for younger children. Asks age-appropriate questions. *Kid Juror Comments*: Really enjoyed the subject, although the production didn't hold their attention as well as they had anticipated. May motivate kids to read. Video. 70 min.; $14.95; Age: 5-8. Warner Home Video.

*** How the Grinch Stole Christmas

A Dr. Seuss tongue-twisting verse with lighthearted music. What Yuletide holiday is complete without this timeless tale of the mean-spirited Grinch and his feeble attempt to steal the yuletide celebration of Whoville? *Adult Juror Comments*: Recommended for every child's library. The music, the characters, and the rhymes are imaginative and engaging. Presents good message about love and giving. "Giving is more important than getting." *Kid Juror Comments*: Dr. Seuss? "He's the best." Kids liked the message and wanted to watch again, right away. It's a winner—well-produced with a meaningful lesson. Video. 26 min.; $12.95; Age: 3-12. Warner Home Video.

* Let's Create for Thanksgiving (Let's Create)

Looking at this American holiday, children are guided in creating art projects that relate to their heritage and are fun to make. *Adult Juror Comments*: A good range of craft techniques, but lacks dialogue between the instructor and kids. Tells the Thanksgiving story from the Pilgrims' perspective, which may be objectionable to Native Americans. Projects are instructional rather than creative. *Kid Juror Comments*: Songs were fine, but some thought it was too long. Video. 50 min.; $24.95; Age: 5-12. Let's Create, Inc.

** Little Angels: The Brightest Christmas (Golden Tales - Hallmark)

Similar to the popular TV show, "Touched by an Angel"—but for children. A team of child angels helps children in need by guiding and guarding them and showing them that they are not alone. *Adult Juror Comments*: Promotes admiration and love of family and neighbor. A positive story that emphasizes values such as helping others and believing in oneself. Plot is predictable and the production has some audio problems. "It's a lot like a folktale." *Kid Juror Comments*: Enjoyed it. Would watch again. "I learned to help people who need it and to give to the poor." "I know how those kids felt. They were scared." "The angels were respectful and helpful." "It does make you wonder if angels are real." "I loved the angels." Video. 45 min.; $12.98; Age: 5-8. Golden Films.

* Mouse on the Mayflower

Set sail with the tiniest Pilgrim for a music-filled voyage to the land of the free in a Rankin-Bass animated Thanksgiving holiday treat. Features the voices of Tennessee Ernie Ford and Eddie Albert. Some religious overtones. *Adult Juror Comments*: While music and animation are fine, the historical information contains inaccurate references to Native Americans that may be close to offensive and lack sensitivity. *Kid Juror Comments*: Younger kids did not understand the concepts, which are best for eight- to ten-year-olds. Video. 46 min.; $12.98; Age: 6-12. Artisan/Family Home Entertainment.

** Noel

Poignant tale of a magical Christmas-tree ornament that comes to life. As it is passed down from one generation to another, we see the wonder, joy, and spirit of Christmas. *Adult Juror Comments*: This touching Christmas theme makes a colorful family movie with classic appeal. Tugs at the heart while subtly teaching the meaning of Christmas. Deals with separation, loss, and death. Noel clearly has pathos. Contains Christian overtones. *Kid Juror Comments*: Considerable empathy for Noel, whose happiness and sadness were felt deeply by the audience. They fell in love with Noel, and cried when the ornaments were put away. Video. 25 min.; $9.95; Age: 4-7. U.S.A. Home Entertainment.

** Nutcracker on Ice

The Nutcracker, probably the world's most beloved Christmas tale, is performed on ice by Olympic gold medalists Oksana Barol and Viktor Petrenko. *Adult Juror Comments*: An introduction to this classic by Tchaikovsky. Those who love figure skating or ballet will particularly enjoy it. The costumes are beautiful, and the skating is admirable. Perfect for family viewing or music appreciation. *Kid Juror Comments*: Spellbound by the talent displayed. Girls enjoyed this more than boys. Act II is more enthralling than Act I. Some kids wandered off, but returned for the peek backstage at the end. "The skating is cool." Video. 110 min.; $14.98; Age: 6-12. Twentieth Century Fox Home Entertainment.

** Passover at Bubbe's

Spring is here, and it's time to celebrate "Passover at Bubbe's." From the creators of the award-winning *Chanuka at Bubbe's* comes this puppet cast once again. *Adult Juror Comments*: Attempts to cover too many concepts and becomes confusing. Promotes strong family values. Stimulates discussion about religions, language, culture. Addresses the history and traditions of Passover. Older kids will understand content best. *Kid Juror Comments*: Some kids wanted to learn more about Passover and start preparing to celebrate. Hebrew-speaking audience liked hearing the prayers they've learned. They wanted to watch it again, but non-Jewish kids had a difficult time understanding the subject. Video. 30 min.; $19.95; Age: 4-8. Monterey Home Video.

** Pee Wee's Playhouse Christmas Special

This wild holiday has many visiting celebrities stopping by to wish Pee Wee a merry Christmas. Includes Annette Funicello, Frankie Avalon, Magic Johnson, Cher, Joan Rivers, Oprah Winfrey, Whoopi Goldberg, Little Richard, k.d.lang, and Zsa Zsa Gabor. *Adult Juror Comments*: Pee Wee's very clever, and original approach teaches kids good social behaviors. This may be a little dated, but it's still very clever. Lots of gags, though some humor may be above children's understanding. *Kid Juror Comments*: Great, especially for those at the younger end of the recommended age range. Video. 48 min.; $12.95; Age: 5-8. MGM/UA Home Entertainment.

** Rudolph the Red-Nosed Reindeer (Christmas Classics)

Remember how the North Pole's favorite reindeer saves Christmas? Puppetmation with narration and singing by Burl Ives. *Adult Juror Comments*: Still a good story with entertaining, colorful presentation. Addresses questions of fitting in, peer acceptance, and differences. An appealing non-Christian tale for Christmastime. *Kid Juror Comments*: Who's the greatest? Santa and Rudolph, who's very childlike. Younger kids were afraid of the snowmonster. Video. 53 min.; $12.98; Age: 4-8. Artisan/Family Home Entertainment.

** Santa Claus Is Coming to Town (Christmas Classics)

Holiday favorite told and sung by Fred Astaire, with the voices of Mickey Rooney as Kris, and Keenan Wynn as Winter. Features the Westminster Children's Choir. *Adult Juror Comments*: Good story, good values. It still holds up. "As an adult, I remember what a lasting impression it made on me as a child." Lacks continuity. *Kid Juror Comments*: Loved the songs and sang them afterwards. "The part with the warlock was bad. It could really happen." Video. 53 min.; $12.98; Age: 4-8. Artisan/Family Home Entertainment.

* Santa Experience, The (Rugrats)

The talkative toddlers and their families share Christmas in a mountain cabin and plot to trap Santa. *Adult Juror Comments*: This funky story has Santa coming to a family, telling them to be good. The jokes are more suitable for adults than children. Camera work is creative. The characters are rather one-dimensional and sometimes obnoxious. "I cringed throughout." *Kid Juror Comments*: For these children, the children in the video were most interesting. Some wanted to watch it again. Video. 25 min.; $9.98; Age: 5-10. Paramount Home Entertainment.

* Santa's First Christmas

 Santa himself recalls his first bumbling attempt to deliver toys to every child in the world, and what he's done to create one of the smoothest-running operations today. *Adult Juror Comments*: This story is definitely weird. Good music, but the language is difficult for the audience. Lacks cultural diversity, has poor role models, and the production value is mediocre. "It's too smart-alecky." *Kid Juror Comments*: Shifting between past and present complicated the narrative and made it difficult to understand. The plot is best understood by older kids. Video. 25 min.; $9.98; Age: 5-8. BMG Home Video.

** Scooby-Doo! and the Witch's Ghost (Scooby-Doo)

 Scooby-Doo and the gang go sleuthing into the supernatural at a haunted house in New England, where they learn a good lesson about judging people by appearances. *Adult Juror Comments*: Wholesome, healthy entertainment. Good plot, music mysteries, and clues. Teaches kids not to be fearful and to "Use your brain to unravel the mystery. "Scooby's team is diverse and positive." *Kid Juror Comments*: Kids loved the animation and caught the lesson of "Don't judge people by their appearance." "Scooby and Shaggy always help each other when they're in trouble." "I relate to Shaggy because I'm a scaredy-cat." Video. 70 min.; $19.96; Age: 5-11. Warner Home Video.

* Silent Mouse

Live-action film reveals the true story behind the creation of the beloved carol "Silent Night." Narrated by Lynn Redgrave, the video features remarkable photography and splendid music performed by Europe's acclaimed choirs and orchestras. *Adult Juror Comments*: Nicely produced. Creatively teaches how to turn a bad situation into a good one, with a little luck and the help of friends. Little diversity. Humorous, cute holiday video, but the narration is sometimes distracting. The mouse is adorable. *Kid Juror Comments*: The mouse as the main character and storyteller was wonderful. "It kind of changed my thinking about 'Silent Night.' " They did not like how the priest was represented. Video. 50 min.; $19.95; Age: 5-10. Interama, Inc.

** Snow White Christmas (Hallmark Hall of Fame)

Beautiful Snow White and her comical little companions embark on a thrilling quest to thwart the Wicked Queen's malicious magic. Includes new characters, delightful songs, and animated fun. *Adult Juror Comments*: "Content was sort of a jumble of other tales made into a new fairy tale." May be useful for stimulating discussion about good versus evil, caring about others, and doing things for others. The stepparent and older women are negatively stereotyped. *Kid Juror Comments*: "This is not the real Snow White." Thought the wicked queen was cool. It was scary for younger kids. "I liked when her mommy and daddy kissed her to wake her up." "I liked how the giants liked everyone." Video. 46 min.; $9.98; Age: 5-8. Artisan/Family Home Entertainment.

** Squanto and the First Thanksgiving (American Heroes and Legends)

True story about a Native American from colonial Massachusetts who was sold into slavery in Spain. Years later, he returns to America and teaches the Pilgrims how to survive the difficult years at the Plymouth colony. Narrated by Graham Greene. Music *Adult Juror Comments*: Excellent. Makes a wonderful addition to any child's collection. Somewhat slow-moving, but the information is compelling. "This will become a holiday regular for our classroom." *Kid Juror Comments*: Learned a lot of things about Thanksgiving that they did not know before. They enjoyed the production even though they thought it was slow. Video. 30 min.; $8.95; Age: 5-12. Ablesoft.

Chapter Three • Elementary

** Stories from the Jewish Tradition (Children's Circle)

A wealthy merchant learns the meaning of Hanukkah when he sues a peddler's family for savoring the smell of his wife's pancakes from a window. *Adult Juror Comments*: This is a terrific collection of Jewish stories, well-produced and authentic. Both the live action and the illustrations are also well done. The Hanukkah pictures are particularly beautiful. Whether or not one is Jewish, it has appeal. *Kid Juror Comments*: Those who were Jewish found it particularly interesting, and even those who weren't were fascinated by learning about the stories. Some parts were too slow. Video. 34 min.; $14.95; Age: 5-10. Scholastic/Children's Circle.

*** Tailor of Gloucester, The
(The World of Peter Rabbit and Friends)

The Tailor of Gloucester is exhausted and ill with fever. Yet he still hasn't finished making the beautiful silken coat for the Mayor's wedding on Christmas day. *Adult Juror Comments*: This beautiful production has exquisite animation and captivating artistry, faithful to the original story. The music is soothing yet lighthearted. It may encourage reading the original books. A jurors' favorite. *Kid Juror Comments*: Charmed with the story and the production even though it's somewhat slow. They knew the accents were English, but stayed with it and didn't have a difficult time understanding. All of the kids wanted to watch this again. Video. 30 min.; $14.95; Age: 3-12. Goodtimes Entertainment.

* To Grandmother's House We Go (Mary-Kate and Ashley)

Mary-Kate and Ashley's Christmas odyssey involves two light-hearted crooks who claim to be Santa's elves, a ransom demand, a mother's love, a million-dollar lottery ticket, and a would-be Santa and his reindeer. *Adult Juror Comments*: Cute, simple, at times thought-provoking. Filled with slapstick humor. The criminals are too nice. The stunts appeal to this age group. Lacks cultural diversity and has some profanity. Poor role models such as running away and stealing money. *Kid Juror Comments*: Loved silly, slapstick humor. The twins are endearing to children, their adventures compelling. Even boys liked this one. "I liked when they smashed their piggy banks." "Running away isn't good." "I could watch it a million times." Video. 89 min.; $14.95; Age: 5-10. Warner Home Video.

* Trollies Christmas Sing-Along, The (The Trollies)

The Trollies celebrate Christmas in this delightful sing-along. The Trouble Trollies try to ruin Christmas by attempting to steal the Christmas tree, but the Trollies thwart them again. *Adult Juror Comments*: Recommend viewing with an adult. The bad behavior of the Trouble Trollies needs a filter for discussion. One character hits another. There is more focus on the "bad Trollies" than the positive characters. *Kid Juror Comments*: Kids watched this only intermittently. Video. 30 min.; $12.98; Age: 4-8. PPI/Peter Pan, Inc.

Age 5-8

Video

Holiday

* Turkey Caper, The (Chucklewood Critters)

In celebrating Thanksgiving, the Chucklewood Critters learn about the Pilgrims, the Indians, and how friendships develop. The cubs, unsure of two strangers who enter the forest, face some touchy moments while making friends with the newcomers. *Adult Juror Comments*: Demonstrates cooperation and care for wildlife. Animals are all respectful toward each other. Language is age-appropriate. Sometimes choppy. Portrayals of Native Americans are stereotypical. Production value is mediocre. *Kid Juror Comments*: Liked the talking animals and learning about Thanksgiving, but did not maintain their interest. Probably little repeat viewing value. Video. 25 min.; $9.98; Age: 3-8. Unapix/Miramar.

** Twas the Night Before Christmas (Christmas Classics)

A gentle retelling of the all-time favorite Christmas tale. *Adult Juror Comments*: This rather mediocre production has attractive outdoor scenes. Portions were omitted, which may be disconcerting to children familiar with the poem. Background music is repetitive, the pace is slow, no cultural diversity. *Kid Juror Comments*: Didn't like the reindeers arguing, although it provided an opportunity to discuss conflict resolution. Video. 27 min.; $12.98; Age: 4-8. Artisan/Family Home Entertainment.

*** Twelve Days of Christmas, The (Animated Classics)

Ever wonder how that silly Christmas carol, "The Twelve Days of Christmas," got started? When Sir Carolboomer sends his bumbling squire to steal the Christmas list of Princess Silverbelle, he grabs the answers to the king's crossword puzzle instead. *Adult Juror Comments*: Good story line, silly adaptation of the "story behind the song." Makes for good family viewing. *Kid Juror Comments*: Exceptional animation and offbeat plot. Captured and held their attention throughout. Video. 30 min.; $14.95; Age: 5-8. Goodtimes Entertainment.

*** Ugly Duckling's Christmas Wish, The

This animated adaptation of Grimm's fairy tale features an outcast duckling who wishes to find a place to belong. *Adult Juror Comments*: Good story for a child expecting a new sibling. Has a happy ending, and it's full of sad, joyful, and angry emotions. Raises issues of homelessness, loneliness, friendship, difference, and family. Encourages one to be nice to all people and animals. *Kid Juror Comments*: Everyone watched this twice. They loved the happy ending. Kids empathized with the ugly duckling and the girl with the same wish. "You shouldn't run away from home." "It teaches you not to be mean." "It was sad in parts." Video. 70 min.; $9.99; Age: 4-8. Anchor Bay Entertainment.

* Visit with Santa, A

A group of children visit Santa at the North Pole and discuss the holiday traditions and sing Christmas songs. In the process, they discover a wonderful secret: Santa will visit as long as children believe in him. *Adult Juror Comments*: Entertaining, cheerful, and colorful. Addresses Christmas traditions worldwide. Interview style lacks child appeal. Little diversity. Good motivation for discussion about materialism. Promotes idea that "Christmas is about giving." *Kid Juror Comments*: The always enjoyable Santa and sing-along. Prompted discussion about the meaning of Christmas. Video. 30 min.; $12; Age: 4-8. Thurston James.

** White Christmas (White Christmas)

Dorothy, whose only wish is to have a white Christmas, is whisked off to the magical world of Weatherland by Santa, who is touched by Dorothy's unselfish plea. Includes Bing Crosby's classic song, "White Christmas." *Adult Juror Comments*: This entertaining, different twist to the classic story has lots of action and stimulates the imagination. The female lead is strong, but other characters are gender-stereotyped. *Kid Juror Comments*: Enchanted. Enjoyed the animation. Encouraged them to use their imaginations. "It was the best. I always wanted to know what was coming next." Kids wanted to watch again. Video. 26 min.; $12.98; Age: 5-8. Sony Wonder.

** You're Invited to Mary-Kate & Ashley's Christmas Party (You're Invited to Mary-Kate and Ashley's)

You're invited to join the twins as they ring in the Yuletide with style. *Adult Juror Comments*: Delightful. Presents Christmas as a time for love and joy. Shows positive results when friends help each other and promotes family traditions. Some felt it lacked substance and the girls' behavior was stereotypical. *Kid Juror Comments*: Enjoyed watching the twins ski and play in the snow. They sang along to the songs. Prompted a discussion about family Christmas vacations. All the kids wanted to bake cookies afterwards. "The best part: seeing Santa as the delivery man." Video. 30 min.; $12.95; Age: 5-8. Warner Home Video.

Age 5-8

Video

Holiday

Category—How-To

** Breadtime Tales

How does bread become bread? Follows three young bakers who show how to bake bread. *Adult Juror Comments*: The written instructions (included) are useful in extending the lesson into an activity. It was interesting to watch the baking process. Good for teaching life skills. *Kid Juror Comments*: Eager to bake their own bread afterwards. Youngest members of the audience wandered. Moves a little slowly. Video. 30 min.; $12.95; Age: 3-8. Karol Media, Inc.

** Juggle Time

Learn confidence while learning to juggle in slow-motion by using scarves. Three colorful scarves are included in package. *Adult Juror Comments*: Good instructional program. Age-appropriate with clear directions. The singing can become a little annoying and very silly. Nice pace. *Kid Juror Comments*: The rhyming and music were very annoying. Content was for older kids, but the format was for younger ones. A few parts were hard to follow. Video. 30 min.; $16.95; Age: 5-12. Jugglebug.

** Karate for Kids II: Intermediate (Karate for Kids)

The second video in the award-winning three-part series. The upbeat music keeps the work-out fast and fun. *Adult Juror Comments*: Best-suited for children who already have a basic knowledge of karate, since the moves are a little fast. Karate instructors did not encourage use unless accompanied by professional instruction. *Kid Juror Comments*: Boys participated aggressively. Video. 30 min.; $9.95; Age: 5-12. Bright Ideas Productions.

** Kids Get Cooking: The Egg

Celebration of food and cooking teaches about recipes, experiments, crafts, and more. *Adult Juror Comments*: Good for teaching kids how to find their way around the kitchen. Instructions clear and child-centered. The food itself is nothing extraordinary but will appeal to most. *Kid Juror Comments*: "This is cool." Liked the idea of cooking for themselves and learning new items. Didn't like the puppets that kept interrupting the show. "I learned how to tell the difference between a hard-boiled egg and fresh one." Video. 30 min.; $14.95; Age: 4-10. Kidvidz.

* Kids' Guitar 1 (Kids' Guitar)

Three easy guitar lessons introduce children to the guitar and to basic music theory. Teaches basic techniques, strumming, and eight popular songs. *Adult Juror Comments*: Good instructional program. Meets a need for inexpensive guitar lessons and is well-paced. Appropriate for a music class or on your own. Even adults interested in learning the guitar enjoyed this. *Kid Juror Comments*: Those who already expressed an interest in learning how to play the guitar enjoyed this the most. They thought the directions were clear and the language suitable for them. Video. 90 min.; $24.95; Age: 6-12. Homespun Tapes.

** Let's Create Art Activities (Let's Create)

Teacher Ann Felice motivates kids while doing imaginative projects. Fosters respect for nature, the environment, and peers. *Adult Juror Comments*: Presents clear ideas that encourage creativity. Best used in a setting where children can follow along with their own project or with teachers inspired to do the projects. Presentation somewhat patronizing. *Kid Juror Comments*: The projects were so exciting that children did not want to sit through the demonstration before starting the experiments. A little too long. Video. 51 min.; $24.95; Age: 5-10. Let's Create, Inc.

** Let's Create for Halloween (Let's Create)

How to create seven Halloween projects. *Adult Juror Comments*: Good ideas and illustrations for arts and crafts projects, ideal for holiday programs with teachers or parents as group leaders. Well-produced. Catchy music. *Kid Juror Comments*: Variety of projects. A lot of things they'd like to make throughout the year. Video. 65 min.; $24.95; Age: 5-12. Let's Create, Inc.

* Let's Create Fun Jewelry for Boys & Girls (Let's Create)

Create rings, medallions, and pins from everyday items for yourself or as a gift for someone else. *Adult Juror Comments*: Good crafts instruction. Clear directions with interesting history included. Some projects require adult supervision and a list of needed materials. Stopping the tape in order to catch up with the instruction is useful. *Kid Juror Comments*: Some were anxious to try some of the ideas; others were not interested at all. Boys were more interested than they thought they would be. Video. 60 min.; $24.95; Age: 6-14. Let's Create, Inc.

Age 5-8

Video

How-To

** Look What I Found: Making Codes and Solving Mysteries (On My Own Adventure)

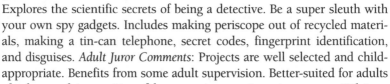

Explores the scientific secrets of being a detective. Be a super sleuth with your own spy gadgets. Includes making periscope out of recycled materials, making a tin-can telephone, secret codes, fingerprint identification, and disguises. *Adult Juror Comments*: Projects are well selected and child-appropriate. Benefits from some adult supervision. Better-suited for adults with no background in art. Use of language is sometimes inaccurate. *Kid Juror Comments*: Interested in the subject, but some kids thought it dragged a bit. Not interested in watching again. Video. 45 min.; $14.95; Age: 5-10. Gilbert Page Associates.

** Look What I Made: Paper Playthings and Gifts (On My Own Adventure)

A variety of things to make and enjoy. Get out the scissors, paper, and tape. Imagine your kids' pleasure when they make a bouquet of flowers, a party piñata, and hats or even a newspaper hammock from watching this video. *Adult Juror Comments*: Excellent for teaching crafts. Better suited to adults with no background in art. *Kid Juror Comments*: Ingenious activities. Wanted to see it over and over. Video. 45 min.; $14.95; Age: 6-12. Gilbert Page Associates.

** Magic of Martial Arts, The: Power Without Violence

Master Eastwest, a playful martial artist, teaches kids the ethics of how to use karate…and when not to use it. Magic tricks, jokes, and music mix with interactive karate instruction. Includes self-defense and non-violent conflict resolution techniques. *Adult Juror Comments*: Entertaining, well-produced, many positive messages. Emphasizes using karate skills only to defend yourself and even then, only enough to ward off an attacker and give you a chance to get away. Great music. Good diversity. *Kid Juror Comments*: Enjoyed the combination of magic and karate, especially the boys. Kids danced along and predictably, followed the viewing with play kicks. Certainly stimulated discussion about studying karate and how you can't learn it by just looking at a video. Video. 45 min.; $14.99; Age: 6-10. Magic of martial arts productions.

* My First Party Video (My First)

How to create a party, based on the kids book series. *Adult Juror Comments*: Presents fun party ideas. Requires adult supervision for younger kids. Safety orientation is age-appropriate. Parents will appreciate the quality instruction. The cooking segment shows only girls participating, no boys. Sometimes patronizing. *Kid Juror Comments*: Liked the suggestions and wanted to try the activities. They did, however, want to see more kid interaction in the video. "Some of the food looked yucky." Video. 45 min.; $12.98; Age: 5-12. Sony Wonder.

** Paws, Claws, Feathers & Fins (A Kid's Guide to Pets)

Generally, kids receive little preparation for living with and caring for pets. This program helps families make appropriate choices in pet selection, and emphasizes both the joys and the responsibilities of living with a pet. *Adult Juror Comments*: Practical information about every aspect of having a pet. Shows children speaking about and working gently with animals. Can be broken into segments to absorb the material. Teaches gentleness and responsibility. Could be useful for families. *Kid Juror Comments*: Eager to discuss their pets following their viewing. "We talked about being gentle, kind, and caring for our pets." It's very age-appropriate, and the children appreciate the new information. Video. 30 min.; $14.95; Age: 5-12. Kidvidz.

** Piggy Banks to Money Markets (A Kid's Guide to Dollars and Sense)

American children spend over $6 billion annually, but have a limited understanding of money and how it works. Presents the ins and outs of earning, saving, and spending. *Adult Juror Comments*: Clear, informative, lively, and believable presentation of some complex topics. Shows how some children make mistakes and try again. Should stir an interest in saving, investing, keeping records, and enterprise. Good diversity. *Kid Juror Comments*: Prompted a lot of discussion about personal experiences with allowances, garage sales, savings, and money in general. "It would be great to earn my own money." Kids were fascinated and wanted to watch it again. Video. 30 min.; $14.95; Age: 5-12. Kidvidz.

*** Squiggles, Dots and Lines

Ed Emberly presents his drawing alphabet as a tool for kids to unlock their creativity. The on-camera kids share stories, make cards and books, create a giant mural, and get ready for a party. *Adult Juror Comments*: Simple production with good ideas and an excellent introduction to drawing. *Kid Juror Comments*: Wanted to try their hand at drawing right away. Video. 25 min.; $14.95; Age: 5-12. Kidvidz.

* Ukulele for Kids, Parts One and Two

Child-friendly lessons give kids an early start on music-making. Ginger, a lovable dog puppet, helps Marcy teach ten basic chords, plus ear training, music theory, strumming techniques, and several popular songs, including "Skip to My Lou." *Adult Juror Comments*: Good production that appeals to a special audience. Some jurors felt that the dog puppet was too babyish. *Kid Juror Comments*: Not surprisingly, those more interested in music were most interested. "The ukulele is difficult to play." Video. 100 min.; $39.9; Age: 6-10. Homespun tapes.

Category—Music

* Anastasia Sing-Along

 Features sing-along songs from the movies *Anastasia, Ferngully: The Last Rainforest*, and *On the Riviera*. Invites kids to follow along with the words on the screen and join in the chorus with familiar characters. *Adult Juror Comments*: Having "Anastasia" on the cover is a bit misleading. Different clips vary in production quality. Requires being able to read quickly. Some of the older clips were not very appealing. *Kid Juror Comments*: Loved the chance to sing along, especially when they learned new songs. Girls liked this better than boys. Popo the Puppet was a big hit, as was Shirley Temple and the dog from "Anastasia." Video. 25 min.; $14.98; Age: 5-8. Twentieth Century Fox Home Entertainment.

** Bangin' and Sangin'

 Master percussionist Billy Jonas performs original and well-known songs. Using unique one-man-band instruments he's created from recycled objects, Billy inspires audience participation. *Adult Juror Comments*: Well-produced, simple production. High energy and positive attitude. "Billy is a unique entertainer. It's fun for kids to see this different perspective on music." Combines music for older kids along with those for younger ones. *Kid Juror Comments*: Enthusiastic. Kids loved it; they danced and moved spontaneously. "I want to learn more about playing the drums." "I like it because he bangs on things a lot." "I didn't know it was possible to break dance to a kid's song." "Recycling can be fun." Video. 41 min.; $19.99; Age: 4-9. Ivy Classics, Inc.

** Beethoven Lives Upstairs (Classical Kids)

A young boy develops a special friendship with Beethoven, watches as he creates and rehearses the Ninth Symphony, and is invited to its premiere performance. *Adult Juror Comments*: Demanding story respects and challenges its audience. Adults expressed a need for more stories like this. Beautifully told. Promotes lessons in kindness, friendship, and differences. *Kid Juror Comments*: Attractive story about the boy who befriended Beethoven. "More, more." "I could watch it again." They liked the costumes and the period setting. Video. 52 min.; $18.98; Age: 6-12. Children's Group, The.

* Brass, The (Tune Buddies)

Explores the brass family of instruments and how brass instruments always play a major role in musical compositions. Investigates how brass instruments make their big brassy sound through a simple vibration. *Adult Juror Comments*: Well-produced. Introduces a variety of brass instruments and gives demonstrations of how each works. Narrator is very silly and uses pretty advanced vocabulary. Demonstrations are well selected to illustrate a point. Highly educational. *Kid Juror Comments*: Funny and informative. Some kids responded well, others didn't. They enjoyed the marching band and the host. "I learned how to blow through my mouth like I was blowing on a horn." "It makes me want to join the school band." "We learned a lot." Video. 23 min.; $11.95; Age: 5-8. Warner Bros. Publications.

** Dr. Seuss's My Many Colored Days (Notes Alive!)

Engaging Dr. Seuss story features colorful 3-D animation of a child and dog experiencing their feelings through color and music. Narrated by Holly Hunter; music score by Richard Einhorn; performed by the Minnesota Symphony Orchestra. *Adult Juror Comments*: Too slow, too long, style is stiff. Enhances pride in individuality and self-expression. Teaches communication skills using emotions. Beautiful music, but cuts to the orchestra distract from the story. *Kid Juror Comments*: Good production, though some parts lost their attention. Some students clapped, swayed, and danced along. Others found it boring and confusing. "The music people are not fun." "Made us think about how our hearts feel." Video. 45 min.; $19.95; Age: 5-8. Minnesota Orchestra Visual Entertainment.

** Dr. Seuss's My Many Colored Days (DVD) (Notes Alive!)

Follow the adventures of a child and a dog as they share everyday emotions expressed through color and melody. Based on the book, *Dr. Seuss's: My Many Colored Days*. Includes a behind the scenes tour and an interactive quiz game of 22 questions and facts. *Adult Juror Comments*: Top notch production quality that includes animation and a live orchestra concert. Music fits well with animation. Emotions fit well with accompanying music: from glee and joy, to the blues and downright sadness. Suitable for varied ages and cultures. *Kid Juror Comments*: Kids enjoyed the animation and the music, clapping along to the fast-moving parts. "It values that everyone has bad moods sometimes." "Afterwards, we wanted to talk about our feelings." DVD. 60 min.; $24.95; Age: 4-10. Minnesota Orchestra Visual Entertainment.

** Fred Penner: What a Day!

Fred Penner discovers a magic photo booth with songs about fun, friendship, and life. *Adult Juror Comments*: Jurors liked using music and songs to stimulate happiness in a concert format. The story line didn't hold together. *Kid Juror Comments*: Fun and engaging, but younger children lost interest. It's better suited for school-age viewers than preschool. Video. 28 min.; $10.98; Age: 3-13. Children's Group, The.

* Getting to Know the Instruments (Tune Buddies)

The tuneful chef introduces the beautiful menu of the musical families of instruments and their key instruments. The chef's musical cooking adventure gives kids a taste of what the brass, percussion, strings, and keyboard families are all about. *Adult Juror Comments*: Whimsically introduces musical instruments. Teaches kids about different instruments in a fun way. They use a cake recipe to get the instruments in an orchestra together. Narrator uses language incorrectly. More educational than entertaining. *Kid Juror Comments*: Challenged their knowledge base. "It made us think about the wide range of instruments available." "It was silly too." Those interested in music enjoyed it; those who didn't lost interest. Video. 24 min.; $11.95; Age: 5-8. Warner Bros. Publications.

** I Dig Dirt

Highlights a fascinating display of really big earth-movers in action. Winner of a CINE golden eagle. Catchy music by Grammy-winning Jeff Tyzik. *Adult Juror Comments*: The first part is quite good. Honesty in presenting fascinating machinery in action, but the trickery at the end contradicts that. The kids' narration and hosting is well done, especially the interview with female driver. *Kid Juror Comments*: Fascinated by variety of machinery, the size comparison, and ways to play in the dirt. Enjoyed the kids' narration. Kid scores were high across the board. It's a bit long and sophisticated for younger ones. Video. 30 min.; $12.95; Age: 3-8. Dreams Come True Productions.

** Is Not, Is Too! (Cathy and Marcy's Song Shop)

Cathy and Marcy lead children and adults in singing, signing, dancing, and yodeling. While children listen to a variety of instruments including the hammer dulcimer, mandolin, and banjo, they're invited to play along at home on their air guitars. *Adult Juror Comments*: Active, well-selected songs stimulate creative interaction. The production is simple and pleasing. Kudos for including sign language. Although this is directed at children, it's useful for adults too. *Kid Juror Comments*: Enjoyed the interaction and caught on quickly. They learned some new songs that they soon sang, especially the younger ones. Video. 30 min.; $14.95; Age: 4-8. Community Music, Inc.

*** Joe Scruggs in Concert

Upbeat tunes, unbeatable lyrics, lively puppets, and larger-than-life props and characters make this show a non-stop family frolic. *Adult Juror Comments*: Joe's songs are wonderfully imaginative; visuals are fun and attractive. *Kid Juror Comments*: Very singable. Asked to watch it often. Video. 51 min.; $14.95; Age: 3-8. Shadowplay Records & Video.

** Joe's First Video

Combines animation, live action, and irresistibly enchanting songs that create a musical masterpiece in a class by itself. Features Joe Scruggs. *Adult Juror Comments*: Wonderful music video for kids. Very age-appropriate. *Kid Juror Comments*: Wanted to watch again. Video. 31 min.; $14.95; Age: 3-8. Shadowplay Records & Video.

** Keyboards, The (Tune Buddies)

Hosts Snack Upright and Sammy Swing and the Tune Buddies Gang tickle the ivories in this keyboard family adventure. Classical melodies, jazz, and digital rock 'n' roll are played on the different kinds of keyboards. *Adult Juror Comments*: Imaginative production. Introduces instruments through a dream. Depicts a wide range of keyboard instruments and introduces a variety of musicians and music styles including jazz, digital organ, and pipe organ. Educational, fun, and entertaining. *Kid Juror Comments*: Interested, actively engaged. "I brought out my toy piano and played along, and my friends danced." "I'd like to learn to play the piano." "I liked the pipe organ." "This would be a good program for my music class at school." Video. 25 min.; $11.95; Age: 5-8. Warner Bros. Publications.

*** Learning Basic Skills: Music by Hap Palmer

Teaches color, and letter and number recognition to Hap Palmer's best-loved songs. Includes "All the Colors in the Rainbow," "Marching Around the Alphabet," "A Pocketful of B's," and "30 Second Challenge." *Adult Juror Comments*: Hap Palmer's music is fun, funny, intelligent, entertaining, and realistic. He knows how to reach kids. Shows great respect for cultural diversity. *Kid Juror Comments*: They were excited to hear the first letter of their name sung in the alphabet song. Video. 24 min.; $19.95; Age: 4-8. Educational Activities, Inc.

* Let's Keep Singing (Sing Along with John Langstaff)

Draws children into the wonderful world of music-making with master music educator and Pied Piper John Langstaff. Designed for children watching alone or in groups. *Adult Juror Comments*: Song selection is good. Adults wanted more explanation and movement instructions. This is better-suited to classroom than home use. *Kid Juror Comments*: Not very attractive and only sporadically held their attention. Video. 45 min.; $19.95; Age: 5-8. Langstaff Video Project.

Age 5-8

Video

Music

** *Madeline and the Dog Show (Madeline)*

Scrubbed and perfumed, Genevieve, Madeline, the girls, and Miss Clavel line up to register for the show. Genevieve cannot enter. She has no pedigree. Delightfully animated and filled with music, fun, and adventure. *Adult Juror Comments*: Excellent adaptation of the classic book with colorful, entertaining characters. Strong female role models. *Kid Juror Comments*: Infectious. Girls enjoyed it more than boys. They sang and hummed afterwards. It stimulated their interest in the books. Video. 26 min.; $12.95; Age: 4-12. Sony Wonder.

** *Monkey Moves*

Walk like a woo woo. Roll like a baboon. Based on the work of Dr. Moshe Feldenkrais, designed to help children develop balance, coordination, and motor skills while moving to music. Music by Paul McCandless. *Adult Juror Comments*: Applause for the concept of teaching different ways to exercise and making goofy animal sounds. Thought the speaker was awkward. *Kid Juror Comments*: Enjoyed exercising with this video. Liked the imaginative approach. "I'm building muscles by doing this." Three-year-olds may have trouble watching the video and doing the exercises at the same time. Video. 26 min.; $19.95; Age: 3-9. Rosewood Publications, Inc.

** *Move Like the Animals*

Roll like a cat. Crawl like an alligator. Based on the work of Dr. Moshe Feldenkrais, it helps children develop balance, coordination, and motor skills while moving to original music. *Adult Juror Comments*: Clever and thoughtful production. The information about animal movement is as appealing as the performances themselves. Instrumentation is excellent and well-paced. Adults appreciated that the kids can be understood when they're speaking. *Kid Juror Comments*: The originality—participating with the musical performances—was quite successful. They thought the performers were energetic and appealing and wanted to share this video with friends so they could do it again. Video. 24 min.; $19.95; Age: 3-8. Rosewood Publications, Inc.

** *Music and Magic (Positive Music Videos for Today's Kids)*

Contains seven original songs set to video in a fast-paced style. Kevin Anthony sings "Positive Music Videos for Today's Kids." Strong, upbeat music with messages that promote self-esteem. *Adult Juror Comments*: Capitalizes on kids' interest in fast-paced programming. Some songs are better than others, and sometimes the messages get lost in the snazzy presentation. Good diversity, but too much emphasis is on the adult singers. *Kid Juror Comments*: Enjoyable, especially the bubbles. "My two-year-old daughter loved it." Video. 30 min.; $12.95; Age: 5-11. Bright Ideas Productions.

** Musical Max and Other Musical Stories (Children's Circle)

Animated stories include the antics of a lively fiddle, a woman who would rather play trombone than clean her house, and a girl who travels to Africa to play her spirited violin. *Adult Juror Comments*: Stories true to the original book and have wonderful voices and music. Shows equal gender balance. *Kid Juror Comments*: The female characters were particularly attractive. Seems more suited to ages three to seven. Video. 37 min.; $14.95; Age: 5-8. Scholastic/Children's Circle.

* On the Day You Were Born (Notes Alive!)

 Debra Frasier's award-winning book comes alive with bold three-dimensional animation and sights and sounds of the world-class Minnesota Symphony Orchestra. Features Steve Heitzeg. *Adult Juror Comments*: Stunning, gentle production, combines music and animation in an intriguing combination of creative writing and fine art. The interviews and deconstruction of the tape is fascinating. Especially appeals to new-age philosophy. Moves slowly. *Kid Juror Comments*: Excellent artist interviews. Enjoyed learning how the video was made and, for the most part, loved the music. "I wanted to hear what the writer had to say." Some little ones were put to sleep. Video. 30 min.; $19.95; Age: 5-8. Minnesota Orchestra Visual Entertainment.

** Percussion, The (Tune Buddies)

An ace reporter is on the beat to drum up information on the instruments that make up the percussion family. He explores how percussion instruments keep the beat for all other instruments and covers rock, jazz, classical, and ethnic rhythms. *Adult Juror Comments*: Cute presentation, covers variety of percussion instruments. Channels kids' natural tendency to bang on things into constructive knowledge. Creative venue for introducing the drums and rhythm instruments. *Kid Juror Comments*: Had a great time watching. "I like pretending I was playing the drums with the man." "I think I'd like to have drum lessons." "We learned that one type of percussion instrument helps the speed of the band, and the other makes the melody." Video. 28 min.; $11.95; Age: 5-8. Warner Bros. Publications.

*** Sammy and Other Songs from Getting to Know Myself

 Nice examples of children stretching, jumping, and discovering the joy of moving. Covers awareness of body image and the body's position in space and body movements. *Adult Juror Comments*: Well-produced. Gives pleasant, clear demonstrations of movement concepts and body parts. Insights for a child that enhances their self-image. Good cultural diversity. Song lyrics are shown on-screen, encouraging readers to sing along. *Kid Juror Comments*: Much fun. They sang along when they could. Video. 30 min.; $19.95; Age: 3-9. Educational Activities, Inc.

Age 5-8

Video

Music

*** Sing 'n Sign for Fun

 Gaia and a group of hearing and deaf children perform seven upbeat songs with American Sign Language, teach signs for greetings and the manual alphabet. Signed, voiced, and open-captioned for total communication. *Adult Juror Comments*: Thoughtful production introduces sign language through singing. Songs are hip and portray a sense of hope. Shows good friendship-making skills and concern about global issues. Requires repeat viewing to learn signing. Good diversity. *Kid Juror Comments*: Wonderful music, singing, and finger spelling. Asked many questions about being deaf. Prompted discussion about believing in one's self, respecting others, differences, and making friends. Girls enjoyed Gaia. Video. 42 min.; $14.95; Age: 5-8. Heartsong Communications.

*** Sing Along, The (Cabbage Patch Kids)

All songs from the Cabbage Patch series with on-screen lyrics. *Adult Juror Comments*: Helps kids realize that their thoughts, dreams, and feelings are okay, and encourages self-esteem. The characters accurately depict children's attitudes. The doll figures are cleverly manipulated to show movement and expression. *Kid Juror Comments*: How do the Cabbage Patch Kids work together, maintain their friendships, and have fun? A good discussion on that. The child jurors sang along with the song selections. Everyone's favorite part was the clubhouse. Video. 30 min.; $12.98; Age: 5-8. BMG Home Video.

** Strings, The (Tune Buddies)

The undercover musical detective is out to solve the "Concert Hall Caper" and find out if the strings are guilty of making beautiful music. He investigates the key instruments in the string family as he searches for the missing violin string. *Adult Juror Comments*: Informative, whimsically produced. Inspires further inquiry into string instruments. Using a mystery story as a means of exploring the instruments is a cute touch. A wide variety of people demonstrate the various instruments. *Kid Juror Comments*: Funny and educational. Kids liked the detective story format. "The host PJ is a little weird." "The instruments were interesting, especially the violin." "I'd like to learn more about orchestras." Video. 25 min.; $11.95; Age: 5-8. Warner Bros. Publications.

Chapter Three • Elementary

* Tales & Tunes: Spooky Tales & Tunes (Tales & Tunes)

 Haunting new collection of stories and songs from the creators of the award-winning Baby Songs. Great assortment of cartoons, live-action, and sing-along songs for ages two to eight. *Adult Juror Comments*: Surely not appropriate for the age group indicated by the supplier, because it's too scary for kids under five. The resolution of fears in "Spooky Dreams" is well-done. "Monsters in the Morning" is clever. *Kid Juror Comments*: Some children under five were uncomfortable, while others liked it. Older kids enjoyed it and found it wasn't as scary as they thought it was going to be. They related to the events as similar to their everyday life and found them funny. Video. 30 min.; $12.98; Age: 3-8. Anchor Bay Entertainment.

* Tales & Tunes: Sports Tales & Tunes (Tales & Tunes)

 Cartoons, live-action antics, and songs bring out the "good sport" in everyone. Includes "Follow That Baseball," "Yes You Can," "Let's Play Ball," and "Teamwork." *Adult Juror Comments*: Humor is very appropriate for this age. The material varies in quality, though. One storylike section, although predictable, has an emotional appeal. Others are somewhat repetitive, and approach is superficial. *Kid Juror Comments*: Related to the subject. Some children joined in singing along with it. Video. 30 min.; $12.98; Age: 4-8. Anchor Bay Entertainment.

** Teddy Bears' Jamboree, The

 Music pioneers Gary Rosen and Bill Shontz perform live for 10,000 fans and their teddy bears. Filled with zany humor, superb harmonies, instrumental versatility, and inventive lyrics. Invites audience to sing along with the Rosenshontz Group. *Adult Juror Comments*: Live family concert features delightful music by accomplished musicians whose music is filled with positive lyrics. Content and performers are engaging. Lyrics and melodies are simple to remember. *Kid Juror Comments*: Easy to sing along. Because it's long, might be best used in segments. Liked watching the kids dance together with their teddy bears. Video. 62 min.; $9.95; Age: 4-9. Stories to Remember.

** Tickle Tune Typhoon: Let's Be Friends

Twelve joyful songs from the Typhoon's three award-winning albums come alive with dance and colorful costumed characters. Includes "Let's Be Friends," "My Body Belongs To Me," and "Hug Bug." *Adult Juror Comments*: Songs are compelling and fun, but it's too slow. It's a videotaped production of a live concert that loses its energy in the translation. Great diversity and skill at playing instruments. *Kid Juror Comments*: Sang and danced along. Characters very appealing, especially the dancing veggies and the Tooth Fairy. Some thought the music was too loud and hard to hear the words. "The Hokey Pokey was my favorite." "That man played the drums with his feet!" Video. 58 min.; $14.95; Age: 3-9. Just for Kids Home Video/Celebrity Home Entertainment.

** Veggie Tales: A Very Silly Sing-Along! (Veggie Tales)

Sing yourself silly with Bob the Tomato, Larry the Cucumber, and all their veggie buddies in this silly collection of favorite tunes from the Veggie Tales series. *Adult Juror Comments*: Amusing as well as interesting. Excellent colors and sound quality. Songs in Spanish make it more challenging. Helps teach rhythm and musical scale. "Hairbrush song was like Gilbert and Sullivan for vegetables." Contains Christian-based content. *Kid Juror Comments*: Music was fun and catchy. Imaginative production. "I liked the Spanish." But overall, it did not hold the children's attention as well as the Veggie Tales with stories. Video. 30 min.; $12.99; Age: 4-8. Big Idea Productions, Inc.

* We're All Americans

Celebrate diversity with songs about connections, community, growing up with love and trust, understanding differences, and healing social wounds. *Adult Juror Comments*: Interesting and unusual. A little preachy and long. Technically well-done, but the excitement of a real concert is not conveyed. "Makes one think of issues of race and work ethics. Teaches good values—do your best, be kind and love one another." *Kid Juror Comments*: "I liked listening and singing to the music." Not a lot of action. Presentation gets boring for kids after a few songs. Sometimes kids couldn't hear the performers' voices. Multicultural cast is appealing. Video. 51 min.; $19.99; Age: 5-8. Charles R. Rothschild.

*** Wildlife Symphony (Reader's Digest)

Combines classic symphonies with stunning footage of animals as they frolic, prance, and dance in their own inimitable way. Shows lions at play, insects at work, wildlife in the rainforest, and dolphins in the sea. *Adult Juror Comments*: Has beautiful cinematography, and it's funny but long. It's great to listen to as well as watch. Sparks an interest in nature, insect world. *Kid Juror Comments*: Kids like the images of animals. Some were mesmerized when viewing. Some were surprised to find there was no narration. Kids related different animal traits to themselves. They said it was "relaxing." Video. 48 min.; $29.99; Age: 6-12. IVN Entertainment.

** Woodwinds, The (Tune Buddies)

 Introduces the woodwind family, from the soft sounds of the flute or clarinet to the jazzy roar of the saxophone. Explores the diversity and sound range of the different families of woodwind instruments in the format of a musical treasure hunt. *Adult Juror Comments*: Simple production. Introduces kids to woodwind instruments with informative demonstrations using a treasure hunt theme. Corny host, at times tends to talk down to the kids. Portrays only Europeans or Americans. *Kid Juror Comments*: Some liked it, others didn't. "Everybody was very nice helping solve the clues." "It was okay. The clues were hard to figure out." "My friends in band will like it." "All the kids starting band in sixth grade would love it, I think." Video. 23 min.; $11.95; Age: 5-8. Warner Bros. Publications.

*** Zin! Zin! Zin! A Violin (Reading Rainbow)

 LeVar finds out how orchestra members combine their sounds and work as a team. Demonstrates creativity, expression, rhythm, dance, and self-expression as a joint effort. Explores rhyming, melodies, math, and the interrelationship. *Adult Juror Comments*: Great introduction to music. Frank discussion of the hours of practice, pressure, and hard work. Balances a variety of musical information and stimulates interest in music while informing children. A delight. *Kid Juror Comments*: Great, great, great. Discussed strings, brass, and horns. "I want to be a musician." "I like the flute and the French horns." "The 'Stomp' part was cool." After watching, kids got out instruments and made their own orchestra. Video. 28 min.; $19.95; Age: 5-8. Reading Rainbow/GPN.

Age 5-8

Video

Music

Category—Nature

*** *Adventures in Asia (Really Wild Animals)*

A wild magic carpet ride around Asia: cuddly giant pandas in Southern China, hairy orangutans in Borneo, huge manta rays in the Red Sea, and close-knit elephant families in India. *Adult Juror Comments*: Packed with information from various locations. The music captured kids' attention. The jokes sometime detract from the information they are trying to convey. Some explanations are not particularly clear. *Kid Juror Comments*: Likable host, good show, fine mix of animation and live action. Children got a kick out of the animals' humor. Even the three-year-olds loved it. Girls were more attentive than boys. Video. 40 min.; $14.95; Age: 3-12. Nat'l Geographic Home Video.

*** *Amazing North America (Really Wild Animals)*

From the frozen Arctic to the Florida Everglades, the animals of North America are on parade: alligators patrolling the swampy waters of the Okefenokee, ground squirrels battling rattlesnakes in the Wild West, and many other encounters. *Adult Juror Comments*: Visually interesting, entertaining, and well-paced. Scored high with jurors. Humor sometimes gets in the way of information. Organization is a little confusing. Suitable for home or school use. *Kid Juror Comments*: Scored high. Music helped capture their interest. Fills a much-needed gap of nature videos designed specifically for kids. Prompted discussions about animals in different regions. Video. 47 min.; $14.95; Age: 5-12. Nat'l Geographic Home Video.

*** *Animals & Me: Eating (Animals & Me)*

Satisfies children's curiosity about wildlife. Entertaining and educational. Narrated by children. Features chimpanzees, bears, and elephants, along with exotic sounds and music. *Adult Juror Comments*: Excellent, realistic photography, content, and presentation. Stands out for polish and high standards. Narration effective and natural. *Kid Juror Comments*: "I liked the elephants eating." "It's fun watching the bears catch fish." "This movie gets all happies." (Happy faces on the evaluation tool.) Video. 30 min.; $14.95; Age: 3-8. Small World Productions.

** *Antlers Big and Small (Mother Nature)*

Examines nearly a dozen different cousins of the deer family in their forest habitats of the great North American Wilderness. *Adult Juror Comments*: Lots of information. Uses real-life footage (somewhat dated) of animals in their natural habitat. Appeals to older kids as well. Great learning tool. Some adults objected to the reference to the animals' mating practices. *Kid Juror Comments*: Fascinating and humorous. Those who like animals were most attentive. The footage looked slightly faded. Video. 25 min.; $12.95; Age: 6-12. Discovery Communications.

Chapter Three • Elementary

** Babes in The Woods (Mother Nature)

Baby animals in nursery habitats ranging from pouches to telephone poles, and from around the world as they learn and grow. Includes newborn koalas, kangaroos, and cranes, small key deer, noisy woodpeckers, and a Canadian gosling. *Adult Juror Comments*: Good footage though slightly faded. Interesting choice of animals. Informative and engaging without being didactic, although language is more suitable for older kids. Wonderful prelude for a trip to the zoo. *Kid Juror Comments*: Held their attention and was the right length, with the right selection of animals. Dated, slow-moving, and not upbeat when compared to other current nature titles. Video. 25 min.; $12.95; Age: 5-8. Discovery Communications.

*** Bear Cubs, Baby Ducks, and Kooky Kookaburras (Geokids)

Uncle Balzac guides Sunny and Bobby into the world of baby animals: baby turtles, bear cubs, penguin chicks, a lost zebra, and even a peek at stingrays. *Adult Juror Comments*: Respect for nature and the environment. Music is terrific. The mix of live action, graphics, and animation enhances literacy. *Kid Juror Comments*: "This is the best video we saw." The children sang along, clapped, asked questions, and jumped out of their seats with excitement. They loved the animal pictures drawn by the children. Great pace. Works best with younger audience. Video. 33 min.; $14.95; Age: 1-10. Nat'l Geographic Home Video.

* Big Horse

Loving and respectful survey of the role big horses have played in human history: on farms, in industry, and even wartime. Features Percherons, Belgians, and Clydesdales. *Adult Juror Comments*: Appealed most to kids who love horses. Stimulated further inquiry. A good learning tool with simple production values, though it's a little slow-paced. Narrator annoyed some children. *Kid Juror Comments*: Didn't like seeing the animals roughed up. Liked the foals and seeing people taking good care of the animals. Video. 30 min.; $19.95; Age: 5-8. Big Horse Productions.

** Biggest Bears!, The

Stunningly photographed in Alaska, with a young narrator. Explores myths about grizzlies, the biggest bears. *Adult Juror Comments*: Outstanding nature for educational value. Excellent child narrator, wonderful photography. Environmental values emphasized. *Kid Juror Comments*: Children enjoyed learning about different types of bears. "I liked watching the bears catch the fish. They must be very fast." Video. 30 min.; $14.95; Age: 4-9. Bullfrog Films.

** *Born to Be Wild (Owl/TV Video)*

Many, many funny, furry, fuzzy animals: monkeys, bears and chimps. Follows a mother koala and her baby, who is tracked by a radio implant, and observes Quing-Quing and Quan-Quan, the endangered giant pandas, at lunch. *Adult Juror Comments*: Excellent use of animation to provide information that would be difficult to show live. Also enjoyable are the children who interview researchers about working at the zoo. Some concern about the safety of being around wild animals. *Kid Juror Comments*: Kids were fascinated with the information about animal behavior. Enjoyed seeing how the animals care for their young. The pandas were everyone's favorite. Video. 28 min.; $11.98; Age: 4-13. The Children's Group.

** *Bringing Up Baby (Mother Nature)*

Visits animal babies at wildlife nurseries and their proud parents. A lost sea lion finds its mother, and a mama coyote rescues her pups when she senses a cougar nearby. *Adult Juror Comments*: Excellent photography and well-chosen background music. Good variety of birds and mammals. Alliteration in narration is overdone. *Kid Juror Comments*: Stimulated discussion about how many birds used regurgitation methods of feeding their young. "Cute cubs. I liked finding out how babies live." Video. 25 min.; $12.96; Age: 5-8. Discovery Communications.

** *Business of Beavers, The (Mother Nature)*

Visits a beaver lodge and the family. Also explains the importance of beavers to the forest habitat. *Adult Juror Comments*: Interesting close-up of habitat, habits, and the lives of beavers. Exceptional learning potential to expand vocabulary. A little slow-moving for those not fascinated by beavers. *Kid Juror Comments*: Sat through the entire video, but weren't interested in seeing it again. Video. 25 min.; $12.95; Age: 5-8. Discovery Communications.

** *Castaways of Galapagos (Mother Nature)*

Who occupies the remote Galapagos Islands? The legendary 500-hundred pound Galapagos tortoise, amazing marine iguanas, the graceful flamingos, awkward blue-footed booby birds, and the albatross. Stunning wildlife scenes. *Adult Juror Comments*: Informative and beautiful, helps link past and present in a true island adventure of the most natural kind. At times the vocabulary is far too advanced. *Kid Juror Comments*: Educational. Remembered the animal names. One six-year-old said, "These are the animals I like the best. The kind we don't have in Wisconsin." Some wanted to watch it again immediately. Video. 25 min.; $12.95; Age: 5-8. Discovery Communications.

** Cool Cats, Raindrops, and Things That Live in Holes (Geokids)

 Sunny is shocked that bushbabies sleep in hollow trees. Uncle Balzac explains that many animals make their homes in holes. This episode features "Cool Cats," a rhythm-and-blues tribute to the feline family. Created by Hank Saroyan. *Adult Juror Comments*: Great cinematography, fine characters, and clever songs. But tries to do too much, for example, by squeezing in a phonics lesson. *Kid Juror Comments*: Enjoyed seeing animals they don't usually see. Humor is inappropriate and over their heads at times. Video. 33 min.; $14.95; Age: 4-7. Nat'l Geographic Home Video.

*** Creepy Creatures & Slimy Stuff (Owl/TV Video)

Takes a curious look at slugs, snakes, and other slimy stuff. From the rain forest to the desert, explores the weird and wonderful world of scorpions, frogs, eels, and bats. *Adult Juror Comments*: Informative, with clever animation and excellent cinematography. Narration and dialogue easy to follow. Songs have excellent audio quality. Low-key presentation. *Kid Juror Comments*: Ready to watch it again. "My six-year-old girl loved it!" Video. 30 min.; $11.98; Age: 4-13. The Children's Group.

** Curious Cougar Kittens (Mother Nature)

 Birth of two cougar kittens in the high country of Utah. Mom protects and teaches her playful, adventurous kittens. Dated, washed-out footage, slow narration, not upbeat enough. *Adult Juror Comments*: Much information in an educational format. Intimate view of the daily life of cougar kittens. *Kid Juror Comments*: Enjoyed the cougar antics, particularly when they tried to get the turtle out of its shell. Asked to see it a second time. Asked good questions and wanted books about cougars. Video. 25 min.; $12.95; Age: 5-8. Discovery Communications.

*** Deep Sea Dive (Really Wild Animals)

 Explores the last great frontier on earth, the magnificent oceans, from surface to sea floor. Great whales, friendly dolphins, scary sharks. Features award-winning cinematography by National Geographic Magazine. Narrated by Dudley Moore. *Adult Juror Comments*: Fabulous footage. Informative yet entertaining. Songs are smarmy and predictable, but also meaningful. Worthy message: "Keep waters clear." *Kid Juror Comments*: A pleasure. Liked the fast pace, new information, the humor, and the music. Laughed and screamed with delight. Afterwards, discussed their knowledge about some of the animals. Video. 40 min.; $14.95; Age: 5-12. Nat'l Geographic Home Video.

** *Desert Animals (See How They Grow)*

The desert is home to a tiny tarantula, gerbil, tortoise, and gecko, and gives them a sunny start on their life adventures. Narrated by baby animals themselves, so to speak. *Adult Juror Comments*: Most of the photography is staged— not in the natural habitat. Good introduction to a variety of desert animals. Slow-moving but thorough and includes little-known facts. *Kid Juror Comments*: It was fun to hear the animals talk about themselves. Liked the animal voices and the tarantula's jokes. "I liked the animation that shows how each animal grows and changes." Not interested in viewing it again. Video. 30 min.; $12; Age: 4-7. Sony Wonder.

** *Dr. Zed's Brilliant Science Activities (Owl/TV Video)*

Dr. Zed's hands-on introduction to the magic of science through simple tricks and activities. Test the principles of flying, create colorful molecular art, discover the power of a finger, and take a close-up look at optical illusions. *Adult Juror Comments*: Lively suggestions for projects that kids can do with adults as an introduction to scientific concepts. Somewhat dated and slow-paced. Good diversity. Production quality lacks clarity at times. *Kid Juror Comments*: Wanted to watch it again. Learned a lot, even though a few didn't understand Dr. Zed's explanations. Video. 30 min.; $11.98; Age: 4-12. The Children's Group.

** *Exploring the Rain Forest (Redbook Learning Adventures)*

 Delightful songs and film clips of the rain forest, featuring Fluffy Duffy and friends who explain why the rain forest is worth protecting. *Adult Juror Comments*: Conveys important information clearly. Songs are repetitive and at times long, although the repetition helps learning. Some also thought that the mix of fantasy and reality didn't work well. *Kid Juror Comments*: Danced along and liked the songs. Re-enacted the spaceship blastoff. Definitely watch this again. It's most suitable for four- to seven-year-olds. Video. 30 min.; $12.98; Age: 4-7. Anchor Bay Entertainment.

** *Flying, Trying, and Honking Around (Geokids)*

 With help from Uncle Balzac, Sunny and Bobby learn about different birds and find out why most birds fly and why other animals can't. Wacky Francisco Flamingo flaps past with Flamingo Facts and introduces counting, phonics, and rock 'n' roll. *Adult Juror Comments*: Incredible animal footage and facts, but overall it's not clear who the audience is. Individual segments suitable for different ages. Video jumps from offering fairly complex animal facts to teaching the alphabet. Why? *Kid Juror Comments*: Really excited about the topic, but found the presentation confusing. Lost their interest when the information wasn't suitable for their age and ability. Video. 33 min.; $14.95; Age: 3-8. Nat'l Geographic Home Video.

* Good Neighbor Ground Squirrel (Mother Nature)

 Visit to a den where a mother squirrel hibernates and has pups. Explains the amazing alarm system of squirrels when a badger, a coyote, and a hawk threaten them. *Adult Juror Comments*: Interesting information about different species and habitats. Jurors enjoyed the female narrator, since most nature programs have male voices. Some footage appears washed-out. *Kid Juror Comments*: Appreciated the educational information, such as learning there are more species of squirrels than the backyard variety they're familiar with. Too long for audience. Video. 25 min.; $12.95; Age: 5-8. Discovery Communications.

* Henry's Amazing Animals: Animal Hunters
(Henry's Amazing Animals)

Join the fun-filled musical safari as animal numbers introduce your preschooler to the numbers zero through ten. *Adult Juror Comments*: Humorous, beautifully produced, excellent cinematography. Provides factual, educational information. Some objected to graphic hunting and feeding scenes where animals eat other animals. Henry's sarcasm and behavior is irritating. *Kid Juror Comments*: Said they'd watch it again and recommend it to their friends. Most thought the scenes involving animals eating animals were disgusting but cool. "Why do only the female lions hunt?" "I like the archer bug—he's an excellent hunter." Video. 30 min.; $9.95; Age: 5-9. DK Vision and Partridge Films.

** Henry's Amazing Animals: Animal Talk
(Henry's Amazing Animals)

 How do worker bees direct traffic? Why do zebras talk with their ears? Explores how extraordinary wildlife from all around the world communicate. *Adult Juror Comments*: Beautiful. Interesting information. For example, bowerbirds build blue nests to attract the female. Animated narrator is sarcastic and disrespectful—shouting at another character who doesn't speak his language and makes fun of him. *Kid Juror Comments*: Loved it. Cool. Interesting. They'd watch again. "I'd watch it 200 times." "I learned that lots of animals talk differently." "I want to know more about my dog." "There are so many kinds of animals." They enjoyed narrator's humor. Video. 30 min.; $9.95; Age: 4-7. DK Vision and Partridge Films.

** In the Company of Whales

Observes whales, the largest animals to ever live on earth, powerful creatures of extraordinary grace and intelligence, masters of their realm for more than 30 million years. *Adult Juror Comments*: High scores. Great visuals, an excellent introduction to the subject even though some parts were very slow and too technical for kids. *Kid Juror Comments*: Those interested in animals and nature really enjoyed this. Others found it too long and some words hard to understand. "I would love to swim with them." Video. 55 min.; $19.95; Age: 5-12. Discovery Communications.

Age 5-8

Video

Nature

** Jungle Animals (See How They Grow)

Illustrates how the lush jungle offers a perfect place to grow up for a little scorpion, alligator, snail, and two tiny tigers. *Adult Juror Comments*: Good combination of animation and live action, with excellent photography and music. "Makes learning fun." Humor is more appropriate for adults than children, and it's slow-moving. *Kid Juror Comments*: Enjoyable, appealing most to those interested in nature. Video. 30 min.; $12.98; Age: 3-8. Sony Wonder.

** Let's Create a Better World (Let's Create)

How to create environmentally sensitive art projects with recyclable materials that are usually thrown away. *Adult Juror Comments*: Jurors liked the focus on reduce-reuse-recycle-respect. Children need to be attentive while watching the demonstrations. For classroom setting or at home with an adult helping. Focus does not encourage independent creativity. *Kid Juror Comments*: Interest in the activities, especially paper-making. Good tool for children who need a little nudge in the creative area. Video. 70 min.; $24.95; Age: 5-12. Let's Create, Inc.

*** Little Duck Tale, A

 This tender, heartwarming story portrays the true-life adventures of "Chibi" and his duckling brothers and sisters as they struggle for survival in downtown Tokyo. Children will find joy in this tale of determination and triumph. *Adult Juror Comments*: Absolutely fabulous story, perhaps a wee bit too long. Shows a great role model for the mother, engaging an international community of support for her. *Kid Juror Comments*: Kids loved this. Much to our surprise, even the boys did. They stayed with it even though it's long. They were anxious to retell the story to their parents. Video. 55 min.; $14.95; Age: 5-12. Discovery Communications.

* New World of the Gnomes, The

Produced in cooperation with the World Wide Fund for Nature, emphasizes respect for the planet while enjoying the amazing adventures of the gnomes. *Adult Juror Comments*: Well-produced, simply animated, but colorful. Creates an awareness for endangered species and environment. Conveys some anti-human sentiment and shows some stereotyping. Language is sometimes too advanced for kids. *Kid Juror Comments*: Appealing fantasy story about little people in a happy society with animal friends where everyone helps and promotes goodness. They didn't always understand what was happening. Video. 26 min.; $14.95; Age: 5-8. B.R.B. Internacional, S.A.

Chapter Three • Elementary

** Orca Whales & Mermaid Tales (Mother Nature)

An intimate look at huge orca whales and mysterious manatees, once thought to be mermaids. Explains the orca's fascinating blowhole and watches a manatee calf swimming just hours after it's born. *Adult Juror Comments*: Well-produced. Respectful and inspiring story with beautiful cinematography. Contains lots of information, well-paced, with interesting narration. It's a little dense with information. *Kid Juror Comments*: "The kids really sat and watched this video." The entire program kept their attention, and they wanted to watch again. Some language and terminology were way over their heads. Video. 25 min.; $12.95; Age: 4-12. Discovery Communications.

** Penguins in Paradise (Mother Nature)

Penguins in their coastal paradise of Patagonia, waddling on land and gliding underwater. Introduces their neighbors, cormorants, and sea lions. *Adult Juror Comments*: Well-produced nature video. "If you enjoy nature documentaries, you'll enjoy this one." Informative with a good ecology message. Some graphic images are below-average. *Kid Juror Comments*: Liked learning about the penguins. What kept their attention was how funny they seemed. Generated a lot of discussion about animals and the environment. "People should help penguins by not polluting." Video. 25 min.; $12.95; Age: 5-8. Discovery Communications.

** Sea Animals (See How They Grow)

An underwater wonderland becomes the cradle of life for the fast-growing little ray, pipefish, cuttlefish, and the hermit crab. *Adult Juror Comments*: Opportunity to learn about new animals and their habitat. Suitable for use in a classroom or for learning at home. Narration is lively, though some language is too advanced for preschoolers. Tends to be a little preachy and moves slowly. *Kid Juror Comments*: Those interested in animals enjoyed this the most. It held the attention of the older children best. Prompted discussion after about sea creatures and their environment. Video. 30 min.; $12.98; Age: 3-8. Sony Wonder.

** Springtime Toddler Tales (Mother Nature)

From mountaintops to treetops, proud parents nurture their springtime toddlers: bison calves, elephant seal pups, black bear cubs, pelicans, and more. They all explore, grow and learn. *Adult Juror Comments*: Lovely footage of animal young. Only occasionally does the narration become cloying and anthropomorphic. Otherwise, it's inviting and informative. A good teaching tool for classroom use or in the home. *Kid Juror Comments*: Okay, but they thought the birth scenes were "sort of gross." They said they learned a lot of new things. Video. 25 min.; $12.95; Age: 5-8. Discovery Communications.

** *Swinging Safari (Really Wild Animals)*

Leads young viewers deep into wildest Africa. Spin, National Geographic's animated globe-on-the-go host, is the safari guide. He shows what it's like to live with animals in the wild. *Adult Juror Comments*: Captivating, entertaining, and educational, with disappointing photography that looks several generations old. Good pace, songs range from corny to sappy. Introduces concepts about the food chain and endangered animals. Lion segment occurs twice. *Kid Juror Comments*: Children generally respond well to animal videos, and this was no exception. They liked Spin, the scenes from old movies, the pace, and the humor. Video. 40 min.; $14.95; Age: 4-10. Nat'l Geographic Home Video.

*** *Totally Tropical Rain Forest (Really Wild Animals)*

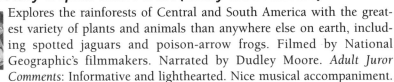

Explores the rainforests of Central and South America with the greatest variety of plants and animals than anywhere else on earth, including spotted jaguars and poison-arrow frogs. Filmed by National Geographic's filmmakers. Narrated by Dudley Moore. *Adult Juror Comments*: Informative and lighthearted. Nice musical accompaniment. Well-executed, well-organized introduction to the rain forest. "Gives you all the information you ever wanted to know." *Kid Juror Comments*: Got a kick out of all the bugs and weird animals and enjoyed learning how animals survive. It made them want to study bats. The humor tends toward the sarcastic, but the kids respond well to that. It's more entertaining than they expected. Video. 40 min.; $14.95; Age: 5-12. Nat'l Geographic Home Video.

** *Trailsigns North: Poop, Paw & Hoof Prints*

Teaches how to read trail signs that animals leave in the wilderness. Trail guide Eric, his friend Max, and the animated Mambo Moose transport the viewer to the spectacular Alaskan wilderness. Contains rare footage of animals in their habitats. *Adult Juror Comments*: Print material about identifying animals by their poop is hard to find. The innovative approach here teaches a lot about animals and their habitats. Provides a new approach to identifying animals in the wild. Eric and Maxwell are good role models. *Kid Juror Comments*: Appealed most to kids with a special interest in animals and trail signs. The title was distracting to some. It held their interest once they get into it. There was the occasional "gross" remark. Video. 25 min.; $14.95; Age: 4-8. Paragon Media.

Chapter Three • Elementary

** Tree Animals (See How They Grow)

Shows how a baby chameleon, stick insect, fruit bat, and buzzard take to the trees to climb, crawl, and fly their way into young adulthood. *Adult Juror Comments*: Encourages appreciation for nature and environmental awareness. Having the animals speak is unrealistic and not believable. Makes a good prelude to field trips to the library, zoo, or wilderness. "I like its simplicity. Even I learned something." *Kid Juror Comments*: Most enjoyable: the part about the chameleons. They were intrigued by how and what they ate. Good length. Shows variety of animals that interested the kids. They especially liked learning how animals grow to adulthood. Kept their interest. Video. 30 min.; $12.98; Age: 4-9. Sony Wonder.

** Wet and Wild (Owl/TV Video)

 Explores the coral reef off the coast of Kenya, swimming alongside the dolphins, getting close to penguins, visiting a trawler, and observing the effects of pollution on sea otters. An educational and entertaining journey. *Adult Juror Comments*: Shows wonderful variety of sea life and people. Refreshing to have an elderly expert on-camera. Well-produced with excellent cinematography. *Kid Juror Comments*: It was cool to have child narrators. They liked learning about survival and wanted to see it again. Provoked an interest in aquariums and sea life. "It's great when the kids interview the adults." "I liked the starfish facts." Video. 30 min.; $11.98; Age: 5-12. Children's Group, The.

** When Goats Go Climbing (Mother Nature)

 Mountain goats cavorting high on craggy peaks and enduring a harsh snowstorm. Young goats climb and play on the day they're born. Points out their amazing vision. *Adult Juror Comments*: Makes a good teaching tool for classroom or at home. Well-produced, informative, and appropriately paced. The scenery is stunning. Engaging and educational for a child motivated to learn. Vignettes are particularly well-done. *Kid Juror Comments*: Favorites, among many: the baby goats. They laughed and said they learned something about how animals survive. Appealed most to kids interested in animals. Video. 25 min.; $12.95; Age: 5-8. Discovery Communications.

*** *Wonders Down Under (Really Wild Animals)*

Travels to the *land down under* to learn about Australia's unusual animals. Leaping kangaroos, paddling platypuses, and cuddly koalas make this immense island their home. Dudley Moore is the voice of Spin, National Geographic's animated host. *Adult Juror Comments:* Entertaining and informative. Moore's cheerful narration is superb. Fascinating footage is enhanced by helpful commentary that is sometimes corny. Confusing when some animals are shown but not discussed. *Kid Juror Comments:* Children enjoyed the humorous comments and the fast pacing. A good tool for further discussion. Kids wrote volumes afterwards about what they learned. They wanted to watch it again immediately. Video. 40 min.; $14.95; Age: 4-10. Nat'l Geographic Home Video.

*** *World Alive, A*

Profiles the myriad creatures of the planet, their activities and interactions. Has a dramatic musical score. Narrated by James Earl Jones. *Adult Juror Comments:* Well-produced, shows an excellent selection of wildlife. Footage of animals in their habitats is extraordinary. *Kid Juror Comments:* Attractive colors and pictures. Called out the animal names when they saw them. "Great because we saw animals all around the world, even some we didn't know about!" Evoked questions about the food chain and animals eating each other. Video. 25 min.; $14.95; Age: 5-12. Sea Studios.

*** *Worlds Below, The*

Herds of sea lions, snowstorms of plankton, starfish in motion, and majestic underwater forests. A newborn seal swims among wave-swept rocks. Vast submerged plains in the mysterious depths. *Adult Juror Comments:* Beautifully produced with excellent cinematography. Well-constructed. *Kid Juror Comments:* Captivating for kids interested in animals and the sea. Video. 48 min.; $19.95; Age: 5-12. Sea Studios.

** *Zoo Food with Grandpa Nature*
(Grandpa Nature's Kids Collection)

Grandpa Nature and his kids lead a behind-the-scenes tour of the zoo. Comedian Jonathan Winters is the voice of Grandpa Nature. Many original songs. *Adult Juror Comments:* Well-produced with interesting music and photography. Opportunities to introduce concepts about life cycles. Science portrayed in an original manner that's suitable for home and school. *Kid Juror Comments:* Used by some parents and teachers as a preview to a field trip to the zoo. Kids were eager for their visit afterwards. "I wanted to see more magic." Video. 32 min.; $12.95; Age: 5-8. Milestone Media, Inc.

Chapter Three • Elementary

* Zoofari!

Have you ever wanted to go on a safari? To discover and marvel at the splendid variety of animals? Join Sir Arthur Blowhard and his assistant Smythe on a zoofari, exploring the wonders of nature's creatures, big and small, up-close and personal. *Adult Juror Comments*: Contains lots of good information. Children are always interested in seeing real animals. The music is too loud at times. An inside look at animals in captivity. Hosts reflect old colonial stereotypes, and the presentation is a bit shallow. *Kid Juror Comments*: Okay, although they thought sequences were too long for younger kids. "Too bad they're all in a zoo." "The lions seem so sad." Video. 32 min.; $14.95; Age: 3-8. White Tree Pictures, Inc./Venture Enter Group.

Category—Special Interest

*** Ashok by Any Other Name

Ashok wants to change his ethnic-sounding name to something more American. Addressing ethnic pride, this speaks to those with unusual names, and to anyone who feels a need to change in order to fit in. *Adult Juror Comments*: Good topic, suitable for this age. Good script, mediocre production values. Storytelling format is not what children are accustomed to, but it works. Supports tolerance and ethnic diversity. It would be helpful for an adult to help facilitate. *Kid Juror Comments*: Appreciated the lesson and were somewhat uncomfortable with the topic. They enjoyed the history lesson at the end and the "meet the authors" section. Video. 45 min.; $29.95; Age: 6-12. Aims Multimedia.

** Astronomy 101: A Family Adventure

For those that have looked at the night sky and wondered what is really up there, join Michelle and her mother as they explore the night sky together. *Adult Juror Comments*: Use of mother-and-daughter team was refreshing. Showing women in science is an intelligent move. Effectively combines information and entertainment in a visually compelling format. *Kid Juror Comments*: Enjoyed the pictures of the night sky and the stars. Some information was much too complicated and technical for the children. Students who are star watchers enjoyed it the most. Video. 25 min.; $14.95; Age: 6-14. Mazon Productions Inc.

*** Barry's Scrapbook: A Window into Art

Barry Louis Polisar hosts a visual and musical tour through the world of art. Features hands-on art projects using recycled materials and interviews with artists and songs. *Adult Juror Comments*: Has high learning potential that engages children's thinking skills, teaches collage-making, deals with textures, and relates instruction to art seen in museums. Polisar and the museum narrator were effective speakers. Shows minority artists. *Kid Juror Comments*: Learned some important things about art. Participated eagerly, answering questions and anxiously wanting to try the projects. They enjoyed seeing the artists at work. Video. 40 min.; $19.95; Age: 5-14. ALA Video/Library Video Network.

** Big Aircraft Carrier, The (Real Life Adventures)

Offers a behind-the-scenes look at flight operations and life on board a floating city of six thousand crew members. Music, child narration, and voice-over of pilots enhance this tour. *Adult Juror Comments*: Good production, clearly presented, and shows cooperation. It's well-paced and informative and has an excellent female role models. "Kids should love this." *Kid Juror Comments*: Impressed by the size of the aircraft carrier and it functions. Kids enjoyed seeing different pilots and planes and how they take off. Video. 40 min.; $14.95; Age: 5-8. Little Mammoth Media.

*** Big Aquarium, The (Big Adventure Series)

Visit the largest freshwater aquarium in the world in Chattanooga, TN. Shows hundreds of fish and animals from various habitats, divers feeding fish, and looks behind-the-scenes at the control center, the veterinarian, and the research lab. *Adult Juror Comments*: Wonderful footage of a wide variety of aquatic plants, animals, and fish. Eye-catching and informative. This would be a great tool for ocean studies. Fosters an appreciation for aquatic life as well as interest in unique species. *Kid Juror Comments*: Colorful, scientific, cool. Great animals. "I loved the colors of the fish." Showed people working with the animals. "I'd like to work there." Video. 48 min.; $14.95; Age: 5-8. Little Mammoth Media.

* Big Boats Li'l Boats (Adventures with My Uncle Bill)

Josh, his friends, and Uncle Bill explore all kinds of boats and ships. Introduces the captain, shows the engine room, and visits the wheel house. *Adult Juror Comments*: Interesting and varied boat footage. Informative, well-paced, and well-produced, though they go a little overboard with the talking in unison. *Kid Juror Comments*: It's a little long for this age group. Kids didn't understand the connection to Uncle Bill. His character was unnecessary and detracted slightly from the general message. Video. 29 min.; $14.95; Age: 3-8. Paragon Media.

*** Big Park, The (Big Adventure Series)

Explores Yellowstone National Park, its wildlife, and the people who preserve it. Explains how animals are monitored and how the wolf program safeguards an endangered species. Shows firefighters and rescue helicopters and discusses geothermal systems. *Adult Juror Comments*: Educational but needs supplementary explanation. Teaches a lot about parks. Explanations are educationally sound and authentically depicted. Beautiful scenery. Pace is a little slow. *Kid Juror Comments*: Mixed reaction. Kids said they wouldn't want to sit at home and watch it, but they would in school. The narrator spoke too fast and was difficult to understand. It made them want to visit a park. They loved the images of the bubbling water. Video. 48 min.; $14.95; Age: 6-11. Little Mammoth Media.

** Big Plane Trip, The (Real Life Adventures)

Offers a behind-the-scenes look at the operations of an international flight from a child's point of view, with a child narrator, lively music, and graphics. *Adult Juror Comments*: Informative. Shows all the jobs on airlines. Child narrator asking questions works well in the format. Lots of technical information and detail. A little long for audience to watch all in one sitting. *Kid Juror Comments*: The narration helped the children understand the presentation. Younger children lost interest when the information became too technical. They enjoyed the scenes in Switzerland. Video. 45 min.; $14.95; Age: 5-10. Little Mammoth Media.

** Big Renovation, The (Big Adventure Series)

Shows a home renovation from the ground up, including demolition, framing, plumbing, electrical wiring, and heating, ventilating, and air conditioning. Visits the architect, builder, an entomologist, a tile factory, and a sawmill. *Adult Juror Comments*: While the explanations are good, it moves too slowly. Content is straightforward, easily understood, presented in a safe and wholesome setting. Young people learn about safety and following proper procedures around construction sites. *Kid Juror Comments*: "I learned how it takes a lot of people and materials to build a house." Too long, but they liked seeing the finished house and the steps it took to get there. Uses technical terms beyond kids' comprehension. Video. 48 min.; $14.95; Age: 6-10. Little Mammoth Media.

Age 5-8

Video

Spec Int

*** Big Space Shuttle, The (Big Adventure Series)

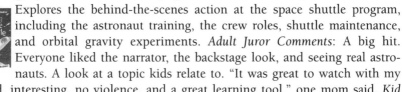

Explores the behind-the-scenes action at the space shuttle program, including the astronaut training, the crew roles, shuttle maintenance, and orbital gravity experiments. *Adult Juror Comments*: A big hit. Everyone liked the narrator, the backstage look, and seeing real astronauts. A look at a topic kids relate to. "It was great to watch with my child, interesting, no violence, and a great learning tool," one mom said. *Kid Juror Comments*: Captured kids' interest and motivated further inquiry into the subject. Kids liked it because it was real. They particularly enjoyed the launch. "Everything in it is great." "I liked seeing the girl scientists." Video. 50 min.; $14.95; Age: 6-10. Little Mammoth Media.

** Big Zoo, The (Real Life Adventures)

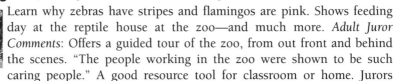

Learn why zebras have stripes and flamingos are pink. Shows feeding day at the reptile house at the zoo—and much more. *Adult Juror Comments*: Offers a guided tour of the zoo, from out front and behind the scenes. "The people working in the zoo were shown to be such caring people." A good resource tool for classroom or home. Jurors objected to all the commercials at the start. *Kid Juror Comments*: Impressed by seeing what the different animals eat and how the zookeepers take care of everything. They wanted to go to the zoo afterwards. "I like the real pictures; they made me want to go to the zoo." Video. 45 min.; $14.95; Age: 5-8. Little Mammoth Media.

* Built for Speed

Follows a stock car driver and her two young friends in an action-packed day at the stock car races. Explains how a race car differs from a regular car. *Adult Juror Comments*: Those interested in stock cars may find this appealing. It's simply produced and has poor sound quality. Includes female drivers, but it makes light of car crashes despite discussion of safety. *Kid Juror Comments*: The racing segments were exciting, and why not? "Girls can drive fast and get paid for it?" asked one child. Video. 30 min.; $14.95; Age: 5-10. White Tree Pictures, Inc./Venture Enter Group.

* Come Fly with Us

This sing-along musical has on-camera kids that fly on barnstormers and seaplanes and with the famous Blue Angels demonstration daredevil team. Tours a flight museum and visits a Boeing 747 cockpit. *Adult Juror Comments*: Good music and scenery, but the material is redundant and the production quality is mediocre. Lacks cultural diversity. *Kid Juror Comments*: General enthusiasm, although a few left during the screening. Those interested in planes were engaged. Video. 30 min.; $14.95; Age: 5-8. Paragon Media.

** *Everything You Ever Wanted to Know about Planes, But Didn't Know Who to Ask*

Many interesting facts about planes, from landing gear to flaps, from de-icing to the speed of sound. Shows painted planes with designs from the Simpsons, Disney characters, creatures of the sea, and wild animals. *Adult Juror Comments*: Production is age-appropriate and interesting. Kids will enjoy learning about the variety of planes and how they fly. *Kid Juror Comments*: Appealed most to kids who are fascinated about planes or travel. Others could take it or leave it. Boys enjoyed this more than girls. Video. 20 min.; $9.95; Age: 4-8. Just Planes Videos.

** *Fireman Jim's Amazing Rescue Rigs*

Entertaining, educational video about fire trucks and other rescue vehicles. Includes six safety messages including 911; fire prevention; stop, drop, roll; fire drills at home; etc. Firefighters and kids teach lessons. *Adult Juror Comments*: A nice blend of action and instruction. Lots of lights, sirens, and smoke. Jim is a friendly and informative role model. Overall, gives viewer a sense of confidence. Useful in the home, classroom, and community. *Kid Juror Comments*: Kids love watching the rescue vehicles "on the move," the sights and sounds captivated them. Children relate to the straight facts. They like Fireman Jim and the kids' commentaries. "I want to know more about fires, so I can be safe." Video. 30 min.; $14.95; Age: 5-8. Multimedia Group, The.

** *Good Enough to Eat (Because Natural Is Fun)*

So you want to make organic chicken soup? Visit the warehouse, kitchen, the produce aisle, the butcher, and meet people working at the market. *Adult Juror Comments*: Good presentation of interesting information and concepts about the food industry. Production quality is mediocre, making it difficult to watch. *Kid Juror Comments*: After viewing this, when children went to the grocery store, they spoke about the behind-the-scenes activities. Video. 30 min.; $12.95; Age: 4-8. Karol Media, Inc.

** *How a Car Is Built, with IQ Parrot*

Follows the nine-mile Ford Mustang assembly line and observes how workers and high-tech machines transform giant rolls of steel into gleaming new cars. *Adult Juror Comments*: Simply produced but clear. Presentation is long and sometimes technical. Comparing a mustang horse with the Mustang car was well-done. Safety demonstrations were convincing. "I learned a lot and enjoyed the old assembly-line footage." *Kid Juror Comments*: Kids liked the idea of comparing an assembly line to a river. Commented on how the people work together and on the many people needed to build a car. "It takes a long time to build a car, and teamwork to get the job done." Video. 30 min.; $14.95; Age: 5-12. Think Media.

Age 5-8

Video

Spec Int

** How a Tugboat Works, with IQ Parrot

Kids board a tugboat and watch it dock the Queen Elizabeth II, using hand signals, whistles, and ropes. Includes rare footage of early tugboats. Demonstrates teamwork and the success of tiny tugs pulling off Herculean tasks. *Adult Juror Comments*: Well-presented with interesting camera angles and editing. Contains lots of little-known information in great detail. Most suitable for special-interest groups. Encouraged searching out more information in books. *Kid Juror Comments*: Repeat viewing strongly supported. Boys and girls liked it equally and wanted to go for a ride on a tugboat. "I liked seeing a boat that's longer than three football fields." It's too long for younger kids. Video. 28 min.; $14.95; Age: 5-8. Think Media.

* How It's Done - Episode #1 - From Roller Coasters to Ice Cream (How It's Done)

Discover fascinating facts about how everyday things in factories and farms. Detective Howie Dunn undertakes a behind-the-scenes investigation to solve the mystery of "how it's done." *Adult Juror Comments*: Presents good information in an interesting way. A useful educational tool, although too fast-paced and lacking in serious detail. Jurors did not care for the puppet character. *Kid Juror Comments*: Sought more information about the subjects that the program just begins to cover. Brought up more questions than answers. "I liked the part about baseballs best." Video. 32 min.; $9.99; Age: 5-10. Anchor Bay Entertainment.

* How It's Done - Episode #2 - From Baseball Bats to Potato Chips (How It's Done)

Investigates "The mystery of the missing oranges" and squeezes out some juicy facts. Visits a baseball bat factory for a look at how a piece of wood is turned into a real swinger. *Adult Juror Comments*: Begins to answer a lot of "why and how" questions. The live action sections are fine, but the puppetry is awkward. Adults thought the presentation was mediocre and slow. The packaging cover is somewhat misleading. *Kid Juror Comments*: Favorite segment: how the yo-yo works. They wanted to learn more. Howie Dunn's humor was just right for them. They learned some new things, and some wanted to take home the video and share with their parents. First graders enjoyed the puppet. Video. 34 min.; $9.99; Age: 5-10. Anchor Bay Entertainment.

Chapter Three • Elementary

*** I Dig Fossils

A family learning adventure uncovers 300-million-year-old fossils close to home. As nine-year-old Scott and his dad embark on a real-life adventure, Scott explains how fossils are formed as they hunt for treasures. *Adult Juror Comments*: Fascinating topic with excellent material. Informal science education, as well as good father and son role models. Safety and legal issues are well addressed. Scott is energetic, involved, and believable. Provokes an interest in history. *Kid Juror Comments*: Appealing child narrator. Made them curious about hunting for fossils. Some were disappointed when they didn't immediately find any in their back yard. Video. 24 min.; $14.95; Age: 5-12. Mazon Productions Inc.

*** Janey Junkfood's Fresh Adventure!

This Emmy award-winning video features rap music, juggling, and splashy graphics. Guides kids through the confusing food marketplace and gets them off the junk food track. *Adult Juror Comments*: Informative, thoughtful, and entertaining. The children were realistic and the adults funny. Quality nutrition information is offered. Well-produced, though the audio falters throughout. Using original ideas for delivering complex concepts. *Kid Juror Comments*: Enjoyed the rap music, the on-camera kids, and the comedic parts. They understood the information presented about healthy eating and talked about it afterwards. Video. 28 min.; $24.95; Age: 5-12. Foodplay Productions.

** Jazz (Miss Christy's Dancin)

Incorporating ballet, tap, and modern dance, Christy introduces children to the basics of jazz dancing. *Adult Juror Comments*: Has good descriptions and good warm-up exercises. Teaches dance vocabulary in a simple way. Uses contemporary music and encourages group performances. Recommended by dance professionals as an adjunct to regular classes. *Kid Juror Comments*: Girls responded best. A favorite for those with an existing interest in dance. The kids liked watching the students dancing in the ending. Video. 30 min.; $12.98; Age: 6-12. PPI/Peter Pan, Inc.

** Kid to Kid: Staying Safe!

Features Dr. Loretta Long of Sesame Street exploring strategies for staying safe, at home, at play, on the street, and on the Internet. *Adult Juror Comments*: Good production. Touches on a lot of topics briefly. Encourages assertiveness and problem-solving. Demonstrates how knowledge is applied. Shows good diversity. Kidnapping scene is frightening. *Kid Juror Comments*: Focused and intent. "It shows us how to stay safe." "Sometimes the narrator spoke too fast." Kids related to the characters. "They were kids just like us." "I feel safer walking to school now." "It taught me to be smart." Video. 25 min.; $16.99; Age: 6-10. Daniel Productions.

** *Kids Love Trains (Kids Love)*

 Travel on steam trains, freight trains, big and small trains, fast and slow trains, an orange train, a snowplow train, and even a Santa train. A look at what it takes to make the trains run on time. Includes songs by Red Wagon Music. *Adult Juror Comments*: Well-produced with catchy songs and good visuals that reinforce the information. The child narrators enhanced the production, though some of the dialogue was too fast. *Kid Juror Comments*: Liked the songs, some of which were familiar. Kids with a passion for trains got their fill. It inspired the kids to play with trains afterwards. Video. 30 min.; $14.95; Age: 3-8. Acorn Media Publishing Inc.

*** *Kids' Kitchen: Making Good Eating Great Fun!*

 A child's cookbook comes to life as a juggling nutrition magician and her kitchen crew of multi-ethnic schoolchildren create kids' favorite nutritious and delicious snacks without cooking. Includes an animated depiction of the food pyramid. *Adult Juror Comments*: Offers creative, original ideas for presenting complex nutrition information to children. Important information that can be pretty boring is well-presented. It's well-paced for discussion during and after. Can easily be broken into segments. *Kid Juror Comments*: Enjoyed watching the kids on-screen make snacks they could relate to. It's sort of corny, but they still wanted to watch it again. Video. 45 min.; $34.95; Age: 5-10. Foodplay Productions.

** *Let's Get a Move On*

 Millions of families move each year. Teaches how to survive the impact of changing places, saying goodbye, and adjusting to new people, new situations, and new spaces. *Adult Juror Comments*: Great video for kids who are anxious about moving. Kids in video are realistic and talk about the concerns of most kids: Will I make new friends? Will I like my new house? Will I learn my way around the new town? Great diversity. *Kid Juror Comments*: Kids learned that moving is not a scary event. "I liked how it told you it might be different in your new home, but you can make new friends and it might take a while." " I don't want to move." "What happens if you don't like the new place?" Video. 30 min.; $14.95; Age: 4-10. Kidvidz.

* Lots and Lots of Trains, Volume I (Lots and Lots of Trains)

 Shows a great variety of live-action trains—big trains, little trains, steam, diesel, freight, and passenger trains—new trains, fast trains, slow trains, city, country and mountain trains, toy trains, even trains that blow through snow. *Adult Juror Comments*: Not particularly stimulating. Great shots of trains, but a little too long and repetitive. Appeals to avid train fans. No insights into types of trains or railroad history. Trains from different countries are not identified. Appropriate music. *Kid Juror Comments*: Wanted more information about trains. It was a little boring. "I didn't like it because it didn't tell me enough about the trains." "I wanted to know where the trains were going." Video. 30 min.; $14.95; Age: 5-10. Superior Promotions/Home Video, Inc.

* Max and Felix

Max applies his talents as a skateboard daredevil, master carpenter, spellbinding storyteller, and champion fisherman. Felix photographs the disastrous and hilarious results. *Adult Juror Comments*: Theme of friendship is well-represented throughout the story. Price is considered too high for a program only eleven minutes long. Designed to suit a narrow age bracket. *Kid Juror Comments*: "It's funny and easy to figure out." "I really like the story about the porch." "It's interesting and silly too." Video. 11 min.; $29.95; Age: 3-8. Aims Multimedia.

* Nathalie's First Flight (Just Planes for Kids)

 Before the plane takes off, Nathalie tours a maintenance facility where planes are repaired. During the flight, she explores the cabin, cockpit, and galley. Includes tips on preparing for a plane trip. *Adult Juror Comments*: Provides a good introduction to planes and flying with spectacular views. Leisurely paced. Vocabulary is too technical and beyond the understanding of the audience. The on-camera talent lacks zest. *Kid Juror Comments*: Those who like airplanes enjoyed this most; some others lost interest. It's a great introduction for a child who's never flown before. Video. 32 min.; $14.95; Age: 4-8. Just Planes Videos.

* New Soccer for Fun and Skills (New Games Video)

 These games encourage players to improve and develop soccer skills and team building. *Adult Juror Comments*: Offers some excellent game strategies, although advanced and experienced soccer players will find it too basic. Offers suggestions for safe, non-competitive, cooperative play. *Kid Juror Comments*: Kids thought it had good ideas for beginning players, but experienced soccer players thought it talked down to them. Video. 24 min.; $29.95; Age: 6-12. New Games.

** Open Your Heart America
(Learn to Sing and Sign with Gaia)

Gaia introduces American Sign Language with an inspiring song for children that also features a homeless woman. Encourages activism and a renewed spirit in America. Part two teaches how to sign the song. *Adult Juror Comments*: This is a little corny but appealing. At times it talks down to kids. The songs are well-selected and not overbearing in delivering an uplifting message. Length is right for this audience. *Kid Juror Comments*: Enjoyed learning sign language, and most kids wanted to see it again right after the first screening. Most imitated signing and remembered a few signs. "It's different and may help someone." Video. 20 min.; $12.95; Age: 6-12. Heartsong Communications.

*** Scholastic's Magic School Bus for Lunch, The
(Scholastic's Magic School Bus)

Arnold doesn't have to go on a field trip. He accidentally swallows his miniaturized classmates and becomes the field trip! Better than an amusement park, Arnold's digestive system is full of surprises. *Adult Juror Comments*: Provides an outstanding tool for teaching complicated concepts in science. Factual but fun, clever, lively, and entertaining. Children gain an understanding of the digestive system in an imaginative manner. *Kid Juror Comments*: Girls and boys alike of varying ages enjoyed this. Kept their attention throughout and encouraged questions during and afterwards. Video. 27 min.; $12.95; Age: 4-12. Scholastic Entertainment.

*** Scholastic's Magic School Bus Gets Lost in Space, The
(Scholastic's Magic School Bus)

Janet drives the whole class crazy when she joins Ms. Frizzle's class on a field trip and gets them lost in outer space. When the navigational system breaks down, Janet is the only one with the knowledge to save them. *Adult Juror Comments*: A wonderful adaptation of the book. Well-produced. Most kids are fascinated with the Magic School Bus book series. *Kid Juror Comments*: Laughter and smiles throughout. Asked to watch it again. Kept their attention, and they felt they learned something about space. Video. 30 min.; $12.95; Age: 5-12. Warner Home Video.

** Sheep Crossing

Using equal fact and fun, program explores the world of sheep and wool. Features real people, especially children who work with sheep, enhanced with graphics and music. *Adult Juror Comments*: Has a limited audience, but would be very good for research or if a child had a special interest in sheep. Focus on wool became a bit boring. Music is distracting. Initially, it is not clear who is being referred to—a person or a sheep. *Kid Juror Comments*: The level of interest was surprising. "My friends and I would like to see more about sheep." Seeing the sheep being sheared upset them until they learned it doesn't hurt. They enjoyed the new baby sheep. "I'm going to work on a sheep farm when I grow up." Video. 27 min.; $14.95; Age: 5-8. Great White Dog Picture Co.

*** Sign and ABC's (Sign Language for Kids)

Focus on the alphabet, the most important tool developed by humans. Teaches the written, spoken, and American Sign Language (ASL) alphabets, introduces spelling and teaching the signs for eighty-eight words. *Adult Juror Comments*: Nice pacing allows for review, but still challenging. Very well executed. Wonderful exposure to sign language. This can be used in the classroom or at home. "It demonstrated that everyone can learn to sign." *Kid Juror Comments*: "It was funny." "It taught me a lot of signs. I would like to learn more." Kids tried to converse in sign after the video. The skits and the gestures intrigued them. Video. 50 min.; $14.98; Age: 5-10. Aylmer Press.

** Sign Songs (Sign Language for Kids)

Learning sign language offers benefits for hearing kids even if they never use it. Improves reading and motor skills and appreciation of different cultures. Hosted by Ken Lonnquist, from the National Theater of the Deaf. *Adult Juror Comments*: This is a good idea, but the signing is too fast for young children to track. Some songs are simply wonderful and can be used to build enthusiasm for learning to sign. Animation lacks appeal. It's probably best used in segments. *Kid Juror Comments*: The music and the signing were interesting. Younger ones lost attention quickly. "This is a grown-up movie." Video. 29 min.; $19.98; Age: 3-10. Aylmer Press.

** Sign-Me-a-Story

Linda Bove, from Sesame Street, introduces children to American sign language, teaching simple signs and acting out familiar tales. *Adult Juror Comments*: Well-conceived production. Provides an introduction to sign language, with a short lesson before each story. Well-sequenced. Linda Bove is excellent. Offers opportunity for discussion on being hearing-impaired. Slow-paced. *Kid Juror Comments*: Liked the music and wanted to watch it again. Many recognized Linda Bove from Sesame Street. They are inherently interested in learning sign language and wanted to try it afterwards. Video. 30 min.; $14.98; Age: 3-8. Sony Wonder.

*** Sing, Dance 'n Sign (Gaia)

Get your feet and fingers in motion and join Gaia and the Kidsign Club kids for a musical adventure with sign language. Gaia spins her magical ribbons into Handlandia, a world where everyone can sign—even trees and animals. *Adult Juror Comments*: Outstanding. Bright costumes and sets. Music stimulated dancing and singing. Generates understanding and tolerance of others. Positive and fun. Great way to introduce sign-language. Includes a study guide. *Kid Juror Comments*: Kids were enthusiastic and motivated even though they thought it was too fast. "I wanted it to slow down so I could practice." "I loved all the magic ribbons and the songs." "I want to learn the ABC's in sign language." "The elf made dancing fun." Video. 51 min.; $14.95; Age: 4-12. Heartsong Communications.

** Tap (Miss Christy's Dancin)

Introduces children to tap-dancing, an American-originated form of dance noted for developing coordination, balance, rhythm, and speed. *Adult Juror Comments*: Music and pace are appropriate for kids. Has good warm-up exercises and a good introduction to basic tap steps. Instruction is clear, but dance professionals suggested using the video as a supplement to regular instruction, not instead of. *Kid Juror Comments*: Discovered that it was far more difficult to learn the steps than they thought. Those familiar with tap said it lacked depth of instruction. Yet, "It's more fun than ballet." Video. 30 min.; $12.98; Age: 6-12. PPI/Peter Pan, Inc.

* There Goes a Boat (Real Wheels)

What child isn't thrilled to see jet planes landing on an aircraft carrier? Join a visit to a variety of ships, from passenger ships to submarines. *Adult Juror Comments*: Good information with an emphasis on safety. Subject is appealing to kids, but this is too technical. Presenting military ships and missiles as toys was disturbing. *Kid Juror Comments*: Okay, particularly the boys. Video. 35 min.; $9.95; Age: 5-8. Warner Home Video.

** *There Goes a Bulldozer (Real Wheels)*

Construction foreman explains machines associated with heavy construction—from jackhammers to bulldozers with close-ups of sights and sounds surrounding a construction crew at work. *Adult Juror Comments*: Good information with good demonstrations. Good opportunity to examine different careers in construction. Shows little diversity. *Kid Juror Comments*: The slapstick humor really went over. They related the information in the video to their own experiences. Some wanted to see it again. Boys enjoyed it more than girls did. Video. 35 min.; $9.95; Age: 3-8. Warner Home Video.

** *There Goes a Fire Truck (Real Wheels)*

Features fire equipment operated by professionals. Fireman Dave shows kids what it's like to be a firefighter and demonstrates how the equipment works. *Adult Juror Comments*: Colorful visually, but there's a great deal of information to absorb all at once. May stimulate further inquiry. Shows little ethnic cultural diversity and hardly any women are practicing firefighters. *Kid Juror Comments*: Stimulated play imitating fire trucks. They were fascinated by the yellow fire trucks at the airport and wanted to go to a fire station after viewing this. Video. 35 min.; $9.95; Age: 3-8. Warner Home Video.

* *There Goes a Police Car (Real Wheels)*

Behind-the-scenes look at police officers and their equipment from horses to motorcycles, helicopters to special radios. *Adult Juror Comments*: Contains good information. Most felt the slapstick approach to the encouragement of respect for police officers was inappropriate. Officer's gear was captivating, but using "bad guys" was inappropriate. Lacks cultural and gender diversity. *Kid Juror Comments*: The live-action section scored high. They wanted to watch it again. One boy noticed the use of the word "policemen" and said, "I told you girls can't be police." Video. 35 min.; $9.95; Age: 5-8. Warner Home Video.

* *There Goes a Race Car (Real Wheels)*

Shows race cars and the people behind them, from behind-the-scenes pre-race preparation to crossing the finish line. Examines unusual types of racing. *Adult Juror Comments*: Fast-paced and interesting. The accident scenes tend to glamorize danger. Points out the importance of safety. Toyota endorsement is prominent. Some parts are too technical for this audience. Hosts are pretty silly. *Kid Juror Comments*: "My eight-year-old son loved it." (As did most of the boys.) It's most suitable for a special-interest audience. Video. 35 min.; $9.95; Age: 5-8. Warner Home Video.

* There Goes a Spaceship (Real Wheels)

Visits the Kennedy Space Center and Space Camp and explores the challenges of living in space. Looks at what it takes to be a NASA astronaut. *Adult Juror Comments*: Good introduction to the study of space and space travel. However, the promotional advertising is objectionable. *Kid Juror Comments*: Kept their attention. Most suitable for kids interested in the subject. Video. 35 min.; $9.95; Age: 5-8. Warner Home Video.

** There Goes a Train (Real Wheels)

Offers a close-up look at the world of trains, from steam engines to locomotives. Explores the many functions of today's trains, including the caboose. *Adult Juror Comments*: Well-produced. Use of real people is a plus. Filled with information, though it starts out slowly. Good safety messages. *Kid Juror Comments*: Enjoyable, though a little long. Video. 35 min.; $9.95; Age: 5-8. Warner Home Video.

** There Goes a Truck (Real Wheels)

Take a ride through the exciting world of trucks. Safe inside the cab, kids feel the exhilaration of operating everything from sanitation trucks to the super truck that transports the NASA space shuttle. *Adult Juror Comments*: Tends to be rather silly, a little too long, and too technical. Featuring both female and male drivers brought kudos from jurors. The recycling message is good. Shows some unsafe behavior. *Kid Juror Comments*: Kids definitely enjoyed this more than the adults. They liked the realistic sounds and the silly humor. "Be careful around a truck!" Real footage and sounds are a plus. Video. 35 min.; $9.95; Age: 5-8. Warner Home Video.

* There Goes an Airplane (Real Wheels)

Shows how airplanes are used for many different purposes, from passenger planes to "the fastest planes of all"—fighter jets. Visits the deck of an aircraft carrier and watches jet fighters takeoff and land at high speed. *Adult Juror Comments*: Appealing for those interested in planes. Shows little gender or ethnic diversity. Fast-paced action is just right for young children. Shows a good variety of planes. *Kid Juror Comments*: "Boys were glued to the screen." The humor went over some children's heads. Descriptions were too difficult for this age range and delivered too fast. Video. 35 min.; $9.95; Age: 5-8. Warner Home Video.

* When I Grow Up I Wanta Be...an Astronaut
(When I Grow Up I Wanta Be...)

 Twelve children train for and conduct a space shuttle mission with astronaut Bob Springer as their mentor at U.S. Space Camp. Gives an overview of the history of space exploration. *Adult Juror Comments*: Well-produced, it answers a lot of questions. Shows good cultural mix and girls play important roles. It is best suited for kids who have an interest in this subject. Tends to be too long. *Kid Juror Comments*: "This is good for people who want to be astronauts." "I like that girls get training." Some kids thought it was too long. "It shows kids of all colors." A good starting point for talking about careers in space. Video. 45 min.; $19.95; Age: 5-10. Five Points South Productions.

** When I Grow Up I Wanta Be...Vol. 1
(When I Grow Up I Wanta Be...)

 Seven children perform in real-life settings as a jockey, zoo veterinarian, fire and rescue worker, auto racer, and jet fighter pilot. Special appearance is made by the Blue Angels. *Adult Juror Comments*: Appealing and educational. Stimulated kids thinking about their particular talents, interests, and career aspirations. Shows little diversity. *Kid Juror Comments*: Kids liked this. "I enjoyed it because it shows that you can be anything you would like to be." "It made me think about what I want to do." "I am too little to think about it right now!" Kids talked about what they wanted to be when they grew up. Video. 44 min.; $19.95; Age: 5-10. Five Points South Productions.

** Whistlepunks & Sliverpickers (I Can Do It! Video Field Trips)

 Puts girls and boys in the driver's seat while they explore forests by planting trees, operating enormous machines, driving big trucks, milling lumber, and building a house. Shows skilled women and men working together. *Adult Juror Comments*: Provides good information on forestry and logging. Creatively presented with interesting photography. Unfortunately, the packaging appeal is somewhat misleading. Useful for classroom study about trees or home. *Kid Juror Comments*: One class had just completed studying machines and related to the subject particularly well. Shows good gender role models. Video. 30 min.; $18.95; Age: 3-9. I Can Do It! Productions.

Age 5-8

Video

Spec Int

** *You Can Fly a Kite (You Can Video Series for Children)*

 Demonstrates teamwork while playing in the magical world of kites. Teaches how to build and fly a kite, kite history, and introduces young champion kit flyers. *Adult Juror Comments*: Kids on-screen are very natural. It's well-paced. Photography of kite flying competition is compelling. Not much cultural diversity. *Kid Juror Comments*: "Cool. I especially liked the team flying." Wanted to build a kite immediately. A little long for younger kids. Video. 30 min.; $12.95; Age: 5-8. Blackboard Entertainment.

Age 5-8

Video

Spec Int

Chapter Four

Middle School (Ages 8-12)

By Irene Wood

High-quality videos are seldom available for children between the ages of eight and twelve. When the first blush of innocence and credulity begin to fade, and before the world-weary sophistication of adolescence has yet to bloom, a black hole appears on the television screen. It is the absence of videos and CD-ROMs designed to capture the interest of this age group.

The plethora of productions for younger children—visits to farm animals, learning about the world beyond their own home—has been disdainfully dismissed as "too babyish." This age group is often captivated by a weekly television series or, in a rush to grow up, lured to the pounding immediacy of MTV. At the same time, children's intellects are being challenged (we hope) by the demands of schoolwork. Kids at this age are also becoming more interested in the adult world and the emotional experiences they're exposed to as they grapple for a better understanding of life. They are forming close friendships (gaggles of giggling girls) and gaining more independence (gangs of after-school sports enthusiasts), especially in a society of more and more working and single-parent households in which children are increasingly left on their own. That is why this book is a perfect opportunity to introduce some high-quality viewing that can meet both educational and personal needs.

The best videos and CD-ROMs are characterized by accurate and well-developed content, up-to-date authenticity, well-written scripts, and sharp production values. Moreover, children's media must convey to its audience a respect for their intelligence and imagination. Since children like to watch others their age, or older, in familiar or unusual situations, they appreciate captivating dramas, problems that are solved through perseverance and consideration for others, and portrayals of times, places, and events from which they can learn about a larger world outside their own environment.

Titles such as *Bully Smart* and *Stranger Smart* give older children valuable, concrete guidance for dealing with common social issues they may encounter. These programs also give parents and kids a chance to talk about people or incidents that might trouble children in their daily lives. Students looking for better ways to survive in school will appreciate tips in programs such as *Amazing Insect Warriors* or *Why is the Sky Blue*. Personal interests are addressed by *The Blue Angels: In Pursuit of Excellence* and *Nancy Drew: Stay Tuned for Danger* among others. The middle years often include music lessons and, that bane of kids' existence, practicing. The *Meet the Musicians* series brings perspective to the perplexities of learning an instrument and engages the student's interest in the larger context of music appreciation. *Beethoven Lives Upstairs* CD-ROM offers a wonderful introduction to Beethoven and an imaginary hero. The babysitting instructional tape and the *Babysitters Club* series are perfectly suited to girls between the ages eight to twelve. The first title prepares them to handle their first paying job as well as increasing their sense of accomplishment, while the others are appealing entertainment that explore friendships and problem-solving in the familiar milieu of girlfriends.

Family-oriented feature films, whether the tried-and-true *Please Don't Eat the Daisies* or the more recent *Keeping the Promise* let children experience human relationships in unfamiliar and unusual family situations. *Cyrano* and *Black Beauty* acquaint children with sensitivity to some stalwart works of literature in fine productions. *Bizet's Dream* is a multidimensional work which introduces the music of this 19th Century composer, the creative process, and a young girl's evolving relationships in a creative, spectacularly produced drama.

Just as the world of eight- to twelve-year-olds is expanding, so too are the opportunities to offer imaginative, eye-opening, mind-stretching media for these children. The following videos and CD-ROMs represent an excellent array of productions that touch on the interests and needs of "middle-age" children.

Irene Wood is the current manager of Brennemann Library at Children's Memorial Hospital in Chicago and the former editor of Media Reviews for Booklist, *a publication of the American Library Association. She holds a MLS from the University of Washington.*

Format—CD-ROM

Category—Education/Instruction

** Devils Canyon: A Dinamation Adventure (Time Blazer)

Cyberaptor, a mechanical creature that interfaces with a time-travel device, malfunctions and strands its creator, Dr. Cope, in a pre-historic jungle. Your mission is to rescue Dr. Cope from the past after you take a training program. *Adult Juror Comments*: Interesting approach that is engaging, entertaining, and educational. Supplementary materials include membership card and website information. Requires patience on the part of the player. *Kid Juror Comments*: Challenging. Kids enjoyed it, particularly activities similar to "real-life" undertakings, such as the time and the patience needed to pick out a fossil. Some children were frustrated initially, but went back to play the game later. CD-ROM. WIN/MAC; $39.95; Age: 8-12. Paragon Media.

** Disney's Adventures in Typing with Timon & Pumbaa (Disney's Learning Series)

Kids build essential typing skills, including finger placement, speed, and letter recognition, while getting plenty of laughs from Timon and Pumbaa in this wild and wacky adventure. *Adult Juror Comments*: Wonderful and entertaining way to introduce keyboard and typing skills. "What better way than through this amusing yet educational method?" One parent asked to take it home so she could learn to type herself. *Kid Juror Comments*: Some kids liked the characters, but not the typing. If they stick with it, they can learn a lot. "It taught me where to put my fingers." "It's dumb; it says 'let's work on posture.'" Kids loved getting the certificates. Some thought it was boring. CD-ROM. WIN/MAC; $29.99; Age: 8-12. Disney Interactive.

*** Easy Book Deluxe

Draws children into the world of creative storytelling by printing out double-sided books in four sizes—from mini to poster size. Includes spell-checker, thesaurus, text-to-speech, and sound. *Adult Juror Comments*: Installs easily. Straightforward and simple to operate, fun and creative. The child determines content. Motivated kid jurors to write a book and gain design experience. Best for kids comfortable with the computer. *Kid Juror Comments*: Kids thought it was a lot of fun. Several kids made a book of their own using this. "This is awesome." Their favorite part was making a finished book. Some parts were hard to access. Kids liked the science fiction, fairytale, and comic book formats. CD-ROM. WIN; $14.95; Age: 8-12. Sunburst Technology/Houghton Mifflin.

** *Geometry World*

 Interactively explores geometric principles. Creates tessellating patterns, tangram designs, and symmetric figures. Uses a Geoboard and geometric programming tool to create and explore plane figures. Two great adventures. *Adult Juror Comments*: Easy to install, difficult to operate, interesting variety. Good visual quality. Excellent tool for use in conjunction with classroom instruction or for motivated kids, on their own. Stimulating and diverse. Good review for older kids. *Kid Juror Comments*: Kids needed help with difficult parts. Some areas were very difficult—formula for area of triangles, obtuse angles. Good visuals, graphics. Some parts were particularly fun: tangrams, drawing with symmetry. Kids liked the adventure. CD-ROM. WIN/MAC; $39.95; Age: 10-18. Cognitive Technologies Corp.

** *Grammar Rock (Schoolhouse Rock)*

Imagine...children mastering the building blocks of language through rock music. Kids rock out to the Emmy award winning rock video grammar lessons from ABC's Saturday morning lineup. Includes over twenty grammar activities at three skill levels. *Adult Juror Comments*: Very engaging and rewarding. Excellent learning tool. Involves children creatively. Great for home learning. The videos are a bit dated. Program had some glitches and locked up on slower computers. *Kid Juror Comments*: Scored high with kids. A "lifesaver." "It makes learning boring stuff fun." The music videos were the high point of the program. Kids liked printing out their own silly stories. Students familiar with the cartoons had an advantage. CD-ROM. WIN/MAC; $39.95; Age: 7-12. Learning Company.

** *Hot Dog Stand: The Works*

Players are challenged to successfully manage their own small business with this simulation program. Creates a stimulating learning environment that practices critical math, problem-solving, and communications skills. *Adult Juror Comments*: Offers a unique perspective on learning. Good graphics and support materials. Easy to install. Explores challenging and new business concepts such as backward planning and market values. Repetition of setting up business becomes boring over time. *Kid Juror Comments*: Funny animation. Kids liked seeing how well they could forecast sales. Boys seemed to be more interested in content than girls. They realized how much planning was involved and still enjoyed the game. Setting up each business is repetitious. CD-ROM. WIN/MAC; $14.95; Age: 10-16. Sunburst Technology/Houghton Mifflin.

Age 8-12 · CD-ROM · Edu/Instru

*** *I Spy Spooky Mansion*, See Page 167.

*** *Indian in the Cupboard, The*

Based on the book and the critically acclaimed movie. Explores the Iroquois culture, crafts, and adventures in a beautifully rendered woodlands environment. *Adult Juror Comments*: Treats the Native American culture with respect, although in a Hollywood fashion. Installation instructions were inadequate for some. *Kid Juror Comments*: Kids liked this. "My twelve-year-old, who normally does not play computer games, spent an entire evening enthralled with this game." CD-ROM. WIN; $22.95; Age: 8-12. Virgin Interactive.

*** *Jumpstart: Adventures 3rd Grade (Jumpstart)*

 An activity-filled curriculum-based program blending the core subjects for third grade, including language arts, math, science, history, music, and art. Offers an adventure in an educational game format. *Adult Juror Comments*: Enormously successful at integrating facts, skills, learning, and problem-solving. The story is absorbing, the robots are fun, and each puzzle gives a reward. Clear instructions, helpful hints. Adult assistance is helpful to get started. *Kid Juror Comments*: Kids enjoyed the variety of activities, the graphics, and the songs. They were engaged and challenged to build upon skills they have already. Might test a child's attention span. Their favorite parts were robot, different rooms, going back in time. CD-ROM. WIN/MAC; $40; Age: 7-10. Knowledge Adventure.

** *Jumpstart: Adventures 6th Grade (Jumpstart)*

 Launches media-savvy tweens into a brain-building mission with console-style games and over 4,000 curriculum challenges. Builds knowledge of language arts, math, ancient history, geography, and science. *Adult Juror Comments*: Easy to install. Content is really good, but actual play is poorly explained. Instructions not very clear. Sometimes skips or repeats words. Challenging. Far above the level of sixth grade. *Kid Juror Comments*: Good but difficult. Kids got frustrated. "The program was very hard." Kids found it difficult to move around, but thought it contained interesting information. Enjoyed the "Save the Rain Forest" section. CD-ROM. WIN/MAC; $20; Age: 10-14. Knowledge Adventure.

Age 8-12

CD-ROM

Edu/Instru

*** Jumpstart: Typing (Jumpstart)

Using an Olympic metaphor, this program helps kids build important keyboarding skills that prepare them for the computer-dominated world. Contains more than thirty "extreme keyboarding" techniques such as rock-climbing and snowboarding. *Adult Juror Comments*: Great format, age-appropriate. Different levels offer adaptability. It was surprising how much children learned during the evaluation session. It makes you want to type. Helps develop motor skills. Does not offer the opportunity to correct work. *Kid Juror Comments*: Overall, kids enjoyed it. They couldn't wait to play. "It's just plain fun, and I'm learning to type." "I like the snowboarding game." "I liked winning gold medals without help." Kids had technical problems with this. CD-ROM. WIN/MAC; $30; Age: 7-11. Knowledge Adventure.

* Lenny's Time Machine (Lenny's)

All about people and culture in challenging multilevel games, puzzles, creative activities, and facts. Players create scenes while learning about music, science, art, and leisure. *Adult Juror Comments*: Arcade-style game. The historical selections seem trite, offering only one screen of "facts" for each time period. Adults experienced some technical difficulties. Even the company's technical support agreed the instructions are poor. *Kid Juror Comments*: Some kids loved it. Others were intrigued at first, but didn't stay with it. Others found it challenging once they got the hang of it. Held the interest of kids well over eight-years-old. CD-ROM. WIN; $49.99; Age: 7-12. Virgin Interactive.

** Make a Map (Learning Ladder)

Creates maps that turn into 3-D cities that you can "get into your car and drive through." Teaches geography, map-making, and basic orienteering. Develops map reading, critical thinking, problem-solving, spatial relationships, and community awareness. *Adult Juror Comments*: Fun game that helps to develop a sense of direction and geography. Driving the car was difficult at first. Sarcasm is used throughout. It could be frustrating for younger children. *Kid Juror Comments*: Kids enjoyed making their own maps and driving. "I liked learning geography." The crashing aspect of the car was initially very frustrating, because it was hard to control. CD-ROM. WIN/MAC; $39.95; Age: 8-12. Panasonic Interactive Media.

*** Math Blaster: 4th Grade (Blaster Learning System)*

 Good story, superior graphics and sound, interesting characters, and a wide range of play at various levels of difficulty. Includes addition and subtraction, multiplication and division, fractions, decimals and complex numbers. *Adult Juror Comments*: Very user-friendly and appealing to kids. Excellent developmental program for audience. Develops cognitive and problem-solving skills. Well-organized. Program adapts to child's abilities. Offers good rewards. Too fast for first-time users. *Kid Juror Comments*: They loved the "mental math" section and the problem-solving. "Awesome." "This is a fun way to practice. Can we keep it?" "I had screams of delight and students jumping for joy when they got answers correct." "Great special effects." CD-ROM. WIN/MAC; $20; Age: 8-12. Knowledge Adventure.

*** Math for the Real World*

Kids try out their math skills in a "real" context. They join a band and travel on a ten-city road tour across the United States while solving practical math problems such as purchasing music equipment, food, and gas. *Adult Juror Comments*: An offbeat, challenging way to learn math. Teaches logic, fractions, time, money, charts, maps, volume, weight, measurement, patterns, and more. Wow! Easy to install and operate. *Kid Juror Comments*: Kids loved making music videos and getting chased by the press. The math games are challenging as well as age-appropriate. Also, kids worked together. Their other favorite parts were building roads and getting food. CD-ROM. WIN/MAC; $20; Age: 10-14. Knowledge Adventure.

** Phonics Game, The (The Phonics Game)*

A systematic teaching tool disguised as a game. Interactive technique teaches sounds and rules of phonics and spelling while students engage in competitive play. Learning is reinforced by CD-ROM games and audio tapes. *Adult Juror Comments*: Appropriate, accurate, and fun. Personalizing the phonics rules makes them easier to remember. Video was a little stilted. Little diversity. Can be used in classroom or home, but needs adult guidance. *Kid Juror Comments*: "I learned a lot." "It's easy to learn when you don't realize you're being taught." Children were delighted to be able to read words more easily after the first time. They commented on how "old" it looked. "They all liked being called 'Mega Stars.'" CD-ROM. WIN/MAC; 60 min.; $284.85; Age: 8-12. A Better Way of Learning, Inc.

** Pre-Algebra World

A highly interactive program to develop math skills. Master fractions in the stock market, a pizza parlor, and an art gallery. Learn estimation and rounding in a basketball court. Uncover prime numbers in an archaeological dig. *Adult Juror Comments*: The program consists of good drill and practice activities. Great for students in fifth and sixth grade before pre-algebra. Simple. Easy to install, but difficult to move around to different games. *Kid Juror Comments*: Well-produced program that some kids found easy and colorful. They liked practicing skills they learned in math. "It was fun to shoot basketball." "We liked the pizza parlor." "My mom would like me to have it." CD-ROM. WIN/MAC; $39.95; Age: 10-13. Cognitive Technologies Corp.

** Reading Blaster 4th Grade (Blaster Learning System)

Six villains vanish in Dr. Dabble's spooky mansion. Join a daring hunt while mastering reading comprehension. Contains 75 stories at three levels of difficulty. Includes parent tips by the director of the National Reading Diagnostics Institute. *Adult Juror Comments*: Fun, colorful, user-friendly, and age-appropriate program. Covers wide range of curriculum. Well-thought out for reading skills practice. No problems or glitches detected. Offers a fun way to learn. *Kid Juror Comments*: Makes learning fun for kids. "This software has great graphics." "I liked the castles, monsters, and mysteries." "I learned some new words." "This is a very creative program." CD-ROM. WIN/MAC; $20; Age: 8-12. Knowledge Adventure.

*** Reading Blaster 5th Grade (Blaster Learning System)

Challenging game within a mystery environment. A large selection of vocabulary words accompanied by talking word lists ensures a unique experience each time. Contains an easy-to-use editor. *Adult Juror Comments*: Builds and reinforces vocabulary in a challenging way. Good visuals, cute characters, positive feedback. A variety of increasing difficulty levels with easy operation. Requires active thinking. "This will get kids' brains working." *Kid Juror Comments*: Kids liked being the detective and solving the mystery. Most enjoyed the anagram game, which required thinking of new words before their opponent did. "Great list of words." "I like the funny characters. They made learning fun." CD-ROM. WIN/MAC; $20; Age: 9-12. Knowledge Adventure.

*** Sky Island Mysteries (Thinkin' Things)*

Teaches vital skills like giving priorities to different tasks, draws conclusions based on observation and logic. Communicates through a mix of words and pictures. Allows opportunities to solve fourteen mysteries on four different islands. *Adult Juror Comments*: Great games using problem-solving skills. Difficult at times but excellent. Beautiful graphics, challenging and fun, good quality. Offers educational problem-solving, using games. Somewhat slow-starting. Takes time to install, but it's easy. *Kid Juror Comments*: Kids found it challenging and difficult. They really liked the graphics and the opening music. They liked the "worm" character and enjoyed all the game levels, which challenged their different skills. The airplane game was a favorite. CD-ROM. WIN/MAC; $29.95; Age: 8-12. Edmark.

** Type to Learn*

 Program has taught over 15,000,000 people to master keyboarding and has undergone a major overhaul. Remains educationally sound with new games, voice prompts, graphics, and other features. *Adult Juror Comments*: Format makes a great tutorial, except the drill section is boring and the graphics are out-of-date. Best for beginners on the keyboard. Follows the child's progress and gives constant feedback. *Kid Juror Comments*: Instructions are easy to follow, but kids found this extremely boring. They enjoyed the sound effects. "Helped me learn typing skills." "Told me when I made a mistake and kept track of how I was doing." "I'm telling my friends about this program." CD-ROM. WIN; $24.95; Age: 8-14. Sunburst Technology/Houghton Mifflin.

** Year 2000 Grolier Multimedia Encyclopedia (Year 2000 Grolier Multimedia Encyclopedia)*

A fast, easy-to-use learning tool. It has 59 thousand articles, 15 thousand images, 12 hundred maps, and much more. *Adult Juror Comments*: An easy-to-install, easy to navigate program filled with lots of useful and interesting information. Jurors wondered why the browser paths were not established during the set up. Good audio and video. "Enjoyed the 'media' section." *Kid Juror Comments*: Appealing. Encourages critical thinking skills. "I got stuck, but I kept going through lists. I wanted to know more!" "The human body was awesome." "You have to spell correctly to find stuff." Kids didn't like switching disks. CD-ROM. WIN/MAC; $59.99; Age: 8-18. Grolier Interactive.

Age 8-12

CD-ROM

Edu/Instru

Category—Family

* Croc: Legend of the Gobbos

Invites the player to help Croc, the crocodile, rescue his peace-loving friends from the grasp of the evil magician, Baron Dante. Features five different 3-D worlds, including volcanoes, forests, ice glaciers, and underwater caves. *Adult Juror Comments*: Excellent graphics, nice activities, easy to use. Fairly straight forward and amusing, with a cute, animated character. Low levels of interactivity. Objects on screen were much the same. "This program offers plain old good fun." *Kid Juror Comments*: Kids liked the characters and the graphics. Easy for kids to install. Movement is sometimes hard to control. "Cool game if you like adventure and fantasy." "The Gobos are cute." "Croc can jump really far." CD-ROM. WIN; $49.98; Age: 8-12. Twentieth Century Fox Home Entertainment.

* Laura's Happy Adventure (Playmobil PC Game Series)

 Enter an enchanted world with Laura, who discovers a mysterious diamond and is swept away on adventures. Features over twenty hours of gameplay. *Adult Juror Comments*: Technically demanding, requires Pentium with 64 RAM. Uses keyboard commands instead of mouse— frustrating for user accustomed to mouse. Slow loading. Pace and challenge doesn't match what kids are up to. Not very imaginative. *Kid Juror Comments*: Kids were impressed with the graphics, but it moved slowly and their interest dropped. Suitable for younger kids, but they should anticipate technical problems. Kids wanted more challenges. "They need to make the stories more interesting." CD-ROM. WIN; $24.99; Age: 8-12. Ubi Soft Entertainment.

*** Nancy Drew: Secrets Can Kill (Nancy Drew)

An interactive mystery game that challenges girls to solve a murder as they become the famous teenage girl detective, Nancy Drew. Players must find hidden clues, solve brain-teasing puzzles, collect inventory items, and interrogate suspects. *Adult Juror Comments*: Installation difficult. Impressive production with hidden puzzles that make it very challenging. Great content, wonderful music, excellent graphics. Highly rated. Presents a problem, gives tools to solve it, stimulates curiosity and creativity. *Kid Juror Comments*: Cool. Kids had fun, and it was easy to use. "All of our friends are asking us about this and want to play." Girls love company motto, 'For girls who aren't afraid of a mouse.'" "I have a waiting list of intermediate-age girls who want to play." CD-ROM. WIN; $34.95; Age: 8-14. Her Interactive.

** Nancy Drew: Stay Tuned for Danger (Nancy Drew)

Interactive game that challenges players to solve a mystery by role-playing the famous teenage detective, Nancy Drew. Players must find hidden clues, solve brain-teasing puzzles, collect inventory items, and then interrogate the suspects. *Adult Juror Comments*: Well-produced, excellent graphics. Lacks installation instructions. Good plot and fun use of the computer-generated characters. Encourages critical thinking skills to solve the mystery. Death theme bothered some. *Kid Juror Comments*: Kids liked it, and thought their friends would too. "My favorite part was working with my friends to remember all the clues we found." "It was fun being a detective." "I didn't like the death threats." "We learned how to solve mysteries." CD-ROM. WIN; $29.99; Age: 8-12. Her Interactive.

** Tale of Orpheo's Curse, The (Are You Afraid of the Dark?)

Encourages kids to use their wits to explore Orpheo's haunted theater and unravel the mystery ghost tale. Distinguished by its sophisticated storytelling design, it features a variety of rich graphic styles and the cast of the TV show. *Adult Juror Comments*: Multiple layers of engagement. A little scary, but intriguing. Allows children to explore on their own and finish the story. "Essentially a non-violent video game." High quality graphics. *Kid Juror Comments*: Interesting, interactive, and fun. Younger kids needed help from adults or older kids to play. One eleven-year-old said, "Absolutely thumbs up." CD-ROM. WIN; $59.99; Age: 8-12. Viacom New Media.

Category—FLM

*** Dear America: Friend to Friend (Dear America)

Based on the book series, offers an opportunity for girls to form friendships with fictional young women from American history via non-online chatting technology. Interactions include Circle of Friends game, Player's Diary, and Instant Message Window. *Adult Juror Comments*: Easy to use, though doesn't allow user to save a spot for later return. Provides opportunities to practice interpersonal skills through hypothetical situations. Having historical background on each character provides an interesting catch. *Kid Juror Comments*: Girls loved it, particularly the secret diary of each character. "I liked making the characters do different things and solve their problems." "It was really awesome learning about these girls. We really seemed to have conversations with them." CD-ROM. WIN; $30; Age: 8-12. Knowledge Adventure.

Category—Music

** Beethoven Lives Upstairs, See Page 180.

Category—Nature

* Everglades Journey 2.0
(Trekinteractive Young Naturalist Series)

Explores the Everglades National Park and its ecosystem. Filled with vivid photographs and field-guide facts about the wetlands, hiking, and canoeing of this spectacular park. Quick Time 2.1 is required. *Adult Juror Comments*: Easy to load and play. Child tour guides are appealing. Supports environmental responsibility. "It's just like a resource book on a CD-ROM." Photos and sound quality are okay, not great. Offers no verbal or audio instruction. *Kid Juror Comments*: Liked the sounds and songs of the animals, bugs, and snakes. Child can move at his or her own pace. Written factual information suitable for older children, while camping and canoeing sections are more appropriate for younger ones. CD-ROM. WIN/MAC; $24.95; Age: 8-12. T.I. Multimedia.

** Nature: Virtual Serengeti (Nature: Virtual Serengeti)

Adventure and learning combine in this photo safari for kids that is loaded with videos, photos, and animated maps. *Adult Juror Comments*: Riveting presentation, especially the navigation compass. Video clips offer real, 360 degree perspectives. Users are driven to explore and learn. Some had difficulty with the set up and found the pace too slow. Correct answers are not provided. *Kid Juror Comments*: Slow to start. Cool graphics. Lots of interesting information. "I wanted things to really speed up." "My favorite part was answering questions in the journal." "I liked traveling by jeep and in the airplane." Images are sometimes fuzzy. CD-ROM. WIN/MAC; $29.99; Age: 8-12. Grolier Interactive.

** Secret Paths in the Forest (Secret Paths)

A friendship adventure for girls, where characters need help with feelings and friendship. Girls help the characters by going on a quest through the wilderness where they solve puzzles that reveal secret stones with hidden messages that offer help. *Adult Juror Comments*: Well-designed, easy to use. Beautiful graphics. Looks at typical real-life problems and social interactions. Good diversity. Moves pretty fast at times. Challenging adventure with beautiful graphics and sound effects. *Kid Juror Comments*: Easy to use, directions could be better. Girls thought it was cool because it was humorous and difficult. "I liked their stories. When I got something right, my heart bounced." "I thought it was very cool." CD-ROM. WIN/MAC; $29.95; Age: 8-12. Purple Moon Productions.

*** Wide World of Animals (ABC World Reference)*

Comprehensive geographical approach to over 600 animals. Combines breathtaking imagery with fascinating information and statistics on mammals, birds, reptiles, amphibians, and fish from around the world. Offers panoramic views of animals' habitats. *Adult Juror Comments*: Ingenious, delightful learning tool. High-quality production captures children's love of animals while teaching geography, geology, and botany. Amazing soundtrack. *Kid Juror Comments*: Kids loved it. They found it full of information and fun to play. Best suited for the upper end of recommended age range. "Terrific for the home with many-aged siblings." CD-ROM. WIN/MAC; $39.95; Age: 8-12. Learning Company.

** Yellowstone Journey, See Page 180.

Format—Video/DVD

Category—Education/Instruction

*** Adventures in the Great Stone Balloon
(Adventures in the Great Stone Balloon)

In this adventure video and activity book, Martha Lambert and her balloon crew take an imaginative ride to learn about dinosaurs. They help prepare a dinosaur picnic, speak to Mother Earth about why dinosaurs are extinct, and create stories. *Adult Juror Comments*: Creative, absorbing, engaging. Excellent animation and production. Fascinating to watch, listen to, and think about. Challenging and interactive. Greatly respects children and their abilities. Reading, writing, and imagining are explored. *Kid Juror Comments*: Good and funny. Appealing to both boys and girls, but especially to kids who are already reading. "The singing was good. Mother Earth was cute." "I liked when the dinosaurs fell over and died." "We sang along with the dinosaur song." Video. 51 min.; $19.95; Age: 7-10. A Full Service Imagination.

*** Ancient Egypt (Ancient Civilizations for Children)

Travel to ancient Egypt, a civilization that began along the Nile River over five thousand years ago. These early people advanced civilization by building pyramids and temples, establishing a vast trading system, and developing hieroglyphics. *Adult Juror Comments*: Holds your interest from beginning to end. Flows well from one subject to the next. Topics appealing, very informative, good videography and format. "Provides accurate and factual information in an age-appropriate fashion." Aesthetically pleasing. *Kid Juror Comments*: "It was gross when they talked about taking the brains out. It was cool seeing inside the tombs." Kids complained about the captions, but learned a lot from them. Got them thinking about Egyptians and other cultures." Video. 23 min.; $29.95; Age: 8-12. Schlessinger Video Productions.

Age 8-12

Video

Edu/Instru

** *Baby-Sitting: The Basics & Beyond (Kids 101)*

The fairy good-sitter teaches new baby-sitters about feeding, diapering, avoiding accidents, and entertaining children. Includes a question-and-answer session on preventing and handling emergencies. Ideal for new parents or future baby-sitters. *Adult Juror Comments*: Teaches good baby-sitting practices in an appealing way. Contains safety information that few programs offer. Good pace, sparkling special effects, and true stories. Important information and high-quality presentation. Great discussion-starter. *Kid Juror Comments*: Much better than taking a baby-sitting class. Kids liked the fairy good-sitter. "It's great for an older sibling." "I liked that there were examples of good things to do." "Makes sense." Video. 30 min.; $14.95; Age: 8-12. Carpool Productions.

*** *Big Airshow, The*, See Page 182.

** *Big Auto Plant, The*, See Page 182.

*** *Big Boom, The*, See Page 183.

** *Big Train Trip, The*, See Page 184.

*** *Brett the Jet*, See Page 184.

* *Bully Smart (Street Smart)*

Teaches a four-step personal safety-system to deal with bullies. The children represented go to school fearing a bully and are instructed on how to deal with him. *Adult Juror Comments*: Good advice for kids. Emphasizes self-esteem and personal safety. Best watched with parent or adult. Offers a lot of material for discussion. Lacks cultural diversity. *Kid Juror Comments*: Kids recognized the incidents from the video in their daily lives and thought the advice given was good. They commented, "Maybe bullies shouldn't watch it, or they might get some new ideas and techniques to attack others." Video. 32 min.; $19.95; Age: 8-12. PFS Streetsmart.

** *Cooperative Group Games (New Games)*

A useful video for teachers and group leaders. The twelve games teach and reinforce basic skills in math, English, creativity, teamwork, listening, and other things. Useful for children of various ages. These games are also for coed P.E. programs. *Adult Juror Comments*: Kids are obviously having a lot of fun. Offers teachers and group leaders of elementary age kids a simple, clear presentation of new ideas for interactive physical activities. Sound and video quality are not great. Great diversity. *Kid Juror Comments*: "It's hard to hear what the leader is saying." Kids learned new games they've not seen before. "Can we go out and play these games?" "Good to watch when you're bored." Video. 30 min.; $29.95; Age: 7-11. New Games.

** *Dance! Workout with Barbie,* See Page 185.

** *Extremely Goofy Movie, An,* See Page 186.

** *Girl's World, A (Girl's World, A)*

 This real-life adventure takes girls on an exciting day of fun, friendship, and discovery as they explore the worlds of Annie, a horse vet; Karen, an artist; and Suzanne, a jet pilot. *Adult Juror Comments*: This video shows great role models for young girls. Unfortunately, the sound level is so low at times that you can't hear what's being said. Highly motivating. It offers a clever look at occupations that will inspire any young girl. *Kid Juror Comments*: Boys and girls alike enjoyed learning more about various careers, especially the pilot and the glass-blower. They were inspired. "It's good to see girls with strong careers." It's too bad the sound is so poor at times. Video. 45 min.; $14.95; Age: 8-12. Laurie Hepburn Productions.

** *How Much Is a Million? (Reading Rainbow)*

 LeVar explores ways of counting large numbers as he talks to people who share grouping and estimating techniques. This episode helps viewers visualize how much are a million, a billion, and a trillion. *Adult Juror Comments*: Good presentation of intangibles. Beginning moves slowly, but overall quality is visually exciting and well-paced. Format is wonderful for parent-child interaction. Very practical application. Description of a million is quite understandable. *Kid Juror Comments*: Discussion and illustrations helped to understand numbers. "Children particularly enjoyed the crayons being manufactured at the crayon factory and related to estimating how many supplies were needed." "I liked how many gold fish go into the stadium." Video. 28 min.; $19.95; Age: 7-10. Reading Rainbow/GPN.

** *Hurricanes and Tornadoes (Weather Fundamentals)*

Hurricanes and tornadoes, the most destructive storms on Earth, fascinate us because of their awesome force. In this program, students study both phenomena from their early formation to the full-blown maturity that wreak havoc on land. *Adult Juror Comments*: Live clips of storm are very dramatic. Narration makes concept easy to understand. Good multicultural cast, but not all are skilled. "Fascinating facts and experiments kept the subject lingering in your mind." "Makes a lasting impression." *Kid Juror Comments*: Kids liked the fast pace and the visual excitement. They liked the live action footage of the real storms. "I learned a lot about the weather." Video. 23 min.; $29.95; Age: 8-12. Schlessinger Video Productions.

** In Tune with Brass (Instrumental Classmates)

Introduces the major brass instruments and explains the parts of the instruments that make the sounds. Instruments are heard individually, and the role each one plays is demonstrated. Series sold as a five-video set only. *Adult Juror Comments*: Accurate and challenging introduction to brass instruments. Well-produced. Covers key facts and an impromptu quiz. Little cultural diversity except mention of many important African American musicians. "Pretty dry presentation." *Kid Juror Comments*: Enjoyed the slapstick-surfer narrator. They joined in without prompting when he invited them to "try and buzz." Enjoyed the band. "Made me feel like marching." "Not many African American children." Enthusiasm dropped off at the end. Video. 30 min.; $149.95; Age: 8-12. Warner Bros. Publications.

** In Tune with Keyboards, See Page 189.

** In Tune with Percussion, See Page 190.

** In Tune with Strings, See Page 190.

** In Tune with Woodwinds, See Page 190.

*** Jet Pilot

Takes an in-depth look at what it takes to be a jet pilot from pilot training to cockpit controls, from how hand signals are used to communicate between ground crew and pilot to the importance of the maintenance operations. *Adult Juror Comments*: Informative and well-written. Doesn't talk down to children. Explains the process of flying a jet. The photography was excellent: "The aerial photography made me feel I was in the cockpit flying my own jet." *Kid Juror Comments*: Engaging. Kids learned that they need to go to college to become a pilot. Motivated discussion about female pilots and those of varied ethnic backgrounds. Appealed to girls as well as boys. "Do pilots make money having so much fun?" Video. 30 min.; $12.95; Age: 6-12. BC Entertainment.

*** Mrs. Katz and Tush, See Page 192.

* Our Disappearing World Forests (Think About It)

Features a talking computer who leads children to look at the complex issues surrounding our vanishing forests. In interviews, experts assess research data. *Adult Juror Comments*: Encourages critical thinking. Information provided is very instructive without being overly technical. Exemplifies cooperative learning. The talking computer was not well received, and the acting scored particularly low. *Kid Juror Comments*: Just okay. They liked the ecosystem poster. Could be useful for further research about forests. Video. 27 min.; $19.95; Age: 8-12. Paragon Media.

__ Rhythms of Peace 2,__* See Page 194.*

*__** Rope Around the World,__* See Page 195.*

*__*** Shaman's Apprentice, The,__* See Page 196.*

** Skill Games (New Games)

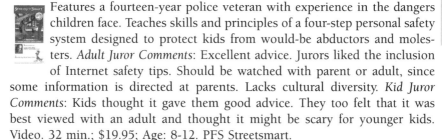

Teaches developmental skills that promote learning and social skills. Included are physical skills like throwing, catching, running, plus social experiences like cooperation, teamwork, inclusion, and fun! *Adult Juror Comments*: Not entertaining, but offers good instruction for non-competitive games. Mediocre production values. Producer is respectful of children's questions and takes time to really listen. Encourages teamwork and good sportsmanship. Lacks diversity. *Kid Juror Comments*: Kids learned new games, but need to watch it again to learn how to play them. They were not motivated to watch it at first. "Good directions given on how to play." "We need to show our gym coach this." Video. 30 min.; $29.95; Age: 7-12. New Games.

*__** Snow Jam,__* See Page 197.*

** Stranger Smart (Street Smart)

Features a fourteen-year police veteran with experience in the dangers children face. Teaches skills and principles of a four-step personal safety system designed to protect kids from would-be abductors and molesters. *Adult Juror Comments*: Excellent advice. Jurors liked the inclusion of Internet safety tips. Should be watched with parent or adult, since some information is directed at parents. Lacks cultural diversity. *Kid Juror Comments*: Kids thought it gave them good advice. They too felt that it was best viewed with an adult and thought it might be scary for younger kids. Video. 32 min.; $19.95; Age: 8-12. PFS Streetsmart.

*__*** When Aunt Lena Did the Rhumba,__* See Page 200.*

Category—Family

** *102 Dalmatians,* *See Page 201.*

*** *Adventures of Flower the Arson Dog,* *See Page 202.*

** *Air Bud: World Pup,* *See Page 202.*

*** *Alice in Wonderland*

Daydreaming Alice chases the White Rabbit into the magical, madcap world of Wonderland with its kaleidoscope of off-the-wall characters. Alice goes to a wild tea party, meets the Queen of Hearts, and is tricked into playing a curious croquet game. *Adult Juror Comments*: Whimsical, magical adventure with terrific animation and memorable score. An entertaining introduction to classic literature, plus Walt Disney explaining animation. Promotes diversity: "Everyone is different, and that is O.K." *Kid Juror Comments*: Really taken with the fantasy. "I would like to dream like that." "It told a very funny story of things that we can't see here in this world." "We also get bored with school and want to go exploring." They even said they would like to read the book. Video. 75 min.; $22.99; Age: 7-12. Buena Vista Home Entertainment/Disney.

*** *All Dogs Go to Heaven,* *See Page 203.*

** *Alley Cats on Strike,* *See Page 204.*

* *Alvin and the Chipmunks Meet Frankenstein* (Alvin and the Chipmunks)

 While working at a movie studio as the featured performers, Alvin and his brothers enjoy many attractions, including Dr. Frankenstein's castle. When the Chipmunks meet the Frankenstein monster, the ensuing experience is touching and illuminating. *Adult Juror Comments*: Well-produced. Lots of intertwining plots. Teaches message about not judging people by how they look. A bit scary in the beginning. Contains some inappropriate destructive behaviors. *Kid Juror Comments*: Enjoyed, would watch again. "It was kind of scary in some parts." "I sleep with a teddy bear too, just like Theodore." "It's a little confusing." "The chipmunks are so cute. I love the way they talk." "The monster was nice to the kids." Video. 78 min.; $19.98; Age: 8-12. Universal Studios Home Video.

** Anastasia

 Spectacular animated story about a lost Russian princess and her quest to find her true identity. Features celebrity voices and spellbinding music, including "Once Upon a December." *Adult Juror Comments*: This production combines adventure, sensitivity, history, music appreciation, and a strong female role model. Some Rasputin scenes are graphic and extremely frightening. *Kid Juror Comments*: Boys and girls alike loved this. Boys loved the revolution. Girls loved the relationship issues. Kids liked the glimpses of history. They asked, "Which parts are real and which aren't?" Kids thought Rasputin was too "monsterish." Video. 94 min.; $26.95; Age: 8-12. Twentieth Century Fox Home Entertainment.

* Animal Antics (America's Funniest Home Videos)

Shows hilarious antics of wild and family animals, from giraffes to pot-bellied pigs. *Adult Juror Comments*: Based on the TV show, features home videos by amateurs with slap-stick and adult humor. Starts out funny, but gets pretty repetitive. Borderline animal exploitation. Funny. "I laughed out loud." *Kid Juror Comments*: Some liked it, others didn't. "It's cruel to roll a dog down a bowling alley." "I like the funny things the animals do." "It was funny to see the dog chase the laser beam." "My favorite part was when the sheep gave the man a hard time." Video. 51 min.; $14.95; Age: 8-12. E-Realbiz.

** Animals Are People Too, Volume 1

 Teaches empathy for animals and appreciation for their individual intelligence by showing colorful clips of animals interacting with humans. Helps to address anxieties children may have toward animals. *Adult Juror Comments*: Entertaining, funny. Shows how animals affect humans. "It's amazing to learn about the range of activities that animals can learn." Animals are harnessed into unnatural gear such as scuba diving equipment, skis, and false eyelashes that bothered many. *Kid Juror Comments*: Appealing. "I'll be looking for the husky who rides the Harley." "I didn't know the Taco Bell dog was a girl." "My favorite part was the rat. I bet mine could learn those tricks if I spent time with him." "I couldn't believe a dog could go scuba diving." Video. 30 min.; $9.95; Age: 8-12. Questar, Inc.

Age 8-12

Video

Family

Age 8-12

Video

Family

** *Animals Are People Too, Volume 2*

Hosted by Alan Thicke and his golden retriever who meet amazing animals like a canine cancer survivor, a chimp that co-starred with Tarzan, and many more. Includes a tour of an emergency room for animals and shows the advances in animal health care. *Adult Juror Comments*: Warm, lovable stories, endearing pet antics. Good narration. Demonstrates the rewards of patience, training and hard work. Could stimulate an interest in the responsibilities of keeping a pet. Nice mix of domestic and wild animals, feathers and fur. *Kid Juror Comments*: Excited to see animals in a new context. "We knew that animals help people, but we had no idea how many ways." "This is better than Candid Camera." "My brother would like to have a smart dog make his lunch too." "I wish MY dog was trained like that." Video. 47 min.; $9.95; Age: 8-12. Questar, Inc.

** *Animals Are People Too, Volume 3*

Hosted by Alan Thicke and his golden retriever, Max, who meet amazing animals. Features a skydiving dachshund, a musical elephant that paints, skateboarding pigs, and many more. Includes a visit to an elephant hospital and the seals at Sea World. *Adult Juror Comments*: Informative, entertaining. Interactions between people and animals are touching. Promotes sensitivity and a sense of wonder towards animals. "How can animals be so human?" Scenes of activities that endanger the animals' lives provoked questions. *Kid Juror Comments*: Universally amused by the animal antics. "I think everybody will like it really a lot." "The people that made this movie really care about animals and should get a million dollars." "I liked it because it tells facts about animals. Also it's funny." Video. 47 min.; $9.95; Age: 8-12. Questar, Inc.

** *Animals Are People Too, Volume 4*

Hosted by Alan Thicke and his golden retriever, Max, who meet amazing animals like Eddie the canine star of "Frasier," acrobatic cats, killer whales that seem to understand language, and many more. Includes extremely photogenic lizards and heroic dogs. *Adult Juror Comments*: Delightful. Good visuals and sound track. Engaging animal portraits and stories. Encourages kids' observational skills. Encourages respectful attitude towards animals. "I believe it could help a child overcome a fear of animals." *Kid Juror Comments*: Cute little animal stories. Fun, moved along, peppy. "It was neat and scary when the trainer rode the nose of the killer whale." "I didn't know iguanas got that big. I can't imagine loving them." "I liked the lizards living in the dresser." Video. 47 min.; $9.95; Age: 8-12. Questar, Inc.

** Animals Are People Too, Volume 5

Hosted by Alan Thicke and his golden retriever who meet amazing animal celebrities, such as a dog who's a dancer, a cat supermodel, and dogs who work with special needs children. Includes a trip to an elephant hospital and a visit with a cat therapist. *Adult Juror Comments*: Informative, wholesome entertainment. Reinforces good behavior by watching animals make gains and achievements. "It keeps moving and never lets you get bored." Younger viewers might need to be cautioned against playing with non-domesticated animals. *Kid Juror Comments*: Kept their interest. "It showed people helping animals with problems, and animals helping people with problems." "I will watch it over and over — whenever I want to feel good." "I liked the dogs dancing and getting married." Video. 47 min.; $9.95; Age: 8-12. Questar, Inc.

*** Anne Frank's Diary

An animated adaptation of the famous diary written by young Anne Frank during the Jewish Holocaust, chronicling her family's days in hiding from the Nazis. *Adult Juror Comments*: Artistically magnificent. Exquisite artwork and realistic detail. Excellent account of the treatment of Jews during WWII. Animation makes it easier for children to connect to WWII than documentary style. Handles issues of young womanhood. *Kid Juror Comments*: Impressed them. "The characters were believable; we could feel their fears." "I could see how she felt jumpy and confused." "We want to learn more about WWII." "You should teach kids that this really happened so it won't happen again." Video. 88 min.; $19.95; Age: 8-14. Globe Trotter Network SA.

*** Aristocats, See Page 207.

* Baby-Sitters and the Boy-Sitters, The (The Baby-Sitter's Club)

Mishaps and mayhem ensue when the boys decide to start their own baby-sitting club. Is there room for two clubs in one town? *Adult Juror Comments*: This is perhaps a little middle-class idealistic but does address appropriate issues for children of this age. Well-produced and fun. Shows little diversity. *Kid Juror Comments*: Kids enjoyed this, particularly the girls. Well-produced, well-acted. Boys and girls interacting shows positive gender awareness and role models. "There was no meanness; everyone gets along." "It was a little too much like a TV sitcom." Video. 30 min.; $14.95; Age: 7-14. Warner Home Video.

Age 8-12

Video

Family

** Baby-Sitters Remember, The (The Baby-Sitter's Club)

 In this episode, the Baby-Sitters share their funniest and fondest memories and celebrate their unique friendship. *Adult Juror Comments*: Funny. Lightly presents issues of contemporary life, offers positive role models who take responsibility, earn money, and cooperate with one another. Will appeal most to young girls. *Kid Juror Comments*: Kids related to this story, particularly the girls. Not very appealing to the boys. Addresses issues that concern girls at this age such as how to establish lasting friendships. Video. 30 min.; $14.95; Age: 7-14. Warner Home Video.

*** Bach's Fight for Freedom (The Composers' Specials)

This fictional story shows Johann Sebastian Bach struggling for the freedom to compose music. Bach argues passionately that the only master you can serve faithfully is your own heart, and he recognizes a kindred soul in a ten-year-old assistant. *Adult Juror Comments*: Great story. Gives an impression of what 18th-century life was like. Characters are exaggerated to adult eyes, but appealing to children. Well-produced. Bach's compositions made wonderful background music. *Kid Juror Comments*: Kids loved everything about it, from the costumes to the sets to the story. Pleasantly presented insights into Bach's music. A little long for the younger kids. Video. 53 min.; $19.95; Age: 8-12. Devine Entertainment Corp.

* Balloon Farm, See Page 212.

* Billboard Dad (Mary-Kate and Ashley)

 When two sisters team up to find a new love for their newly single Dad, it's a fun-loving California adventure gone wild. *Adult Juror Comments*: Good entertainment geared to girls. Shows the twin's concern for their father's happiness. Adults objected to too much attention on sex, negative comments about the boys, and unsafe actions such as skateboarding into the pool. *Kid Juror Comments*: Enlightening for single-parent kids. Enjoyed watching the twin's antics, attire, hobbies, and abundance of just about everything. They liked how they took care of their Dad and caught the bad guy. Most would watch it again. Definitely a girl movie. Video. 90 min.; $19.98; Age: 8-12. Warner Home Video.

*** Bizet's Dream (The Composers' Specials)

Fictional story of the friendship between composer Georges Bizet and his twelve-year-old piano student, Michelle, who is captivated by the story of the gypsy, Carmen, heroine of Bizet's opera. *Adult Juror Comments*: Exquisite production, a wonderful introduction to Bizet's music, the creative process, and the relationship between art and life. Great family viewing. *Kid Juror Comments*: Good story. Held children's attention. Kids enjoyed discovering a story line based on real life or parallels to life. They liked the music, dancing, and costumes. Girls particularly enjoyed it. Video. 53 min.; $19.95; Age: 8-12. Devine Entertainment Corp.

** Blue Angels, The: In Pursuit of Excellence

Offers a behind the scenes look at the U.S. Navy's Flight Demonstration Team, from "on the ground" to "inside the cockpit." Shows how people's passion sets the stage for accomplishment. *Adult Juror Comments*: Creative, esthetically pleasing with spectacular shots of flight formations from the air and ground. Sophisticated vocabulary is well explained. Encourages teamwork, trust, cooperation, and pursuing one's dream. *Kid Juror Comments*: Liked the live-action shots and child narrator. "It was great to go into the cockpit, training area, and take-off area." "I felt like I was there." Kids liked seeing men and women working together, developing trust. "There was a lot to learn." Video. 60 min.; $15.95; Age: 8-12. Dreams Come True Productions.

*** Booker

 Set in the 1860s south, Booker is the impassioned story of the boy who struggled through slavery to found the Tuskegee Institute. Through the eyes of nine-year-old Booker T. Washington. Stars LeVar Burton, Shelly Duvall, Judge Reinhold. *Adult Juror Comments*: Well-acted and produced; a realistic depiction of the institution of slavery and its dehumanizing process. Values education as a precious commodity. Shows how through education one achieves true freedom. Also shows not all white people were evil. *Kid Juror Comments*: Kids enjoyed it. When Booker reads to his class, they commented, "I couldn't believe slaves were not allowed to read." Realistic, kids couldn't believe how the children had to work. "Black people were treated badly, both as slaves and when freed." Video. 60 min.; $14.95; Age: 8-12. Bonneville Worldwide Entertainment.

** Boyd's Shadow

 This story tells of a lonely boy and his invisible friend, Shadow, who coaxes Boyd into confronting a scary hermit. Boyd learns valuable lessons about the healing quality of friendship and the power of a smile. *Adult Juror Comments*: Simple story, moderately paced. Good message with a happy ending. The acting falls short. Shows some poor role models such as spanking. The sister's behavior is atrocious in the beginning, but she makes a turnaround, somewhat unbelievable, at the end. *Kid Juror Comments*: Kids identified with the prejudice shown toward the hermit. When he turns out to be nothing but a misunderstood old man, they were relieved. They enjoyed the messages about friendship. Video. 45 min.; $19.95; Age: 7-11. Horizon Film and Video.

*** Bridge to Terabithia*

 Jesse Aarons, a shy fifth grader, learns about love when he strikes up a friendship with the new girl in town. Together they create a fantasy world they call "Terabitha," set in a pine forest near their farms. *Adult Juror Comments*: Thoughtful and intriguing. Well-produced. True to the original book. Deals realistically with problems. A great story about differing values and finding common ground. Addresses friendship, moving away, and death. Somewhat dated presentation. *Kid Juror Comments*: Great story, sad ending. Slow at the beginning, but it held the kids' interest. Story looks "real," not like Hollywood-perfect. "It is good to be nice to a new kid." "It showed that girls can do a lot." "Some characters were disrespectful." Video. 60 min.; $14.95; Age: 8-12. Bonneville Worldwide Entertainment.

** Brink, See Page 216.

*** Bug's Life, A, See Page 216.

*** Can of Worms (Disney Channel)

A smart, inventive teenager is convinced he doesn't belong on Earth and identifies better with imaginary aliens about whom he spins elaborate stories. Rental only. *Adult Juror Comments*: Terrific. Humorous production with cool special effects. Demonstrates good conflict resolution skills. Presents lessons about accepting differences in individuals. "Fun science fiction story focuses on teenage misfit." *Kid Juror Comments*: Enjoyed it. Would watch again and recommend to their friends. "The alien dog was a hoot." "Good story about dealing with peer pressure." "It makes kids think about consequences for their behavior." Video. 84 min.; rental only; Age: 8-14. Buena Vista Home Entertainment/Disney.

** Chess Kids

 Documentary profiles the best young chess prodigies from all over the world including the actual child from *Searching for Bobby Fischer*. *Adult Juror Comments*: Clear, entertaining portrayal of tournament chess. Respectful of children's critical thinking skills. Seeing kids from other cultures playing chess is appealing. It's interesting to see how they communicate despite the language barriers. *Kid Juror Comments*: Kids were surprised at how interesting it was. "I liked trying to figure out where the children were from." They liked seeing the only girl chess player beat several people. "Felt like I was at a world chess tournament." Some found it boring. Video. 51 min.; $14.95; Age: 8-12. Lynn Hamrick Productions.

Age 8-12

Video

Family

** *Claudia and the Missing Jewels (The Baby-Sitter's Club)*

Claudia's jewelry designs are a huge hit at the Stoneybrook Crafts Fair, and she's on the road to fame and fortune. When her jewelry vanishes, the Baby-Sitters set off to solve the mystery. *Adult Juror Comments*: Good story, promotes values about friendship, but the presentation is very middle-class and promotes stereotypes. *Kid Juror Comments*: Very popular with middle-school girls. They thought that it was realistic and that making jewelry was "cool." Video. 30 min.; $12.95; Age: 7-14. Warner Home Video.

** *Claudia and the Mystery of the Secret Passage (The Baby-Sitter's Club)*

A note found in the secret passage at Mary Anne and Dawn's house leads Claudia and her friends on an adventure. Will they be able to settle an ancient feud, or does only danger await them? *Adult Juror Comments*: Acting good, music lively. Successfully translates the popularity of the "Baby-Sitters" book series and portrays the characters well. Advertisements at the beginning of the tape are objectionable. *Kid Juror Comments*: Girls loved this. Boys did not want to watch. Children liked how this promoted being nice to siblings. Video. 30 min.; $14.95; Age: 7-14. Warner Home Video.

*** *Courage Mountain*

Fifteen-year-old Heidi leaves her beloved grandfather, her childhood sweetheart, and her cherished Swiss mountains to attend boarding school in Italy. When World War I breaks out, the girls escape and embark on a daring trek across the frozen Alps. *Adult Juror Comments*: Everyone enjoyed this. Great role models—caring, brave, and intelligent. Conveys a can-do attitude. Stimulates curiosity and creativity. Girls liked it better than boys. *Kid Juror Comments*: Great. Learned a lot about the war and life in an orphanage. "A little scary, but exciting." "The people looked old-fashioned, this must have been long ago." Kids learned not to judge people by how they look. Video. 105 min.; $14.95; Age: 8-12. MGM/UA Home Entertainment.

** *Cyrano (Theatre Adventures)*

Antwerp's Blauw Vier Theatre performs this adaptation of Edmond Rostand's classic story. Cyrano, thinking his nose is too large, and Christian, thinking he's not intelligent enough, combine efforts to woo Roxanne with the written word. *Adult Juror Comments*: The filming of a stage production makes a slow-moving video by most standards. Good acting, costumes, sets. Addresses love, duty, and self-esteem. The backstage section was interesting. *Kid Juror Comments*: Kids found it extremely slow-moving and noted the lack of diversity. They enjoyed learning about technical aspects. "I liked the poetry in the letters. The ending is very sad; Cyrano should have told Roxanne he loved her." Video. 101 min.; $27; Age: 8-15. Globalstage.

** Dawn and the Dream Boy (The Baby-Sitter's Club)

 It's love at first sight when Dawn meets Jamie Anderson. She's sure that Jamie would be a "dream date" for the Sweetheart Dance. Does Jamie feel the same way? *Adult Juror Comments*: Entertaining and appealing for pre-teen girls. Realistically portrays girls' interests. Smooth but unrealistic conflict resolution. Only affluent suburban families are represented. Some jurors objected to the story and the gender stereotyping. *Kid Juror Comments*: Most all of the girls ages nine through twelve liked it and would watch it again. Some kids were visibly embarrassed by the referrals to boy and girl crushes. Video. 30 min.; $12.95; Age: 9-12. Warner Home Video.

** Dawn Saves the Trees (The Baby-Sitter's Club)

 When the city plans to build a road through the local park, Dawn leads the Baby-Sitters in a fight to save the trees. The group is ready to do anything, but has Dawn gone too far? *Adult Juror Comments*: Enjoyable. Encourages reading and activism in a way that bridges generations. The Baby-Sitters are clever and intelligent. They don't just turn on the TV. Offers good humor for both girls and boys. *Kid Juror Comments*: Girls enjoyed this more than the boys. They liked the actresses selected to portray the characters they're familiar with from the books. Realistically portrayed issues they deal with. Video. 30 min.; $14.95; Age: 7-14. Warner Home Video.

*** Dear America: Picture of Freedom, A (Dear America)

 Twelve-year-old Clotee is a slave who works in the "Big House" of a Southern plantation. Clotee has secretly taught herself to read and write. In the face of grave danger, she bravely works to help free her people. *Adult Juror Comments*: Excellent production. A great springboard for examining American history. Values of courage and conviction. "A very touching story." Best viewed with an adult because of dramatic portrayals of period violence. A slave is whipped. *Kid Juror Comments*: Engaging. Kids would watch it again. "I learned that singing spirituals is like Morse code." "I learned about the underground railroad." "Clotee risked her life for the others." "She was brave." "I liked how she wrote in her journal." Video. 30 min.; $14.95; Age: 8-12. Scholastic Entertainment.

*** Degas and the Dancer (The Artists' Specials)

The 19th-Century French painter, Edgar Degas, paints to survive. Initially, he scorns painting dancers but gets caught up in a ballerina's life and becomes interested in a ballerina named Marie. They reveal their hopes and fears to one another. *Adult Juror Comments*: Worthwhile story, beautifully produced. Degas is shown as a self-centered old man whose art is more important than people. Marie's influence improves his behavior. Prompts the question, "Does being a genius give you license to treat others badly?" *Kid Juror Comments*: "I learned about what it takes to be an artist." "I liked the way they all taught each other something. The painter taught her that if you don't make a mistake, you'll never learn. She taught him not to be so grouchy and have respect for others." Video. 55 min.; $19.95; Age: 8-12. Devine Entertainment Corp.

* Duke, The, See Page 227.

*** Edison: The Wizard of Light (Inventors' Specials)

Thomas Edison's research in moving images is disrupted by a scruffy lad, Jack. Edison recognizes something of himself in the boy and takes him in. Together Edison and Jack pursue the dream of the motion picture. *Adult Juror Comments*: Inspiring. Excellent balance between history, science, and imagination. Time-period clips enhanced visual and cognitive understanding. Promotes a healthy respect for intelligence and inquiry. It's a great way to introduce inventors and science. *Kid Juror Comments*: Children were riveted, entertained, and informed. They loved the set of Edison's shop. "I liked how it told how the inventions were made." "I didn't know that the first movies didn't have sound." Video. 54 min.; $19.95; Age: 8-12. Devine Entertainment Corp.

* Enchanted Tales: A Tale of Egypt (Enchanted Tales)

Plucked from the Nile by the daughter of Pharaoh, Moses grows up as the favored friend of Pharaoh's son Ramses. After witnessing the cruel treatment of the Israelites, Moses discovers his true identity and his destiny. *Adult Juror Comments*: Interesting dialogue and musical interpretations will captivate students' attention. Religious overtones. Animation not synchronized with audio, and transitions between scenes are difficult. Violent scenes are pertinent to the story and are excessive. *Kid Juror Comments*: Best viewed with an adult. "There is a lot of fighting." "After the first miracle, I saw that God was trying to get the Pharaoh to change his mind." "We learned about how brave Moses was." Video. 48 min.; $9.98; Age: 8-12. Sony Wonder.

** Families of China, See Page 230.

** Families of Puerto Rico, See Page 230.

* Family Follies (America's Funniest Home Videos)

Features home videos from the television show America's Funniest Home Videos showing the silly behavior of kids, moms, and dads. *Adult Juror Comments*: Funny antics, juvenile. Adults shoving their spouse's face into the wedding cake or kids putting straws in sleeping siblings' mouths brought about safety concerns. Typical of home videos, some clips are unclear. Editing is well-done. *Kid Juror Comments*: Kids were thoroughly entertained. "We laughed so, so much." "The parents were silly." "I could relate when the girl hit the piñata and it hit her dad accidentally." "I thought I was watching my family videos." "My friends would laugh hysterically." Video. 53 min.; $14.99; Age: 9-12. E-Realbiz.

** Famous Fred, See Page 231.

*** Fantasia 2000, See Page 231.

** Far from Home: The Adventures of Yellow Dog

A boy and his dog, lost in the wilderness, fight for survival in an emotional tale of friendship and courage. *Adult Juror Comments*: Appealing animal story, visually driven. Good family interaction and respect for nature, with examples of survival skills. Depicts the outdoors as both gentle and rugged. Children are never underestimated. Contains some strong language. *Kid Juror Comments*: Kids clapped when the dog returned. Lots of things going on make this story a little complicated to follow. Led to discussion of literature-related themes and realism of the adventure, and to "practice what you are." Some kids thought it was slow. Video. 81 min.; $19.98; Age: 8-12. Twentieth Century Fox Home Entertainment.

*** Ferngully: The Last Rainforest, See Page 232.

** Flash (Wonderful World of Disney)

Tells an inspirational story about the bond between a boy and his horse. They overcome the odds when the boy's grandmother dies, and the boy and his horse seek out his father. *Adult Juror Comments*: Good production with beautiful music and scenery. "Addresses difficult topics such as death and running away with sensitivity." "Inspires viewers to face obstacles in their lives." "Somewhat slow-moving at times and intensely emotional." *Kid Juror Comments*: Riveted. Asked to watch it again. "My favorite part was when the horse knocked the boy into the water." "It was really sad when the boy had to sell his horse to pay for his grandmother's funeral." "My horse-lover friends would love this." Video. 90 min.; $14.99; Age: 7-12. Buena Vista Home Entertainment/Disney.

** Frankenstein (Theatre Adventures)

Masterful stage production combined with vivid costumes and sets in Stage One's live performance and adaptation of Mary Shelly's "Frankenstein." Filmed and edited by the BBC. *Adult Juror Comments*: High-quality production with excellent sound, sets, lighting, acting. Starts slow. True to the book. The story, by definition, is scary and creepy. Stimulated a discussion about lightning and energy. *Kid Juror Comments*: Kids varied in their response to this. The genre, filming a stage production, is not engaging for all. Most enjoyed learning about the technical aspects of the production and enjoyed learning that "a lady wrote it." They liked the monster. Video. 96 min.; $27; Age: 8-15. Globalstage.

** Getting Even with Dad

A small-time crook thinks the only way he can go straight is with money from one last heist. But his son catches on, and concocts a plan to make him do time—as a dad. Stars Ted Danson and Macaulay Culkin. *Adult Juror Comments*: Reinforces the idea that "the clever, ethical child can reform his wayward parent"—placing a lot of questionable responsibility on children. Laudable for addressing parental negligence, but offers little challenge. Reinforces gender stereotypes. *Kid Juror Comments*: The kids related to Timmy. Some discussed their similar experiences. Kids liked the action, the smart boy, and the funny parts of the story line. Video. 108 min.; $14.95; Age: 8-14. MGM/UA Home Entertainment.

*** Girl of the Limberlost

Elnora Comstock is determined to attend high school. Although her widowed mother thinks it's a "foolish dream," Elnora is comforted by free-spirited naturalist Mrs. Porter. Based on the book by Gene Stratton Porter. *Adult Juror Comments*: Excellent. Great example of showing rather than telling a story. Characters demonstrate perseverance, dedication, forgiveness, and striving for acceptance. Views a turn-of-the-century farming community and environmental concerns from that time period. *Kid Juror Comments*: Kids liked Elnora's tenacity and curiosity. "The people were so real." "I think Elnora did a good job of helping her mom and growing up." "I liked the way Elnora wasn't afraid to touch things like snakes and bugs." Appeals to both boys and girls. Video. 111 min.; $19.95; Age: 8-12. Bonneville Worldwide Entertainment.

** Goldrush: A Real Life Alaskan Adventure (Wonderful World of Disney)

A woman sets out on an expedition in the wilds of Alaska in search of gold in the early 1900s. *Adult Juror Comments*: Great tool to show a strong, assertive woman's role during the gold rush time period. Promotes an inner drive to overcome obstacles by demonstrating physical strength, endurance, and business sense. Beautiful cinematography of Alaskan landscape. *Kid Juror Comments*: Enjoyed learning how gold was mined and how people dressed and acted during the 1900s. Their favorite part was finding the cabin in the snow and the woman winning her mine back in the end. Portrayed the human spirit and the importance of persistence. Video. 89 min.; $14.99; Age: 8-18. Buena Vista Home Entertainment/Disney.

** Goofy Movie, A

Goofy bonds with his teenage son Max on a cross-country road trip, but ends up having a rock 'n roll misadventure on the way. *Adult Juror Comments*: Clever blend of traditional kids and music video culture. Fast moving. Goofy is a popular cartoon character so kids tend to enjoy him immediately. Slapstick comedy sinks to low level teen humor. Rudeness and disrespect are shown as acceptable behaviors. *Kid Juror Comments*: Kept them entertained and interested throughout. "Awesome music." "Goofy is goofy." Related to Max very well—maybe too well: "I think school is boring too." "I figured out that other kids like different things than their parents do." Video. 78 min.; $22.99; Age: 8-12. Buena Vista Home Entertainment/Disney.

*** Handel's Last Chance (The Composers' Specials)

James, a Dublin street kid, is enrolled in an upper-crust school where he is treated like an outsider. He is befriended by Handel and chosen as a principal choirboy for the "Messiah." Handel rescues Jamie. The "Messiah" is a huge success. *Adult Juror Comments*: Beautifully produced. Provides an excellent introduction to the "Messiah," with a wide range of humor, music, values, and historical commentary. Shows how new friends support one another. Somewhat harsh and scary at times and moves rather slowly. *Kid Juror Comments*: They thought it was amusing, and that it looked realistic. "I enjoyed the boy's singing." Kids enjoyed conflict with bullies. "I liked when Handel tells Jamie, 'Listen to the voice deep inside your heart.'" Video. 51 min.; $19.95; Age: 8-12. Devine Entertainment Corp.

Chapter Four • Middle School

* Haunted Mask (Goosebumps)

Shy, quiet, Carly Beth is a target for everyone's teasing and practical jokes. One Halloween, she finds a wonderfully spooky mask that has her tormentors scared and running. When she refuses to take her mask off, strange things happen. *Adult Juror Comments*: The message is positive: developing self-awareness and the value of friends and family. But the moral is almost lost in the frightening scenario. Jurors objected to manipulating the viewers' emotions. *Kid Juror Comments*: Kids like the thrill quotient, the pace, and the visuals. "The talk is mean and ugly, but the effects were awesome." Kids liked the transforming mask. More sophisticated kids were bored; younger kids were scared. Video. 44 min.; $14.98; Age: 8-12. Twentieth Century Fox Home Entertainment.

* Heidi (Shirley Temple)

Shirley Temple plays the spirited young heroine in the classic novel on which the movie is based. Although the orphan is forced to live with her gruff grandfather, he eventually comes to adore her. *Adult Juror Comments*: Cute and charming. Offers examples of honesty, an assertive role model, strong characters, and families. Contains some religious content—prayer, singing, and schooling. Has some unfavorable stereotypes. *Kid Juror Comments*: Enjoyed by girls more than boys. Dated; some kids saw the nuns dressed in traditional habits from the back and thought they were some kind of "bad guy." Could be a springboard for reading the book. Video. 88 min.; $14.98; Age: 7-11. Twentieth Century Fox Home Entertainment.

*** Horse Sense

Eleven-year-old Tommy goes to visit his older and wealthy cousin in the big city. But the when the older boy misbehaves, he is sent out to his young cousin's ranch where he learns a little "horse sense"…and the two help each other grow. *Adult Juror Comments*: Great movie, enjoyable and realistic. Many touching moments and many scenes that can be used to show coping skills. Strong important themes—family, hard work, responsibility—are brought across with appropriate humor. *Kid Juror Comments*: Completely engrossed them, didn't miss a beat. "Good acting, nice plot." "It made me want to think about my life. Do I help others, or do think mostly about myself?" "The girlfriend is a brat! She needs a reality check!" "I didn't know about wild horses." Video. 89 min.; $14.99; Age: 8-14. Buena Vista Home Entertainment/Disney.

Age 8-12

Video

Family

* Huckleberry Finn

Ron Howard is Huck in this classic Mark Twain story of life on the Mississippi. *Adult Juror Comments*: Sophisticated content contains some aggressive language and physical interactions. Issues of slavery, abuse, name-calling, and theft are big topics for this age. It's too frightening for younger viewers though the content has historical value. *Kid Juror Comments*: Children who lack information on this period in history were confused about issues like slavery-versus-freedom concepts that are key to this film. Kids discussed how the father and son treated each other. Video. 77 min.; $14.98; Age: 9-13. Twentieth Century Fox Home Entertainment.

* Imaginaria

 A computer animation odyssey for kids with colorful, playful imagery and music by award-winning composer Gary Powell. Upbeat, playful, interactive, it requires kids to use their imaginations. *Adult Juror Comments*: Fantastic and sophisticated program. Exquisitely matched sound and computer graphics. Jurors voiced concern over some violent imagery and the extra-fast pace. *Kid Juror Comments*: Kids thought this was "weird." They weren't interested in watching it again. Video. 40 min.; $9.98; Age: 7-12. Unapix/Miramar.

** Incredible Genie, The

 Simon is a brainy but bashful 13-year-old who could use a best friend. That best friend turns out to be a 4,000-year-old genie. Together, they use "hocus pocus" to rouse up some adventure and trouble. *Adult Juror Comments*: Action-packed and full of suspense. Fantasy theme reinforces messages about wishes and friendship. Slightly campy and predictable, but fun anyway. Addresses issues regarding peer pressure. Contains some profanity. Adults loved it. *Kid Juror Comments*: "Cool. Everyone loves a fairy tale." Kids wished it was a true story. They talked about wishes, believing that "only clear wishes can be granted." "I liked when the Genie changed Simon into a king." They liked how conflict is handled. Video. 91 min.; $9.99; Age: 8-12. Paramount Home Entertainment.

*** Iron Giant, The (The Iron Giant)

 Features all-star cast, including Jennifer Aniston and Cloris Leachman, in a story of a young boy and a 50-foot robot who discover the power of friendship and learn rewarding lessons. *Adult Juror Comments*: Heartwarming, feel-good, child-centered parable which delivers a message about anti-violence and hope. Military stereotyping generated discussion. Excellent animation. Contains violence that is relevant to telling the story. *Kid Juror Comments*: Enjoyed the rural Maine setting. Felt sorry for the Iron Giant. Some were glued to the screen. "Hogarth was afraid of the Iron Giant, but he saved him anyway." "It showed how to be friendly to someone who is different from you." Video. 86 min.; $22.95; Age: 8-12. Warner Home Video.

Age 8-12

Video

Family

** It's Not Always Easy Being a Kid

Young Charlie struggles to regain his self-esteem after failures at school. He's encouraged to aim at real accomplishment instead of trying to "be cool" by smoking. *Adult Juror Comments*: Production is heavy-handed in delivering messages about not smoking. Tends to rely heavily on narration. Audio is difficult to understand. Uses puppets as positive role models, but they tend to be fairly preachy. *Kid Juror Comments*: Children enjoyed the puppets. This is suitable for early adolescents who are dealing with peer pressure. However, using the Tortoise and Hare fable as a smoking metaphor is a confusing way to deliver the message. Video. 15 min.; $19.95; Age: 7-10. Judy Theatre, The.

** Jacob Have I Loved

A 16-year-old girl (Bridget Fonda) wishes she can leave her isolated Chesapeake Bay community and escape the shadow of her beautiful and talented twin (Jenny Robertson). A turn of events moves her from jealousy to self-realization. *Adult Juror Comments*: Beautiful production, great scenery. Helps audience focus inward and think about their own interactions with others and why they behave the way they do. Respectful of children's abilities; speaks openly about the destruction of hate and jealousy. *Kid Juror Comments*: Very appealing title on a subject not often talked about—twins not liking each other. Parts are sad; the girl kept getting ignored and left alone. "I liked when the girl was with her dad." "I like movies about kids having adventures." Video. 60 min.; $14.95; Age: 8-12. BWE Entertainment.

* James and the Giant Peach

A literary, imaginative tale about a little boy who journeys to a wondrous city "where dreams come true." *Adult Juror Comments*: A frightening representation of the book, with nightmarish imagery, extremely cruel adults, and violent fights between insects. Beautiful production that combines live action and animation. Intense and not suitable for all kids. *Kid Juror Comments*: Kids liked this even though they found it scary. One child had nightmares afterwards. Some were inspired to read the book. Kids enjoyed the vibrant characters. Video. 79 min.; $19.99; Age: 7-12. Buena Vista Home Entertainment/Disney.

** Jessi and the Mystery of the Stolen Secrets (The Baby-Sitter's Club)

When club secrets are mysteriously leaked to outsiders, the Baby-Sitters go undercover to find the culprit. Bumbling detective work makes things worse. Can the girls solve the mystery or is it the end of the Baby-Sitters Club? *Adult Juror Comments*: Good plot and entertaining production. It deals with issues, such as privacy, that children this age can relate to. Good discussion-starter. *Kid Juror Comments*: Kids loved this. Captures this age group's attention. Kids enjoy the story and the characters. Boys enjoyed it as well as girls. Video. 30 min.; $14.95; Age: 7-14. Warner Home Video.

** Jet Pink (The Pink Panther Cartoon Collection)

Clear the funway. It's an all-out "air-farce" as the Pink Panther tries to earn his military wings and go from top cat to Top Gun. Buckle up for a close encounter with an alarming clock, a hapless house painter, and a gang of gunslingers. *Adult Juror Comments*: Well-produced. Clever, entertaining even though it's predictable. The best value of cartoons is their zaniness. Action-packed. Does feature variety of cartoon violence and unsafe behavior. There is hitting, falling, and lots of sight gags. *Kid Juror Comments*: Kids thought it was extremely funny. They got a kick out of the creative problem-solving, brainstorming, and imagination. "I want to watch it again." They loved when the Pink Panther was painting everything pink while the painter was painting it blue. Video. 51 min.; $12.95; Age: 7-12. MGM/UA Home Entertainment.

*** Johnny Mysto: Boy Wizard

Aspiring magician Johnny Mysto can't get his magic to work, until he receives a mysterious ring from his hero, the Great Blackmoor. Johnny makes his sister disappear with his new magic, and must travel back in time to find her. *Adult Juror Comments*: Engaging. Well-produced. Introduces King Arthur tale. "This is a 'toe-gripper,' full of magic, adventure, mystery, suspense, and humor." "Encourages thinking and recall." Contains some profanity and lacks diversity. *Kid Juror Comments*: Kids were mesmerized. "When the magic ring glowed, it was awesome." Motivated kids to want to learn more. "I want to know more about Merlin." "The magic tricks were great." Kids would definitely watch it again. "My friends would love this." Video. 87 min.; $9.99; Age: 8-12. Paramount Home Entertainment.

** Johnny Tsunami, See Page 243.

** Johnny Tsunami, See Page 243.

** Journey Begins, The (Tell Me Who I Am)

Contains original stories, captivating music, and positive messages for the entire family. Traces the time-travel adventures of Nia, an African princess, and her magical pet, Funzi the Fuzzwuzz, as they learn about famous African-American heroes. *Adult Juror Comments*: Appealing, cute characters, good story, great music. Presents positive African-American historical figures. Good preparation for learning science, history, language, and black history. "Best part is when they tell what's real and what's not." *Kid Juror Comments*: The music was a hit. The story confused them when it jumps between past and present. Kids like the ending that explains what was real and wasn't. Most kids liked the game "Tell Me Who I Am" and the music even if they couldn't understand all of it. Video. 35 min.; $19.9; Age: 7-12. Kid Positive.

*** *Kayla: A Cry in the Wilderness (DVD)*

Pubescent Sam befriends a wild dog. Pressure to destroy the dog strains Sam's family. The townspeople fear the dog, because wild dogs kill livestock. Kayla wins over the townspeople by leading Sam's sled to victory in the annual race. *Adult Juror Comments*: "Full of life's lessons with examples of both positive and negative interactions. A real conversation starter to help kids understand the many changes all children encounter." Some violence and killing of animals. *Kid Juror Comments*: Drama and excitement made it good. Wind and nature sounds are good. "We want to know more about Canada." "I liked seeing the boy get past his hurt and accept a new family." Video. 86 min.; $19.99; Age: 10-18. Questar, Inc.

*** *Keeping the Promise*

A young boy stays alone in the wilderness protecting his family's land claim until they can reunite. As weeks turn into months, Matt is transformed when Penobscot Indians befriend him. Based on a novel by Elizabeth George Speare. Stars Keith Carradine. *Adult Juror Comments*: Well-produced. Shows the respect, honor, and friendship in relationships between American pioneers and Native Americans. Examines hardships early settlers endured, and the responsibilities a 13-year-old faces with bravery and maturity. *Kid Juror Comments*: Enjoyed sounds, scenery, and learning how the Indians lived. "I could see what life was like then." "I learned why the Indians hated white people—because they killed them." "Made me think about how I would act if I was left alone." Video. 98 min.; $29.95; Age: 8-18. Questar, Inc.

*** *Keeping the Promise (DVD)*

Thirteen-year-old Matt is left alone in the wilderness of Maine in 1768 to protect his family's claim. He is befriended by Penobscot Indians who teach him how to survive. Special DVD features give background information and questions for discussion. *Adult Juror Comments*: Moving story, well–produced, and enhanced with DVD capabilities. "The DVD feedback option is wonderful for promoting discussion." "The ease of going from scene to scene was a great benefit." Good historical information and author's biography. *Kid Juror Comments*: Liked the adventure story. DVD features easy to operate for most. "I liked the way we could go back to different sections, like when they were shooting arrows." "It showed a lot about hunting and building a cabin." "Matt got along with the Indians." DVD. 102 min.; $24.95; Age: 8-12. Questar, Inc.

Age 8-12

Video

Family

** *Kid Cop*

Determined to follow in his father's footsteps, eleven-year-old Peter Hanson wants to be a policeman. He helps his Dad's former partner, Frank, solve local crimes along with his crime-fighting partner, Lisa. *Adult Juror Comments*: Lots of action. Well-produced. Provides good role models for conflict resolution and helping. Interesting story. Lacks cultural diversity. No weapons are used even though it's about cops. Encourages critical thinking. *Kid Juror Comments*: Captivating. Motivated interest in the work of detectives. "I want to be a conflict manager." "I learned to stand up for myself." "I liked how the boy solved problems for the grownups." "It made me laugh at the antics of the criminals." Video. 93 min.; $9.99; Age: 6-12. Paramount Home Entertainment.

*** *Kiki's Delivery Service*

The night comes for Kiki, an aspiring young witch, to follow her dream and embark on the experience of a lifetime. She discovers that the confidence she needs to overcome the challenges of growing up is within herself and not in her magic. *Adult Juror Comments*: Charming. Positive role models, great cinematography. Deals with typical issues for young people such as acceptance by peers and showing kindness. Shows how goals can be reached if one doesn't give up. "Best I've seen in a long time." *Kid Juror Comments*: Engaging. Lots of discussion followed the screening. Kids related to Kiki trying to reach her goal and failing along the way. "It's hard to know what you want to be." "I liked the song, 'If I can make life better, then I'm going to fly.'" Video. 103 min.; $19.99; Age: 8-12. Buena Vista Home Entertainment/ Disney.

*** *Knight in Camelot, A (Wonderful World of Disney)*

Whoopie Goldberg stars as a modern-day scientist who's flung back in time to 6th century England, where her attempts to make "improvements" produce comical results. *Adult Juror Comments*: Captivating. An enchanting story for children and families to share. Beautifully produced. Accurate portrayal of medieval England's culture and social structure. Models the values of courage, honor, equality, and respect with a touch of humor. *Kid Juror Comments*: Riveted. Would definitely watch again. "I would love to travel back in time." "I noticed that the Nobles were unkind to the Serfs, but that's how it really was." "I want to read the Mark Twain book that the story is based on." "The castle was awesome." Video. 88 min.; $14.99; Age: 8-12. Buena Vista Home Entertainment/Disney.

** Kristy and the Great Campaign (The Baby-Sitter's Club)

Kristy and the Baby-Sitters hit the campaign trail for a new girl who they think is terrific, but a little shy. When they offer to manage her campaign, the question is, "Does Kristy really want Courtney to win or her opponent to lose?" *Adult Juror Comments*: Good story line but predictable. Appeals to girls more than boys. Interactions are gender-stereotyped. *Kid Juror Comments*: Kids familiar with the books liked it although they thought parts were corny. Video. 30 min.; $12.95; Age: 7-10. Warner Home Video.

*** Larger Than Life

They say an elephant never forgets, but this is an elephant you'll never forget. Vera, a four-ton bundle of fun, brings a trunk full of love, laughter, and excitement to this adventure. Stars Bill Murray and Janine Garofalo. *Adult Juror Comments*: Humorous, enjoyable story that is visually appealing and a little offbeat. Offers insights into humane animal treatment, training, and transporting an elephant. Scenes with Hispanics and Indians were poorly done. Some sexual innuendo and exaggeration. *Kid Juror Comments*: "It was fun, slow at times." "We liked when Bill Murray started being nice to the elephant." Kids appreciated the creative camera angles, and made note that all the main characters were white. Good script, age-appropriate. Video. 93 min.; $14.95; Age: 7-12. MGM/UA Home Entertainment.

* Last Winter, The

A ten-year-old country boy learns to accept change and his family's decision to move to the city. *Adult Juror Comments*: Contains mature themes on moving, death, and young love. Contains some profanity, nudity, a sub-plot of marriage between cousins, and a mother who shoots a deer to show her glee with a new shotgun. We recommend it be shown with adult supervision. *Kid Juror Comments*: Kids had mixed reactions to this. Some thought it was "weird" and did not like it. Children though the story was sad, but it made them talk about loss, grief, and fear of change afterwards. Kids' response varied according to their maturity. Video. 103 min.; $92.98; Age: 8-12. Twentieth Century Fox Home Entertainment.

*** Leonardo: A Dream of Flight (Inventors' Specials)

Family drama stars Brent Carveras as Leonardo da Vinci, the 15th-century genius obsessed with flying, and David Felton as Roberto, the young boy he takes under his wing. *Adult Juror Comments*: Interesting story, quality production, visually appealing. Historically accurate. Introduces the concept of flight. Presents the reality of what it's like to be a genius. Suitable for use in a classroom and for home viewing. *Kid Juror Comments*: Terrific. Kids wanted to learn more about Leonardo da Vinci. Several did independent research on da Vinci after watching this. "I learned a lot." "This was better than any of the books I have read about Leonardo." Video. 48 min.; $19.95; Age: 9-14. Devine Entertainment Corp.

Age 8-12

Video

Family

** *Les Miserables (Animated Classics Collection)*

Against a vivid backdrop spanning 40 of the most exciting years in French history, Victor Hugo's timeless novel springs to life. A tale of love and sacrifice, sin and redemption, and one man's struggle to make a place for himself. *Adult Juror Comments*: Well–produced; however, the story is confusing and difficult to follow. Understanding causes of conflict in French society after the French Revolution is required to understand the story line. May encourage further study. *Kid Juror Comments*: Led to history discussion and possible desire to read the original text. Kids asked clarification questions. "These are famous stories we should know." "Showed how to treat others." Video. 60 min.; $19.95; Age: 8-14. Just for Kids Home Video/Celebrity Home Entertainment.

* *Life with Louie: The Masked Chess Boy (Life with Louie)*

Louie discovers he's got a knack for chess, but hides his identity at the all-school tournament. Share the fun as Louie inspires his pals to reach for their dreams without worrying about what other kids say. *Adult Juror Comments*: Although the characters are stereotyped and sarcastic, it addresses an issue that almost all children face—peer pressure. It's almost too exaggerated, bordering on being demeaning. It stereotypes "smart" kids. *Kid Juror Comments*: Children liked the cartoon and enjoyed how Louie and his father came together in the end. May provoke an interest in learning to play chess. Boys liked Louie in a mask. Some voices were hard to understand. Video. 21 min.; $5.98; Age: 7-11. Twentieth Century Fox Home Entertainment.

** *Liszt's Rhapsody (The Composers' Specials)*

Set in Budapest in 1846, this program celebrates the inextinguishable flame of genuine talent shown by a free-spirited eleven-year-old gypsy boy who inspires a frustrated Franz Liszt to reach his own potential. *Adult Juror Comments*: Introduces classical music through a biographical sketch of a composer's life with a fictional side involving a child co-star thrown in. Quality production, beautiful costumes and sets. Historical characters are well-presented. A little slow-moving. *Kid Juror Comments*: Kids had mixed reactions to this. Some thought it was boring, had an uninteresting plot, and that only kids interested in music would like it. Those interested in piano or violin music enjoyed learning about Liszt. They enjoyed the child character. Video. 49 min.; $19.95; Age: 8-12. Devine Entertainment Corp.

** Little Ghost

Twelve-year-old Kevin meets a 300-year-old eleven-year-old ghost named Sofia. They partner up to help Sofia save her castle from being turned into a health spa and get Kevin's mom's evil boyfriend out of their lives forever. *Adult Juror Comments*: A light-hearted, appealing tale for both adults and kids. Prompts social and emotional problem-solving common in single parent families. Kevin and Sofia resolve their problems without losing a sense of kindness, respect, or honesty. *Kid Juror Comments*: Enjoyed the story. Cheered when Kevin and Sofia won against the mom's boyfriend. Kids related to issues such as feeling left out when the single parent pursued a career or introduced a potential new parent. They liked the happy ending. Video. 88 min.; $9.99; Age: 8-12. Paramount Home Entertainment.

*** Little Lord Fauntleroy

A poor boy discovers he is heir to a vast fortune. He goes to live with his miserly grandfather and brings joy to all who know him. Eventually, he softens even the old man's heart. Based on the classic novel by Frances Hodgson Burnett. *Adult Juror Comments*: A heart-wrenching story for boys. The compassion and kindness of the main character is refreshing. Plot is clear and moves along smoothly. Contains historically accurate costumes with updated language. Exemplifies entertainment with a message. *Kid Juror Comments*: Held kids' attention. They enjoyed learning a few things about this time period and setting. "They showed how being a kind, good, and friendly person pays off. And, they did it in a fun way." "I liked it and can't wait to watch it again." Video. 100 min.; $14.98; Age: 7-12. Twentieth Century Fox Home Entertainment.

*** Little Match Girl

Recast in the future, this classic story sensitively recounts the trials of a poor, homeless little girl. Narrated by F. Murray Abraham, animated and directed by Michael Sporn. *Adult Juror Comments*: Good story line, illustrates the trials of being homeless, though not accurately reflecting conditions of homeless people today. Offers simplistic solutions. Has its light moments and good repeat viewing value. It's too scary for children under six. *Kid Juror Comments*: Kids liked the movie, although some misinterpreted the plot. They thought it was a happy movie even though it had its sad parts. Afterwards, they discussed ways they could help the homeless in their own community. Video. 28 min.; $9.98; Age: 8-12. Artisan/Family Home Entertainment.

** Little Mermaid II, The: Return to the Sea, See Page 248.

*** Loretta Claiborne Story, The (Wonderful World of Disney)*

  A young woman overcomes profound social and physical hardships to become a celebrated African-American athlete. *Adult Juror Comments*: Bright and inspirational. Timeless message of unselfish love that can be watched time and again. "An action show, not in the typical sense, but because of the action it makes you want to take action to believe in people." *Kid Juror Comments*: Responded with great empathy. "We need to watch more movies like this so we can show more respect to special people." "They did a great job with this true story." "It made me sad but very happy." "When it's this good, it deserves a good rating." Video. 90 min.; rental only; Age: 8-14. Buena Vista Home Entertainment/Disney.

* Love Bug, The, See Page 249.

* Mail to the Chief (Wonderful World of Disney)

 A middle-school boy strikes up an on-line friendship with someone bearing the screen name of "Average Joe," only to discover that he's corresponding with the President of the United States. *Adult Juror Comments*: Humorous production that dumbs down the political characters. Kenny is a nerd who is down-to-earth with realistic troubles. Draws parallels between the presidential advisors and the hero's peers putting pressure on both of them. Values clear thinking. *Kid Juror Comments*: Enjoyable. Shows how even when kids tell the truth sometimes their parents don't believe them. "It made me want to check out political sites and learn more about politics." The audio was hard to understand at times. Video. min.; rental only; Age: 8-14. Buena Vista Home Entertainment/Disney.

*** Marie Curie: More Than Meets the Eye (Inventors' Specials)

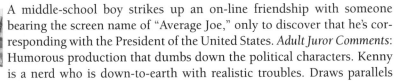 The Boudreau sisters are determined to aid the war effort by catching German spies. Madame Curie is a prime suspect. She is in fact helping save lives through her research, and the sisters learn that curiosity is essential to science and life. *Adult Juror Comments*: Excellent use of historical fiction as a teaching tool. Made kids think, debate, and form their own opinions. Nice web of humor, mystery, and facts that catch the imagination. Brings scientific discovery to children's level. *Kid Juror Comments*: Kids enjoyed learning how X-rays were discovered, about important women in science and World War I in France. "I liked figuring out all the pieces of the story." "It looked scary, but it ended up to be a good thing. It made science fun." Video. 54 min.; $19.95; Age: 8-12. Devine Entertainment Corp.

** Mary Anne and the Brunettes (The Baby-Sitter's Club)

Mary Anne likes Logan Bruno. So does Marci, the most popular girl in the eighth grade. Will Mary Anne lose Logan because she's too shy? *Adult Juror Comments*: Addresses teen-agers' dating behavior. Story line is rather trite, predictable, and shows gender stereotyped "boy-crazed" characters. Jurors objected to the commercials at the beginning of the tape. *Kid Juror Comments*: Kids enjoy the Baby-Sitters, regardless of the stereotyped behaviors. It addresses issues they relate to, and they find it funny. Some objected to the reference to the "beautiful blond hair" and said, "Boo talks down to us." Video. 30 min.; $14.95; Age: 8-14. Warner Home Video.

*** Mary Cassatt: American Impressionist (The Artists' Specials)

Painter Mary Cassatt's tidy life in Paris is disrupted when her brother's family arrives. Soon, she finds herself inspired and uses the children as models. An introduction to Degas leads to fame. *Adult Juror Comments*: Superb, professional production. Endearing cast brings to life an adult storyline that allows for thought and evaluation. Portrays discrimination against women and the social undercurrents of the late 1800s at a level that children can understand. *Kid Juror Comments*: Authentic, interesting, and funny. "The paintings and actors are fun to see and watch." "I liked it when the kids got into the paint fight." "Costumes and hairdos were great for that time." "It showed me a different world." Video. 56 min.; $17.98; Age: 8-14. Devine Entertainment Corp.

*** Mary Poppins, See Page 251.

* Midas Touch, The

Everything Billy Bright touches turns to gold because of a power he acquires when he enters a rundown mansion. There, a mysterious lady grants him one wish, and suddenly money is no longer a problem for Billy. *Adult Juror Comments*: Excellent production quality with interesting special effects. Greed versus generosity theme. Inappropriate language used throughout such as "stupid, shut up, and idiot." Relationship with grandmother was tender and caring. *Kid Juror Comments*: Kept kids in suspense. Slap-stick humor appealed to the kids. "It was cool the way things transformed into gold; it looked realistic." "The kids and the bad guys weren't respectful of one another." They liked the tree house. Would watch again. Video. 92 min.; $9.99; Age: 9-13. Paramount Home Entertainment.

Age 8-12

Video

Family

** *Miracle in Lane 2 (Disney Channel)*

 A 13-year-old boy is determined to win a trophy like his athletic older brother. Along the way, he teaches everyone around him exactly what it means to be a true winner. Rental only. *Adult Juror Comments*: This is the story of a young boy overcoming a great many obstacles to participate in an action sport he loves. Addresses how his whole family deals with his disability. Some adult innuendoes such as the kids finding massage oil in their parents' bedroom. *Kid Juror Comments*: Enjoyable. Held their attention. They found it sad, but exciting, and related to the characters. "I learned about the disease called spina bifida." "It's a story that shows people working together." Video. 89 min.; rental only; Age: 8-12. Buena Vista Home Entertainment/Disney.

*** *Mulan*

Mulan is a young girl who doesn't follow tradition. When her aging father is ordered into battle, she disguises herself as a soldier and takes his place in the army and joins a comedic troop led by Captain Chang. *Adult Juror Comments*: Wonderful music and great animation. Inspirational story with a lot of humor dispersed throughout. Thematic topics include family unity, working hard, and fighting for what is important. *Kid Juror Comments*: Enthralled. Would watch again and recommend to friends. "I liked learning about the Chinese culture, and I'd like to go there someday." "It makes me wonder about girls in other cultures." "Mulan was strong and brave." Video. 88 min.; $22.99; Age: 7-12. Buena Vista Home Entertainment/Disney.

*** *Murder She Purred: A Mrs. Murphy Mystery*, See Page 255.

*** *My Dog Skip*

  When Willie Morris receives a Jack Russell Terrier for his tenth birthday, he and his canine companion (Skip) turn bullies into friends, tangle with hapless moonshiners, and win the affections of the prettiest girl in school. *Adult Juror Comments*: Full of coming-of-age themes with plenty for kids to talk about: love, loss, creativity, and growing up. Good representation of the forties. Brings up civil rights issues. *Kid Juror Comments*: Kids were attentive to the issues presented. "It showed how a boy could love a dog so much." The ending is very sad, most felt that the dog didn't need to die. "Friendship is important even between people and their pets." Video. 95 min.; $22.96; Age: 8-18. Warner Home Video.

** New Adventures of Spin and Marty, The: Suspect Behavior (Wonderful World of Disney)

A mystery adventure about two mischievous boys whose wild imaginations lead to more exciting adventures than they ever imagined. Rental only. *Adult Juror Comments*: Entertaining. Well-produced. Fun, suspenseful murder mystery that provokes thought and inquiry. Encourages children to stand up for what they believe in. Has some mature themes and name-calling. *Kid Juror Comments*: Engaged. Liked the music. "It's like a kid's 'Mission Impossible.'" "It was like an adult story, but with good language and characters." "It teaches kids not to jump to conclusions or to blame others for something they didn't do." Video. 88 min.; rental only; Age: 8-12. Buena Vista Home Entertainment/Disney.

** New Swiss Family Robinson, The (Wonderful World of Disney)

Jane Seymour and David Carradine star in this contemporary version of the Robinson family who are setting sail for Australia. Along their voyage, the family squares off against modern day pirates, survives a shipwreck, and washes ashore a deserted island. *Adult Juror Comments*: Good adventure. Deals with sensitive subjects such as growing up and sexuality. Contains some violence such as hitting. Reinforces resolving family conflict. "Makes you wonder how your own family would handle the situation." *Kid Juror Comments*: Story held children's interest. "The natural settings, animals, and characters are great." "It was neat how they built their house and had to learn to live alone on the island." "Too much teen-age love stuff." The story is sometimes confusing. Video. 89 min.; $14.99; Age: 8-12. Buena Vista Home Entertainment/Disney.

*** Newton: A Tale of Two Isaacs (Inventors' Specials)

Like a comet blazing across the night sky, Isaac Newton's original theories on celestial movement and gravity jolted the Royal Academy in 1683. His young scribe finds even the greatest men must overcome personal tragedies to achieve success. *Adult Juror Comments*: Engaging historical fiction. An example of how mathematics, curiosity, and problem-solving interrelate. Biographical content on Newton is personal and easy to understand. Demonstration of Newton's laws of motion is wonderfully done. *Kid Juror Comments*: Kids enjoyed problem-solving and solutions that relate to their own perspective. Liked the proverbial apple falling on Newton's head, which gave him the idea of gravity. "The science scenes were neat." "I liked the costumes and the sets." Video. 51 min.; $19.95; Age: 8-12. Devine Entertainment Corp.

** Noah (Wonderful World of Disney)

A cut-rate general contractor, a mid-level executive in heaven, and a kind-hearted pet shop owner find themselves unlikely cohorts in this contemporary version of the biblical patriarch who built an ark and filled it with animals. Stars Tony Danza. *Adult Juror Comments*: Well-produced, humorous, encourages moral and spiritual thinking and reflection. The concept that adults can change their behavior and continue to learn the values of children is very appealing. Contains some sexual innuendoes. *Kid Juror Comments*: Kids enjoyed it, loved all the animals. "I was glad when the dad finally went to his son's ball game." "I didn't like the kissing." "The ark was really cool." "Everyone in the town was his family." Video. 89 min.; $14.99; Age: 8-14. Buena Vista Home Entertainment/Disney.

* Nuttiest Nutcracker, The (The Nuttiest Nutcracker)

Set during a snowstorm, lonely and distraught teen-aged Marie sits by the window waiting for her parents to arrive. As she closes her eyes and begins to fall asleep, the fun-filled, madcap adventures begin. *Adult Juror Comments*: An unusual twist on a familiar tale. Fascinating use of computer graphics and choice of music. Basic good versus evil theme. Places value on helping others. Shows some unsafe behavior such as the king on a ladder, and has some sexual innuendoes. *Kid Juror Comments*: Story is hard to follow at first, but it held their attention. Cute, silly. Some kids thought it was way too slow; others loved it. "I liked the puns, the humor, and the sound effects." "My little brother would really like this." Video. 48 min.; $14.95; Age: 5-9. Columbia Tristar Home Entertainment.

*** Our Favorite Bears (Game Warden Wildlife Journal)

Dedicated to the men and women who protect bears and their habitat. Tells about black bears in Arizona, grizzlies in Wyoming, newborn cubs in Ontario, and the polar bear police in Manitoba. *Adult Juror Comments*: Well-produced, interesting, appeals to adults and kids. Raises good questions about environmental issues. Good diversity shown. "Respects what people are doing to save bears." *Kid Juror Comments*: Enjoyable. "I didn't know that dogs were used to train bears." "I never knew there were polar bear police in Canada. That would be a cool job." "My favorite part was the scene with the cute bear cubs." Video. 40 min.; $12.95; Age: 8-12.Creative Street.

** *Our Lips Are Sealed (DVD)*

Mary-Kate and Ashley Olsen have to join the witness protection program and travel halfway around the world to escape the mob. Once in Australia, it's a struggle to keep quiet about their real identities. Action, laughs, super spies and surfer guys. Adult Juror Comments: Very appealing. Clever story with almost cartoonish comedic style. Tasteful clothes, clean language, and even the bad guys have a certain restraint. Has educational value: teens learn to keep their mouths shut. DVD features include outtakes and trailers. Kid Juror Comments: Girls liked it best. "It's a junior chick flick with action." Got everyone doing Australian slang and accents. All enjoyed the scenery and soundtrack. "The music was put in just the right spots." "There were a lot of kids and action, just a great movie." DVD. 90 min.; $24.98; Age: 8-14. Warner Home Video.

*** *Outback Grand Prix and Other Stories,* See Page 258.

*** *Party with Zoom,* See Page 259.

** *Passport to Paris (Mary-Kate & Ashley Olsen)*

Mary-Kate & Ashley go to Paris to visit their grandfather. They fall in love with France and fall head-over-heels for two French boys. *Adult Juror Comments*: Well-produced, beautifully illustrates Paris. Story presents a theme of young love in an appropriate manner. Shows how kids can make a difference in the lives of others. Some found the stereotyping of white middle-class kids who love to shop annoying. *Kid Juror Comments*: Kids enjoyed it. "My friends will really like this." "Riding the motor scooter through Paris looks like fun." "It was cool when grandpa changed his attitude in the end." "I like the way it showed lots of different people working together." Video. 80 min.; $19.96; Age: 9-12. Warner Home Video.

** *Peanut Butter Solution, The (Les Productions La Fête)*

An eleven-year-old hero investigates a haunted house and gets so frightened that all of his hair falls out. A magic recipe to make his hair grow back produces astonishing results. *Adult Juror Comments*: Challenging and imaginative tape with an interesting and creative plot. Challenges children's critical thinking skills. Technical qualities are low, uses the word God as an expletive throughout. Kidnapping scene could scare young children. *Kid Juror Comments*: Kids laughed and talked about the program. The children thought that the plot developed slowly, but the excitement at the end was enjoyed by all. Kids said they would recommend it to friends. Some may have difficulty with the French-Canadian accent. Video. 90 min.; $29.95; Age: 7-12. Productions La Fête.

Age 8-12

Video

Family

*** *People*

 PEOPLE Cara and her lovable grandfather embark on a journey of imagination that brings them face to face with the wonderful variety of people in the world. Based on Peter Spier's book. Music by Al Jarreau, Chaka Kan, Grover Washington Jr, Vanessa Williams. *Adult Juror Comments*: Original. Deals with the difficult topic of divorce. The content is rendered sensitively, yet makes its point about celebrating diversity and cultural differences with positive stereotyping. Varied animation styles. "Flashes of brilliance." *Kid Juror Comments*: Great music. Kids loved it. Fast-paced animation style appeals to kids more than adults. Kids liked the rap music section with Heavy D a lot. Kids relate to characters, dialogue, and the topics discussed. "Cara was goody-goody." Video. 54 min.; $12.95; Age: 8-12. Stories to Remember.

** *Perfect Game*

A young boy and his rag-tag baseball team are determined to overcome all odds and be winners. Stars Edward Asner and Patrick Duffy. *Adult Juror Comments*: Inspiring, uplifting, and engaging story of a come-back softball team. The ending reinforces the idea that winning at any cost is a bad philosophy. Has good believable characters with some mild gender stereotyping. Contains some profanity. *Kid Juror Comments*: Kids were engaged by the whole story and the characters. "It was about real people that play baseball—like me!" "I liked when the kids says 'I love this game' after he hits a home run." Video. 97 min.; $19.99; Age: 8-12. Buena Vista Home Entertainment/Disney.

** *Pete's Dragon,* See Page 260.

*** *Peter Pan (Cathy Rigby),* See Page 261.

** *Phantom of the Opera (Animated Classics Collection)*

 For generations, this story of love, music, and madness has inspired countless retellings on the stage and on film. Gaston Leroux's immortal novel leaps from the page to the screen in this animated adaptation. *Adult Juror Comments*: Rather simplistic production. Plot is confusing in parts. Introduces children to opera. The phantom captures children's interest; full of drama, excitement, and the triumph of good over evil. *Kid Juror Comments*: "Exciting, scary, and fun to watch." Kids familiar with story liked the production. It did not appeal to all the children. The killing of the cat was unnecessary and disturbing. Discussion about phantom followed. Video. 60 min.; $19.95; Age: 8-14. Just for Kids Home Video/Celebrity Home Entertainment.

** Pinocchio (Theatre Adventures)

This is an adaptation of a stage production of the classic tale of Pinocchio, the wooden puppet. Performed in the style of commedia dell'arte, Professor McNamer and sidekick Preston host the play with behind-the-scenes commentary. *Adult Juror Comments*: True to the original, it addresses the story's place in Italian history. However, this genre—videotaping stage productions—does not have high appeal to children. Appears to be too schoolish. Shows good diversity. *Kid Juror Comments*: Some children liked the production, but found the story line confusing. Some found it boring. It led to a discussion about responsibility. "I like the colorful artwork, costumes, music, and humor." "I didn't like the masks on the characters." Video. 94 min.; $27; Age: 7-12. Globalstage.

* Please Don't Eat the Daisies (Family Treasures)

When sudden fame goes to a drama critic's head, it's up to his family to get his feet back on the ground in this light and frothy comedy that generates laughs for all. *Adult Juror Comments*: This old-fashioned story has many elements and wholesome values, but is somewhat dated. The four brothers are mischievous characters. *Kid Juror Comments*: Kids didn't get some of the social interactions. They liked the part with the kids the best. Video. 111 min.; $14.95; Age: 8-12. MGM/UA Home Entertainment.

*** Pocahontas, See Page 262.

*** Pocahontas II Journey to a New World, See Page 263.

** Pooch and the Pauper, The, See Page 263.

** Pride, Prejudice and Fudge (Little Dogs on the Prairie)

A new animation series featuring the antics of a cast of prairie dogs from the Old (not too old!) West. Packed with zany stories and original songs designed to entertain and present children Bible-based values. *Adult Juror Comments*: Very positive and funny. Good animation and sound. Cute prairie dogs are an indirect way to teach children how to behave and treat one another. Well-suited for Christian families. "The adult who viewed it with us was in stitches." *Kid Juror Comments*: Got the jokes and learned the lessons. "It would be even funnier to watch it again." "Sometimes we don't treat people very well, but we learned that it is wrong." "I've been mad for silly things before." "If we were grading, we would say 100 percent." Video. 35 min.; $14.99; Age: 9-14. Fancy Monkey Studios.

Age 8-12

Video

Family

** Quick and the Fed, The (Reboot)

Dot is partially erased by a magnet. Bob races against time to return her to normal, a difficult task made worse by the hostile dragons, knights, and skeletons of a descended Game Cube. *Adult Juror Comments*: Filled with sophisticated humor, good computer-generated animation, and suspense. Contains scary images and characters, lots of sword fighting, combat and destruction. Filled with computer-related jokes. *Kid Juror Comments*: Kids enjoyed this. They liked the jokes. Kept their attention. Kids were eager to discuss what went on afterwards. Video. 25 min.; $12.95; Age: 8-12. U.S.A. Home Entertainment.

*** Ready to Run, See Page 266.

*** Real Macaw, The

  Tells about a 150-year-old parrot with an attitude. The parrot and a teenage boy head out in search of buried treasure so that they can save the boy's grandfather from having to move into a retirement home. *Adult Juror Comments*: Exciting, well-polished, and believable story, wonderful scenery. Encourages problem-solving skills, honesty, assertiveness and respect for elders. *Kid Juror Comments*: Enchanting. Kids were fascinated by the pirates, tropical islands, and talking parrots. They wanted to hunt for treasure themselves. "It showed me how kids can help solve problems without doing bad things." Video. 92 min.; $19.95; Age: 8-13. Paramount Home Entertainment.

* Rebecca of Sunnybrook Farm, See Page 266.

*** Rembrandt: Fathers and Sons (The Artists' Specials)

  The successful painter, Rembrandt, takes on a young Jewish studio apprentice. The boy's struggle to achieve his own goals leads Rembrandt to defy artistic convention with his painting, "The Night Watch." *Adult Juror Comments*: Highly emotional and poignant production. Rich tapestry of art, history, and human nature woven together with forgiveness, responsibility, and commitment. Provides a window to the world of the past. Presents Jewish traditions in a positive way. *Kid Juror Comments*: Excellent artistic video with an appealing and sad story. "The people were the story. It showed the Jews relating to Christians very well." "I liked Rembrandt. I liked it when he made faces." "I want to learn more about art." Video. 53 min.; $17.98; Age: 8-14. Devine Entertainment Corp.

* Return of Tommy Tricker, The (The Stamp Traveller)

Tommy Tricker and his friends are out to free Charles Merriweather, the mysterious lad held prisoner on a famous Bluenose stamp. But, Charles turns out to be a girl—his sister Molly. *Adult Juror Comments*: It helps to have seen the first Tommy Tricker film to understand the story. The acting and dialogue are somewhat stilted, the production awkward, and the plot is unclear. "I liked the time travel and focus on problem-solving by the children." *Kid Juror Comments*: "It didn't make sense. I think they were trying to find a kid on a stamp that was stolen." Kids thought that characters were mean to one another. There is a scene with a kid urinating on a pole that bothered some. "Time traveling through stamps is cool." Video. 97 min.; $14.98; Age: 8-12. Productions La Fête.

*** Return to the Secret Garden

  Although Katherine has everything going for her, a close friendship eludes her until she arrives at Misselthwaite Manor in England. With her sickly cousin and a boy named Timothy, she unravels a mystery and discovers what friendship really means. *Adult Juror Comments*: Excellent family viewing. Pleasing, beautiful production. Delightful way of showing the value of friendship. Contemporary treatment of the classic may be more appealing to today's children. Good introduction into upper class English lifestyle. *Kid Juror Comments*: Awesome. "Interesting, funny, and cool." "I like adventure. I know how the kids felt." "I liked how the movie looked and sounded—especially the flute part." "The garden was supposed to be alive." "Showed that a garden can grow with friendship." Video. 90 min.; $12.95; Age: 8-12. Feature Films for Families.

* Road to El Dorado, The

 Two con men seek riches and glory as they search for the legendary El Dorado, the City of Gold. Their friendship develops through the action and deception that occurs on the well-traveled path to easy fortune. *Adult Juror Comments*: Interesting mix of humor and greed. Con men lie, cheat, and gamble without much consequence. Yet their friendship wins out over their selfishness. Superior sound track and animation. Loosely depicts early Europeans in the New World. Some profanity. *Kid Juror Comments*: Good adventure story. Unusual and interesting. "Sound was awesome and current. We tried listening for individual instruments." "Friends trust each other even if they make a mistake." The Aztecs tried to sacrifice some people, but the heroes refuse it. Video. 89 min.; $24.99; Age: 8-12. Dreamworks.

** Robin Hood, See Page 268.

** Robin of Locksley (Hallmark Hall of Fame)

After his parents win the lottery, archery and computer whiz Robin McCallister is put in Locksley, a private boys school. Disgusted by the rich bullies there, he concocts a brilliant, daring plan to help a poor classmate. Stars Sarah Chalke. *Adult Juror Comments*: Clever version of Robin Hood story with good use of characters. Excellent production quality. Addresses ethics in a high-tech world. Shows compassion. *Kid Juror Comments*: Appeals to action-oriented children. They found it interesting placing an old story in a contemporary setting. It piqued their interest in the Internet and archery. Video. 97 min.; $9.98; Age: 10-16. Artisan/Family Home Entertainment.

** Rookie of The Year

When a young boy's broken arm heals, he finds he can throw a baseball with awesome speed. Soon he's in the major leagues on his way to the World Series. *Adult Juror Comments*: Fun fantasy. Contains some socially inappropriate actions, such as insults from the coach in the opening scene, the mother punching her boyfriend and saying, "I should have killed him." Overall, enjoyable, nicely paced; girls and boys both like this. *Kid Juror Comments*: Children liked this very much. One girl in the group said, "I liked the characters even though it's a 'boy' story." Video. 103 min.; $14.98; Age: 8-12. Twentieth Century Fox Home Entertainment.

** Rossini's Ghost (The Composers' Specials)

Reliana is transported back in time to a theatre in which Rossini is about to launch "The Barber of Seville." Invisible to everyone but Rossini, Reliana watches her grandmother and a friend fight over the composer and the opera's disastrous premiere. *Adult Juror Comments*: Beautifully done, lovely costumes and sets. Filled with facts and information. The story depends a lot on the background narration and is sometimes confusing. Somewhat didactic in presenting history and meaning of the opera. Good friendship models. *Kid Juror Comments*: Stimulated children's interest in the opera and William Tell. "I like the line 'friends are like money—hard to get and easy to throw away.'" "I liked the ghost." Girls liked it more than boys, especially the romantic climax. Video. 52 min.; $19.95; Age: 8-12. Devine Entertainment Corp.

** Ruby Bridges (Wonderful World of Disney)

In 1960, six-year-old Ruby scores well on her scholastic tests, and is chosen to be the first African American to integrate a local school. She is exposed to racism for the first time. With support of teachers and friends, she becomes a moral inspiration. *Adult Juror Comments*: "Moved me to tears." A complex subject for this age, but explained well. Informs kids of the changes in this country over the years, with a knowledge of segregation and integration. The abusive crowd scenes are a bit scary. Emphasis on religion. *Kid Juror Comments*: "The subject was very sad, and there were a lot of mean-spirited people, but Ruby was strong and wanted to learn more despite their prejudices." Teaches kids about equality in this country. Video. 89 min.; $14.99; Age: 8-12. Buena Vista Home Entertainment/Disney.

** *Rugrats in Paris: The Movie (Rugrats).*

Stu Pickles is summoned to work at Paris' newest amusement park, and the Rugrat kids learn valuable lessons in courage, loyalty and true love and find that fun is the same in any language. *Adult Juror Comments*: Well produced, action packed story. Good example of contemporary animation. Pure fun. Heartwarming story speaks to children of one-parent households. Bathroom humor offends some adults but is developmentally on-target. *Kid Juror Comments*: Riveted. Kids were on the edge of their seats and full of laughter. "This was really funny." "Jessica can be mean but she's just a little kid and doesn't know any better yet." "The Rugrats remind me of my little brothers." Video. 78 min.; $14.95; Age: 8-12. Paramount Home Entertainment

*** *Saintly Switch, A (Wonderful World of Disney)*

An aging NFL quarterback and his troubled marriage move to New Orleans. In their new house, the kids discover magic and switch their parents' souls. Appreciation is gained as the couple discovers what it is like to walk in the other's shoes. *Adult Juror Comments*: Excellent production quality, funny story— touching and enjoyable. "What a wonderful way to explore who does what and why." "Paves the way for discussion of gender stereotyping." Contains reference to voodoo. *Kid Juror Comments*: Loved it and would watch again. "It was so funny, especially seeing the father pregnant." "That couldn't really happen, but I laughed a lot." "The dad was great." "It's important to listen." "The best part was the spooky attic scene." Video. 88 min.; $14.99; Age: 8-12. Buena Vista Home Entertainment/Disney.

*** *Salt Water Moose*

A young boy's lonely summer turns into the adventure of a lifetime when he comes to the aid of a moose stranded on a nearby island. Timothy Dalton and Lolita Davidovich star in this courageous and heartwarming tale set along the northeastern coast. *Adult Juror Comments*: Good story. Lots of appeal. Supports children's sense of adventure and need for accomplishment. Deals with issues of divorce and equality in sports. Conflicts are handled well. Female character is strong, athletic, smart, and willful. *Kid Juror Comments*: Kids liked this, both the boy and the girl in film, and the girl's relationship with her father. Some boys wanted to buy it. Said one child juror, "Dreams do come true." Video. 90 min.; $14.95; Age: 8-14. Artisan/Family Home Entertainment.

Age 8-12

Video

Family

** Sand Fairy, The

 This story from the BBC tells the tale of children who discover a troll in the sand who will grant them their wish for a day. Teaches children about appreciating what they have. *Adult Juror Comments*: Entertaining, but a little too long. Good movie for discussion about choices and their consequences. Costumes, sets, music, and especially the puppet, were wonderful, serving the period accurately. Has gender stereotypes, lacks cultural diversity. *Kid Juror Comments*: "The Sand Fairy was cool." The kids in the movie were great actors." At times it was hard to understand what the children were saying because of their accents. "Are Sand Fairies real?" "You have to be careful about wishes." "Can we read the book?" Video. 139 min.; $29.98; Age: 6-10. Twentieth Century Fox Home Entertainment.

** Sandlot, The

Kids spend a summer during the '60s playing baseball, noticing girls, and finding out what's really behind that fence. *Adult Juror Comments*: Nice male-bonding story. Fails to include girls in sports. However, girls and boys enjoyed it equally. Talks about some real-life teen issues with harsh realities—feelings, hopes, and dreams. The characters work out their problems without violence. *Kid Juror Comments*: The kids laughed, squealed, tittered, and watched in stunned silence throughout the entire movie. They loved that the story provided thinking opportunities. Video. 101 min.; $14.98; Age: 8-12. Twentieth Century Fox Home Entertainment.

** Scooby-Doo and the Alien Invaders, See Page 271.

*** Seal Morning (DVD)

The discovery of a baby seal brings Rowena, an orphaned teen girl, together with Miriam, her recluse aunt. Soon their tiny cottage becomes a refuge for a menagerie. Set in the 1930s on a remote part of the desolate English coastline. *Adult Juror Comments*: Appealing natural relationships in wildlife. "Encourages people to consider their effect on the environment." Scenes introduce death by killing of animals. Depicts a non-traditional family as they solve daily problems. "It has something for everyone." *Kid Juror Comments*: "You should be nice to others and take care of animals." "Not good; threats of killing the dog and seals." "We like seeing animals in videos; they make it funny and interesting." "Most of our friends would like it, because of the seals and the geese." Video. 103 min.; $19.99; Age: 8-18. Questar, Inc.

** *Secret Garden, The - CBS/Fox*

Mary Lennox, a recently orphaned little girl, is sent to live with her uncle in his oppressive house on the Yorkshire moors. Through the companionship of new friends, they bring life back to the estate and find new strength in themselves. *Adult Juror Comments*: Well-produced, unusual plot. Looks at different cultures; handles universal themes of neglect, boredom, loneliness, friends, and overcoming adversity. *Kid Juror Comments*: Kids thought the pace was too slow. The overall setting is somber, and they thought the girl character was rude. Girls ages four to five enjoyed it best. The British accent was difficult for some. "Looks like a play, not a movie." Video. 107 min.; $14.98; Age: 7-12. Twentieth Century Fox Home Entertainment.

** *Secret Garden, The - MGM/UA*, See Page 271.

*** *Secret Garden, The - Warner Bros.*

One of the best-loved of all children's tales blooms anew in this enchanting version of Frances Hodgson Burnett's turn-of-the-century classic. Brought together at a country house, Mary, Colin, and Dickson discover a locked garden and bring it to life. *Adult Juror Comments*: Kids identify with characters on many levels—losing parents, being part of a family, and learning to understand feelings. Wonderful, universal story. Content is appropriate to this audience. Stimulates students' creativity. *Kid Juror Comments*: Kids are inspired and moved by the emotions present in each of the characters. "No matter what your problems are, you can overcome them." "It must have been taped in a big garden. It was neat." "Awesome, it was the best video ever." Video. 102 min.; $19.98; Age: 7-12. Warner Home Video.

** *Shadow of the Knight*

Johnny and his baby dragon named Yowler are learning the old Celtic ways with Johnny's grandfather. When the Dark Knight escapes from the fairy's magic spell to mercilessly hunt for Yowler, Johnny uses his quick thinking to save them both. *Adult Juror Comments*: Great suspense, delightful, enchanting. Fairy tale in a contemporary setting. Shows how the fear of the unknown can lead to prejudice. Addresses death of a loved one, medieval history, castles, and Celtic myths. The dark knight is scary. *Kid Juror Comments*: Pretty predictable. The dragon wasn't very realistic. They liked how the boy outmaneuvered the Dark Knight. Generated discussion about the social worker taking Johnny after his grandfather dies. "The boy loved his grandfather." Video. 91 min.; $9.99; Age: 8-12. Paramount Home Entertainment.

* Shiloh 2: Shiloh Season (Shiloh Season)

Shiloh is everything young Marty Preston wants in a dog, and a lot more. Through Shiloh's unselfish example, Marty risks everything to turn an enemy into a friend. *Adult Juror Comments*: Well-produced. Addresses emotionally potent topics such as alcoholism, gun use, dog attacks, and a car crash. "Offers potential for in-depth discussion." Best when viewed with an adult. Shiloh is adorable. Shows good conflict resolution role models. *Kid Juror Comments*: Kids had mixed responses. "It was a little scary." "When the Judd started to like Marty, it stopped being so scary." "My friends would all like the dog." "The bad guy's drinking and being mean is just part of showing how bad guys can turn good." Video. 96 min.; $19.96; Age: 10-14. Warner Home Video.

*** Sky Is Gray, The (The American Short Story Collection)

From Ernest J. Gaines, author of *The Autobiography of Miss Jane Pittman*, comes a deceptively simple yet emotionally complex tale of what it is like to be black in Louisiana during the 1940s. *Adult Juror Comments*: A wonderful opportunity for discussion of some very enormous issues—racism, respect, tolerance. Very realistic—music and setting are great. Excellent teaching tool. *Kid Juror Comments*: "Kind of slow, but real good." "No one moved a muscle during the entire video." "Really good movie." Video. 46 min.; $24.95; Age: 6-12. Monterey Home Video.

** Smart House, See Page 273.

*** Sports Illustrated for Kids, Vol. 1 (Sports Illustrated for Kids)

The approach here—"sports as a metaphor for life"—teaches children about responsibility, self-control, and the importance of teamwork. Features Grant Hill, Brett Favre, and Mia Hamm. *Adult Juror Comments*: A great motivational tool. Presents idea that "Hard work equals positive results" and "Learn from your mistakes." The "ask-the-athlete" format makes it real. Provokes an interest in athletic careers for both genders. Fast, entertaining pace. *Kid Juror Comments*: Students were hooked from the beginning—no wiggles, chatting, or inappropriate behavior. They truly enjoyed the program. "It's neat that the kids talked to pros about their games and other things like food and hobbies." It's fun to watch. Video. 50 min.; $14.98; Age: 8-12. Twentieth Century Fox Home Entertainment.

Age 8-12

Video

Family

*** Sports Illustrated for Kids, Vol. 2 (Sports Illustrated for Kids)*

The "sports as a metaphor for life" approach teaches kids about responsibility, self-control, and the importance of teamwork. Volume 2 features Derek Jeter, Venus Williams, and Steve Young. *Adult Juror Comments*: Practice makes perfect. Shows excellent attitudes from positive role models. The athletes' personal lives led to a discussion about hobbies, ability, and endurance. Presents the idea "Take pride in what you do." Excellent production quality. *Kid Juror Comments*: Presents a variety of sports, such as karate and snowboarding. Kids appreciate the honesty of athletes having hard times. "It's nice to know about women in sports." Offers good advice about practicing, teamwork, and working hard to be your best. Video. 50 min.; $14.98; Age: 8-12. Twentieth Century Fox Home Entertainment.

** Stacey Takes a Stand (The Baby-Sitter's Club)*

Stacey is tired of juggling life between two cities. The Baby-Sitters rescue Stacey, reminding her that home is where the heart is. *Adult Juror Comments*: Presents an issue that is significant for many children—pulls of divorced parents and living part-time with both parents. Lively, appealing. Shows children talking things out, offering emotional support, enjoying differences, and problem-solving. *Kid Juror Comments*: Kids liked this, especially the girls. They thought the program could help diffuse the stress of divorced parents. They wanted to see it again. Some felt it was a little corny. Video. 30 min.; $14.95; Age: 7-14. Warner Home Video.

** Stacey's Big Break (The Baby-Sitter's Club)*

Stacey's new career as a fashion model means endless fittings and photo shoots and no time for her friends. Will Stacey choose modeling or her life as one of Stoneybrook's favorite Baby-Sitters? *Adult Juror Comments*: Simple story, but addresses issues relevant to this age group. Girls' values are rather superficial. Contains a lot of gender stereotypes. Some objected to Stacey's pursuit of a modeling career. *Kid Juror Comments*: Kids thought this was okay, but noted that "nobody talks like that." Video. 30 min.; $14.95; Age: 7-14. Warner Home Video.

Age 8-12

Video

Family

** Stay Out of the Basement (Goosebumps)

Margaret's dad starts acting weirdly, spending all his time in the basement. Strange sounds leads to exploration of their father's spooky secret. *Adult Juror Comments*: Sharing a scary experience with another helps children address their fears. In this program, siblings related well to each other by resolving conflicts together. It's full of scary scenes, and the father's behavior is strange. *Kid Juror Comments*: Kids jumped at the chance to watch Goosebumps. It held their attention, especially the eight-year-olds. They liked the plant food that the dad created and seeing the kids help each other. Video. 44 min.; $14.98; Age: 8-12. Twentieth Century Fox Home Entertainment.

** Stories and Other Legends from Other Lands

Folklore beautifully illustrated in styles typical of the country of origin: Germany, Ireland, Israel, and Yugoslavia. *Adult Juror Comments*: Amusing. Great for studying folk tales. Exposes viewer to different myths. Illustrations beautifully represent each story, as does the ethnic music. Contains some nudity and inappropriate behavior such as killing the neighbor's cow. *Kid Juror Comments*: Provoked discussions about wealth and animal rights. Introduced kids to some new stories. Kids were bothered by the name-calling and stealing. "People are not always nice to each other." Video. 23 min.; $19.95; Age: 8-12. Nat'l Film Board of Canada.

** Summer of the Colt (Les Productions La Fête)

On a magnificent ranch in Argentina three children from Buenos Aires visit their grandfather. Explores the sorrows and joys of growing older. *Adult Juror Comments*: Addresses its message with sensitivity while keeping the audience's attention. Shows a beautiful and touching story with some slower moments that allow for reflection. Some jurors objected to the breast-feeding scene. *Kid Juror Comments*: One child watched several times over one weekend. Some kids were bothered by a lip-sync problem. The breast-feeding scene was uncomfortable for some kids. The toilet scene brought about uncomfortable laughter. Video. 96 min.; $19.95; Age: 8-14. Productions La Fête.

* Summer of the Monkeys

Based on the award-winning novel by Wilson Rawls. A twelve-year-old boy, Jay Berry Lee, encounters four runaway circus monkeys who prove to be clever troublemakers. *Adult Juror Comments*: This coming-of-age story deals with a boy's misbehavior and selfishness and his transformation, bringing his family closer together. Insight into a rural family, their community, and their values. The grandfather plays an inspiring role. *Kid Juror Comments*: Learned about the importance of goals, family, and sacrifice. Enjoyed the monkeys' antics and showed some concern about the aggressive behavior of the boy and his peers, and the treatment of the boy's dog. Video. 90 min.; $19.99; Age: 7-11. Buena Vista Home Entertainment/Disney.

Age 8-12

Video

Family

** *Swan Lake Story: A Dance Fantasy, The (Children's Cultural Collection)*

 This classic ballet, performed by the State Ballet of Oregon in a spectacular outdoor setting, tells the romantic story of a young maiden who is turned into a swan by an evil spell, which can only be broken through a pledge of eternal love. *Adult Juror Comments*: Introduces children to the music of Tchaikovsky and dance. Beautifully produced with breathtaking outdoor scenes. The orchestra sounds good, but the performers are not polished. Can lead to a discussion about fairy tales. *Kid Juror Comments*: Girls liked this ballerina and prince tale better than boys. All the kids liked the music. The younger children will benefit from adult guidance. Kids familiar with dance enjoyed this best. Video. 38 min.; $19.98; Age: 8-12. V.I.E.W. Video.

** *Switching Goals*

 Mary-Kate and Ashley Olsen star as soccer-playing sisters, one as a tomboy and athlete, the other a boy-crazy fashion plate. They mischievously trade teams by trading places. Schemes, mix-ups, and action are part of this game. *Adult Juror Comments*: Pokes fun at the need to win and offers the message that honesty is the best policy. The parents learn a lesson about lying, and children learn that parents make mistakes too. "Be yourself. Real friends will accept you." Shows little diversity. *Kid Juror Comments*: Enjoyable, funny, appealed to girls more than boys. Kids liked the lessons about compromise, hard work, and sportsmanship. "You shouldn't lie when you get into trouble." Kids loved the idea of having a twin to switch places with. Video. 85 min.; $19.96; Age: 7-12. Warner Home Video.

*** *Sword in the Stone, The,* See Page 277.

** *Take My Brother Please! (Clarissa Explains It All)*

 Contains two episodes, "Darling Wars" and "Brain Drain," featuring Clarissa and her brother Ferguson at their bickering best. Includes a "Sibling Survival Guide" video. *Adult Juror Comments*: Clarissa is a positive girl role model. The content is believable and cute. The negative behavior between siblings does not find solutions, but might lead to discussion. Demonstrates realistic family issues about intelligence and responsibility. *Kid Juror Comments*: Kids liked this. They thought the actors behaved as if they were really brother and sister. Video. 60 min.; $14.98; Age: 8-12. Paramount Home Entertainment.

Age 8-12

Video

Family

** Tale of Pigling Bland, The
(The World of Peter Rabbit and Friends)

Pigling Bland is off to find a job in the market. Getting there is not as easy as he anticipates. *Adult Juror Comments*: Good production, excellent animation. Retains charm and spirit of original artwork while making it accessible to a contemporary audience in terms of pace, mood, and captivating characters. Elements of this story are very confusing. *Kid Juror Comments*: Kids liked this. They discussed the issue of the license needed for a pig to be on the road afterwards. Kids wanted to read the book afterwards. "That was a nice story." Video. 30 min.; $14.95; Age: 7-12. Goodtimes Entertainment.

* Tarzan

Based on Edgar Rice Burroughs' story, Tarzan is orphaned, then adopted by gorillas. He develops the instincts and prowess of a jungle animal. Later, Tarzan meets Jane, another human, and his two worlds become one. Songs by Phil Collins. Adult Juror Comments: Lush animation and good bits of humor. Colonial safari hunters drawn at their worst. Intense fighting and violence punctuate fast-paced story. Violence may be necessary on African plains, but it's still scary. Kid Juror Comments: Frightened younger viewers. Older kids were excited, wanted to act like gorillas and swing from trees. "The jungle was scary." "The people were bad and had guns." Sound track too loud at times. "'Terk' was very funny." Video. 88 min.; $19.98; Age: 10-14. Buena Vista Home Entertainment/Disney.

** Thirteenth Year, The, See Page 280.

* Thunderbirds Are Go

Zerox, a 21st-century spacecraft, is leaving earth's atmosphere, bound for Mars, with five men aboard. The craft disappears and the Tracy team launches an exciting rescue mission in space. *Adult Juror Comments*: Dated, a bit primitive for some audiences. Opening sequence is slow-moving. The women's roles appear superficial. Appeals most to boys with special interests. *Kid Juror Comments*: Girls said, "This is boys' stuff; they like these kinds of movies with rockets and fights." Favorite parts: jet-docking the shuttle, puppets. Video. 94 min.; $19.98; Age: 7-12. MGM/UA Home Entertainment.

** Tiff, The (Reboot)

After an argument, Bob and Dot become insufferable. One scheme after another to rekindle their friendship fails, until a dangerous encounter forces the two to work together and they learn to respect each other's point of view. *Adult Juror Comments*: A computer-generated update of the Jetsons, complete with updated means of resolving conflict that includes the use of guns. Family seems almost human. *Kid Juror Comments*: Kids liked this a lot. They liked the characters and the way it looks. "The video shows how friends can like each other better and how it's important not to take sides and be mad at one another." Video. 25 min.; $12.95; Age: 8-14. U.S.A. Home Entertainment.

** Tower of Terror (Wonderful World of Disney)

A washed up journalist teams up with his niece to solve a haunting Hollywood mystery about five partygoers who disappeared from an elevator on Halloween in 1939. Their ghosts are trapped in the remains of the Hollywood Tower Hotel. *Adult Juror Comments*: Entertaining action and suspense. Based entirely on ghosts with good plot twists. "Jealousy is presented as a wasteful and harmful emotion." Viewers identified with feelings of inadequacy and giving yourself a second chance. *Kid Juror Comments*: The kids worked together to figure out the spell and fix the elevator. "Some kids might want to look up witchcraft to put a spell on siblings." "I know this is real because there is a ride at Disney World about this." Video. 88 min.; $14.99; Age: 8-12. Buena Vista Home Entertainment/Disney.

* Toy Story

Newcomer Buzz Lightyear crash-lands in Woody's world, igniting a rivalry that lands them in the hands of Sid, the toy-torturing boy next door. By working together and recognizing their friendship, they manage to survive. *Adult Juror Comments*: Includes some bizarre behaviors by the neighbor boy, such as blowing up toys. Additionally, Sid's behavior goes unnoticed by his parents, exemplifying bad parenting as well. His resolved behavior change is not credible. Nostalgic in other ways. *Kid Juror Comments*: Kids enjoyed the screening. Parts were scary for some who asked, "Turn it to a different part. This is naughty." Most children would never consider abusing their toys, but this could influence them to do so. Video. 81 min.; $26.99; Age: 8-12. Buena Vista Home Entertainment/Disney.

** Toy Story 2 (Toy Story)

In this sequel, while Andy is away at camp, Woody is toy-napped by a greedy collector, and Buzz Lightyear and his friends embark on a rescue mission. Features the voices of Tom Hanks, Tim Allen, and many new characters. Animated. *Adult Juror Comments*: Enchanting, full of adventure, great special effects. Imaginative. Addresses what real friendship is. Pokes fun at stereotypes. Jessie is a strong female role model. It's neat for kids to imagine what their toys think about them. *Kid Juror Comments*: Yes! "I laughed through the whole thing." "The chase scene in the baggage area of the airplane was great." "Even my mom and dad would like this." "I liked the first 'Toy Story,' but this one was better because it has a girl in it." Video. 92 min.; $19.98; Age: 8-12. Buena Vista Home Entertainment/Disney.

Age 8-12

Video

Family

*** *Treasure Seekers, The*

Based on a classic story by English author, Edith Nesbit. Set in early 1900 England, five motherless children struggle to save their inventor father from financial ruin, but their efforts end in disaster. Happily, his promising invention saves them. *Adult Juror Comments*: Well-produced, appeals to adults and kids. Facing adversity, poverty, and disgrace, a family discovers that love, respect, togetherness, and perseverance lead to success and joy. Challenges materialism and offers hope for resolving problems. *Kid Juror Comments*: Appealing, engaging. They like how it gave insight into English culture and how kids showed respect to adults. "I am going to go home and hug my mom and dad." They noticed that the big sister was mean, but fair. The lesson learned was "Pay your debts." Video. 97 min.; $29.95; Age: 8-18. Questar, Inc.

*** *Treasure Seekers, The (DVD)*

 Depicts the struggle a motherless family of five endures to save their inventor father from financial ruin. Disasters occur despite support from outsiders. DVD features include a scene index and information on Victorian England and author Edith Nesbit. *Adult Juror Comments*: Captivating story, good material for showing different lifestyles attainable by choice. DVD questions for discussion are a good addition to the movie, help encourage problem-solving. Charming depiction of Victorian England with background info on DVD. *Kid Juror Comments*: "It was an exciting story. The kids were fun." "The father's invention was interesting. I didn't know it could take six years to invent something." "I liked how they talked: would you like a spot of tea?" "I would love to watch it again." DVD. 108 min.; $24.95; Age: 8-12. Questar, Inc.

*** *Trumpet of the Swan*, See Page 284.

* *Underground Adventure (Oz Kids)*

 What begins as an innocent bus trip for Frank, the Wizard's son, turns into a wild underground ride for all the kids as they encounter dragonettes, merry-go-round mountains, an enormous teddy bear, and more. *Adult Juror Comments*: Addresses fear and feelings. Offers lessons in grammar, science, and geography. Displays some negative and disrespectful attitudes and stereotypes. Language and thinking skills vary in age-appropriateness; difficult to determine proper age audience. *Kid Juror Comments*: A bit long. Sometimes weird or doesn't make sense. One character calls her brother a dummy several times. "I liked the vegetables when they ran." "I liked when the little boy saved the other children and then returned home safely." Video. 64 min.; $12.95; Age: 7-12. Paramount Home Entertainment.

*** Vincent and Me (Les Productions La Fête)

Jo hopes to learn to paint like Vincent van Gogh. A mysterious European art dealer buys a few of her drawings and tries to sell them as original van Goghs. *Adult Juror Comments*: Excellent production, funny, and with an engaging approach to art and children. Sensitive portrayal of a character as deaf. Vincent is perfectly cast. The detective is good, too. Resourcefulness is valued. *Kid Juror Comments*: Attentive audience explained scenes to each other while watching. Kids said they'd watch it again. They enjoyed the drawing and learning about Vincent van Gogh. Girls thought the character Jo was a "show-off." Video. 100 min.; $19.95; Age: 7-13. Productions La Fête.

* Voyage to the Bottom of the Sea

A routine scientific expedition to the North Pole turns into a race to save mankind when a polar ice cap is on fire and threatens the world. A submarine is sent to the rescue. Cast includes Peter Lorre, Barbara Eden, and Frankie Avalon. *Adult Juror Comments*: Though dated, the story is exciting. Underwater photography is excellent. It sparks an interest in science, modern submarines. Contains some aggressive language and behaviors and characters that smoke. *Kid Juror Comments*: Kids really liked the story line and special effects, especially boys. "I was really nervous and excited to see what happened at the end." "The submarine was cool, but the squid looked fake." Video. 106 min.; $14.98; Age: 8-12. Twentieth Century Fox Home Entertainment.

** Welcome to the Dead House (Goosebumps)

Josh and Amanda reluctantly move to a new town where there are strange things going on. Is it a chemical spill that is the cause, or something more sinister? Based on the first Goosebumps book. *Adult Juror Comments*: Chilling scary stuff. Formulaic, but good quality. Fun to watch because it doesn't take itself too seriously. Appropriate content for audience, and well-produced. Unique catch at the end. May provoke an interest in kids to read the books. *Kid Juror Comments*: "Scary, spooky, creepy." Captured kids' attention. Kept them in suspense. Audience couldn't believe that the family stayed together. They liked this better than the book. "It just really scared me." Video. 42 min.; $14.98; Age: 8-12. Twentieth Century Fox Home Entertainment.

** Werewolf of Fever Swamp, The (Goosebumps)

A young boy sets out to discover the mystery behind the werewolf legend in his new town of Fever Swamp. *Adult Juror Comments*: Creates opportunity to discuss fears, fact versus fiction, and werewolves. Content is tasteful yet scary. Has some stereotypes, but shows them as flawed. *Kid Juror Comments*: Good and scary without being "real." Great effects such as the use of fog. "I like spooky videos." "I liked the book better." "The ending is great because you don't really know what's going to happen." Video. 46 min.; $14.98; Age: 8-12. Twentieth Century Fox Home Entertainment.

Age 8-12

Video

Family

** Winning London (Mary-Kate and Ashley)

The Olsen twins jet to London to represent their high school in an international competition of the Model United Nations and have the time of their lives. *Adult Juror Comments*: Up-to-date with interest appeal, especially for pre-teen and early teen girls. Good travel photography; nice scenes of London. Shows cultural differences and promotes understanding of diversity. Wholesome romance, popular music. Fun entertainment. *Kid Juror Comments*: Big hit with the girls. "It is good for anyone to see. No violence, just some tricks and a lot of fun." They understood there was a debate, but for the most part liked seeing the cute guys. "The filming was fast. We actually felt like we were there." Video. 90 min.; $19.96; Age: 8-12. Warner Home Video.

*** Winslow Homer: An American Original (The Artists' Specials)

  War-weary artist Winslow Homer retreats to the countryside to paint, but his sanctuary is invaded by two children. Together, they bury the ghosts of the past to move forward with their lives. *Adult Juror Comments*: Super family video. Interesting, historically accurate, and educational. Subtle story and paintings are woven together well. Makes the viewer believe it's really 1874 in New York. Creativity balances the theme of the horrors of war. *Kid Juror Comments*: Found it engrossing and entertaining. "It was funny and sad, interesting, and about war." "The way the artist worked was great, how he saw things and painted them." "I liked the kids messing with the man, and the boy and girl being sweet on each other." Video. 49 min.; $17.98; Age: 8-14. Devine Entertainment Corp.

** Wishbone: A Tail in Twain (Wishbone)

Kids have an end-of-summer adventure and learn about the power of stories. Wishbone, as Tom Sawyer, has an adventure with Huck Finn in this tale based on Mark Twain's *The Adventures of Tom Sawyer*. *Adult Juror Comments*: Interesting and creative. Well-produced with excellent sets. Good way to introduce classic books to kids today. However, some of the scenes between present time and Tom Sawyer's are questionable and confusing. *Kid Juror Comments*: Kids related to the characters seeking adventure in this story. "Makes me want to go out and read the story by Mark Twain." They objected to the scene with the knife. Video. 60 min.; $19.95; Age: 8-12. Lyrick Studios.

** *Wishbone: A Terrified Terrier (Wishbone)*

Joe's loyalty is tested when he is invited to hang out with older and more popular kids. War tests the character of Wishbone as Henry Fleming, in a story based on Steven Crane's *The Red Badge of Courage*. *Adult Juror Comments*: Tension of new friends versus old friends is handled well. Resolution works for audience. Contains explosions and killings though not gratuitously. Civil War enactment provides authenticity. Excellent handling of a difficult subject. *Kid Juror Comments*: Kids loved how the dog conveys emotion. They especially liked the behind-the-scenes section showing how Wishbone tries to solve the problem. Video. 25 min.; $12.95; Age: 8-12. Lyrick Studios.

*** *Wishbone: A Twisted Tail (Wishbone)*

A crime wave that hits the Oakdale neighborhood causes kids to be more careful about choosing new friends. Wishbone, as the orphan Oliver Twist, is trapped by a web of crime in London. *Adult Juror Comments*: Well-developed plot and character development. Good blend of past and present, of literature and values. Suitable humor for this age group. Somewhat confusing. *Kid Juror Comments*: Kids enjoyed this, especially those familiar with the Charles Dickens novel. A favorite segment: the trial of the dog. Good discussion followed the video. Video. 30 min.; $12.95; Age: 8-12. Lyrick Studios.

** *Wishbone: Bone of Arc (Wishbone)*

Contains two parallel stories. One shows Samantha as the heroine of the boys soccer team, with Wishbone as her ally. In the other, Joan of Arc leads the French army against the English in Mark Twain's "Joan of Arc" with Wishbone as Louis de Conte. *Adult Juror Comments*: Two stories with parallel themes are somewhat confusing to viewers. They're still entertaining and stimulate an interest in the classic tale. Slow-paced. *Kid Juror Comments*: "It was a good movie, and I recommend it." "Now I'd like to read the book," quotes one child juror. Some kids thought the language was "dorky." Video. 30 min.; $12.95; Age: 8-11. Lyrick Studios.

** *Wishbone: Frankenbone (Wishbone)*

David's got trouble on his hands when he adds a little spark to his science fair project. Meanwhile, Wishbone, as Dr. Frankenstein, unleashes a monster in this version of Mary Shelly's *Frankenstein*. *Adult Juror Comments*: This is quite an imaginative adaptation of the classic story. It switches between a contemporary story and the classic tale, which is a bit confusing. Still, it's appealing. *Kid Juror Comments*: Just scary enough. At times, the vocabulary is a little difficult for the target audience. "Encouraged me to find a book about the lady who wrote the book." Video. 20 min.; $12.95; Age: 8-11. Lyrick Studios.

Age 8-12

Video

Family

* Wishbone: Homer Sweet Homer (Wishbone)

Based loosely on the ancient Greek tale *The Odyssey*. The kids refuse to give up when developers come to destroy Jackson Park and their favorite tree. Wishbone, as Odysseus, never gives up the heroic quest to save his home. *Adult Juror Comments*: Wishbone is sensitive to environmental issues. Both kids and adults are portrayed as smart and caring. Transition between today and Ancient Greece is confusing. Adults objected to this version of the classic story because they felt it was demeaning. *Kid Juror Comments*: Kids like the dog's imagination and cute clothes. The ecology message was confusing. Even so, both boys and girls laughed most of the time. The vocabulary and ancient Greece history was way over their heads. Video. 30 min.; $12.95; Age: 8-12. Lyrick Studios.

** Wishbone: Salty Dog (Wishbone)

Samantha leads Joe and David into a dangerous adventure while searching for gold. Based on Robert Louis Stevenson's *Treasure Island*. *Adult Juror Comments*: Well-produced, unique concept. The idea of adventure and danger is well presented. Children love the explanation of how special effects are achieved. *Kid Juror Comments*: Kids thought it was exciting. They especially liked the ending that showed how the special effects were created. They absolutely love the dog, Wishbone. It inspired kids to read the original story. Video. 25 min.; $12.95; Age: 8-12. Lyrick Studios.

** Wishbone: The Prince and the Pooch (Wishbone)

Based on the *Prince and the Pauper*. Joe coaches Emily's T-ball team and Wishbone plays both parts in this adaptation of a Mark Twain novel, ending up in major trouble. *Adult Juror Comments*: Although he's a dog, Wishbone has a fanciful imagination. His literary adventures also include a moral theme. The costumes are great, but the bumbling girls baseball team is overdone. Some objected to this interpretation of the classic story. *Kid Juror Comments*: Kids laughed a lot. They loved the animals and thought the dog was appealing. Many were familiar with the *Prince and the Pauper*, but the adult leader had to point out the connection. This assumes familiarity with the original story. Video. 30 min.; $12.95; Age: 8-12. Lyrick Studios.

Age 8-12

Video

Family

** *Wishbone: The Slobbery Hound (Wishbone)*

Based on Sir Arthur Conan Doyle's *The Hound of the Baskervilles*. After Wishbone is falsely accused, he and the kids team up as detectives to prove his innocence. Wishbone, as Sherlock Holmes, investigates an alleged canine criminal. *Adult Juror Comments*: The simultaneous stories, contemporary and original, meld literature with current events. "It's wild." The combination of classic stories with present day characters is sometimes confusing. Wishbone's imagination, voice, and wit are fantastic. *Kid Juror Comments*: Kids like this, especially the dog as a detective hero. It's funny and weird at the same time. They liked the computer a lot. Some viewers had trouble following the plot. It was confusing to go back and forth between the simultaneous stories. Video. 30 min.; $12.95; Age: 8-12. Lyrick Studios.

*** *Yeh-Shen: A Cinderella Story from China*

This is the original Cinderella, 1000 years older than the European version we all know and love. It won the "Children's Book of the Year" award from the Library of Congress. *Adult Juror Comments*: Mystical, marvelous, creative, and thrilling twist to a classic story. Characters present positive images, and it gives insight into another culture. Artistic elements are excellent overall. Teaching ideas are endless from folk tales to cultural study. *Kid Juror Comments*: Kids were enamored by the characters and the story. They wanted to see it again. Good discussion-starter. One viewer, an adopted child, took offense at the orphan being called "worthless and good-for-nothing." Video. 25 min.; $9.98; Age: 7-12. Twentieth Century Fox Home Entertainment.

** *You Lucky Dog, See Page 290.*

** *Young Magician, The (Les Productions La Fête)*

Pierrot, a twelve-year-old boy, who is passionate about magic, discovers that he has powers of telekinesis that he can't control. While learning how to harness his powers, he is called on to save an entire city from a huge bomb blast. *Adult Juror Comments*: Wonderful, creative entertainment. Witty production with good character development and relationships. Adult role models are not so good. "All kids wish they had magic powers." Adults objected to lack of attention given to safety issues. *Kid Juror Comments*: Kids like the story. Dubbing was distracting at first, but viewers got caught up in the story and it soon became a non-issue. Video. 99 min.; $14.98; Age: 7-12. Productions La Fête.

* *Zenon: Girl of the 21st Century, See Page 294.*

** Zeus and Roxanne

Zeus is a little roughhouse dog, and Roxanne is a special dolphin under study by marine biologist Mary Beth. The unexpected relationship that develops between the two animals brings together Mary Beth and Terry, Zeus' owner, and their families. *Adult Juror Comments*: Well-rounded and funny. Real life accuracy, keeps interest. Good morals and values. Good use of humor. Some unsafe behavior shown (no helmets for bicycling, motorcycling, and skating) and some questionable humor (dog relieves himself on the bad guys). *Kid Juror Comments*: Exciting and funny; believable story. Overall good video and sound. More suited for girls than boys. "I liked Zeus putting the bad guys in and out of the water." "I liked it when Zeus was riding Roxanne." "It teaches us to be good to dolphins." Video. 98 min.; $9.94; Age: 8-14. HBO.

** Zoom: Best of the 70s, See Page 294.

Category—FLM

** Dr. Dolittle, See Page 295.

Category—Holiday

* Angel Doll, The

Based on the novel by Jerry Bledsoe and set in small-town North Carolina in 1950, during the height of the polio epidemic. Two boys set out to get an angel doll for one of their sisters and find the true meaning of Christmas. *Adult Juror Comments*: Well-produced, great story line, full of emotion, poignant ending. Main characters exhibit strong moral character. Christianity is respected. Except for some questionable scenes with boys looking down a woman's bosom, great family movie. *Kid Juror Comments*: Favorable responses with strong reactions to the mature themes. "It moved along, not fast or slow, but just right to keep you interested." "It was sad for me to watch some parts." "It made us realize how lucky we are." "Looked like real life." Video. 96 min.; $19.95; Age: 8-12. Angel Doll Productions, LLC.

** Arnold's Christmas (Hey Arnold!)

During Arnold's hip and urban Christmas, tough Helga has the holiday all figured out—cash, presents, and getting what you wish no matter what. But, Christmas Eve finds Arnold searching for ways to help a man reunite with his daughter. *Adult Juror Comments*: Entertaining. Contains some inappropriate wisecracking. Promotes good social values such as sacrifice, selflessness, charity, and the positive results that come from helping others. Shows good cultural diversity. *Kid Juror Comments*: Children identified with many parts of the story. Both boys and girls liked Arnold as well as the other characters. It motivated a discussion about the benefit of giving and leads to greed. Kids' favorite part is when he got his daughter back. Video. 37 min.; $12.95; Age: 8-12. Paramount Home Entertainment.

* Christmas Reunion

After being orphaned, Jimmy moves in with his callous grandfather, who because of his own grief, cannot accept Jimmy into his heart. Feeling unwanted and isolated, Jimmy sets off on a mystical journey with a very special guide, Santa. *Adult Juror Comments*: Good story, well-produced. Deals with difficult issues—prejudice, gypsy culture, class struggles, abandonment, acceptance. Stresses independent thinking. Pace is awkward for this complex story line. *Kid Juror Comments*: Kids liked the story and the period costumes and sets. They didn't like the negative portrayal of gypsies, and the presentation seemed too muddled for complete understanding. Video. 88 min.; $12.95; Age: 10-16. Saban Entertainment.

** Dawn and the Haunted House (The Baby-Sitter's Club)

Dawn is convinced that Claudia's strange behavior has something to do with the haunted house on the hill and the spooky woman who lives there. Can the Baby-Sitters club help solve the mystery? *Adult Juror Comments*: Promotes friendship and caring. Offers positive messages in the dialogue between mother and daughter about the need for tutoring. Discusses reluctance to admit to having learning problems. Contains gender stereotypes. *Kid Juror Comments*: Kids familiar with the book series liked the story most. They especially liked the haunted house, but thought it unfair to tell stories about the old lady to scare people. Video. 30 min.; $14.95; Age: 7-14. Warner Home Video.

** Easter Storykeepers, The (Storykeepers)

In the dark days of Roman persecution, Christian Storykeeper, Ben the Baker, and his friends spread the tale of Easter and of Jesus' death and resurrection. This action-packed story teaches faith, family values, and the history of Easter. *Adult Juror Comments*: Raises good philosophical questions and moral dilemmas. Usefulness as history depends on the viewer's religious beliefs. Includes an oddly accented African family. Contains some violence, such as scenes of Rome burning, attacking people, crucifixion. *Kid Juror Comments*: Kids were enthralled and full of questions about the Romans and the Christians. Provides a discussion-starter for moral issues without being preachy. "It showed us how to be good." Their favorite part was Jesus rising from the dead. Video. 70 min.; $14.98; Age: 8-12. Twentieth Century Fox Home Entertainment.

Age 8-12

Video

Holiday

** Little Drummer Boy

 A lonely little boy discovers the greatest gift of all on a winter's night in Bethlehem. Narrated by Greer Garson with songs by the Vienna Boy's Choir. *Adult Juror Comments*: This classic tale represents good values. It's well–produced, though somewhat dated, and more diverse than other Christmas tapes from this era. *Kid Juror Comments*: Kids enjoyed it. They were sad when the lamb starts to die. Kids liked the creatures and seeing the various cultures. Video. 27 min.; $12.98; Age: 7-12. Artisan/Family Home Entertainment.

* Prancer

A wounded reindeer and a precocious eight-year-old girl form an everlasting bond in this tender holiday drama about true devotion and friendship. An enchanting film filled with heart and gumption. *Adult Juror Comments*: A unique holiday story with real-life issues. Shows a lack of concern for safety when the girl hangs onto the side of a moving car, climbs onto the roof, wrestles a gun away from her dad. The father's behavior is awful. His change, unbelievable. *Kid Juror Comments*: Kids related to the girl and her problems with her dad. They commented that she had a lot of freedom and did things "they certainly would get in trouble for." Their favorite part was the ending, when Prancer flew away with Santa. Video. 103 min.; $14.95; Age: 7-10. MGM/UA Home Entertainment.

** Scooby-Doo! and the Witch's Ghost, See Page 305.

** Scrooge

Albert Finney plays Ebenezer Scrooge, who is persuaded by ghosts to change his penny-pinching ways. Great musical score by Leslie Bricusse. *Adult Juror Comments*: Potentially scary ghost scenes are handled well. Great score and cast, beautiful production design. This classic tale has classic appeal. Some language is too difficult to understand. *Kid Juror Comments*: Dated. Some children found the movie to be a bit slow. However, the high drama and ghosts held their interest. Most kids lost interest during the musical sections. Video. 113 min.; $14.98; Age: 8-12. Twentieth Century Fox Home Entertainment.

* To Grandmother's House We Go, See Page 307.

Age 8-12

Video

Holiday

Category—How-To

* How to Play the Spoons: Music from the Kitchen

 Takes you through the basics of the age-old art of playing the spoons. "Spoon Man" demonstrates two methods of playing—thumbs and pointer—and correct wrist technique. *Adult Juror Comments*: Presentation is rather dry, narration not compelling. Instructions are pretty good and address ten styles of music. Sets were not interesting. The historical background on spoons shows diversity and encourages hands-on learning. *Kid Juror Comments*: Limited appeal. Boring to some. Others were interested enough to try playing the spoons. "Spoon Man talks too much." "I never knew you could do that with spoons." "I would like to see other people play the spoons." Video. 30 min.; $19.95; Age: 8-12. Spoon Man, Inc.

* How to Study for Better Grades

 From the editors of World Book Encyclopedia, contains concise and easily understood strategies for building successful study skills. Produced in a hip, easy-to-follow style. *Adult Juror Comments*: Helpful for kids having trouble in school. Somewhat dated approach, though. No mention of the Internet or computers. Many ideas are presented. Sequences are long. May be more effective if the child doesn't try to process it all at once. *Kid Juror Comments*: Well-organized. Covers many curriculum-based concepts. Encourages kids to think, reason, and question. Kids liked the music, but thought it was too long. They did not remember all of the study techniques afterwards. Video. 45 min.; $24.95; Age: 10-13. Creative Street.

*** Look What I Grew: Windowsill Gardens (On My Own Adventure)

Shows kids how to make nature come alive anywhere, anytime. Gives clear demonstrations that lead to "growing your own supper." Includes making a terrarium, growing your personal indoor salad garden, and writing a garden journal. *Adult Juror Comments*: Instructions are clear and child-oriented. Has potential to stimulate learning about this subject. Because many projects require a sharp knife, we recommend adult supervision. "So many ideas, it's hard to remember them all." *Kid Juror Comments*: Kids were eager to participate in the activities. Their curiosity level was high. Video. 45 min.; $14.95; Age: 7-12. Gilbert Page Associates.

** Magic of Martial Arts, The: Power Without Violence,
See Page 312.

Age 8-12

Video

How-To

Chapter Four • Middle School

* My First Magic Video (My First)

Teaches how to create a magic show. Based on the popular "My First Book" series. *Adult Juror Comments*: Well-produced, child oriented. Safety is emphasized. Interactivity is not encouraged, however, and the focus is more on crafts than magic. It requires a lot of cutting and gluing. The adult instruction is dry and often dull. *Kid Juror Comments*: Kids liked it, but said that it moved too fast to learn the tricks. One older child said she would have preferred seeing kids do the activities. Video. 45 min.; $12.98; Age: 8-12. Sony Wonder.

** Secrets of Magic with Dikki Ellis

Dikki Ellis shares his special blend of comedy and magic as well as the actual secrets of how to do magic tricks. Presents basic performing tips to build skills and confidence, followed by step-by-step instructions. *Adult Juror Comments*: Has great potential for involvement and fun. Helps to have the materials ready beforehand so kids can learn along with video. "Ellis offers some valuable and fairly sophisticated hints on presentation." *Kid Juror Comments*: This video includes a lot of information. Some students took notes in order to remember everything. "Let's do that trick." Kids wanted to learn more original magic tricks in addition to those shown in the video. Video. 30 min.; $14.95; Age: 8-12. Video Vacations.

Category—Music

** Beethoven Lives Upstairs, See Page 314.

** Meet a Friend of Scott Joplin (Meet the Musicians)

Stars Dennis Kobray as a friend and fan of Scott Joplin, whose "Maple Leaf Rag" and "The Entertainer" helped break down racial barriers of the Post-Reconstruction South. Despite the obstacles, Joplin helped create ragtime music. *Adult Juror Comments*: Informative and entertaining. Good resource for music teachers. Introduces a difficult time in history, particularly for African-Americans. Quality sound and good music. Age appropriate presentation of material for target age group. *Kid Juror Comments*: Worthwhile. Enjoyed the pictures of Joplin and old black and white footage of the times. "We would like to hear more ragtime music." "The narrator encouraged us to listen for the beat, rhythm, and melody." "We learned a lot about Joplin." Video. 55 min.; $24.95; Age: 8-12. Meet the Musicians.

** *Meet George Gershwin (Meet the Musicians)*

 Set in New York City during the Roaring Twenties, Gershwin's music emerges from the melting pot of the recent immigrant styles of music. His story reflects optimism and can-do spirit. Dennis Kobray performs many of Gershwin's best known pieces. *Adult Juror Comments*: Good concept, accurate and suitable information. Portrays Gershwin's drive and hard work to succeed. Good sound and images. Geared more for education than for entertainment. "This will be appreciated most by music lovers." *Kid Juror Comments*: Kids with an interest in music loved it. "The music was beautiful." "We couldn't believe how much we learned in 58 minutes." "Gershwin explained everything so we could understand." "We loved how we could read the words to the songs." Video. 58 min.; $24.95; Age: 8-12. Meet the Musicians.

** *Meet Johann Sebastian Bach (Meet the Musicians)*

 Brings this 18th century composer to life with performances on the clavichord, harpsichord, and grand piano. Set at the close of the Baroque era when Bach's music was considered by peers as old-fashioned and overly embellished. Starring Dennis Kobray. *Adult Juror Comments*: Displays time period well. Bach is brought to life as a human with the same impulses and feelings as we all have. "I loved seeing the different classical instruments and the insights into his process of composing." More instructional than entertainment. *Kid Juror Comments*: Found Bach and his life music interesting. "Better than reading a book to learn about Bach." "Kinda like a school lesson, only more fun." "The music sounded great! You could hear the differences between the harpsichord and piano." Video. 52 min.; $24.95; Age: 8-12. Meet the Musicians.

** *Meet Ludwig Van Beethoven (Meet the Musicians)*

 A biography of Beethoven featuring his most famous works and his struggles with hearing loss, an exploitive father, and the limiting role of musicians in France. His story stresses overcoming adversity and believing in oneself. Starring Dennis Kobray. *Adult Juror Comments*: Comprehensive, informative, well-paced. Doesn't have much action or scene changes. Basically a one man show. Provides a musical tour through history. The narrator's monologues interweave nicely with piano excerpts. Most suitable for educational use. *Kid Juror Comments*: Slow. Kids who like music liked this best. "Enjoyed learning about Beethoven and how he became a great musician, and that was neat." "It seemed real." "Beethoven was a different, newer kind of composer." Inspiring to anyone with a handicap. Video. 56 min.; $24.95; Age: 8-12. Meet the Musicians.

Age 8-12

Video

Music

** Meet Wolfgang Amadeus Mozart (Meet the Musicians)

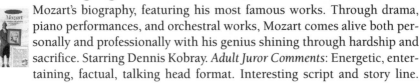

Mozart's biography, featuring his most famous works. Through drama, piano performances, and orchestral works, Mozart comes alive both personally and professionally with his genius shining through hardship and sacrifice. Starring Dennis Kobray. *Adult Juror Comments*: Energetic, entertaining, factual, talking head format. Interesting script and story line. Language is age-appropriate. Information is accurate and suitable. Costumes and styles authentic. More educational than entertainment. *Kid Juror Comments*: Kids interested in music were most responsive. They enjoyed learning about Mozart. "He was not buried by himself. He got sick and died early." "I liked learning about old instruments." "The music was good." "It's not the kind of video I'd watch again." Video. 54 min.; $24.95; Age: 8-12. Meet the Musicians.

* Nutcracker: The Untold Story (Notes Alive!)

Based on the original E.T.A. Hoffman tale, this Tchaikovsky classic is told in rhyme combined with 3-D animation of Maurice Sendak's illustrations, a live ballet performance, and music by the Minnesota Symphony Orchestra. *Adult Juror Comments*: Lovely production, bright, lively images—captivating. The format, changing from live action to animation, makes the story confusing. Shots of the orchestra are somewhat disembodied from the action scenes. Language is too complex for the audience. *Kid Juror Comments*: Kids loved Sendak's animation, particularly the mice. Children under eight found it hard to follow. Some vocabulary was too advanced for them to understand. "Pretty to look at." Kids loved the battle scenes. Video. 50 min.; $19.95; Age: 8-12. Minnesota Orchestra Visual Entertainment.

*** Sousa to Satchmo (Marsalis on Music)

Wynton Marsalis shows how John Phillip Sousa's European-style orchestra is transformed into an American band. Ragtime and raggin' changed its beat to become New Orleans' jazz. Includes performances of Sousa's, Scott Joplin's, and Louis Armstrong's music. *Adult Juror Comments*: Top-notch production, full of information. Music is great. History is interesting, showing relationship of past to present. Blends visuals and content well. Involves kids throughout. *Kid Juror Comments*: Kids enjoyed this, especially those interested in music. They liked learning the history of bands and orchestras. Video. 54 min.; $19.98; Age: 8-12. Sony Classical.

*** *Tackling the Monster (Marsalis on Music)*

Wynton refers to practicing music as "the large monster" and has a strategy for slaying this monster. With cellist Yo-Yo Ma, he shows young musicians how to practice new or difficult pieces. Together they play a thrilling jazz improvisation. *Adult Juror Comments*: Excellent material that is practical information for kids. Has great ethnic representation. Relates the benefits of practice and its effects to everyday life. Shows good intergenerational and ethnic mix. *Kid Juror Comments*: Kids liked the interaction between Yo-Yo Ma and Marsalis, especially those interested in music. Kids liked watching other kids practice. Video. 54 min.; $19.98; Age: 8-12. Sony Classical.

*** *Why Toes Tap (Marsalis on Music)*

Using Tchaikovsky's original and Ellington's jazz arrangement of "The Nutcracker," Wynton demonstrates how composers use rhythm to express a wide variety of emotions. With simple instruction, Wynton teaches how to swing with the music. *Adult Juror Comments*: Marsalis is excellent. He interacts well with children and makes use of excellent sports' analogies. Shows good multicultural diversity. "I enjoyed it immensely." *Kid Juror Comments*: Kids enjoyed this. It held their interest, especially those with a music background. There was too much verbalization for some. Video. 54 min.; $19.98; Age: 8-12. Sony Classical.

Age 8-12

Video

Music

Category—Nature

** Amazing Insect Warriors (Bug City)

Imagine an astonishing wasp that can stun a cockroach and hypnotize it, or a beetle that frightens a large mouse. See how these fascinating warrior insects use everything from camouflage to chemicals in order to survive in their world. *Adult Juror Comments*: Amazing cinematography. Outstanding close-ups of insects. Graphics and models enhance the descriptions. Information about the invincibility of beetles was excellent. The puppet narrator was juvenile. *Kid Juror Comments*: Interesting and really fun." Did not like the puppet narrator. "This will help my research on insects." "Army ants were fascinating." "How did they get those pictures of bugs inside their nests?" Video. 23 min.; $12.95; Age: 8-12. Schlessinger Video Productions.

** Animals of the Amazon River Basin

Stained like tea from the forest's fallen leaves, the Rio Negro is one of the world's great rivers. This program explores the Amazon River basin in Brazil's rain forest and the extraordinary wildlife in the area. *Adult Juror Comments*: A beautiful documentary with great educational value, sophisticated narrative, and great camera work. Has quality and depth in an accurate and sensitive presentation. Shows how quiet the world is in the animal kingdom. *Kid Juror Comments*: Referring to the KIDS FIRST! happy-sad face evaluation tool, kids said, "This movie only gets happies from us, no frowns or angries." Kids loved the weird frog and other animals they hadn't seen before. They wanted to see it again. Video. 29 min.; $29.95; Age: 8-12. Aims Multimedia.

** Coral Reef, The: A Living Wonder (Nature's Way)

Coral reefs are living animal colonies, very important to the tropical ocean ecosystem and an integral part of the cycle of life as home to thousands of fish and invertebrates. *Adult Juror Comments*: Young viewers will find the pace a bit slow. Contains gorgeous visuals, though the narration is not as compelling. New words on the screen help kids learn new concepts. Excellent education value for learning about oceans. *Kid Juror Comments*: Kids felt this was a little academic and had limited repeat play value. They all thought the information was interesting and well-presented. The word prompts were helpful. Video. 16 min.; $29.95; Age: 9-16. Aims Multimedia.

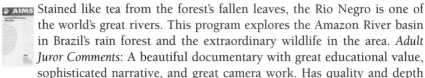

** Why Is the Sky Blue? (Why Is the Sky Blue?)

 How fast is lightning? Why are sunsets red? What's the difference between a hurricane and a tornado? Host Spencer Christian guides kids through a series of more than 40 frequently asked questions and their answers about the wonders of weather. *Adult Juror Comments*: Beautiful cinematography. Fast moving. There was not enough time for responding to the questions. Explanations are thorough, factual, and interesting. "It made me want to find out more about the phenomenon of weather." *Kid Juror Comments*: Kids liked the time lapses in the weather shots. The format makes it seem really long. "I wanted to know more about the jet stream and high and low pressure." Some said they would not watch again because they already knew the answers. Video. 23 min.; $12.95; Age: 8-12. Schlessinger Video Productions.

Category—Special Interest

* Alice in Wonderland/A Dance Fantasy (Children's Cultural Collection)

 Alice, the Mad Hatter, the Cheshire Cat, and the Queen are brought to life by the Prague Chamber Ballet. Creatively interprets timeless children's stories and tales through a medley of dance, music, and theater. *Adult Juror Comments*: This is a beautiful and abstract production with excellent sets and costumes. It's very sophisticated in content and its musical score. It's extremely scary for younger kids. The teacher is stiff and hard-edged. Offers stereotypes of good and evil. *Kid Juror Comments*: Appeals most to children who appreciate and relate to dance or to those who are intrigued by the Alice in Wonderland story. Video. 27 min.; $19.98; Age: 8-12. V.I.E.W. Video.

** Big Submarine, The (Big Adventure Series)

 Voyage under the sea with the crew of a giant Trident submarine. See what it's like to live underwater for months at a time. Discover how submarines work. Visits the bridge, the kitchens, and more. *Adult Juror Comments*: Good presentation, easy to understand. Child narrators enhance appeal. Offers limited information about nuclear technology. Little diversity shown in terms of race or gender. *Kid Juror Comments*: Presentation is a little long. Kids enjoyed seeing the behind-the-scene shots of a real submarine. They commented about the teamwork that was represented. Video. 40 min.; $14.95; Age: 7-12. Little Mammoth Media.

*** Dare to Dance

Chronicles three young girls' passion for ballet. Explores the joys and challenges of class and performance. Interviews with instructors, parents, and professional dancers are informative and inspirational. *Adult Juror Comments*: Beautifully presented, displays the dedication required. An unusually sensitive, honest, and appealing introduction to the dance world. Profiles some talented youngsters. Provides accurate information for kids interested in pursuing dance as a career. *Kid Juror Comments*: Girls who have studied dance loved it. They felt it was a true picture of what it is like to study dance and why dancers work so hard. "They're just like us, and they can do all those beautiful steps." Video. 40 min.; $19.95; Age: 8-16. Paragon Media.

** Kid to Kid: Staying Safe! See Page 341.

*** Sing, Dance 'n Sign, See Page 346.

** Smart about Strangers (Smart about Strangers)

Takes a positive approach to developing children's awareness of stranger dangers. Shows children how to recognize and avoid dangerous situations or escape from them. *Adult Juror Comments*: Well-produced, though simple. Lighting and audio is sometimes a problem. Language is suitable for audience. Empowers kids to keep themselves safe. Encourages parents to address a difficult subject with their children. *Kid Juror Comments*: Kids would tell their friends about it. "I liked practicing the double-arm grab. It's the easiest move for me." "I thought this was very helpful information." Some kids commented that the instructions were difficult to hear. Video. 23 min.; $19.95; Age: 7-12. Rikabi Productions, LLC.

*** This Old Pyramid (Nova: Adventures in Science)

Egyptologist, Mark Lehner, and stonemason Roger Hopkins test clever and bizarre theories about pyramids by building one. Tours hidden tombs and passageways of the Great Pyramid of Giza and shows computer re-creations of sites. *Adult Juror Comments*: Well-presented with good narration. Provides an excellent exercise in problem-solving, critical thinking, and a fascinating contemporary look at the question "How were the pyramids of Egypt built?" *Kid Juror Comments*: Excellent. Kids learned a lot about building methods. They liked learning about the pyramids. It has great educational value, more so than its entertainment value. A bit long. Video. 90 min.; $19.95; Age: 10-14. WGBH.

Chapter Five

Junior and Senior High School (Ages 12-18)

By Allan J. Brenman and Adelaide Vinneau

Although today's teens are far less controlled by their parents than their parents' or grandparents' generation, they also have more responsibility. Teens today have more financial obligations, are entrusted with the care of younger siblings, and shop and prepare meals for their families. Eighty per cent of teenage girls do their family's laundry! Nevertheless, they remain adolescents and filter information through the mind of a teenager. They are romantic, idealistic, and naive as well as cynical, rebellious, jaded, and over-marketed.

A teen's world revolves around the pressures of acceptance, self-image, popularity, the opposite sex, defying authority, and a sense of identity. While making the journey toward maturity, their friends become the center of their lives and their families take a back seat. A desire for independence and autonomy develops as adolescents question, challenge, and frequently reject their parents' lifestyles and values. Teens struggle with questions about themselves: "Who am I? What kind of person should I be? How do I make and keep friends? How do I get along with the other sex? What do I really believe in?" In this chapter, you will find programs that expand their experiences, introduce them to new ideas and attitudes, and give them insight into unknown territories such as those portrayed in *City Boy*, *Journey*, *Two Soldiers*, or *The Great Dictator*.

Teens are primary targets for marketing many products, from entertainment to clothes, sports equipment, computers, and soft drinks. Businesses recognize the financial clout of the teenage population and target them relentlessly. Teenage girls spent more then $80 billion in 1998. In the process, they are learning to make informed choices and become discriminating consumers. On a different level, they also are learning to use logical and sophisticated reasoning skills and are absorbing new ideas as they develop a wider view of the world. They need guidance, encouragement, and the resources to do that. Among such resources are some titles found in this chapter: *The Digital Field Trip to the Rain Forest*, *In Search of Human Origins: The Story of Lucy*, or *How the West Was Lost*.

Television that addresses common adolescent issues helps them learn new ways of handling their problems and of feeling less awkward, alone, and different. Typically, adolescents function like an adult one moment and like a child the next. Teens crave guidance from adults even while they are verbally rejecting it. Videos and CD-ROMs that address relationships, struggle for independence, insecurities, fitting into a peer group, substance abuse and sexuality help them deal with their own dilemmas. Programs such as *Self Esteem and Drugs*, *The Boyhood of John Muir*, *Working It Out: A Survival Guide for Kids*, or *Life Begins* help develop healthy attitudes and opinions.

We also know that teens have access to more information more readily than ever before. They are more computer savvy than most of their parents and teachers will ever be. Teenage girls use computers and the Internet as much as boys do. Both genders respond to music, humor, positive attitudes, and integrity. Many CD-ROMs teach skills in a fashion that it's hard to separate the fun from the learning. Among these are *New Millennium World Atlas Deluxe*, *Mission to Planet X: Internet Coach*, *Encarta Encyclopedia Deluxe 99*, and *Astro Algebra*. These excellent educational programs are both compelling and entertaining. Dozens of others like them are summarized and evaluated below.

Allan J. Brenman is a staff psychologist at Bradley Hospital in Providence, Rhode Island. He has both a Doctorate and a Masters of Education with a concentration in interactive media from Harvard University. Adelaide Vinneau is the Director of the Nashville, Tennessee YWCA's Domestic Violence Program.

Format—CD-ROM

Category—Education/Instruction

*** Algebra World

Highly interactive math-building tools covering equations, ratios, percentages, variables, geometry, and negative numbers. Kids solve a mystery while exploring these math challenges. Has three skill levels and a user-tracking feature. *Adult Juror Comments*: Good teaching tool for difficult concepts. Program offers activities covering skills such as problem-solving and introduces algebraic concepts. Puzzles are difficult. Excellent 3-D graphics, great music. *Kid Juror Comments*: Challenging and fun on different levels. Made kids think and come up with solutions. Kids enjoyed the graphics. "I like building my own shapes." "I didn't know algebra was fun." The different levels are really useful. CD-ROM. WIN/MAC; $39.95; Age: 12-18. Cognitive Technologies Corp.

** ASL Sign Language, Volume One: Vocabulary, Grammar and Sentences (American Sign Language CD-ROM Series)

Designed to teach American Sign Language skills, this program is simple to use and has all the features of state-of-the-art multimedia software. *Adult Juror Comments*: Impressive. A superior instructional program, exceptionally informative. Adults thought children would need to have some motivation to learn sign language in order to enjoy this. Responsive, gives constant positive feedback. Installation difficult. *Kid Juror Comments*: Children were intrigued and kept going back to this. The video section can be slowed down to see the hand movements clearly. A great tool that could be used in conjunction with live instruction. CD-ROM. WIN; $95; Age: 12-18. Sign Enhancers, Inc.

*** Astro Algebra (Mighty Math)

Covers major algebraic topics in a game format. Includes negative integers, equivalent expressions, ratio and proportions, exponential notation, and inverse operations. *Adult Juror Comments*: Awesome. Outer space setting is very imaginative and visually stimulating. Great graphics and sound. Presents algebra painlessly, with positive reinforcement. Challenging content. Excellent teaching tool. Particularly helpful for slow learners. *Kid Juror Comments*: Much fun with this program. They were challenged and motivated and thought it was fantastic! "I liked solving the problems at the space station." "If you like math, you'll love this." "It was cool, fun and taught me stuff." CD-ROM. WIN/MAC; $29.95; Age: 10-18. Edmark.

*** Digital Field Trip to the Rainforest, The
(The Digital Field Trips)

Explore the Blue Creek Rain Forest Reserve in Belize, Central America with hundreds of photos, videos, and interactive activities. Learn about the world's rain forests, the diversity of plants and animals, and the importance of vital ecosystems. *Adult Juror Comments*: Excellent learning tool, kid-friendly, easy to use. Contains good reference material that is educational and entertaining. Information on vegetation, strata, water cycles using diagrams, charts and graphs. A superior program. *Kid Juror Comments*: Lots of good information. Kids enjoyed learning the geography lessons, especially when video was used. They liked the monkeys and other animals, but eating bugs was their favorite part. "The more games the better, because they make me think." CD-ROM. WIN/MAC; $49; Age: 11-18. Digital Frog International, Inc.

*** Digital Field Trip to the Wetlands, The
(The Digital Field Trips)

Virtual reality technology allows users to visit the wetlands in Algonquin Park, Canada. Hundreds of photos, videos, animations, and engaging interactivities make it perfect for nature enthusiasts, students, or anyone interested in nature. *Adult Juror Comments*: Easy to use, no glitches, covers many different disciplines. Well-produced with excellent learning and reference tools. Presents useful information through reading, visuals, and memorization. *Kid Juror Comments*: Enjoyed the web game, field trip, and vacation. "I liked finding animals in the bog, looking around at the scenery, and playing the game." A resourceful, informative program with good graphics, video, and audio. "Makes learning fun." CD-ROM. MAC; $49; Age: 10-18. Digital Frog International, Inc.

** Digital Frog 2, The

Teaches frog dissection, anatomy, and ecology with full-color photographs, full-motion video, narration, and detailed animations—including 3-D. Interactive map, context-sensitive help, and definitions make it fun and easy to use. *Adult Juror Comments*: Interesting alternative to a real dissection, with good graphics. "It helped me understand what we were doing in my biology class." It doesn't tell what the user did wrong. *Kid Juror Comments*: Very easy. "It was great." "I could go up to the menus at any time to change areas." "I liked how it showed a heart and then a smaller section and a smaller section and then the pumps for the heart." "Helped me understand my biology class." CD-ROM. WIN/MAC; $85; Age: 12-18. Digital Frog International, Inc.

*** Encarta Encyclopedia 98 Deluxe

State-of-the-art multimedia encyclopedia provides top-quality information with current and authoritative content, dynamic multimedia features, and links to the Internet. *Adult Juror Comments*: A wealth of information. Excellent tool for researchers. Easy to use. Cross-referencing makes it appropriate for older kids. Excellent resource with great graphics. Includes Web site links. Lightning-fast. *Kid Juror Comments*: Marvelous virtual tours of ruins and hieroglyphics, collages, time lines, and the links to the Internet. Highlights included the maze game and the interactive world languages. Perfect tool for junior researchers. CD-ROM. WIN; $69.95; Age: 8-Adult. Microsoft.

*** Encarta Encyclopedia Deluxe 99 (Encarta)

 A powerful learning resource helps users find more information through an interface to the Internet. Engaging multimedia features and content. Comes with a research organizer that's useful for research, writing, and homework. *Adult Juror Comments*: Very good. Extremely easy to use. Excellent reference resource. "A lot more fun than looking it up in the library." Great maps, graphics, and sound. Ability to go on-line provides cutting-edge opportunities for student research. *Kid Juror Comments*: Unbelievable, awesome. Kids were clamoring to use it. Makes research painless and fun. Very few topics they could not find. Information is clear and concise. "Unbelievable, how could we live without it?" CD-ROM. WIN; $69; Age: 8-18. Microsoft.

*** Encarta Virtual Globe

Comprehensive world atlas offers an excellent geographic reference guide for home or school use. Delivers the highest-quality detailed maps, up-to-date statistical data, and the richest cultural information of any atlas in any medium. *Adult Juror Comments*: Outstanding atlas/encyclopedia with fantastic links to the Internet. Great for social studies use. The "name that place" game increases map skills. Fabulous geography resource. *Kid Juror Comments*: Loved the animal sounds, the "flying views," music, and the videos. Biggest drawback: lacks sound with geographical descriptions. Kids under ten needed help to play. CD-ROM. WIN; $54.95; Age: 10-18. Microsoft.

Age 12-18

CD-ROM

Edu/Instru

*** Excel@ Middle School (Excel@)

A personalized study system with lesson plans, tutors, and a study planner designed to help middle school students master core academic subjects. Includes algebra, science, history, geography, and English. *Adult Juror Comments*: Fabulous, well-produced. Great visuals and good music. Simple format, lots of nifty plug-ins. Challenging content. Contains an attached encyclopedia and access to the Internet. Great for self-motivated students. *Kid Juror Comments*: Easy to use. Report writing, grammar, vocabulary, and speed reader especially useful. A learning tool that most thought they'd use often. "It made it fun to learn." "Makes doing schoolwork easier." Visual images in the study section are outstanding. CD-ROM. WIN/MAC; $40; Age: 11-16. Knowledge Adventure.

* Impact: Ground Zero

Examines the massive impact of an asteroid that many scientists believe collided with Earth and wiped out the dinosaurs 65 million years ago. Also introduces the astronomers who scan the skies for dangerous objects heading our way. *Adult Juror Comments*: Factual but dry presentation. Quality varies. Jurors had difficulty installing and experienced audio difficulties. Content is interesting, but narration long-winded. Classic example of turning a theory into a fact. *Kid Juror Comments*: The images were fine, but scientists were difficult to hear. Found it boring and difficult at times. "I liked the picture of the meteors and asteroids and the link to the Internet." Kids enjoyed the quiz about asteroid impact. CD-ROM. WIN/MAC; $24.95; Age: 12-18. Bamboole.

* Internet Coach for Netscape Navigator

Multimedia tutorial and on-line reference tool walks the user step-by-step through the Internet. A one-click menu makes navigation a snap. All Netscape features are simply explained and demonstrated. *Adult Juror Comments*: Direct and straight-forward learning tool. Useful to Internet newcomers. Simple language is used in a rather dry format with cute characters. Doesn't necessarily make the Internet look interesting. Best for real beginners. *Kid Juror Comments*: Useful learning about the Internet, but not interesting for those with previous Internet experience. Kids enjoyed the cartoon demonstration. CD-ROM. WIN/MAC; $28.95; Age: 12-18. APTE, Inc.

*** Life Begins

Provides parents with a new way to teach human conception through birth. Lockout program allows parents to customize material to the age of their child. *Adult Juror Comments*: Effective, well–organized, and indexed. Tastefully done, good visuals. Good teaching and resource tool. Blocking of inappropriate material works well. Delivers strong message about responsible sexual behavior. We experienced technical problems. *Kid Juror Comments*: Some kids were embarrassed. Elicited interesting comments and questions, such as, "I wish we had this when I was in eighth grade." "I liked seeing the baby grow." Discussion of motherhood followed viewing. Error screen came up too often. CD-ROM. WIN/MAC; $69.95; Age: 12-18. Quality Multimedia, LC.

* Mission to Planet X: Internet Coach

Simulates the Internet, with the latest multimedia technology. Using a game format, players are challenged to reach the mysterious planet X as they learn to surf the Web. *Adult Juror Comments*: Great idea, but hard to follow their method of searching the Internet. Kids loved the puzzles. At times frustrating: the icons and text are hard to read, and the instructions are difficult to follow. *Kid Juror Comments*: Kids loved the puzzles and visual effects, especially the pictures of planets. Boys stayed interested the longest. This complex puzzle had mixed success holding children's interest. The kids found it too slow, and it skipped around too much. CD-ROM. WIN/MAC; $38.95; Age: 12-18. APTE, Inc.

** New Games Training CD-ROM, The (New Games)

Combining the best features of previous "New Games" books and videos, this CD-ROM provides a guide to developmental skills, safety issues, game adaptations, and more. *Adult Juror Comments*: Navigation is easy. Provides thorough explanations and visual aids. However, specific games do not identify a target audience. The film clips were interesting and helpful. Good for training student group leaders. *Kid Juror Comments*: Liked it and would play some of the games that they learned. "These would be cool to play at a church picnic." "The detective game looks like fun." "The film clips showing the games were neat." "These games encourage people to work together." CD-ROM. WIN/MAC; $39.95; Age: 12-18. New Games.

Age 12-18

CD-ROM

Edu/Instru

*** New Millennium World Atlas Deluxe

Create your own global journey with in-depth geographical information and a sophisticated 3-D map that helps define the constantly changing world. Tools provided for creating maps and organizing information. *Adult Juror Comments*: Filled with interesting articles. Detailed coverage about cultures, history, physical geography, even selecting a college. Visual representation of the world is well done. Easy to operate. *Kid Juror Comments*: Best segment: mapmaking, travel information, and notebook guide. "Really colorful. Makes an excellent educational resource and reference tool." Easy to use. Atlas contains information perfect for school reports. CD-ROM. WIN; $44.95; Age: 12-18. Rand McNally New Media.

** Ramagon Interactive Construction Kit

Makes use of animated building pieces. The kit allows children of all ages to use their imagination to formulate and build their own creations. Their work comes alive with movement and sound. *Adult Juror Comments*: Content is interesting, challenging, creative. Exceptionally confusing and difficult to install. After watching instruction videos, adults still couldn't get it to do what they wanted. Made the children want to play with real Tinkertoys afterwards. *Kid Juror Comments*: Every single kid needed help to install. Experienced users had to reset computer to use it. Boys responded to it better than girls. "We liked the way the shapes moved around the screen and choosing our own colors." "I liked adding my own things." CD-ROM. WIN; $24.95; Age: 8-18. El-Ko Interactive.

*** Space Station Alpha: The Encounter (Time Blazer)

You are a mission specialist on Space Station Alpha. Your top-secret mission is to board and investigate an alien spacecraft to determine its origin and mission. A prototype spacesuit aids you as mission control guides you through the spaceship. *Adult Juror Comments*: Excellent graphics. Slow at beginning. "One of the most interesting approaches to acquiring and using information." Good repeat-use value. Includes supplementary materials such as a membership card and Web site information. *Kid Juror Comments*: "Fun stuff." Kids liked the images, the sounds, and the movement. Challenging, but required patience. Kids tended to speed through until they got hooked. Kids had more success and enjoyment when playing in small groups. CD-ROM. WIN/MAC; $54.95; Age: 10-18. Paragon Media.

*** World Book 1998 Multimedia Encyclopedia

Learn, achieve, and succeed. Two CDs contain all the articles from the print World Book Encyclopedia and features 360-degree views, interactive simulations, videos, animation, photographs, illustrations, and audio. Allows access to the Internet. *Adult Juror Comments*: Easy to install. Clear and concise. An excellent resource with solid, current content. Well-designed to answer questions, encourage browsing, or explore new topics. Switching CDs is a slight nuisance. It's a complete multimedia encyclopedia. *Kid Juror Comments*: Tremendous way to use the computer. "This program would help me do my homework." Kids love the facts, images, monthly events, and going to the Internet. "I learned all about bears, even the football team." Program kept kids interested. CD-ROM. WIN; $69.95; Age: 8-18. IBM Multimedia.

Category—Family

** Kuba, the Classic Push to Play CD-ROM Game

Based on the European hit board game that uses marbles, the object is to push seven neutral marbles, or all of your opponent's marbles, off the playing board. Offers play options over a local area network, modem, or anywhere through the Internet. *Adult Juror Comments*: Can improve eye-hand coordination, attention span, and memory. Teaches teamwork. Shows ways to view a problem as a challenge and opportunity. Similar to playing checkers. Can be played with a friend or on the Internet. *Kid Juror Comments*: Great family game. Ranges from easy to hard. Strategy takes a while to figure out. "I liked winning." "The computer played really well. It beat me a lot." Kids liked the music and the special effects with the realistic graphics. CD-ROM. WIN/MAC; $19.99; Age: 10-18. Patch Products, Inc.

* Nancy Drew: Message in a Haunted Mansion
(Nancy Drew Interactive Mysteries)

Nancy Drew is invited by a friend to San Francisco to assist in the renovation of a Victorian mansion. Mysterious accidents keep throwing the renovations off schedule. Is it unsettled spirits at work? Assume the identity of the super-sleuth to find out. *Adult Juror Comments*: Easy to install. Two levels of play. Some games are difficult to play due to precision required of cursor. Great at combining critical thinking and cognitive problem-solving. Offers insight into San Francisco's architecture. *Kid Juror Comments*: Some enjoyed it, others found it too slow. "Good mystery without too many easy giveaways." "Too girly." "Lacks creepy ambiance." "The tile puzzle was very frustrating because you had to maneuver the pieces perfectly." "Cool old house and good clues." CD-ROM. WIN; $29.99; Age: 8-14. Her Interactive.

Age 12-18

CD-ROM

Family

*** Nickelodeon Director's Lab

Turns kids' computers into a complete "production studio," allowing them to draw, compose music, create animation, and record their own voice. Create from scratch or adapt familiar elements from the Nickelodeon Network. *Adult Juror Comments*: Good content, would have been fabulously successful if not for technical problems. Does very complex functions that require prior knowledge of video editing. Must have a sound card for certain functions, helps to have a microphone. *Kid Juror Comments*: Some kids adored it, thought it was absolutely great. Their reaction depends on their interest in the subject. "Wonderful for budding producers." It allows kids to create their own short videos. CD-ROM. WIN; $54.95; Age: 8-18. Viacom New Media.

Category—Special Interest

** Elite Darts

Features cricket, baseball, and ten other games. The player may choose from four different boards in a basement, sports bar, English pub, or pool hall. *Adult Juror Comments*: Challenging with multiple levels of difficulty. "Stimulating, requires fine motor skills and good problem-solving skills." "A 'ghost' hand holds the dart, allows the player to gauge how to point and throw it." "It's really fun." *Kid Juror Comments*: Mixed reviews. Too easy for some, challenging for others. Has limited sound effects and choice of wallpapers. "Rooms look like something adults would like, not kids." "The best part is the competition." It was difficult to navigate with the mouse. CD-ROM. WIN/MAC; $19.99; Age: 12-18. Patch Products, Inc.

Format—Video/DVD

Category—Education/Instruction

** Edgar Allan Poe: A Journey in Verse
(The Master Poets Collection)

The master of American poetry created some of the most striking and moving imagery ever created. These various recitals of his poems bring to life the phrasing and lyricism that forever changed the landscape of poetic verse. *Adult Juror Comments*: Good teaching tool for poetry studies. Well-produced; clear cinematography and audio. Good examples given to illustrate various poetic styles and functions. *Kid Juror Comments*: Appealed to those who had an interest in poetry or Poe. Appreciated the costumes and settings. "It helped me to understand the content of his poems because it related Poe's poetry to his life experiences." Video. 34 min.; $24.95; Age: 13-18. Monterey Home Video.

** Foodplay: This Is Your Life!

Combines thought provoking drama and humor to help teens see through media messages, build positive bodies, and improve their eating habits. Comes with a teacher's activity book. *Adult Juror Comments*: Fast-paced, right mix of slapstick humor and important facts. Simply produced. Content holds kids' interest and is well balanced. Thought-provoking, accurate information given in teen terms. Great discussion material for both adults and kids. *Kid Juror Comments*: Funny and inventive. Gives kids a lot to think about. "At first I thought it was boring, but then I found myself laughing and really listening." "This is way better than a parent or teacher lecture!" Video. 54 min.; $179; Age: 10-15. Foodplay Productions.

*** Invention / 3 Volumes

Celebrates great inventions that have altered our world, including the marvels of simple gadgets such as the mousetrap. Looks behind the scenes at enterprising people whose tenacity and ingenuity stimulate creativity in everyone. *Adult Juror Comments*: Stimulating program for teens, with excellent graphics. Motivates an intergenerational discussion. Occasionally contains some dated material. Shows women as positive role models. *Kid Juror Comments*: Among the favorite segments: "Popular Science" segments from the 1940s, the timed dog food dispenser, and the interviews with the inventors. Section on carbon dating interested them the most. A big hit with boys! Video. 300 min.; $59.95; Age: 12-18. Discovery Communications.

** Life by the Numbers, Vol. 1: Seeing Is Believing
(Life by the Numbers)

The world of mathematics plays a pivotal role in creating fantastic illusions, from special effects to Renaissance paintings to the fourth dimension. *Adult Juror Comments*: Teaches how to use numbers in a fun way. It's a good tool for those interested in numbers and math. It's more informative than entertaining though it's visually, musically, creatively, and cognitively appealing. *Kid Juror Comments*: Flashy presentation, excellent production that connects math to life. Some kids got lost in parts, but enjoyed the sections that they understood. "Opened up another world for mathematics. It inspired me to research the fourth dimension." Video. 57 min.; $19.95; Age: 12-18. Monterey Home Video.

** Mastering Asthma: A Family's Guide to Understanding

 Follows the diagnosis and treatment of asthma in the daily lives of three children of different ages, addressing common questions and teaching mastering skills. Teaches parents to become active partners by offering practical, everyday tips. *Adult Juror Comments*: Good overview of asthma that blends factual information and dramatic delivery of information. Suitable for family viewing as well as for school groups to understand their friends who have asthma. Comforting for parents as well as children. *Kid Juror Comments*: Very informative. "I want my mom to see it." "What about grown-ups, do they have it too?" Helps to reduce fear of asthma. "I'd like to learn more about medicine and science." Video. 20 min.; $34.95; Age: 7-Adult. A.A. Pediatrics.

** Tell-Tale Heart

This faithful adaptation Poe's best known short story explores murder, madness, and betrayal in a compelling study of a man driven by his own demons to take the life of another. *Adult Juror Comments*: Using a dramatic-reading style, honors Poe's story with integrity. Doesn't dumb down the language. Michael Sollazzo's portrayal as the psychotic murderer is sensitively portrayed. The gruesome details are left to the imagination of the viewer. *Kid Juror Comments*: Probably not a video that teens will pick up without some persuasion. None were overly enthusiastic about it. All agreed they would have liked more action. It held their attention but didn't captivate them. Video. 25 min.; $24.95; Age: 14-18. Monterey Home Video.

* To Walk with Lions

The story of the last years of George Adamson, 30 years after the Academy Award-winning film "Born Free," in his quest to rehabilitate lions born in captivity in spite of poachers, politics and his own personal demons. *Adult Juror Comments*: Complex and involved. A personal look at a very private man. Seamless cinematography, beautiful scenery, superb acting. Harsh documentary style, gruesome in parts. Presents real-world issues in real-world terms: racism, alcohol, wildlife, greed, poverty. *Kid Juror Comments*: Overall strong response. "It was interesting. I have never seen a movie like this before." "Very adult movie. It made me feel like an adult. But I wish there had been a cute teenage boy in it." "I didn't like it that George gets killed at the end." Video. 108 min.; $9.98; Age: 15-18. Twentieth Century Fox Home Entertainment.

*** Walking with Dinosaurs

Computer graphics and animatronics depict dinosaur life and their beginnings 220 million years ago in this BBC production narrated by Kenneth Branaugh. *Adult Juror Comments*: Great! Wow! Great special effects. Combining puppets and animatronics is fascinating and well-done. "Discovery Channel meets *Jurassic Park*." "I'm definitely more interested in dinosaurs since I watched this." *Kid Juror Comments*: Cool! "I know tons more about dinosaurs now." "I didn't know there were no ice caps at the poles during the Jurassic period." "Some scenes depicting dinosaurs eating one another were gross." "I felt like I was there." Video. 180 min.; $29.98; Age: 8-18. Twentieth Century Fox Home Entertainment.

*** Witness: Voices from the Holocaust

Some of the earliest recorded testimonies and rare archival footage provide school-age viewers with a uniquely personal introduction to the Holocaust. Jews, resistance fighters, American POWs, and child survivors tell stories in their own words. *Adult Juror Comments*: An intense, chilling reminder of the catastrophe. Compelling and challenging, excellent document for teaching history. Powerful and touching. Marvelous editing. Stimulates inquiry and reflection. Humanizes history. *Kid Juror Comments*: "I think it presented touchy material in a positive and informative way." "Actual stories helped give a better understanding of the Holocaust." "Interesting but too long." "This seems to be happening again in Kosovo." Video. 86 min.; $29.95; Age: 12-18. Stories to Remember.

** Working It Out: A Survival Guide for Kids
(The Personal Safety Series)

Every day, children are faced with issues involving peers that directly affect their personal safety. This program takes a no-nonsense look at peer-related issues. *Adult Juror Comments*: A serious and practical approach to real issues faced by kids. Addresses difficult concepts with role-playing sections that answer important questions. Implied issues are scary. "Not particularly enjoyable, but contains excellent information." *Kid Juror Comments*: "Now I know what to say to that jerk at school." Kids related to many of the situations. Adult intervention to help discuss the heavy material is useful. Some thought the acting was stilted and not very realistic. Video. 30 min.; $19.95; Age: 10-18. PSI Productions.

Age 12-18 · **Video** · **Edu/Instru**

Category—Family

* All Creatures Great and Small

James Harriot left World War II a shaken man, but the country veterinarian learned peace through his remarkable ability to heal animals. Based on a true story. Stars Christopher Timothy, Robert Hardy, Peter Davison, and Carol Drinkwater. *Adult Juror Comments*: Lovely story with solutions to problems returning veterans face, such as family tensions and dealing with difficult people. Set in rural England in 1946. Slightly unsafe behavior. *Kid Juror Comments*: Story okay, but the pace too slow. They had difficulty relating to the setting and WWII period. Some scenes evoked giggles. There is little repeat viewing value for this age. Video. 94 min.; $19.98; Age: 12-18. Twentieth Century Fox Home Entertainment.

** Ashpet: An American Cinderella (From the Brothers Grimm)

This humorous version of Cinderella, set in American South, provides a way for children and adults to explore values, self-esteem, and sibling rivalry. *Adult Juror Comments*: Many opportunities to compare this with other versions of the classic tale. Jurors responded favorably to the Southern setting and the period costumes. They thought the ending was not as powerful as other versions. *Kid Juror Comments*: Girls enjoyed this best. The World War II setting was somewhat confusing. Several kids thought it ended too abruptly with little explanation. Ten to twelve-year-olds loved it. "The African-American lady told a good story." Video. 25 min.; $29.95; Age: 8-18. Davenport Films.

* Author, Author!

Al Pacino plays a playwright living in New York with five children and stepchildren. Parental role reversal occurs when the mother leaves the household and the father's commitment to the children pulls together an unlikely new family structure. *Adult Juror Comments*: The father and children relate to each other in extraordinary ways. Addresses separation and divorce. Contains some profanity, gender stereotypes, and sexual overtones. "Wild and crazy family but still charming." Dated approach to topic. *Kid Juror Comments*: Deals with family crisis in a way children can understand. The child characters appealed most to children experiencing similar situations. Kids enjoyed seeing Al Pacino as a young actor. Video. 109 min.; $14.98; Age: 12-18. Twentieth Century Fox Home Entertainment.

* Beverly Hills Family Robinson (Wonderful World of Disney)

Marsha Robinson, host of a TV cooking show, takes her family on a working vacation. While there, pirates hijack their yacht. Their dysfunctional family ends up healing when faced with extreme survival circumstances. *Adult Juror Comments*: Honors family values with a comical approach to "the bad guys." While the idea of fixing the family's broken down relationships is good, all the horrible behavior to show their dysfunction is overdone. Great setting. *Kid Juror Comments*: Kids liked the ideas about modern versus primitive living and loved the tree house. "I wish we lived in a tree house like that." They related to the lack of quality time the family spent together prior to their island experience. Video. 89 min.; $14.99; Age: 12-14. Buena Vista Home Entertainment/Disney.

*** Black Stallion Returns, The

 Alec pursues his beloved horse, Black, who's been kidnapped by his original owner. Alec's mystical bond with Black makes him "the one fated rider" for the film's big race. *Adult Juror Comments*: Lots of action, backed with excellent photography. A wonderful portrait of a boy and the emotional ties with his horse. Sensitive and respectful treatment of other cultures. The death scene may bother some children. *Kid Juror Comments*: Terrific. Video. 125 min.; $14.95; Age: 6-18. MGM/UA Home Entertainment.

*** Black Stallion, The

 A shipwreck leaves Alec and a wild Arabian stallion stranded on a desolate island. Their survival forges a lasting bond of friendship. *Adult Juror Comments*: An uplifting and spirited story with strong humanistic appeal. Every turn of events leads to a positive outcome. Vivid settings. *Kid Juror Comments*: Children adored this film. They loved the horse and the adventure. Opening segment is great. They were spellbound. Exciting story, held their attention longer than expected. Video. 117 min.; $14.95; Age: 4-18. MGM/UA Home Entertainment.

** Boyhood of John Muir, The

Dramatic feature tells the early story of Scottish emigrant John Muir, known today as the founder of the Sierra Club and Yosemite National Park, and as America's first great spokesman for the wilderness. *Adult Juror Comments*: Teaches about early conservation efforts. Portrays a strongly patriarchy society and religious narrow-mindedness. Addresses family relationships and perseverance. Scenery is awe-inspiring. *Kid Juror Comments*: Most boys knew who Muir was. "History brought to life—Bravo!" Shows how different cultures meet and clash. Strictness of Muir's father prompted discussion about parental behavior. Video. 78 min.; $29.95; Age: 12-18. Bullfrog Films.

Age 12-18

Video

Family

** *Breaking Away*

This Academy Award-winning comedy portrays four friends coming to terms with life after high school. Highlights Indiana University and world-class cycle racing. *Adult Juror Comments*: Well-produced. Funny, well-written, and a pleasure to view. Presents timeless themes such as teens struggling to make decisions regarding their future. Teaches perseverance. Contains some profanity. Accurately depicts peer pressure. *Kid Juror Comments*: Pretty good. Kids cheered at the end. Kids commented about the graphic language and appreciated that it shows how teens think and try to fit in. "Excellent music; it kept my attention." "I am much more interested in cycling now." Video. 101 min.; $14.98; Age: 12-18. Twentieth Century Fox Home Entertainment.

*** *Chicken Run*

Cooped-up chickens try to break out into a free-range lifestyle assisted by a boasting American rooster who's escaped from the circus. Voice talents by Mel Gibson, Miranda Richardson, and Julia Sawalha and animation by Aardman Animations. *Adult Juror Comments*: Entertaining for all. Cute story, comedic aspects, and colorful claymation make an excellent production. A not-so-obvious remake of *The Great Escape*. Great discussion starter for business, politics, assertiveness, persistence, and teamwork. *Kid Juror Comments*: A big hit. "It's silly and fun, but it taught us to look for different ways to solve problems." "The chickens were like real people, with good expressions and human voices." "I learned what prison must be like." Video. 89 min.; $26.99; Age: 8-18. Dreamworks.

** *Children's Favorites: Legends (Children's Favorites)*

Five classic legends come to life with colorful, spirited animation. The lyrical story of Syrinx, Daedalus the artful craftsman of Greek mythology, plus three stories: "The Sufi Tale," "The Flying Canoe," and "Paradise." *Adult Juror Comments*: Beautiful, sensitively rendered. The first four stories contain no language, only music. Some nudity and abstraction. May need explanation of background and cultural context. *Kid Juror Comments*: Most suitable for older children or children with more sophisticated tastes in art and animation. The abstract presentation was hard for some to follow, but others found it "neat," "cool." "I loved the music." Video. 44 min.; $19.95; Age: 13-18. Nat'l Film Board of Canada.

** City Boy

Nick, a 17-year-old orphan, leaves Chicago in search of his identity, and unexpectedly finds romance and a home in a majestic forest. He soon finds himself torn between his love for Angelica and loyalty to his boss. *Adult Juror Comments*: Appealing teen portrayal. Nick is an orphan with emotional problems related to his past. He overcomes many difficulties, a dishonest friend, a handicapped hand, fear of fire and ignorance about nature, and helps save the day. Some mild violence. *Kid Juror Comments*: Kids enjoyed the story. Stimulated discussions about loyalty, environment, and tenacity. Audio and video are poor at times. Kids discussed importance of choices they make and the friends they choose. They related to Simon being a phony and a "jerk." Video. 110 min.; $19.95; Age: 10-16. Bonneville Worldwide Entertainment.

*** Court Jester

Framed by the pageantry of 12th-century England, Danny Kaye sings, dances, and clowns, yet still finds time for dangerous duels with swordsmen and rescuing damsels in distress. A delightful comedy. *Adult Juror Comments*: Contains some questionable language. Appeals to entire family. Presents a rather nasty view of the English upper class in another time period. Wit and humor throughout. "Kids enjoyed, so did I, we all laughed out loud." *Kid Juror Comments*: Great humor, but kids definitely thought it was too dated. "I liked the sword fighting." Characters think their way through problems. "I liked when the witch hypnotized the jester. That was funny." Video. 101 min.; $14.95; Age: 8-18. Paramount Home Entertainment.

** Creature Comforts

Four short films from Nick Park, creator of "Wallace and Gromit." Features the Academy Award-winning "Creature Comforts" about zoo life. *Adult Juror Comments*: Delightful, creative, challenging. Connection between hell and non-payment of contracts is illogical. Wonderfully produced in claymation format. Shows anatomically correct clay man. English accent is difficult. "Handbag" is unsuitable for anyone. *Kid Juror Comments*: Sophisticated humor was above the level of many kids. Non-English-speaking kids didn't get it at all. Most loved the claymation. Some watched it several times. Anatomically correct clay guy brought snickers. "Best clay-animation I've seen." Video. 33 min.; $14.98; Age: 12-18. Twentieth Century Fox Home Entertainment.

Age 12-18

Video

Family

* Curse of the Lost Gold Mine

Adventure and greed in the mountains of British Columbia, Canada. Recounts the legend of the Indian named Slumach and the search for his lost gold mine. *Adult Juror Comments*: Good mystery. Part of the legend includes scenes of hangings and shootings. As much a tale of justice as a tale of an expedition to find gold, though the re-enactment is hokey. Can provoke a discussion about values. *Kid Juror Comments*: Enjoyed the spooky mystery, though portrayal of the Indians was inappropriate. Kids found the story line confusing. Initially it sparked their interest, but didn't deliver. Video. 50 min.; $19.95; Age: 12-18. Superior Promotions/Home Video, Inc.

* D.P. (The Short Story Collection II)

 On the barren German landscape after World War II, a lonely black orphan boy discovers the only other black he has ever seen—an American Army soldier. *Adult Juror Comments*: Very slow-moving and difficult to follow. Did not engage children despite excellent historical information and acting. Pictures some racist behaviors. Story line is hard to follow. "You really feel for the little boy in this movie." *Kid Juror Comments*: Despite the awards this show has won, it had almost no appeal to our child jurors. Dull and depressing. Showed people of different races making fun of each other. Film looks dated. Video. 55 min.; $24.95; Age: 13-18. Monterey Home Video.

** Dancing on the Moon (Tales for All)

Thirteen-year-old Madeline suspects that she is from another planet. One summer afternoon finds Madeline and Freddy swimming at two different areas of the beach. A storm comes up and suddenly nothing will ever be the same. *Adult Juror Comments*: Cute but somewhat disconnected. Reinforces concepts about being yourself, standing up for your beliefs, and treating others with respect. The situations Madeline faces are realistic and believable. *Kid Juror Comments*: Pleasant though slow-moving. Kids liked the computer graphics, the imaginary friend, and the toy dog. Offers ideas about mortality. "It was easy to understand, especially for kids in junior high." They enjoyed the imaginary pet. Video. 92 min.; $29.95; Age: 11-14. Productions La Fête.

** *Degrassi High (Degrassi)*

 Addresses friendship, love, death, pregnancy, rumors, rebellion, drinking, divorce, death, and more. Ensemble cast presents a unique teenage view of high school and the challenges of growing up. *Adult Juror Comments*: Well-produced, addresses controversial issues, slightly dated. Portrays the reality of high school years and a window into the life of a pregnant teen. Language and format are targeted to teen audience. Good diversity shown. *Kid Juror Comments*: Encourages kids to talk to friends about things that they are going through. Offers thoughts about divorce from a teen's perspective and insight into the life of a pregnant teenager. "Why didn't they show the viewpoint of the guy who got her pregnant?" Video. 180 min.; $39.95; Age: 12-18. WGBH.

** *Degrassi Junior High (Degrassi)*

 Visits a school in a class by itself and confronts issues about friendship, puberty, rumors, sports, studies, and more. Presents a unique view of life from a teen's point of view. *Adult Juror Comments*: Touches on serious subjects, using appropriate language and stories. Cause and effect are dealt with in a way kids this age can relate to. Addresses sexism and prejudice. Some programs should be viewed with adults to explain health and social issues. *Kid Juror Comments*: Made kids question what they would do in a similar situation and opened discussions about serious, controversial topics. "Seemed to focus on the popular kids." Program seems slightly outdated and moves too slowly for older kids. Video. 180 min.; $39.95; Age: 12-15. WGBH.

** *Dralion (Cirque du Soleil Presents)*

The renowned Cirque du Soleil takes viewers on an awe-inspiring journey of the senses. Acrobats and comedians from a variety of cultures perform dazzling acts together. *Adult Juror Comments*: Colorful, artistic. Good sound and lots of action; operatic music is captivating. Shows graceful men and very strong women. Sometimes the scope is too broad, and 90 minutes is a little long. Generates interest in the performance arts. *Kid Juror Comments*: Most were intrigued by the fantastic physical acts, lighting, and costumes. "I want to know how they did some of the stuff they did like flying." "I bet they practice all the time." "I couldn't understand the language." Video. 89 min.; $22.96; Age: 8-18. Columbia Tristar Home Entertainment.

Age 12-18

Video

Family

*** *Einstein: Light to the Power of 2 (Inventors' Specials)*

A fictional friendship between an African-American girl and the renowned physicist, who encourages her to fulfill her potential and defend her rights. *Adult Juror Comments*: Intergenerational story motivates, stimulates, even inspires. School problems such as grades, peer pressure, and race relations are treated in an intriguing format. Offers potential for further discussion. Exceptionally executed. *Kid Juror Comments*: Enthusiastic. "I like what Einstein tells the girl about being a minority." Einstein is portrayed as a champion, mentor, teacher. Provoked inquiry into his life and work. Eye-opener for kids regarding race relations in the 1950s. Video. 55 min.; $19.95; Age: 8-18. Devine Entertainment Corp.

** *Fantastic Voyage (Fantastic Voyage)*

Medical and scientific specialists and their submarine-like craft are reduced to microscopic size in order to enter the bloodstream of a top scientist, travel to his brain and hurriedly remedy the blood clot that threatens his life. *Adult Juror Comments*: Great way to teach about parts of the human body through an experiential window. Its spy appeal keeps older kids' attention. Good role models for overcoming difficulties. As a science fiction film, it's slightly outdated. *Kid Juror Comments*: Offers a good adventure that isn't too suspenseful. Kids liked how it showed the inside the human body, the red and white blood cells, arteries and veins. "I want to ask my science teacher about the things that we saw." Video. 101 min.; $14.98; Age: 8-18. Twentieth Century Fox Home Entertainment.

*** *Fly Away Home*

Wonderful adventure of a thirteen-year-old girl and her estranged father who discover what families are all about when they adopt orphaned geese and teach them to fly. *Adult Juror Comments*: Charming, wholesome movie with powerful acting by likable characters. Without being overly sentimental, shows how parent and child can reconcile differences. Inspiring insights into flight, migration, death, and self-strength. *Kid Juror Comments*: Students were moved and touched by the family's commitment to the geese. "It was a wonderful movie, beautifully filmed." "Kids thought some parts were unrealistic, such as the game warden and army guys. Good discussion followed the viewing. Video. 107 min.; $14.95; Age: 7-18. Columbia Tristar Home Entertainment.

Age 12-18

Video

Family

*** Galileo: On the Shoulders of Giants (Inventors' Specials)

Galileo uncovers mysteries of the universe while dealing with financial problems, an unemployed brother, and a jealous rival. He finds unlikely support from a Medici son. The pair struggles for intellectual freedom while they invent the telescope. *Adult Juror Comments*: Very informative and stimulating. Opens further inquiry into Galileo's theories about planetary motion. Excellent production quality, great settings, good acting. Offers insight on social conditions and issues. *Kid Juror Comments*: Kids enjoyed learning about Galileo's experiments to track the movement of stars and planets. Appreciated the realistic sets and costumes. "It showed us how everybody can think alike and still be wrong, as well as how society punishes creative ideas. Video. 57 min.; $19.95; Age: 8-18. Devine Entertainment Corp.

** Giant of Thunder Mountain, The

This exciting family adventure features Richard Kiel as the giant who must overcome an evil carnival operator, the prejudice of a small town, and a 1,500-pound grizzly bear. *Adult Juror Comments*: Good acting, good story, dealing with differences by showing the damage that prejudice can inflict on both society and an individual. Production well-paced for kids. *Kid Juror Comments*: Exciting. Older kids gave it an all-star. Held everyone's attention straight through till the end. Under-fives were scared when the bear appeared. "The pictures were great." Video. 88 min.; $19.95; Age: 10-18. American Happenings.

** Good Morning Miss Toliver

A captivating look at Presidential Award-winner Kay Toliver, who combines math and communication-arts skills to inspire and motivate her East Harlem Tech students. *Adult Juror Comments*: An upbeat and inspiring portrait of a dedicated and creative teacher. Miss Toliver is a role model for students and teachers, offering excellent ideas for teaching math to all students. "This is a must-see for teacher training." *Kid Juror Comments*: Everyone wished they had a teacher with Miss Toliver's qualities. They enjoyed seeing how math can be interesting, relevant, and not just scary. Led to a discussion about inner-city schools and their students. Video. 27 min.; $24.95; Age: 10-18. Fase Productions.

** Great Books: Frankenstein, The Making of the Monster
(Great Books)

Entering the dark, mysterious world of Mary Shelley, this video helps to understand why her brooding masterpiece continues to fascinate and frighten. Shows how classic literature has shaped our lives and continues to influence our thinking. *Adult Juror Comments*: Well-produced and intellectually stimulating. Best-suited for older children with sophisticated critical thinking skills. *Kid Juror Comments*: Very interesting, informative, and easy to understand. "It kept me intrigued." Video. 50 min.; $19.95; Age: 14-18. Discovery Communications.

Age 12-18

Video

Family

*** Great Books: Le Morte D'Arthur (Great Books)

 Visit the possible site of Camelot and learn the connection between Sir Thomas Mallory's 15th century masterpiece and George Lucas's "Star Wars" trilogy. *Adult Juror Comments*: Excellent production, with clear narration appropriately paced. Offers insight for high school students who are familiar with the history and legend of King Arthur. Presentation is a bit wordy. *Kid Juror Comments*: "It's not acting; it's history." Eighteen-year-olds were fascinated with use of different time periods to relate a story to our own era. Explanation of armor and "Star Wars" segments were particularly well done. Video. 50 min.; $19.95; Age: 14-18. Discovery Communications.

*** Great Dictator, The

Chaplin's brilliant lampoon of the Third Reich features Charlie in a dual role as a Jewish barber and the Hitlerian dictator. *Adult Juror Comments*: This classic lacks the production quality and special effects kids are accustomed to today. Yet it addresses important concepts—Nazism, oppression of Jews, and military aggression. Demands critical thinking skills and requires advance preparation. *Kid Juror Comments*: Young adults with some understanding of World War II benefited most from this story. Kids felt that much preparation was needed to really understand this film, although some liked the comedy as fair value on its own. Video. 126 min.; $19.98; Age: 12-18. Twentieth Century Fox Home Entertainment.

** Hello, Dolly!

Barbra Streisand stars as the famous matchmaker Dolly Levi, who sets out to get Walter Matthau for herself. Lavish musical production features great songs by Jerry Herman. *Adult Juror Comments*: Good family entertainment. This classic Broadway musical with elaborate sets and choreography also exemplifies the predictable humor of the genre. Loaded with subtle sexual innuendoes and gender-stereotyped behavior. *Kid Juror Comments*: Appealing costumes and fashions, but thought the story did not apply to their lives. Girls enjoyed this more than boys. Video. 146 min.; $14.98; Age: 12-18. Twentieth Century Fox Home Entertainment.

*** Joseph: King of Dreams

Based on the Old Testament story about the rivalry between Joseph and his brothers. The brothers sell Joseph into slavery to the Egyptians in bitter response to their father's favoritism. After he becomes an Egyptian king, Joseph forgives his brothers. *Adult Juror Comments*: Top-notch animation and music. Stresses teamwork and individuality. "It encourages forgiveness among friends and family." Contains biblical references and shows good diversity. *Kid Juror Comments*: Kids wanted to know more about the story of Joseph. "Joseph could tell what was going to happen by listening to his dreams. That's cool!" "I liked it when Joseph showed forgiveness to his brothers who sold him into slavery." Video. 75 min.; $24.99; Age: 8-18. Dreamworks.

** Journey (Hallmark Hall of Fame)

Devoted grandparents pick up the pieces that their restless daughter leaves behind, teaching how family is all about the people who love you. Stars Jason Robards, Brenda Fricker, and Meg Tilly. *Adult Juror Comments*: Inspirational and attractive production. Contemporary subject matter deals with difficult emotional issues about abandonment. Slow-moving, serious, and thoughtful. *Kid Juror Comments*: Favorite sections: the grandfather's picture-taking and the grandmother's handling of the children. Video. 99 min.; $14; Age: 12-18. Artisan/Family Home Entertainment.

*** Kayla: A Cry in the Wilderness (DVD)

When young Sam befriends a wild dog, the townspeople, fearing it will kill their livestock, pressure his family to destroy it. DVD features include information on Quebec and author Elizabeth Van Steenwyk, a scene index, and questions for discussion. *Adult Juror Comments*: Excellent picture quality, great story, pleasing dialog. DVD extras are wonderful and easy-to-use, should motivate further study. "I could see lots of areas of inquiry for kids: wild dogs, exploration, sledding, dog training, music, carpentry." *Kid Juror Comments*: Especially liked the interactive material. "Everything was wonderful, but I wanted more." "It was interesting to know about the author because I might like to read some of her other books." "We loved the story. We laughed, we cried, and we cheered." DVD. 96 min.; $24.95; Age: 10-18. Questar, Inc.

*** Little Horse That Could, The

 This real-life story tells about a little horse with a big heart and the young woman, Carol Kozlowski, who trains and competes with him. Carol takes you behind the scenes to see all that is involved in caring for and training a champion. *Adult Juror Comments*: Beautifully filmed, slow-moving, yet interesting. Provides insight about horse competition. Horse's point of view is an unusual touch. Teaches a valuable lesson about not giving up and working toward personal goals. *Kid Juror Comments*: Horse-lovers were totally captivated. They learned respect and delight for these amazing animals. As the story unfolded, their enthusiasm grew. "I liked learning how to take care of horses." Video. 60 min.; $12.95; Age: 8-18. Dreams Come True Productions.

** Little Princess, The (Shirley Temple)

In Shirley Temple's first Technicolor musical, she goes from a snooty prep-schooler to a servant when her rich father dies. Based on the novel by Frances Hodgson Burnett. Song-and-dance routines with Arthur Treacher. *Adult Juror Comments*: Adults enjoyed this for nostalgic reasons—it is familiar. Offers complex messages regarding death, poverty, and hope. Some children will have difficulty relating to the historical time period. Its fairy tale appeal is timeless. *Kid Juror Comments*: Children politely watched, but said they would not have selected it on their own. It was difficult to follow, and many got very restless. They liked the happy ending, compared the movie version to the book, and asked questions about boarding schools. Video. 93 min.; $14.98; Age: 7-18. Twentieth Century Fox Home Entertainment.

*** Miracle at Midnight (Wonderful World of Disney)

In Nazi Germany, the Germans are about to impose a final solution to the Jewish population. Facing impossible odds, a group of Danes risk their lives to smuggle Jews out of the country. *Adult Juror Comments*: Compelling story. Excellent production. Haunting story depicting some of the worst treatment bestowed on mankind. Compassionate, honest, and scary view of racial hatred and the families and non-Jewish friends who risked their lives to support the Jews. *Kid Juror Comments*: Kids found it really interesting. It helped explain the choices people had to make during this time. "I hope this will never happen again." "I would have saved my friends too." "The people who risked their lives were really brave." Video. 88 min.; $14.99; Age: 12-18. Buena Vista Home Entertainment/Disney.

*** Miracle Worker, The

The inspiring story of how a determined teacher helped the profoundly challenged Helen Keller overcome her disabilities to become a celebrated international leader for the disabled. *Adult Juror Comments*: Fabulous! Loved it. Great enrichment story suitable for a wide audience. Strong inspirational message for those with physical impairment. Provocative drama promotes feelings of respect and understanding. *Kid Juror Comments*: Enthralled. Great. "I related to this story because my grandfather is blind." "The superimposed images of her hands were very effective." "My favorite and most inspirational part was when she learned the meaning of words." Video. 89 min.; $19.99; Age: 8-18. Buena Vista Home Entertainment/Disney.

* Mozart's the Magic Flute Story
(Children's Cultural Collection)

 Mozart's great opera "The Magic Flute" narrated in English and sung in its original German. Performed by the famous Gewandhaus Orchestra of Holland. *Adult Juror Comments*: Good narration, costumes, staging, and cinematography. Offers children a suitable introduction to opera. The story is difficult to follow. *Kid Juror Comments*: Enjoyable, especially for those interested in music. Even teen-age boys responded reasonably well. Music teachers thought performance was mediocre. Video. 42 min.; $19.98; Age: 10-18. V.I.E.W. Video.

* Mr. Headmistress (Wonderful World of Disney)

Con-man Tucker dresses up as Ms. Bascombe, the headmistress of an all girls' boarding school. He doesn't count on the bond he soon forms with his students. *Adult Juror Comments*: Humorous and appealing. Doesn't always portray teachers, students, and education positively. Shows cooperation, honesty, teamwork, and how restoring relationships takes work. Most of the young girls are miserably unhappy and self-absorbed. *Kid Juror Comments*: Exciting. "I think people of many ages would find it funny. We loved it." Kids loved the field hockey game. There was some unsafe behavior like the thugs hitting each other. "Made me laugh even though it was predictable." "The ending made me feel good." Video. 89 min.; $14.99; Age: 12-18. Buena Vista Home Entertainment/Disney.

Age 12-18

Video

Family

** Mrs. Doubtfire

How far would an ordinary father go to spend more time with his children? Watch as this divorced dad goes to extreme measures in this comedy starring Robin Williams and Sally Field. *Adult Juror Comments*: Excellent. At times painful, poignant, and ultimately triumphant. Illustrates in a humorous fashion some of the best and worst adult behaviors that occur during a divorce. Adults loved it. Contains a lot of profanity. *Kid Juror Comments*: "I could relate because I know a lot of kids who have gone through divorce in their families." "Robin Williams is so funny!" "I liked the creative idea of the father pretending to be a woman." "It covers a really serious topic in a funny way." Video. 125 min.; $14.98; Age: 12-18. Twentieth Century Fox Home Entertainment.

*** MVP: Most Valuable Primate

A sign-language-speaking, hockey-playing chimp skates away with the affections of an entire town—and helps two young kids find the courage to become champions. *Adult Juror Comments*: Fantastic. Wonderful story involving feelings and attitudes. Virtues from honesty to perseverance are personified, rather than preached. The characters play the story straight instead of wholesale slapstick. Sends a clear message of acceptance. *Kid Juror Comments*: Won them over, every one. Definitely would watch again. "Funny, crazy, exciting, terrific. Hilarious in places." Portrayal of hearing-impaired sister impressed them. "Even if you are different, you can still do things." "I want to learn sign language." Video. 93 min.; $24.98; Age: 8-16. Warner Home Video.

* My Date with the President's Daughter
(Wonderful World of Disney)

Hallie, the daughter of the president, only wants to be a normal kid and go on her first date. Duncan, a shy teen, asks her out and their date turns into an adventure that could seriously damage their relationship as well as national security. *Adult Juror Comments*: Humorous, appealing to teen audience. Well–produced, though it incorporates a lot of heavy metal music and is filled with chase scenes. Provides insight into the possibilities of being a prominent politician's child. *Kid Juror Comments*: Kids could relate to Hallie. "She just wants to be a regular kid like me." "Some of the music was loud, like headache music. It bothered me." "It was funny when the characters lost the secret service men." "It shows some unsafe behavior at the party." Video. 88 min.; $14.99; Age: 10-18. Buena Vista Home Entertainment/Disney.

*** *National Velvet (Family Entertainment)*

With excellent performances and exhilarating footage of horse racing, this cherished story of a small girl who realizes her big dream—first prize in England's National Steeplechase—remains enchanting. Stars Elizabeth Taylor, Mickey Rooney. *Adult Juror Comments*: Classic film shows healthy family interactions and excellent female role models. Mickey Rooney plays a weak character who grows stronger with the family's trust in him. The horse and race scenes are stunning. *Kid Juror Comments*: Gripping. The older ones were particularly interested in following the specifics of the plot. Horse-lovers were thrilled. Video. 124 min.; $14.9; Age: 5-18. MGM/UA Home Entertainment.

** *Oklahoma!*

Rodgers and Hammerstein's landmark musical is brought to the screen with all the spirit and energy of the Broadway production. Oscar-winning score. *Adult Juror Comments*: Classic with adult themes about marriage, sex, love, death, suicide, and politics. Very dated approach, with great music, costumes, and phony sets. Contains potential theme of sexual assault. Shows women as vain and simple. *Kid Juror Comments*: Corny and hokey. Limited action and a lame love story. Some liked the songs and dancing. Others couldn't get into it. Led to a discussion about western settlements as well as traditional theater. Video. 145 min.; $19.98; Age: 12-18. Twentieth Century Fox Home Entertainment.

** *One Fine Day*

Two single parents agree to share babysitting for the day when both their kids miss a school field trip resulting in twelve hours of misadventures and one unexpected twist. Stars Michelle Pfeiffer and George Clooney. *Adult Juror Comments*: Enjoyable, funny, light-hearted comedy and romantic fantasy. Appealing to any parent who has struggled with schedules for children. Contains mild profanity, sexual innuendoes, and gender stereotypes. *Kid Juror Comments*: Hilarious, believable, good acting. Kids commented on the single mom stereotyping and "too much cussing." "They shouldn't have shown the lady in her bra." "It taught me to give people a second chance." Video. 109 min.; $14.98; Age: 14-18. Twentieth Century Fox Home Entertainment.

** *Opus & Bill: A Wish for Wings*

Based on the well-known comic strip characters. Opus the Penguin wants to fly like a real bird. In pursuing his desire, he learns to value his natural attributes. *Adult Juror Comments*: Attractive animation, sophisticated comedy with fairly hip attitudes. Contains some adult language. Subject matter is appropriate for older kids or family viewing. *Kid Juror Comments*: Lots of laughs. Parts of the story are confusing, but one thing is clear: the penguin wants to fly. "It talks about how it's okay to be who you are and how we all have something that makes us special." Video. 30 min.; $12.98; Age: 15-18. Universal Studios Home Video.

Age 12-18

Video

Family

Chapter Five • Jr & Sr High School

*** *Our Friend Martin*

The remarkable life of Dr. Martin Luther King Jr., using modern animated characters who travel back in time and meet Dr. King at various points in his career. Approved by the King family. *Adult Juror Comments*: Excellent use of live-action historical footage mixed with animation.

Traces his influence on American history. Graphic images depicting racist behavior is best viewed with adults. Stellar cast, voices of Oprah Winfrey, John Travolta, and others. *Kid Juror Comments*: Impressive. Many were not aware of the content. "This video taught us to respect other people, not hate each other because of color." "It taught me a lot of history, and it was sad." "I liked when they time-traveled." Video. 60 min.; $9.98; Age: 8-18. Twentieth Century Fox Home Entertainment.

** *Phar Lap*

Based on the true story of a New Zealand race horse who becomes the legendary winner of 37 races. *Adult Juror Comments*: Interesting historical plot with great horse-racing scenes. Addressed anti-Semitism and class struggles in Australia. Also portrays the grim aspects of the sport. Foreign accents difficult to understand. *Kid Juror Comments*: "Loved the show; it made me cry." Kids were intrigued when they discovered it was based on a real story, and went on to look up information about horses in Australia and New Zealand. Video. 107 min.; $14.98; Age: 12-18. Twentieth Century Fox Home Entertainment.

* *Prehistoric Pink (The Pink Panther Cartoon Collection)*

Pink Panther goes primeval, helping a dull-witted caveman invent the wheel. He dukes it out with persistent pests, vexing vampires, stubborn stallions, and an annoying astronomer who sends him around the moon in eight out-of-this-world escapades. *Adult Juror Comments*: Contains slapstick violence, but doesn't condone it. Best viewed by kids who understand absurdity and sophisticated humor. Contains some sexual innuendo. The sight gags appeal to all ages. *Kid Juror Comments*: Wonderful. Pink Panther character and the music were great. They pointed out that "duking it out" was inappropriate behavior. Video. 51 min.; $12.95; Age: 8-18. MGM/UA Home Entertainment.

Age 12-18 · **Video** · **Family**

*** Princess Bride, The

 Long ago there lived the beautiful Buttercup and her "one true love," Wesley. They part and lose touch for many years. When an evil prince arranges to marry Buttercup, Wesley returns to battle warriors, giants, and wizards to rescue his true love. *Adult Juror Comments*: A jewel to watch. Humorous, slightly fractured fairy tale with a princess who stands up for herself. Charming sets and period costumes, well-acted and seamlessly edited. Employs extensive vocabulary and a variety of literary devices. *Kid Juror Comments*: Storyteller approach piqued the children's interest and held their attention. They loved the characters. The intelligent princess scored a big hit with her witty retorts. Kids repeated several of the lines over and over after the screening. Video. 98 min.; $14.99; Age: 12-18. MGM/UA Home Entertainment.

* Principal Takes a Holiday, The (Wonderful World of Disney)

Zachery Ty Bryan stars as a rowdy high school senior who must get through the year without any demerits in order to claim his parents' $10,000 graduation gift. An accident befalls the principal and the rowdy senior finds a drifter to stand in. *Adult Juror Comments*: Through the mistakes made by high school students, viewers learn lessons about taking responsibility for their actions and grades. Values diversity. Presents educational and social challenges, encourages kids to be assertive. *Kid Juror Comments*: Kids enjoyed the humor and tricks the characters pulled on each other. Favorite parts: when the principal was covered in red paint and Bill Nye the science guy. Video. 98: min.; $14.99; Age: 12-18. Buena Vista Home Entertainment/Disney.

* Rivers Run, The

Set on a riverboat in Australia at the turn of the century, this epic saga of a family living on the river depicts the strength of family bonds, through good times as well as bad. *Adult Juror Comments*: Beautiful scenery. Story is long and best viewed in segments. Period piece set in Australia that provides a glimpse into life on a river boat. Portrays independence in women and highlights the importance of family ties. *Kid Juror Comments*: Ambivalent. The historical fiction mini-series format made it difficult to watch in one sitting. It's long, and some found it a bit boring. "I thought the scenery was beautiful, but the story moved too slow and it's long." "There wasn't enough action." Video. 210 min.; $24.95; Age: 12-18. Questar, Inc.

Age 12-18

Video

Family

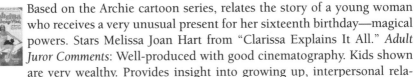

** Sabrina the Teenage Witch (Hallmark Hall of Fame)

 Based on the Archie cartoon series, relates the story of a young woman who receives a very unusual present for her sixteenth birthday—magical powers. Stars Melissa Joan Hart from "Clarissa Explains It All." *Adult Juror Comments*: Well-produced with good cinematography. Kids shown are very wealthy. Provides insight into growing up, interpersonal relationships, making decisions. *Kid Juror Comments*: All the kids responded positively to the script. They enjoyed the romance and the plot. Especially for kids who enjoy high school dramas. Girls related to it better than boys. Video. 91 min.; $14.95; Age: 12-18. Artisan/Family Home Entertainment.

*** Seal Morning (DVD)

 In 1930s England, the discovery of a baby seal brings orphaned Rowena together with her reclusive Aunt Miriam, and soon, more wildlife. Special DVD features include information on the setting and on seals, and suggests questions for discussion. *Adult Juror Comments*: A warm, inviting story presented in a super interactive DVD. The menu items give additional information that is useful for discussion. Wonderful camera work, breathtaking scenes. "A great experience for the whole family to see and share experiences." *Kid Juror Comments*: Watched it attentively, were interested in DVD features. "The index made it easy to find your place." "It has good color and sound. It made everything look real." "I liked it when the seal was 'singing' with the women." DVD. 103 min.; $24.95; Age: 8-18. Questar, Inc.

*** Singing for Freedom
(A Concert for the Child in Each of Us)

A momentous gathering of people from all walks of life sing and dance as they become a powerfully united congregation at a "Sweet Honey in the Rock" concert at Glide Memorial Church in San Francisco. *Adult Juror Comments*: A marvelous family concert, truly inspirational. Aptly captures the group's charisma and musicality. Elementary music teachers thought this was a wonderful introduction to music. Everyone noted how it motivated them to want to get up and dance! *Kid Juror Comments*: Didn't take long for children to get up and sing and dance along. "This is a lot of fun, watching people of all races sing together." Video. 59 min.; $14.98; Age: 5-18. Music for Little People.

*** Soldier Jack (From the Brothers Grimm)*

 Set in rural America after WW II, Jack returns from the war and receives two gifts: a sack that can catch anything and a jar that tells whether a person will live or die. Jack eliminates death from the world, until he realizes what a mistake that is. *Adult Juror Comments*: Excellent production. Scene with devils is too frightening for younger kids. Offers insight about life and death that is suitable for older kids, or younger ones when accompanied by an adult. Provokes interest in Appalachian folk tales. *Kid Juror Comments*: Well-received lesson about how to treat others. Some were familiar with this story. They enjoyed the wartime setting. Video. 40 min.; $29.95; Age: 7-18. Davenport Films.

*** Sounder*

An Academy Award-nominated story about a sharecropper during the Depression. Paul Winfield plays the desperate father who steals for his family. Cicely Tyson plays his wife, Ken Hooks his oldest son. They love, laugh, struggle, and endure. *Adult Juror Comments*: Accurately represents the original book. Has great learning potential and is very respectful of children. Shows that dignity is possible even under oppression. This is a difficult subject that is handled extremely well. *Kid Juror Comments*: Educational and enjoyable. "It made me want to find out more about black sharecroppers." Not all kids were aware of discrimination, and some were taken aback by what they saw. "It was sad, but I learned a lot." Video. 105 min.; $14.95; Age: 8-18. Paramount Home Entertainment.

** That Thing You Do*

Big-hearted comedy about a local rock band that is catapulted into fame when their signature tune hits the top of the charts. *Adult Juror Comments*: Wonderful script, upbeat soundtrack. "Feel good" movie with good pro-social messages such as getting along, cooperation, and respect for others. Contains some profanity, sexual innuendo, and ethnic stereotypes. *Kid Juror Comments*: Kids liked the music. "It made me think about the '60s." "It was great to see the rock band's dream come true." "The recording studio was cool." "It made me think about how men and women should get along." Video. 105 min.; $14.98; Age: 12-18. Twentieth Century Fox Home Entertainment.

Age 12-18

Video

Family

** Three Wishes

Set in the prosperous 1950s, this fatherless family finds magic and kindness when they bring an injured drifter and his dog into their home. There is more to the stranger and his canine companion than meets the eye. *Adult Juror Comments*: Good story, production quality, and character development. Contains adult themes: brief nudity, some sexuality, and fear of losing a child to cancer. Faithfully reflects the time period: characters are white, smoke, and don't wear seatbelts. *Kid Juror Comments*: Sometimes experienced difficulty following storyline, but understood by the end of the movie. "It's touching, both happy and sad." "I want to learn more about the Korean War." Video. 115 min.; $9.94; Age: 14-18. HBO.

** Tim Burton's The Nightmare Before Christmas

Jack Skellington, the Pumpkin King of Halloween Town, decides to spread Christmas joy to the world. But his well-meaning mission unwittingly puts Santa Claus in jeopardy and creates a nightmare for good little boys and girls everywhere! *Adult Juror Comments*: Fun claymation with an incredible amount of attention to detail. Clever story line. Characters are well developed. Some images are creepy and gruesome. Some violent scenes. *Kid Juror Comments*: Enjoyed it. Kids thought the claymation was really cool. "My favorite part was when the boogey man lost his skin and all the bugs came crawling out." "I'd really like to learn more about producing claymation." Video. 76 min.; $22.99; Age: 10-18. Buena Vista Home Entertainment/Disney.

** To the Moon (Nova)

Tells the story behind the Apollo space program, including the walk on the moon in 1969. Introduces the unsung heroes, and shows the dangers, by using a broad range of perspectives in a documentary format. *Adult Juror Comments*: Straight-forward, informative, upbeat with excellent photography and music. A rather dry presentation with lots of data. Space enthusiasts will enjoy it most. Encourages interest in space program and may inspire a space career choice. *Kid Juror Comments*: The images and interviews connected audience to the characters. "The pain of their failures was evident." A good teaching tool about the journey to the moon. Kids liked the diagrams and found the presentation to be rather information rich. Video. 120 min.; $19.95; Age: 10-18. WGBH.

*Tweety and Sylvester

 Sufferin' Succotash! A match made in heaven teams up the lisping pussy-cat Sylvester and the not-so-innocent little canary named Tweety. *Adult Juror Comments*: Tiny canary outsmarts voracious but not-too-bright cat, sometimes by clever ruses, but usually by violent means. Although the violence is of the broad, slapstick variety, it is the constant means of resolving conflict, get what you want, etc. *Kid Juror Comments*: Compared to the superheroes of today, this violence is pretty mild stuff. Kids laughed at the silliness and commented, "We would never do stuff like that." Redeeming virtue—little, weak, smart Tweety always wins. Repetitive. Video. 60 min.; $12.95; Age: 4-18. MGM/UA Home Entertainment.

** Two Soldiers (The Short Story Collection II)

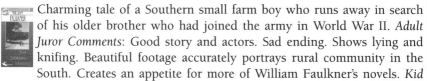 Charming tale of a Southern small farm boy who runs away in search of his older brother who had joined the army in World War II. *Adult Juror Comments*: Good story and actors. Sad ending. Shows lying and knifing. Beautiful footage accurately portrays rural community in the South. Creates an appetite for more of William Faulkner's novels. *Kid Juror Comments*: Retained attention. "The little boy had a lot of freedom for his age." "I liked seeing how people lived in another part of the country." "I'm glad I didn't live there." Best viewed with an adult who can help explain difficult parts. Video. 30 min.; $24.95; Age: 8-18. Monterey Home Video.

*** Wallace and Gromit: A Close Shave (Wallace & Gromit)

Academy Award-winner for Best Animated Short Film. Animator Nick Park's cool claymation couple, Wallace and Gromit, get wrapped up in a sheep-napping yarn. *Adult Juror Comments*: Wonderful family viewing, clever and artistic. The "Britishisms" are odd and a pleasure to watch. Excellent quality will spark interest in claymation. Adults loved this, perhaps even more than children. *Kid Juror Comments*: Good sense of mystery. British humor did not escape the kids. They thought it was clever that the dog never speaks, but relies on facial expressions and physical antics. They loved Gromit, as well as the inventions and gadgetry. Video. 30 min.; $9.98; Age: 8-18. Twentieth Century Fox Home Entertainment.

*** Wallace and Gromit: The Wrong Trousers (Wallace & Gromit)*

Wallace, an eccentric inventor, and Gromit, his ingenious canine, match wits against a mysterious penguin and a sinister pair of trousers in this Oscar-winning animated title. *Adult Juror Comments*: Excellent claymation. Superior mystery story wrapped in a perfectly detailed, miniature set and performed by endearing clay characters. Good for repeat viewing by many age groups. "Wow! I haven't been this impressed in a long time." *Kid Juror Comments*: Perfect entertainment—the story, the characters, the attention to detail, and the wide range of emotions. They were enthralled even in the third viewing. "It's great." They loved Gromit. Video. 29 min.; $14.98; Age: 5-18. Twentieth Century Fox Home Entertainment.

** Windrunner

Greg, a high school senior, finally makes the football team only to find his family is moving to Utah. Greg's father, a former NFL pro, is serving a prison sentence there. A Native American helps him fulfill his dreams. *Adult Juror Comments*: Well-produced, lovely scenery. Shows examples of determination, perseverance, and resolving conflict. "This is a wonderful story full of inspiring moments." Loosely touches on the story of Native American athlete, Jim Thorpe. *Kid Juror Comments*: Enjoyed it, would watch again. "I love the parts about horses and football." "The ghost was a little hard to believe." "I'd like to learn more about Jim Thorpe." "My favorite part was when he forgave his father." Video. 109 min.; $19.95; Age: 10-18. Questar, Inc.

* With Six You Get Eggroll

Doris Day and Brian Keith star in this romantic comedy about coping with kids, marriage, and a newly-created family. *Adult Juror Comments*: Lively and entertaining. It demonstrates individual family members' viewpoints and how they resolve problems to create a healthy family unit. Some funny moments from adult perspective, and still sensitive to youth. Predictable and silly. *Kid Juror Comments*: Kids enjoyed the '60s aspects although they found the story unrealistic and the characters irrational. They learned lessons about being nice to others, especially parents and siblings. "Most families aren't that way now." Video. 95 min.; $9.98; Age: 12-15. Twentieth Century Fox Home Entertainment.

*** *Wizard of Oz, The*

Swooped away from her Kansas farm by a mighty twister, Dorothy and her dog Toto end up in a world of witches and wizards. Dorothy's only hope of returning home is to find the Wizard of Oz. Stars Judy Garland, Ray Bolger, Jack Haley, Bert Lahr. *Adult Juror Comments*: What a delight to watch this timeless classic about courage, love, brains, family, and adventure. Could lead to discussion about society, make-believe versus reality, and the idea of "home." Has value for repeat viewing. Great for entire family. *Kid Juror Comments*: Kids loved the flying monkeys, the scarecrow, the tin man, and Toto." Most have seen it before, but still wanted to watch again and again. Some parts are scary for younger kids. Video. 103 min.; $19.98; Age: 5-18. MGM/UA Home Entertainment.

*** *Your's, Mine and Ours (Family Treasures)*

When a widow and a widower tie the knot, they share 18 children, four bathrooms, and endless domestic hilarity in this "affectionate investigation of American family life at its fallible best." (Hollywood Reporter) Stars Lucille Ball and Henry Fonda. *Adult Juror Comments*: Very funny. Sheds light on the importance of family and the struggles they endure. Wonderful problem-solving skills and sensitive values are demonstrated. Addresses adult ideas more than child's perspective, and uses a sophisticated vocabulary. *Kid Juror Comments*: Appealing. They recognized Lucy. "It's about friendship and love and a big family that learns to get along." Video. 107 min.; $14.95; Age: 8-18. MGM/UA Home Entertainment.

Category—FLM

** *My Fair Lady (My Fair Lady)*

 Henry Higgins teaches Eliza Doolittle how to speak proper English in this classic musical production starring Audrey Hepburn and Rex Harrison. Based on Bernard Shaw's book, *Pygmalion*. *Adult Juror Comments*: Fabulous classic masterpiece. Great music, timeless story, incredible actors. Shows how a person can accomplish anything, if he or she works at it. Promotes self-esteem and gives insight into living conditions of different classes during this time. *Kid Juror Comments*: The songs and the accents held the kids' interest throughout. Girls liked the musical format better than boys. Sparked curiosity about the era and culture. "Everyone has someone in their life who challenges them." Video. 171 min.; $19.98; Age: 12-15. Twentieth Century Fox Home Entertainment.

Category—Foreign Language

** You Can Sign: Volume One
(American Sign Language for Beginners)

A user-friendly program designed for anyone who wants to learn American Sign Language. Lessons focus on common topics applicable to daily life. Viewers are entertained by the Bravo family and guided by deaf instructor, Billy Seago. *Adult Juror Comments*: Uses effective teaching strategies—signs are given in advance, then demonstrated in a realistic environment. Production quality is quite good. Instruction offers a useful resource for any ASL class. Repetition is suitable for beginners. *Kid Juror Comments*: Kids tried to figure out the parts that were only given in sign language, and enjoyed understanding new communication skills. They were fascinated watching family members speak in ASL. Kids wishing to learn sign language will enjoy this most. Video. 82 min.; $29.95; Age: 12-18.Sign Enhancers, Inc.

Category—Holiday

*** Christmas Carol, A

A new version of the holiday classic about Ebenezer Scrooge whose life is radically changed on Christmas Eve by the visits of three spirits—the ghosts of Christmas Past, Christmas Present, and Christmas Yet to Come. Stars George C. Scott. *Adult Juror Comments*: Wonderful, classic story—not too scary. Beautifully produced, wonderful message. Provides thoughtful family holiday entertainment for Christmastime. *Kid Juror Comments*: Engaging, timeless tale tells a good story. Kids enjoyed watching it together with the adults during the holiday season. Video. 100 min.; $14.98; Age: 12-18. Twentieth Century Fox Home Entertainment.

* Christmas Story, A

More than anything, nine-year-old Ralphie Parker wants a "Genuine Red Ryder Carbine Action Two Hundred Shot Lightning Loader Range Model Air Rifle." Standing between him and the gift of his dreams are two parents opposed to his acquiring a rifle. *Adult Juror Comments*: Situation is timeless. Narrative delivery is well done. Contains strong language, aggression." Appropriateness of promoting a gun as a gift may be troubling. Raises issues of peer pressure and deep, deep emotions. *Kid Juror Comments*: Provocative, especially among boys. Many felt their parents would act the same if they asked for a gun. The 1940s setting evoked discussion about different values and points of view. Long. Inappropriate for younger kids. Video. 95 min.; $14.95; Age: 10-18. MGM/UA Home Entertainment.

* Ebenezer

A Wild West setting for the Charles Dickens' classic, *A Christmas Carol*, featuring Jack Palance as Scrooge, the most greedy and mean-spirited crook in the West. Ghosts of Christmas past, present, and future open Scrooge's eyes to love and friendship. *Adult Juror Comments*: Staging of this Christmas classic takes place in the "Old West," complete with bar scenes, brothels, smoking, cussing, fighting, etc. Ebenezer comes around in the end, but the process of getting there presents lots of negative and adult images. *Kid Juror Comments*: Almost all children knew the story and preferred the more familiar version. Half liked this, half did not. "I liked seeing people happy at the end." "My favorite part is seeing Ebenezer with the past, present, and future ghosts." Video. 94 min.; $14.95; Age: 14-18. Plaza Entertainment.

* Jingle All the Way

A father is desperate to buy his son that "must-have" holiday toy. In a frantic last-minute shopping spree he is pitted against a stressed-out postal carrier, a sleazy Santa, and lots of other parents. Stars Arnold Schwarzenegger as dad. *Adult Juror Comments*: Very thin, many negative messages and stereotypical behavior. The children behaved better than the adults. *Kid Juror Comments*: "There's too much fighting." "Some pictures were too fake." "Little kids shouldn't see the drinking part." "The adults didn't treat each other well." Middle-class kids related best, at-risk kids didn't relate to this at all. Video. 90 min.; $19.98; Age: 10-18. Twentieth Century Fox Home Entertainment.

*** Miracle on 34th Street (Family Feature)

Six-year-old Susan has doubts about childhood's most enduring miracle—Santa Claus. Although she doesn't expect anything from Santa this year, she gets the most precious gift of all: something to believe in. Based on the 1947 classic. *Adult Juror Comments*: Charming, well-acted and well-produced. The child star is excellent. While some items are unreal, the story is so strong that it suspends reality. Opens avenues for discussing human relationships and adult interactions. *Kid Juror Comments*: The best. Entirely held kids' attention. Made them feel sad and then happy. "Pretty cool even though it is old." Video. 113 min.; $14.98; Age: 6-18. Twentieth Century Fox Home Entertainment.

Age 12-18

Video

Holiday

* Olive, The Other Reindeer

When a small dog named Olive learns that Blitzen is injured and Christmas may be cancelled, she jumps at the chance to join Santa's reindeer team. Based on the delightful, best-selling children's book. *Adult Juror Comments*: An adult satire with a moral: "Do your best and help those around you strive to do their best too." "It isn't what I call a holiday treat for children; the language is verbally abusive, and actions by the characters are violent." *Kid Juror Comments*: "I cheered and worried about the main character, Olive." "It is easy to understand Olive, who is caring and wants to help." "The mailman was a nasty man; mean to everyone." "I think it's okay to show that not all people have good intentions." Video. 46 min.; $14.98; Age: 10-18. Twentieth Century Fox Home Entertainment.

** Pink Christmas, A

A blue Christmas appears to be in store for the Pink Panther, alone, cold, and hungry on a Central Park bench in New York City. He sets out in search of a meal, concocting a wild array of hare-brained ploys and disguises along the way. *Adult Juror Comments*: Pink Panther's a perennial favorite that's light and entertaining with good music. His antics don't make him the best role model all the time, but in the end, he does show how cooperation helps. Little diversity. *Kid Juror Comments*: The Pink Panther is fun, wholesome, and entertaining. They asked to watch this program again. Video. 27 min.; $9.95; Age: 5-18. MGM/UA Home Entertainment.

Category—Nature

** Dances with Hummingbirds

Get close to the lightning-fast hummingbirds in their dance of life, accompanied by traditional American, Flamenco, and Andean musical compositions. Naturalist Michael Godfrey describes the feeding, nesting, and courtship behavior of hummingbirds. *Adult Juror Comments*: The visual music program is separated from the informational portion, which was a wonderful way to present this program. Bird enthusiasts will drool over this title. *Kid Juror Comments*: "It was cool." Kids liked it, although they found it a bit overwhelming. Some were mesmerized. Kids decided that they wanted a hummingbird feeder afterwards. Video. 31 min.; $19.95; Age: 8-18. Ark Media Group, LTD.

Age 12-18

Video

Nature

*** *Little Creatures Who Run the World*
(Nova: Adventures in Science)

 Travel to rain forests and deserts with naturalist Edmund Wilson to observe the world of ants. Close-up photography shows ordinary ants and their unusual cousins. Wilson teaches the benefits of cooperation by observing these creatures. *Adult Juror Comments*: Excellent production, interesting and informative. Good music, outstanding photography and content. Presents the message that "working together builds strength." "Offers more science than I can teach in five days." *Kid Juror Comments*: Wonderful and informative. Kids never dreamed there was so much to know about ants. It made them want to study ants. "Bugs are cool!" Video. 60 min.; $19.95; Age: 8-18. WGBH.

** *My First Nature Video (My First)*

Answers nature questions. Kids discover how much fun nature can be by planting seeds, making creepy-crawly traps, and growing a miniature garden in a bottle. *Adult Juror Comments*: Inspires young minds to explore nature. Asks questions, presents problems, and challenges each child at his or her own level and ability. Some projects require equipment, assembling materials, and tasks that need adult assistance. *Kid Juror Comments*: Children were eager to do the activities at home. They enjoyed learning new things and wanted to share with their classmates or friends. "My sister would like this too." Video. 40 min.; $12.98; Age: 6-18. Sony Wonder.

*** *People of the Forest: The Chimps of Gombe*
(The Discovery Video Library)

Trace 20 years of love and rivalry by a tribe of chimpanzees from the forests surrounding Lake Tanganyika, based on the research of naturalist Jane Goodall. Intricate tapestry of emotion and drama, narrated by Donald Sutherland. *Adult Juror Comments*: Great program. Well-produced, excellent cinematography. *Kid Juror Comments*: Enthusiastic, especially those who love animals. Stimulates a lot of discussion about the subject. Video. 90 min.; $19.95; Age: 5-18. Discovery Communications.

Age 12-18

Video

Nature

* Spirits of the Rainforest (The Discovery Video Library)

 Discover an environment containing more species of animals than any other part of the world. Encounter six-foot river otters. Boat down uncharted rivers. Share the magic of the Machiguenga Indians whose lifestyle has changed little since the Incas. *Adult Juror Comments*: Gorgeous nature documentary and lush footage offers excellent geography lessons. Stimulated interest in the spiritual link between people and their environment. The hunting section was bothersome to some. Native dialogue seems contrived. *Kid Juror Comments*: A top favorite among children interested in rain forests and the environment. Video. 90 min.; $19.95; Age: 13-18. Discovery Communications.

*** Wild India (The Discovery Video Library)

 The culture of India once enjoyed a mutually respectful relationship with nature. The British Raj introduced hunting parties, and a growing population threatened India's animals. Traces efforts to preserve the nation's environment and wildlife. *Adult Juror Comments*: Beautiful documentary. Stimulating, thoughtful, and interesting. Background music is lively, and the terminology is quite sophisticated. This is a marvelous resource. *Kid Juror Comments*: Peaceful, rich, and revealing. Older children enjoyed the classical music accompaniment. Suitable for both classroom and home use. Video. 90 min.; $19.95; Age: 13-18. Discovery Communications.

Category—Special Interest

*** Daredevils of the Sky (Nova: Adventures in Science)

 Ever wanted to fly like a bird and soar in the wind? Stunning photography of dizzying aerobatic stunts puts the viewer in the pilot's seat for snap rolls, loops, humpty bumps, and hammerheads. It's fantastic fun at 200 hundred miles an hour. *Adult Juror Comments*: Interesting presentation, with applications that apply to math and physics. Covers the history of aviation and aerobatics, and features two female flyers. *Kid Juror Comments*: "My eleven-year-old son loved this." Kids who are interested in flying got a real kick out of this. They were surprised how much they learned. Lengthy for this age. Video. 60 min.; $19.95; Age: 12-18. WGBH.

Age 12-18

Video

Spec Int

*** *How the West Was Lost (3 Tapes)*

Documentary about the struggle for the American West and the tragic deci-mation of five Native American nations—the Navajo, Nez Pierce, Apache, Cheyenne, and Lakota. They didn't just fight for territory, they fought to pre-serve a way of life. *Adult Juror Comments*: A wonderful and moving story. Slow-moving, but worth every moment. Suitable for adults as well as older children, particularly those whose history lessons have not offered accurate information about Native Americans. *Kid Juror Comments*: Children appreciated the archive photography and were in awe of the landscape. Led to discussions about the injustice done to Native Americans. Kids thought the interviews and music became repetitive. Video. 300 min.; $79.95; Age: 12-18. Discovery Communications.

*** *In Search of Human Origins, Episode 1: The Story of Lucy (Nova: Adventures in Science)*

 Anthropologist Don Johanson may have solved the mystery of the missing link between man and ape in finding the remains of a tiny female, named Lucy, who is over three million years old. Travel back in time through re-creations of Lucy's world. *Adult Juror Comments*: Excellent introduc-tion to anthropology and human evolution. Invitingly framed as a mystery or thriller, captures the excitement through its portrayal of life long ago. *Kid Juror Comments*: Informative, exciting reenactments held kids' atten-tion. Suitable for kids curious about anthropology, evolution, and the history of mankind. Video. 60 min.; $19.95; Age: 14-18. WGBH.

*** *Living and Working in Space: The Countdown Has Begun*

 Features interviews with today's space professionals—a space doctor, the "lunar lettuce man," and designers of space clothing and Mars vehicles. *Adult Juror Comments*: Excellent informal science education, captivating concept, well-developed. Executed with polish, verve, and imagination. Gender representation is non-traditional. Vocabulary is somewhat tech-nical and advanced. *Kid Juror Comments*: Captured kids' interest in space and life's new directions and possibilities. Strong gender and ethnic role models were a plus for kids. Space enthusiasts were thrilled with this. Video. 60 min.; $29.95; Age: 12-18. Fase Productions.

** Math...Who Needs It?

Stars Jaime Escalante, the math teacher who inspired the movie nominated for an Academy-award, *Stand and Deliver*, and his students at Garfield High in Los Angeles. Bill Cosby and Dizzy Gillespie make guest appearances. *Adult Juror Comments*: Inspiring, humorous, and enlightening with stimulating narrative. Suitable for high school students or family viewing. *Kid Juror Comments*: Admired Jaime Escalante. Skeptical about it at first because it was about math, but most actually liked it. Everyone felt it was best-suited for older students. Video. 58 min.; $19.95; Age: 8-18. Fase Productions.

* Self-Esteem and Drugs (Voices from the Front)

Frank testimonials from teens with chemical-dependency problems and discussion of the impact on their self-esteem. Fast-moving, MTV-style, designed to be hard-hitting but teen-friendly. *Adult Juror Comments*: Very realistic on the challenges and peer pressure experienced by teens. Positive role models are represented. Recommend using with adult intervention. "I'd love to see all the programs in this series." *Kid Juror Comments*: Well-received, though they said it's not something they would choose to watch on their own. Video. 30 min.; $39; Age: 13-18. Attainment Company, Inc.

** Total Teen Fitness with Doctor

A *Total Teen Fitness* offers an entertaining exercise video for teens, which is a complete workout accompanied with nutritional messages, anti-drug and alcohol tags, and self-esteem-boosting lyrics. Features a culturally diverse group of kids. *Adult Juror Comments*: Graphics are well done. Carries a strong message regarding the need for a healthy lifestyle. Accompanied by an excellent poster for holistic health. Delivers appropriate messages about nutrition. *Kid Juror Comments*: Motivating. Enjoyed the graphics, but found the humor a little corny. The material is repetitive. Video. 30 min.; $19.95; Age: 12-18. Archer, Searfoss & Associates, Inc.

** Where's the TV Remote? American Sign Language Video Course (The Beginning American Sign Language Video Course)

Have you ever lost your TV remote? Join the amusing search while learning household signs, as the Bravo family looks for theirs. The remote may be lost, but Billy Seago makes sure that you aren't. *Adult Juror Comments*: Makes learning sign language easy and pleasant. Connecting the signing to a real-life story is a fabulous way to teach sign language. Best viewed with adult guidance. An adequate but not particularly imaginative production. *Kid Juror Comments*: Learning sign language is interesting. They liked the story and new concepts. After viewing, they used sign language throughout the day. Video. 30 min.; $49.95; Age: 5-18. Sign Enhancers, Inc.

Age 12-18

Video

Spec Int

Chapter Six

Parenting (Adult)

By Karen Kurz-Riemer

What do dog training, tae bo, and parenting have in common? Videos and CD-ROMs are available to make learning the task easier. Whether housebreaking puppy, doing an aerobic workout, or caring for a newborn, the video revolution has created a new format for how-to and self-help instruction. Most parents would acknowledge there is probably no task more challenging than raising children, and an ever-expanding number of videos and CD-ROMs are available to help. Yet perhaps no endeavor is as emotionally charged, culturally influenced, and intensely personal as parenting. Those who would take on the daunting challenge of instructing parents must reflect current research on child and parent development, convey their messages in accessible and engaging formats, and allow for cultural and religious differences in parenting styles. That's a tall order. Videos such as *About Us: the Dignity of Children*, hosted by Oprah Winfrey, offer an insight into a child's world and excellent diversity.

Moreover, public awareness of how research can inform parenting has been heightened by media coverage of neuroscience findings that the structure of the human brain is affected by the quality and range of life experiences, most dramatically from birth to age three. Although not always reflecting the latest in child development research, the "correct" advice to parents has changed dramatically over the years. During the 1950s, parents were told to feed their babies on a four-hour schedule, to formula-feed rather than breast feed because formula was more "modern" and nutritious, and not to hold their babies too much or respond too promptly to their cries for fear of spoiling them. No longer.

We now rely on videos such as *Baby Matters*, *The First Years Last Forever*, and *Ten Things Every Child Needs*, which reinforce current thought about how individual babies differ—sometimes widely—from what was previously thought. These videos inform us that feeding infants when they are hungry is a more reliable way to ensure their healthy growth, that breast milk is generally the most nourishing food for babies, and that babies whose dependent needs are met are not "spoiled," but are more likely to be emotionally secure and eager to learn.

In addition to communicating current theory and "best practice" to parents, it is important that parenting programs speak and write in clear language, without professional jargon, which conveys respect for parents' intelligence and experience. Parents and children featured in such programs should be diverse by education, income, race, and age. Fathers and grandparents should be as visible as mothers. Useful messages should be offered as suggestions or strategies, not prescriptions. They ought to reflect practical knowledge and awareness of the difficulties in raising children in two-parent as well as single-parent families. *Let's Go Potty* and *Exercise with Daddy & Me* are two examples of videos that promote thoughtful parenting. It helps if programs explain the rationale behind their proposed techniques.

"Talking heads" are among the least interesting formats for instructional purposes. Parenting programs that use action shots of parents and children, interspersed with occasional featured experts, are more appealing to most audiences. In *The Touchpoint Series*, Dr. T. Berry Brazelton exemplifies how graphics and print add to the clarity and aesthetic appeal. In recognition of the serious and challenging work of parenting, "cutesy" approaches that patronize or minimize the dignity of children or parents should be avoided. At the same time, a sense of humor and a creative approach to the presentation strengthens the impact of the message. Since parenting is as much an emotional experience as it is intellectual, programs that address both means of perception are more powerful than programs that focus on one level over the other.

Just as there is no single "right way" to raise children, there is no parenting video that appeals to all parents. *Finding Quality Child Care* supports the idea that parenting practices vary by cultural and individual belief systems. Our interactions with children echo the conscious or unconscious memories of our own childhood experiences and the positive and negative behavior of our own parents and caregivers. If a program can help us focus on our hopes and dreams for our children and give us information about the potential impact of various parenting practices, it will help us make more informed parenting choices. Effective parenting programs take into account the perspectives of diverse parents and diverse children, while conveying their research-based and practical messages clearly, creatively, and respectfully.

Karen Kurz-Riemer served as a consultant to the government of Singapore and the state of Hawaii in beginning a program similar to Minnesota's Early Childhood Family Education (ECFE) program with which she was involved for 20 years. ECFE is a nationally recognized model for its parenting education program. Ms. Kurz-Riemer has a master's degree from Chicago's Erikson Institute for Advanced Study in Child Development.

Format—CD-ROM
Category: Education/Instruction

* Active Parenting Today

 Develop courage, responsibility, and self-esteem in your child, using Active Parenting principles. Contains an hour of video, illustrating styles of parenting, effective non-violent discipline skills, and logical consequences. *Adult Juror Comments*: Content is very good with realistic lessons that are valuable to any parent. The presentation lacks appeal. The video clips are only a few inches in diameter, the narrator is dull, and it lacks flexibility, forcing constant review of some segments. CD-ROM. WIN; $39.95; Age: Adult. Active Parenting Publishers.

*** Baby Matters (Parenting Solutions)

 Good resource for parents to track prenatal care, medical data, child's developmental process, milestones, family tree, histories, and photos of their child's life from prenatal to babyhood. *Adult Juror Comments*: Knowledgeable, beneficial program. Provides links to authoritative Web sites. Presented in an easy-to-understand format that allows structured and unstructured data entry. "A wonderful way to document the growth and development of your child." Designed for adult use. CD-ROM. WIN; $29.95; Age: Adult. Parenting Solutions.

Format—Video/DVD
Category—Education/Instruction

* ABC's of Teaching ABC's, The

 How to teach the alphabet while going about daily activities. Puts parents back into the picture by encouraging them to act as their child's first teacher. *Adult Juror Comments*: Supports concept of "parents as children's first teachers," showing how kids learn through everyday activities. Adults felt there was too much pressure placed on kids to learn without having fun. Some phonics' information is inaccurate. Video. 14 min.; $14.95; Age: Adult. SOS Videos.

*** About Us: The Dignity of Children

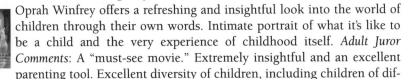

Oprah Winfrey offers a refreshing and insightful look into the world of children through their own words. Intimate portrait of what it's like to be a child and the very experience of childhood itself. *Adult Juror Comments*: A "must-see movie." Extremely insightful and an excellent parenting tool. Excellent diversity of children, including children of different abilities. Beautifully choreographed, scripted, and edited. Opens your eyes and your heart. Video. 94 min.; $19.98; Age: Adult. Steeplechase Entertainment.

*** Baby's World, A

Examines early child development and processes that transform infants into walking, talking human beings. Each episode looks at different human characteristics, tracing development through the first years of life. *Adult Juror Comments*: An extraordinary series rich with information. "Wonderful survey on cognitive and motor development in the first three years of life." Beautiful photography. Features diverse group of children and families. Adults had some safety concerns. Video. 180 min.; $39.95; Age: Adult. Discovery Communications.

** Day One: A Positive Beginning

Practical tips for parents and caregivers to create positive environments, from birth, to promote children's fullest mental, physical, and emotional development. Used by hospitals, birthing centers, and parenting education programs. *Adult Juror Comments*: Well-organized. Text is sophisticated, clearly presented, and articulated. Good sound, excellent visuals, good diversity, but too wordy. Parenting advice is appropriate with easy to implement suggestions. Delivery lacks impact and appeal. Video. 30 min.; $125; Age: Adult. New Horizons for Learning.

* Discipline Makes the Difference (Successful Parenting)

No one method of discipline works with all children, and no one method works every time. This video presents a range of alternatives that teach responsible behavior and self-control without damaging a child's self-esteem. *Adult Juror Comments*: Good examples of each disciplinary technique, with ways to proceed in a positive manner. Some thought portions were disrespectful, such as using the "time-out" chair. Low production and audio quality. Video. 17 min.; $49.95; Age: Adult. Active Parenting Publishers.

Parenting

Video

Edu/Instru

** First Years Last Forever, The

Hosted by actor Rob Reiner. New research in brain development reports vital importance of the relationship between caregiver and child in the critical first years of life. Discusses bonding and development, communication, health, and nutrition. *Adult Juror Comments*: Cohesive, informative, with good balance between narration and visual presentation. Sophisticated but not highbrow. Good for new parents. Lacks minority professionals speaking. "Makes me want to have another baby." Video. 30 min.; $5; Age: Adult. I Am Your Child.

* Make Way for Baby!

Focuses on the prenatal stimulation research done by Dr. Beatriz Manrique. Teaches pregnancy care, fetal development, calisthenics, and stimulation before birth that helps form a closer bond between parents and baby. *Adult Juror Comments*: Good message about connecting emotionally and physically with fetus early in pregnancy. Well-organized, contains useful prenatal health information though some claimed benefits are highly speculative. Background music is at times intrusive. Video. 55 min.; $19.95; Age: Adult. Amphion Communications.

** New Idea for Special Education, A

 Designed for parents, educators, and other professionals working with children with special needs. Sensitively produced, offers guidance and valuable resources. Includes information about new regulations regarding placement, discipline, and referral. *Adult Juror Comments*: Good basic guide. Stresses importance of finding a teacher or administrator to help guide parents through the process. Respectful. Presents the law clearly. "Professional content is excellent." Video. 45 min.; $49.95; Age: Adult. Edvantage Media, Inc.

* Playtime for Babies

An interactive play program to assist baby's sensory and physical milestone development. Features a mother playing with her baby while focusing on visual, tactile, hearing, strength and movement milestones. Adult Juror Comments: Practical and useful information, particularly for first-time parents. Effective examples of play techniques and positive modeling for warm interaction. Lack of father/male caregiver reinforces gender biases. No cultural diversity shown. Video. 28 min.; $15.95; Age: Adult. Baby playtime.

* Playtime for Newborns

An interactive play program to assist baby's sensory and physical milestone development. Features a mother playing with her baby while focusing on visual, tactile, hearing and strength movement milestones. Adult Juror Comments: Basic information presented in a positive, loving way. Safety concerns and cautions may not be stated strongly enough or could be lost on those who do not read well. Slow pace. Jurors particularly enjoyed information on infant massage. No diversity shown. Video. 26 min.; $15.95; Age: Adult. Baby Playtime.

** Straight Talk about Autism with Parents and Kids

 Features interviews with autistic children and their parents. One video looks at early childhood, and the second investigates adolescent issues. Areas covered include communication difficulties, social skills, transition, and difficulty of diagnosis. *Adult Juror Comments*: Emotional insight and encouragement to those working with autistic children and teens, stresses potential of the individual. Creative and resourceful ideas on how to develop socialization situations. Reverberates with experience of daily life. Not a kid title, although may be used with teen-agers who have autistic siblings or for sensitivity training. Video. 79 min.; $129; Age: Adult. Attainment Company, Inc.

*** Touchpoint Boxed Set

 Dr. T. Berry Brazelton, a leading pediatrician, guides new parents through every stage of parenting from pregnancy through toddler-hood. He helps parents understand and advance their child's development. *Adult Juror Comments*: Excellent video for new parents. Deals with major concerns. Shows great diversity. Brazelton points out the behaviors parents can identify as cues to their child's continuous changes. Fathers were delighted to hear the explanations and reassurances. Video. 45 min.; $39.95; Age: Adult. Pipher Films, Inc.

** What Children Need in Order to Read

 Provides research-based information on the skills needed by children for success in reading, including knowledge of the alphabet, sound structure of language, and the pleasure of books. Resource for anyone working with young children. *Adult Juror Comments*: This is not really a teaching video, but contains a discussion about reading. Presentation is rather dry. Combines commentary with singing and reading by children. Suitable for teachers, librarians, or parents interested in helping their child read. Video. 30 min.; $35; Age: Adult. Debeck Educational Video.

Parenting

Video

Family

Category—Family

*** Miracle of Life, The (Nova)

 Offers an incredible voyage through the human body as a new life begins. A dramatic breakthrough in science and cinematography makes it possible to film the development of the first stages of life from fertilization to embryo to fetus to childbirth. *Adult Juror Comments*: Outstanding production, beautifully filmed. Assumes viewers have some scientific language background. "I would feel comfortable watching this with my own child to explain the process of reproduction. It's a great tool to encourage conversation." *Kid Juror Comments*: Perfect for a child-development class. Excellent depiction of the birth process and the body's functions. "Couldn't take my eyes off it." Encourages tenderness and affection as part of sexuality. Some may be uncomfortable with the live birth at the end. Video. 60 min.; $19.95; Age: 16-Adult. WGBH.

Category—How-To

*** Caring for Your Newborn (Health Answers for Parents)

 This educational, entertaining video answers the most frequently asked questions for new parents. Uses lighthearted vignettes to present situations all parents encounter. Four pediatricians discuss each topic. *Adult Juror Comments*: Comprehensive information, clearly presented, addresses primary concerns. Shows involvement of both parents in infant care. Organized so viewer can easily return to specific area. "Though not high-tech, it works well." Humor is suitable. Video. 40 min.; $19.95; Age: Adult. A.A. Pediatrics.

** Exercise with Daddy & Me

 Amusing program for dads looking for ways to relate to their babies. Offers ways for father and baby to interact through movement, music, and massage. Features a group discussion on fatherhood. Instructors are a registered nurse and a pediatrician. *Adult Juror Comments*: Well-done, visually appealing, good pace. Useful if adults will interact with baby in the ways shown in video. Little cultural diversity. Great ideas for engaging fathers. Instructions on how to hold baby properly are not very clear. Video. 50 min.; $19.95; Age: Adult. My Baby and Me Exercise.

Party Games (Action Games)

Teachers, parents, and caregivers can utilize these games for an entertaining, non-competitive experience. All children are winners. *Adult Juror Comments*: Delightful ideas for easy, inexpensive games. Information about the skills these activities help cultivate. Simply produced with captions that emphasize certain points. Little diversity. Useful for both parents and providers. Video. 25 min.; $14.95; Age: Adult. Action Games.

** *Three R's for Special Education, The*

Practical guide designed for parents of children with special needs. Professionals and experienced parents explain how to advocate on behalf of such children. Discusses parental rights, legal underpinnings, and processes of special education. *Adult Juror Comments*: Empowering, helpful, and reassuring. Offers an excellent resource targeted for parents of children with special needs. Discusses financial issues. Thorough and careful presentation for parents of children with special needs. Video. 60 min.; $50; Age: Adult. Edvantage Media, Inc.

Category—Music

** *Babies Make Music (Lynn Kleiner Series)*

Early childhood music pioneer Lynn Kleiner shows how musical interactions can be delightful and easy, even for parents with no music background. She uses a variety of activities including massage rhymes, lullabies, games, songs, and dances. *Adult Juror Comments*: Easy to follow, enjoyable, very rhythmic, good for language development. Encourages parents to interact with their child using songs and activities. "As a parent, I thought the video was a good teaching tool." Repeats songs so you can learn them easily. This is really designed for parents though kids enjoyed the puppets and watching babies and children on-screen. Some made animal noises along with the puppets and danced. Some didn't want to watch it at all. Video. 52 min.; $14.95; Age: Adult. Headbone.

** *Making Music with Children: Ages 3-7*
(Making Music with John Langstaff)

John Langstaff demonstrates ways to introduce children to music. Includes singing games, rhythm and movement activities, and music from different cultures. Suitable for teacher training or parent education. *Adult Juror Comments*: Explanations are clear and understandable. Respect for children is evident. Shows diverse group of children. Useful for a non-musical adult who is interested in singing with kids. Video. 59 min.; $24.95; Age: Adult. Langstaff Video Project.

** Making Music with Children: Ages 7-11
(Making Music with John Langstaff)

John Langstaff demonstrates easy, effective ways to engage children in music. Includes rhythm and movement games for building orchestras out of household objects. Lyrics and music are included. *Adult Juror Comments*: Quite useful for music teachers preparing to teach new songs to a class. Best when viewed and used a few songs at a time. Excellent information, but the speaker lost the audience's interest quickly. Video. 59 min.; $24.95; Age: Adult. Langstaff Video Project.

* Songs and Fingerplays for Little Ones

Teaches hand and body movements to accompany seventeen songs. A day-care provider engages and entertains children at the same time. *Adult Juror Comments*: Delightful selection of songs and fingerplays, in appropriate sequencing from easy to difficult. Best used as a teaching aid. Adult caregiver is an excellent role model, showing understanding for child reluctant to participate. Video. 30 min.; $14.95; Age: Adult. Clever Productions.

Category—Parenting

** Baby 'n Me Workout

An exercise program that helps moms get back in shape, with developmental stimulation and massage for your baby. Appropriate for babies six to eight months in age. *Adult Juror Comments*: Clear instructions that explain the exercises with careful demonstrations including warnings, suggestions, and encouragement. Lots of hugs and kisses. Well-suited for the physical needs of new moms. "Didn't like the music, but think it's good for babies." Video. 65 min.; $14.95; Age: Adult. On the Job Productions.

** Effective Discipline: How to Raise a Responsible Child
(Active Parenting Today Video Library)

Teaches discipline skills that help develop cooperation and responsibility. Encourages use of logical consequences. *Adult Juror Comments*: Information is clear and concise. Good resource for parents with practical, down-to-earth information. Teaches decision-making skills and positive problem-solving. Sample role-play scenarios bring the messages to life. Video. 28 min.; $49.95; Age: Adult. Active Parenting Publishers.

** From Wibbleton to Wobbleton

Features storyteller Sally Jaeger sharing lap rhymes, finger plays, songs, and lullabies with babies and their parents. Gives parents and caregivers a repertoire of activities to soothe and entertain baby anywhere, anytime. *Adult Juror Comments*: Cute. Teachers and babies are adorable. Depicts familiar songs as well as introducing new ones. "This should be in the baby bag given to new moms by the hospital." Respectful, though the "coochie-coochie coo" tone was bothersome. Slow-moving. Video. 40 min.; $14.95; Age: Adult. 411 Video Information.

* Let's Go Potty

Designed to reinforce parenting skills necessary to successfully toilet train a baby. Demonstrates patient, positive guidance and addresses how impatience leads to child abuse. *Adult Juror Comments*: Thorough but dry production. Follows logical progression through all aspects of toilet training. Basic principals are sound. Narrator is hard to understand. "As a pediatrician, I would have liked more explanation about working with resistant learners." Video. 22 min.; $19.95; Age: Adult. Parenting Resources, Inc.

* Playtime for Creepers

An interactive play program to assist baby's sensory and physical milestone development. Features a mother playing with her baby while focusing on baby's visual, tactile, hearing, strength, balance, coordination, and movement development. *Adult Juror Comments*: Well-organized with a clear structure. Provides parents with helpful, age-appropriate information. A fun way to spark interaction between parent and baby. Lacks cultural diversity. Video. 30 min.; $15.95; Age: Adult. Baby Playtime.

* Playtime for Toddlers

An interactive play program to assist baby's sensory and physical milestone developments. Features a mother playing with her baby while focusing on developing motor skills, strength, balance, coordination, and movement. *Adult Juror Comments*: Upbeat, simple, informative, and fun presentations. Cheerful and positive. Shows age-appropriate play activities for adults who spend time with young children. Gives both verbal and visual instructions. Lacks cultural diversity. Video. 32 min.; $15.95; Age: Adult. Baby Playtime.

Chapter Six • Parenting

** *She Said Yes: The Unlikely Martyrdom of Cassie Bernall*

Columbine victim Cassie Bernall had once been on the same destructive path as her killers. This video tells the story of the steps her parents took to put the troubled teen back on track. *Adult Juror Comments*: Well-produced. Encourages parents to take a proactive role with their kids. Meaningfully shows how a teen can positively influence the life of a peer. Contains Christian content. Some jurors experienced audio problems. Video. 35 min.; $89.95; Age: Adult. Active Parenting Publishers.

* *Sidestepping the Power Struggle: How to Redirect Your Teen's Misbehavior (Active Parenting of Teens Video Library)*

Identify your teens' goals when they misbehave and avoid power struggles. Solve problems with teens. Watch other parents set guidelines for parties and dating. *Adult Juror Comments*: Applicable to all parents of teens. Preventive measures are discussed with techniques to avoid a power struggle before it starts. The included brochure augments the video. The video itself is not comprehensive, and the rapid pace diminishes its effectiveness. Video. 28 min.; $49.95; Age: Adult. Active Parenting Publishers.

*** *Ten Things Every Child Needs*

Explains how our earliest interactions influence a child's brain development. Expounds on ten basic topics: interaction, touch, stability, safety, self-esteem, quality childcare, play, communication, music, and reading. *Adult Juror Comments*: Positive and motivating information. Intersperses interviews with video segments and live action clips of children. Outstanding resource for parents both young and mature. Assertions are supported with examples, "like watching a '60 Minutes' segment." Video. 60 min.; $14.95; Age: Adult. Consumervision, Inc.

** *What Your Child Needs on Order to Read* (*What Your Child Needs in Order to Read*)

With the insights and advice of acclaimed reading expert, Marilyn Jager Adams, parents are introduced to tools and strategies to prepare children for reading success. *Adult Juror Comments*: Well-produced. Good continuity. Information is thorough, but a bit theoretical. Terms and explanations are not always appropriate for a lay audience. Shows realistic activities with children. Video. 30 min.; $14.99; Age: Adult. Time Life Home Video.

Chapter Six • Parenting

Category—Special Interest

** Breakthrough: How to Reach Students with Autism

A hands-on, how-to program for teachers and parents, featuring "Teacher of the Year" Karen Sewell. Sewell demonstrates the rigorous but compassionate program she has developed over her career, making significant progress with a four-year-old student. *Adult Juror Comments*: Excellent, helpful information on living with an autistic child. Shows the benefits of early intervention and what the future holds. Quality production offers specific techniques showing problems, progress, and completion. Video. 26 min.; $59; Age: Adult. Attainment Company, Inc.

** Finding Quality Childcare
(The Parents' Survival Video Series)

Easy-to-follow tips with solid guidelines for assessing the quality of any childcare program. Recommends what to look for and which questions to ask. Experts address health, curriculum, safety, and more. Includes quality checklist. Adult Juror Comments: Comprehensive observations and descriptions of different types of child-care. Providers, consultants, center directors, and parents provide information and sound advice. Well-produced, easy to follow. Video. 45 min.; $19.95; Age: Adult. Quartet Creative Series.

* Parenting the Gifted Child, Part I and II
(Parenting the Gifted Child)

Is your child gifted? Video explains the characteristics of gifted children and offers parenting tips. *Adult Juror Comments*: Covers the current knowledge on gifted children. Presentation is basically a videotaped lecture. Defines giftedness as based on child's test scores. Could be beneficial to parents, teachers, and administrators. Video. 96 min.; $39.95; Age: Adult. Nichols Galvin Productions.

** Taming the Strong-Willed Child

Family psychologist John Rosemond shares six reliable tips for taming the strong-willed child. Various scenes demonstrate both appropriate and inappropriate methods of interacting with such children. *Adult Juror Comments*: Simple production with content that is respectful of children. Ideas are consistent with current theory, translated into action. Appropriate for group use. Includes follow-up activities. Jurors had trouble using the words "taming" and "obey." Video. 24 min.; $19.95; Age: Adult. Parent Power Productions.

Indices

Multi-Cultural/Diversity

Indices

Titles Best for Boys

Dealing with Problems, Conflict Resolution

Conflict Resolution

Indices

Conflict Resolution

Indices

Index by Title

Indices

Index by Title

Index by Title

Indices

Indices

Indices

Index by Title

Indices

Y

Z

Index by Title

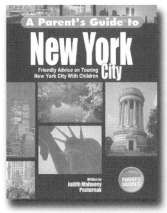

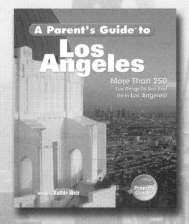

APPLICATION FOR MEMBERSHIP

Coalition for Quality Children's Media
www.kidsfirstinternet.org

Please help support the CQCM's efforts to teach children and parents how to critique media so that they can select what is appropriate and what is not. This includes recognizing what is violent, discriminatory, or age-appropriate.

- **Individual ($25/yr.):** Receive a subscription to our online email newsletter, a FREE KIDS FIRST!®-endorsed video and a FREE video rental at Hollywood Video.
- **Retailer ($50/yr.):** Receive a subscription to our online email newsletter; a FREE KIDS FIRST!®-endorsed video; a FREE video rental at Hollywood Video; KIDS FIRST!® endorsement stickers.
- **Organization ($100/yr.):** Receive a subscription to our online email newsletter for all of your staff members; a FREE KIDS FIRST!®-endorsed video; 10 FREE video rental at Hollywood Video.

Sign me up:

Name:_____

Company/organization:_____

Street:_____

City:_____

State:_____Zip:_____

Phone:_____Fax:_____

Email address:_____

URL:_____

__ I would like a subscription to CQCM's email newsletter.
Mail this application along with your payment to
Coalition for Quality Children's Media/ KIDS FIRST!®
112 W. San Francisco St.,
Suite 305A
Santa Fe, NM • 87501
505.989.8076
505.986.8477(fax)
admin@kidsfirstinternet.org

Membership Dues:_____

Payment type
__ Check __ Credit card (Visa/Mc)

cc#:_____

expiration date:_____